EXECUTIVE
ESSENTIALS

EXECUTIVE ESSENTIALS

THE COMPLETE SOURCEBOOK FOR SUCCESS

MITCHELL J. POSNER

AVON
PUBLISHERS OF BARD, CAMELOT, DISCUS AND FLARE BOOKS

Because the English language lacks a generic singular pronoun that indicates both "he" and "she," it has been customary to use the masculine pronoun to refer to either sex. Although I've tried to use terms that encompass both sexes wherever possible, I have often resorted to the generic masculine pronouns for the sake of style, readability, and succinctness. With the obvious exception of things like "choosing a necktie," all the material in this book applies to both men and women.

Note: All prices, product information, addresses and telephone numbers are included to aid the reader, but are subject to change without prior notification. The author and publisher are not responsible for any loss, damages or other consequences resulting from such changes.

EXECUTIVE ESSENTIALS: THE COMPLETE SOURCEBOOK FOR SUCCESS is an original publication of Avon Books.

AVON BOOKS
A division of
The Hearst Corporation
105 Madison Ave.
New York, New York 10016

Cover design by Gribbitt! Ltd.
Book design by Joyce Kubat

First Avon Printing: March 1982
First Revised Edition: November 1987

AVON TRADEMARK REG. U.S. PAT. OFF. AND IN OTHER COUNTRIES, MARCA REGISTRADA, HECHO EN U.S.A.

Printed in the U.S.A.

OPM 10 9 8 7 6 5 4 3 2 1

CONTENTS

Introduction   1

PART I
PUTTING TIME ON YOUR SIDE

1. A short course in saving time   7
The time log and how to use it; planning effective time
management

2. Tackling the time-wasters   15
Meetings; telephone interruptions; the tyranny of the urgent; procrastination; lateness; ineffective delegation; poor planning; taking
on too much; your body, your mind, and your schedule

3. The paperwork problem   37
Too much paperwork; the symptoms, culprits, and cure

4. Tools to save time and eliminate paper with   51
Planners, diaries, and appointment calendars; how to use checklists
to save time; suggested reading

PART II
COPING WITH THE
INFORMATION EXPLOSION

5. The data deluge   65
What "information overload" can do to you; how executives get
(and sometimes don't get) the news they need

6. Information ecology: getting the most in the least time   71
The screening process: the first glance, skimming, previewing,
screening nonprint media; the cure for IOA (Information Overload
Anxiety); developing your own media mix

7. Using your head   83
The unlimited potential of the human brain; cognitive skills: reading
better, listening better; note taking; memory aids

8. Information gathering   103
How to choose business magazines, newsletters, all-news radio;
research: the personal reference library; databases; on-line services

9. Appendix to Part II   139
Guides to major English-language business periodicals and all-news
radio stations

PART III
LIFE IN THE FAST LANE:
EXECUTIVE HEALTH

10. Your health and your job   153
Drugs in the workplace; smoking; health and the executive woman;
physical examinations

11. Stress: a user's guide to bodily wear and tear   161
Stress: definitions, misconceptions, and causes; personal stressors;
distressors; what stress can do to you; warning signs; stress-related
diseases; burn-out; stress reduction and relaxation techniques

12. Use it or lose it: exercise for executives   189
What is "in-shape"?—flexibility, strength, muscle mass, endurance;
aerobic exercise; exercise and weight control; exercise and mood;
tips for a proper workout; heart check guide; where to work out;
working out where you work; the home gym

13. A lean course in nutrition   199
The nutrients: carbohydrates, proteins, fats, and vitamins; minerals;
water; the "bad boys" of nutrition: sugar, salt, and cholesterol

14. The physiology of job performance   213
The basic performance factors: light, body comfort, heat, cigarette smoke, drugs, noise, and desk fatigue; the "far-out" factors that may—or may not—affect your performance: biorhythms, the weather, negative ions, altitude, pollen, and smog; waking up fresh; burning the candle at both ends: how much sleep, food, and exercise you really need; staying alert

15. Healthy hardware   225
A guide to exercise equipment; cardiovascular and strength training; eyeguards; braces; suggested reading

PART IV
WINNING

16. The success scriptures and what you can learn from them   233
How to choose a success book: who the writers are and what they promise; how they get to you: inspiration, motivation, and imagination—the psychology of the pep talk; success material for women

17. What every businessperson ought to know something about   245
What it takes: a thumbnail sketch of the successful executive personality; delegating; modifying behavior; methods of leadership; risk taking; negotiating; public speaking; arguing; a guide to management theories and current fads; management by objective (MBO); Japanese management techniques; the Absolute Theory of Management; statistics

18. Power: out of the closet   287
Power and job dependence; the tactics of power; the ethics of power; playing the power game; company politics

19. Learn and earn: executive education   297
Why you can't afford to stay out of school; seminars: who gives them, why they are popular, how to select them, how to get your company to pay; attending the seminar and getting the most out of it; the big names in the seminar field; how to evaluate a seminar; the CEU (Continuing Education Unit): what's it worth?; selecting a

school and a program: the MBA; the MS; the Ph.D.: the EMBA; the glamour courses; teaching your way to the top; what you should know when you get out of school; who gets ahead; the influence of family background, education, cognitive skills, race, etc. on success

PART V
MOVING THROUGH
THE JOB JUNGLE

20. Do you sincerely want to be a corporate executive?   329
191 ways an executive fills his day, or what executives do; self-analysis; the good life

21. Narrowing the field   333
Deciding on the kind of job you really want; the job outlook for the eighties, and the prospects for the executive; recent trends

22. A look at your entire career   343
The corporate career atlas; recent changes in the traditional career path; other career trends

23. Roadblocks   355
Getting fired: what to do about it, severance, outplacement; mergers and acquistions; what to do when the takeover comes; the bright side of mergers; the transfer notice; where the grass is greener: a study of the quality of life in major US metropolitan areas and abroad

24. The hunt   377
A philosophy of job hunting; how to talk to a headhunter and what to do when one doesn't call; finding the opportunities; evaluating a job offer; personnel agencies and job counselors; how to pick an employment agency; creative job hunting tactics

25. The one-two punch: résumés and interviews   395
Getting through the door in an envelope, or all about résumés: importance, format, general points on writing; the interview: preparing for the interview, protecting yourself, responding to ten questions interviewers love to ask, knowing what to listen and look for during the interview; passing the chemistry test: rapport with an interviewer; the corporate snoop: privacy and the job hunt; references on request

26. Appendix to Part V   409
The activities and responsibilities of the executive, an in-depth
survey

PART VI
GETTING YOUR SHARE:
EXECUTIVE COMPENSATION

27. What everybody wants   419
What are you after? What is the company after? What does Uncle
Sam want?

28. How much?   423
Salary factors; computing your compensation; the cash or incentive
bonus; pay-for-performance policies; the golden parachute; the
bonus formula

29. Perks   439
Insurance plans; medical plans; pension plans; profit sharing; deferred compensation; future value incentives: stock options and performance options; top-of-the-line perks: company loans, cars, estate
planning, executive dining, housing, club memberships; the new
perks: health programs, domestic partners, child care, kidnap insurance; vacations; flexible compensation; trends

30. Making your best deal: the bargaining table   459
Your position in the negotiations; preparation; protocol; what to
bargain for; compensation planning forms

PART VII
THE OFFICE ARSENAL

31. The office of the future   467
What it is and what it means to you; the growth of office automation: its advantages; what you should know about the modern office

32. The computer   475
The components; the software program; the personal computer; the
benefits of a computer; operating systems software; executive guide
to applications software; inside the PC; compatibility; pitfalls;
glossary

33. Peripherals   505
Other developments in office automation; the electronic typewriter;
the memory typewriter; output devices; modems; input devices;
add-on boards

34. Electronic duplication and storage   515
Copiers: types and features, the economics, a copier efficiency
checklist; micrographics; types of microforms

35. Telephones   529
The principal devices; the executive workstation; things to remember
about telephone service; OCCs; suggested reading

36. Communications and electronic mail   535
The basic methods; teletype services; facsimile; teleconferencing;
voice mail; computer based message systems (CBMS); trends in electronic mail; in defense of paper

37. Office security   547
The basic equipment; types of security systems; computer security;
fire detection; buying security equipment

38. The office environment   559
The open office: its history and its variations, the reasons for its
growth, what to do if you must work in one; your needs versus the
company's; the office landscape and office automation; the business
life of plants: office greenery

39. The automated office; surviving in style   573
Convincing your boss to modernize the office; a basic plan for introducing office automation; adjusting to the office of the future;
trends to watch; recommended reading

40. Personal accessories and opportunities: executive style   581
Stationery, business cases, calculators, pens; the executive wardrobe;
wardrobe coordinators; an at-a-glance guide to personal appearance

PART VIII
ON THE ROAD: WHAT THE TRAVEL GUIDES DON'T TELL YOU

41. Getting there by air   **603**
Alternatives to the business trip (Is a trip really necessary?); on-line travel services; things that go bump on the flight, on-board options, special meals; seating, first class/business class/future class; clubs; determining whether your company should own its own plane; preparing a corporate jet analysis; knowing how to survive a plane crash; required papers for international travel; international currency regulations; how to go to a trade show

42 Travel bummers   **643**
Air sickness, jet lag, water, food, medical care; what to take with you; losing things

43. Are you a target? terrorism and American executive   **653**
Are you a potential victim? reducing the risks; hardware; a prevention checklist; nonlethal weapons; suggested reading

Afterword   **673**
Putting it all together

Index   **674**

The preparation of this book required the assistance of business executives and academic experts too numerous to mention. However, I would like to thank several people in particular for the valuable advice, assistance, patience and support: Frederic B. Poneman, International Trading Group; Warren Berman, J&W Supply, Inc.; Harriet Berman; Beverly Hanger; Special thanks to Marlene Shama for her thorough research and keen insights; Marian Cohen for her major contribution to Parts V and VI; to Karen Lucic, PhD., for her help with the revisions in the 1987 edition; and to my wife Renee Z. Posner, whose help on this project transcends that which can be put into words.

INTRODUCTION

On becoming an observer of the American business scene, I quickly reached a conclusion that is undoubtedly shared by a large segment of the business community: Success is not simply a matter of keeping one's nose to the grindstone, or a reward for years of unwavering loyalty and devotion to the firm. Proof that I am not alone in this view lies in the sizable and sustained audience for books on how to manipulate, dominate, intimidate, or otherwise aggravate one's way to the top. And books on how to look, dress, decorate, and impress for success.

Executive Essentials is not a book about one of these areas. It is an attempt to help you evaluate all of them—and then some. My goal is to identify and fill those "knowledge gaps" that, if left open, could create serious consequences in your career. These are the areas and issues that have a critical impact on the overall effectiveness and success of an executive, but are not generally taught (in some cases, are completely ignored) in colleges, business schools, and executive training programs. Like it or not, we are talking about knowledge that often makes the difference between success and stagnation.

I've tried to separate the wheat from the chaff, eliminating useless examples, anecdotes, redundancies, interviews with "Bill C.," and other kinds of fluff that authors use to stretch a single subject into a book. The result is a comprehensive source book that treats each topic in a straight-to-the-point manner.

Executive Essentials is organized into eight parts that correspond to the basic subjects on which we are least enlightened:

Time management. Time is surely the executive's most precious commodity. This section shows you how to recognize where you are wasting time and why, and what you can do to avoid squandering it.

Information management. Knowledge reaches us through the communications environment, and that environment is being flooded—and increasingly polluted. Trying to keep abreast can result in a loss of time, energy, and concentration. Yet no executive can afford to risk closing himself off. The modern businessperson has to learn to *select* what to read, listen to, and watch—and, at the same time, exploit one's mental potential to the fullest. This section shows you how to screen information and how to improve your cognitive abilities, so that you can take in more in less time and process it more effectively.

Attitudes, insights, and key personal skills. An American business cliché is that success is merely a matter of a winning attitude, with a dash of inspiration thrown in. You'll learn how you go about developing that winning attitude. Also, how to negotiate, delegate, take risks, speak in public, play the power game, and much more. In this part of the book there's advice on executive education and information about a few successful but relatively little-known approaches to more effective management, such as Japanese techniques and the Absolute Theory of Management.

Health. Success has as much to do with dependability, stamina, and vitality as it does with knowledge, ability, and skill. Poor health will slow one's career advancement; it happens more than most people realize. Beset by fatigue, stress, illness, depression, and other problems, many executives are perceived as health risks and, therefore, poor prospects for promotion. This section is not about how to pamper yourself—I'll assume that you are prepared to go flat out to get to the top. Rather, it's about how to take care of yourself now that you're traveling at a fast pace while carrying a heavy load.

Career paths. This is not a how-to-get-a-job guide for the unemployed or for the kid just out of college. The fact is that in today's business environment, the market for talent is open, freewheeling, and treacherous. It's also rife with opportunity. Even the executive who has a secure, enjoyable position with excellent potential must consider the ever-changing job picture and how it might affect him. This section is designed to provide you with the basic rules by which the job-changing game is played among accomplished executives. I hope that it'll entice you to remain always "available," and that it will also provide insurance against the unthinkable—the sack—which happens even to the best of us.

Compensation. Okay, so money isn't the only factor important to a job decision. But why accept less than what you are worth? You might think you have a good reason for doing so: Be advised that there are very few good reasons around. Remember, nobody is happy at a job if he feels he's being shortchanged or taken advantage of. And there's more to compensation than just a salary. What about "perks" and tax advantages? This section is designed to help you determine what you should be getting and what is available in the way of compensation, and to help you go about getting it without risking all.

Home base: your office. Mission Control for some, The Fortress of Solitude for others. Whatever the purpose your office serves, its design and operation is about to change. The office of 1992 will bear little resemblance to that of 1982. With the increased emphasis on office productivity, there's a good chance that you'll be seeing most of these changes long before the end of the decade. Many innovations are being introduced already, and more will be phased in over the next few years. You have two choices: Regard the automated office as sheer gimmickry, toys of eggheads that do no more than help secretaries type faster; or recognize and learn to capitalize on the vast potential of the modern office. And if you don't think you've got the time to work toward greater efficiency, effectiveness, and output, don't assume the competition thinks likewise. This section will tell you (1) what the office of the future is all about, (2) what are its assets and its drawbacks, (3) how to introduce office automation, and (4) how your job will be affected. Above all, you'll be well versed in the latest devices, their functions, and the accompanying lingo so that you won't be at the mercy of the equipment salesperson or, worse, some wiseacre from data processing.

The field: doing business away from home. Whether it's undertaken to buy, sell, make contacts, or generate goodwill, a trip requires preparation if it is to yield maximum results. The less affected you are by travel problems that upset schedules, health, and performance, the better. Some people learn to avoid nuisances through experience; others never quite manage to cope. Wouldn't you rather be briefed on how to "travel smart" than learn by making all the possible mistakes?

I've organized this book into sections with short chapters and subheadings, so a quick review of any of the topics covered is easy. You may even wish to clip out or photocopy a page or two for your desk or bulletin board. *Executive Essentials* was written to be used.

If I've done my job well, this book should help you identify and clarify the problems you face at work—and provide many of the solutions required to meet the challenges of business in the eighties.

PART I

PUTTING TIME ON YOUR SIDE

"The past is gone; the present is full of confusion; and the future scares hell out of me!"
David Lewis Stein

1
A SHORT COURSE IN SAVING TIME

Don't underestimate the importance of effective time management. *The executive is judged by what he accomplishes, not by how many hours he puts in.* If you decide to work ten hours a day, it should be because you have a full ten hours of work to be done. More often than not, we fill ten hours with what should take us only eight. This pattern will not go unnoticed, and will undoubtedly be frowned upon.

Since there are an unlimited number of ways to waste time—Are you sure you should be reading this book now? Is there something more important to attend to?—there are countless ways to improve the situation. What you've got to do is figure out exactly where you are wasting time, and then start doing something about it. The ways in which people waste time seem obvious when you read them from a list, but because we are often unaware of them in our own lives and jobs, self-analysis is in order.

Some advice on this subject is pure common sense. There are also several creative, innovative, and even downright ingenious time-saving methods that are worth exploring.

Let's face it: It is very difficult to change behavior. So if you choose to follow the suggestions in this chapter, go easy on yourself. Don't attempt to turn your life upside down to save an hour. At least, not all at once.

HOW TO SEIZE THE TIME

Every writer and consultant on time management presents a plan of some sort. No matter what the approach, each plan can be boiled down to five basic steps:

1. *Formulate a work plan.* How do you intend to spend your day?
2. *Complete a time log.* How did you actually spend your day?
3. *Do an analysis.* What went wrong? What went right? Major problems?

4. *Find solutions.* Formulate strategies to eliminate the problems, improve your work plan, and devise an efficient routine.
5. *Implement.* The hard part. Putting your plans and strategies into effect.

FORMULATE A WORK PLAN

Plan your day. Make a list, and be specific. Note down activity and how much time you intend to allocate to it, either as a percentage of the work day or as actual time in minutes—or both.

Rank the activities in order of priority using a simple rating system such as the numerical one devised by noted time management consultant R. Alec Mackenzie:

1 = important and urgent
2 = important, not urgent
3 = urgent, not important
4 = routine

COMPLETE A TIME LOG

There are several steps involved:

MAKE ONE   Devise your own, or try the simple five-column chart of Fig. 1.

FILL IN ABSOLUTELY EVERYTHING YOU DO   Professors Thomas Bonoma and Dennis Slevin* refer to the contents of a time log as *work incidents.* They define a work incident as "any change in what you are doing." This sensible approach leaves little room for fudging by not recording such things as reading a newspaper article. An interruption is defined by the professors as "any unprogrammed incident." Don't forget to record the nature and duration of every work incident and interruption while it is still fresh in your mind.

MAKE COMMENTS   Anything that comes to mind about the incident: complaints; frustrations; ways in which this incident or interruption could have been eliminated or expedited.

STICK WITH IT   Keep this log for a minimum of three days. A week or two is ideal. Obviously, it is unwise to pick a week you know will be atypical, because the results will not be as useful. However, don't use the excuse of "waiting for the typical week" to delay doing the log. If your work schedule changes after you complete the log, you can always start another time log.

---

*Thomas V. Bonoma and Dennis P. Slevin, *The Executive Survival Manual* (Belmont, CA: Wadsworth Publishing Co., 1978), p. 14.

Time of Day	Activity	Duration	Priority Rating	Comments

Fig. 1. Sample time log
If you like, leave a space at the top for goals and objectives.

DO AN ANALYSIS

There are several methods, but the goal is the same for each—to locate the incidents that waste your time, and those you could deal with more effectively. Most important, you want to make certain that you are making progress toward achieving your objectives by allocating time to activities according to their priorities.

In order to do this, you've got to rate your daily activity. My favorite rating system is in the time log designed by William C. Giegold and included in his text *Strategic Planning and the MBO Process* (New York: McGraw-Hill, 1978).

Giegold employs a columnar rating system. One column is for *control*, a measure of how much time is spent on planned or unplanned activity; one is for *usage*, a measure of the priority of the activity; and one is for personal *satisfaction*. Each column is rated separately, and then they are combined for an overall "Effectiveness Rating," or ER. The three aspects of the rating system are weighed according to the individual's needs *(see* Fig. 2).

Time period	Activity	Ratings			Comments and suggestions for improvement
		A	B	C	
8:00					
8:30					
9:00					
1:00					
1:30					
2:00					
2:30					

Rating codes (See Note 1)

   Column A: 1 = planned 2 = unplanned
   Column B: 3 = urgent 4 = important 5 = unimportant 6 = routine 7 = imposed
   Column C: 8 = satisfied 9 = dissatisfied

Effectiveness Rating for the day (See Note 2)

      A = percent of time rated "1" in Column A _____
      B = percent of time rated "4" in Column B _____
      C = percent of time rated "8" in Column C _____

$$\frac{A + B + C}{300} = \text{Effectiveness rating} \quad \underline{\hspace{2cm}}$$

NOTES ON USE OF THE TIME LOG

Note 1: Give every activity a rating in all three columns. Column A provides a measure of *control* of your time. Column B provides a *usage* measure. Column C is a subjective measure of your *satisfaction* with the way your time was spent.

          Column B may contain more than one digit. For instance, you may rate this morning's 10:00 meeting with the boss as a 357—urgent, unimportant, and imposed. Likewise, an activity may be a 34, urgent and important, or a 35, urgent but unimportant.

Note 2: The Effectiveness Rating (ER) is a combined score on control, usage, and satisfaction. Each rating, A, B, and C may vary from zero to one hundred. The formula for ER obviously weights these three factors equally. You may adjust these weights as you see fit, depending on the nature of your problem. For example, if your job is composed of unplanned activities or emergencies—typical of a fire fighter or trouble-shooter—there is little point in downgrading your ER just because "That's the job." In such a case, your formula for ER might be $\frac{B + C}{200}$.

          Whatever formula you choose, *stay with it* so as to preserve a uniform basis for measuring changes in effectiveness.

Fig. 2. Daily time log and effectiveness rating

From *Strategic Planning and the MBO Process,* by William C. Giegold. Copyright © 1978 by McGraw-Hill, Inc. Used with permission of McGraw-Hill Book Company.

If you prefer, you can use the "1 to 4" rating system described earlier, the one used for formulating a work plan. If you choose to do so, add the number 5 to indicate "not urgent, not important"—an incident with so low a priority that it is virtually wasted time.

Compare the amount of time allocated to each activity with the actual time spent. Did the high-priority items receive the most attention? Were the activities carried out with maximum effectiveness?

If you look carefully at your analysis, you will see that the specific time management problems are of two basic types:

> *tangibles.* The kind you are likely to record in the log: telephone interruptions, drop-in visitors, a disorganized desk.
> *intangibles.* These problems stem from attitude and personality quirks, and they are difficult to pin down. The evidence of such problems will probably turn up in the "Comments" column of the log. Statements like "Just couldn't get started today" or "I'm such a nice person—it always gets me in trouble" are often an indication that something below the surface is affecting your ability to control your own time.

FIND SOLUTIONS

Now that the problems are self-evident, what should you do about them? Once again, Bonoma and Slevin have reduced the problems to elegant simplicity. There are, they say, two basic ways to save time:

> *Work faster.* This includes all solutions that involve increasing your speed and working ability.
> *Do less.* This covers all methods of eliminating unnecessary tasks and streamlining the work load.

This section of the book is filled with all sorts of strategies and suggestions for saving and managing time. But they are all variations on one or the other—doing less or working faster.

Time	Action	Priority	Comment, Disposition, or Results
Goals: 1. _____ 4. _____ 2. _____ 5. _____ 3. _____ 6. _____		Date: _____	
		1 = Important and urgent 2 = Important, not urgent 3 = Urgent, not important 4 = Routine	Delegate to _____ . Train _____ to handle. Next time ask his recom- mendation. Consolidate, eliminate, or cut time. Other.
8:00			
8:30			
9:00			
9:30			
10:00			
10:30			
2:00			
2:30			
3:00			
3:30			
4:00			
4:30			
5:00			
5:30			
Even-ing			

Fig. 3. Daily time analysis
(above and opposite)

Reprinted, by permission of the publisher, from *The Time Trap*, by R. Alec Mackenzie, © 1972 by AMACOM, a division of the American Management Associations (pp. 26-27). All rights reserved.

Instructions for the Daily Time Analysis

1. Enter the date and list the goals for the day in terms of results, not activities. (Include the agenda in the time allocated for a sales meeting, *not* just the meeting itself.)
2. Record all significant activities in terms of results during each 15-minute period. Do not wait until noon or the end of the day. The major benefit is lost.
3. Answer the following questions immediately after the completion of the daily time log.

Questions

1. Did setting daily goals and times for completion improve my effectiveness? If so, why? If not, why not?
2. What was the longest period of time without interruption?
3. In order of importance, which interruptions were most costly?
4. What can be done to eliminate or control them?
   a. Which telephone calls were unnecessary?
   b. Which telephone calls could have been shorter or more effective?
   c. Which visits were unnecessary?
   d. Which visits could have been shorter or more effective?
5. How much time was spent in meetings?
   a. How much was necessary?
   b. How could more have been accomplished in less time?
6. Did I tend to record "activities" or "results"?
7. How many of my daily goals contributed directly to my long-range objectives?
8. Did a "self-correcting" tendency appear as I recorded my actions?
9. What two or three steps could I now take to improve my effectiveness?

2

TACKLING THE TIME-WASTERS

When executives fill out time logs or talk about time management, a number of common time-wasters usually emerge. These problems are encountered by almost every manager at one time or another. What follows are a few suggestions on how to solve them.

MEETINGS

The business community has a love-hate relationship with its meetings. They can be great fun; they can be excruciatingly boring. They can be very productive—or they can be the biggest time-wasters of all. Despite the following insights and advice, I must point out that I have yet to find an executive who claims to be in complete control of meetings or his meeting time.

REDUCING THE NUMBER
AND DURATION OF MEETINGS

LOG YOUR MEETINGS   See which ones can be eliminated, and which can be cut down. Of course, it isn't always up to you.

AVOID COMMITTEES UNLESS YOU THINK THEY HAVE AN IMPORTANT PURPOSE   Committees = meetings; therefore, fewer committees = fewer meetings. Dissolve committees when they have accomplished their purpose.

NEVER CALL A MEETING UNLESS THERE IS NO ALTER-NATIVE   If there is another way to deal with a situation, pursue it. Almost anything is more efficient, whether it be letter, conference call, or doing the job yourself. Meetings are required only when group action is necessary.

DON'T GO UNLESS YOU HAVE TO   If it's unimportant, skip it altogether. If it's important, ask yourself if *you* have to be there. Is there someone else you can send? You'll find ways to duck the real sleepers,

15

saying, "I wasn't informed," or "There is a conflict in my schedule, and it's an appointment I can't change." Tell someone to tape the meeting so you can be sure to be brought up to date. Chances are, if it's not worth going to, it's not worth listening to, either. But jump around on the tape to get the gist of it, or ask a trusted colleague where the meat of the meeting lies, and listen to that.

PREPARING FOR A MEETING

BRING THE MEETING INTO FOCUS IN ADVANCE   Know what you hope to accomplish. Set priorities.

SET TIME LIMITS   When will it start? When will it end? Sometimes you won't finish, and will have to schedule another meeting. Nobody wants that, so they will all push to finish on time. But if you leave it open-ended, the meeting will tend to fill as much time as it has been allotted. By the way, start on time. Don't wait for anyone—well, almost anyone. If a VIP is late, use your charm, and tactfully tell him that it sets a bad example and to please be prompt in the future.

USE CHECKLISTS   Prepare a checklist for yourself. Perhaps make a version that you can give out to participants.

CHOOSE THE TIME AND PLACE WITH CARE

DEAL WITH POTENTIAL INTERRUPTIONS IN ADVANCE

IMPROVING MEETINGS

MAKE SURE THERE IS AN AGENDA, AND STICK TO IT   Try to get someone else to keep saying, "Let's move on," or "Let's stick to the agenda," unless you have real command of groups. Otherwise, you come off sounding like a nerd who wants to go by the book when one of the senior execs is telling everyone "the one about the one-legged sailor." Nevertheless, the agenda is not for nurds only. It really makes a difference in reducing wasted time and increasing efficiency.

IF YOU HAVE NOTHING TO CONTRIBUTE AND NOTHING IMPORTANT TO LEARN, STAY AWAY   And if you have done your part and feel that you are no longer needed, split. If it's your meeting, excuse anyone who is no longer needed. This way *you won't waste the time of others*, and they will respond better when you *do* need them.

EVERYONE AT THE MEETING SHOULD BE THERE FOR A PURPOSE   If this is the case, and it should be, make sure you involve everyone. This will help curtail boredom and make sure no one holds back a valuable contribution.

ENCOURAGE PEOPLE TO LISTEN

16

BE FIRM BUT TACTFUL IN DEALING WITH PROBLEM PERSON-
ALITIES:

The Negative Element
The Over-aggressor
The Introvert
The Attention Seeker
The Non Sequitur Specialist
The Lobbyist
Mr. Cool
Mr. Showbiz
The "Dirty Laundry" Man
The Bleeding Heart
The Devil's Advocate

ENCOURAGE THOSE WHO HELP THE MEETING PROGRESS:

Mr. Initiative
The Good Humor Man
The Opinion Leader
The Clarifier
The Elaborator
The Acid Tester
The Scrutinizer
The Compromiser

TELEPHONES

How ironic that a device that has saved the business community so
much time and money, eliminating unimportant correspondence and
business trips, has turned out to be the biggest time-waster of all.

As with the automobile, TV, and most other technological advances,
the danger lies in overuse.

THE DISEASE: TELEPHONE ABUSE

WE TALK TOO MUCH   At work, the phone is primarily a business
tool. It should be treated as such. Our calls last much longer than they
should.

WE CALL TOO OFTEN   Picking up the phone at the slightest whim is
a serious offense against your valuable time. It breaks your train of
thought and your work flow, and exposes that much more of your time
to situations you do not completely control. The party at the other end
may put you on hold, put you off, confuse you, abuse you, and mislead
you.

WE ARE UNABLE TO REGULATE THE INCOMING CALL PATTERN
If you are like most executives, you have at least two bosses—your immediate superior and the phone. When the phone summons, you answer. Ridiculous!

WE LACK THE SAVVY TO CUT A PHONE CALL SHORT AND BE NICE AT THE SAME TIME

THE CURE: CUTTING TELEPHONE TIME

By now you've probably figured out how to solve a few of these problems. Time management experts agree on how best to cut down on phone interruptions.

CALL LOG   Record incoming/outgoing; party/nature of call; length; time of day. Do this for a solid week, or for several days a week over a two- or three-week period. You'll be shocked at how much time you spend talking to your buddies about getting together over the weekend, and at how long it takes you to complete a call that was intended to get a simple yes or no answer to something.

CALL CLUSTERS   Placing and receiving calls is an activity unto itself. Block out a period of time each day for placing calls and, if possible, for receiving them. Some prefer early morning. Others late afternoon before quitting time. Or you can have two periods, early A.M. and late P.M. Calls that fill this period of clustered activity are not interruptions.

CALL SCREENING AND CALL-BACK   This requires a secretary. When you do not wish to be interrupted, tell your secretary to have the party call back, or take the number so that you may return the call when it is more convenient. Of course, make a priority list of individuals whose calls you will take under any circumstances. If this list is very long, then you are not being selective enough. If you trust your secretary's cordiality in requesting that an important person allow you to return his or her call, so much the better. A priority list should reflect urgency, not just rank. Only a very privileged few should have carte blanche access to your time.

Often, your secretary can provide the caller with the information required, thus eliminating the need for a call-back. If she says, "Perhaps I can help you," in many cases the caller will turn elsewhere to seek the information he's looking for and will therefore tell your secretary, "Never mind, I'll call so-and-so instead"; or "Never mind, I'll go look it up."

If you answer your own phones: Lots of executives prefer to answer their own phones. It allows them to maintain contact with what's going on at all levels of their business and gives their business associates a feeling of accessibility to the top. If you feel this way, by all means follow through, but remember that it will cost you in time. One compromise is a daily period for incoming calls: Have a secretary say that you take calls personally between nine and ten each morning. You'll get your share of inane calls, but at least they won't interrupt anything else.

SET THE TONE OF THE CONVERSATION AT THE START   Cut the bull and get down to it. If you start with pleasantries, you are opening Pandora's box. After the how-are-you's, say, "The reason I'm calling is ... " In some cases a simple "How are you?" is too much, because he'll actually tell you, in detail. There are those social critics who say our culture is in a sorry state when people ask how you are and don't really want to know. They may be right. My solution is don't ask if you don't want to know. If you say, "This'll only take a minute," then only take a minute. Don't be afraid to say, "Listen, Bill, I have only about five minutes to talk. If you need more time, let's talk later." Then, if the guy starts running off at the mouth, you have an out. "As I said, Bill—I'm in quite a rush, so let's continue this another time." One rule: Be nice! (But also be firm.)

Again, there are exceptions. Salesmen and politicians often claim that "talking it up" is part of their approach. They feel uncomfortable saying, "Hi. The reason I'm calling is to sell you a seventy-five-thousand-dollar computer." Okay. If you must chat, do so. But be aware of the problem and don't overdo it. Incidentally, I know several salesmen who use the straight-ahead "I'm out to sell you" approach quite effectively.

LEARN HOW TO CLOSE THE CALL   End it when you've accomplished the purpose. Don't be afraid to cut it off. Unless you are a shrink or a priest, you are not a confessor. A great trick (this will blow my cover) is to press the receiver button or cradle down while you are talking a blue streak. The other party won't be upset at you, because he'll think he's been cut off. He probably won't call back if it's just to make idle chatter. But safeguard against it by alerting your secretary to pick up the phone and tell him you've stepped away from your desk. Don't tell this to all your friends or it'll never work again.

DON'T DIAL YOUR OWN CALLS   Impersonal? Stuffy? Yes, but it's also a great time-saver, because frequently the person isn't in, or you've reached the wrong party and you must be transferred, or you're put on hold. To some, the words "Mr. Doe? Please hold. Mr. Smith calling" sound very impressive. Some others will be annoyed. But since you know who you want to reach, you are in control.

GET IT TOGETHER FIRST   Take a few minutes and outline, mentally or on paper, what you want to say or find out. Get the main points in so that you don't forget and have to call back.

PAY ATTENTION   Listen. Take notes if necessary. Get it right the first time. You'll sound more alert and attentive. You'll be more productive. And you won't have to call again to "double check." The "double-check" is, 80 percent of the time, simply a cover phrase for inattention or feeblemindedness.

DON'T KEEP PEOPLE WAITING   Their time is valuable, too. If you do it to them, they'll do it to you. It's a bad pattern to start. If you are victimized, hang up. If your party doesn't call back, try again later. It's less humiliating than wearing your neck out by cradling a phone in it, and it frees you to go back to your work.

CONSIDER THE NEW DEVICES   Don't go gadget crazy, but there is a wide range of telephone accessories—answering devices; automatic dialers; speaker phones; call timers; wireless phones—and many of them can be helpful. This will be discussed in a later chapter.

THE BEST WAY TO ELIMINATE
INTERRUPTIONS: THE HIDEOUT

If you've got some money to spend:

RENT A SMALL APARTMENT NEAR YOUR HOME OR OFFICE   Don't give out the address or phone, except to those who may need to reach you in an emergency. Or don't install a phone. If you carry a beeper, then you can call in when needed. Perhaps your company can cover the rent.

RENT A HOTEL OR MOTEL ROOM   This has certain advantages over an apartment. You can rent it only when you need it; besides, you get the use of room service, pool, sauna, and other conveniences, especially relaxing when you are holed up for several days.

RENT AN OFFICE FROM ANOTHER COMPANY   Just a small 9 x 12 where no one knows you and no one cares.

If you don't have money to spend:

WORK AT HOME A DAY OR TWO A WEEK   But don't tell many people, or you'll get those calls at home.

WORK IN YOUR CAR   Drive it to a secluded spot, take a clipboard and a pocket dictation unit, and you're all set.

USE THE LIBRARY   Great place. Everyone minds his own business and you are unlikely to get into distracting conversations.

IF YOU ARE REALLY HARD UP, TRY THE REST ROOM   Several

executives I know consider this the place for mind-busting reading and thinking. A bathroom stall has an inner-sanctum feeling.

RELIGIOUS RETREAT HOUSES For a very reasonable fee you can stay at a rectory or some such place. Your room will be stark, but the setting is usually idyllic country beauty and the atmosphere is very calming.

SUGGEST THAT YOUR COMPANY DESIGNATE AN EMPTY OFFICE AS A QUIET ROOM Unfortunately, it may not be vacant when you need it the most.

THE PERMISSIBLE INTERRUPTION: THE BREAK

Stopping work because of a drop-in visitor, phone call, or other distraction is clearly unproductive. But regular, self-imposed breaks can be extremely valuable. Research has shown that short interruptions leading to higher recall of material. Five- to ten-minute breaks are best.

THE TYRANNY OF THE URGENT

"We live in constant tension between the urgent and the important," wrote Charles Hummel. "The problem is that the important tasks rarely must be done today, or even this week. The urgent task calls for instant action—endless demands pressure every hour and day."*

You have your day planned, and it's beautiful. Everything's rolling along on schedule; everything's going to get done. Then it hits: the urgent; the unexpected. The crisis. Suddenly the day is no longer beautiful. The meetings get canceled. Paperwork is put aside. Those important calls never get made. Your excuse? "There was an emergency and I had to deal with it."

The lure of the crisis is almost irresistible, because it demands your immediate attention. But in retrospect, it is the high-priority items that count. The real danger in such a situation is that the urgent matters tend to assert priority over the important, instead of the other way around.

There's not much you can do about this except exercise good judgment: *Think before you throw things aside to attend to a "crisis."* Can you let the crisis work itself out? Is there someone else who can handle

---

*Charles Hummel, *Tyranny of the Urgent* (Chicago: Intervarsity Press, 1967) quoted in R. Alec Mackenzie's *Time Management* (Greenwich, NY: Alec Mackenzie and Associates, 1976), p.58

it? What will be the repercussions if you let a crisis persist versus the repercussions if you interrupt your priorities?

PLAN AHEAD It's amazing how many problems can be avoided when you have considered in advance how to deal with them. Keep careful records and thorough notes to avoid forgetting anything that is routine now, but could turn into a crisis if neglected until the last minute. More often than not, the roots of crisis lie in routine tasks.

DON'T PANIC Under pressure, the natural thing to do is to act to eliminate whatever is exerting the pressure. But remember—the thing causing the pressure isn't necessarily the most important thing you could be attending to at the time. Once you realize that urgency is not necessarily synonymous with priority, you will feel less pressure.

FORMULATE CONTINGENCY PLANS Whenever you are involved in something the outcome of which is uncertain (that covers just about everything), consider what you will do if it doesn't work out as you plan. Developing contingencies involves time and effort, but the consequences can be grave if you don't have them to fall back on. And as a result of your efforts to come up with a contingency, you might discover a new and better way of doing things.

PROCRASTINATION

I put off writing this section for quite a while. No kidding. But if any area requires biting the bullet, procrastination is it. Management experts have few pearls of wisdom to offer here, and the reason is apparent to any amateur analyst: *Procrastination is primarily a psychological problem,* symptomatic of some glitch in our personalities. In some people the result is a general problem, while in others, just a tendency to postpone certain tasks or responsibilities.

Depressed people procrastinate a lot. Those who hate to say no will often put off that nay-saying phone call.

If procrastination is a truly debilitating problem that has been affecting your performance, you must do something about it before it's too late.

You might consider one of the many methods of self-improvement, from TM to psychotherapy. You choose.

FOR RELIEF OF MILD PROCRASTINATION SYMPTOMS

In many cases procrastination is far less serious than a personality disorder. It is merely the bad habit of putting off something unpleasant, or what grandma would call "just plain laziness." Here, time management experts such as Alan Lakein and Edwin Bliss have been helpful with a few clever little strategies for psyching yourself up (or out?) and plowing into action. Here are the best:*

DIVIDE AND CONQUER If you have taken to procrastinating because of the sheer awesomeness of the task before you, break it up into smaller, less unwieldy jobs that don't leave you weak in the knees. Once you start accumulating small victories and accomplishments, you'll be on your way. Momentum is the buzzword for this feeling.

This method is referred to by Bliss as the "Salami Technique" (because you slice up the task like a salami) and by Lakein as the "Swiss Cheese Method" (because you bore small holes in the big job). Cute.

THE BALANCE-SHEET METHOD This method, so named by Bliss, is essentially an exercise in self-humiliation. This may be just what the doctor ordered. Get a sheet of paper and make a balance sheet. One side of the sheet is for all the wonderful things that will result if you do this job now. The other side is for listing all the reasons why you're putting it off. If there are solid, concrete reasons for postponing the job, they will show up clearly. But if you are simply procrastinating, the reasons for putting if off will look pretty silly when compared with the benefits of completing it. If the balance sheet fails to reveal good reasons for doing the job now, you should question whether the job is worth doing at all. Nothing saves time like eliminating work.

The chief advantage of this method is in seeing all the lily-livered, lame excuses you have for procrastinating. The effects are often very dramatic. Executives have been known to go to their windows and shout, "Man the battle stations," "I've not yet begun to fight," or, my favorite, "Whatever could be done tomorrow should be done today."

BITE THE BULLET Unfortunately, as time management expert Michael LeBoeuf points out, the "divide and conquer" technique won't help you when you are putting off a one-shot task like firing your secretary; I don't recommend firing someone over a week's time, five minutes a day. And when you've got to report disappointing sales figures to your boss, there doesn't appear to be much sense in bothering with the "balance sheet" method. You have to do it, and you needn't waste time convincing yourself.

Biting the bullet is for the time when you must be bold. It's not so bad. Everyone jumps into a cold swimming pool once in a while.

PRIORITIZE Do the important things first. Learn to assign priorities and organize your work so that you give the greatest and most immediate attention to the most important jobs. If you've got to take the heat because something isn't done, at least make sure it's minor. You want to be known as someone who always comes through on the big

---

*Reprinted, with permission, from *How to Get Control of Your Time and Your Life,* by Alan Lakein, Copyright © 1973 by Alan Lakein. Published by David McKay.

ones. That's where you make your reputation—not by accomplishing lots of little things that don't matter much.

AVOID THE PERFECTIONISM TRAP   That's when you never finish anything because you are never satisfied. If you are obsessive about a project, it could be that you are trying to delay moving on to the next—more difficult or unpleasant—task. Or trying to put off the discomfort associated with being judged on your work.

The way to avoid this is to set standards of performance, both at the company level and the individual level. "In our company, we don't want memos that are great works of literature," says one chief executive. "We discourage even the excessive correction of typos in interoffice communication. On the other hand, I get terribly annoyed at the sight of a misspelled word or outdated statistics on an important report. If it happens often, I'll call the perpetrator on the carpet."

Know how good the job must be, and when you reach that level, move on. The points you might gain for that little bit extra might very well be offset by a reputation for being slow and unable to let go of something.

DO IT RIGHT THE FIRST TIME   So many things must be done a second or third time simply because there is a lack of understanding between you and your superiors about what the project is all about. Make sure you get it straight. And keep the lines of communication open throughout the project.

If you find that you are doing things over because you have overlooked items the first time around, you might consider using checklists and taking better notes. If you plan to rely on your memory, make sure it's reliable.

SET DEADLINES   It is difficult to conceptualize a task without placing it in some sort of time frame. You can set a deadline for practically anything. Use every means, including the above techniques, to get things in on time.

LATENESS

Lateness has become an epidemic in a country where punctuality is considered a virtue. In some cultures lateness is not only accepted, but encouraged. But in the United States, it has always been an indication of poor character. "Punctuality" appears on every school child's report card.

So why are there so many Johnny- and Janey-come-latelys in the U.S.? Perhaps, like other puritan ethics, punctuality is considered old-fashioned. If adultery is on the rise, what chance does being on time have?

There could be other reasons. The deterioration of essential services in some of our larger cities makes it difficult to get something or somebody to another place. And the proliferation of the computer—intelligence that never sleeps—means that traditional time limits, such as those set for banking and regular mail deliveries, have less meaning.

Do not be fooled into thinking that being late will have no consequences. Nobody likes to be kept waiting. And during the time a person spends waiting for you, he is likely to be thinking about all your negative traits. He will not be in a good frame of mind when you arrive.

Remember the days when the person would worry about your well-being when you were late, because it was "not like you"?

Being prompt has class. It shows respect for others and is just plain good business. When you arrive is as much a part of your initial impression as what you are wearing.

HOW TO BE ON TIME

ASSUME AND PREPARE FOR THE WORST This is Murphy's Law applied to lateness. If it takes ten minutes to get somewhere, allow more time than that. You just never know when they will start construction on Washington Street, or when a truck will turn over on the freeway. Sure, if things go smoothly, you might arrive early. But if you think that this will make you look overeager, you can always stop into a nearby coffee shop and read or do some light work. (Always carry some reading and/or light work with you—not only for the times when you arrive early, but also for the times *you* are kept waiting.)

DEFINE YOUR TERMS If you mean "around three," make it clear that you mean "approximately three," "between 2:30 and three," etc., not "exactly three." Giving an approximate time of arrival is usually acceptable when the other party is at home or in his office and there is always something to do until you arrive. It is not okay if the person has a tight schedule—for example, another appointment at 3:30.

IF YOU ARE GOING TO BE LATE, CALL

IF YOU HAVE TROUBLE GAUGING TIME, USE A TIMING DEVICE THAT SIGNALS WHEN YOU MUST GO And follow it religiously. Many of the newer electronic watches come with alarm functions. So do many pocket calculators.

LEARN HOW TO END A PREVIOUS ENGAGEMENT IN SUFFICIENT TIME This is not as simple as it sounds. It involves setting priorities, because you may wish to keep a less important party waiting while you finish up with a more important one. Don't do this often. Most VIPs will respect your desire to be prompt in meeting with your next visitor. If you are late, the person cooling his heels will feel that you don't consider his time as valuable, and he will reflect that perception in his dealings.

AVOID, AT ALL COSTS, MEETING SOMEONE IN FRONT OF SOMEPLACE   If one of you is late, the other will be obliged to stand there waiting. It is difficult, if not impossible, to make use of that time.

IN ADVANCE, FIGURE OUT HOW MUCH TIME AN APPOINTMENT WILL TAKE   Then, allow at least 30 percent more. This applies even to getting out of the house in the morning. One industrial psychologist told me that I would be amazed at how many people are late because they spent ten minutes wrestling with a cowlick, trying to hide a blemish, or picking out a tie. Naturally, people don't confess to such things, so they are forced to lie, making some incredible remark about the traffic.

IF YOU SEE THAT YOUR SCHEDULE IS TOO TIGHT, CHANGE IT IN ADVANCE   Give yourself some room.

START LEAVING A MEETING BEFORE IT'S TIME TO LEAVE   You need a few extra minutes to work your way out the door. If you wait to the last minute to say, "I must be going," you may find yourself sitting back down to hear the last few points the party was saving for the end.

LEARN YOUR ENVIRONMENT   How long does it take to get there? By bus? Rail? Cab? Get the lowdown on making time from the natives. For example, New Yorkers know that you've got to allow time to hail a cab, as well as time to reach your destination. In the rush hour, or in the rain, getting a cab can take almost as long as the ride itself.

DON'T MAKE PROMISES THAT YOU CAN'T KEEP   Be realistic. And if you see that you have overcommitted yourself, let the parties involved in on the situation.

AVOID REPEAT PERFORMANCES   If you are late for a meeting once, don't let it happen again with the same party. Such behavior tends to form patterns. The sooner you break it, the better. What's more, the other party will form a pattern of his own, and begin to classify you as "always late." Once he does, that reputation will be very hard to break.

IF YOU ARE ABSOLUTELY HOPELESS

CARRY A BEEPER   And have your secretary beep you before each appointment.

ASK THE OTHER PARTY IF HE WOULD MIND CALLING TO RECONFIRM ON THE DAY OF THE APPOINTMENT

PSYCH YOURSELF OUT   You'll need the help of your secretary: Have her set appointments for you. Sometimes you will be given the actual time of the appointment. Sometimes you will be given a time that is anywhere from five to fifteen minutes early. This unpredictable schedule will keep you on your toes. You will never know whether you are arriving early or on time. So it will be tough to cheat.

IDENTIFY THE UNDERLYING PSYCHOLOGICAL REASONS FOR CHRONIC LATENESS:

- fear of being early and having nothing to do
- poor judgment of time
- disorganization
- lack of respect for the other party
- little value placed on promptness
- "subconscious" reasons, such as lateness as a form of aggressive behavior

How far inside yourself you need to go in order to solve this problem is something only you can determine. Base your decision not only on the severity of the problem, but on the potential damage to your career. In some situations lateness does not matter as much as in others. A film star who is constantly late on the set will eventually cost the studio many thousands of dollars in resulting production schedule overruns. Very few can afford to do this repeatedly and expect to work. But in some professions, only deadlines are important—not punctuality.

INEFFECTIVE DELEGATION

The ability to delegate is an essential ingredient of effective time management. Many of us feel that we got where we are on our own merits and are therefore reluctant to place even a tiny sliver of our fates in someone else's hands. Then there are those who are arrogant enough to believe that nobody else can do the job. Often, this is just a way of masking an insecurity—the fear of being shown up. When this problem is taken to extremes, we can wind up victims of *reverse delegation*, in which we take on the work of subordinates.

All of these attitudes are distinct liabilities. There is virtually unanimous agreement that without some form of delegation, proper use of time is impossible. Equally important is the *skill* of delegating. It's one thing to decide to delegate tasks and responsibilities. It's quite another to make it work.

HOW TO DELEGATE

FIND THE RIGHT PERSON FOR THE JOB The right person isn't always the most obvious, the most available, or even the most qualified. There may be someone highly motivated, with lots of drive, who will get excited about the task. Often, such a person will outperform a more experienced person who might be passive or even resentful about the task.

ONCE YOU'VE CHOSEN THE PERSON, MAKE SURE HE IS PROPERLY OUTFITTED   Supply aids to doing the job well—resources, contacts, advice, a budget.

MAKE SURE YOU ARE ON THE SAME WAVELENGTH   What exactly is it you want done? What is your subordinate's accountability? What are the limits and breadth of his responsibility? Make it all clear at the beginning. It will save you a lot of heartache.

STROKE   Give credit where and when it is merited. It's simple human nature: People like to receive recognition for a job well done. But you should mean it. Insincere praise backfires, because the subordinate will think you are being obsequious, or substituting praise for a raise or bonus.

TRUST   Give your delegatee a vote of confidence. Understand that he may disagree with you, or even go wrong. That's the chance you take. Outwardly demand perfection; but remind yourself nobody's perfect, and don't be unreasonable.

BEWARE OF REVERSE DELEGATION   This occurs when the person you are delegating the job is able to get *you* to do the job. Sometimes it's that one adorable, sweet, lovable person you just can't say no to. Sometimes it's the one who says he needs advice, who flatters you into helping him by making you feel needed. If you're not careful, you'll wind up doing his work as well as your own—and praising him for its quality. Know where to draw the line.

ACCEPT RESPONSIBILITY   That is one thing you cannot delegate. It's your decision to assign the task, and you have got to take the heat. Funny how these things work. If you are called in to get praise heaped upon you, it always looks gracious to say, "Well, I had some terrific help," or "My staff deserves most of the credit," or "It was a team effort." But if you get called on the carpet and say, "Well, it was Spofford's fault, he's so sloppy," or "I'm having trouble getting a competent staff together," you are digging yourself a big hole in which you may get buried. Better off getting your head bloodied. The cowboys in the boardrooms love the spirit of the rugged individualist, the leader. Don't overdo it by taking the rap for everything, though.

BE A NICE PERSON   Remember Captain Bligh? Well, this ain't the navy, and you're not at war. When you want something done, ask; don't bark orders. Be courteous to those who treat you with respect. Just because you are a higher-up in your company doesn't mean that you are worth more as a human being. The only time you should pull rank is when being nice doesn't work. You'll know when that happens, and it won't be often.

LAY YOUR CARDS ON THE TABLE   Don't hold back. Make sure your subordinate knows what is expected, and how to go about it. If there are certain caveats connected with the task, such as keeping something confidential or avoiding a confrontation with Mr. X, say so. If possible, say why you want this job done, how it fits into your overall scheme, and what the consequences will be. The more your appointee knows, the less often he'll have to say to others, "I'll have to get back to you on that one." It also allows him to think on his feet.

Occasionally I receive calls from business associates to discuss the price of a service and the person delegated to speak with me is empowered only to make *the offer*, not to negotiate; in fact, quite often he doesn't know what kind of compromise his boss would accept. Not only does that annoy me, but it makes him look like a lackey, and I quickly demand to speak to the boss. You can bet that this gentleman resents his boss more than he resents me.

FOLLOW UP   Make sure that the job gets done—on time, correctly. Don't leave your subordinate hanging. It's a good idea to set a time to discuss the job with him. I've been in situations in which I tried to discuss a particular job with a superior and was told, "Handle it." So I would. Six months later, the guy would barge into my office, his blood pressure so high I could hear the blood coursing through his veins, to tell me that I hadn't done that job right, and what was the matter with me. *He* was to blame.

LEAVE THE GUY ALONE   You gave him the job, now let him do it. If you trust him—and if you don't, what's he doing on your staff?—give him the chance to prove himself.

GO SLOW   It takes years to acquire the judgment to delegate effectively. For your sake and his, go slow with every subordinate. Don't start dumping stuff on him out of the clear blue. Let him know that you want to start delegating, ask him how he feels about it, and control the flow. Give him a chance to get in the groove.

BE SELECTIVE IN WHAT YOU DELEGATE   Ask yourself if the task at hand is an appropriate one for delegation. Delegation can be overdone, possibly creating the impression that you don't want to get your hands dirty.

DELEGATE IN ADVANCE   Let the subordinate know what kinds of things you'll be wanting him to handle, rather than waiting for the job to come along and prompt the thought, "Aha, this is just what I want to give to Arnold. Send him in." Arnold will be more prepared if he knows what kind of work has his name on it.

DON'T JUST DELEGATE THE DULL OR THE DIRTY   Some guys think that subordinates exist primarily to do their busy-work. They save all the plums for themselves. This is such a rotten way to do things, nothing more need be said. If you delegate some of the more stimulating and challenging jobs, it will be easier to get top-drawer performances from your staff.

POOR PLANNING

This problem is self-evident, and symptomatic of the entire time management problem. Objectives? Formulate them carefully and clearly. Priorities? Set them. Planning? Always plan. This is primarily an analytical function—learning to deal with certain variables, assigning values to them, putting them in order, and identifying the essence of the task. You learned this in school if you took philosophy, mathematics, logic, or any science. It's just that nobody told you it had anything to do with everyday business. If you learned anything in college, you learned to be critical of fallacious arguments; of unethical policies; of ineffective strategies. So, use your mind.

TAKING ON TOO MUCH

This problem is almost always self-generated, and it is intimately bound up with attitudes toward work. Often, we have a desire to "make up for lost time," or feel that by taking on that much work, we will get ahead that much faster. Whether it is driving ambition, a healthy success orientation, or an insecurity or need for approval, the effect is often the same—taking on too much at once. Realize that *the amount of things that one is handling at any given time often bears no fruitful relationship to overall productivity.* Don't overburden yourself; you'll end up doing lots of things in a mediocre manner, but nothing well.

SYMPTOMS

Overeagerness to assume new tasks translates into some behavioral quirks at the job:

POOR ESTIMATION OF TIME   We want to take on this job so badly that we underestimate how much time it will take, or how much time we'll need for the other tasks we have. Research has shown that, on the whole, jobs take longer than most executives estimate they will take. So allow more time—*give yourself a cushion*, even if you have to pass on something in order to create that cushion.

HYPERRESPONSIVITY   That's when you respond to all and everything that comes your way. It's nice to champ at the bit, but don't overdo it. And if you do take on something, *give what is needed or what is asked for.* Don't overwork the assignment. *Volume is often a negative rather than a positive, because the superior has to cope with unnecessary detail and increased paperwork.*

POOR PRIORITIZING You can't decide what's most important, so you approach everything with equal weight.

JUST CAN'T SAY NO

Like procrastination, this is largely a personality problem, and a serious one. The inability to say no is obviously a major root cause of another time-waster, "attempting too many things at once."

MAJOR CAUSES

LACK OF CONFIDENCE AND ASSERTIVENESS You may wish to engage in assertiveness training, TA, est, or whatever you feel will help you become more confident and self-assertive.

BEING TOO NICE One of the more positive aspects of our Judeo-Christian culture is the overall emphasis on being "nice," being generous, and helping thy neighbor. But this may be taken too far, leading to a distorted view of what it means to be a nice person and continual effort to go to great lengths to avoid offending people.

If you are a nice, cooperative, helpful person, there is no reason to feel that you betray that self-image every time you say no.

THE NEED TO FEEL USEFUL Many executives encourage others to ask for help solely because of the ego boost it gives. This signifies insecurity.

THE DESIRE TO AVOID CONFRONTATION AND/OR UNPLEAS-ANTNESS Saying yes is so much easier. And less risky.

MAJOR SOLUTIONS

In this book we can't examine these personality problems in depth, but we can attack this particular hangup in a few practical ways:

IF YOU ARE THINKING "NO," DON'T HESITATE Say it right away, before your ambivalence betrays you and gives someone a chance to apply pressure. A quick "no" will often convey that it's useless to argue or brown-nose.

EXPECT TO SAY NO SEVERAL TIMES A DAY—THIS IS YOUR SOLEMN RIGHT When it happens, you won't be surprised and tinged with guilt, because you've already come to terms with it.

BE CIVIL, POLITE, AND UNDERSTANDING Find alternative ways

of helping others with their problems, such as referrals or suggestions on how they might handle the problems themselves.

DON'T GET DEFENSIVE AND MAKE EXCUSES   Easier said than done, but try. Being defensive is so common in business circles that even when you aren't being defensive, people will accuse you of it. Be nice, but be firm. And never waver.

IF YOU WANT TO SAY NO AND CAN'T THINK OF A VALID REASON, EITHER DON'T OFFER ONE OR REMAIN SILENT UNTIL YOU CAN THINK OF ONE   Saying "yes" to fill a void is the real sucker's way out.

THE UNIVERSAL ANTIDOTE: YOUR SENSE OF HUMOR

A funny is great when you are in a tough spot. If you are trying to get someone to leave your office, it's always better to send him out laughing. If you can't say a flat-out "no" to a person, why not disarm him with a witticism?

But what if you aren't funny, or have a tendency to put your foot in your mouth? What if you overdo it—too much sarcasm? The results can be fatal. So if you can't do the humor thing well, don't do it at all. Practice at home.

SCHEDULING: THE TO DO LIST

The need to sketch out a plan for the day's activities is so obvious it hardly needs mentioning. As schoolkids we wrote down our home-work assignments at the end of each day as a reminder. And most executives write reminders in their diaries, calendars, and planners.

REMINDING IS DIFFERENT FROM PLANNING

So from now on, when you scribble in your list of things to do, keep these points in mind:

SET PRIORITIES   Take several minutes to consider what must be done tomorrow and what is most important in the long run. You'll need this information to schedule your day sensibly.

SCHEDULE   Have a deliberate order for your tasks. Try to tackle the most important things first.

BEWARE OF THE "SMALL THINGS" SYNDROME   Don't fill up precious time with a collection of small things to get out of the way before taking on the major jobs. It's the easiest way to eat up your day without accomplishing anything significant. Contrary to the opinions

---

of most management experts, though, I think it's okay to warm up with a little thing—something that will sharpen your mind, get you in focus, and give you a sense of accomplishment without taking up much time—in short, an aid to psyching yourself up. Example: a short, clever "complaint" letter. A goodwill note to a client. Or compute your sales record, when you know all along it's going to be sensational.

LOOK FOR THINGS TO DELEGATE   Just because an item appears on your To Do list doesn't mean that *you* have to do it. It simply means that you must see that it *gets done*. If at all possible, find somebody else.

YOUR MIND, YOUR BODY, AND YOUR SCHEDULE

"Each person with a little introspection can begin to sense his own inner timing—hunger contractions, the chill of dropping temperature, the quality of fresh vigor, emotional ebullience or anxiety and irritation. An hour-by-hour evaluation of mood, alertness, and sensations will begin to give each person the shape of his daily changes."*

Nobody in the business community is likely to argue with you if you were to point out that every individual has a different personality, intellectual approach, and perception of the environment in which one works. To a large degree, this diversity is what makes a successful company tick. However, most of us do not realize that there are significant differences in physiological functioning from individual to individual. Not everyone is "sharp" at the same time; not everyone is able to sustain complete concentration for hours. Some can go fifteen minutes at a stretch, but do it several times a day. Some are intellectually useless after two P.M. And some don't have any real energy or drive until mid-morning.

These physiological differences are due to a wide variety of variables—hormonal, genetic, nutritional, metabolic, biochemical, sleep related, and environmental. *The important thing is that you should become aware of your own patterns.* Careful scrutiny of the time log should help. When making entries, note your mood (grouchy/feeling great; confident/dull; mind wanders/sharp/focused) and your physical feelings (sluggish; tired; bloated from lunch; energized, relaxed, calm). Patterns will emerge that reflect your energy levels, mental and physical peaks, and the kinds of activities that have positive or negative effects.

*From *Body Time: Physiological Rhythms and Social Stress* by Gay Gaer Luce, Copyright © 1971 by Gay Gaer Luce. Reprinted by permission of Pantheon Books, a division of Random House, Inc.

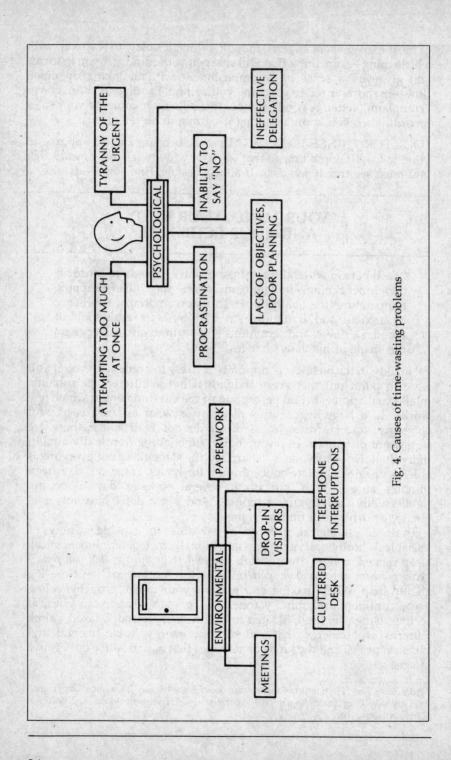

Fig. 4. Causes of time-wasting problems

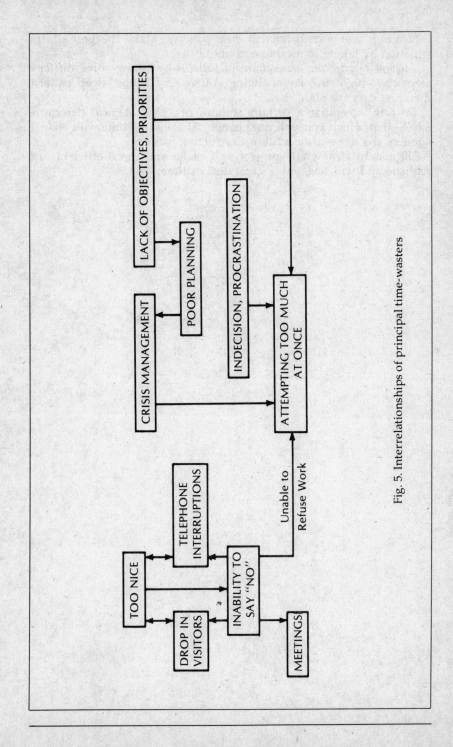

Fig. 5. Interrelationships of principal time-wasters

Structure your activity around these patterns. Make the best of the situation by taking them into account.

Attempt to alter the more awkward patterns by taking some difficult steps that might involve changing your eating habits, sleep pattern, diet, and exercise plan.

Do both, accepting a certain amount of "physiological determinism"—that which you will not change. At the same time, you change some of the more distasteful or destructive patterns.

Ultimately, this whole project will make you more efficient and realistic and will save you a great deal of time.

3
THE PAPERWORK PROBLEM

Everyone agrees that there is simply too much paper floating around the American business community. If the pile on your desk or in the mail won't tell you, take a long look at the way things are done in your office.

SYMPTOMS

Copier consciousness. One "coffee boy" told me that by parking his coffee-and-donuts wagon by the copier of a large office, he did a larger business than he did during coffee breaks. Take a look at your bills for paper, toner, and repair if you need confirmation of this tale.

Formulosis. I'm not sure who invented the standard form, but I'll bet his or her intention was to *reduce paperwork*. And in fact, if forms are used properly, they will save time and paper. Unfortunately, the federal government has managed to turn a bright idea into a blight—and many companies have followed suit. Are there standard forms in your firm that leave you at a loss to explain their value?

Typing backlog. Does the wait to get something typed remind you of the wait for gasoline in the summer of '79? If so, it could be that your typists are slow, inefficient, or overloaded with work, but it could well be because they are processing too much unnecessary wordage. The belief is that typing equals official and businesslike. But remember there are times when a handwritten note has more class and warmth. Use the phone more often. With the cost of a page of typing over $12, a phone call, unless it's to Peking, is almost certainly going to be cheaper and faster.

Reading yourself to sleep in your own office. Do you find that the most useless, irrelevant information crosses your desk, requiring your initials? You probably assume it's coming from the higher-ups. Maybe. But maybe it's some exec trying to make points by showing how on-top-of-things he is. If you'd rather he keep his statistics on paper clip usage and his Vince Lombardi-type "win" pep talk quotes to himself, say so.

You can't always get what you want. You ask for an important file. But you get a file that is worthless. Or a file so thick that it takes fifteen minutes to find what you're looking for—and you with only three minutes to read it. Files shouldn't be like gold mines, where you have to move tons of useless earth to find a precious little bit of ore. Files should be like bank vaults, holding only the stuff that counts.

Clerical glut. Is everyone's nephew or niece working at your place during the summers and after school? How many clerks do you need, anyway? They may be busy filing and all, but what if they are spending all day processing unproductive paper? Better check.

Document fever. Documents, reports, and memos about everything. Are they really necessary? Especially if they're thick, reports impress people; they show that the author did lots of work. But reports should have an objective—one achieved as efficiently as possible. *That's* what should be impressive.

Too many files. We run out of space, we buy more files. Right? A waste of space, a waste of money. If you have a business that necessitates a steady increase of its volume of filed material, consider the many space-saving alternatives, such as micrographics and microforms (see Chapter 34), or frequently purge the files of obsolete or other unnecessary paper.

THE PAPER TEST: SHOULD THIS PAPER BE CREATED?

---

1. *What is its purpose?*
2. *How will it be used, and where is it going?* Perhaps a call or a short memo would work better.
3. *Do I plan to put the right amount of information in the document?* Too much is waste of time and paper. Too little means that you may have to do it all over again, but more thoroughly.
4. *Is it redundant?* Can the information be found elsewhere with little time and effort?
5. *Is this the best time?* Or will you have to summarize the situation again later?

---

6. *Can this task be accomplished in a paperless manner?*
7. *What happens to the paper after it is read?* If you have ideas, include them: "File under . . ." or "You may discard," for example.
8. *Can we do without this?* The bottom line.

THE CULPRITS

The Creator.* In principle, there's nothing wrong with someone creating paperwork. But if the person is on a power trip, thinks he's the literary light of the office, or, even worse, is insecure enough to think that his work will be evaluated by the volume of paper he produces, he's a serious problem.

Trevor Bentley has isolated three types of dementia that, personified, result in uncontrolled paper.

Memo Man. Inarticulate, so uses memos to cover it up.

Bookworm. Likes words and numbers. Compulsive about writing everything down. This is the guy who used to copy every word the teacher said in class, but usually didn't do so hot.

The Copier Freak. To some, copiers are like motorcycles, fast cars, or even drugs. They love using them, and they'll use any excuse. They love the bright yellow-green light, the moaning noise, the smell of the chemicals.

The Reader. He's got to read absolutely everything that crosses his desk. He's afraid he'll miss something. As a result he is not selective in his reading and wastes lots of time. He subscribes to mailbags full of magazines, newsletters, and brochures, making for lots of clutter.

The Checker. Has to check and double-check everything before it goes out. Finding errors isn't always cost effective. Sometimes it takes more time than it's worth. How important is a typo in an interoffice memo? Years ago someone invented spot checking and sampling. It works quite well to keep people on their toes—and their work accurate.

The Converter. He takes statistics broken down by month and breaks them down by year. If he doesn't like metric, he'll convert to pounds, inches and quarts. He's a specialist in the kind of work known as NVA—No Value Added.

The Filer. This is usually a team effort. First there's *the one who creates*

---

*This "paperworker" and the others that follow were so named by Trevor J. Bentley in *Information, Communication, and the Paperwork Explosion* (Maidenhead, England: McGraw-Hill, 1976), pp. 15–30.

---

the file in the first place. Then there's *the person who actually does the filing*. The file maker often uses a system that only he can understand, or that follows rules of logic so obscure that the clerical staff would have to be trained at Scotland Yard to follow the clues. The file "stasher" takes the blame for lost files when it is often not his fault. Or, on the other hand, he may file an item under a heading that an executive might never think of checking. It is estimated that 20 percent of all clerical activity is spent in filing, 15 percent in retrieving.

The Destroyer. This is the one who goes too far. The joy of clearing a paper-filled desk, of moving through documents and consigning most of them to the wastebasket, gives him or her the exhilarating feeling of a job well done. Often, however, items that are important to others get pitched, because *the destroyer, in his zeal, forgets to check with others.* If there is something in dispute that requires referral to written documentation, keep the document away from a destroyer.

The Fountain of Knowledge. This one can be very dangerous—the person who feels personally slighted if he doesn't know absolutely everything going on in the office. "Why wasn't I told?" is his favorite expression. Often, he will go to improper lengths to find out what's going on, reading communications of a confidential nature, for instance, or glancing over memos on someone's desk when that person is at lunch or a meeting.

THE CLUTTERED DESK

Before I suggest to you what should be on your desk, or even what a desk is for, let's dwell on what to remove from your desk. For this exercise you will need:

- *at least one large trash can.* If you are into recycling paper, get a smaller can as well for nonpaper items.
- *a table or other large surface.* You will need this to sift through the mountains of junk that you probably have in and on your desk.
- *file folders*
- *file cabinet,* if your desk drawer doesn't have one built in
- *a few storage boxes*

Scan for known garbage. This is junk mail, candy wrappers, last week's papers and last month's magazines, and anything else that is sitting on your desk which you have already sentenced to become part of a landfill. Just remind yourself that it feels so good to throw things away! Savor the experience; enjoy it to the fullest.

Now you should feel euphoric and ready to move on to the next step.

Dump everything from the top of your desk onto the table or other surface, and add the contents of your desk drawers. Obviously, be careful with vases, full ashtrays, etc. Disgusting, isn't it, all that junk?

Eliminate. When in doubt, throw it out. Believe me, you don't need most of what is there unless you've been extremely vigilant already. And if that is the case, your desk isn't cluttered, so you don't need to do this exercise. Sorry.

Sort. Now you've thrown out what's not needed, *make piles according to category.* There are several ways to do this sorting procedure: by subject, by category, or by recent/dated. You will be filing from these piles. Some of the material may belong in your desk drawer file for ready access; other material is to be kept for records only and will probably not be needed, except in the case of such events as an IRS audit or an insurance claim.

File. Yes. But as you hit each file folder, make sure that nothing in it can be pitched. Over 90 percent of filed material over a year old is never referred to. If it's legal and/or financial, you might want to hold on to it. If not, throw it out.

ORGANIZING YOUR DESK

A desk is a work space, or, more accurately, a work tool. It should be styled that way and not as a storage depot for papers, food, books, what-have-you. Your desk should contain only those things specifically related to your day's work, and items you will use to enhance overall performance.

Do not put things on your desk because you feel that you will be reminded to attend to them. This doesn't work. Soon a pile of things not to be forgotten develops and the pile must be sifted to find that item—that is, if you remember to look for it. Another hitch: If the memory-jogging effect does succeed, it is likely to distract you or break your train of thought, because every time you look up, there's that paper beckoning to you.

Purge your desk of various useless items. It's not a museum, a window display, a souvenir shop, a trophy case, a photography exhibit, a retrospective of the past ten years of your life, or your equivalent of King Tut's tomb. Therefore, remove various awards, gift paperweights, pen-and-pencil sets that you don't use, too many pictures, etc.

LEGEND FOR AUTHORITY TO DISPOSE	LEGEND FOR RETENTION PERIOD
AD—Administrative Decision	AC—Dispose After Completion of Job or Contract
ASPR—Armed Services Procurement Regulation	AE—Dispose After Expiration
CFR—Code of Federal Regulations	AF—After End of Fiscal Year
FLSA—Fair Labor Standards Act	AM—After Moving
ICC—Interstate Commerce Commission	AS—After Settlement
	AT—Dispose After Termination
INS—Insurance Company Regulation	ATR—After Trip
	OBS—Dispose When Obsolete
ISM—Industrial Security Manual, Attachment to DD Form 441	P—Permanent
	SUP—Dispose When Superseded

*After Disposed   **Normally   †Govt. R&D Contracts

TYPE OF RECORD	RETENTION PERIOD YEARS	AUTHORITY
ACCOUNTING & FISCAL		
Accounts Payable Invoices	3	ASPR-STATE, FLSA
Accounts Payable Ledger	P	AD
Accounts Receivable Ledgers	5	AD
Authorizations for Accounting	SUP	AD
Balance Sheets	P	AD
Bank Deposits	3	AD
Bank Statements	3	AD
Bonds	P	AD
Budgets	3	AD
Capital Asset Record	3*	AD
Cash Receipt Records	7	AD
Check Register	P	AD
Checks, Dividend	6	
Checks, Payroll	2	FLSA, STATE
Checks, Voucher	3	FLSA, STATE
Cost Accounting Records	5	AD
Earnings Register	3	FLSA, STATE
Entertainment Gifts & Gratuities	3	AD
Estimates, Projections	7	AD
Expense Reports	3	AD
Financial Statements, Certified	P	AD

Fig. 6. Records retention timetable
This table can be used as a guide to how long to save records.
(*through page 46*)

From "Records Retention Timetable" (New York:
Electric Wastebasket Corp., 1977). Reprinted courtesy of
Electric Wastebasket Corp., New York, NY 10036.

TYPE OF RECORD	RETENTION PERIOD YEARS	AUTHORITY
Financial Statements, Periodic	2	AD
General Ledger Records	P	CFR
Labor Cost Records	3	ASPR, CFR
Magnetic Tape and Tab Cards	1**	
Note Register	P	AD
Payroll Registers	3	FLSA, STATE
Petty Cash Records	3	AD
P & L Statements	P	AD
Salesman Commission Reports	3	AD
Travel Expense Reports	3	AD
Work Papers, Rough	2	AD

ADMINISTRATIVE RECORDS

Audit Reports	10	AD
Audit Work Papers	3	AD
Classified Documents: Inventories, Reports, Receipts	10	AD
Correspondence, Executive	P	AD
Correspondence, General	5	AD
Directives From Officers	P	AD
Forms Used, File Copies	P	AD
Systems and Procedures Records	P	AD
Work Papers, Management Projects	P	AD

COMMUNICATIONS

Bulletins Explaining Communications	P	AD
Messenger Records	1	AD
Phone Directories	SUP	AD
Phone Installation Records	1	AD
Postage Reports, Stamp Requisitions	1 AF	AD
Postal Records, Registered Mail & Insured Mail Logs & Meter Records	1 AF	AD, CFR
Telecommunications Copies	1	AD

CONTRACT ADMINISTRATION

Contracts, Negotiated. Bailments, Changes, Specifications, Procedures, Correspondence	P	CFR
Customer Reports	P	AD
Materials Relating to Distribution Revisions, Forms, and Format of Reports	P	AD
Work Papers	OBS	AD

CORPORATE

Annual Reports	P	AD
Authority to Issue Securities	P	AD
Bonds, Surety	3 AE	AD
Capital Stock Ledger	P	AD
Charters, Constitutions, Bylaws	P	AD

TYPE OF RECORD	RETENTION PERIOD YEARS	AUTHORITY
Contracts	20 AT	AD
Corporate Election Records	P	AD
Incorporation Records	P	AD
Licenses - Federal, State, Local	AT	AD
Stock Transfer & Stockholder	P	AD

LEGAL

TYPE OF RECORD	RETENTION PERIOD YEARS	AUTHORITY
Claims and Litigation Concerning Torts and Breach of Contracts	P	AD
Law Records - Federal, State, Local	SUP	AD
Patents and Related Material	P	AD
Trademark & Copyrights	P	AD

LIBRARY, COMPANY

TYPE OF RECORD	RETENTION PERIOD YEARS	AUTHORITY
Accession Lists	P	AD
Copies of Requests for Materials	6 mos.	AD
Meeting Calendars	P	AD
Research Papers, Abstracts, Bibliographies	SUP, 6 mos. AC	AD

MANUFACTURING

TYPE OF RECORD	RETENTION PERIOD YEARS	AUTHORITY
Bills of Material	2	AD, ASPR
Drafting Records	P	ADt
Drawings	2	AD, ASPR
Inspection Records	2	AD
Lab Test Reports	P	AD
Memos, Production	AC	AD
Product, Tooling, Design, Engineering Research, Experiment & Specs Records	20	STATUTE LIMITATIONS
Production Reports	3	AD
Quality Reports	1 AC	AD
Reliability Records	P	AD
Stock Issuing Records	3 AT	AD, ASPR
Tool Control	3 AT	AD, ASPR
Work Orders	3	AD
Work Status Reports	AC	AD

OFFICE SUPPLIES & SERVICES

TYPE OF RECORD	RETENTION PERIOD YEARS	AUTHORITY
Inventories	1 AF	AD
Office Equipment Records	6 AF	AD
Requests for: Services	1 AF	AD
Requisitions for Supplies	1 AF	AD

PERSONNEL

TYPE OF RECORD	RETENTION PERIOD YEARS	AUTHORITY
Accident Reports, Injury Claims, Settlements	30 AS	CFR, INS, STATE
Applications, Changes & Terminations	5	AD, ASPR, CFR
Attendance Records	7	AD
Employee Activity Files	2 or SUP	AD
Employee Contracts	6 AT	AD

TYPE OF RECORD	RETENTION PERIOD YEARS	AUTHORITY
Fidelity Bonds	3 AT	AD
Garnishments	5	AD
Health & Safety Bulletins	P	AD
Injury Frequency Charts	P	CFR
Insurance Records, Employees	11 AT	INS
Job Descriptions	2 or SUP	CFR
Rating Cards	2 or SUP	CFR
Time Cards	3	AD
Training Manuals	P	AD
Union Agreements	3	WALSH-HEALEY ACT

PLANT & PROPERTY RECORDS

Depreciation Schedules	P	AD
Inventory Records	P	AD
Maintenance & Repair, Building	10	AD
Maintenance & Repair, Machinery	5	AD
Plant Account Cards, Equipment	P	CFR, AD
Property Deeds	P	AD
Purchase or Lease Records of Plant Facility	P	AD
Space Allocation Records	1 AT	AD

PRINTING & DUPLICATING

Copies Produced, Tech. Pubs., Charts	1 or OBS	AD
Film Reports	5	AD
Negatives	5	AD
Photographs	1	AD
Production Records	1 AC	AD

PROCUREMENT, PURCHASING

Acknowledgements	AC	AD
Bids, Awards	3 AT	CFR
Contracts	3 AT	AD
Exception Notices (GAO)	6	AD
Price Lists	OBS	AD
Purchase Orders, Requisitions	3 AT	CFR
Quotations	1	AD

PRODUCTS, SERVICES, MARKETING

Correspondence	3	AD
Credit Ratings & Classifications	7	AD
Development Studies	P	AD
Presentations & Proposals	P	AD
Price Lists, Catalogs	OBS	AD
Prospect Lines	OBS	AD
Register of Sales Order	NO VALUE	AD
Surveys	P	AD
Work Papers, Pertaining to Projects	NO VALUE	AD

TYPE OF RECORD	RETENTION PERIOD YEARS	AUTHORITY
PUBLIC RELATIONS & ADVERTISING		
Advertising Activity Reports	5	AD
Community Affairs Records	P	AD
Contracts for Advertising	3 AT	AD
Employee Activities & Presentations	P	AD
Exhibits, Releases, Handouts	2 - 4	AD
Internal Publications	P (1 copy)	AD
Layouts	1	AD
Manuscripts	1	AD
Photos	1	AD
Public Information Activity	7	AD
Research Presentations	P	AD
Tear-Sheets	2	AD
SECURITY		
Classified Material Violations	P	AD
Courier Authorizations	1 mo. ATR	AD
Employee Clearance Lists	SUP	ISM
Employee Case Files	5	ISM
Fire Prevention Program	P	AD
Protection - Guards, Badge Lists, Protective Devices	5	AD
Subcontractor Clearances	2 AT	AD
Visitor Clearance	2	ISM
TAXATION		
Annuity or Deferred Payment Plan	P	CFR
Depreciation Schedules	P	CFR
Dividend Register	P	CFR
Employee Withholding	4	CFR
Excise Exemption Certificates	4	CFR
Excise Reports (Manufacturing)	4	CFR
Excise Reports (Retail)	4	CFR
Inventory Reports	P	CFR
Tax Bills and Statements	P	AD
Tax Returns	P	AD
TRAFFIC & TRANSPORTATION		
Aircraft Operating & Maintenance	P	CFR
Bills of Lading, Waybills	2	ICC, FLSA
Employee Travel	1 AF	AD
Freight Bills	3	ICC
Freight Claims	2	ICC
Household Moves	3 AM	AD
Motor Operating & Maintenance	2	AD
Rates and Tariffs	SUP	AD
Receiving Documents	2 - 10	AD, CFR
Shipping & Related Documents	2 - 10	AD, CFR

Place upon your desk only the item you're working on at the moment. Everything else should be filed or otherwise kept out of sight. When you've finished with it, get rid of it by sending it to the appropriate place. If you will need the item later, file it and make a note under the appropriate space in your planner where you have filed it.

Do not allow periodicals and correspondence to be placed on your desk by others. The in and out boxes are a must, but don't keep them on your desk. Go to the in box only at a specified time each day, so that you aren't tempted to sift through it during working hours. But never neglect it, or the in pile will become a meaningless stack of papers.

THE PERSONAL PAPERFLOW SYSTEM

Now that your desk is uncluttered and organized, the challenge lies in keeping it that way. Remember, just as appearance and apparel make a personal statement, so does the look of your desk. Unless you are a chief exec, your desk should not be too empty: People will think that you are not very busy, which is bad, or that you are obsessively neat, which is worse. You should have work—mail, memos, statistics, orders, etc.—on your desk, but well placed and organized. It is better not to wait until the desk looks like the mailroom, then go on a neatness spree only to watch the piles mount up so that next week you start all over. Stay in control of your paper.

Screen unnecessary paper. Cancel subscriptions to unwanted newsletters, magazines, and catalogs. Get the office manager to bypass you on irrelevant interoffice memos. Have your secretary handle paper that does not require your personal attention.

Try to handle each piece of paper only once. Most time management experts treat this as an absolute. That is of course ridiculous. Some papers will get handled dozens of times with good reason. But don't shuffle paper that can be acted on and disposed of, or passed on to someone else. It is truly amazing how many times a letter can get read before one gets around to writing a simple reply.

Classify paperwork as it comes in. Some recommend three piles: *Immediate Action, Pending,* and *Informational.* And of course, there's the throwaway pile. Vary this according to your own needs—almost everyone has a *To Be Filed* stack. And some add an *Urgent* pile, used only for the projects that must be acted on instantly. This pile should come into being only on occasion.

Spot junk mail before it lures you into reading it. Junk mail has its own language. I offer the following observations as a former author of some high-quality junk mail. Most of you are experts already, so you bear me out:

When they say:	What they are really saying is:
• "Free!"	If we give you something that doesn't cost us much, will you buy something on which we will make much more?
• "You may have already won"	But we won't tell you until you give us a chance to sell you, and then mail in this coupon. Of course, you need not buy anything to win a prize, but if you think it'll help, so much the better. And if you are considering buying, but are not motivated to mail the card, the lure of a prize might push you over the line.
• "An important message"	It's important to us that you read this and respond.

Also watch for the visual cues: odd-shaped envelopes; offbeat printed matter—stamps, wheels, brochures, etc.; return addresses that don't identify the sender.

Shop junk mail quickly—go to the offer card first. This is either a postcard or a card to be stuffed into a provided envelope. This is the bottom line. You will find out in 30 seconds (a) who the offer is from, (b) what is offered, (c) for how much, (d) for how long, (e) length of guarantee, (f) delivery time, (g) payments accepted. If you are interested, then go back and read the stuff. If not, to the basket with it.

When something is no longer "active," but must be kept as a record, file it immediately! Your desk top is not a file cabinet.

CUTTING DOWN ON PAPERWORK

The best way to cut down on paperwork is to locate the people responsible and take them to task. The next best way is to dig in and fight from your own desk.

Put only what is absolutely necessary in writing.

Screen out unnecessary paper. Junk mail. Junk memos.

Cut down on copier use.

Use the telephone. It's faster and cheaper than letters.

Use the dictating machine. Avoid writing out rough drafts of letters or instructions to your secretary. You can speak at 200 wpm with ease, but can write only about 20 wpm. Using a dictating machine saves your secretary's time, too.

Use cassettes. A cassette memo can be recorded even while you are driving or waiting for a plane. Pop it into the mail and the recipient will be able to reuse it afterward.

Throw away even more paper.

4

TOOLS TO SAVE TIME
AND ELIMINATE
PAPER WITH

Although effective time management is primarily a matter of will power, there are a number of products that can be of great help:

PLANNERS, DIARIES,
APPOINTMENT CALENDARS

I know a doctor who relies on the first "freebie" appointment book he receives each year (the drug firms send them) and gets along quite well with it. Then there's the multimillionaire investment manager who has been using the girlie calendar supplied to him by his garage at Christmastime. And the key executive at a major corporation who makes up his own daily forms, has his secretary run off and date 365 of them, and then has them bound.

You should have a planner of some type, but there is little agreement on what is the ideal type for the executive. It's a very personal matter.

Will a specific type contribute to your effectiveness? That depends more on how you schedule and manage your time than on how you record it. Nevertheless, most managers do view the choice of a planner as a considered purchase. Planners appear by the thousands in late fall, and even sooner in the mail-order and ad specialty markets. It seems that any guy with a printing press and a calendar figures he has a chance in this business.

WHAT EXECUTIVES LOOK
FOR IN A PLANNER

The following data is based on a survey conducted by *Business Week*'s new-product development department.

EXECUTIVES PREFER A "PLANNER" FORMAT OVER A SIMPLE DIARY   They view their appointment book as a planning tool, not simply as something in which to record their daily activity. The simple diary format is a carry-over from the original English design.

AESTHETIC APPEAL   A planner is a highly personal tool. It says something about the user; so, naturally, you'll want yours to look good. You have to consult it several times a day; often in front of others.

TIME MANAGEMENT SECTION   Time is the eternal equalizer—everyone has the same number of hours in a day, no matter what one's lot in life. It's how you use it that makes the difference. Apparently, many believe that the proper planner can help them manage time.

PERSONAL DATA PAGE   Here you list credit card numbers, bank account and insurance policy numbers, etc. While the demand for this feature is strong, it is greater in the upper echelons. The reason appears to be that upper level executives tend to involve their secretaries, who then need handy access to basic information, in personal financial matters. Lower level executives often don't use this feature, because they don't want such data lying around.

A BINDING THAT LIES FLAT   The book should lie open on a desk, without the help of hands.

A DOUBLE-RIBBON BOOKMARK   To keep place in two pages at the same time.

"800" NUMBER DIRECTORY   Such numbers can be hard to find, and directories are real time-savers. Many of the toll-free "800" numbers are in service 24 hours a day.

SPACE FOR MOST FREQUENTLY USED NUMBERS

OPTIMAL PAGE LAYOUT:

- *quarter-hour subdivisions*
- *extra space for luncheon engagements*, so one can note all details
- *simple layout;* easy on the eyes, uncluttered
- *proportionally less space for weekends and nights.* The lower on the totem pole, the greater the need for "overtime" space

A PLANNING FEATURE   Space for weekly, quarterly, and yearly planning—and, ideally, a planning calendar for five years ahead, plus last year's calendar for reference.

WHAT EXECUTIVES DO NOT WANT IN A PLANNER

Many diaries are filled with such things as air distance charts, postage rates, census and business statistics, and other extraneous reference materials. All these features do is make the book thicker and more expensive. The fact is, executives don't want this stuff in their planners. *BW* found that most of them don't use it. If an executive wants to know the weather in Hong Kong, he'll contact his travel agent or some other appropriate party. The survey respondents claimed that this kind of data simply served to distract.

When choosing a planner, pick one that will provide quick access to information that is vital to your everyday work.

Since about 85 percent of all your calls are placed to a pool of 30–40 numbers, sufficient space for recording those key numbers is perhaps the most important extra.

TIME LOGS

For several reasons, planners don't contain time logs. First, time logs are highly personal and should be structured by the individual. Second, they are used only for a few weeks at a time. Third, the planner is not a workbook. It is not meant to train people in time management or to function as a means of conducting research. You'll get the most out of your planner if you take the trouble to do a time log first.

POCKET PLANNERS

Executives like flexible covers; space for expenses, notes, and phone numbers; and, as an extra, "800" numbers. Keep the size down, as "thin is in." If you carry it in your jacket pocket, its outline shouldn't bulge through.

SEVERAL GOOD PLANNERS

BUSINESS WEEK EXECUTIVE PLANNER   Taking into account the results of their survey, the *BW* staff has come up with one of the best planners around. Layout, binding, and graphics are all excellent. And it contains just the right amount of supplemental information. It is also competitively priced.

DAYTIMERS   The GM of the planner industry. The largest users of Daytimers are lawyers, accountants, and salespeople, and one look at the format tells you why. The Daytimer is for people who literally must time their day—a godsend for those who bill by the hour, or whose profits are dictated by how many sales calls they can cram into a single day.

The time record section is split into twelve-minute segments. The appointment section is a series of open lines. There is also a "To Be Done Today" planning section.

The ink is eye-ease green, but the paper wasn't meant for anything but a ballpoint. A fountain pen or marker will probably bleed through in the pocket version.

When you buy a Daytimer, you are buying into a system of planning paraphernalia. Pages can be added and deleted, and there is a wide range of formats. You can, in effect, customize your planner.

Recently, Daytimers has expanded its time management accessories to include a wide variety of useful page formats.

Daytimers are very good; to use them is to love them.

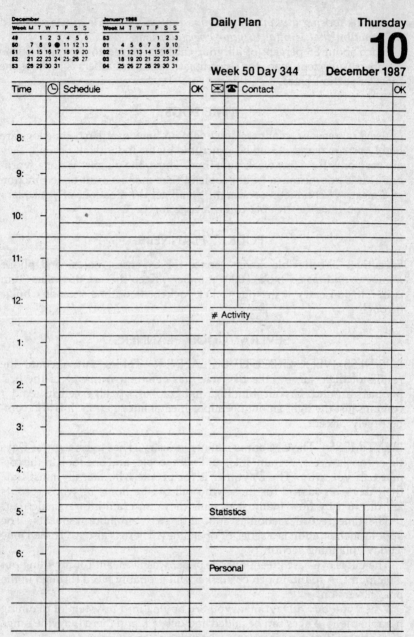

Fig. 7. Page formats of Time/Design management systems:
daily and weekly plans

Period: _____
_____
_____

Day	🕐	Activity	✉	☎	OK
Mon					
Tue					
Wed					
Thu					
Fri					
Sat					
Sun					

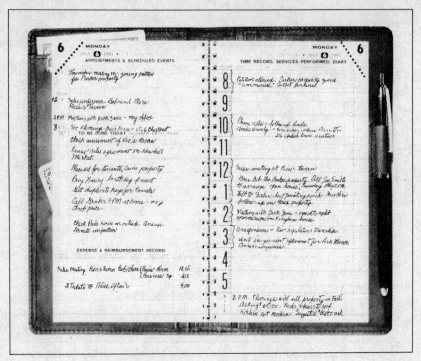

Fig. 8 Illustration of Pocket Daytimer
Courtesy of Daytimers, Allentown, PA 18001

DAYRUNNER A popular planning system by Harper House. The basic planner uses a ring binder and dividers, with pages designed to act as appointment calendars, telephone directories, project-planning sheets, expenses, even pages that keep track of your exercise program. The graphic design of the pages is excellent, very easy on the eyes. The accessory pages are quite expensive, however.

FILOFAX Until a few years ago, Filofax was just another high-quality organizer from Great Britain, on the market for nearly six decades. In 1980, the company changed hands, and since then Filofax has become a phenomenon.

The core of the Filofax system is a six-ring leather binder that can hold appointment pages, address pages, maps, lists, and other inserts.

Daytimers, Dayrunner, Time Design and other time management systems also offer the versatility of inserts, so the success of Filofax is due in part to its classic look and status. You can spend over $500 for an ostrich-skin binder. There are over sixteen different diaries and 150 different forms, allowing the executive to customize the system to taste.

By any reckoning, Filofax is an excellent organizer, but one should be aware that most of its time management features can be obtained for a lower price. As for status, the executive of a rival firm noted that "Filofax is very common now." If it's snob appeal you are after, you might want to look elsewhere.

TIME/DESIGN   A well designed, high quality time management system. It follows the basic concept of a binder and a large selection of custom pages, allowing you to assemble a planner to suit your needs. Time/Design recently received a European design award. The binder, subject dividers and other accessories are of the highest quality, giving the system a certain cachet. Time/Design is very expensive, costing in excess of a hundred dollars.

THE ENGLISH IMPORTS: LETTS OF LONDON AND LEATHERSMITH OF LONDON   The English are diary fanatics, which is not surprising when you consider how long diaries have been available there. In 1816 Charles Letts produced the first Letts Diary or Bills Due Book and Almanack. T. J. & J. Smith Ltd. started competing with Letts in 1839 and now sells its products under the name Leathersmith.

Both firms produce well-made diaries and planners with exquisite bindings and high-quality paper. Most have leather covers, gilt-edged paper, and ribbon bookmarks. In the pocket editions the emphasis is clearly on producing a very slim coat or shirt-pocket diary that is rich looking and does not cause a "bulge." Clearly, the weight is on elegance over utility, since neither company has done much with the page design: a page consists of simple boxes bearing the date or, in some cases, boxes that include lines with time of day. To keep it thin there are between three and seven days to the page, depending on the model.

The leather desk versions are beautiful and have much more space. Matching address books are available at additional costs. Letts has a "Timeplan" system that includes a desk planner with a useful time management section. It is very nearly identical to the *Newsweek* planner. The desk versions start at $20. Pocket versions start at $4.

For name of nearest dealer, contact:

Letts of London, Ltd.
400 Oser Avenue
Hauppauge, New York 11787

Leathersmith of London Ltd.
3 East 48th Street
New York, New York 10017

TIME MANAGEMENT SOFTWARE   If you are a personal computer user, you might consider a time management software package to help you keep track of tasks, priorities and appointments. Among the best are Prime Time from Wiseware which is one of the few programs that goes beyond gimmickry and actually assists you in following basic time management principles. One of its best features is the ability to keep the to-do list current; it automatically carries an uncompleted task forward so you don't have to go back through old to-do lists; you can also plan ahead and keep track of activities delegated to specific individuals.

Other programs with time management features are Lotus Metro, Sidekick and Travelling Sidekick, and Control Center, which is designed to work with the Time/Design system.

A unique organization program called Tornado Notes from Micro Logic Corp. actually simulates a stack of paper. You can spontaneously jot down a series of random notes on a computerized scratch pad; when you return to your "pile" of notes you can skim, sort, search and edit. The idea is to eliminate the need for little scraps of paper and to enable you to create a "freestyle" note-taking system that is fast and simple.

CHECKLISTS

Getting it right the first time is an important time-saver, and that often means not leaving anything out the first time. Any aid in doing a thorough job will save you time. One such aid is the checklist. Checklists serve several purposes:

They let you get a view of the entire job before you. All steps written out, one after the other.

At a glance, you can see how far you've gone and what remains.

Checklists serve as memory joggers, reminding you to complete tasks that might have slipped your mind.

A completed checklist, with dates and figures filled in, is an excellent record.

Checklists facilitate communication with superiors. Once approved, they signify that there is agreement on what it is you are supposed to be doing.

Checklists can make you look good at meetings. You'll be prepared and can help keep the group on track. If someone overlooks something, you'll be able to remind him about it.

HOW TO MAKE A CHECKLIST

WRITE DOWN, IN LIST FORM, ALL THE THINGS THAT YOU MUST DO   Show the list to your boss, secretary, and other interested parties for additions and other suggestions. You may wish to have someone else do the first draft. A checklist is a blueprint of your thinking, and if yours does not meet with approval by the boss, you may be open to some criticism. If you can, ask the boss to draft a checklist.

DO A STRAW POLL OF EVERYONE INVOLVED   You'll come up with a long list of items to be included.

ADVERTISING AND SALES PROMOTION FUNCTIONS

The purpose of this questionnaire is to enable you and your management to determine whether your advertising and sales promotion functions are being performed economically and effectively. It should also assist you in determining when to obtain the services of an advertising agency.

Advertising

1. Does your firm provide quality workmanship and efficient service, which are bases for your advertising? ☐ Yes ☐ No
2. Has your firm established an advertising program? ☐ Yes ☐ No
3. Have you considered these determinants of advertising:
   a. The nature of your business? ☐ Yes ☐ No
   b. Company objectives (strategy)? ☐ Yes ☐ No
   c. Industry practice? ☐ Yes ☐ No
   d. The media used? ☐ Yes ☐ No
4. Is your advertising program primarily of a continuous nature? ☐ Yes ☐ No
5. Do you use noncontinuous advertising to:
   a. Prepare your customers to accept a new product? ☐ Yes ☐ No
   b. Suggest new uses for established products to your customers? ☐ Yes ☐ No
   c. Bring special sales to your customers' attention? ☐ Yes ☐ No
6. Do you use your advertising to pave the way for your sales representatives by making your company and product well known? ☐ Yes ☐ No
7. Have you developed an advertising budget showing the outlay of funds for advertising? ☐ Yes ☐ No
8. Do you use standard advertising ratios for your line of business or type of industry as guides? ☐ Yes ☐ No
9. Is your company's advertising set as a percentage of projected sales? ☐ Yes ☐ No
10. Have you decided to spend the major portion of your company's total advertising outlay on one of your products and to give only incidental advertising to others? ☐ Yes ☐ No
11. Do you vary your advertising expenditures seasonally? ☐ Yes ☐ No
12. Is your company's advertising truthful and in good taste? ☐ Yes ☐ No
13. Has your firm obtained assistance from suppliers and trade associations concerning your advertising program? ☐ Yes ☐ No

Fig. 9. Sample checklist
(above and next page)

From *The Dow Jones-Irwin Business Papers,* by Tate, Megginson, Scott, and Trueblood, Copyright © 1977 by Dow Jones-Irwin. Reprinted by permission of Dow Jones-Irwin.

14. Are you attempting to measure the results of your advertising?
    □ Yes □ No
15. Before an advertisement is composed, do you consider what you expect the advertising to do for your firm?   □ Yes □ No
16. In planning your ads, do you use these pointers:
    a. Identify your store completely and clearly?   □ Yes □ No
    b. Select similar illustrations?   □ Yes □ No
    c. Select a printing typeface and stick to it?   □ Yes □ No
    d. Develop easily read copy?   □ Yes □ No
    e. Use coupons for direct mail advertising response? □ Yes □ No
    f. Get the audience's attention in the first five seconds of a television or radio commercial?   □ Yes □ No
17. Check which of these tests you use for immediate-response ads:
    □ Coupons to be returned to your store?
    □ Letters or phone requests referring to the ads?
    □ Split runs by newspapers?
    □ Sales made of the particular item?
    □ Checks on store traffic?
18. Do you attempt to evaluate the relative effectiveness of each of your advertising media?   □ Yes □ No

Sales Promotion
19. Check which of these sales promotion techniques you use:
    □ Special displays
    □ Premiums
    □ Contests
    □ Free samples
    □ Free introductory services
    □ Demonstration products
20. If you are a retailer, are your window and counter displays changed frequently?   □ Yes □ No
21. If you are a manufacturer, are you using trade shows? □ Yes □ No
22. Are your sales representatives furnished with:
    a. Good sales kits?   □ Yes □ No
    b. Up-to-date promotional materials?   □ Yes □ No
    c. Catalogs?   □ Yes □ No
23. If you are selling two or more products, are you promoting them:
    a. Jointly?   □ Yes □ No
    b. Separately?   □ Yes □ No

Using an advertising agency
24. Are you aware that most newspaper advertising is developed by creative skills possessed by the newspaper staff?   □ Yes □ No

SUGGESTED READING

Time management books are incredibly redundant; the biggest waste of time would be to read more than one of them cover to cover. If you must look at several, read one and skim the others. Otherwise, you'll wind up reading over and over about time logs and telephone interruptions.

Here are some of the best books on saving time:

How to Get Control of Your Time and Your Life, by Alan Lakein (New York: New American Library, 1974)

The one and only. This book talks about time and your entire life. It is only partly a tips book. It is also motivational, and very helpful if you are in the "it's-time-to-make-a-new-start" mood. Lakein is recognized as the leading authority on time management.

Getting Things Done, by Edwin Bliss (New York: Charles Scribner's Sons, 1976)

Ed Bliss is also a well-known expert on time management. His book is very practical and to the point. It consists of short, pithy sections on each of the principal time management issues.

The Time Trap, by R. Alec Mackenzie (New York: AMACOM, 1972; out of print)

A perennial business best-seller, this book teaches the subject from a manager's point of view. It is well researched through both personal and academic investigation and provides some valuable insights into effective time management in the corporate structure.

Working Smart, by Michael LeBoeuf (New York: McGraw-Hill, 1979)

This book reads like an amalgam of the better parts of all the foregoing books. It is eminently practical, offering the most in-depth analysis of problems and possible solutions. LeBoeuf covers personal as well as business life. He has obviously lifted time management tips from other popular works on the subject, but he does come up with some creative approaches of his own. While not quite as "inspiring" as Lakein's book, it is the best written.

The Dow Jones-Irwin Business Papers, by Curtis E. Tate, Jr., Leon C. Megginson, Charles R. Scott, Jr., and Lyle R. Trueblood (Homewood, IL: Dow Jones-Irwin, 1977; out of print)

A different type of time management book, this is just a bunch of checklists and forms—but they are helpful. Some of the checklists in the book can be applied to your business just as they are. Others will have to be modified. In any event, you'll see what a checklist is and how it functions, and the ones in the book will serve as a good foundation upon which to build your own. In addition, the question-naires included in this book serve as an excellent way to learn some valuable management techniques by identifying the variables that you must confront in many different situations.

PART II

COPING WITH THE INFORMATION EXPLOSION

"Try to know everything of something,
and something of everything."
Henry Peter, Lord Brougham

5

THE DATA DELUGE

In *Future Shock*, author Alvin Toffler* points out that ideas have been estimated to enter and leave our awareness at a rate twenty to one hundred times faster than they did a hundred years ago. Scientists suggest that although a large portion of our brain is, theoretically, underutilized, especially in the area of perceptual and reasoning ability, the typical individual is approaching the upper limits in his ability to assimilate and process information. In short, our circuits are overloaded.

A breakthrough in microcircuitry, computer science, or semiconductors can revolutionize an entire industry. Firms spring up overnight and go bankrupt or get gobbled up just as quickly. As a businessperson, you have the special problem of trying to maintain the efficiency of a system, of a routine, while at the same time being on the lookout for ways to update and, if necessary, jettison the status quo.

A look at any of the major business magazines reveals that editorial coverage has been expanded in recent years in the areas of global affairs, science and technology, social and environmental issues, and even religion. Everything affects business, and business effects everything. Because the American economy is the world's most powerful, with the most advanced communication systems, business here affects the whole world, and international business in turn affects the American economy.

You cannot just watch the stock markets, the trade publications, and the markets that you work in. But *while information is expanding rapidly, and the need for its consumption increasing, the amount of time available for such activity is not increasing to keep up with it.* Already, most successful executives spend their leisure time trying to catch up on important reading and viewing.

HOW WE REACT NEGATIVELY
TO "INFORMATION OVERLOAD"

Toffler has characterized various responses. They are nothing more than simple stress symptoms applied to the information problem, but that stress is what makes the responses so marked.

The Denier. Overwhelmed by the information explosion the denier refuses to accept any more. He blocks out certain realities and often clings to the philosophy that the old way is still the best way, the tried-and-true way. In the current business environment, this attitude will lead to disaster. Unless you are a demigod at your corporation, the very embodiment of success, this static approach will make you a sitting duck for anyone with any foresight.

The Specialist. Unable to absorb and master the material being shot at him, or uninterested in doing so, this person picks a narrow field and learns all he can to keep pace: knows a lot about a special thing instead of a little about a lot of things. While the specialist's approach to survival may not be the best prescription for a full, diverse life, it is not a bad strategy for executive survival in a society that has great use for specialists in highly complex fields—provided, of course, that your particular field of expertise remains in demand. A single innovation may wipe out your turf in one stroke. And then where are you? So the specialist, as he prospers, must cast a wider net and absorb information to keep his options open. Since the degree of interrelatedness of all fields of business is increasing, everything affects your specialty. So you must keep track, if only superficially, of events outside your area.

The Reversionist. The Denier, when confronted with rapid change, clings to the status quo. The Reversionist turns tail and tries to dredge up the past in some sort of absurd defense against the future through use of nostalgia. If this is you, see a shrink; take a rest from your job. One doesn't often encounter this type in business, because, unless he is an officer through family clout or ownership, he just can't last.

The Supersimplifier. Just as the name implies, he is the reductionist, simplifying complex information, turning grey areas into black and white, moral ambiguities into simple rights and wrongs. It takes great intellectual ability to see the essence of a chunk of information and simplify it, boiling it down to a few essential facts. But the supersimplifier attempts to do this with his defense mechanisms, not his intellect. He is drowning in a sea of facts, and he must simplify in order to comprehend and to survive. This person can be dangerous, because when you've used all your powers of analysis and concentration to come to grips with difficult issues, he will stand up in the meeting and brush it all aside with some rinky-dink platitude. The real trouble is that many of your colleagues would rather swallow his bromides than dig into the meat of the issues.

To Toffler's list I add one of of my own:

The Information Junkie. This one realizes the extent of what is taking place in terms of the information explosion and makes an energetic, if utterly unrealistic, attempt to keep up with it all. He buys every newspaper, magazine, book, and newsletter he can get his hands on, and saves each one because he can't bear to throw it out unread, fearing that he might be missing something. Often, such a person doesn't enjoy the process of learning new things, because he is so frantic about it. While reading one thing, he thinks about what's next. This behavior can apply to television, movies—any and all media. I know someone who listens to an all-news station for hours at a time, even though the entire news report repeats itself every half hour. Why? "Because," he says, "something might happen after I've heard the news the first time." Now, regular listening makes sense, but continual monitoring? You may know him as the person who holds up everyone's plans for Sunday because he has got to get through the entire Sunday paper before leaving the house.

Not only does he continually acquire the same information several times in different forms; he will also become very boring, because he is not taking in another very valuable kind of information—the kind that comes from being around people. As Voltaire said, "The multitude of books is making us ignorant." That was in the eighteenth century, before shopping centers and bookstore chains.

In coping with the information explosion, it's quality, not quantity, that counts. Digest a smaller amount of material that is richer in information, not a gluttonous amount filled with starchy nonsense.

Enjoy what you read. And by no means must everything you absorb have a specific purpose. You can learn a lot about how to survive in the corporate world from reading *War and Peace.* But read it because it's a good book, not because of some work-related benefit.

COPING

Become an "information ecologist." Keep your environment free of unhealthy elements: Screen out unreliable information, word pollution, redundancy, irrelevance.

- Identify material worthy of your attention.
- Develop the discipline to discard the unworthy.
- Learn to seek out and home in on the pertinent facts and figures.
- Discard all else.

Make greater use of your mental potential. Do just what the IBM boys do when their computers are no longer up to the job—increase capacity, speed, power, and storage capability. You can upgrade the same functions of your own brain by learning to:

- read more efficiently
- increase your brain's retentiveness
- reduce stress that might be negatively affecting your performance
- improve your work environment for improved performance
- sharpen your listening skills and note-taking ability.

Learn new information-gathering techniques. Most of us are still gathering information in the same manner we learned in school. Many alternatives exist, some of them the result of recent innovations. Here is a list of principal information sources:

- data bases
- business libraries
- microfilm/microfiche
- video/audio cassettes
- magazines
- books
- radio
- television
- reference services

HOW EXECUTIVES GET THE NEWS

CURRENT EVENTS AND HARD NEWS

NEWSPAPERS AND MAGAZINES   Most executives rely exclusively or in part on:

- *The New York Times*
- *The Washington Post*
- *The Wall Street Journal*
- *USA Today*
- Local dailies
- *Time*
- *Newsweek*
- *U.S. News and World Report*

TELEVISION   A survey reported in *Industry Week* found that only 40 percent of managers and professionals watch TV news, mostly because of "not being home for it."

ALL-NEWS RADIO   In this format there is no programming other than hard-news reports, wire services, and features. It is very popular among executives, especially during "drive time," a radio-biz term for 7–9 A.M. and 4–6 P.M., when people are on their way to work or home and have their car radios turned on. This time slot is the radio equivalent of TV's prime time.

BUSINESS NEWS

In order of preference, according to *Industry Week*'s survey:

- *The Wall Street Journal*
- *Business Week*
- *Forbes*
- *Fortune*
- *The Economist*

Note: This is a ranking of the publications based not on their excellence, but on their use as a primary source of news. Since *Business Week* is the only domestic weekly, it seems logical that it would be at the top of the list of business magazines.

OTHER NEWS SOURCES

CONSUMER MAGAZINES   Executives do not appear to allot much time to the reading of consumer magazines, although it is apparent from other readership surveys that many subscribe to them.

NEWSLETTERS   These are popular, especially among upper level executives. Financial newsletters, especially those dealing with investments and tax planning, are popular, as are association and industry newsletters.

CATALOGS   Many executives scan the catalogs they receive in the mail; they are helpful in gauging marketing trends and consumer preferences, as well as pricing structures.

On the average, executives spend one-third of their day reading. But studies recently conducted here and in Britain suggest that most executives do not read enough to keep pace, that they are not well informed, and that they understand the spoken word far better than the written.

Part of the problem is an overreliance on several passive information-gathering methods:

NEWS GATHERED BY STAFF   This includes news summaries prepared by staff members, and information gleaned from subordinates who point out important news as it happens. Unfortunately, news and information relayed by others eliminates the intuitive and creative insights of the executive himself. Chances are, given the same article, a topflight executive will pick up on a few things that others will miss. In addition, the brain has a tendency for us to "file" seemingly unimportant things that are called forth later on. If one never scans the relevant material, one misses the opportunity to make associations and connections.

CLIPPING SERVICES An efficient way of monitoring press coverage on a particular subject, individual, or company. For a fee, a clipping service scans newspapers (in some cases, magazines as well) for mention of any name or subject you wish. The articles are then clipped, appropriately underlined to call relevant data to your attention, and sent to you. One drawback is that many of the ideas you get each day are sparked by bits of information that have overtly little or nothing to do with a particular name or subject. So by relying on a clipping service, your focus could become too narrow.

There are clipping services in most major cities. Look under "Clipping Bureaus" or "Clipping Services" in the Yellow Pages.

CONFERENCES AND SEMINARS Pleasant (if you're lucky), great for making contacts, but often insufficient in scope and depth. Large meetings attract many publicity hounds who are more interested in self-aggrandizement or in riding a hobbyhorse than in providing valuable information.

DATABASES See Chapter 8.

Good judgment is a most important requirement for a successful executive; yet most fail to exercise that judgment in gathering information.

6

INFORMATION ECOLOGY: GETTING THE MOST IN THE LEAST TIME

By estimate, the number of books and scientific papers is doubling every eight years. We can't possibly read everything we wish to read. *The act of selecting worthwhile reading material is as big a time-saver as reading very fast*, if not bigger.

SCREENING PRINTED MATTER

Let's begin with a typical situation. A book or magazine arrives at your desk. What do you do?

THE FIRST GLANCE

TITLE   This should tell you something. But it doesn't always.

AUTHOR   When reading a book or article, do note the author's name. If you like how and/or what he writes, next time you spot the name, you'll have good reason to invest time in reading the material; and chances are you'll know something about it even before you read it.

Use the trash can. If you don't want to read something, throw it away— now. Or give it away. But get rid of it. Otherwise, you might, in a moment of weakness, decide to read it. It's like wasting an hour or two watching something on TV that you know is trash, and feeling crumby afterward because you wasted the time. Reading material can also be a "vast wasteland." The printed word, contrary to what your grade-school teachers and school librarians may have told you, is not sacred.

IF IT'S A BOOK

CONTENTS   This is a good place to begin your survey. Lately publishers and writers have begun using the contents page as a means of selling a book, so it may promise more than the book delivers; rarely does it promise less. If you don't see what you want, it's probably not in there.

DUST JACKET   Sometimes the jacket blurbs give you a good idea about what's inside. A quote from a critic or authority you know and respect may help you decide. If not, ignore the quotes. Comments and introductions are a big part of the book business; often, someone will write an introduction or comment about someone else's book merely to keep in the public eye. While most do not lie about their opinions, neither are they likely to be unprejudiced. Dust jackets often include an upbeat capsule description of the book's subject matter and summarize the author's credentials. Unfortunately, the intention is usually to advertise the book rather than describe it, so the jacket often oversells.

INDEX   Scan it quickly. You'll get a more thorough idea of the subjects covered and the author's point of view, as well as a good idea of what other authors or experts are invoked. When you pick up several books on management and see in the index that huge passages are devoted to "Drucker, Peter, on management," you have to at least ask yourself whether you should be reading Drucker's books instead. A quick scan of the book in question will tell you whether you'd rather get the subject matter in another author's style, or from another's perspective.

PREFACE OR INTRODUCTION   This is usually written *after* the book and often provides a good idea about what is coming in terms of the author's goals and point of view, and/or it summarizes the contents. Do not read the acknowledgments during the screening period. Besides, most first authors dedicate most of that space to thanking wives, parents, children, lovers.

IF IT'S A MAGAZINE

In magazines for general audiences, articles assume the reader has little or no prior knowledge, so there must be some introductory material on the subject. If an article in such a magazine is just a few pages long, it rarely goes beyond the basics. So if you are well versed in the subject, you won't learn anything new. If the article is long, skim to see if there is some new material or in-depth analysis that might be of some value.

For example, in a period no longer than several weeks, *The Wall Street Journal, Business Week, Forbes, Fortune*, and *U.S. News and World Report* all ran articles on recent trends in the movie business, based on a conference and a reporting of studio earnings. *The Wall Street Journal* broke it first (unsurprisingly, because they are a daily), and the others followed suit with one- or two-page items covering essentially the same information. (The exception was *Forbes*, which did an in-depth study of motion picture financing and marketing techniques and how Hollywood is changing, in an article that included pictures and graphs.) One of the news versions of this item would have been sufficient to get the gist, and a look at the *Forbes* article would have been worthwhile.

IF IT'S A NEWSLETTER OR TRADE JOURNAL

Prior knowledge is assumed, so authors waste little time on preliminaries. Article length is not a reliable screening method here. *Give special attention to pictures, graphs, and diagrams.* These are used to illustrate or make a point. If there are many of them, you can get a good idea of what the article is about, and the information contained therein. The inclusion of just one illustration could be misleading, because authors wanting to add eye appeal often throw in a visual that has little to do with the text.

SKIMMING

The key to skimming is to (a) move your eyes in broad sweeps, very rapidly, one line at a time, and (b) look for key words, words that are outstanding or significant that convey the general ideas of the text. The uses of skimming:

A QUICK LOOK AT SOMETHING IMPORTANT   If you are really under the gun, but you can't possibly attend that meeting without some familiarity with the report, skim it. But remember that at best, skimming will provide half as much comprehension. So it's a sort of gamble if you really must "own" that material.

WEEDING OUT THE BULL   Skimming will help you decide which parts of a book, magazine, article, or report you will go back and read. You will be able to pick out the digressions, the "fluff" paragraphs, the meaningless quotes, and the spoon-feeding.

CHECKING FOR REDUNDANCY   In my opinion, redundancy is one of the biggest problems in coping with the information explosion. Frankly, some parts of this book contain information you may have seen elsewhere. Don't bother reading them! Key words can be an excellent clue.

Example: In 1979, the AFL-CIO had a convention during which (1) George Meany made his resignation speech, (2) President Carter spoke, and (3) the labor policies for the troubled times ahead were discussed. Fine; you read all about it in a newspaper or magazine.

Then you picked up another magazine, and it contained an article on labor. You saw the words "AFL-CIO Convention" and knew that much of what followed chronicled what was done and said there. The item was straight news, so you skipped it; you already knew what was done and said. Then you came upon an editorial and skimmed it to find the editorial meat. You skipped the tedium of reading who said what all over again.

The act of skimming is subjective. Not everyone will pick out the same key words or form exactly the same opinions about the material.

PREVIEWING

Like skimming, previewing is a screening and time-saving method; but it is a bit more methodical. It serves two main purposes: (1) preparing you for a second, more conventional reading, familiarizing you with the material; (2) searching out the essential elements of the material. When you must familiarize yourself with a report before the big meeting, previewing is far better than skimming, although doing both is ideal. Previewing is recommended by experts for material that is critical, technical, and lengthy; skimming works better for general, light reading.

- *Read the beginning of the material.* At least the first two paragraphs.
- *Read all the section, subsection, chapter, and subchapter headings.* Nonfiction books are filled with more and more subheadings and divisions, because it's been found that people like their information in smaller packages. Maybe it's because people can read an entire section whenever they've got a free moment. Whatever the reason, the numerous section headings are flags to the content of the material.
- *Read the first sentences of subheadings and paragraphs that catch your eye.*
- *Read anything marked "summary."*
- *Read eye-catchers like underlined, italicized, bold-type, or capitalized portions.* One exception: In previewing, stay away from footnotes. Often quite fascinating, they are not critical, or they would be part of the text.

QUALITY

There is a lot of reading material being passed off as new, significant, or controversial when in reality it is old, banal, and tiresome. When reading, be on the alert for empty words, sift them out and do not read the sentences that surround them. A few danger signs of poor workmanship:

IRRELEVANT HISTORICAL PASSAGES   When you're reading about the advantages of electronic typewriters, do you really want to know who invented the manual in 1817?

MEANINGLESS QUOTATIONS FROM IMPORTANT PEOPLE   We have all seen politicians in action. Do you think that they are the only VIPs that speak and say little? Very often an author will interview an expert for some insight. If the interviewee has nothing to say, it looks bad for him and makes the interviewer uncomfortable. So he often obliges with some articulate but essentially no-value-added drivel.

OUT-OF-DATE MATERIAL   Who wants yesterday's papers?

FLUFF   Articles and even books often have to meet length requirements. Thin books tend not to sell as well as thick ones. Magazines must fill the space they have blocked out for articles. Sometimes an author gets carried away with his ability and just keeps on writing. The result tends to be fluff. I could be a wise guy and fluff up this section to three times the size, but then I would be having fun at your expense. (See? I already added another three lines!)

EXAMPLEMANIA   Teach by examples. Illustrate by examples. All our teachers did it, and taught us to do it. But unless examples are worthwhile, they just waste space. Many authors overdo it.

FAULTY ANALOGIES   Some analogies just don't work.

FALSE ARGUMENTS   Circular reasoning, faulty generalizations, etc.

OVERUSE OF STATISTICS   Sometimes they help build an argument. That's good. Sometimes they are signals from the author: "Look at me, I'm thorough. I'm accurate. I'm scientific. I back up what I say!" That attitude breeds lots of numbers mixed in with words. Too many statistics = ZZZZZ.

Save only what you can use. If there is an article you want to read after skimming the magazine, save the article by tearing it out. Throw away the magazine; eliminate temptations.

SCREENING NONPRINT MEDIA

TELEVISION

Our ability to screen television programs is perhaps the best developed of all screening techniques (no pun intended). This is because we can't accumulate every television program. We must make choices. How do we do this?

- *Familiarity.* Programmers like to build audience loyalty. They do this by giving you just what you've come to expect. The only time they depart from their norm is when the ratings slip. So the more successful a show, the more consistent it will be. This allows you to make a guess as to which shows will be "message," which exposé.
- *Program guides.* Recent years have seen an increase of specials at the expense of series. Program guides do a reasonable job of summarizing a show.
- *Reviews.* Increasingly, television programs are being reviewed in the press and on radio—and on television itself. Fortunately, these reviewers seem to have no loyalties to the stations or networks for which they work.
- *TV skimming and previewing.* Flipping the dial. Watching the first ten minutes, etc. We all know how to do it.

The most important aspect of TV screening: When you've concluded that something isn't worth watching, DON'T WATCH!! Remember that TV news is redundant. The same items are repeated on news broadcasts throughout the day. A film report from Iran may start out on "Today" or "Good Morning America," with portions of it appearing on local news and the whole thing shown again on the network evening news. If the first few seconds of the film and voice-over are exactly the same, you know you've got a rerun.

VCR   VCRs, or videotape recorders, make selecting a TV program a bit easier, since you can tape a show and watch it later, or tape it while watching another show at the same time. All the more reason to be on your guard against garbage. The newer VCRs offer some help with a "preview" mode. This is a fast-forward mode that allows you to jump ahead and view segments in fast action. The drawback here is that you don't get any intelligible audio, so it's often difficult to determine what is going on. But help is on the way: Several companies have announced devices that speed up picture *and* audio in a manner that allows you to see *and* hear clearly.

RADIO

Listen to the radio for news. If nothing new has developed since the last time you wached the TV news, you can afford to skip TV—unless you are happily addicted to the little color stories and features.

AUDIO CASSETTES

These can be skimmed, although not as easily as print. If your tape machine has a "cue" feature:

1. Listen at regular intervals.
2. Be sensitive to "silent spots" that occur when the speaker pauses excessively, or stops to listen to a question from the audience. Using the "cue" device, you can chop off as much as 30 percent of the listening time in silent spots.
3. Preview the tape. Listen to the first five minutes to determine:
   a. The nature of the tape. Who is the main speaker?
   b. Is it a conference? A prepared speech? A professionally produced tape?
      - Conferences recorded "off the cuff" are hard to skim because they are largely unstructured and poorly organized.
      - Prepared speeches usually have a structure to them. See if you can lock into the structure. If you can, you'll know where the speaker is going and be able to skip his examples, asides, sick jokes, etc.
      - Professional tapes are easiest to skim. They have introductions and summaries and are often divided into small listening sections. You can easily jump ahead and/or replay parts of the tape, according to your need.

ON USING YOUR INTUITION

Screening is, to a large degree, intuition. The decision to buy a book and read it is not as easy to pin down. Many times you will decide to read or listen to something that on the surface seems silly, simplistic, or boring—but you have a feeling that it will turn out to be "special" in some way.

On the other side of the coin, anxiety over missing something may cause you to buy something wasteful. I have a lawyer friend who decided to "get into" real estate. He can't resist buying a real estate book, even though he invariably reports that the book contains "nothing new." He has hundreds of real estate books cluttering his bookshelves.

If in doubt, wait. Put it off for an hour. Or several days. And look again.

I.O.A.

The information explosion clearly has lots of people at wit's end. As a relief from what the prominent organizational psychologist Warren Bennis calls "Information Overload Anxiety" (I.O.A.), he has proposed "the Fat-Free Daily Reading Diet." To my way of thinking his diet is a bit lean, but I think the leanness is a deliberate attempt on Bennis's part to shock us into perceiving how little we need in order to get by.

THE FAT-FREE DAILY READING DIET

according to Bennis*

- **Newspapers** *The Wall Street Journal.*

- **News magazines** Limit one. Prefers *Newsweek.*

- **General Culture and Ideas** *Vogue, The Listener,* the Sunday *New York Times.* Beware of the Sunday *Times.* It can cause "terminal I.O.A." if the entire contents is attempted.

according to me

Add one local paper.

Read one selectively, skim one or two others. No preferences.

Agreed.

---

*From Warren G. Bennis, "A Prescription for Information Overload Anxiety" (*Technology Review,* June/July 1979), pp. 12–13, 88. Reprinted by permission.

- **Reference**   Random House Dictionary, National Directory of Addresses and Phone Numbers.

  There are several first-rate unabridged dictionaries. And why put a limit on reference works? The limit should be on the amount of time spent reading them. See the "personal reference library" section of Chapter 8 for recommended works.

- **Management and Business** *Business Week*, for its timeliness and concise coverage.

  Agreed. But skim *Forbes* and *Fortune* for important and relevant features. Mags like *Inc.*, *Venture*, and *Free Enterprise* tend to be a bit fluffy.

- **Science and Technology** *Scientific American* "gives the specialist too little and the nonspecialist too much." Bennis prefers *New Scientist*, from England.

  Problematic; depends on your background and special interest. *New Scientist* is good. So is *New Products and Processes*, published by *Newsweek.* It is unlikely that you will read any publication in this category cover to cover. Skim *Science 81*, *Psychology Today*. If you are involved with computers, be careful not to overdo it with technical and trade mags.

- **Other Items**   Monthly Economic Report, free from Morgan Guaranty Trust Co.; Statistical Bulletin, free from Metropolitan Life Insurance Company; *Manas* (philosophy/ideas); *Brain/Mind* (psychology/behavior).

  Stock, bond, and commodity market analyses, free from major brokerage houses like Merrill Lynch and Smith Barney. Limit: one or two magazines and one or two newsletters of your choice. If you find *Manas* or *Brain/Mind* too heavy, why not choose a mag or two for recreational reading? *Smithsonian*, *Natural History*, *Harper's*, *Quest*, *Sports Illustrated*, *Esquire*, or the irrepressible *New Yorker* are a few suggestions. And by all means, make time to read through an occasional book— but choose carefully.

DEVELOPING YOUR OWN MEDIA MIX

Managing the format and flow of information is really an offshoot of management. So you should begin by logging your "information time." Using the following list, log just how much time is spent daily in gathering information from each of these categories. Be specific. At the end of the day, evaluate your activities and set priorities. Are you spending too much time on *Sports Illustrated?* Not enough on *The Bank Credit Analyst?* Perhaps you aren't reading enough. Whatever the case, use the log results to construct a media-mix plan in which you allot time to specific information activities. Always take into account the flow of material. If it's a weekly magazine, when does it arrive? If it's a TV program, it has a specific viewing time. (If you have a video recorder and you tape the show, when will you watch it?) If it's a tape, book, or magazine, is it borrowed? When must it be returned? After a short time, patterns will form naturally. And you will better understand and control your own methods of coping with the information explosion.

MEDIA LOG

Date	Time	Type of Media	Title	Priority	Comments (Value; sections read, etc.)
9/3	8:15 – 9:00	magazine	_Business Week_	important	valuable article on German consumer mkt in Int'l Business. Spent too much time on article about skiing and book reviews.
9/3	3:10 – 3:30	magazine	_People_	unimportant	Read while waiting to see doctor. Next time, bring important reading to doctor's office!

Fig. 10. Sample media log
Use this format, or design one of your own.

Magazines

business
news
consumer
special interest

Television

business related
educational
general entertainment
social issues oriented
    entertainment
public affairs
religious
news

Radio

news
public affairs
self-improvement features
religious

Books

business
technical
general nonfiction
fiction
history
case studies

Audio cassette/Videocassette

business conferences
business courses
self-improvement
business book condensations
fiction and nonfiction
    book condensations
magazines on tape

Databases

statistics
abstracts
newswires
newsletters
full text articles

Fig. 11. Media checklist
This list can be used in planning your own media mix.

7

USING YOUR HEAD

All the craziness caused by information overload serves to underscore a fascinating paradox: We have trouble coping with the tremendous amount of information bombarding us from our environment, but in reality our brains are far from overloaded.

In fact *our brains have virtually unlimited potential.* If you feel intimidated by the office computer, just remember that next to your brain, that computer is like comparing the rubbing together of two sticks to the operating of a nuclear reactor. The human brain far outclasses even the largest computer in versatility and complexity.

Peter Russell, in his stimulating and useful *The Brain Book,** gives a few examples of the brain's capacities and capabilities. A brief summary:

- *Storage.* The brain can store 1,000 bits of new information per second from the moment of birth to old age with room to spare. Recent research indicates that we may remember everything that happens to us.
- *Recognition.* The brain can recognize a face in less than a second. No computer can do that.
- *Miniaturization.* Are you amazed by those pictures of powerful computer chips no bigger than a fingertip? Well, even with such miniaturization, a computer that could do all the brain could do would weigh more than ten tons and would be too large to fit in Carnegie Hall.

The brain is still the best thinking machine we know.

So, why the problem? Scientists estimate that we use only a small percentage of our brains. These estimates range from one to ten percent, and Russell puts the figure at an even smaller .1 percent or less. Some believe that geniuses of Einsteinian magnitude are capable of using perhaps a little more of their brain's capacity. Imagine what they could do with 50 percent.

We have never been properly taught how to use the brain. We don't know how it works, how to get the most out of it, or the kind and form

*From Peter Russell, *The Brain Book.* Copyright © 1979 by Peter Russell. Reprinted by permission of the publisher, Hawthorn Books, a Division of Elsevier-Dutton Publishing Co., Inc.

of information that it responds to best. There is still a great deal that we don't know about the brain, but we have learned a lot since today's adults were in grade school. What follows are some tips on how to improve your brain's ability to absorb, process, and retain information.

READING BETTER

Many books have little to offer in the way of new information and are poorly written to boot. It is therefore understandable that one would not want to spend the same amount of time reading a business or technical book, newsletter or office paperwork as one would spend reading Shakespeare, John Cheever, Thoreau, or even Peter Drucker.

One way in which executives cope is to learn what must be read and what can be skimmed. The difference is like that between food and vitamins. Food is to be savored and enjoyed; vitamins are gulped down, as quickly and painlessly as possible.

Another popular solution to the reading problem, besides skimming, is rapid reading. Before we see just how this can help you and how you can learn the technique, consider what we have learned about reading in recent years:

MYTH	*TRUTH*
• *Words are read one at a time.*	We read for meaning, so we fixate on phrases—groups of words that convey meaning.
• *500-plus wpm is impossible.*	Still some controversy, but it does appear likely that we can read faster than 500 wmp.
• *A fast reader can't really appreciate what he reads.*	This is a matter of degree. A good reader knows that he shouldn't read everything as fast as possible, but as fast as comfortable. If you read at a rapid rate, appreciation of the material can actually be improved: There is less boredom, more rhythm to the reading process, and less muscular fatigue.

- *High speeds mean lower comprehension.*

Wrong. Faster speeds mean less starting and stopping, and therefore greater concentration. Seeing a greater amount of words in less time enables one to get a more comprehensive overview and better perspective on the material. Thus there is a better chance of perceiving order and association—further aids to comprehension and memory.

- *Average reading speeds are best.*

Nonsense. Average does not mean natural. Everyone, from health food freaks to auto buffs, knows that statistics on national averages don't always denote something positive. An average is just a mathematical term; it doesn't tell us much about individual capacities. And when it comes to reading, average speeds reflect abnormally slow speeds resulting from inadequate teaching methods—the Jugheads in the sample who pull the average down.

PROBLEMS ASSOCIATED WITH READING

Rapid reading involves unlearning inadequate techniques as much as it does learning useful new ones. Here are some of the problems that may be slowing you down, and what can be done about them.

BACK-SKIPPING OR REGRESSION   Going back over words and phrases. This is unnecessary and useless. It is primarily the result of apprehension and in no way aids comprehension. The experts try to cut this out completely.

SLOW FIXATION   Your eyes stay with a word grouping longer than they should. This problem is tackled by training you to increase your speed, spending about one quarter-second on each fixation, and also learning to take in more words per fixation.

VISUAL WANDERING   Eyes wander off during reading. This is eliminated by vastly increasing speed, much in the way that a trainer builds intensity and concentration in athletes by moving them through a workout at a faster pace. It's also like watching a comedian: If he tells his jokes fast enough, he can keep your interest even if only half his jokes are good, because if you hate one, there's usually a good one not far behind. We tend to wander off our reading when we hit slow or boring spots, but if we're moving fast enough, we tend to wander off course less. There is almost always better material not far ahead.

CONSCIOUS REGRESSION   Reading something over again on purpose, because you didn't think you got it the first time. Once you learn to read properly, your comprehension will improve and you won't be doing this. But you might occasionally pause at some point to think about an unusually difficult concept. Reading something over doesn't provide anything new.

ALTERED BREATHING AND SUBVOCALIZING   While reading, many of us breathe as if we are speaking out what we read; or we may actually vocalize the words as they are read, usually (but not always) at an inaudible level. If you move your lips when your read, or feel activity in your larynx, you've got one of these problems. Your reading speed then tends to be limited by how fast you can speak.

RAPID READING

The average reading speed of the American executive is 200-250 words per minute. This is slower than college level. In today's business climate it is unacceptable, since you will have difficulty reading as much as you should. A slow reading rate can hold you back considerably. Here are the pros and cons of rapid reading:

CON	PRO
• *The rapid-reading firms make exaggerated claims.* Evelyn Wood, the Coca-Cola of the industry, claims to have taught more than ten million people to read three to ten times faster with improved comprehension. Most experts on reading believe our maximum reading speed is between 800-1200 wpm. (After that, they say, you're skimming, with great loss in comprehension.)	Many academics are short-sighted, claiming that the maximum reading speed is 600 wpm—until shown otherwise.
• *They teach skimming, not reading.*	They teach both. And skimming is a very useful skill.

• *Rapid reading takes the joy out of reading.*	Some rapid-reading experts deny this outright. Others say that you needn't speed-read everything. If you would rather read poetry or the Bible more slowly, do so.
• *Rapid reading emphasizes speed over comprehension and retention.*	Speed is essential for good comprehension and retention. The reader gets a better view of the whole because he sees more in less time; thus he can place things in context and see patterns that will enable him to remember.

Both sides have their points, which makes it that much more difficlt to decide whether or not to take a rapid-reading course, or, if you have already done so, to continue reading in this manner. Most courses emphasize two principal benefits: increased speed and comprehension.

SPEED   This is highly subjective. Some people have the ability to read faster than others. One thing is clear—almost everyone can improve reading speed. Is it actually beneficial to do so? Again, that depends on you—and on what you read. Several reading teachers I have spoken to point out that what many people really need is remedial reading, not speed reading, because they lack the basic reading skills. Speed reading will be of little benefit to these people.

COMPREHENSION   Recognition of words and sentences is not the same as understanding the ideas they are communicating. And understanding is different from remembering. Therefore, what counts is how fast you can grasp what you are reading, not how fast your eyes can move down the page. And you must be able to retain what you've understood so it doesn't leave you two pages later. There is a good indication that in this regard the words-per-minute come-on is bunk. If your ability to read outstrips your ability to comprehend, you are not accomplishing anything. And if your ability to comprehend something does not include some means of fixing the ideas in your memory, you will not be able to make much use of what you've read. *Speed must vary with material, because the material will determine how long it will take you to grasp its contents.*

Some time ago a Columbia University reading teacher prepared a one-page test for a roomful of speedreading graduates. He was amazed to discover they read at speeds of almost 6,000 words a minute. To be sure they understood what they read, he asked them to do it again—in fact, two more times. Their average quickly parachuted to about 1700 wpm, still extremely impressive. Then the teacher told them the sad fact: What they read had absolutely no meaning. The teacher had stitched together a page of pure mumbo-jumbo, taking two lines from one magazine article and then two lines from another—all the way down the page.

—"Faster, Faster," by Randall Poe, in
Across the Board, February, 1978

THE BASIC PRINCIPLES OF RAPID READING

INCREASE THE NUMBER OF WORDS PER FIXATION   In order for the eyes to see a moving object in focus, they must move. If the object is still, the eyes must be still. And since words are still, the eyes must stop, at least micromomentarily, to allow them to focus on the words.

So the eyes don't move smoothly across the printed page, like an express train, but rather in a series of jumps and stops, like a local train rushing to get back on schedule. The jumps take very little time, but the stops take more. Using your train analogy, it's as if the ride between stations was very short, because the stations are so close together, but the time spent at each stop is long. In speed-reading lingo, these stops made by the eyes on words or groups of words are called *fixations*. These fixations take place between one-quarter and one-half second.

A main principle of speed reading is *to train the eye to see more words per stop*—a whole phrase perhaps, instead of one or two words—and that will result in faster reading.

USE PERIPHERAL VISION IN READING   We do see out of the corners of our eyes, and although whole words and phrases gathered in by our peripheral vision may not be in focus enough so that they may be read conventionally, they do cue us to what is coming next. Reading specialists believe that they can train people to be able to absorb the words that are captured by their peripheral vision, and also to increase the scope of peripheral vision to take in more words—from above and below as well as from the sides.

INCREASE THE NUMBER OF FIXATIONS PER SECOND   Studies indicate that the eye can register five words per one-hundredth of a second. Specialists have been successful in reducing fixation time at least to the faster end of the acceptable range, one quarter-second. Obviously, this increases speed.

SPOT REDUNDANCY IN PRINTED ENGLISH   Our brain can recognize letters and even words by seeing just parts of them—shapes, curves, and only a few key letters instead of all. In addition, many words and phrases can be omitted from written material without loss of meaning.

The principles that form the basis of all speed-reading techniques are without a doubt valuable and, if practiced, will increase your speed and comprehension.

Applying the principles

1. *To some degree, the manner in which you read is a habit.* And habits are hard to break. You must retrain yourself to read. This is tough, and it's the best reason for going to a speed-reading course; it will force you to break old habits. If you are doing it on your own, practice for a few minutes before reading.

2. *Once you learn the principles, use them.* People have a tendency to slip backward to old patterns developed as a child.

3. *Satisfy yourself.* Forget words-per-minute. If you feel comfortable with your reading and comprehension, and have sufficient time to finish all the material, that's just fine.

Using the basic principles, rapid-reading experts make lots of money teaching people to read faster.

WHAT THEY DO

- Eliminate regression and back-slipping.
- Increase number of fixations per second.
- Expand area of fixation.
- Increase motivation.
- Teach previewing, skimming, and other aids that help you cut down on the sheer volume of reading material.
- Make greater use of peripheral vision and the redundancy factor in reading.

HOW THEY DO IT

- *High-speed training.* If you drive at 90 mph for a few hours, when you come back down to 70, it'll feel like its pretty slow, even if 70 was fast by comparison to your usual 55. The reading teachers go for broke, pushing you to break boundaries even to the point of telling you to move your hand, eyes, across the page as fast as physically possible and turning the pages as fast as you can. This encourages the reader to take in more with his eyes, to break the habit of reading at a set pace, and to use the right side of the brain in the reading process (when we read left to right, the material seen in the right visual field goes to the left side of the brain). When you read fast, both sides of the brain are brought into play more readily. High-speed training also improves the ability to pick out key words—often the only things you ever see when you do this exercise. High-speed training helps break the subvocalizing habit because you are forced to read much faster than you can subvocalize.
- *Visual guides.* Some kind of pointer—your finger or a book mark, etc. By learning to follow the pointer, back-skipping can be eliminated. The visual guide can also increase speed, because as we increase the movement of the pointer, the eyes will tend to go

along with it. By altering the pattern of the pointer's movement on the page, we can expand the focus of the fixation and thereby increase speed and comprehension.

- *Breathing exercises.* Regular, even breathing is best for reading, and the experts use exercises in which awareness of breathing takes precedence over speed and comprehension.
- *Metronome training.* This can establish a smooth rhythm. It also helps build speed.
- *Motivational training.* What you get when you cross an Evelyn Wood with a Vince Lombardi. People at these courses get geared up for speed. Sample lessons do more than just hook the person into taking the course. The small accomplishment of experiencing an increase in reading speed in just one night makes us hungry: Students return with a burning desire to read faster. Of course, instructors must keep students aware of the basic fact that it is the responsibility of the individual student to put the technique into practice. Many claim that the motivational aspect of these courses is far more productive than are the actual techniques. Certainly, the charged atmosphere and constant "take it to the limit" evaluations are what make these courses more effective than study-at-home cassette and workbook courses offering the same techniques.
- *Computer software.* There are several software programs designed to improve reading speed and comprehension. Among the better packages is Smart Eyes, a software learning program published by Addison-Wesley of Reading, Massachusetts. It is a practical, useful program that lets you practice on your own text if you wish.

LISTENING BETTER

Listening is unquestionably the weakest link in the communications chain. Poor listening ability can hurt your career more than just about anything else.

Very little that is heard is actually remembered. Even less is understood. As with reading, the problem is not with our cognitive capacities. We are capable of absorbing and reacting to hundreds, even thousands of auditory bits each second. And good listening is not a matter of hanging on every word. We hear on many levels—phrases, sentences, sounds, tones and intonations—complemented by nonverbal cues such as gestures and facial expressions.

The failure, says noted communications expert Tony Schwartz, is not in the listening, but in the failure to *attend* to what we hear. Again, this is analogous to reading, where the problem is not in reading the words, but in how we process what we read.

The business world is filled with poor listeners. It's tough enough to communicate with peers, but this problem pales by comparison to the difficulty of communicating downward. There is evidence that as much as 80 percent of an original item of information is lost in three sequential downward transmissions.

There is little that can compare to the exhilaration of beginning a response to a speaker by reeling off a lucid summary of what he has just said. It is a great way to shower respect and laudation on the speaker—or a great way to begin to cut his argument to pieces. The choice is yours. Either way, good, careful listening is so rare you are bound to be remembered.

HOW TO BE A BETTER LISTENER

PREPARE   Familiarize yourself with the subject to be discussed. Be fresh, well rested, and comfortable. This will minimize distractions and help you pay close attention.

PUT THE SPEAKER AT EASE   Make sure that the speaker is comfortable, and look and act interested. If the speaker is comfortable and feels that the listener is receptive, he'll do a better job.

LISTEN WITH COMMITMENT   Listening to someone is not just a matter of placing yourself within earshot. It is an act of will, and you may have to work at it. In the business world it is said that the higher up you go, the harder you must work to listen to others.

MAINTAIN A GOOD MENTAL ATTITUDE   Be open-minded, interested, and empathetic. Try to see the subject from the speaker's point of view. If you are unable or unwilling to do this, you are probably wasting your time.

KNOW YOUR BIASES AND PREJUDICES   While self-examination alone doesn't often change a person, it is important to be aware of one's own biases and prejudices. You will be more alert, and therefore better able to keep those biases under control and prevent them from interfering with your listening ability. Let's be frank. If you are one of those who think that, say, women are not as smart as men, you should be listening extra carefully and attentively when a woman speaks to you. You must try to compensate for your tendency to devalue—on account of her sex—anything she says.

Value judgments apply to occupations, life-styles, and geographical areas as well as to sex, race, and religion. For example, many people are suspicious of so-called experts, or specialists in a given field. Others prefer to hear the word from an expert than from a dynamic professional speaker. There are those who care little about the speaker's credentials or communications skills as long as he seems trustworthy. Where do you stand? Ask yourself how receptive you will be to the speaker because of such prejudgments.

CONCENTRATE Most people start out paying close attention. After a while, that attention drops off, and then increases again toward the end of the listening period. Try to hear more than just the beginning and the end of what someone is saying by staying with him during the bulk of the talk.

DON'T LET YOURSELF GET DISTRACTED Once you get used to the sound of the speaker's voice and to the accompanying gestures, and get a rough idea of what he is saying, there is a tendency to seek out some other object of attention. It could be anything from the newspaper on your desk, to a hangnail, to admiring someone's looks. This will obviously interfere with your reception ability. Another key source of distraction is your own thoughts. Whether reflections on what has just been said or just simple daydreaming, your thoughts can interfere with the listening process. Try to focus on what is being said, keeping your inner thoughts at bay.

It is not easy to cut out distractions, especially if the speaker is dull. If this is the case, try to cut him off, get him to cut it short, or make a conscious decision not to listen. Don't let the situation get away from you, because giving in to distractions is a bad habit, and you may find yourself doing it to an important speaker or someone with something very worthwhile to say.

LISTEN CRITICALLY Look for specious arguments, poor logic, improper assumptions, half-truths, and inaccurate statistics. This will keep you sharp and involved in the listening process. And if by chance you find yourself on an opposing side, you'll have accumulated enough ammunition to torpedo the speaker.

TRY TO ISOLATE THE MAIN POINTS Many people have difficulty getting to the point. They give all sorts of examples, faulty analogies, and anecdotes that are off the topic. Zero in on the main points. That the speaker's mind is cluttered or muddled doesn't mean yours must follow suit. Good listening means separating the grain from the chaff.

WATCH FOR NONVERBAL CUES Social scientists tell us that much of what is communicated is expressed in a nonverbal manner—by tone of voice, facial expressions, and gestures. While there are several good books purporting to teach you how to interpret body language, you already know a great deal. For example, when you see a speaker clenching and unclencing his fists, what does that tell you? All you really have to do is be observant.

TAKE AN ACTIVE ROLE Give feedback whenever possible. Let the speaker know that you understand, that you are following him. Or that you don't and aren't. Ask for more information when needed.

SEEK OUT A GOOD LISTENING POST You should be comfortable too. Find a seat or location where all the information is available to you without strain. In a lecture situation, that might mean you should be in the center of the room, or up front, or just away from the window and the noise from the street.

DELAY FORMULATING YOUR ARGUMENTS   The most common listening problem is that the would-be listener is preparing his reply while the speaker is talking. This is the chief reason why so little actual listening takes place. If you can't repeat what the speaker has just said to his satisfaction, you haven't been listening, and your reply, whatever it is, will carry less credibility.

DON'T INTERRUPT   Rude. Boorish. Breaks the speaker's train of thought. And makes it tougher to follow his thread.

HOLD YOUR TEMPER   Something that was said got you angry? That doesn't automatically entitle you to take the floor. Besides, few people can think or speak clearly when they are fighting mad. Sit on it until your turn comes.

DON'T TALK TOO MUCH   Many of us love to hear ourselves. But that is not the purpose of a discussion. You already know what you think. Express yourself only when appropriate. When you've made your point, give the other person a chance to respond.

GO EASY   When you are criticizing or arguing, be careful. Unless you are going for a knockout, you don't want to put the other person on the defensive to the extent that he tightens up or gets angry. Communication then breaks down. You may win the battle, but lose the war.

HOW TO AVOID COMMON LISTENING TRAPS

Listening is *the* basic skill for negotiation, arguing a point, and carrying out orders. Here are a few suggestions that will safeguard against costly mistakes:

WHEN YOU HAVE JUST LISTENED TO SOMETHING OF VITAL IMPORTANCE, REPHRASE IT ACCORDING TO YOUR UNDERSTANDING   Repeat it to the source to check whether you have it right. Say, "So what you're saying is . . ." or "Let me see if I understand you correctly. . . ."

WHEN YOU MUST ACCEPT AND CARRY OUT AN ORDER THAT YOU DISAGREE WITH, MAKE SURE YOU HAVE IT RIGHT   First, you often become so involved with your counter-argument that you may miss the details of the order. And second, if you carry out an order improperly because you didn't hear it right, it could be taken for a rebellious act, since you are already on record as a dissenter. *In many cases an inverse relationship exists between the degree of excitement generated by something you've just been told, and the level of comprehension of that information.* When you get particularly worked up about something, make sure you have the facts right and any instructions clear.

WHEN YOU FIND SOMETHING BORING, DON'T STOP PAYING ATTENTION   It may be boring because you are lost, not because the information is dull or irrelevant. Besides, a boring speaker can at any moment become lucid and start spitting out important information.

NOTE TAKING

Most business people take crumby notes. Either they attempt to capture every word on paper, missing the sense of the whole they would get from relaxing, listening to, and watching the speaker; or they take haphazard, poorly organized, sketchy notes, which are of little or no value when they are needed. Many executives eschew taking notes, undoubtedly because they think it's bad for their image.

Just like school, isn't it? In high school or college, poor notes mean poor study and mediocre grades. But this is the real world, where a B— can cost thousands of dollars. At a crucial meeting, a tête-à-tête with your boss, lawyer, or accountant, you've got to nail it right.

WHY CONVENTIONAL NOTE TAKING IS INEFFICIENT

WE WASTE TIME WRITING WORDS THAT WON'T HELP US RECALL THE CONTENT   And then waste time rereading those unnecessary words. Learning-methods specialist Tony Buzan estimates that these words account for over 90 percent of note taking.

WE SPEND TOO MUCH TIME SEARCHING FOR THE KEY WORDS THAT CONVEY MEANING AND IMPORTANT CONCEPTS   This is difficult and time consuming, because key words are mixed in with all those irrelevant words and phrases. With these words few and far between, it is hard to form the associations and connections between the key words and their concepts. Psychologists believe such associates are necessary for learning and memory.

WHILE WE ARE BUSY TAKING NOTES, WE RISK MISSING MUCH OF WHAT THE SPEAKER IS SAYING   Since nine out of ten words are useless, we should be able to take good notes in one-tenth the time of verbatim note taking.

In spite of all this, note taking is worthwhile. Whether or not you consult your notes afterward, items that are written down are six times as likely to be remembered as those that are not. Good note taking is a method of encoding information and organizing it in the way most useful for you. If you do it right, you should have time to jot down interpretations and inferences. When you return to your notes, they should immediately draw your attention to what is important.

Some recent innovations based on learning research can make the task a great deal easier.

THE MIND MAP

A mind map is simply a means of taking notes that is more in accord with the modes of association and memory utilized by the brain.

The brain responds to organization. It thrives on it, searches for it. And if the material is not organized, the brain seeks to impose its own order. Mind maps allow material to be more easily, rapidly, and clearly organized.

The higher the percentage of key words in the notes, the higher the recall. Mind maps involve the recording of only key words and ideas. This reduces bulk wordage and insures that the words written are rich in meaning. Maps also aid comprehension of the material by forcing one to listen actively in order to extract the key words and concepts.

The brain is aided in its associative ability if the words and ideas are clustered together visually. A mind map allows you to write key words near related ideas. With conventional linear notes, ideas often appear in the chronological order of their presentation. If the speaker is disorganized or skips around, so do the notes.

The brain will more easily retain that which is visually interesting or outstanding. The mind-map method completely rejects the grade-school concept of neat, orderly notes. With conventional notes, every page looks the same. Not so with mind maps, since the note taker is encouraged to vary sizes, shapes, colors, and images used. When pictures work better than words, they are used.

We respond more readily to that in which we become more involved. Mind maps are the antithesis of mindless copying. They are engaging, original, and fun. You are actively involved in creating a highly personal set of notes. And since the process is less time consuming, it's easier to pay attention to what's being said.

HOW TO MAKE MIND-MAP NOTES

Put central ideas at the center of the page. Mind maps should be organized in an organic manner, like cells. The nucleus—the main idea—is at the center, and as we move away from it, we encounter more specialized organs. Some time management planners such as Dayrunner have special pages for mind maps.

Use key words. Print the words rather than using script. Use lower case except where added emphasis is desired.

Use lines and arrows to link related or associated concepts. The best way is to write the key words on separate lines, and then connect those lines with other lines. If you run words together in a given line, you'll quickly close up the map and run out of room to add more key words to their proper places. The idea is to leave the map open-ended at all times, so that you can put a key word in its proper place even if a central concept comes at the end of the talk.

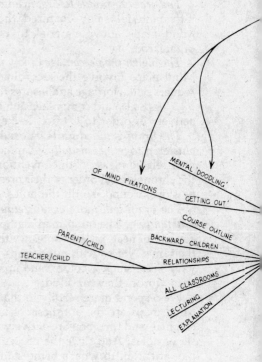

Fig. 12. Sample mind map
This map outlines the many uses of mind maps,
as detailed in Tony Buzan's book.

From *Use Both Sides of Your Brain*, by Tony Buzan, p. 103.
Copyright © 1974 by Tony Buzan. Reprinted by permission
of the publisher, E. P. Dutton.

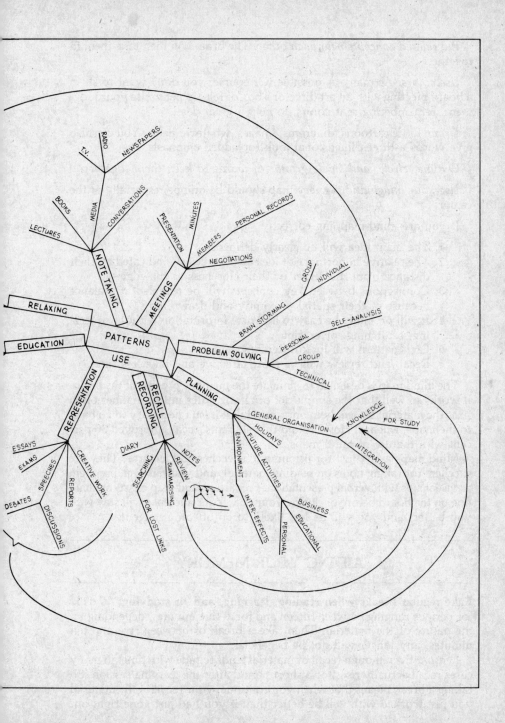

Put related concepts near each other. The brain will then take them in together.

Use colors. As many as possible. Of course, you don't want to sit in a board meeting with an art director's box of felt-tip pens. Use your judgment, remembering that colors do help a great deal.

Draw. Little cartoons, diagrams, images, whatever helps. You can also give words a three-dimensional look for added emphasis.

Outline, circle, and shade groups of words to keep them together.

Use your imagination. Every map should be unique, especially at the center.

If you are mind-mapping correctly:

1. The main idea will be clearly defined.
2. The relative importance of ideas will be clearly indicated by their distance from the center or their closeness to the edge.
3. Connections between key concepts will be revealed at a glance because of their spatial proximity and drawn links.
4. It will probably be easy to add new information without squeezing, scratching, or erasing.
5. Each pattern will look different.
6. Recall and review will be more effective and take less time.

The mind map is designed to simulate the memory process of the brain. It works so well that the simple act of taking notes in this manner often fixes the material so deeply in one's mind that it isn't necessary to go back to the maps. Michael Howe found that students' recall improved 50 percent with the use of mind maps.

Mind maps aren't just for listening to speeches and lectures. They are excellent for taking notes on reading material, and you can even use them as visual aids with verbal presentation. Prepare a mind-map chart, or chalk one on the board before or during your talk. Your audience will stay with you better, and you will be less likely to go off on a tangent.

AIDING YOUR MEMORY

Take regular breaks when reading, learning, and/or studying. Work for periods ranging between fifteen and forty-five minutes, depending on the nature of the material. Then take a break of between five and ten minutes; any longer will not be beneficial.

Reason: Even though recall of material tends to fade with time, in many cases recall actually rises for a short period after the learning session. So taking a break means that when you continue, your recall of the material you just worked with will be better than if you had just gone right on.

It may save you lots of time in looking back over what you just read.

Another reason: In any learning situation, the beginning and the end of a session are remembered better than the rest. So if you break up the sessions into smaller ones, you have more sessions and thus more beginnings and ends.

Before beginning, plan the time and work schedule in advance—and stick to it. Remember what the break is for. Breaking too often or too long means too little time spent on the material to make any real sense of it or to allow you to get an overview. Very long work sessions, on the other hand, will defeat your purpose.

Reason: At certain times you'll feel that you are really rolling along, and that there is no need for a break. Actually, it has been found that interrupting people at times like this, when they are very much involved in their work, leads to even greater recall. If you go by the clock and not by your subjective mood, you won't fall into the habit of skipping breaks.

Another reason: When you get absorbed in your work, you may have a sense of profound understanding and insight into what you are reading. You may not think a break is necessary. But what we are talking about here is *remembering.* And as both Buzan and Russell are quick to point out, *understanding something and remembering it are two different things; they don't necessarily go hand in hand.*

During the breaks, rest, relax, get some air; take a total rest from the type of material you've been working on. If you merely switch to something similar, you will not get the full benefit of the rest.

Reason: During the rest period the mind will organize and condense what it has learned. Let it do that unimpeded by still more material.

When returning to work, spend a minute or two going over the previous material. This may seem ridiculous, since you stopped only five or ten minutes ago, but it has been found that such a review acts as a warm-up. It brings the material into focus, and gets you set to begin anew.

But isn't the habit of taking breaks considered a time-waster? Yes, it is, in the negative form discussed in my section on time management; but those breaks are the result of distractions or procrastination. Here we are talking about breaks that serve a very specific purpose, and that must be performed with discipline according to a planned routine. Do not decide to take a break just because a phone call has come in. Rather, use your ten-minute break to make phone calls; have your secretary tell the caller that you will get back to him later (when you take your break).

Apply these same memory-aiding principles to oral communications. You've probably heard the adage "First tell them what you are going to say, then say it, and finally, tell them what you've said." This makes sense in light of what we know about our memory patterns.

1. Give the most important information during periods of high recall for the auditor—ideally, at the beginning and at the end of your talk.
2. Use high-recall periods to summarize, preview the next portion of your talk, or drive home the key concept.
3. If your talk is much longer than fifteen minutes, take a short break (tell your listeners how long). Or simply stop to pour some coffee, etc. Try this even in a conference or meeting when you have the floor.

Make your ideas stand out. Exaggerate an idea or otherwise embellish it. In reacting, you can underline, make colorful notes and doodles, and think about how the idea is unique.

Reason: Research has shown that we tend to remember elements that stand out from things around them.

Associate. Association is a basic memory tool utilized by the brain, which makes all sorts of connections between things that are remembered. Research has shown that the context and the environment in which the information is learned or experienced play a very important role.

Take stock of your surroundings and situation and associate these with the material you are learning.

Try to form clear associations between ideas.

Organize.

LOOK FOR A PATTERN, RULE, OR PRINCIPLE THAT MAY GOVERN OR APPLY TO OR UNITE THE MATERIAL YOU ARE TRYING TO REMEMBER   There is evidence that the mind attempts this involuntarily, because it is a basic strategy for memory. Help it along voluntarily. The better the organization, the easier the memory.

BREAK UP LARGE AMOUNTS OF MATERIAL INTO SMALLER CHUNKS   Find some classification or means or organizing them that will break them down. A common example is to break down major markets into smaller chunks by geographic regions.

Visualize. *Visualize what you want to remember, whether it be a graph, a face, or a warehouse shelf.*

Reason: We take in through our eyes most of what we learn. And although many scientists believe that we have some capacity for a "photographic" memory, the ability remains latent. We are so unaccustomed to forming mental pictures of things, places, and people that we have failed to develop that ability, or allowed it to atrophy.

Be more aware of your surroundings and try to picture them with eyes closed. Do the same for other senses. Imagine smells, noises, touches that you've recently experienced. Awaken these lost abilities. Note how often children do it. Research has shown that children are better than adults at remembering what they have seen. Children rely more on what they see of the physical world than on symbols like words and numbers.

8

INFORMATION GATHERING

"Knowledge is of two kinds," wrote Samuel Johnson. "We know a subject outselves, or we know where we can find information upon it."

Knowing a subject is the direct outgrowth of experience. And for experience there is no substitute. But the next best thing is knowing where to look for the best information gathered through the experience of others.

CHOOSING A BUSINESS MAGAZINE

GENERAL BUSINESS PUBLICATIONS

LOOK AT A FEW COPIES FIRST   Borrow them from friends or pick them up around the office or in waiting rooms. I would suggest buying an issue or two off the newsstand, but that doesn't make much sense pricewise: Often, a trial subscription is just a few dollars more than the price of several issues. If you can't find a few issues to look at, but you have a feeling that this magazine is for you, take a trial subscription that can be canceled for a full refund. Then look at the first issue; if you're not satisfied, write "cancel" on the invoice and mail it back. Do not pay the bill out of laziness. You don't want useless magazines cluttering your house or office. They will seduce your attention and take valuable reading time away from better information sources.

GET A FIX ON THE EDITORIAL POLICY   Something should emerge from reading the magazine. Is it very newsy? Or does it concentrate on case studies, dealing with contemporary business issues by giving examples of how successful companies deal with them? Does the content seem weighted in terms of marketing information, or is it geared more toward finance? How about approach: Does it assume too much knowledge or experience on your part, or, perhaps, too little?

If you are still confused, just drop a note to the publisher asking for a summary of readership statistics. This will tell you who reads the magazine, where he works, how much he makes, what his interests are, etc. You can get an idea of the target audience, and then determine whether you stand to benefit from a magazine geared toward such a group. I know many male executives who read *Redbook* and the *Ladies Home Journal* because it puts them in touch with a market that is primary for their products, and there are women who read *Playboy*, *Esquire*, and *Sports Illustrated* for similar reasons. Thus, even consumer magazines can function as business magazines.

IS IT FUN TO READ?   Style is important, because some people prefer the bare facts and others like anecdotes, or articles with a sense of humor. Some magazines give the pros and cons of an issue; others take one side or the other. Since even business-related reading should be enjoyable, pick magazines you like to read. But keep their strengths and weaknesses in mind and try to compensate for the latter in other ways.

FREQUENCY   Monthly or weekly or daily? You'll have to plan your reading schedule accordingly.

TECHNICAL AND TRADE PUBLICATIONS

Follow procedures for general publications, and take a good look at who writes the articles and who publishes.

Are the writers and contributors industry experts or those working in industry? Or are they staff writers?

Although staff writers are more objective, they are often novices in the industry and are unable to dig out the truly useful or "inside" information.

Many periodicals are published solely as a vehicle for advertisements; the features don't say much about anything. Some executives rely on advertisements as a source of information and as a way of keeping in touch with the competition. If this is your bag, then such a publication is worthwhile. A general rule: If the mag is free or very cheap, it is advertiser supported and thus laden with ads.

Sometimes a trade journal is not published by an independent company, but is the publishing arm of a national organization or a lobby of some sort. Thus it may carry a strong editorial bias; keep this in mind.

CHOOSING A NEWSLETTER

Newsletters are a multimillion-dollar industry. They are usually very expensive to subscribers, but very inexpensive to produce. This translates into big profits. Why do people pay $100 and more for a four-page, single-color report with no fancy paper or pictures? The primary reason is advice—and newsletters can be a valuable and convenient way to get information. The newsletter concept is predicated on the principle that the advice found in it is the sole property of those who subscribe to the letter; in a sense, it is an extension of the consultant idea. Some newsletter writers go to great lengths to support this notion, setting up "hotline" phone numbers to provide daily updates of the advice provided in the newsletter, and holding seminars around the country from time to time to which newsletter subscribers are invited free or at a reduced rate.

The concept gained momentum on Wall Street. Various analysts supply their stock market tips and picks each week to eager but confused traders, speculators, and investors. Some of the analysts—such as Jim Dines, author of the *Dines Letter*, and Joseph Granville—have been so successful with this activity that it has become primary rather than secondary. The current Cinderella of the field is entrepreneur Howard Ruff, a former actor, whose *Ruff Times* newsletter, combined with books and a syndicated TV show, grosses several million dollars. Ruff is not a stock expert; he counsels people on prudent investment strategies in these troubled times.

Newsletters exist covering all kinds of things—diamonds, gold, art, tax shelters, inflation, etc. Since the circulation is small and the information highly specialized, supposedly worth a great deal of money in potential profits or savings, the newsletters seem worth the price even at a hundred or two hundred bucks. But simple arithmetic will tell you that any one of these that catches fire will net the author a pretty sum. So the lure to publish is often irresistible, and many newsletters in the field simply do not provide truly expert advice, privileged information, or hot tips. Some don't even provide sound advice, and when their subscribers go broke after a few months of following the letter's suggestions, they eventually disappear from the scene. The author? Well, he's made a couple of hundred thousand, so he's okay.

Newsletters can be a valuable and convenient way of getting information. Or they can be a rip-off. The key is learning to choose wisely.

Choose a newsletter on the basis of a strong recommendation from a savvy investor. Preferably, one who is rich. Ask how long he has been a subscriber, whether he has followed the advice in the letter, and how it has all turned out. Even if he hasn't chosen to follow the advice, can he tell you how accurate the author's predictions were?

Ask for a sample copy and look it over carefully. If the author declines to send you one, forget it. Any reputable newsletter writer worth his salt will be glad to do so.

Take advantage of the trial subscription approach. A newsletter that costs $225 per year is hardly an impulse purchase for most people. So the newsletter publisher will often offer a trial rate of, let's say, eight weeks for $35. Of course, the publisher isn't losing any money on this deal, but you can get a reasonable chance to assess the worth of the letter for a lot less expense than that of a full year's subscription.

Evaluate the basic investment philosophy of the writer and the soundness of his analytical techniques. Most newsletter writers will provide some background concerning their approach and outlook. If you think it sounds suspicious, don't waste your money. You'll have trouble working up the resolve to act on the advice.

Consider the credentials of the author—and don't be misled by good PR. Getting one's name in a magazine or newspaper doesn't make anyone a leading expert, no matter what the PR and advertising boys write. Judge the author by his performance in his field, not on his shrewdness in hiring a PR person and the size of his budget committed to advertising and PR.

Remember that past performance is in the past. Many newsletter ads point out that if you invested just $1,000 in 1975 according to Charles H. Nurd's advice, you'd be worth $59,963 today. Impressive? Yes. So you buy the man's newsletter, follow his advice, and lose all your dough in the next three months. Charles will be quick to note that he can't be right all the time, but that those who invested with his system in '75 are still ahead. The SEC requires that a caveat be printed at the bottom of such ads. It's there for a reason.

Watch out for hard sell. A newsletter publisher doesn't waste time following subscription leads outside the special field that the letter deals with. But he will pound away at the potential audience, trying to turn the prospect into a subscriber. If you are in his target audience, he will try to make you feel that you will be left behind and left out, and will lose time and lose money if you don't subscribe. Most of the time you'll be offered a money-back guarantee. If you subscribe, but are not satisfied, avail yourself of the guarantee.

Take advantage of on-line databases such as *Newsnet* (see section on databases).

MONITORING ALL-NEWS RADIO

This is an excellent news source. Major news, weather, and sports are repeated about every 20 minutes. With the exception of a late-breaking story, the items don't vary much with each 20-minute report. So a quick listen several times a day is good, but sticking with the station for another go-round of the same items is a waste of time and will drive you crazy. Many stations set particular times for reports, such as business news, featuring stock market quotes and gold settings, etc. Some of the time is filled with quickie movie reviews and consumer tips and inflation fighter information, with things like how to get the most for your money when buying chocolate syrup. All things considered, this is a good way to get concise and up-to-the-minute news; and, best of all, you can assimilate it while you are doing something else. In general, *radio is the most accessible of all information sources.* A survey revealed that during the major blackout in the Northeast in 1977, 77 percent of those surveyed listened to radio, and 95 percent of the respondents rated radio's performance good to excellent.

Another survey shows that 49 percent of all business executives rely on radio as the first source of news in the morning, ahead of newspapers (42 percent) and TV (8 percent). It is also the primary source of news during the day.

See the All-News Radio Guide in the Appendix to Part II. It gives the stations in the U.S. that carry this format. Check a newspaper or your hotel desk for the location of the station on the dial. Note: The guide gives format only; quality and tone of the news may vary widely from station to station.

RESEARCHING: SKILLS AND RESOURCES

Research skills are among the most underrated skills of executives. Anyone who has ever watched a Senate hearing knows the value of having done one's homework. Research helps you:

- defend your position
- attack the positions of others
- formulate sound strategies
- uncover potential pitfalls and opportunities
- sound much more knowledgeable than you are

There are two basic reasons why some executives don't research well: They are intimidated by the apparent complexity of the information-seeking process; and research takes time.

This is also why superiors may turn the job over to you. If you can research things more quickly and thoroughly than your peers, you will have more time available for more creative and innovative tasks and will also gain a reputation as a person who has his act together.

Know your research sources:

- libraries
- databases
- private research organizations
- public or nonprofit research organizations
- reference book publishers
- nonbook research sources

Libraries are still the primary and least expensive source of information. The hang-ups: You have to leave your office and go there; material is on a first-come, first-served basis, so it might not be there when you want it; you can't take reference books outside the library; in large part, libraries operate on limited budgets, and their reference sources aren't always up to date.

Databases are an excellent investment if your company can afford a service and you use it enough to justify the cost. There's a full discussion of databases later in this chapter.

Many other public and private research sources are enormously useful. It's just a matter of knowing which research organization to contact for what kind of information.

The best way to begin solving this research problem and many others is to compile your own research library. Remember, books are tax deductible. And if it's a simple fact or statistic you need, a call to the publisher of the appropriate reference book will often suffice.

THE PERSONAL REFERENCE LIBRARY

Not every little need for data or a statistic should send you or your secretary scurrying to the library. It is a very good idea to have some basic business information at your fingertips. You expect other professionals, like your doctors, lawyers, and accountants, to depend on reference works. Why not you, the manager?

The best reference books for business and industry (a) are expensive and (b) become outdated quickly. But many companies willingly pick up that tax-deductible tab.

Here is my suggestion for a basic business reference library. To this list add reference works specific to your industry or profession.

Where To Find Business Information, by David M. Brownstone and Gorton Carruth (New York: John Wiley & Sons, 1982)

A super book, worth every penny it costs. It is clearly organized and easy to use. International in scope, it provides information on English language publications, including the name and address of the publisher of each book or periodical listed, the complete title, price, frequency of publication, and range of subjects covered. The Source Finder subject index appears to have been written with the executive in mind: It is one of the few with subject headings that make sense to people in business. This book won't give you any specific data on a subject, but it will save you a great deal of time in finding what you are looking for. And it can help you make your research much more complete.

The Dow Jones-Irwin Business Almanac, edited by Sumner N. Levine (Homewood, Illinois: Dow Jones-Irwin) Annually.

A useful compendium of hard statistics, business facts, names and addresses, and other useful bits of information that appear to have been pulled from various sources.

Business Services and Information, the Guide to the Federal Government, by Management Information Exchange, Inc. (New York: John Wiley & Sons)

This book attempts to organize by topic the tremendous volume of business information available from the federal government. It is very worthwhile and will undoubtedly be used often once you acquire it. There are a few problems: Any book like this is outdated the instant it goes to press, and there is little the book can do to reduce the headaches that come from dealing with the federal bureaucracy. Often, in your quest for data, you will be directed to an office in a division of a federal agency, only to be told that it no longer makes the data available.

A Deskbook of Business Management Terms, by Leon A. Wortman (New York: AMACOM, 1979)

A dictionary of management terms. Great for finding impressive terms to spice up reports and speeches, or for diciphering those used by others. The listings are very brief; they do little more than define the word or phrase.

Publications of the Baker Library, Harvard Business School:

Baker Library, one of the nation's finest business libraries, makes a number of its publications available to the public. Among them is a short book called *Business Reference Sources: An Annotated Guide for Harvard Business School Students.* It is a good, concise bibliography that includes the call numbers by which the books are shelved in the Baker Library. Other bibliographical books include *Business Intelligence and Strategic Planning* and *Executive Compensation;* and each of a series of twenty "mini-lists," 2–6 pages long, suggests where to look first for information on a particular business topic.

For a complete listing and order form, contact:
Publications Office
Baker Library
Harvard Business School
Soldiers Field
Boston Massachusetts 02163

A Researcher's Guide to Washington, by Washington Researchers
This book is not simply a list of what is available; it is intended to help you through the Washington maze. Included: a complete GSA phone directory, a directory of over 1,500 key statistical personnel, a list of every government document room and what is in each, and some valuable tips on how congressional committees function and how to get information from their researchers. Contact:
Washington Researchers
910 Seventh Street, NW
Washington, D.C. 20006

Guide to American Directories (Coral Springs, Florida: B. Klein Publications)

This guide lists over 6,000 directories. Use it to locate the directory you need. You can then contact the publisher if your need is just a matter of one or two listings. Or you can get the directory from the library. The book is also an excellent "shopping guide" for your company, because the staff can go through it and decide which directories are worth ordering. Contact:

B. Klein Publications
P. O. Box 8503
Coral Springs, Florida 33065

The Encyclopedia of Associations (Detroit: Gale Research Company)

Lists and briefly describes over 13,000 organizations in the United States. Besides data on membership and a statement of the objectives of each listed organization, this encyclopedia defines specific research interests and projects and lists personnel who can be of assistance. Such organizations are an excellent reference source, because one of their principal functions is to compile and disseminate information for and about their constituencies. Contact:

Gale Research Company
Book Tower
Detroit, Michigan 48226

Ulrich's International Periodicals Directory (New York: R. R. Bowker)

Trade journals and magazines are an excellent source of information. More than 60,000 of them are listed here by subject, and they are cross-referenced by title. Most libraries carry this one. Contact:

R. R. Bowker Company
1180 Avenue of the Americas
New York, New York 10036

National Information Center for Educational Media:

NICEM puts out several indexes, one each for educational films, educational video tapes, and educational audio tapes. Nonbook media can be the superior source of information in many cases, and the index offers the most complete list. The *16mm Educational Films Index* comes in four volumes. Contact:

National Center for Educational Media
University of Southern California
University Park
Los Angeles, California 90007

Dictionary of Business and Economics, by Christine and Dean S. Ammer (New York: Free Press)

My favorite of the business and economics dictionaries on the market, because it is the most up to date and the best written. Such books are usually written by eggheads, and I have trouble understanding them. Dean S. is the academician. Christine is a professional lexicographer with a great deal of experience in writing encyclopedias, dictionaries, and other reference works; it shows. This book is clear, well-organized, and intelligently cross-referenced. It is also a good buy. Free Press is a division of Macmillan, so the book should be widely available.

Research Centers Directory (Detroit: Gale Research Company)

In any business it is worthwhile to get the jump on the competition. When it comes to research, there is often a big lag between the completion of a study and the publication of the data in a place meant for consumption by the executive. An aggressive businessperson goes right to the source. This directory lists those sources—a few thousand university and nonprofit research organizations. Use this book to find the research groups that might be working in your field of interest, select one person in each group to contact (this is important; don't just write the lab), and you just might see such a connection result in a relationship of mutual benefit. You can also use this directory to select organizations to do research specifically for you or your firm. Since they are nonprofit and often rely on highly trained but low-paid students, they can usually do the job for much less than a private research facility that services the business community.

Industrial Research Laboratories in the United States (New York: Jacques Cattell Press)

This book lists labs serving business and industry, the recent publications by each lab, and their relevant personnel. These labs see every firm as a potential client and will often bend over backward to help you. Contact:
Jacques Cattell Press
R. R. Bowker Company
1180 Avenue of the Americas
New York, New York 10036

International Directory of Published Market Research (New York: Undine Corporation)

Over 4,000 listings. Studies are categorized according to the British Industrial Classification System. This book is a must for any company thinking of striking out in a new direction, whether it be new-product development, expansion of an existing line, a new-service business, or import-export. Contact:

Undine Corporation
575 Madison Avenue
New York, New York 10022

Exhibits Schedule, Annual Directory of Trade and Industrial Shows (New York: Successful Meetings Magazine)

The most complete list available. Includes trade shows here and abroad, classified by industry, geographic area, and date. The only hitch—the book is an annual and becomes worthless after that year. Contact:

Exhibits Schedule
Successful Meetings Magazine
633 Third Avenue
New York, New York 10017

The National Directory of Addresses and Telephone Numbers, edited by Stanley Greenfield (New York: Bantam Books)

Has over 50,000 useful phone numbers nationwide. These include local and federal agencies, freight lines, communications services, etc.

Survey of Buying Power (New York: Sales and Marketing Management Magazine)

This survey includes data on American cities with populations of over 40,000, and on foreign countries. It concentrates on consumer income, buying patterns, and purchasing power. Contact:

Sales and Marketing Magazine
633 Third Avenue
New York, New York 10017

THE DATABASE

A database is nothing more than a compilation of information stored electronically and usually accessed through a computer. It is almost certain that you have already used databases, for many reference works commonly found at the library, such as the *Thomas Registry* and the *Business Periodical Index*, are nothing more than printed and bound versions of databases. You or your office may have compiled your own custom database of clients, inventory or mailing lists using a database management software program designed for your microcomputer. Such databases are not generally accessed from a remote computer by telephone line and as such are called "off-line" databases.

In this section we will focus on on-line databases, which are banks of information stored in a large computer in some remote location. Such on-line databases have become a primary source of information gathering because they are fast, efficient, current and generally cost-effective. In addition, many databases are interactive, *i.e.*, they allow you to take action, such as booking a plane reservation or ordering a reprint of an article.

INDUSTRY OVERVIEW

The database industry is made up of those firms which compile and maintain a database, often called the database producer, and the company that makes it available to the consumer for a fee, usually called the vendor. The vendor gives you a phone number for your computer to call and a code number to log into the database. It charges you fees and collects the money, turning over a portion to the producer.

ADVANTAGES

Speed. On-line databases are fast, much faster than a librarian with a card catalog.

Accuracy. The database never forgets where it puts things, and that "Mc" comes before "M" in alphabetizing.

Currentness. Directories, annuals, indexes are published only periodically. But a good database will be up to date as of a few days ago.

Less redundancy. It will be easier to avoid reading the same data several times, since the computer will give you a side-by-side listing of related materials.

DISADVANTAGES

Terminals. You can take a book or magazine on the bus . . . but a terminal? Well, you can at least make a hard copy to take with you.

Limited availability of intact items. If you need the entire article exactly as it originally appeared, you won't always find it in the database. This will present a problem in preparing a letter to the editor or replying to allegations in the article you're seeking.

The point of view of a third party. Database managers take great pains to insure a complete and sensible abstracting procedure. But it always comes down to an individual or a small group deciding what is worth going into the database and what is not. What looks minor to an abstractor, may be a touchstone for a brilliant idea when read by you.

Cost. There are equipment costs, hookup costs, time costs, and telephone line fees.

Language barrier. Programmers are making tremendous strides in developing languages that make it possible for the layman to communicate directly with the computer. But when it comes to databases, there are still some problems. Sooner or later you will find yourself mired in a "Who's on first" conversation with the electronic brain, and you'll call for help (which, incidentally, is usually graciously provided).

Concept barrier. How are items classified? Would you look for the Ayatollah under Iran? Islam? OPEC? all three? A database comes with a thesaurus, or a kind of index to help you cross-reference. Also, the computer will scan its banks for related items—even, for example, items in which the word *Ayatollah* appears in the title.

Nevertheless, I had tremendous difficulty finding "jet lag" in one of the largest databases. It wasn't under "aviation," or "medicine," or "travel," or "airlines," or any other category I could think of. I gave up, although I'm sure it's in there somewhere.

USES OF THE DATABASE

Planning. The database is useful when preparing forecasts and projections, designing new-product-entry programs, and doing industry analyses, because the base provides a large number of statistical and editorial items on the industry and consumer markets.

Marketing. The base assists in developing strategies by providing information on market forces, competitors, and buying trends.

Public relations. You can order up information for a speech, or a letter to the editor, or to your congressperson. And you can monitor the press coverage of your company and industry.

Administrative. Keep track of all issues affecting the successful administration of your company, from labor statistics, and reports of union activities to business and economic indicators and national affairs.

International affairs. Keep abreast of business, social, political, and economic developments in current and potential import or export markets.

Finance. Economic trends, stock market figures, banking information, money-market statistics, industry performance figures, all at your fingertips.

Government. Keep track of tax incentive programs, key legislation affecting your business, and other government activities.

General information. Who, what, where, when, why, how . . .

Sports. Settle arguments, win bets.

DATABASE SERVICES

There are dozens of databases, and the number could well be in the hundreds by the time this book is published. Many enterprising entrepreneurs hope to strike it rich by assembling and selling access to very specialized databases in advertising and finance, as well as technical and professional fields. These firms will probably seek you out through ads in trade publications and direct mail.

On-line databases generally fall into several categories:

Encyclopedic databases offer reference information on a wide variety of subjects.

Specialized databases offer information on a specific subject or group of subjects, generally too obscure or technical to be included in an encyclopedic database.

Information utilities is a catch-all term for companies that were formed to market a variety of on-line sevices to personal computer users. Such services might include everything from reference material, stock quotes to discount merchandise, recipes and restaurant reviews.

On-line special services aren't really databases, but are included here because they use the same basic methods to provide their services. Examples include *MCI Electronic Mail* and *Western Union*.

A Guide to Popular Business Database Services

Dialog   One of the earliest databases, Dialog is actually a grouping of over 250 smaller databases for which Dialog acts as the vendor. The databases under the Dialog umbrella comprise one of the largest and most comprehensive encyclopedic databases. It provides access to summaries of articles and reports, detailed financial data and directory listings on companies, statistics, full-text articles and newswires—from a pool of over 100 million items.

Like most databases, you are charged for the time you spend on-line, by the minute or the hour. The prices vary according to the actual special database you access. For example, the World Patents Index charges $175 per hour, while you pay only $36.00 per hour for access to U.S. Census statistics through the Cendata database.

Knowledge Index is another service of Dialog designed for a more general user who requires access to a more limited set of databases. True, the amount of available data is much less, but in return the user pays a lower price, currently a flat rate of $24.00 per hour, plus a one-time fee of $35.00 which entitles you to 2 hours of free search time (a $48.00 value). This is a good deal, because all of the databases available on the *Knowledge Index* cost far more than $24.00 per hour. The only catch is that the hours of access are decidedly "off-peak," *i.e.*, evenings and weekends, and that you must use your free two hours of search time within the first 30 days of membership.

Dialog Information Services, 3460 Hillview Avenue, Palo Alto, CA 94304; 800-3 DIALOG

Newsnet   This is a database that specializes in newsletters. Newsletters are generally more expensive than magazines because they don't carry advertising and are meant for very limited circulation. The concept behind *Newsnet* is to provide the user with a kind of index to several hundred newsletters, so you can search through current and back issues. You pay only for the time it takes to search for and read the information on the specific topic. You avoid costly subscription fees for newsletters that carry articles that are irrelevant to you, and you save time in scanning and turning pages as you browse through them.

Beware, however, that some newsletter publishers see this as a way for the reader to avoid paying for the information, and allow *Newsnet* to be used as an on-line index only. If you want to read the copy, the cost goes up significantly, and in some cases, you may have to become a subscriber, or at least pay a fee to receive the information in hardcopy form.

An intriguing *Newsnet* service is called *NewsFlash.* This service involves giving *Newsnet* a series of key words or phrases, called your *NewsFlash* profile. As *Newsnet* adds new material to its database, it electronically watches for data that matches the "profile." Each time you log on, *NewsFlash* will tell you what it has flagged in its database since you last went on-line. In a sense, then, the *NewsFlash* service is doing an automatic search for you while you are off-line. Its like an electronic clipping service, and can be very useful in keeping up-to-date. The service includes monitoring of UPI (not available on standard Newsnet). The cost is $.37 per item found (sometimes called a *hit*).

Newsnet, Inc., 945 Haverford Road, Bryn Mawr, PA 19010; 215-527-8030 inside Pennsylvania; 800-345-1301 outside Pennsylvania.

Dow Jones News/Retrieval Service   Long an acknowledged leader in business and financial information services, Dow Jones has put together one of the best databases for the businessperson. The Dow Jones News/ Retrieval Service is an offspring of their highly specialized stock market and trading information services.

The service includes over thirty databases, which are divided into six groups or tiers: Business and Economic News Services; Quotes; Text-Search Services; Financial and Investment Services; General News and Information Services; Mail Service and Free Consumer Newsletter.

The *Business and Economic News Services* is derived primarily from the *Dow Jones News Service, The Wall Street Journal* and *Barron's,* including highlights of the last five editions of *WSJ,* and selections from stories published in the past 90 days.

The *Text-Search Services* will take you back to 1979 for articles in the *WSJ* and *Barron's* and the *Dow Jones News Service.* In addition, the full text edition of every WSJ is available since January 1984.

Quotes covers various types of stock quotes including current and historical, *Dow Jones Averages,* a quote service offering news items related to a stock as well as its price, and a service called TRACK which automatically keeps tabs on items of related interest, according to a user profile.

Financial and Investment Services offers detailed financial information on companies listed on the New York and American Stock Exchanges, and access to a database of information abstracted from the public disclosure statements required by the Securities and Exchange Commission.

SCHEDULE 1-A DATABASE RATES
Connect time rates **include** all royalties paid to Database Suppliers.
No start-up fee. No minimum charge.

FOOTNOTES: * *Not available through the dialog classroom instruction program*
　　　　　▲ *Citation*　　● *Full text database*　　‡ *Forthcoming*

Database (Supplier)	On-line Connect Time Rates		Off-line Print Rate Per Record	On-line Type Rate Per Record
	Per Minute	Per Hour		
ABI/INFORM® (Data Courier)	$1.35	$ 81.00	$ .60	$ .50
ACADEMIC AMERICAN ENCYCLOPEDIA (Grolier Electronic Publishing)	.75	45.00	.25●	
ADTRACK™ (Kingman Consulting Group, Inc.)	1.58	95.00	.25	.25
ADVERTISED COMPUTER TECHNOLOGIES™ [ACT I] (Data Courier)	1.60	96.00	1.00	.75
ADVERTISED COMPUTER TECHNOLOGIES™ [ACT II] (Data Courier)	1.60	96.00	.60	.40
AEROSPACE DATABASE (American Institute of Aeronautics and Astronautics, Technical Information Service [AIAA/TIS])	1.30	78.00	.25	.20
AGRIBUSINESS U.S.A.SM (Pioneer Hi-Bred International, Inc.)	1.60	96.00	.60	.50
AGRICOLA 1970 to Present (U.S.D.A. Technical Information Systems)	.65	39.00	.20	.10
AGRIS INTERNATIONAL (Food and Agriculture Organization)	.75	45.00	.15	
AIM/ARM (The Center Vocational Education, Ohio State University)	.42	25.00	.10	
AMERICA: HISTORY AND LIFE (ABC-Clio Information Services)	1.08	65.00	.15	
AMERICAN BANKER (American Banker, Inc.)	2.00	120.00	.25	
AMERICAN MEN AND WOMEN OF SCIENCE (R.R. Bowker)	1.58	95.00	.40	
AP NEWS (Press Association)	1.40	84.00	.25●	
APTIC (U.S. Environmental Protection Agency)	.90	54.00	.20	10
AQUACULTURE (NOAA/EDIS/LISD)	.58	35.00	.15	.10
AQUATIC SCIENCES & FISHERIES ABSTRACTS (NOAA/Cambridge Scientific Abstracts)	1.45	87.00	.45	.40
ART LITERATURE INTERNATIONAL [RILA] (International Repertory of the Literature of Art and J. Paul Getty Trust)	.80	48.00	.15	
ARTBIBLIOGRAPHIES MODERN (ABC-Clio Information Services)	1.00	60.00	.15	
*　ARTHUR D. LITTLE/ONLINE (Arthur D. Little, Inc.)	1.50	90.00	.20▲	
			100.00●	
ASI (Congressional Information Service, Inc.)	1.50	90.00	.25	
A-V ONLINE (Access Innovations)	1.17	70.00	.20	
BIOBUSINESS™ (BioSciences Information Service and Information Access Co.)	1.95	117.00	.35	.25
BIOGRAPHY MASTER INDEX (Gale Research Company)	1.05	63.00	.65	.55
BIOSIS PREVIEWS® 1969 to Present (BioSciences Information Service)	1.40	84.00	.34	.24
BLS CONSUMER PRICE INDEX U.S. Bureau of Labor Statistics)	.75	45.00	.50	.50
BLS EMPLOYMENT, HOURS AND EARNINGS (U.S. Bureau of Labor Statistics)	.75	45.00	.50	.50
BLS PRODUCER PRICE INDEX (U.S. Bureau of Labor Statistics)	.75	45.00	.50	.50
THE BOND BUYER (Bond Buyer, Inc.)	2.00	120.00	.25	
BOOK REVIEW INDEX (Gale Research Company)	.80	48.00	.25	.25
BOOKS IN PRINT (R.R. Bowker)	1.08	65.00	.20	
BUSINESS & INDUSTRY NEWS (Predicasts)	2.20	132.00	.78	.68
BUSINESS SOFTWARE DATABASE (Data Courier Inc.)	1.50	90.00	.90	.90
BUSINESSWIRE (Business Wire)	1.40	84.00	.25	
*　CA SEARCH 1967 to Present (Chemical Abstracts Service)	1.50	90.00	.35	.23
CAB ABSTRACTS (Commonwealth Agricultural Bureaux)	.92	55.00	.35	.25
CANADIAN BUSINESS AND CURRENT AFFAIRS July 1980 to Present (Micromedia Ltd.)	1.20	72.00	.20	
CANCERLIT (U.S. National Library of Medicine (NLM)	.60	36.00	.20	.05
CAREER PLACEMENT REGISTRY (Career Placement Registry, Inc.)	1.58	95.00	1.50	1.00
CENDATA™ (U.S. Bureau of the Census)	.60	36.00	.20●	
CHASE ECONOMETRICS (Chase Econometrics)	1.25	75.00	1.00	1.00
CHEMICAL BUSINESS NEWSBASE [CBNB] (Royal Society of Chemistry)	1.83	110.00	.60	.54
CHEMICAL EXPOSURE (Science Applications International Corporation)	.75	45.00	.15	
*　CHEMICAL INDUSTRY NOTES (Chemical Abstracts Service)	1.83	110.00	.35	.23
CHEMICAL REGULATIONS & GUIDELINES SYSTEM (CRC Systems, Inc.)	1.17	70.00	.90	
*　CHEMNAME™ (DIALOG Information Services, Inc. and Chemical Abstracts Service)	2.63	158.00	.32	.18
*　CHEMSEARCH™ (DIALOG Information Services, Inc. and Chemical Abstracts Service)	2.63	158.00	.32	.18
*　CHEMSIS™ 1967 to Present (DIALOG Information Services, Inc. and Chemical Abstracts Service)	2.63	158.00	.32	.18

Fig. 13. An excerpt from current database listing
(*through page 121*)

From DIALOG Information Services Inc.
Palo Alto, CA. Reprinted by permission.

Database (Supplier)	On-line Connect Time Rates Per Minute	Per Hour	Off-line Print Rate Per Record	On-line Type Rate Per Record
* CHEMZERO (DIALOG Information Services, Inc. and Chemical Abstracts Service)	$2.63	$158.00	$.32	$ .18
CHILD ABUSE AND NEGLECT (National Center for Child Abuse and Neglect	.58	35.00	.10	
CHRONOLOG® NEWSLETTER (DIALOG Information Services, Inc.)	.25	15.00	.15•	
CIS (Congressional Information Service, Inc.)	1.50	90.00	.25	
* CLAIMS™/CITATION 1947 to 1970 (IFI/Plenum Data Inc.)	1.58	95.00	50.00	50.00
* CLAIMS™/CITATION 1971 to Present (IFI/Plenum Data Inc.)	1.58	95.00	20.00	20.00
CLAIMS™/CLASS (IFI/Plenum Data Inc.)	1.58	95.00	.10	
* CLAIMS™/COMPOUND REGISTRY (IFI/Plenum Data Inc.)	1.58	95.00	.15	
* CLAIMS™/REASSIGNMENT & REEXAMINATION (IFI/Plenum Data Inc.)	.92	55.00	.50	.25
* CLAIMS™/U.S. PATENTS 1950 to 1970 (IFI/Plenum Data Inc.)	1.75	105.00	.50	.25
* CLAIMS™/U.S.PATENT ABSTRACTS 1971 to Present (IFI/Plenum Data Inc.)	1.75	105.00	.50	.25
* CLAIMS™/U.S. PATENT ABSTRACTS WEEKLY IFI/Plenum Data Inc.)	1.75	105.00	.50	.25
* CLAIMS™/UNITERM 1950 to Present (IFI/Plenum Data Inc.)	5.00	300.00	.50	.25
CLINICAL ABSTRACTS 1981 to Present (Medical Information Systems)	1.15	69.00	.25	.10
COFFEELINE™ (International Coffee Organization)	1.08	65.00	.20	.20
* COMMERCE BUSINESS DAILY (Commerce Business Daily, U.S. Department of Commerce)	.90	54.00	.25•	
COMPENDEX® (Engineering Information, Inc.)	1.80	108.00	.47	.35
COMPUTER DATABASE™ (Information Access Company)	1.60	96.00	.55	.50
CONFERENCE PAPERS INDEX (Cambridge Scientific Abstracts)	1.40	84.00	.40	.30
CONGRESSIONAL RECORD ABSTRACTS (National Standards Association)	1.60	96.00	.25	.15
CONSUMER DRUG INFORMATION FULL TEXT (American Society of Hospital Pharmacists)	.58	35.00	.30•	.20•
CORPORATE AFFILIATIONS (National Register Publishing Company [NRPC])	1.40	84.00	1.25	1.25
CRIMINAL JUSTICE PERIODICAL INDEX (University Microfilms International)	1.10	66.00	.25	.20
CRIS/USDA (Current Research Information System, U.S. Department of Agriculture)	.67	40.00	.15	
CURRENT TECHNOLOGY INDEX (Library Association (London))	$1.15	69.00	.25	$.25
D & B — DONNELLEY DEMOGRAPHICS (Donnelley Marketing Information Services)	1.00	60.00	12.00	10.00
D & B — DUN'S ELECTRONIC DIRECTORY OF EDUCATION (Dun & Bradstreet)	1.00	60.00	.45	.45
D & B — DUN'S ELECTRONIC YELLOW PAGES—CONSTRUCTION DIRECTORY (Dun & Bradstreet)	1.00	60.00	.20	.20
D & B — DUN'S ELECTRONIC YELLOW PAGES—FINANCIAL SERVICES DIRECTORY (Dun & Bradstreet)	1.00	60.00	.20	.20
D & B — DUN'S ELECTRONIC YELLOW PAGES—INDEX (Dun & Bradstreet)	.58	35.00	.05	
D & B — DUN'S ELECTRONIC YELLOW PAGES—MANUFACTURERS DIRECTORY (Dun & Bradstreet)	1.00	60.00	.20	.20
D & B — DUN'S ELECTRONIC YELLOW PAGES—PROFESSIONALS DIRECTORY (Dun & Bradstreet)	1.00	60.00	.20	.20
D & B — DUN'S ELECTRONIC YELLOW PAGES—RETAILERS DIRECTORY (Dun & Bradstreet)	1.00	60.00	.20	.20
D & B — DUN'S ELECTRONIC YELLOW PAGES—SERVICES DIRECTORY (Dun & Bradstreet)	1.00	60.00	.20	.20
D & B — DUN'S ELECTRONIC YELLOW PAGES—WHOLESALERS DIRECTORY (Dun & Bradstreet)	1.00	60.00	.20	.20
D & B — DUN'S FINANCIAL RECORDS^{SM} (Dun & Bradstreet)	2.25	135.00	74.00	74.00
D & B — DUN'S MARKET IDENTIFIERS® 10+ (Dun's Marketing Services)	1.67	100.00	2.00	2.00
D & B — INTERNATIONAL DUN'S MARKET IDENTIFIERS® (Dun's Marketing Services)	1.67	100.00	2.00	2.00
D & B — MILLION DOLLAR DIRECTORY® (Dun's Marketing Services)	1.67	100.00	2.00	2.00
DATABASE OF DATABASES (M.E. Williams, Inc.)	.80	48.00	.20	
DE HAEN DRUG DATA (Paul De Haen International, Inc.)	1.10	66.00	.30	.25
* DIALINDEX (DIALOG Information Services, Inc.)	.75	45.00	N/A	
DIALOG PUBLICATIONS (DIALOG Information Services, Inc.)	.25	15.00	.15	
DIALOG® QUOTES AND TRADING (Trade Plus)	.60	36.00		
DISCLOSURE® II (Disclosure Information Group)	.75	45.00	11.00	7.00
DISCLOSURE™ FINANCIALS (Disclosure Information Group)	.75	45.00	11.00	7.00
DISCLOSURE™ MANAGEMENT (Disclosure Information Group	.75	45.00	11.00	7.00
* DISCLOSURE/SPECTRUM OWNERSHIP (Disclosure Information Group)	1.00	60.00	25.00	25.00
DISSERTATION ABSTRACTS ONLINE (University Microfilms International)	1.20	72.00	.25	.25
* DOE ENERGY (U.S. Department of Energy)	1.30	78.00	.25•	.25
DRUG INFORMATION FULLTEXT (American Society of Hospital Pharmacists)	.80	48.00	.35•	.25•
ECONOMIC LITERATURE INDEX (American Economic Association)	1.25	75.00	.15	
EI Engineering Meetings® 1982 to Present (Engineering Information, Inc.)	1.80	108.00	.47	.35
ELECTRIC POWER DATABASE (Electric Power Research Institute)	1.10	66.00	.35	.35
EMBASE 1974 to Present (Elsevier Science Publishers)	1.40	84.00	.33	.44
ENCYCLOPEDIA OF ASSOCIATIONS (Gale Research Company)	.90	54.00	.75	.75
ENERGYLINE® (Environment Information Center, Inc.)	1.80	108.00	.35	.30
ENVIROLINE® (Environment Information Center, Inc.)	1.80	108.00	.35	.30

Database (Supplier)	On-line Connect Time Rates		Off-line Print Rate	On-line Type Rate
	Per Minute	Per Hour	Per Record	Per Record
ENVIRONMENTAL BIBLIOGRAPHY (Environmental Studies Institute)	$ 1.00	$ 60.00	$ .15	
ERIC (National Institute of Education, Educational Resources Information Center)	.50	30.00	.14	.10
EVERYMAN'S ENCYCLOPEDIA (Learned Information Ltd.)	.70	42.00	.90●	.80●
EXCEPTIONAL CHILD EDUCATION RESOURCES (Council for Exceptional Children)	.58	35.00	.15	
FACTS ON FILE® (Facts on File, Inc.)	1.00	60.00	.25●	●
FAMILY RESOURCES (Nat. Council on Family Relations & Inventory of Marriage & Family Literature Proj.)	.95	57.00	.25	.25
FEDERAL INDEX (National Standards Association)	1.50	90.00	.20	
FEDERAL REGISTER ABSTRACTS (National Standards Association)	1.25	75.00	.20	
* FEDERAL RESEARCH IN PROGRESS (National Technical Information Service)	.80	48.00	.20	.20
FINANCIAL TIMES COMPANY ABSTRACTS (D-S Production Limited)	1.20	72.00	.85	.80
FIND/SVP REPORTS & STUDIES INDEX (National Standards Association)	1.30	78.00	.25	.25
FINIS: FINANCIAL INDUSTRY INFORMATION SERVICE (Bank Marketing Association)	1.30	78.00	.30	.20
FLUIDEX (BHRA, The Fluid Engineering Centre)	1.15	69.00	.28	.18
FOOD SCIENCE & TECHNOLOGY ABSTRACTS (International Food Information Service)	1.25	75.00	.25	.15
FOODS ADLIBRA™ (General Mills)	1.05	63.00	.15	.10
FOREIGN TRADE & ECON ABSTRACTS (Netherlands Foreign Trade Agency)	1.30	78.00	.30	.25
* FOREIGN TRADERS INDEX (U.S. Department of Commerce)	.90	54.00	.25	.25
FOUNDATION DIRECTORY (The Foundation Center)	1.00	60.00	.30	
FOUNDATION GRANTS INDEX (The Foundation Center)	1.00	60.00	.30	
GEOARCHIVE (Geosystems)	1.25	75.00	.30	.15
GEOREF (American Geological Institute)	1.45	87.00	.45	.40
GPO MONTHLY CATALOG (U.S. Government Printing Office)	.58	35.00	.10	
GPO PUBLICATIONS REFERENCE FILE (U.S. Government Printing Office)	.58	35.00	.10	
GRADLINE (Peterson's Guides, Inc.)	1.00	60.00	.95	.95
GRANTS (Oryx Press)	1.00	60.00	.30	
HARVARD BUSINESS REVIEW (John Wiley & Sons, Inc.)	1.25	75.00	.20▲ 7.50●	
HEALTH PLANNING & ADMINISTRATION (U.S. National Library of Medicine)	.60	36.00	.20	.05
HEILBRON (Chapman & Hall Ltd.)	1.58	95.00	.85	.65
HISTORICAL ABSTRACTS (ABC-Clio Information Services)	1.08	65.00	.15	
ICC BRITISH COMPANY DIRECTORY (Inter Company Comparison, Ltd.)	1.20	72.00	.25	.25
ICC BRITISH COMPANY FINANCIAL DATASHEETS (Inter Company Comparison, Ltd.)	1.60	96.00	4.00▲ 8.00●	4.00▲ 8.00●
INDUSTRY DATA SOURCES™ (Information Access Company)	1.25	75.00	.30	
INFORMATION SCIENCE ABSTRACTS (IFI/Plenum Data Company)	1.17	70.00	.35	
INSPEC 1969 to Present (The Institution of Electrical Engineers)	1.60	96.00	.46	.36
INSURANCE ABSTRACTS (University Microfilms International)	.92	55.00	.15	
INTERNATIONAL LISTING SERVICE (International Listing Service, Inc.)	1.50	90.00	2.00	2.00
INTERNATIONAL PHARMACEUTICAL ABSTRACTS (Amer. Society of Hospital Pharmacists)	1.15	69.00	.38	.27
INVESTEXT (Business Research Corporation)	1.60	96.00	4.50●	4.50●
IRS TAXINFO (Internal Revenue Service)	.60	36.00	.10●	
ISMEC (Cambridge Scientific Abstracts)	1.40	84.00	.40	.30
LABORLAW (Bureau of National Affairs)	2.00	120.00	.70	
LC MARC (U.S. Library of Congress)	.75	45.00	.15	.10
LEGAL RESOURCE INDEX™ (Information Access Company)	1.50	90.00	.20	.10
LIFE SCIENCES COLLECTION (Cambridge Scientific Abstracts)	1.45	87.00	.45	.35
LINGUISTICS AND LANGUAGE BEHAVIOR ABSTRACTS (Sociological Abstracts, Inc.)	1.10	66.00	.30	.25
LISA (Library Association Publishing)	1.25	75.00	.25	.25
MAGAZINE ASAP™ (Information Access Company)	1.40	84.00	3.50	3.50
MAGAZINE INDEX™ (Information Access Company)	1.40	84.00	.20	.10
MAGILL'S SURVEY OF CINEMA (Salem Press, Inc.)	.90	54.00	.20	
MANAGEMENT CONTENTS® (Information Access Company)	1.50	90.00	.55	.48
MARQUIS PRO-FILES (Marquis Who's Who, Inc.)	1.30	78.00	.45▲	.35▲ 1.00●
MARQUIS WHO'S WHO, INC. (Marquis Who's Who, Inc.)	1.58	95.00	.50▲ 2.50●	.40▲ 2.50●
MATERIALS BUSINESS (Metals Information)	1.45	87.00	.30	.25
MATHSCI® (American Mathematical Society)	1.20	72.00	.46	.32
MCGRAW-HILL BUSINESS BACKGROUNDER (McGraw-Hill)	1.60	96.00	1.80●	
MEDIA GENERAL DATABANK (Media General Financial Services)	1.00	60.00	2.00	1.50
MEDLINE 1966 to Present (U.S. National Library of Medicine)	.60	36.00	.20	.05
MENTAL HEALTH ABSTRACTS (IFI/Plenum)	1.10	66.00	.20	.10
MENU™ THE INTERNATIONAL SOFTWARE DATABASE™ (The International Software Database Corp.)	1.00	60.00	.15	
METADEX (American Society for Metals)	1.50	90.00	.30	.20
METEOROLOGICAL & GEOASTROPHYSICAL ABSTRACTS (American Meteorological Society, NOAA)	1.58	95.00	.15	
MICROCOMPUTER INDEX™ (Database Services, Inc.)	.75	45.00	.15	.15
MICROCOMPUTER SOFTWARE & HARDWARE GUIDE (R.R. Bowker Company)	1.00	60.00	.25	.10
MIDDLE EAST: ABSTRACTS & INDEX (Northumberland Press)	.92	55.00	.25	
MIDEAST FILE 1979 to Present (Learned Information, Ltd.)	1.25	75.00	.30	

Database (Supplier)	On-line Connect Time Rates		Off-line Print Rate	On-line Type Rate
	Per Minute	Per Hour	Per Record	Per Record
MLA BIBLIOGRAPHY (Modern Language Association)	$ .92	$ 55.00	$ .15	
MOODY'S CORPORATE NEWS—INTERNATIONAL (Moody's Investors Service, Inc.)	1.60	96.00	1.00	1.00
MOODY'S CORPORATE NEWS—U.S. (Moody's Investors Service, Inc.)	1.25	75.00	.25	.25
MOODY'S CORPORATE PROFILES (Moody's Investors Service, Inc.)	1.00	60.00	4.00	4.00
* NATIONAL FOUNDATIONS (The Foundation Center)	1.00	60.00	.30	
NATIONAL NEWSPAPER INDEX™ (Information Access Corporation)	1.40	84.00	.20	.10
NCJRS (National Criminal Justice Reference Service)	.59	35.00	.30	.10
NEWSEARCH™ (Information Access Corporation)	2.00	120.00	.20	.10
NONFERROUS METALS ABSTRACTS (British Non-Ferrous Metals Technology Center)	.75	45.00	.20	.10
NTIS (National Technical Information Service, U.S. Department of Commerce)	1.15	69.00	.25	.25
NURSING & ALLIED HEALTH (CINAHL) (Cumulative Index to Nursing & Allied Health Literature Corp.)	.90	54.00	.25	
* OAG ELECTRONIC EDITION (Official Airline Guides, Inc.)	1.00	60.00	N/A	
OCCUPATIONAL SAFETY AND HEALTH (NIOSH) (U.S. Nat. Institute for Occupational Safety and Health)	.95	57.00	.30	.25
OCEANIC ABSTRACTS (Cambridge Scientific Abstracts)	1.45	87.00	.45	.40
ONLINE CHRONICLE (Online, Inc.)	.58	35.00	.30●	.15●
ONTAP® ABI/INFORM (Data Courier, Inc. & DIALOG Information Services, Inc.)	.25	15.00	N/A	
ONTAP® AGRICOLA (Dialog Information Services, Inc. & U.S.D.A. Technical Information Systems)	.25	15.00	N/A	
ONTAP® BIOSIS PREVIEWS (BioSciences Information Service & DIALOG Inform. Services, Inc.)	.25	15.00	N/A	
ONTAP® CA SEARCH™ (DIALOG Information Services, Inc. & Chemical Abstracts Service)	.25	15.00	N/A	
ONTAP® CAB ABSTRACTS (Commonwealth Agricultural Bureaux & DIALOG Inform. Services, Inc.)	.25	15.00	N/A	
ONTAP® CHEMNAME™ (DIALOG Information Services, Inc. & Chemical Abstracts Service)	.25	15.00	N/A	
ONTAP® CLAIMS (IFI/Plenum Data Co. and DIALOG Information Services, Inc.)	.25	15.00	N/A	
ONTAP® COMPENDEX (Engineering Information Inc. & DIALOG Information Services, Inc.)	.25	15.00	N/A	
ONTAP® D & B DUN'S MARKET IDENTIFIERS® (Dun's Marketing Services)	.25	15.00	N/A	
ONTAP® DIALINDEX™ (DIALOG Information Services, Inc.)	.25	15.00	N/A	
ONTAP® EMBASE (Elsevier Science Publishers and DIALOG Information Services, Inc.)	.25	15.00	N/A	
ONTAP® ERIC (Educational Resources Information Center & DIALOG Information Services, Inc.)	.25	15.00	N/A	
ONTAP® FOOD SCIENCE & TECHNOLOGY ABSTRACTS (International Food Information Science and DIALOG Information Services, Inc.)	.25	15.00	N/A	
ONTAP® INSPEC (The Institution of Electrical Engineers & DIALOG Information Services, Inc.)	.25	15.00	N/A	
ONTAP® INVESTEXT® (Business Research Corporation)	.25	15.00	N/A	
ONTAP® MAGAZINE INDEX (Information Access Corporation & DIALOG Information Services, Inc.)	.25	15.00	N/A	
ONTAP® MEDLINE (U.S. National Library of Medicine & DIALOG Information Services, Inc.)	.25	15.00	N/A	
ONTAP® PsycINFO (American Psychological Association & DIALOG Information Services, Inc.)	.25	15.00	N/A	
ONTAP® PTS MARKETING AND ADVERTISING REFERENCE SERVICE (MARS) (Predicasts & DIALOG Information Services, Inc.)	.25	15.00	N/A	
ONTAP® PTS PROMT (Predicasts, Inc. & DIALOG Information Services, Inc.)	.25	15.00	N/A	
ONTAP® SCISEARCH (Institute for Scientific Information and DIALOG Information Services, Inc.)	.25	15.00	N/A	
ONTAP® SOCIAL SCISEARCH (Institute for Scientific Information and DIALOG Information Services, Inc.)	.25	15.00	N/A	
ONTAP® TRADEMARKSCAN™ (Thomson and Thomson & DIALOG Information Services, Inc.)	.25	15.00	N/A	
ONTAP® WORLD PATENTS INDEX [WPI] (Derwent Publications Ltd. and DIALOG Information Services Inc.)	.25	15.00	N/A	
PACKAGING SCIENCE & TECHNOLOGY ABSTRACTS 1981 to Present (International Food Information Service)	1.15	69.00	.25	.25
PAIS INTERNATIONAL (Public Affairs Information Service, Inc.)	1.15	69.00	.30	.20
PAPERCHEM (Institute of Paper Chemistry) (Non-Subscriber)	1.45	87.00	.35	.25
PAPERCHEM (Institute of Paper Chemistry) (Subscriber)	1.05	63.00	.25	.15
PATLAW (Bureau of National Affairs, Inc.)	2.00	120.00	.70	
P/E NEWS (American Petroleum Institute's Central Abstracting and Indexing Service) (Non-Subscriber)	1.60	96.00	.35	.25
P/E NEWS (American Petroleum Institute's Central Abstracting and Indexing Service) (Subscriber)	1.60	96.00	.25	.15
* PETERSON'S COLLEGE DATABASE (Peterson's Guides, Inc.)	.90	54.00	.25	
PHARMACEUTICAL NEWS INDEX (Data Courier, Inc.)	2.10	126.00	.55	.55

| | On-line Connect Time Rates | | Off-line Print Rate | On-line Type Rate |
| | Per Minute | Per Hour | Per Record | Per Record |
Database (Supplier)				
PHILOSOPHER'S INDEX (Philosophy Documentation Center)	$ .92	$ 55.00	$ .15	
POLLUTION ABSTRACTS (Cambridge Scientific Abstracts)	1.40	84.00	.40	.30
POPULATION BIBLIOGRAPHY (University of North Carolina, Carolina Population Center)	.92	55.00	.10	
* PsycALERT (American Psychological Association)	.92	55.00	.20	
PsycINFO (American Psychological Association)	.92	55.00	20	.35
PTS AEROSPACE/DEFENSE MARKETS & TECHNOLOGY (Predicats) (Non-subscriber)	2.50	150.00	.78	.68
PTS AEROSPACE/DEFENSE MARKETS & TECHNOLOGY (Predicats) (Subscriber)	1.85	111.00	.68	.58
PTS ANNUAL REPORTS ABSTRACTS (Predicats)	1.90	114.00	.68	.58
PTS F&S INDEXES 1972 to Present (Predicats)	1.90	114.00	.33	.28
PTS INTERNATIONAL FORECASTS (Predicats)	1.90	114.00	.48	.38
PTS INTERNATIONAL TIME SERIES (Predicats)	1.90	114.00	.40	.35
PTS MARKETING AND ADVERTISING REFERENCE SERVICE [MARS] [MARS] (Predicats)	2.50	150.00	.68	.58
PTS NEW PRODUCT ANNOUNCEMENTS [NPA] (Predicats)	2.10	126.00	1.80●	.60●
PTS PROMT (Predicats)	1.90	114.00	.58	.48
PTS REGIONAL BUSINESS NEWS (RBN) (Predicats, Inc.)	2.10	126.00	.58	.48
PTS U.S. FORECASTS (Predicats)	1.90	114.00	.48	.38
PTS U.S. TIME SERIES (Predicats)	1.90	114.00	.40	.35
PUBLISHERS, DISTRIBUTORS, AND WHOLESALERS (R.R. Bowker Company)	1.10	66.00	.30	.20
RELIGION INDEX 1975 to Present (American Theological Library Association)	.80	48.00	.17	
REMARC (Carrollton Press, Inc.)	1.42	85.00	.35	.25
RILM ABSTRACTS (City University of New York, International RILM Center)	1.08	65.00	.15	
SCISEARCH® 1974 to Present (Institute for Scientific Information) (Non-subscriber)	2.65	159.00	.25	.20
SCISEARCH® 1974 to Present (Institute for Scientific Information) (Subscriber to print)	1.05	63.00	.25	.20
SOCIAL SCISEARCH® (Institute for Scientific Information) (Non-subscriber)	1.75	105.00	.35	.30
SOCIAL SCISEARCH® (Institute for Scientific Information) (Subscriber)	1.15	69.00	.35	.30
SOCIOLOGICAL ABSTRACTS (Sociological Abstracts, Inc.)	1.00	60.00	.30	.20
SOVIET SCIENCE AND TECHNOLOGY (IFI/Plenum Data Inc.)	1.08	65.00	.50	.40
SPIN® (American Institute of Physics)	.80	48.00	.25	.10
SSIE CURRENT RESEARCH (Smithsonian Scientific Information Exchange)	1.55	93.00	.30	.10
STANDARD & POOR'S REGISTER — BIOGRAPHICAL (Standard & Poor's Corporation)	1.40	84.00	1.50	1.50
STANDARD & POOR'S REGISTER — CORPORATE (Standard & Poor's Corporation)	1.40	84.00	1.50	1.50
STANDARD & POOR'S CORPORATE DESCRIPTIONS (Standard & Poor's Corporation)	1.42	85.00	3.50	3.50
STANDARD & POOR'S NEWS June 79 to June 85 (Standard & Poor's Corporation)	1.42	85.00	.25	
STANDARD & POOR'S NEWS July 85 to present (Standard & Poor's Corporation)	1.60	96.00	.25	
STANDARDS AND SPECIFICATIONS (National Standards Association, Inc.)	1.08	65.00	.30	.20
SUPERTECH (EIC/Intelligence, Inc.)	1.80	108.00	.35	.30
TEXTILE TECHNOLOGY DIGEST (Institute of Textile Technology)	1.08	65.00	.15	
THOMAS NEW INDUSTRIAL PRODUCTS™ (Thomas PublishingCompany, Inc.)	1.60	96.00	.50	.50
THOMAS REGISTER ONLINE™ (Thomas Publishing Company, Inc.)	1.67	100.00	1.50	1.50
TRADE & INDUSTRY ASAP™ (Information Access Company)	1.40	84.00	3.50●	3.50●
TRADE AND INDUSTRY INDEX™ 1981 to Present (Information Access Corporation)	1.40	84.00	.20	.10
* TRADE OPPORTUNITIES (U.S. Department of Commerce)	.75	45.00	.25	
* TRADE OPPORTUNITIES WEEKLY (U.S. Department of Commerce)	.75	45.00	.50	
* TRADEMARKSCAN® (Thomson and Thomson)	1.65	99.00	.45	.35
TRINET COMPANY DATABASE (Trinet, Inc.)	1.50	90.00	1.60	1.60
TRINET ESTABLISHMENT DATABASE (Trinet, Inc.)	1.50	90.00	.50	.50
TRIS (U.S. Department of Transportation)	.75	45.00	.15	
TSCA INITIAL INVENTORY (DIALOG Information Services, Inc. & Environmental Protection Agency)	.75	45.00	.15	
ULRICH'S INTERNATIONAL PERIODICALS DIRECTORY (R.R. Bowker)	1.08	65.00	.20	
UPI NEWS (United Press International)	1.42	85.00	.25●	
U.S. POLITICAL SCIENCE DOCUMENTS (NASA Industrial Applications Center)	1.08	65.00	.15	
WASHINGTON POST ELECTRONIC EDITION (The Washington Post Company)	1.45	87.00	.25	.25
WASHINGTON PRESS TEXT FULL TEXT (Press Text™ News Service)	1.15	69.00	.30	.25
WATER RESOURCES ABSTRACTS (U.S. Department of the Interior)	1.40	84.00	.35	.20
WATERNET™ 1971 to Present (American Water Works Association)	1.33	80.00	.20	.10
WELDASEARCH (The Welding Institute)	1.40	84.00	.25	.20
WILEY CATALOG/ONLINE (John Wiley & Sons, Inc.)	1.00	60.00	.20	
WORLD AFFAIRS REPORT (California Institute of International Studies)	1.50	90.00	.25	.10
WORLD ALUMINUM ABSTRACTS (American Society for Metals)	1.20	72.00	.20	.10
WORLD PATENTS INDEX (Derwent Publications Ltd.) (Non-Subscriber)	2.92	175.00	.50	.10
WORLD PATENTS INDEX (Derwent Publications Ltd.) (Subscriber)	1.92	115.00	.25	
WORLD TEXTILES (Shirley Institute)	.92	55.00	.10	
ZOOLOGICAL RECORD (BioSciences Information Services)	1.45	87.00	.26	.20

CHEMDEX/CHEMDEX2

These two chemical dictionary files are companion files to the Chemical Abstracts databases. All compounds cited in the literature from 1972 to date are contained in these files. Each record contains a Registry Number, the molecular formula, Chemical Abstract's rigorous nomenclature for a specific compound, and many common synonyms recognized by Chemical Abstracts Service. The Registry Numbers retrieved are then used as search terms in the CAS77, CAS7276, and CAS6771 files. Search CHEMDEX or CHEMDEX2 by chemical name or fragment, molecular formula, molecular formula fragment, or group or row within a periodic chart.

Prepared by: Chemical Abstracts Service of the American Chemical Society

Printed Publication: CA Substance Index, CA Registry Handbook, CA Index Guide, and CA Formula Index

File Size: Approximately 2.6 million citations

Coverage: 1972 to present

Updating: Quarterly

Cost: $70/computer-connect hour
$.20/citation for offline printing

Chemical Abstracts
see CAS77/CAS7276/CAS6771

Chemical Abstracts Source Index
see CASSI

Chemical Industry Notes
see CIN

Chemical Reactions Documentation Service
see CRDS

CHEMSDI*

Covers information cited in the last six weeks of Chemical Abstracts. This file will contain detailed information about chemical compounds cited as well as the indexing parameters available in CAS77, CAS7276, and CAS6771. CHEMSDI can be used as a current awareness file for both new compounds and new developments in chemical and related fields.

Prepared by: Chemical Abstracts Service of the American Chemical Society

Coverage: Last six weeks

Updating: Every 2 weeks

Cost: $70/computer-connect hour
$.20/citation for offline printing

*Available 1981

Christian Science Monitor
see MONITOR

CIN

Chemical Industry Notes contains citations to business literature in the chemical industry, including pharmaceutical, petroleum, paper and pulp, agriculture, and food industries. Subject coverage includes production, pricing, sales, facilities, products and processes, corporate activities, government activities, and people. Covers over 80 U.S. and non-U.S. publications.

Automatic SDI service is available on this file.

Prepared by: Chemical Abstracts Service of the American Chemical Society

Printed Publication: Chemical Industry Notes

File Size: Approximately 52,000 citations per year

Coverage: 1974 to present

Updating: Weekly

Cost: $75/computer-connect hour
$.20/citation for offline printing

CIS

Covers publications emanating from the work of committees and subcommittees of the U.S. Congress: hearings; committee prints; House and Senate

Fig. 14. A sampling of databases from SDC Search Services
Reprinted by permission.

Also included is access to the Forbes Directory Issues, Securities Research highlights from Merrill Lynch, and Standard and Poor's company profiles.

General News and Information Services includes a dictionary of financial and economic terms, a database for company stock quote symbols, a medical/pharmaceutical database, movie reviews, news, sports and weather reports, on-line transcripts of *Wall $treet Week*, and a discount merchandise service.

Mail Service and Free Customer Newsletter consists of a free newsletter with useful information for the *Dow Jones News/Retrieval Service* users, and access to *MCI Mail*, an electronic mail service discussed below.

The standard membership kit costs $29.95, and includes five hours of unrestricted connect time. There is also a Blue Chip and Executive Membership package providing different combinations of free connect time and usage discounts. Beyond that usage charges vary with the time of day, the tier you access, and the speed of your modem.

MCI Mail An electronic mail service which offers several alternate types of mail delivery. Instant Letter is simple. You type your message into the system, and the addressee can see it instantly if he or she is also an MCI mail user.

An *MCI Letter* is the next best thing. You enter the letter into the system, and MCI transmits it to their postal center nearest the addressee, where it is printed as a hard copy and posted by regular mail. Or, you can have the letter hand-delivered through MCI's *Overnight Letter* service.

An even faster (and much more expensive) service is the *Four-Hour Letter*. Hand delivery in (you guessed it) four hours.

Telex If you know the party's telex number, you can send an MCI letter via the telex system without having a terminal of your own. Especially useful for communicating overseas, where telex is much more prevalent.

Charges are based on the number of characters in your message and the type of service. The annual subscription fee is currently $18.

Western Union offers two basic services, *Easylink* and *InfoMaster*.

Easylink is an electronic mail service which puts you in touch with practically every member of the Western Union network, including over a million and a half telex users and 110,000 on-line users. It offers mail methods similar to that of *MCI*. Mailbox message stores your message in a central computer which can be accessed by another *Easylink* user. Western Union offers several additional features in connection with this service that might be worth considering if you decide you need electronic mail, so it is worth a call or a note to them for an explanation.

In addition, *Easylink* can transmit your message via *Telex*, *Mailgram*, *Cablegram*. A hardcopy can be mailed from a post office near the message destination through the *Computer Letter* service or *E-Com*, a similar service offered by the *U.S. Postal Service*. You can also access an *InfoCom* station. *Infocom* is a private telex service, usually set up between branch offices of the same company. If the company agrees to receive your incoming message, *Easylink* will let you tap into an *InfoCom* station.

InfoMaster is a superb information system which gives the user access to over 700 databases from 16 different vendors. This is known as a *gateway* service, and the principal advantages are that (a), you needn't learn a separate set of commands, phone numbers and search methods for several different database services and (b), you don't have to worry about whether or not the database service you choose will meet your data needs.

Easylink charges by the type of service and message-length (measured in half pages). InfoMaster is more complicated. There is an on-line charge by the minute, a charge for a "successful" search, and charges for additional sets of headings, abstracts, and full text. Nevertheless, the service is quite reasonable and in line with other data retrieval services.

Official Airlines Guide   Essentially the electronic edition of a travel industry bible listing schedules and fares for virtually every flight and every airline. You can also determine the nearest airport to your destination and take advantage of 24-hour telephone assistance which in my experience is quite good. The OAG on-line service goes one better by giving you hotel and auto rental information, as well as an on-line reservation system which allows you to book a flight and, if you wish, be issued a ticket by Thomas Cook travel agency.

It is a terrific service, especially if you don't have a travel agent of your own or if you don't trust the airline reservations agent (or can't get through on the telephone). However, some short-term promotional fares can elude the database, and some flights can only be booked through Thomas Cook.

When you do purchase a ticket through the system, the Cook agency does more than print your ticket. You can communicate with them and make special requests, and they do guarantee you the lowest possible fare, regardless of what the *OAG* on-line says it is.

If you have ever overpaid for an airline ticket, it should be easy to see how quickly this service can earn back the cost. There is a $50 initial charge which gives you free usage for a month. After that, there are no monthly or annual charges, just a usage fee. And if the session results in a booking (or a cancellation) the usage charges are waived. This is a good deal.

Several of the other services offer access to the *OAG* system, but in most cases it costs a little more than going direct. Still, you might find it more convenient to use *OAG* in that fashion.

Other on-line services are listed in the accompanying table. Several, such as *CompuServe* and *The Source*, are very popular among general computer users, but offer information and services also of interest to business users.

Vendors of On-Line Services

AT&T   1 Speedwell Ave., Morristown, NJ 07960
(800) 367-7225
- AT&T MAIL (electronic message service)
  - ☐ Software costs $85 for MS-DOS, $550 for Unix; 40 cents for up to 400 characters, 80 cents for up to 7,500 characters
  - ☐ 24-hour connection time
  - ☐ Hard copy can be mailed to user
  - ☐ $2 monthly fee

BYTE INFORMATION EXCHANGE   1 Phoenix Mill Lane, Peterborough, NH 03458
(603) 924-9027
- BIX (conference service)
  - ☐ $25 registration fee plus hourly rate
  - ☐ Prime time: 7 a.m.—6 p.m. weekdays, $12 per hour; off-hours: 6 p.m.—7 a.m. weekdays, plus weekends and holidays, $9 per hour
  - ☐ Electronic mail
  - ☐ General business information
  - ☐ Scientific and technical information
  - ☐ Special interest groups
  - ☐ Program libraries

BRS INFORMATION TECHNOLOGIES   1200 Route 7, Latham, NY 12110
(800) 345-4BRS
- BRS/SEARCH SERVICE
  - ☐ System down every day 4 a.m.—6 a.m. (Eastern time), Sundays 2 a.m.—9 a.m. (Eastern time)
  - ☐ $75 annual fee and an hourly rate of $35 plus royalties, and telecommunications cost; or users may subscribe, pay a monthly fee plus an hourly rate, royalties, and telecommunications cost
  - ☐ Electronic mail
  - ☐ General business information
  - ☐ Scientific and technical information
  - ☐ Special interest groups
- BRS BRKTHRU
  - ☐ System down every day 4 a.m.—6 a.m. (Eastern time), Sundays 2 a.m.—9 a.m. (Eastern time)
  - ☐ Rates depend on database and time of day
  - ☐ General business information
  - ☐ Scientific and technical information
  - ☐ Special interest groups
- BRS AFTER DARK
  - ☐ System down weekdays 4 a.m.—6 p.m. (Eastern time)
  - ☐ Hourly rates from $6 to $31 an hour depending on database, royalties, and telecommunications cost
  - ☐ $12 per month minimum
  - ☐ General business information
  - ☐ Scientific and technical information
  - ☐ Special interest groups

COMPUSERVE INC.   500 Arlington Center Blvd., Columbus, OH 43220
(800) 848-8199 inside U.S.
(614) 457-0802 inside Ohio, outside U.S.
- COMPUSERVE INFORMATION SERVICE
  - ☐ 24-hour connection time
  - ☐ Cost varies depending on connection time, duration, and transfer rate

☐ Prime time: 8 a.m.—6 p.m. weekdays; off-hours: 6 p.m.—8 a.m. weekdays, all weekend
☐ Hard copy can be mailed to user
☐ Electronic mail
☐ General business information
☐ Current stock market quotes
☐ Historical stock market information
☐ Current news wire/news retrieval
☐ Scientific and technical information
☐ Special interest groups
☐ Program libraries
☐ Links to MCI Mail

COMSHARE INC. Wolverine Tower, 3001 S. State St., Ann Arbor, MI 48104
(313) 994-4800
• EDVENT II (listing of education seminars)
☐ $60 per hour
☐ Minimum charge of $60 per month
☐ System down one night a week, depending on the system; shuts down daily 5 a.m.—7 a.m., Saturday nights, and Sunday mornings
☐ Allows users to link to Microseek, gateway to W/Information Gateway

DIALOG INFORMATION SERVICES INC. 3460 Hillview Ave., Palo Alto, CA 94304
(800) 3-DIALOG
• DIALOG
☐ Access through (800) DIALNET, Telenet, or Tymnet
☐ $25 annual service fee or commitment contract plus connect charges ranging from 40 cents to $2 per minute, depending on database; commitment contracts begin at $3,000 per year and include discounts on hourly charges and service fees for volume users
☐ Charges per record displayed range from 10 cents to over $1, depending on database
☐ 10 cents to over $1 for off-line printing
☐ System available 136 hours per week
☐ Electronic mail service
☐ General business information
☐ 20-minute-delay stock market quotes
☐ Partial historical stock market information through Media General Database
☐ 48-hour-delay news wire/news retrieval
☐ Scientific and technical information
☐ Gateway to *Official Airline Guide*
• KNOWLEDGE INDEX (an off-hours service)
☐ (800) 3-DIALOG, customer support
☐ $24 per hour for telecommunications and connect charges for all databases; $35 one-time start-up fee includes manual, 2 hours free connect time, and password
☐ Available hours: Mon.—Thurs., 6 p.m.—5 a.m.; Fri., 5 p.m.—midnight; Sat., 8 a.m.—midnight; Sun., 3 p.m.—5 a.m.
☐ Electronic mail service
☐ General business information, $12 per hour
☐ Scientific and technical information
☐ Access to outside services through Dialog Link software
☐ Other services include education, government publications, legal information, magazine index, newspaper index, medical, mathematic, psychological, and reference information

DOW JONES & COMPANY INC. P.O. Box 300, Princeton, NJ 08543
(800) 257-5114 outside New Jersey
(609) 452-1511 inside New Jersey, California, and Alabama

- **DOW JONES NEWS/RETRIEVAL**
  - ☐ Access through Telenet and Tymnet
  - ☐ $49.95 one-time connect; $12 annual service fee after first year
  - ☐ Additional charges: 90 cents per minute, prime time, and 20 cents per minute, off-hours, for most databases; top charge for database is $1.20 per minute, prime time
  - ☐ Prime time: 6 a.m.—6 p.m. (Eastern time); off-hours: 6 p.m.—4 a.m.
  - ☐ Electronic mail service
  - ☐ General business information
  - ☐ Current stock market quotes
  - ☐ Historical stock market information
  - ☐ Current news wire/news retrieval
  - ☐ Full text of the *Wall Street Journal*

GENERAL ELECTRIC INFORMATION SERVICES CO. 401 N. Washington St.,
Rockville, MD 20850
(301) 340-4000

- **GENIE**
  - ☐ (800) 638-9636, ext. 21
  - ☐ $35 per hour for 300 and 1,200 bps, prime time, and $5 per hour for 300 and 1,200 bps, off-hours; $10 surcharge for 2,400 bps
  - ☐ Prime time: 8 a.m.—6 p.m.; off-hours: 6 p.m.—8 a.m. weekdays, all day Saturday and Sunday, and national holidays
  - ☐ Electronic mail service
  - ☐ General business information
  - ☐ Historical stock market information
  - ☐ Scientific and technical information
  - ☐ Special interest groups
  - ☐ Program libraries
  - ☐ Other services: American Airlines travel service, *Grolier's Encyclopedia,* CB simulator

GENERAL VIDEOTEX CORP. 3 Blackstone St., Cambridge, MA 02139
(800) 544-4005 outside Massachusetts
(617) 491-3393 inside Massachusetts

- **DELPHI**
  - ☐ (617) 576-0862 for direct access, also access through Datapac, Telenet, or Tymnet
  - ☐ 16 cents per minute prime time, direct, or 11 cents per minute off-hours, direct; 29 cents per minute prime time, network, or 12 cents per minute off-hours, network
  - ☐ $49.95 lifetime membership
  - ☐ Prime time: 7 a.m.—6 p.m.; off-hours: 6 p.m.—7 p.m.
  - ☐ Electronic mail
  - ☐ General business information
  - ☐ 15-minute-delay stock market quotes
  - ☐ Current news wire/news retrieval
  - ☐ Special interest groups
  - ☐ Program libraries
  - ☐ Can link to other services

MCI DIGITAL INFORMATION SERVICES CORP. 2000 M St. N.W., Suite 300,
Washington, DC 20036
(202) 293-4255

- **MCI MAIL**
  - ☐ (800) MCI-2255 customer service
  - ☐ From 1 to 500 characters at 45 cents, or from 501 to 7,500 characters at $1
  - ☐ $18 annual subscription fee
  - ☐ Two types of accounts: Basic account, no fee; Advanced account, $10 per month for frequent users, includes forwarding features, easier editing, and scan features

☐ Printing charges: $30 for 4-hour delivery, limited to major cities; $8 for overnight delivery; $2 through U.S. Post Office (priority messages, terminal to terminal are $1)
☐ Electronic mail service
☐ Current stock market quotes through Dow Jones, at Dow Jones rates
☐ Gateway to CompuServe, DEC All-in-1, and IBM PROF

MEAD DATA CENTRAL INC.   P.O. Box 1830, Dayton, OH 45401
(800) 227-4908

- **LEXIS**
  ☐ $125 per month subscription charge per location; $30 per hour telecommunications and connect time for WATS, $35 per hour for network
  ☐ 30 percent discount in nonpeak hours
  ☐ Charges per search range from $10—$19 for files in legal database alone; $3 minimum charge for searches in Medis, included in Lexis; $30 maximum charge for searches in Lexpat, the patent database, and for combined searches
  ☐ 2 cents per line for off-line printing plus $15 handling charge
  ☐ Prime time: 7:30 a.m.—7:30 p.m.; off-hours: 7:30 p.m.—7:30 a.m.
  ☐ General business information (included in Nexis)
  ☐ Financial analysis reports
  ☐ Current news wire/news retrieval
  ☐ Scientific and technical information
  ☐ Gateway to Dialog with custom terminals
  ☐ Lexis alone includes federal and state case law, law reviews, government documents, Lexpat, libraries of case law
- **MEDIS** (included in Lexis and Nexis, also available separately)
  ☐ $30 per hour connect and telecommunications charge; $3 to $12 per search for Lexis and Nexis users
  ☐ $10 per hour through WATS for Medis only; $15 per hour through network
  ☐ $10.95 for 1 to 19 searches on Medis alone; discounts available for users performing over 180 searches per month
  ☐ $4.55 to $6.25 for Medline searches
  ☐ $50 one-time registration fee for private individuals; $10 per month for monthly subscribers; free to hospitals
  ☐ Available 24 hours every day
  ☐ 1 cent per line for off-line printing
  ☐ Clinical information
- **NEXIS** (included in Lexis)
  ☐ $50 per month subscription fee
  ☐ $30 per hour connect and telecommunications charge
  ☐ $7 for single search; up to $23 for combined searches
  ☐ Prime time: 7:30 a.m.—7:30 p.m.; off-hours: 7:30 p.m.—7:30 a.m.
  ☐ General business information
  ☐ Financial analysis reports
  ☐ Current news wire/news retrieval
  ☐ Scientific and technical information

NATIONAL ON-LINE CLASSIFIED INC.   1465 Andrews Lane, East Meadow, NY 11554
(516) 481-9222

- **ADNET SERVICE** (a help-wanted and situation-wanted service)
  ☐ 24-hour connection time
  ☐ $10 per year, includes a free listing for 8 weeks; daily display of job costs $4; connection time cost is $9 per hour during the day and $4 per hour at night
  ☐ Night hours are 6 p.m.—7 a.m. (Eastern time), including weekends and holidays
  ☐ Electronic mail

NEWSNET INC. 945 Haverford Road, Bryn Mawr, PA 19010
(215) 527-8030 inside Pennsylvania
(800) 345-1301 outside Pennsylvania

• NEWSNET
  ☐ Access through (215) 668-2035 for 300 bps, (215) 668-2645 for 1,200 bps, also through Telenet and Tymnet
  ☐ Cost varies, depending on connection time, duration, and transfer rate
  ☐ $15 monthly fee
  ☐ Prime time: 8 a.m.—8 p.m. (Eastern time); off-hours: 8 p.m.—8 a.m. (Eastern time)
  ☐ General business information
  ☐ Current stock market quotes
  ☐ Current news wire/news retrieval
  ☐ Scientific and technical information
  ☐ Special interest groups
  ☐ Gateway service to TRW, *Official Airline Guide,* Vu/Quote, and Sports Network

SOURCE TELECOMPUTING CORP. 1616 Anderson Road, McLean, VA 22102
(703) 734-7500

• THE SOURCE
  ☐ Access through Telenet or Sourcenet in major cities, or through WATS in outlying regions
  ☐ Cost varies depending on connection time, duration, and transfer rates
  ☐ Hard copy mailed to address at additional cost
  ☐ $10 minimum monthly fee applies toward usage
  ☐ Prime time: 7 a.m.—6 p.m. weekdays; off-hours: 6 p.m.—7 a.m. weekdays, plus weekends and holidays
  ☐ Electronic mail
  ☐ General business information
  ☐ Current stock market quotes
  ☐ Historical stock market information
  ☐ Current news wire/news retrieval
  ☐ Special interest groups
  ☐ Program libraries within special interest groups
  ☐ Links to *Official Airline Guide,* Compustore, and Investext

TELEBASE SYSTEMS INC. Easynet Division, 134 N. Narbarth Ave., Narbarth, PA 19072
(215) 296-1793 inside Pennsylvania
(800) 841-9553 outside Pennsylvania

• EASYNET
  ☐ Access through (800) EASYNET or through CompuServe or Easylink; high school version available through Addison-Wesley; library version available through Accusearch Inc.
  ☐ $8 per search plus 20 cents per minute teleconnect time (charged only for successful searches) and $2 per abstract; surcharge for some databases
  ☐ Hard copy delivery by Federal Express or U.S. Post Office at extra cost
  ☐ General business information
  ☐ Current stock market quotes
  ☐ Historical stock market information
  ☐ Current news wire/news retrieval
  ☐ Scientific and technical information
  ☐ Special interest groups

TELENET COMMUNICATIONS CORP. 12490 Sunrise Valley Drive, Reston, VA 22096
(800) TELENET
Telenet offers several data communications network products and services, including the Telenet Public Data Network, which provides communications transmission facilities for medium- to large-size companies whose communications traffic isn't large enough

129

to justify a private network. Telenet also sets up private, dedicated networks for customers requiring high-volume data communications. In addition, the firm provides a Telemail electronic mail service for sending messages as well as applications. All major protocols are supported.

**TYMNET MCDONNELL
DOUGLAS NETWORK SYSTEMS CO.**   2710 Orchard Parkway, San Jose, CA 95134
(408) 946-4900

Tymnet offers a public data communications network with access to more than 600 locations in 68 countries. The company also will design and install private networks. In addition, Tymnet offers its Ontyme electronic mail service, its Virtual Net service for connecting public communications networks with private networks, and its Tymstar satellite communications system that ties packet-switching technology to satellite technology.

WESTERN UNION CORP.   1 Lake St., Upper Saddle River, NJ 07458
(800) 442-4803 inside Texas
(800) 527-5184 outside Texas

- **EASYLINK**
  - ☐ Access through (800) 325-4112 for 300 or 1,200 bps, also access through Tymnet and Western Union
  - ☐ Rates vary depending on connection time and character count
  - ☐ Additional fees for hard copy mailed to address: $3.45 first half-page, 50 cents each additional half-page for Mailbox Messages; $8.75 for five pages, 25 cents each additional page for Overnight Documents
  - ☐ $25 annual fee
  - ☐ Prime time: 7 a.m.—midnight (Eastern time) weekdays, except national holidays; off-hours (40 percent discount): midnight—7 a.m. (Eastern time) weekdays, all hours weekends and national holidays
  - ☐ Volume discounts available starting at $1,000 per month
  - ☐ Electronic mail
  - ☐ General business information
  - ☐ Current stock market quotes
  - ☐ Historical stock market information
  - ☐ Current news wire/news retrieval
  - ☐ Scientific and technical information
  - ☐ Links to Easylink in Great Britain, Missive in France, and Telex around the world
- **INFOMASTER** (gateway to more than 700 on-line databases from 16 vendors)
  - ☐ Access by (800) 325-4112 for 300 and 1,200 bps, also access through Tymnet and Western Union
  - ☐ Connect time rates are 15 cents per minute, $9 per hour; $8 basic search fee (applied only with successful searches), plus $6 for each additional set of headings, $2 for each abstract, $6 for each additional full text
  - ☐ Available 24 hours a day, seven days a week

Fig. 15.
Published by permission
InfoWorld, November 3, 1986.

Going on-line As with the purchase of a computer, there are several technical decisions that must be made. While not difficult to fathom, the choice of brands and technical specifications are beyond the scope of this book. Certainly, one should—if possible—determine the specific databases to be used, as this will help when selecting hardware.

What you need is a computer or workstation, a communications device called a *modem*, which can sit outside or be installed into your computer, access to a telephone line, and *communications software* which converts what you type on your computer screen into signals that are transmitted by telephone, and then converts incoming signals to letters, numbers, and graphics which appear on your monitor. There is a wide variety to choose from, varying predominantly by speed, intelligence, ease of use and price.

Access Networks Okay. So you've selected a database service, and done a rough estimate of the cost to use it. And you have your hardware in place. That's it, right? Wrong. There is another link in the chain. The phone number your computer dials does not put you in direct contact with your database. Rather, it connects you with a network which, through technical wizardry, acts as an intermediary, conveying your requests and the replies to and from the database. This service is not free; expect to pay an additional charge for the time spent on the access network. The cost varies with the time of day, database, and speed of your modem, but expect to pay under $20 per hour, and in some cases as little as $6.

There are two types of access methods. The direct dial access is simply one of several phone numbers provided by the database itself. This is usually cheaper since you are not dealing with a third party. *Newsnet, Dialog, MCI*, and *Western Union* are among those with direct dial access telephone numbers.

The other type of access involves independent networks such as *Tymnet, Telenet, Uninet, Datapac* (Canadian) and *Dunsnet.* Generally, such services are a bit more expensive, but if you stick to one, you get used to the procedure and don't have to learn new sets of instructions for each access network or database direct dial. And you can use the same number to access the major databases. When you subscribe to a database, you will be provided with listings of phone numbers of the networks that carry that service, and the direct dial numbers, if any.

Is it worth it? At first blush, databases appear expensive. The access and search charges can add up, and there are usually extra charges for downloading information onto disk in your own computer, should you want to save what you read. In many cases, you will be viewing an abstract, and it will cost more to see the entire item.

If this kind of service is icing on the cake to you, i.e., not essential to your business, you will have a difficult time justifying substantial use of the database. However, it may be much less costly than other methods of information retrieval. A $300 charge for a search may sound like a lot of money, but compared to sending a staff member to a library for several days of manual researching and note-taking with far less accuracy, it could well be a bargain, not to mention the fact that you'll have what you need in a fraction of the time.

Keep in mind. The cost per hour or minute is not always the best way to compare information retrieval charges between different database services. Two services might offer access to the same information, but one might be more efficient, so you can get the job done in far less time. A database costing twice as much per minute might be cheaper in the long run if the less expensive database requires three times as much time to do the same job.

Modem speed. The rate at which your modem transmits data, called the *baud rate*, will affect your costs. If you use a 2400 baud per second (bps) modem instead of a 600bps, theoretically, you could do the same task on-line in one quarter the time. To compensate for potential lost revenue as modems get faster, the databases charge more to transmit at faster rates. In some cases you save a little money with a faster modem. In other cases you don't.

There are many promotional offers available, usually in connection with the purchase of hardware, such as a modem, or communications software. One of the best deals comes with the purchase of the book *On Line* (see below), which includes coupons worth over twenty hours of free connect time (a $350 value) on various databases, assuming, of course, you subscribed to every one. I used the coupon for three databases and the savings easily exceeded the $19.95 cost of the book.

For more on databases. See the section on conferences in which I discuss the related teleconferencing services; also the section on Office of the Future.

Recommended Reading The principal computer magazines periodically run service features about databases. There is currently only one book worth recommending: *"On Line: A guide to America's leading information services"* by Steve Lambert (1985, Microsoft Press, $19.95). This is an excellent book for anyone who wants to know more about databases and telecomputing. Written in clear, non-technical jargon, *On Line* begins with a description of the equipment needed, including the latest in monitors, serial ports, modems and communications software. Lambert discusses the methods of getting your system up and running, and accessing the databases.

The bulk of the book is devoted to a comprehensive guide to the major databases, including costs, methods of access, available information and the basics of how to use the system. The graphics and layout of the book make it easy to follow, and the only real drawback is that unless Microsoft comes out with a revised version, *On Line* is doomed to be out of date. Nevertheless, I don't expect the basics to change much.

On Line is available at bookstores in the computer section or directly through Microsoft Press, 10700 Northup Way, Box 97200 Bellevue, WA 98009, 206-828-8080.

Another valuable book is *How To Look It Up Online* by Alfred Grossbrenner (1987, St. Martin's Press, $24.95). This is a book for people who are serious about using databases; it provides a comprehensive, in-depth analysis of how to use each of the popular databases, and why.

Where Lambert's *On Line* is like a restaurant menu, Grossbrenner's volume is like a cookbook. *How To Look It Up Online* doesn't come with coupons, but could end up saving you hundreds—even thousands—of dollars, because it provides tips on how to conduct information searches quickly and efficiently. Having wasted money looking for information in the wrong database, or following an illogical search procedure, I can attest to the value of Grossbrenner's book in preparing the reader to access a database.

Dow Jones News/Retrieval®

Summary of Information Services
& Price Schedule

Business & Investor Services

//BUSINESS   **The Business and Finance Report**
- Continuously updated business and financial news culled from The Wall Street Journal, The Dow Jones News Service and other news wires.
- The latest news on domestic and international economies.
- Cross references to related information.

//DEFINE   **Words of Wall Street**^{SM}
- Definitions of over 2,000 business and financial terms used by professional investors.

//DJNEWS   **Dow Jones**^{SM} **News**
- Stories from The Wall Street Journal, Barron's, and Dow Jones News Service.
- Stories as recent as 90 seconds, as far back as 90 days.

//DSCLO   **Disclosure® Online**
- 10-K extracts, company profiles and other detailed data on over 10,000 publicly held companies from reports filed with the SEC.

//EPS   **Corporate Earnings Estimator**^{SM}
- Timely earnings forecasts for more than 3,000 of the most widely followed companies compiled by Zacks Investment Research, Inc.

//INSIDER   **Insider Trading Monitor**
- Insider trading information on over 6,500 publicly held companies. Reports on trades made by nearly 60,000 individuals (corporate directors, officers or shareholders with more than 10% ownership).

//INVEST   **Investext®**
- Provides full texts of more than 13,000 research reports from top brokers, investment bankers and other analysts.
- Includes more than 3,000 U.S. and Canadian companies and 50 industries.
- Historical, current and forecasted marketing and financial information.

//KYODO   **Japan Economic Daily®**
- Same-day coverage of major business, financial and political news from Japan's Kyodo News International, Inc.

Figure 16. Summary of Information Services and Price Schedules
Copyright © 1986 Dow Jones News/Retrieval. Reprinted by permission.

//MG   **Media General Financial Services**
- Detailed corporate financial information on 4,300 companies and 170 industries.
- Major categories include: revenue, earnings, dividends, volume, ratio, share-holdings, and price changes.
- Compare 2 different companies or company versus industry data on the same screen.

//MMS   **Economic and Foreign Exchange Survey**^{SM}
- Weekly survey of U.S. money market and foreign exchange trends.
- Median forecasts of monetary and economic indicators.

//QUICK   **Dow Jones**^{SM} **QuickSearch**
- Corporate report drawing information from multiple News/Retrieval sources, searchable with one command.

//SP   **Standard & Poor's Online**®
- Concise profiles of 4,600 companies containing earnings, dividend and market figures for the current year and the past four years.
- Corporate overviews plus S&P earnings estimates for most major companies.

//TEXT   **Text-Search Services**^{SM}
- The Wall Street Journal: Full Text Version. All articles that appeared or were scheduled to appear in The Wall Street Journal since January 1984.
- Dow Jones News. News Service articles and selected stories from Barron's and The Wall Street Journal since June 1979.
- The Washington Post: Full Text Version. Articles that appeared in The Washington Post since January 1984.
- The Business Library. Selected articles from Forbes Magazine, Inc., Financial World and the full text of the PR newswire since January 1985.

//TRACK   **Tracking Service**
- Create and track up to 5 profiles containing as many as 25 companies each.
- Track current quotes (minimum 15 minute delay) and the latest news stories and headlines automatically on the companies in your profiles.

//WSW   **Wall $treet Week**^{SM} **Online**
- Four most recent transcripts of the popular PBS television program Wall $treet Week.

Quotes and Market Averages

//CQE   **Enhanced Current Quotes**
(Minimum 15-minute delay during market hours)
- Common and preferred stocks and bonds.
- Mutual funds, U.S. Treasury Issues and Options.
- News alert.

Note: News alert available on stocks trading on the New York and American stock exchanges and for those listed by NASDAQ.

//DJA   **Historical Dow Jones Averages**^{SM}
- Daily high, low, close and volume available for the last trading year for industrials, transportation, utilities, and 65 composite stocks.

//FUTURES   Futures Quotes

- Current Quotes (10-30 minute delay) for more than 80 contracts from the major North American Exchanges updated continuously during market hours.
- Daily open, high, low, last and settlement prices.
- Daily volume and open interest, lifetime high and low.

//HQ   Historical Quotes

- Daily volume, high, low, and close for stock quotes and composites.
- Monthly stock quote summaries back to 1979; quarterly summaries back to 1978.

//RTQ   Real-Time Quotes

- Stock prices with no delay from the major exchanges, including composites.
- NASDAQ National Market System prices.
- News alert.

Note: News alert available on stocks trading on the New York and American stock exchanges and for those listed by NASDAQ.

Brokerage

//FIDELITY   Fidelity Investor's Express

- Place trades online for listed securities.
- Organize your portfolios and monitor your investments with a Fidelity Investor's Express account.

General Services

//AXP   American Express® Advance

- Statement Information for American Express cardholders.
- American Express travel and shopping services.

//BOOKS   Magill Book Reviews

- Reviews of many recent fiction and non-fiction works with new titles added weekly.

//ENCYC   Academic American Encyclopedia®

- Contains more than 32,000 carefully researched and concisely written articles.
- Updated quarterly.

//MCI   MCI Mail®

- Mail service for sending printed and electronic communications next door or world-wide.

//MOVIES   Cineman Movie Reviews

- Entertaining reviews of the latest releases as well as thousands of movies dating back to 1926.

//NEWS   News/Retrieval World Report[SM]

- Continuously updated foreign and national news from the Associated Press.

//OAG   Official Airlines Guide™

- Schedules, fares, reservations and ticketing for 700 airlines world-wide.
- Hotel and motel information.

//SCHOOL   **Peterson's College Selection Service**^{SM}
- More than 3,000 two and four year colleges and universities.
- Search by size, entrance difficulty, location, cost, financial aid, majors and admissions requirements.

//SPORTS   **News/Retrieval Sports Report**^{SM}
- Continuously updated stories, scores, stats, standings and schedules for most major sports.

//STORE   **Comp-u-store Online**®
- An electronic shopping service of more than 250,000 discounted brand-named products ranging from appliances and sporting goods to gourmet foods.

//WTHR   **News/Retrieval Weather Report**^{SM}
- Three-day Accu-Weather forecasts for more than 80 major U.S. and foreign cities.

Using News/Retrieval

//FYI   **FYI**
- Free online newsletter of News/Retrieval.
- New database announcements and other information of interest to subscribers.

//MENU   **Master Menu**
- A complete listing of the information contained in the service, along with detailed information on how to access each database.

//SYMBOL   **News/Retrieval Symbols Directory**^{SM}
- A comprehensive online listing of the symbols and codes used to access News/Retrieval services.

9

APPENDIX TO PART II

**MAJOR ENGLISH-LANGUAGE
BUSINESS PERIODICALS**

**ALL-NEWS RADIO STATIONS
IN THE UNITED STATES**

MAJOR ENGLISH-LANGUAGE
BUSINESS PERIODICALS

ABA Banking Journal. $20. m (ISSN 0194-5947) ABA Banking Journal, Subscription Department, P.O. Box 466, Village Station, New York, NY 10014

Academy of Management Journal. $38. q (ISSN 0001-4273) Academy of Management Journal. P.O. Drawer KZ, Mississippi State University, Mississippi State, MS 39762

The Academy of Management Review. $38. q (ISSN 0363-7425) Academy of Management Review, P.O. Drawer KZ, Mississippi State University, Mississippi State, MS 39762

Accountancy. $33.38. m (ISSN 0001-4664) Institute of Chartered Accountants in England and Wales, Chartered Accountants Hall, Moorgate Place, London EC2P 2BJ, England

Accounting and Business Research. $12. q (ISSN 0001-4788) Institute of Chartered Accountants in England and Wales, 56-66 Goswell Rd., London EC1M 7AB, England

The Accounting Review. $50. q (ISSN 0001-4826) American Accounting Association, 5717 Bessie Dr., Sarasota, FL 33583

Across the Board. $30. m (ISSN 0147-1554) The Conference Board, Inc., 845 Third Ave., New York, NY 10022

Ad Forum. $48. m (ISSN 0274-6328) Agency File, Inc., 18 E. 53rd St., New York, NY 10022
Name changed to AdWeek with July 1985

Administrative Management. $30. m (ISSN 0884-5905) Dalton Communications, Inc., 1123 Broadway, New York, NY 10010
Formerly Office Administration and Automation; name changed with October 1985

Administrative Science Quarterly. $62. q (ISSN 0001-8392) Graduate School of Business and Public Administration at Cornell University, Mallot Hall, Cornell Univ., Ithaca, NY 14853

Advanced Management Journal. $24. q (ISSN 0036-0805) Advanced Management Journal, 2331 Victory Pkwy., Cincinnati, OH 45206

Advertising Age. $59. w (ISSN 0001-8899) Advertising Age, Circulation Department, 740 Rush St., Chicago, IL 60611

Advertising World. $30. bi-m (ISSN 0163-9412) Directories International, Inc., 150 Fifth Ave., Suite 610, New York, NY 10011
Name changed to International Advertiser with September 1985

AdWeek. $50. 64 times a yr (ISSN 0199-2864) A/S/M Communications, Inc., 820 Second Ave., New York, NY 10017
Formerly Ad Forum; name changed with July 1985. Name changed to Adweek's Marketing Week with September 8, 1986

AdWeek's Marketing Week. $60. 61 times a yr (ISSN 0199-2864) A/S/M Communications, Inc., 49 E. 21st St., New York, NY 10010
Formerly Adweek (National Marketing Edition); name changed with September 8, 1986

Air Transport World. $35. m (ISSN 0002-2543) Air Transport World, Circulation Department, P.O. Box 95759, Cleveland, OH 44101

American Business Law Journal. $20. q (ISSN 0002-7766) Jennifer M. Railing, Dept. of Economics and Business Administration, Gettysburg College, Gettysburg, PA 17325

American Demographics. $48. m (ISSN 0163-4089) American Demographics, P.O. Box 6543, Syracuse, NY 13217

The American Economic Review. $105. 5 times a yr (Mr, My, Je, S, D) (ISSN 0002-8282) American Economic Review, 1313 21st Ave. S., Suite 809, Nashville, TN 37212
May number has added title: Papers and Proceedings of the Annual Meeting of the American Economic Association

American Economist. $8. q (ISSN 0002-8290) Dr. William D. Gunther, Dept. of Economics, University of Alabama, P.O. Drawer AS, University, AL 35486

American Import/Export Management. $25. m (ISSN 0002-886X) North American Publishing Company, 401 N. Broad St., Philadelphia, PA 19108
Name changed to Global Trade Executive with May 1985

American Journal of Agricultural Economics. $65. 5 times a yr (ISSN 0002-9092) Sydney C. James, Secretary-Treasurer, American Agricultural Economics Association, Department of Economics, Iowa State University, Ames, IA 50011

American Journal of Small Business. $27. q (ISSN 0363-9428) University of Baltimore, 1420 N. Charles St., Baltimore, MD 21201

American Printer. $35. m (ISSN 0744-6616) American Printer, Circulation Department, 300 W. Adams St., Chicago, IL 60606

American Shipper. $15. m (ISSN 0160-225X) Howard Publications Inc., 33 S. Hogan St., P.O. Box 4728, Jacksonville, FL 32201

Antitrust Law & Economics Review. $77.50. q (ISSN 0003-6048) Antitrust Law & Economics Review, Inc., P.O. Box 3532, Vero Beach, FL 32960

The Appraisal Journal. $25. q (ISSN 0003-7087) American Institute of Real Estate Appraisers of the National Association of Real Estate Realtors, 430 N. Michigan Ave., Chicago, IL 60611

The Arbitration Journal. $40. q (ISSN 0003-7893) American Arbitration Association, Inc., 140 W. 51st St., New York, NY 10020

AREUEA Journal. See Journal of the American Real Estate and Urban Economics Association

ARMA Records Management Quarterly. $38. q (ISSN 0191-1503) Association of Records Managers & Administrators Inc., 4200 Somerset Dr., Suite 215, Prairie Village, KS 66208

Association Management. $24. m (ISSN 0004-5578) American Society of Association Executives, 1575 Eye St., N.W., Washington, DC 20005

Audio Visual Communications. $13.50. m (ISSN 0004-7562) Media Horizons, Inc., 50 West 23rd St., New York, NY 10010

Automotive Industries. $39.95. m (ISSN 0273-656X) Chilton Co., Chilton Way, Radnor, PA 19089

Automotive News. $50. w (semi-w 4th w Ap, 2d w Je) (ISSN 0005-1551) Automotive News, 965 E. Jefferson, Detroit, MI 48207

Aviation Week & Space Technology. $65. w (ISSN 0005-2175) Aviation Week & Space Technology, P.O. Box 1505, Neptune, NJ 07753

Bank Marketing. $48. m Bank Marketing Association, 309 W. Washington St., Chicago, IL 60606

The Banker. $90. m (ISSN 0005-5395) Financial Times, 102-108 Clerkenwell Rd., London EC1M 5SA, England

The Bankers Magazine (Boston, Mass.). $72. bi-m (ISSN 0005-545X) Warren, Gorham & Lamont, Inc., 210 South St., Boston, MA 02111

Bankers Monthly. $24. m (ISSN 0005-5476) Bankers Monthly, Inc., Tower Suite, 870 Seventh Ave., New York, NY 10019

Barron's. $86. w (ISSN 0005-6073) Dow Jones & Co., Inc., 200 Burnett Rd., Chicopee, MA 01021

Best's Review (Life/Health Insurance Edition). $14. m (ISSN 0005-9706) A.M. Best Co., Inc., Oldwick, NJ 08858

Best's Review (Property/Casualty Insurance Edition). $14. m (ISSN 0161-7745) A.M. Best Co., Inc., Oldwick, NJ 08858

Beverage World. $30. m (ISSN 0098-2318) Keller International, 150 Great Neck Rd., Great Neck, NY 11021

Black Enterprise. $15. m (ISSN 0006-4165) Black Enterprise, Circulation Service Center, P.O. Box 3009, Harlan, IA 51537

Broadcasting. $70. w (bi-w year end issue) (ISSN 0007-2028) Broadcasting Publications, Inc., 1735 DeSales St., N.W., Washington, DC 20036

Brookings Papers on Economic Activity. $25. 2 times a yr (ISSN 0007-2303) Brookings Publications, 1775 Massachusetts Ave., N.W., Washington, DC 20036

Buildings. $35. m (ISSN 0007-3725) Stamats Publishing Co., 427 Sixth Ave. S.E., Cedar Rapids, IA 52406

Bureaucrat. $35. q (ISSN 0045-3544) Bureaucrat, P.O. Box 347, Arlington, VA 22210

Business America. $57. bi-w (ISSN 0190-6275) Superintendent of Documents, U.S. Government Printing Office, Washington, DC 20402

Business and Society. $48. q (ISSN 0007-6503) Warren, Gorham & Lamont, Inc., 210 South St., Boston, MA 02111

Business and Society Review. $56. q (ISSN 0045-3609) Management Reports, Inc., 210 South St., Boston, MA 02111

Business (Atlanta, Ga.). $24. bi-m (ISSN 0163-531X) Business Magazine, College of Business Administration, Georgia State University, University Plaza, Atlanta, GA 30303

Business Economics. $30. 4 times a yr (ISSN 0007-666X) David L. Williams, Executive Secretary-Treasurer, National Association of Business Economists, 28349 Chagrin Blvd., Suite 201, Cleveland, OH 44122

Business History. $18. q (ISSN 0007-6791) Journals Department, Frank Cass & Co. Ltd., 11 Gainsborough Road, London E11 1RS, England

Business History Review. $27.50. q (ISSN 0007-6805) Business History Review, Teele Hall 304, Harvard Business School, Soldiers Field, Boston, MA 02163-0014

Business Horizons. $24. bi-m (ISSN 0007-6813) Business Horizons, Graduate School of Business, Indiana University, Bloomington, IN 47405

Business Insurance. $68. w (ISSN 0007-6864) Business Insurance, 740 Rush St., Chicago, IL 60611

Business Japan. $48. m (ISSN 0300-4341) Business Japan, 41 E. 42nd St., Suite 518, New York, NY 10017

Business Marketing. $25. m (ISSN 0745-5933) Business Marketing, Circulation Department, 740 Rush St., Chicago, IL 60611

Business Month. $32. m (ISSN 0892-4090) Business Month, Circulation Department, 875 Third Ave., New York, NY 10022
        Formerly Dun's Business Month; name changed with March 1987

Business Quarterly. $22. q (ISSN 0007-6996) The University of Western Ontario, 1393 Western Rd., London, Canada N6A 5B9

Business Week. $39.95. w (except 1 issue in Ja) (ISSN 0007-7135) Business Week, P.O. Box 430, Hightstown, NJ 08520

Byte. $21. 13 times a yr (ISSN 0360-5280) Byte Subscriber Service, P.O. Box 328, Hancock, NH 03449

CA Magazine. $30. m (ISSN 0317-6878) Canadian Institute of Chartered Accountants, 150 Bloor St. W., Toronto, Ont. M4W 1G5, Canada

California Management Review. $36. q (ISSN 0008-1256) California Management Review, Graduate School of Business Administration, 350 Barrows Hall, University of California, Berkeley, CA 94720

Canadian Banker. $18. 6 times a yr (ISSN 0315-6230) Canadian Banker, P.O. Box 348, 2 First Canadian Place, Toronto, Ont. M5X 1K1, Canada

Canadian Business. $40. m (ISSN 0008-3100) Canadian Business, 70 The Esplanade, Toronto, Ont. M5E 1R2, Canada

The Canadian Business Review. $24. q (ISSN 0317-4026) The Canadian Business Review, Suite 100, 25 McArthur Rd., Ottawa, Ont., Canada

Chain Store Age Executive with Shopping Center Age. $25. m (semi-m Ja) (ISSN 0193-1199) Executive Offices, Chain Store Age Executive, 425 Park Ave., New York, NY 10022

Chain Store Age General Merchandise Edition. $20. m (ISSN 0193-1350) Executive Offices, Chain Store Age General Merchandise Group, 425 Park Ave., New York, NY 10022
        Name changed to Chain Store Age General Merchandise Trends with January 1985

Chain Store Age General Merchandise Trends. $20. m (ISSN 0193-1350) Executive Offices, Chain Store Age General Merchandise Group, 425 Park Ave., New York, NY 10022
        Formerly Chain Store Age General Merchandise Edition; name changed with January 1985

Challenge (Armonk, N.Y.). $38. bi-m (ISSN 0577-5132) Challenge, 80 Business Park Dr., Armonk, NY 10504

Chemical & Engineering News. $44. w (ISSN 0009-2347) Director, Business Management Division, ACS, P.O. Box 57136. Washington, DC 20037

Chemical Marketing Reporter. $65. w (ISSN 0090-0907) Schnell Publishing Company, Inc., 100 Church St., New York, NY 10007

Chemical Week. $49. w (ISSN 0009-272X) McGraw-Hill Inc., 1221 Ave. of the Americas, New York, NY 10020

Chilton's Automotive Industries. See Automotive Industries

Chilton's Distribution. See Distribution

Chilton's Iron Age Metals Producer. See Iron Age Metals Producer

Coal Age. $30. m (ISSN 0009-9910) Fulfillment Manager, Coal Age, P.O. Box 1513, Neptune, NJ 07753

The Columbia Journal of World Business. $40. q (ISSN 0022-5428) Columbia Journal of World Business, Graduate School of Business, Columbia University, 403 Uris Hall, New York, NY 10027

Communications News. $27. m (ISSN 0010-3632) Communications News, 124 S. First St., Geneva, IL 60134

Compensation and Benefits Review. $50. bi-m (ISSN 0010-4248) American Management Associations, Subscription Services, Box 319, Saranac Lake, NY 12983
        Formerly Compensation Review; name changed with July/August 1985

Compensation Review. $50. q (ISSN 0010-4248) American Management Associations, Subscription Services, Box 319, Saranac Lake, NY 12983
        Name changed to Compensation and Benefits Review with July/August 1985

Computer Decisions. $65. bi-w (ISSN 0010-4558) Hayden Publishing Co., Inc., 10 Mulholland Dr., Hasbrouck Heights, NJ 07604

Computers and People. $18.50. bi-m (ISSN 0361-1442) Berkeley Enterprises Inc., 815 Washington St., Newtonville, MA 02160

Construction Review. $17. bi-m (ISSN 0010-6917) Superintendent of Documents, U.S. Government Printing Office, Washington, DC 20402

The Cornell Hotel and Restaurant Administration Quarterly. $25. q (ISSN 0010-8804) School of Hotel Administration, Cornell University, Ithaca, NY 14853

The CPA Journal. $34. m (ISSN 0732-8435) New York State Society of Certified Public Accountants, 600 Third Ave., New York, NY 10016

Credit & Financial Management. $18. m (bi-m Je-Jl) (ISSN 0011-0973) National Association of Credit Management, 520 8th Ave., New York, NY 10018-6571

Data Communications. $30. m (ISSN 0363-6399) McGraw-Hill Inc., 1221 Ave. of the Americas, New York, NY 10020

Data Management. $16. m (ISSN 0148-5431) Data Management, Circulation Department, 505 Busse Highway, Park Ridge, IL 60068

Data Systems. See Industrial Management & Data Systems

Datamation. $55. semi-m (ISSN 0011-6963) The Cahners Publishing Co., 875 Third Ave., New York, NY 10022

Decision Sciences. $48. q (ISSN 0011-7315) American Institute for Decision Sciences, University Plaza, Atlanta, GA 30303

Direct Marketing. $42. m (ISSN 0012-3188) Hoke Communications, Inc., 224 Seventh St., Garden City, NY 11530

Distribution. $40. m (ISSN 0273-6721) Distribution, Chilton Way, Radnor, PA 19089

DM. See Data Management

Drug & Cosmetic Industry. $20. m (ISSN 0012-6527) Drug & Cosmetic Industry, Circulation Offices, 1 E. First St., Duluth, MN 55802

Dun's Business Month. $32. m (ISSN 0279-3040) Dun's Business Month, Circulation Department, 875 Third Ave., New York, NY 10022
    Name changed to Business Month with March 1987

Economic Development and Cultural Change. $55. q (ISSN 0013-0079) Economic Development and Cultural Change, The University of Chicago Press, 5801 Ellis Ave., Chicago, IL 60637

Economic Outlook USA. $27. q (ISSN 0095-3830) Survey Research Center, Institute for Social Research, University of Michigan, 426 Thompson St., Ann Arbor, MI 48106

The Economist. $85. w (ISSN 0013-0613) The Economist, P.O. Box 904, Farmingdale, NY 11737-9804

Editor & Publisher, the Fourth Estate. $40. w (ISSN 0013-094X) Editor & Publisher Co., Inc., 11 W 19th St., New York, NY 10011

EDP Analyzer. $96. m (ISSN 0012-7523) United Communications Group, 4550 Montgomery Ave., Suite 700N, Bethesda, MD 20814

EFTA Bulletin. q (ISSN 0012-7655) European Free Trade Association, Press and Information Service, 9-11 rue de Varembé, CH-1211 Geneva 20, Switzerland

Electric Perspectives. $27.50. q (ISSN 0364-474X) Edison Electric Institute, Inc., 1111 19th St., N.W., Washington, DC 20036

Electrical World. $15. m (ISSN 0013-4457) Electrical World, P.O. Box 2034, Mahopac, NY 10541

Electronic Business. $50. 23 times a yr (ISSN 0163-6197) Electronic Business, 270 St. Paul St., Denver, CO 80206

Electronic News. $40. w (ISSN 0013-4937) Fairchild Publications, Inc., 7 E. 12th St., New York, NY 10003

Employee Benefit Plan Review. $36. m (ISSN 0013-6808) Employee Benefit Plan Review, 222 West Adams St., Chicago, IL 60606

Employee Benefits Journal. $25. q (ISSN 0361-4050) International Foundation of Employee Benefit Plans, 18700 W. Bluemound Rd., P.O. Box 69, Brookfield, WI 53005

Employee Relations Law Journal. $120. q (ISSN 0098-8898) Executive Enterprises Publications Co., Inc., 22 W. 21st St., New York, NY 10010-6924

Employment Relations Today. $120. q (ISSN 0362-5818) Executive Enterprises Publications Co., Inc., 22 W. 21st St., New York, NY 10010-6924

Energy Journal. $75. q (ISSN 0195-6574) Oelgeschlager, Gunn & Hain, Publishers Inc., 1278 Mass. Ave., Cambridge, MA 02138

The Engineering Economist. $24. q (ISSN 0013-791X) Engineering Economist AITE, 25 Technology Park/ Atlanta, Norcross, GA 30092

Engineering News-Record. $42. w (ISSN 0013-807X) Engineering News-Record, Fulfillment Manager, P.O. Box 2026, Mahopac, NY 10541
    Name changed to ENR with January 1, 1987

ENR. $42. w (ISSN 0013-807X) ENR, Fulfillment Manager, P.O. Box 2026, Mahopac, NY 10541
    Formerly Engineering News-Record; name changed with January 1, 1987

Euromoney. $108. m (ISSN 0014-2433) Euromoney Publications Ltd., Nestor House, Playhouse Yard, London EC4V 5EX, England

Executive Female. $39. bi-m (ISSN 0199-2880) National Association for Female Executives, Inc., 120 E. 56th St., Suite 1440, New York, NY 10022

FE. $33. m (ISSN 0015-1998) Financial Executives Institute, Fulfillment Manager, 10 Madison Ave., P.O. Box 1938, Morristown, NJ 07960
    Formerly Financial Executive; name changed with January/February 1985

Federal Reserve Bank of New York Quarterly Review. Free. q (ISSN 0147-6580) Federal Reserve Bank of New York, 33 Liberty St., New York, NY 10045

Federal Reserve Bank of St. Louis Review. Free. 10 times a yr (ISSN 0014-9187) Federal Reserve Bank of St. Louis, P.O. Box 442, St. Louis, MO 63166

Federal Reserve Bulletin. $20. m (ISSN 0014-9209) Division of Administrative Services, Board of Governors of the Federal Reserve System, Washington, DC 20551

Finance & Development. Free. q (ISSN 0145-1707) Finance and Development, International Monetary Fund Bldg., Washington, DC 20431

Financial Analysts Journal. $36. bi-m (ISSN 0015-198X) Financial Analysts Journal, 1633 Broadway, New York, NY 10019

Financial Executive. $27. m (ISSN 0015-1998) Financial Executives Institute, Fulfillment Manager, 10 Madison Ave., P.O. Box 1938, Morristown, NJ 07960
    Name changed to FE with January/February 1985

Financial Management. $40. q (ISSN 0046-3892) Financial Management Association, College of Business Administration, University of South Florida, 4202 Fowler Ave., Tampa, FL 33620

Financial World. $44.95. semi-m (ISSN 0015-2064) Financial World Partners, 1450 Broadway, New York, NY 10018

Forbes. $45. bi-w (except w 2 weeks in Ap and 2 weeks in O) (ISSN 0015-6914) Forbes Subscription Service, 60 Fifth Ave., New York, NY 10011

Forest Industries. $45. m (semi-m My) (ISSN 0015-7430) Forest Industries, Circulation Department, 500 Howard St., San Francisco, CA 94105

Fortune. $44.50. bi-w (3 issues in O) (ISSN 0015-8259) Fortune, 541 N. Fairbanks Court, Chicago, IL 60611

Frozen Food Digest. $16. q (ISSN 0033-6408) Frozen Food Digest, 271 Madison Ave., New York, NY 10016
    Formerly Quick Frozen Foods; name changed with February 1986

Fueloil & Oil Heat. $14. m (ISSN 0148-9801) Fueloil & Oil Heat, Circulation Department, 10 Canfield Rd., Cedar Grove, NJ 07009
Formerly Fueloil & Oil Heat and Solar Systems; name changed with July 1985
Fueloil & Oil Heat and Solar Systems. $14. m (ISSN 0148-9801) Fueloil & Oil Heat, Circulation Department, 10 Canfield Rd., Cedar Grove, NJ 07009
Name changed to Fueloil & Oil Heat with July 1985
Futures (Cedar Falls, Iowa). $34. m (ISSN 0279-5590) Oster Communications, Inc., 219 Parkade, Cedar Falls, IA 50613

Global Trade. $45. m (ISSN 0884-5484) North American Publishing Co., 401 N. Broad St., Philadelphia, PA 19108
Formerly Global Trade Executive; name changed with March 1987
Global Trade Executive. $45. m (ISSN 0279-4470) Global Trade Executive, 401 N. Broad St., Philadelphia, PA 19108
Formerly American Import/Export Management; name changed with May 1985. Name changed to Global Trade with March 1987
Government Finance Review. $18. q (ISSN 0883-7856) Government Finance Officers Association. 180 N. Michigan Ave., Suite 800, Chicago, IL 60601-7476
Formerly Governmental Finance; name changed with April 1985
Graphic Arts Monthly and the Printing Industry. $55. m (ISSN 0017-3312) Graphic Arts Publishing Co., 875 Third Ave., New York, NY 10022

Handling & Shipping Management. $35. m (2 issues S) (ISSN 0194-603X) Handling & Shipping Management, 1111 Chester Ave., Cleveland, OH 44101
Harvard Business Review. $49. bi-m (ISSN 0017-8012) Harvard Business Review, Subscription Service Department, P.O. Box 3000, Woburn, MA 01888
HCM Review. See Health Care Management Review
Health and Society. See Milbank Memorial Fund Quarterly/Health and Society
Health Care Management Review. $66. q (ISSN 0361-6274) Aspen Systems Corp., 16792 Oakmont Ave., Gaithersburg, MD 20877
Healthcare Financial Management. $45. m (ISSN 0735-0732) Healthcare Financial Management Association, 1900 Spring Rd., Oak Brook, IL 60521
Hotel & Motel Management. $25. 18 times a yr (ISSN 0018-6082) Harcourt Brace Jovanovich Publications, 1 E. First St., Duluth, MN 55802
Human Resource Management. $40. q (ISSN 0090-4848) Subscription Department, John Wiley & Sons, Inc., 605 Third Ave., New York, NY 10158
Human Resource Planning. $30. q (ISSN 0199-8986) Human Resources Planning Society, P.O. Box 2553, Grand Central Station, New York, NY 10163

IEEE Transactions on Engineering Management. Price on request. q (ISSN 0018-9391) Institute of Electrical and Electronics Engineers, 445 Hoes Lane, Piscataway, NJ 08854
Inc. $24. m (ISSN 0162-8968) Inc. Publishing Company, P.O. Box 2538, Boulder, CO 80322
Industrial and Labor Relations Review. $30. q (ISSN 0019-7939) Industrial and Labor Relations Review, Circulation Manager, Cornell University, Ithaca, NY 14853
Industrial Development. $60. bi-m (ISSN 0192-0901) Conway Data, Inc., 1954 Airport Rd., N.E., Atlanta, GA 30341
Bound with: Site Selection Handbook; and, SiteNet Users' Guide

Industrial Distribution. $50. m (ISSN 0019-8153) Technical Publishing, 875 Third Ave., New York, NY 10022
Industrial Management & Data Systems. $89.95. bi-m (ISSN 0007-6929) MCB Publication, Ltd., 198/200 Keighley Rd., Bradford, W. Yorkshire BD9 4JQ, England
Industrial Marketing Management. $76. q (ISSN 0019-8501) Elsevier Science Publishing Co. Inc., 52 Vanderbilt Ave., New York, NY 10017
Industrial Relations. $20. 3 times a yr (ISSN 0019-8676) Institute of Industrial Relations, University of California, Berkeley, CA 94720
Industry Week. $50. bi-w (ISSN 0039-0895) Penton Publishing Company, Penton Plaza, 1111 Chester Ave., Cleveland, OH 44114
Infosystems. $75. m (ISSN 0364-5533) Hitchcock Publishing Company, 25W550 Geneva Rd., Wheaton, IL 60188
Inquiry. $35. q (ISSN 0046-9580) Inquiry, P.O. Box 527, Glenview, IL 60025
Institutional Investor. $150. m (ISSN 0020-3580) Institutional Investor, Circulation Department, 488 Madison Ave., New York, NY 10022
Interavia. $49. m (ISSN 0020-5168) Interavia, 86 Avenue Louis-Casai, P.O. Box 162, 1216 Cointrin, Geneva, Switzerland
Interfaces. $25. bi-m (ISSN 0092-2102) Institute of Management Sciences, 290 Westminster St., Providence, RI 02903
The Internal Auditor. $24. bi-m (ISSN 0020-5745) Internal Auditor, 249 Maitland Ave., Altamonte Springs, FL 32701
International Advertiser. $30. bi-m (ISSN 0163-9412) Directories International, Inc., 150 Fifth Ave., Suite 610, New York, NY 10011
Formerly Advertising World; name changed with September 1985
International Labour Review. $42.75. bi-m (ISSN 0020-7780) ILO Publications, International Labour Office, CH-1211 Geneva 22, Switzerland
International Management (Europe edition). £23. m (ISSN 0020-7888) International Management, Circulation Director, McGraw-Hill House, Maidenhead, Berkshire SL6 2QL, England
International Monetary Fund Staff Papers. $15. q (ISSN 0020-8027) International Monetary Fund, Washington, DC 20431
International Public Relations Review. See Public Relations Quarterly
International Trade Forum. $16. q (ISSN 0020-8957) International Trade Forum, International Trade Centre UNCTAD/GATT, Palais de Nations, 1211 Geneva 10, Switzerland
Iron Age. $42. 24 times a yr (ISSN 0164-5137) Chilton Co., Chilton Way, Radnor, PA 19089
Split into: Iron Age Manufacturing Management; and, Iron Age Metals Producer
Iron Age Metals Producer. $30. 12 times a yr (ISSN 0747-6329) Chilton Co., Chilton Way, Radnor, PA 19089
Continues in part: Iron Age
Issues in Bank Regulation. $28. q (ISSN 0164-7725) Bank Administration Institute, 60 Gould Centre, Rolling Meadows, IL 60008

JEI. See Journal of Economic Issues
Journal of Accountancy. $20. m (ISSN 0021-8448) American Institute of Certified Public Accountants, Inc., 1211 Ave. of the Americas, New York, NY 10036
Journal of Accounting, Auditing & Finance. $64. q (ISSN 0148-558X) Greenwood Press, 88 Post Rd. W., P.O. Box 5007, Westport, CT 06881
Journal of Accounting Research. $35. semi-ann (ISSN 0021-8456) Graduate School of Business, University of Chicago, Chicago, IL 60637
Journal of Advertising. $24. q (ISSN 0091-3367) Charles E. Bradley, Business Manager, Journal of Advertising, University of Wyoming, Box 3275 University Station, Laramie, WY 82071

Journal of Advertising Research. $50. bi-m (ISSN 0021-8499) Advertising Research Foundation, 3 E. 54th St., New York, NY 10022

Journal of Bank Research. $30. q (ISSN 0021-9215) Bank Administration Institute, 60 Gould Center, Rolling Meadows, IL 60008
    Ceased publication with Autumn 1985?

Journal of Banking and Finance. $121.37. q (ISSN 0378-4266) North-Holland Publishing Company, Journal Division, P.O. Box 211, 1000 AE Amsterdam, Netherlands

Journal of Business Communication. $35. q (ISSN 0021-9436) Association for Business Communications, 100 English Bldg., 608 S. Wright St., Urbana, IL 61801

The Journal of Business (Chicago, Ill.). $35. q (ISSN 0021-9398) University of Chicago Press, P.O. Box 37005, Chicago, IL 60637

Journal of Business Research. $134. 6 times a yr (ISSN 0148-2963) Elsevier North Holland, Inc., Fulfillment Department, 52 Vanderbilt Ave., New York, NY 10017

Journal of Business Strategy. $72. q (ISSN 0275-6668) Warren, Gorham & Lamont, Inc., 210 South St., Boston, MA 02111

The Journal of Commercial Bank Lending. $33. m (ISSN 0021-986X) Robert Morris Associates, 1616 Philadelphia National Bank Bldg., Philadelphia, PA 19107

Journal of Common Market Studies. $78.95. q (ISSN 0021-9886) Basil Blackwell, 108 Cowley Rd., Oxford OX4 1JF, England

The Journal of Consumer Affairs. $30. semi-ann (ISSN 0022-0078) American Council on Consumer Interests, 162 Stanley Hall, University of Missouri, Columbia, MO 65201

The Journal of Consumer Research. $56. q (ISSN 0093-5301) Journal of Consumer Research, P.O. Box 70787, Pasadena, CA 91107

Journal of Data Management. See Data Management

The Journal of Developing Areas. $20. q (ISSN 0022-037X) Journal of Developing Areas, Western Illinois University, 900 W. Adams St., Macomb, IL 61455

Journal of Economic Issues. $25. q (ISSN 0021-3624) AFEE/JEI Fiscal Office, Dept. of Economics, University of Nebraska–Lincoln, Lincoln, NE 68588

Journal of Economics and Business. $75. q (ISSN 0148-6195) Journal Fulfillment, Elsevier Science Publishing Co. Inc., 52 Vanderbilt Ave., New York, NY 10017

The Journal of Finance. $40. 5 times a yr (ISSN 0022-1082) New York University, Graduate School of Business, 100 Trinity Place, New York, NY 10006

Journal of Financial and Quantitative Analysis. $38. q (ISSN 0022-1090) University of Washington, Graduate School of Business Administration, Mackenzie Hall, DJ-10, Seattle, WA 98195

Journal of International Business Studies. $35. 3 times a yr (ISSN 0047-2506) Journal of International Business Studies, c/o Tom Beard, University of South Carolina, College of Business Administration, Columbia, SC 29208

Journal of Management. $49. q (ISSN 0149-2063) Production Editor, Journal of Management, Management Area, College of Business Administration, Texas Tech University, Box 4320, Lubbock, TX 79409

Journal of Management Studies (Oxford, England). $142.50. 6 times a yr (ISSN 0022-2380) Basil Blackwell Publisher Ltd., 108 Cowley Road, Oxford OX4 1JF, England

Journal of Marketing. $70. q (ISSN 0022-2429) American Marketing Association, 250 South Wacker Dr., Chicago, IL 60606

Journal of Marketing Research. $54. q (ISSN 0022-2437) American Marketing Association, 250 S. Wacker Dr., Chicago, IL 60606

Journal of Money, Credit and Banking. $28. q (ISSN 0022-2879) Ohio State University Press, 1050 Carmack Rd., Columbus, OH 43210

Journal of Portfolio Management. $125. q (ISSN 0095-4918) The Journal of Portfolio Management, Circulation Dept., 488 Madison Ave., New York, NY 10022

Journal of Property Management. $24.95 bi-m (ISSN 0022-3905) National Association of Realtors, 430 N. Michigan Ave., Chicago, IL 60611

Journal of Purchasing and Materials Management. $20. q (ISSN 0094-8594) National Association of Purchasing Management, Inc., 496 Kinderkamack Rd., P.O. Box 418, Oradell, NJ 07649

Journal of Retail Banking. $64. q (ISSN 0195-2064) Journal of Retail Banking, 1300 N. 17th St., Suite 1200, Arlington, VA 22200

Journal of Retailing. $20. q (ISSN 0022-4359) New York University, 202 Tisch Hall, Washington Sq., New York, NY 10003

The Journal of Risk and Insurance. $40. 4 times a yr (ISSN 0022-4367) College of Business, Univ. of Georgia, Athens, GA 30602

Journal of Small Business Management. $20. 4 times a yr (ISSN 0047-2778) College of Business Administration, Wichita State University, Box 88, Wichita, KS 67208

Journal of Systems Management. $17.50 m (ISSN 0022-4839) Association for Systems Management, 24587 Bagley Rd., Cleveland, OH 44138

The Journal of Taxation. $125. m (ISSN 0022-4863) Warren, Gorham & Lamont, Inc., 210 South St., Boston, MA 02111

Journal of the American Real Estate and Urban Economics Association. $30 (free to members). q (ISSN 0092-914X) American Real Estate and Urban Economics Association, P.O. Box 39114, Washington, DC 20016

Journal of the American Society of CLU. $24. bi-m (ISSN 0007-8573) American Society of CLU, 270 Bryn Mawr Ave., P.O. Box 59, Bryn Mawr, PA 19010
    Name changed to Journal of the American Society of CLU & ChFC with November 1986

Journal of the American Society of CLU & ChFC. $24. bi-m (ISSN 0007-8573) American Society of CLU & ChFC, 270 Bryn Mawr Ave., P.O. Box 59, Bryn Mawr, PA 19010
    Formerly Journal of the American Society of CLU; name changed with November 1986

Journal of the Operational Research Society. $250. m (ISSN 0160-5682) Pergamon Press, Ltd., Subscription Fulfillment Manager, Headington Hill Hall, Oxford OX3 0BW, England

Journal of Urban Economics. $162. bi-m (ISSN 0094-1190) Academic Press, Inc., 1 E. First St., Duluth, MN 55802

Labor Law Journal. $75. m (ISSN 0023-6586) Commerce Clearing House, Inc., 4025 W. Peterson Ave., Chicago, IL 60646

Land Economics. $38. q (ISSN 0023-7639) The University of Wisconsin Press, Journals Dept., 114 North Murray St., Madison, WI 53715

Long Range Planning. $200. bi-m (ISSN 0024-6301) Pergamon Press, Ltd., Subscription Manager, Headington Hill Hall, Oxford OX3 0BW, England

Madison Avenue. $40. m (ISSN 0024-9483) Madison Avenue Magazine, 369 Lexington Ave., New York, NY 10017

Magazine of Bank Administration. $30. m (ISSN 0024-9823) Bank Administration Institute, Publication Office, 60 Gould Center, Rolling Meadows, IL 60008

Management Accounting (New York, N.Y.). $48. m (ISSN 0025-1690) National Association of Accountants, 10 Paregon Dr., Montvale, NJ 07645

Management Decision. $144. q (ISSN 0025-1747) MCB Publications, 198-200 Keighley Rd., Bradford BD9 4JQ, Yorkshire, England

Management International Review. $42. q (ISSN 0025-181X) Betriebswirtschaftlicher Verlag Dr. Th. Gabler, GmbH, 54 Taunusstrasse, D 62 Wiesbaden, W. Germany

Management Review. $28. m (ISSN 0025-1895) American Management Association, Inc., 135 W. 50th St., New York, NY 10020

Management Science. $90. m (ISSN 0025-1909) Institute of Management Sciences, Circulation Dept., 290 Westminster St., Providence, RI 02903

Management Solutions. $25. m (ISSN 0889-0226) American Management Association, Subscription Services, Box 319, Saranac Lake, NY 12983
　　Formerly Supervisory Management (New York, N.Y.); name changed with September 1986

Management Today. £20. m (ISSN 0025-1925) Management Publications, Ltd., 76 Dean St., London W1A 1BU, England

Management World. $22. bi-m (ISSN 0090-3825) Management World, Julia Bradley, Circulation Manager, AMS Building, 2360 Maryland Rd., Willow Grove, PA 19090

Managerial Planning. $32. bi-m (ISSN 0025-1941) Planning Executives Institute, P.O. Box 70, Oxford, OH 45056.
　　Named changed to Planning Review with July 1985

Marketing & Media Decisions. $45. 15 times a yr (ISSN 0195-4296) Decisions Publications, Inc., 1140 Ave. of the Americas, New York, NY 10036

Marketing Communications. $40. m (except Jl.) (ISSN 0164-4343) Media Horizons, Inc., 50 W. 23rd St., New York, NY 10010

Marketing News. $40. semi-m (ISSN 0025-3790) American Marketing Association, Central Services Office, 250 S. Wacker Drive, Suite 200, Chicago, IL 60606

Mass Transit. $30. 11 times a yr (ISSN 0364-3484) Mass Transit, 1191 Rowland St., Riverton, NJ 08077

McKinsey Quarterly. q (ISSN 0047-5394) McKinsey & Co., 55 E. 52nd St., New York, NY 10022

Merchandising. $33. m (ISSN 0362-3920) Gralla Publications, 1515 Broadway, New York, NY 10036

Mergers & Acquisitions. $129. bi-m (ISSN 0026-0010) Mergers & Acquisitions, 229 S. 18 St., Philadelphia, PA 19103

Metropolitan Life Insurance Company Statistical Bulletin. See Statistical Bulletin (Metropolitan Life Insurance Company)

Milbank Memorial Fund Quarterly/Health and Society. $42. q (ISSN 0160-1997) MIT Press Journals, 28 Carleton St., Cambridge, MA 02142
　　Name changed to Milbank Quarterly with Vol. 64, No. 1, 1986

Milbank Quarterly. $55. q (ISSN 0887-378X) Milbank Memorial Fund, 1 East 75th St., New York, NY 10021
　　Formerly Milbank Memorial Fund Quarterly/Health and Society; name changed with volume 64, number 1, 1986

Mini-Micro Systems. $65. m (ISSN 0364-9342) Mini-Micro Systems, 270 St. Paul St., Denver, CO 80206

Modern Office Technology. $40. m (ISSN 0026-8208) Modern Office Technology, P.O. Box 95795, Cleveland, OH 44101

Modern Power Systems. $130. m (ISSN 0260-7840) United Trade Press Limited, UTP House, 33/35 Bowling Green Lane, London EC1R 0DA, England

Money. $31.95 m (ISSN 0149-4953) Money, P.O. Box 14429, Boulder, CO 80322

Monthly Labor Review. $16. m (ISSN 0098-0818) Superintendent of Documents, U.S. Government Printing Office, Washington, DC 20402

Mortgage Banking. $29. m (ISSN 0027-1241) Mortgage Bankers Association of America, 1125 Fifteenth St., N.W., Washington, DC 20005

National Food Review. $11. q (ISSN 0164-3428) Superintendent of Documents, U.S. Government Printing Office, Washington, DC 20402

National Institute Economic Review. $25. q (ISSN 0027-9501) National Institute Economic Review, 2 Dean Trench St., Smith Sq., London SW1P 3HE, England

National Petroleum News. $63. m (semi-m Je) (ISSN 0149-5267) National Petroleum News, 950 Lee St., Des Plaines, IL 60016

National Real Estate Investor. $45. m (bi-m Je) (ISSN 0027-9994) National Real Estate Investor, 6255 Barfield Rd., Atlanta, GA 30328

National Safety and Health News. $25.75. m (ISSN 0028-0100) National Safety Council, 444 N. Michigan Ave., Chicago, IL 60611
　　Formerly National Safety News; name changed with May 1985. Name changed to Safety & Health with January 1987

National Safety News. $25.75. m (ISSN 0028-0100) National Safety Council, 444 N. Michigan Ave., Chicago, IL 60611
　　Name changed to National Safety and Health News with May 1985

National Tax Journal. $30. q (ISSN 0028-0283) National Tax Association-Tax Institute of America, 21 E. State St., Columbus, OH 43215

National Underwriter (Life & Health/Financial Services Edition). $50. w (extra issue Jl, S, O) (ISSN 0028-033X) National Underwriter Company, 420 E. 4th St., Cincinnati, OH 45202
　　Formerly The National Underwriter (Life & Health Insurance Edition); name changed with December 29, 1986

The National Underwriter (Life & Health Insurance Edition). $45. w (extra issue Jl, S, O) (ISSN 0028-033X) National Underwriter Company, 420 E. 4th St., Cincinnati, OH 45202
　　Name changed to National Underwriter (Life & Health/Financial Services Edition) with December 29, 1986

National Underwriter (Property & Casualty/Employee Benefits Edition). $50. w (ISSN 0163-8912) National Underwriter Company, 420 E. 4th St., Cincinnati, OH 45202
　　Formerly the National Underwriter (Property & Casualty Insurance Edition); name changed with December 29, 1986

The National Underwriter (Property & Casualty Insurance Edition). $45. w (extra issue third w N) (ISSN 0163-8912) National Underwriter Company, 420 E. 4th St., Cincinnati, OH 45202
　　Name changed to National Underwriter (Property & Casualty/Employee Benefits Edition) with December 29, 1986

Nation's Business. $22. m (ISSN 0028-047X) Chamber of Commerce of the U.S., 1615 H St., N.W., Washington, DC 20062

NPN. See National Petroleum News

Nursing Homes. $25. bi-m (ISSN 0029-649X) Centaur & Company, 5 Willowbrook Court, Potomac, MD 20854

The OECD Observer. $11. bi-m (ISSN 0029-7054) OECD Information Service, Château de la Muette, 2 rue André-Pascal, F 75775 Paris, Cedex 16, France

The Office. $40. m (ISSN 0030-0128) Office Publications, Inc., 1200 Summer St., Stamford, CT 06904

Office Administration and Automation. $20 m (ISSN 0001-8376) Geyer-McAllister Publications, Inc., 51 Madison Ave., New York, NY 10010
　　Name changed to Administrative Management with October 1985

Oil & Gas Journal. $90. w (ISSN 0030-1388) Oil & Gas Journal, Circulation Services Manager, P.O. Box 1260, Tulsa, OK 74101

Online (Weston, Conn.). $85. 6 times a yr (ISSN 0146-5422) Online, Inc., 11 Tannery Lane, Weston, CT 06883

Operations Research. $65. 6 times a yr (ISSN 0030-364X) Operations Research Society of America, Mt. Royal and Guilford Aves., Baltimore, MD 21202

Organizational Behavior and Human Decision Processes. $176. bi-m (ISSN 0749-5978) Academic Press, Inc., 6277 Sea Harbor Dr., Orlando, FL 32887
　　Formerly Organizational Behavior and Human Performance; name changed with February 1985

Organizational Behavior and Human Performance. $150. bi-m (ISSN 0030-5073) Academic Press, Inc., 111 Fifth Ave., New York, NY 10003
  Name changed to Organizational Behavior and Human Decision Processes with February 1985
Organizational Dynamics. $40. q (ISSN 0090-2616) American Management Associations, 135 W. 50th St., New York, NY 10020

Paper Trade Journal. $30. m (ISSN 0031-1197) Vance Publishing Corp., 400 Knightsbridge Pkwy., Lincolnshire, IL 60069
  Absorbed by: Pulp & Paper
Papers and Proceedings of the Annual Meeting of the American Economic Association. See The American Economic Review
Pension World. $41. m (ISSN 0098-1753) Pension World, 6255 Barfield Rd., Atlanta, GA 30328
Pensions & Investment Age. $80. bi-w (ISSN 0273-5466) Pensions & Investment Age, Circulation Department, 740 Rush St., Chicago, IL 60611
Personnel. $35. m (ISSN 0031-5702) American Management Associations, Subscription Services, Box 319, Saranac Lake, NY 12983
Personnel Administrator. $40. m (ISSN 0031-5729) American Society for Personnel Administration, 606 N. Washington St., Alexandria, VA 22314
Personnel Journal. $36. m (ISSN 0031-5745) A.C. Croft, Inc., P.O. Box 2440, Costa Mesa, CA 92628
Personnel Management. £48. m (ISSN 0031-5761) Personnel Publications, Ltd., 3 New Burlington St., London W1X 2AA, England
Personnel Psychology. $40. q (ISSN 0031-5826) Personnel Psychology, Inc., 9660 Hillcroft, Suite 337, Houston, TX 77096
Petroleum Economist. $122. m (ISSN 0306-395X) Petroleum Economist, P.O. Box 105, 25/31 Ironmonger Row, London ECIV 3PN, England
Planning Review. $50. bi-m (ISSN 0094-064X) The Planning Forum, P.O. Box 70, Oxford, OH 45056
  Formerly Managerial Planning; name changed with July 1985
Plastics World. $50. 13 times a yr (ISSN 0032-1273) Plastics World, Circulation Manager, 270 St. Paul St., Denver, CO 80206
The Practical Accountant. $48. m (ISSN 0032-6321) Warren, Gorham & Lamont Inc., 1633 Broadway, New York, NY 10019
Professional Builder. $35. m (2 issues Je) (ISSN 0361-5316) Professional Builder, 270 St. Paul St., Denver, CO 80206
  Formerly Professional Builder/Apartment Business; named changed with October 1985
Professional Builder/Apartment Business. $35. m (2 issues Je) (ISSN 0361-5316) Professional Builder, 270 St. Paul St., Denver, CO 80206
  Name changed to Professional Builder with October 1985
Progressive Grocer. $44. m (ISSN 0033-0787) Progressive Grocer, 1351 Washington Blvd., Stamford, CT 06902
The Public Interest. $18. q (ISSN 0033-3557) The Public Interest, 10 E. 53rd St., New York, NY 10022
Public Personnel Management. $35. q (ISSN 0091-0260) Personnel Management, 1617 Duke St., Alexandria, VA 22314
Public Relations Journal. $32. m (semi-m S) (ISSN 0033-3670) Public Relations Society of America, Inc., 845 Third Ave., New York, NY 10022
Public Relations Quarterly. $16. q (ISSN 0033-3700) Public Relations Quarterly, P.O. Box 311, Rhinebeck, NY 12573
  Incorporating: International Public Relations Review
Public Relations Review. $31. q (ISSN 0362-8111) Communications Research Associates, Inc., Suite 500, 7100 Baltimore Blvd., College Park, MD 20740
Public Utilities Fortnightly. $78. bi-w (ISSN 0033-3808) Public Utilities Reports, Inc., Suite 2100, Rosslyn Center Bldg., 1700 N. Moore St., Arlington, VA 22209

Publishers Weekly. $89. w (bi-w year end issue) (ISSN 0000-0019) Publishers Weekly, P.O. Box 1428, Riverton, NJ 08077
Pulp & Paper. $50. m (2 issues in N) (ISSN 0033-4081) Circulation Department, Pulp & Paper, 500 Howard St., San Francisco, CA 94105
  Absorbed: Paper Trade Journal
Purchasing. $65. semi-m (ISSN 0033-4448) Circulation Department, Purchasing Magazine, 270 St. Paul St., Denver, CO 80206

The Quarterly Journal of Economics. $60. q (ISSN 0033-5533) MIT Press Journals, 55 Hayward St., Cambridge, MA 02142
Quarterly Review of Economics and Business. $27. q (ISSN 0033-5797) The Quarterly Review of Economics and Business, Bureau of Economics and Business Research, College of Commerce and Business Administration, University of Illinois, Urbana, IL 61801
Quick Frozen Foods. $20. m (except Jl) (ISSN 0033-6408) Quick Frozen Foods, 1 E. First St., Duluth, MN 55802
  Name changed to Frozen Food Digest with February 1986

Railway Age. $30. m (ISSN 0033-8826) Railway Age, Subscription Department, P.O. Box 530, Bristol, CT 06010
The Real Estate Appraiser and Analyst. $25. q (ISSN 0271-258X) The Society of Real Estate Appraisers, 645 N. Michigan Ave., Chicago, IL 60611
Real Estate Review. $54. q (ISSN 0034-0790) Warren, Gorham & Lamont, Inc., 210 South St., Boston, MA 02111
Research & Development. $36. 13 times a yr (ISSN 0160-4074) Research and Development, Circulation Department, Box 5365, New York, NY 10150
Research Management. $50. bi-m (ISSN 0034-5334) Technomic Publishing Co., Inc., 851 New Holland Ave., Lancaster, PA 17601
Restaurant Business. $63. 18 times a yr (ISSN 0097-8043) Restaurant Business, Inc., 633 Third Ave., New York, NY 10017
The Review of Business and Economic Research. $10. semi-ann (ISSN 0362-7985) Division of Business and Economic Research, College of Business Administration, University of New Orleans, New Orleans, LA 70122
The Review of Economics and Statistics. $110. q (ISSN 0034-6535) North-Holland Publishing Co., P.O. Box 211, 1000 AE Amsterdam, Netherlands
Risk Management. $36. m (ISSN 0035-5593) Risk and Insurance Management Society, Inc., 205 E. 42nd St., New York, NY 10017

S&MM. $36. m (bi-w F, Ap. Jl, O) (ISSN 0163-7517) Sales Management, Inc., 633 Third Ave., New York, NY 10164-0563
  Name changed to Sales and Marketing Management with October 7, 1985
Safety & Health. $25.75. m (ISSN 0891-1797) National Safety Council, 444 N. Michigan Ave., Chicago, IL 60611
  Formerly National Safety and Health News; name changed with January 1987
Sales and Marketing Management. $38. m (bi-w F, Ap, Jl, O) (ISSN 0163-7517) Sales and Marketing Management, Subscription Service Department, P.O. Box 1024, South Eastern, PA 19398-9990
  Formerly S&MM; name changed with October 7, 1985
SAM Advanced Management Journal. See Advanced Management Journal
Savings Institutions. $30. m (ISSN 0036-5114) United States League of Savings Associations, 111 E. Wacker Dr., Chicago, IL 60601

Security Management. $30. m (ISSN 0145-9406) American Society for Industrial Security, 1655 N. Fort Meyer Dr., Suite 1200, Arlington, VA 22209

Shopping Center Age. See Chain Store Age Executive with Shopping Center Age

Site Selection Handbook. $60. bi-m (ISSN 0097-3033) Conway Data, Inc., 1954 Airport Rd., N.E., Atlanta, GA 30341

    Bound with: Industrial Development; and, SiteNet Users' Guide

Sloan Management Review. $32. 3 times a yr (ISSN 0019-848X) Sloan Management Review, Alfred P. Sloan School of Management, Massachusetts Institute of Technology, 50 Memorial Dr., Cambridge, MA 02139

Social Security Bulletin. $29. m (ISSN 0037-7910) Superintendent of Documents, U.S. Government Printing Office, Washington, DC 20402

Southern Economic Journal. $44 q (ISSN 0038-4038) Southern Economic Journal, Hanes Hall 019-A, Chapel Hill, NC 27514

Statistical Bulletin (Metropolitan Life Insurance Company). $25. q (ISSN 0026-1513) Metropolitan Life Insurance Company, 1 Madison Ave., New York, NY 10010

Stores. $9. m (ISSN 0039-1867) National Retail Merchants Association, Inc., 100 W. 31st St., New York, NY 10036

Strategic Management Journal. $74.50. bi-m (ISSN 0143-2095) Subscriptions Department, John Wiley & Sons Limited, Baffins Lane, Chichester, Sussex PO19 1UD, England

Supervision. $27.75. m (ISSN 0039-5854) Subscription Department, Supervision, 424 N. 3rd St., Burlington, IA 52601

Supervisory Management (New York, N.Y.). $25. m (ISSN 0039-5919) American Management Associations, Subscription Services, Box 319, Saranac, Lake, NY 12983

    Name changed to Management Solutions with September 1986

Survey of Current Business. $30. m (ISSN 0039-6222) Superintendent of Documents, U.S. Government Printing Office, Washington, DC 20402

Taxes. $80. m (ISSN 0040-0181) Commerce Clearing House, Inc., 4025 W. Paterson Ave., Chicago, IL 60646

Technical Communications. $25. q (ISSN 0049-3155) Technical Communications, 815 15th St., N.W., Washington, DC 20005

Telecommunications. $40. m (semi-m S) (ISSN 0040-2494) Telecommunications, 610 Washington St., Dedham, MA 02026

Telephony. $35. w (except semi-w 2nd week in Ag; 3 times in D) (ISSN 0040-2656) Telephony Publishing Corporation, 55 E. Jackson Blvd., Chicago, IL 60604

Television/Radio Age. $50. semi-m (ISSN 0040-277X) Television Editorial Corporation, 1270 Ave. of the Americas, New York, NY 10020

Textile World. $37. m (ISSN 0040-5213) Textile World, Circulation Manager, 4170 Ashford-Dunwoody Rd., Suite 420, Atlanta, GA 30319

Topics in Health Care Financing. $62.50. q (ISSN 0095-3814) Aspen Systems Corp., Fulfillment Operation, 16792 Oakmont Ave., Gaithersburg, MD 20877

Traffic Management. $45. m (ISSN 0041-0691) Cahners Publishing Company, 275 Washington St., Newton, MA 02158

Training and Development Journal. $50. m (ISSN 0041-0861) American Society for Training & Development, 1630 Duke St., P.O. Box 1443, Alexandria, VA 22313

Training (Minneapolis, Minn.). $42. m (ISSN 0095-5892) Lakewood Publications, Inc., 50 South Ninth St., Minneapolis, MN 55402

Transportation Journal. $50. q (ISSN 0041-1612) American Society of Transportation and Logistics, P.O. Box 33095, Louisville, KY 40232

Trusts & Estates. $49. m (ISSN 0041-3682) Trusts & Estates, Subscription Department, 6255 Barfield Rd., Atlanta, GA 30328

United States Banker. $24. m (ISSN 0148-8848) Kalo Communications, Inc., One River Rd., Cos Cob, CT 06807

Venture (New York, N.Y.). $18. m (ISSN 0191-3530) Venture Magazine Inc., 521 Fifth Ave., New York, NY 10175

Ward's Auto World. $38. m (ISSN 0043-0315) Ward's Communications, 28 W. Adams St., Detroit, MI 48226

World Mining. $40. m (semi-m Jl, O) (ISSN 0043-8707) World Mining, Circulation Department, 500 Howard St., San Francisco, CA 94105

    Merged with: Mining Equipment International; and World Coal, to become: World Mining Equipment

World Mining Equipment. £65. m (ISSN 0746-729X) World Mining Equipment, 27 Paul St., London EC2A 4JU, England

    Merger of: Mining Equipment International; World Coal; and, World Mining. Publication suspended with March/April 1987

World Oil. $24. m (ISSN 0043-8790) World Oil, Circulation Manager, P.O. Box 2608, Houston, TX 77252

ALL-NEWS RADIO STATIONS
IN THE UNITED STATES

From *Broadcasting Cablecasting Yearbook*. Reprinted by permission of *Broadcasting Magazine*.

WERC(AM)	Birmingham AL	WNLC(AM)	New London CT	KDTH(AM)	Dubuque IA
WKRG(AM)	Mobile AL			*WSUI(AM)	Iowa City IA
*WUAL-FM	Tuscaloosa AL			KNIA(AM)	Knoxville IA
WVNA(AM)	Tuscumbia AL	WILM(AM)	Wilmington DE	KOSG(FM)	Osage IA
				KQWC(AM)	Webster City IA
KBYR(AM)	Anchorage AK	*WAMU(FM)	Washington DC		
KFYI(AM)	Phoenix AZ	WTOP(AM)	Washington DC	KBBE(FM)	McPherson KS
KTAR(AM)	Phoenix AZ			KMUW(FM)	Wichita KS
KYCA(AM)	Prescott AZ				
*KUAT(AM)	Tucson AZ	WRHC(AM)	Coral Gables FL	WCMI(AM)	Ashland KY
KNST(AM)	Tucson AZ	WNDB(AM)	Daytona Beach FL	*WEKH(FM)	Hazard KY
KTUC(AM)	Tucson AZ			WKLU(AM)	Midway KY
		WWWQ(AM)	Fort Myers FL	WSJP(AM)	Murray KY
KJEM(AM)	Bentonville AR	WOKV(AM)	Jacksonville FL	*WEKU-FM	Richmond KY
*KLRE-FM	Little Rock AR	WAQI(AM)	Miami FL	*WDCL-FM	Somerset KY
KARN(AM)	Little Rock AR	WINZ(AM)	Miami FL	WHRS(AM)	Winchester KY
KWCK(AM)	Searcy AR	WIOD(AM)	Miami FL		
		WQBA(AM)	Miami FL	WABL(AM)	Amite LA
KPZE(AM)	Anaheim CA	WEBY(AM)	Milton FL	KEUN(AM)	Eunice LA
KLYD(AM)	Bakersfield CA	WNOG(AM)	Naples FL	KPEL(AM)	Lafayette LA
KPMC(AM)	Bakersfield CA	*WMFE-FM	Orlando FL	KAOK(AM)	Lake Charles LA
*KCHO(FM)	Chico CA	WKIS(AM)	Orlando FL		
*KVPR(FM)	Fresno CA	*WKGC-FM	Panama City FL	WWL(AM)	New Orleans LA
KMJ(AM)	Fresno CA	WPLP(AM)	Pinellas Park FL		
KSHO(AM)	Hesperia CA	WQSA(AM)	Sarasota FL	WSDL(AM)	Slidell LA
*KLON(FM)	Long Beach CA	*WFSU-FM	Tallahassee FL		
*KUSC(FM)	Los Angeles CA	WTNT(AM)	Tallahassee FL	WIDE(AM)	Biddeford ME
KFWB(AM)	Los Angeles CA	WFLA(AM)	Tampa FL	WWGT(AM)	Westbrook ME
KNX(AM)	Los Angeles CA	WTTB(AM)	Vero Beach FL		
KDIA(AM)	Oakland CA	WJNO(AM)	West Palm Beach FL	WBAL(AM)	Baltimore MD
KNWZ(AM)	Palm Desert CA			WTRI(AM)	Brunswick MD
				WCBC(AM)	Cumberland MD
KBLF(AM)	Red Bluff CA	WMES(AM)	Ashburn GA		
KQMS(AM)	Redding CA	WGST(AM)	Atlanta GA	WHAG(AM)	Halfway MD
KFBK(AM)	Sacramento CA	WDBS(AM)	Eatonton GA	WNTR(AM)	Silver Spring MD
KSDO(AM)	San Diego CA	WKEU(AM)	Griffin GA		
KGIL(AM)	San Fernando CA	WKEU-FM	Griffin GA	*WFCR(FM)	Amherst MA
				WQRC(FM)	Barnstable MA
*KQED-FM	San Francisco CA	KIZN(AM)	Boise ID	*WBUR(FM)	Boston MA
		KSPD(AM)	Boise ID	WEEI(AM)	Boston MA
KCBS(AM)	San Francisco CA			WEIM(AM)	Fitchburg MA
		WKKD(AM)	Aurora IL	WXJY(FM)	Nantucket MA
KGO(AM)	San Francisco CA	*WSIU(FM)	Carbondale IL		
		WBBM(AM)	Chicago IL	WJR(AM)	Detroit MI
KTMS(AM)	Santa Barbara CA	WLRB(AM)	Macomb IL	WWJ(AM)	Detroit MI
		WTAZ(FM)	Morton IL	WXYT(AM)	Detroit MI
KSMA(AM)	Santa Maria CA	WPOK(AM)	Pontiac IL	*WKAR(AM)	East Lansing MI
*KCRW(FM)	Santa Monica CA	WTAD(AM)	Quincy IL	WDMJ(AM)	Marquette MI
		*WSSR(FM)	Springfield IL		
KCOK(AM)	Tulare CA	WKRS(AM)	Waukegan IL	*KCRB-FM	Bemidji MN
KVEN(AM)	Ventura CA	WFRX-FM	West Frankfort IL	*KSJR-FM	Collegeville MN
KOBO(AM)	Yuba City CA				
				KDAL (AM)	Duluth MN
KVOR(AM)	Colorado Springs CO	*WNIN-FM	Evansville IN	*KMSU(FM)	Mankato MN
KDEN(AM)	Denver CO	WGL(AM)	Fort Wayne IN	*KSJN(AM)	Minneapolis MN
KOA(AM)	Denver CO	WJOB(AM)	Hammond IN		
KCSJ(AM)	Pueblo CO			*KSJN-FM	Minneapolis MN
		KJAN(AM)	Atlantic IA		
WGCH(AM)	Greenwich CT	KJAN-FM	Atlantic IA	*KCCM-FM	Moorhead MN
WPOP(AM)	Hartford CT	WOC(AM)	Davenport IA	KNUJ(AM)	New Ulm MN
WNHC(AM)	New Haven CT	*KLCD(FM)	Decorah IA	*KLSX-FM	Rochester MN
		KMRY(AM)	Des Moines IA	*KLSE-FM	Rushford MN

148

*KGAC(FM)	St. Peter MN
*WIRR(FM)	Virginia-Hibbing MN
KKOZ(AM)	Ava MO
*KBIA(FM)	Columbia MO
KFRU(AM)	Columbia MO
KFMO(AM)	Flat River MO
KHMO(AM)	Hannibal MO
KWOS(AM)	Jefferson City MO
KMBZ(AM)	Kansas City MO
KJEL(AM)	Lebanon MO
*KXCV(FM)	Maryville MO
KRMO(AM)	Monett MO
KRMS(AM)	Osage Beach MO
*KSMU(FM)	Springfield MO
*KWMU(FM)	St. Louis MO
KMOX(AM)	St. Louis MO
KXOK(AM)	St. Louis MO
KOFI(AM)	Kalispell MT
*KUCV(FM)	Lincoln NE
KDWN(AM)	Las Vegas NV
KNUU(AM)	Las Vegas NV
KROL(AM)	Laughlin NV
KOH(AM)	Reno NV
*WEVO(FM)	Concord NH
WKBK(AM)	Keene NH
WEMJ(AM)	Laconia NH
WGIR(AM)	Manchester NH
WASR(AM)	Wolfeboro NH
WJLK(AM)	Asbury Park NJ
KOBE(AM)	Las Cruces NM
KRSN(AM)	Los Alamos NM
*WAMC(FM)	Albany NY
*WSKG-FM	Binghamton NY
WPUT(AM)	Brewster NY
*WBFO(FM)	Buffalo NY
WEBR(AM)	Buffalo NY
WRKL(AM)	New City NY
WVOX(AM)	New Rochelle NY
*WNYC(AM)	New York NY
*WNYC-FM	New York NY
WCBS(AM)	New York NY
WINS(AM)	New York NY
WLIB(AM)	New York NY
WMCA(AM)	New York NY
WOR(AM)	New York NY
*WRVO(FM)	Oswego NY
WLNA(AM)	Peekskill NY
*WXXI(AM)	Rochester NY
WKAL(AM)	Rome NY
WGRC(AM)	Spring Valley NY
*WAER(FM)	Syracuse NY
WFNC(AM)	Fayetteville NC
*KFJM(AM)	Grand Forks ND
*WOUB(AM)	Athens OH
WOMP(AM)	Bellaire OH
*WCPN(FM)	Cleveland OH
WERE(AM)	Cleveland OH
WWWE(AM)	Cleveland OH
*WOSU(AM)	Columbus OH
WMVO(AM)	Mount Vernon OH
WLKR(AM)	Norwalk OH
WKOV(AM)	Wellston OH
KCRC(AM)	Enid OK
KGWA(AM)	Enid OK
*KGOU(FM)	Norman OK
*KWGS(FM)	Tulsa OK
KBND(AM)	Bend OR
*KLCC(FM)	Eugene OR
*KMHD(FM)	Gresham OR
KXL(AM)	Portland OR
WMBA(AM)	Ambridge PA
WNZT(AM)	Columbia PA
*WQLN-FM	Erie PA
WBCB(AM)	Levittown-Fairless Hills PA
KYW(AM)	Philadelphia PA
WCAU(AM)	Philadelphia PA
KQV(AM)	Pittsburgh PA
WMAJ(AM)	State College PA
WTTC(AM)	Towanda PA
WTTC-FM	Towanda PA
WSBA(AM)	York PA
WADK(AM)	Newport RI
WHJJ(AM)	Providence RI
WIS(AM)	Columbia SC
WDAR(AM)	Darlington SC
WKCN(AM)	Dorchester-Brent SC
*KESD(FM)	Brookings SD
*KDSD-FM	Pierpont SD
KCCR(AM)	Pierre SD
*KBHE-FM	Rapid City SD
KQKD(AM)	Redfield SD
*KTSD-FM	Reliance SD
*KRSD(FM)	Sioux Falls SD
*KUSD(AM)	Vermillion SD
KWAT(AM)	Watertown SD
WMDR(AM)	Alcoa TN
WDOD(AM)	Chattanooga TN
WHBQ(AM)	Memphis TN
WLAC(AM)	Nashville TN
KLVI(AM)	Beaumont TX
KHLB(AM)	Burnet TX
*KERA(FM)	Dallas TX
KRLD(AM)	Dallas TX
KURV(AM)	Edinburg TX
KTSM(AM)	El Paso TX
*KUHF(FM)	Houston TX
KPRC(AM)	Houston TX
KTRH(AM)	Houston TX
KMUZ(FM)	La Grange TX
KHJK(AM)	Lockhart TX
KGNB(AM)	New Braunfels TX
KRIG(AM)	Odessa TX
KTNS(AM)	Plano TX
WOAI(AM)	San Antonio TX
KSTV(AM)	Stephenville TX
KTEM(AM)	Temple TX
KRNN(AM)	Terrell Hill TX
*KUER(FM)	Salt Lake City UT
WKVT(AM)	Brattleboro VT
WHWB(AM)	Rutland VT
WCFR(AM)	Springfield VT
WDEV(AM)	Waterbury VT
WENZ(AM)	Highland Springs VA
WHAP(AM)	Hopewell VA
WGH(AM)	Newport News VA
WNIS(AM)	Portsmouth VA
WANI(AM)	Richmond VA
KGMI(AM)	Bellingham WA
*KWSU(AM)	Pullman WA
*KUOW(FM)	Seattle WA
KING(AM)	Seattle WA
KIRO(AM)	Seattle WA
*KPBX-FM	Spokane WA
KXLY(AM)	Spokane WA
*KPLU-FM	Tacoma WA
WHBY(AM)	Appleton WI
WEAQ(AM)	Eau Claire WI
WDUZ(AM)	Green Bay WI
*WGTD(FM)	Kenosha WI
WIZM(AM)	La Crosse WI
WKTY(AM)	La Crosse WI
*WUWM(FM)	Milwaukee WI
WOSH(AM)	Oshkosh WI
WFHR(AM)	Wisconsin Rapids WI
KRSV(AM)	Alton WY
KRAE(AM)	Cheyenne WY
KROE(AM)	Sheridan WY
WCMN(AM)	Arecibo PR
WEKO(AM)	Cabo Rojo PR
*WEUC(AM)	Ponce PR
WKAQ(AM)	San Juan PR
WUNO(AM)	San Juan PR
WIBS(AM)	Charlotte Amalie VI

PART III

LIFE IN THE FAST LANE: EXECUTIVE HEALTH

"The tragedy of life is what dies
inside a man while he lives."
Albert Schweitzer

10

YOUR HEALTH
AND YOUR JOB

Personal health is no longer a personal matter. Corporations lose millions of dollars each year as result of employee illness. It's not only a question of sick pay: A key executive's illness can hold up deals, and result in missed opportunities, confusion, and chaos. More and more, top management is paying close attention to the medical history of its personnel. Your career may suffer if you accumulate a history of health problems, or if you "wear" your problem—obesity or chain smoking, for example. Such conditions signal not only a health risk, but project the image of lack of discipline. Very bad for your reputation.

Most of us are intellectually aware of the tremendous toll a job can take on our health. But it appears that few see the direct connection between physical condition and job performance. "Most executives don't believe that an hour spent on physical fitness is more valuable to the business than one spent at a meeting," says Stan deLisser, president of Executive Health Examiners Group.

What motivates executives to exercise? To some extent, an intelligent desire to reduce the risk of an early death. And executives who wish to remain athletic know the value of regular exercise. But above the demands of work, the pleasures of play, and concern for longevity, vanity is the principal motivating factor.

It's difficult to relate to longevity as a goal—and even tougher to associate the striking of a good business deal with an exercise program. But an exercise program or diet will make a real difference in how you look. Inversely, a potbelly is taken as an indication that fitness is not important to you.

If your life-style includes activities that offer more enjoyment when you are healthy, you have a built-in incentive to shape up, or to stay in shape. But if you are sedentary, you will probably need additional motivation. That's why a sport is so helpful. It provides both a health-related activity and a goal.

All vanities aside, fitness *is* an important component of job success. Just feeling good about yourself will help you, on the job and everywhere else.

What follows in the next five chapters is a frank appraisal of factors that influence executive health, job performance, and longevity—and a basic guide to getting and staying in condition for the big game of life and the daily scrimmages of the business world.

Most job-related health problems are emotional in origin and can be traced to anxiety and stress. Therefore, a large portion of Part III of this book is devoted to the origins of stress, its symptoms, and the methods of controlling it.

DRUGS IN THE WORKPLACE

Illegal drugs are a major problem in American business, affecting white collar and blue collar workers alike. But unless you work in a monastery, you already know that.

Drug abuse makes people unhealthy, leaving them susceptible to a wide variety of diseases as well as sapping energy and impairing performance. Addicts are more likely to be absent and to steal from their employers, not to mention injure themselves and endanger others.

In 1983, the costs to American business was estimated at $60 billion by the Research Triangle Institute. Today, that figure is almost certainly higher.

If you have a drug problem, what can you do about it? And if you are a manager who has to cope with drug abuse among your subordinates, how do you handle it?

No simple answers exist. And it is clearly beyond the scope of this book to discuss the legal and ethical ramifications. However, several basic strategies have emerged from the battlefield as major companies spend millions dealing with this scourge.

THE DANGERS

Drug abuse may induce behavior that threatens the lives of others.

Drugs can impair judgment.

Drug addiction may result in the executive stealing from the company.

An addicted executive may take actions that could hurt the company, compromising company secrets, breaking price and playing favorites.

THE EXECUTIVE ADDICT

How to recognize him. Look for behavioral changes, such as increased absenteeism, mood swings, or unstable work patterns characterized by frantic bursts of energy and slow, lethargic periods. These symptoms are by no means a foolproof method, and you must rely on your instincts. Be even-handed and don't go on a witch hunt, looking to drugs as an excuse to explain away a bad relationship with a worker. Assume an attitude of concern for your subordinate's or colleague's well-being, or you'll never get anywhere.

Then what? Bring up the subject. If you don't have hard evidence, it is going to be difficult to get an admission. But if the employee is lying, it will surface soon enough. Then enlist the help of co-workers, friends and family, together with a counselor. The goal: to get him to admit the problem and agree to seek help.

IMPORTANT ADVICE

Start early. It's good for the company to minimize the damage before it's too late. And it helps the abuser, because the sooner it is discovered the better the chance for successful treatment.

Bring in experienced, outside professional help. Your company should have a clearcut policy on paying for intervention counselors.

Take notes. Assess the executive's performance, documenting its deterioration.

Assure confidentiality. Promise to keep this quiet if the executive agrees to undergo treatment and get the firm to agree to pay for it.

Don't be afraid of the ultimatum. If the executive refuses to accept treatment he will probably be fired.

Don't be big brother. You can't follow the executive home at night. Leave it to spouse, family and friends to assist him there. But encourage them to do so. Strongly.

Compile a good bank of information on where one can get professional help for drug abuse problems in case the executive insists on dealing with the problem on his own, or if your company is unwilling or unable to pay for counseling and treatment.

Make sure your approach is legally sound. Don't be afraid to address the problem squarely, but educate yourself regarding the adequate statutes and regulations. Then make some strict rules regarding the use, possession, selling or providing drugs or alcohol on premises, as well as a regulation regarding reporting to work while under the influence.

Enforce rules and regulations, even where an investigation is required to determine if there has been a violation. This is a very serious matter. Drug tests and rights of privacy are sticky areas and should be discussed with an attorney and perhaps employee representatives.

SMOKING

The Surgeon General has gone public with the fact that cigarette smoke is a health hazard to surrounding nonsmokers as well as the ones who light up. A recent Gallup Poll revealed that 75 percent of Americans believe that smokers should not light up around nonsmokers, and 80 percent believe that workplaces should have restricted smoking areas. This has resulted in a clash between those who feel they have a constitutional right to smoke if they please, and those who would restrict them for the general good.

Nonsmokers outnumber smokers, and complaints have been rising all over the nation, in offices, restaurants, on airliners. At present, only 29 percent of the workforce lights up.

In some cases, smokers can escape total deprivation. A wide range of environmental aids like desktop ionizers, filters and smokeless ashtrays, as well as office systems for cleaning the air are available. Some recent research does indicate that the creativity of smokers diminishes when they are deprived. But before you get too lenient, recognize that smokers are sick 50 percent more than nonsmokers, although the statistics may vary from that figure for your own company.

If your company hasn't already dealt with this problem, it is going to sooner or later. According to the Bureau of National Affairs, a private research organization, the number of U.S. corporations restricting smoking has grown from 8 percent to 36 percent in the past five years. An additional 23 percent are considering the adoption of some regulations. Here are a few suggestions for dealing with this problem and formulating a policy:

Top management must make a commitment to set a firm policy and enforce it.

Take a survey. It would be wise to get a feel for employee attitudes before implementing a policy.

Be aware of local and state ordinances and OHSA safety regulations. Make sure your proposed policies conform.

Check your union agreements and your insurance policies.

Are you going to impose a total ban on smoking or simply restrict it? This is the basic question.

How will you enforce it? Formulate a policy for resolving conflicts.

Have your act together. When you announce the policy, be ready to educate the employees and anticipate the needs and feeling of your workers. You want a healthier environment, but also one in which conflicts between smokers and nonsmokers have been eliminated or at least reduced.

HEALTH AND THE EXECUTIVE WOMAN

Women in the executive suite have no pronounced health problems due to their sex. In fact they are generally healthier. Very few of the chronic "executive diseases" affect women as much as they affect men.

There is some indication that this situation might be changing. More women have entered the work force in recent years, and doctors have begun to see more women afflicted with "executive diseases." But many experts do not expect women to achieve the morbid equality of a male-level disease rate.

Speaking of equality, sex discrimination does add an extra measure of stress for the women executive. So does the problem of sexual advances on the job.

Another stress producer is the conflict that many women feel between career and motherhood. Menstruation is generally not a problem, although it can result in a few extra sick-days.

Strange as it may sound, the most common problems among executive women are dermatological. And women are worse offenders of the rules of good nutrition than men are.

The greatest concern is that women are picking up the bad health habits common in business: alcohol, smoking, sedentary life-style.

As women increasingly find success in the workplace, and reject the notion of being "dependent" on a male, they are placing great demands on themselves. When roles of wife and mother are added to the mix, they may fall victim to what psychologist Harriet Braiker refers to as the Type E-stress cycle, i.e., "everything to everybody." Being a superwoman may well take its toll on a woman's health. For more on this problem, you might wish to read *The Type E Woman: How to Overcome the Stress of Being Everything to Everybody*, by Harriet B. Braiker, Ph.D. (New York: Dodd, Mead & Co., 1986).

OVERVIEW OF TYPES OF EXAMINATIONS

The Standard Examination—The components of this examination, all of which are *tests present in the Comprehensive and Senior Examinations,* are basic procedures to detect the more common chronic diseases such as glaucoma, hypertension, diabetes, heart disease, emphysema and cancer of the colon/rectum plus glandular abnormalities and kidney/liver malfunction. It evaluates major body systems and functions and provides base line data to build an individualized preventive health program. Recommended for age 35 and over.

The Comprehensive Examination—The Comprehensive has additional procedures designed to detect esophagus, stomach, and gallbladder problems more common to people in executive capacities and/or 40 years of age or older. The added procedures, employing contrast media (barium/iodine pills), detect abnormalities such as tumors, cancer and gallstones.

The Senior Examination—This examination focuses on cardiac evaluation and the organs of the abdomen area. We perform a lateral chest x-ray to determine the size and shape of the heart muscle; abdomen x-ray to define the size and position of the liver, spleen, intestines, bladder and kidneys and exercise tolerance EKG. Tolerance testing consists of stressing the heart by exercising on a bicycle ergometer (pedaling against preset resistance) for four or five minutes, then three EKG readings are taken over a five-minute period. Recommended for age 40 and over.

The Periodic Examination—This evaluation omits tonometry screening for glaucoma and the proctoscopic inspection of the Standard Examination but contains all of the other procedures to detect common chronic diseases. Recommended for those under age 35.

Cardiac Stress—The treadmill test is a sophisticated diagnostic tool to help uncover underlying heart disease. It is a predictive indicator of the risk of heart attack. This procedure evaluates the condition of the cardiovascular system and appraises the functional capacity of an individual to perform under stress. Cardiac Stress testing is a succession of uninterrupted and increasing work stages with continuous oscilloscope monitoring of the heart rate. Our physician and a registered nurse are present throughout the testing. Recommended annually for senior executives and those in stressful positions.

Fig. 17. Physical examinations offered by Executive
Health Examiners Group

Reprinted by permission of Executive Health Examiners Group.

STANDARD EXECUTIVE EXAMINATION

Required Time: Approximately 2 Hours

Complete personal and family history
Physical examination of all body systems
X-ray of the heart and lungs (14" x 17")
12-Lead resting electrocardiogram with interpretation
Audiometric Screening
Visual Screening
Tonometry for Glaucoma
Spirometer test of vital capacity
Proctosigmoidoscopy (inspection of the rectum and lower colon)
Stool for occult blood
Hematology:

Red blood count	Hemoglobin
White blood count	Hematocrit
Differential Screening	

SMA-12 Blood Chemistry Analysis plus Triglycerides

BUN (Urea Nitrogen)	SGOT (Oxalecetic Transaminase)
Glucose (Sugar)	LDH (Lactic Dehydrogenase)
Cholesterol	Phosphorous
Calcium	Albumin
Uric Acid	Total Protein
Bilirubin (Total)	Triglycerides
Alkaline Phosphatase	

Urinalysis:

Sugar	Specific Gravity
Albumin	Microscopic

Pap Smear (Women, extra)

Test evaluation, written report and consultation by the examining physician.

Fig. 18. Standard Executive Examination, Executive
Health Examiners Group
Reprinted by permission.

PERIODIC B EXAMINATION

Required Time: Approximately 2 Hours

Complete personal and family history
Physical examination of all body systems
X-ray of the heart and lungs (14" x 17")
12-Lead resting electrocardiogram with interpretation
Audiometric Screening
Vision Screening (near/distant)
Spirometer test of vital capacity
Stool for occult blood
Hematology:

Red blood count	Hemoglobin
White blood count	Hematocrit
Differential Screening	

SMA-12 Blood Chemistry Analysis Plus Triglycerides

BUN (Urea Nitrogen)	SGOT (Oxalacetic Transaminase)
Glucose (Sugar)	LDH (Lactic Dehydrogenase)
Cholesterol	Phosphorous
Calcium	Albumin
Uric Acid	Total Protein
Bilirubin (Total)	Triglycerides
Alkaline Phosphatase	

Urinalysis:

Sugar	Specific Gravity
Albumin	Microscopic

Pap Smear (Women, extra)

Test evaluation and written report by the examining physician.

Fig. 19. Executive Health Examiners Group
Periodic B Examination, for those under 35
Reprinted by permission.

11

STRESS: A USER'S GUIDE TO BODILY WEAR AND TEAR

One sure sign that a thing is popular is that everybody has heard of it but almost nobody is quite sure what "it" is. These days, stress is "it." This product of pressure is commonly equated with nervous tension, probably because we are a pretty wound-up culture. We ingest over five billion doses of tranquilizers to calm ourselves, five billion doses of barbiturates to help us unwind and sleep, and then three billion doses of amphetamines to make us feel perky.

Stress is a term that was once strictly medical and is now so mangled that the definition seems dictated more by the cure than the cause. One thing is certain: The scope of stress extends far beyond simple anxiety. And the sources, signs, and symptoms are far more numerous than most executives imagine them to be.

WHAT IS STRESS?

Basically, stress is the nonspecific response that the body elicits to any demand. This definition by Dr. Hans Selye, one of the leading stress researchers, is obviously very broad. It can be taken to mean simply the wear and tear on the body that comes with living life.

So what's so bad about that? Nothing. In fact, the body is built to handle stress and even, in many instances, thrives on it; many of us function better when demands are made on us. Only when the demands are excessive and/or prolonged or too frequent does stress become dangerous. Stress can also take a great toll when it focuses on a particular organ. Such conditions have become commonplace, especially in the business world.

To distinguish between the natural, constructive form of stress that comes from a competitive environment and excessive stress that overburdens people and does bad things to them, Selye uses two terms: "eustress" for the good, "distress" for the bad. Since this chapter is devoted to counting the ways in which stress can impair your performance and shorten your life—and to finding ways of dissipating that stress—assume I'm speaking of distress unless otherwise noted.

Misconceptions

- Stress is simple anxiety.
- Stress results only from negative occurrences.
- Stress is always bad.

WHAT CAUSES STRESS?

Virtually anything can be a source of stress. Because we differ from one another in our psychological and physical makeup, we differ in our reactions to external events and demands. One man's joy is another man's distress. So, by necessity, any discussion of the causes of stress centers on the *most common* sources—those that elicit stressful responses in many executives. Most experts have by now accepted the future shock theory, which states that the accelerating rate of change, innovation, mobility, and depersonalization of our technologically advanced culture makes each new day a bout with potentially damaging stress. In short, our culture, with its technology, is changing at a rate that outstrips our ability to adapt. Organizational psychologist Jere E. Yates, has produced a chart that effectively summarizes the sources and symptoms of stress that commonly affects the manager.

The origins of stress can be divided into three basic categories: organizational (job-related), social and personal.

ORGANIZATIONAL

According to a survey of 1,400 top managers and 1,200 middle managers conducted for the American Management Association, the four main causes of job-related stress were: heavy workload; the conflict between the required tasks and the desired personal accomplishments; the company's political climate; lack of feedback. The chart clearly demonstrates that most causes of stress are psychological. Noise, crowding, air pollution, and such can take their toll, but the body shows a remarkable ability to adapt to such physical stressors.

Job-related stresses are a bit peculiar. While they are clearly a factor in health problems, they also appear to contribute to job satisfaction. A recent survey by Ruder and Finn found that most executives wouldn't change jobs because of pressure. More often, greater opportunity for fulfillment or challenge is the reason to walk. *The bottom line is that many of the things that we like about our jobs are the very same things that make us sick.*

Let's look at these inverse stressors.

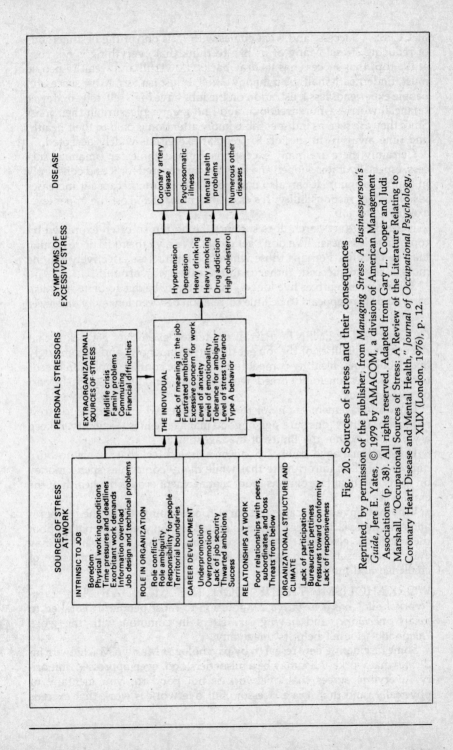

Fig. 20. Sources of stress and their consequences

SOURCES OF STRESS AT WORK

INTRINSIC TO JOB
Boredom
Physical working conditions
Time pressures and deadlines
Exorbitant work demands
Information overload
Job design and technical problems

ROLE IN ORGANIZATION
Role conflict
Role ambiguity
Responsibility for people
Territorial boundaries

CAREER DEVELOPMENT
Underpromotion
Overpromotion
Lack of job security
Thwarted ambitions
Success

RELATIONSHIPS AT WORK
Poor relationships with peers, subordinates, and boss
Threats from below

ORGANIZATIONAL STRUCTURE AND CLIMATE
Lack of participation
Bureaucratic pettiness
Pressures toward conformity
Lack of responsiveness

PERSONAL STRESSORS

EXTRAORGANIZATIONAL SOURCES OF STRESS
Midlife crisis
Family problems
Commuting
Financial difficulties

THE INDIVIDUAL
Lack of meaning in the job
Frustrated ambition
Excessive concern for work
Level of anxiety
Level of emotionality
Tolerance for ambiguity
Level of stress tolerance
Type A behavior

SYMPTOMS OF EXCESSIVE STRESS
Hypertension
Depression
Heavy drinking
Heavy smoking
Drug addiction
High cholesterol

DISEASE
Coronary artery disease
Psychosomatic illness
Mental health problems
Numerous other diseases

Reprinted, by permission of the publisher, from *Managing Stress: A Businessperson's Guide,* Jere E. Yates, © 1979 by AMACOM, a division of American Management Associations (p. 38). All rights reserved. Adapted from Gary L. Cooper and Judi Marshall, "Occupational Sources of Stress: A Review of the Literature Relating to Coronary Heart Disease and Mental Health," *Journal of Occupational Psychology.* XLIX (London, 1976), p. 12.

SUCCESS   Success, and what comes with it, is one of the best methods of reducing stress. Many of us like to think that everything is not rosy at the top, that success has its drawbacks: Powerful and wealthy people must, underneath it all, be unhappy. Well, it just isn't so. Most successful people experience less frustration on the job, have high self-esteem, fewer financial worries, more freedom, and find greater pleasure in their jobs. Since they are seen as indispensable, more attention is paid to their health, and time away from the job for regular exercise is widely accepted.

Certainly there are many exceptions. Some people can't manage success, especially if it is sudden and they are unprepared for it and constantly in fear of losing it. It can also make one less secure, because it increases visibility and responsibility. It's easy for a mistake to cost the upper level executive his job.

Nevertheless, research does support the notion so often expressed by top men in business: "We don't get ulcers. We give them!" The reasoning may be circular. Perhaps those who cope with stress effectively are the more likely to succeed, rather than the other way around.

Successful executives live longer, but that may be due to better medical care. And there appears to be little correlation between longevity and sheer wealth.

GOOD MANAGEMENT   Part of the reason executives get sick is that the positive qualities of the job get distorted somehow, and become ugly and debilitating. Healthy competition can cause conflict; ambition breeds overwork. Responsibility breeds fear and guilt. And time seems to be part of a conspiracy.

Good management is one of the most neglected approaches to stress reduction. In fact, one sure sign of good management is the ability to keep a workload within the limits of manageability.

In a well-managed company, no one should feel that he has to burn himself out. It is unfortunate that while many companies spend money on gyms and health programs, poor management erodes the health of the employees.

Why not have your cake and eat it too? A job with all the pressures and risks necessary to keep you exhilarated and on your toes, but without the pernicious elements that could send you to the cardiac ward. It may even be necessary to change jobs in order to get the right mixture of challenge and moderation.

WORKAHOLISM: THANK GOD IT'S MONDAY   The term "workaholic" has a negative connotation to most people. It is taken to mean *overwork*; and having six letters in common with the word "alcoholic" doesn't help its image any.

Some fascinating new research by psychologist Marilyn Machlowitz indicates that workaholics may be a misunderstood, even oppressed, minority. Everyone agrees that overwork is not good for you mentally or physically, and that it is a stressor. But overwork is work that exceeds

one's tolerance or limits. What about those who have a high tolerance—
or, rather a large *appetite* for work?

Such people don't complain about overwork, because they don't mind
or don't notice. Many love their work and thrive on it, almost to the ex-
clusion of all else. Thus, if you complain about being a workaholic, you
probably aren't one. You are just overworked.

Workaholics are the victims of discrimination for much the same reasons
that other minorities are: They threaten the majority. Workaholics like
their jobs and appear to live satisfied lives. And they don't work solely
to please others. Primarily, they work to please themselves.

WORK OVERLOAD   There is little doubt that being overworked can
harm the executive. There are two basic types of job overload: quantitative, when there is simply too much work to do, and qualitative, when
the work is too difficult. Of course the types are related; if the work is
too difficult it will take longer and probably lead to a larger than normal
backlog. But it is important to get a handle on what is meant by being
"overworked," if you are to find a solution. As for those "workaholics"
who don't complain, they may be having problems even though they appear to thrive on work.

Some workaholics do have serious problems—feelings of inadequacy,
inability to relax—that lie at the root of this behavior. But, according to
Machlowitz, just as many workaholics weave together work and play
almost as a continuum—or two sides of the same coin—rather than as
two separate aspects of life. In such cases, it appears that the rigorous
work load doesn't produce excessive stress. More often, it is a source of
enjoyment.

The real problems lie in one's relationship with family and friends. If
you are always working, neglect is inevitable. Children can suffer from
lack of attention. Workaholism is a primary factor in many broken
marriages.

Machlowitz, in her book *Workaholics*,* offers a diagnostic quiz that
will help you determine if you are a workaholic:

                                                    YES   NO

1. Do you get up early, no matter how late
   you go to bed?
2. If you are eating lunch alone, do you read
   or work while you eat?
3. Do you make daily lists of things to do?
4. Do you find it difficult to "do nothing"?
5. Are you energetic and competitive?
6. Do you work on weekends and holidays?
7. Do you find vacations "hard to take"?
8. Do you dread retirement?
9. Do you really enjoy your work?

---

*Reprinted from Marilyn Machlowitz, *Workaholics*, Copyright © 1980, by permission of
Addison-Wesley Publishing Co., Reading, MA, pp. 17–19.

If you answered "yes" to eight or more questions, you, too, may be a workaholic.

ROLE CONFLICT AND AMBIGUITY Role conflict occurs when an employee is caught between incompatible demands. Ambiguity occurs when the employee isn't given the proper knowledge and instruction on how to do the job. Research has shown that both of these situations can place the individual under unhealthy stress.

CAREER STAGE If an employee feels that he or she has not attained the level that he desires or deserves, the days can be quite stressful. The opposite is also true; stress is created when an employee feels that he has gone too far too fast, that he is a phony, or that he is not adequately prepared to assume the responsibilities of his job, i.e., "in over his head."

RELATIONSHIPS This is an important aspect of executive life. If one has problems in getting on with superiors, subordinates and peers, the resulting stress can be debilitating.

ORGANIZATIONAL STRUCTURE The method by which an employee is evaluated, by which he receives feedback, promotions, and how the organization resolves conflicts and makes decisions may be very difficult for certain executives. Nobody may be directly to blame.

PERSONAL STRESSORS

Certain employees may be more vulnerable because of their ages, changes in life-style, or personal life events. Such stresses can be extremely serious, especially if they are centered around home life. While the office is often perceived as a jungle, the home is considered a source of stability. A stressor that rocks the domestic boat can hurt a great deal. Divorce is an obvious possible source of stress. So is adultery. It appears that many of our moral judgments are attempts to minimize stress-producing events. Respondents to a recent survey considered adultery more immoral than homosexuality, perhaps because adultery is seen as more destabilizing and therefore more stressful.

SOCIAL STRESSORS

Societal attitudes toward work, as well as the feelings of family and friends, may make it difficult for an executive to cope with conflicts. For example, if the subcultural belief among family and friends is "you are not a man if you cannot provide for your family," an out-of-work executive or one struggling to make ends meet may feel very isolated and depressed. In another subculture, friends and family may rally round, providing support until "things turn up."

Overall societal conditions can exacerbate stress. In a recession or in an isolated case of a slumping industry, pressure surely increases on the worker.

ANXIETY AND DEPRESSION

Anxiety and depression are frequently mentioned as symptoms of stress. They can also be a source. Many people simply cannot tolerate high levels of anxiety or deep depression, or they respond to it with negativism. Often, the symptoms can be more of the same, resulting in a physical and mental vicious cycle—and a downward spiral for the victim. This may help explain why relaxation techniques are often so effective against stress. Not only do they attack the *symptoms* by helping the individual to feel relaxed and uplifted, but at the same time they alleviate a major *cause* of stress.

WHAT MAKES SOMETHING A "DISTRESSOR"?

What makes one event or outside influence a stressor, and another simply a run-of-the-mill occurrence, has a lot to do with how you perceive the situation and how you react to it. *In reality, there's no such thing as a stressful situation—only a stressful response.* Here's why some situations cause stressful responses:

INDIVIDUAL DIFFERENCES

Everyone's physiology is different. Say you are in shape. You run five miles a day. For you, a five-mile run is a constructive situation, stressing the heart in such a way as to improve its condition. Your colleague, on the other hand, hasn't done any exercise in years. And he's got angina and hypertension to boot. For him, a five-mile run might mean a stroke. Obviously, a recommendation to run five miles a day can't be applied across the board. You've got to take the individual's condition into account.

It's a good idea to know where you stand. *Learn as much as possible about yourself and how you function.* Otherwise, you can get caught unaware. Everyone is talking about taking more time off because it's good for their health. But suppose you love your job, and it's idleness that sends your blood pressure up and sets your nerves on edge? For you, a long vacation may not be what the doctor ordered. Regular medical examinations to keep you aware of your physical condition are a good idea. In some cases, personality testing may be warranted to help you identify your basic personality traits.

UNPREDICTABILITY

People can put up with even the most annoying and rotten things when they know what to expect. But the very same things can produce stress if they appear unexpectedly.

The flip side of unpredictability is overanticipation. Stress can be caused by anticipation of something unpleasant—having to fire someone or preparing to ask for a raise, for example.

On balance, a regular routine and a well-planned work day can be beneficial, precisely because adherence to a routine cuts down the unexpected. And a sober, sensible analysis of the unpleasantries ahead won't hurt you.

LACK OF CONTROL

It is amazing how much people can endure when they feel in control of a situation. In a now classic study, two groups of workers were subjected to identical irritating noise. The only difference was that the members of one group had buttons with which they could silence the noise at will. Most members of that group chose not to touch the buttons, and so voluntarily worked under the same conditions as the helpless group. But the work output of the group with the *option* to cut the noise was far superior to the group that had no choice.

This doesn't mean that we have to be power-hungry in order to avoid stress. It means that we do better when we feel that we are calling the shots in our lives. Stress can result from the feeling of being at the mercy of the clock, of the bill collector, of the boss. But as the study serves to point out, what is important is not the time, the bills, or the boss, but our perception of the situation.

SOCIAL CONTEXT

Have you ever noticed how you can shrug off your own mistakes when it's witnessed by a casual friend, but the very same gaffe will make you want to crawl under the desk if it happens in front of certain other people? It appears that one's environment and social context are factors in stress.

Culture also plays a role in determining stress. A Brazilian businessperson might do a slow burn if you are a few minutes late for an appointment. To him, you're a stressor. An Arab businessman will most likely spend the time calmly drinking coffee, not feeling slighted in the least. The two react differently due to the differences in cultural conditioning.

Whenever one is in an unknown or openly hostile social or cultural environment, the potential for stress rises markedly. That is why there is such a great need for diplomatic protocol, meetings on "neutral soil," and the like.

WHAT STRESS CAN DO TO YOU

Stress can make you unhealthy and unhappy; it can even kill you. If that isn't bad enough to consider, ponder further: Much of what we do in attempting to alleviate the psychological effects of stress, such as smoke, drink, overeat, and take medication, can also do us in. Fortunately, as we learn more about stress, we become better at identifying the danger signs and symptoms commonly caused by high levels of stress. Unfortunately, by the time many of us take notice of the symptoms and decide to take action, they have already developed into full-fledged diseases.

This section is not intended to turn you into a hypochondriac or a stressphobic (a stress-fearing creampuff). Rather, it is intended to alert you to signs that you may be under excessive stress. This awareness will enable you to monitor the situation closely—and to do something about it should it get out of hand.

Regular physical exams are a must; and you will help your doctor and yourself by calling attention to possible stress-related symptoms.

WARNING SIGNS

THE FIGHT-OR-FLIGHT RESPONSE

This is a common response by the body to a perceived external threat. The body prepares itself to confront the threat or to run from it. The changes that take place in our physiology at this time are quite noticeable:

- breath rate increases rapidly
- blood pressure increases
- muscle tension increases
- heart rate increases
- pupils dilate
- digestion slows or stops
- blood sugar rises
- bowel and bladder control loosens
- perspiration and saliva increase
- adrenaline flow increases
- the senses sharpen

The fight-or-flight response allows us to act more quickly, powerfully, and efficiently to a situation in which having "something extra" might make the difference between our survival and our demise. But two basic situations can turn this key response into a problem:

- The fight-or-flight response is triggered inappropriately. There are times when we believe we are being threatened, but in reality we are not.
- A threat is correctly perceived, but the physical response called for by the fight-or-flight mechanism is inappropriate. Suppose a business associate says something that you take as a threat. Your fight-or-flight mechanism is now switched on. Punching him would be a bad move. Running away is utterly insane. So you basically do nothing but steam. You break a few pencils, perhaps; you call your mate and curse the guy out. But that's it.

Clearly, in our competitive world, the fight-or-flight mechanisms may be triggered too often. And because the physical reactions that the response calls for are socially unacceptable, we are deprived of the most natural outlets for that response. Every fight-or-flight reaction puts a great deal of stress on the body. And being forced to internalize it just makes it worse.

If you find yourself frequently experiencing the reactions associated with the fight-or-flight response, you had better look at what is causing your engine to race.

LIFE CHANGES

Any abrupt change in the status of an individual's life can produce stress. So goes the theory advanced by Drs. Thomas Holmes and Richard Rahe of the University of Washington School of Medicine. Basically, they are saying that health is directly affected by the rate and severity of change in one's life. And there is some evidence that this is true.

Life-change events are potentially harmful because of the *stress* of change, not because the event itself is negative; many life-change events are, in themselves, neutral or downright positive. If it causes a great change, it can cause stress.

Holmes and Rahe have put together a Social Readjustment Rating Scale, which is all the rage in books and magazine articles about stress. It is a list of 43 life events, each of which is assigned a value in terms of Life Change Units. All you do is go through the list looking for events that have taken place in your life over the past year. Tally up the total number of Life Change Units accumulated and you can estimate the probability of illness over the next two years. Simple? Yes. That's why health writers love it. Accurate? Not really.

There are so many factors and variables involved. No distinction is made between eustress and distress: Some of the events on the list may be good for you. And as I pointed out earlier, the major factor in stress formation is not the event itself, but the individual's ability to cope with that event. The Holmes-Rahe list fails to take this into account.

On the positive side, the Social Readjustment Rating Scale can be a valuable tool for increasing your awareness of possible danger points. If you feel you have been having a pretty hard time of late, one look at the rating scale might tell you why. And if you are anticipating having to "work a few things out" in your life, you can prepare to compensate for the possible toll the ordeal could take on your health.

ATYPICAL BEHAVIOR ON THE JOB

When people are under stress, they often do things out of character. It's easy to excuse such behavior by saying "I'm not myself today." We expect that people will understand. And that is why we tend to bend over backward with a subordinate we know to be competent. But whether it be our subordinates or ourselves, the best approach isn't always to look the other way. There are some common behavior patterns that are, in effect, warning lights that something is amiss. It may indeed appear that the individual is "slipping." If recognized early, the problems causing the stress can be confronted and overcome—and you can probably avoid having to fire somebody, or getting canned yourself.

EXCESSIVE ABSENTEEISM   Often an indication of problems at home, low morale or self-esteem, and a general wish to avoid problems, absenteeism is also coupled with depression; we feel like staying in bed and shutting out the world.

PROCRASTINATION   When a worker who is normally "a real go-getter" starts pushing pencils around the desk, it's probably not because he's getting lazy. Something has taken the fight out of him, and he is simply running out the clock—stalling for time, avoiding the challenges he used to eat for breakfast.

POOR TIME MANAGEMENT   People under stress often feel tyrannized or oppressed by time. When you feel that way, often you wind up losing control of your own schedule and work routine.

DEFENSIVENESS   This is perhaps the most common sign of all. But since defensive behavior is so widespread in the business world, it's significance as a sign of something more serious is often overlooked. If an individual starts displaying defense mechanisms that are out of the ordinary, take notice. Be especially on guard for:

Avoidance of reality, either by denying that problems exist ("Relax, there's no problem") or by creating an illusion ("Things are great; everything's going really well").

Excessive suspicion, or xenophobia (fear of that which is foreign). The individual thinks that so-and-so is out to get him, can't be trusted, or is to blame.

NOT CUTTING THE MUSTARD   The quality of work is substandard, or below the individual's normal performance levels. Putting on the pressure may be the worse thing you can do in this situation. If it's a subordinate, try to find out what is going on. If it's you, take stock of the situa-

THE SOCIAL READJUSTMENT RATING SCALE

LIFE EVENT	MEAN VALUE
1. Death of spouse	100
2. Divorce	73
3. Marital separation from mate	65
4. Detention in jail or other institution	63
5. Death of a close family member	63
6. Major personal injury or illness	53
7. Marriage	50
8. Being fired at work	47
9. Marital reconciliation with mate	45
10. Retirement from work	45
11. Major change in the health or behavior of a family member	44
12. Pregnancy	40
13. Sexual difficulties	39
14. Gaining a new family member (e.g., through birth, adoption, oldster moving in, etc.)	39
15. Major business readjustment (e.g., merger, reorganization, bankruptcy, etc.)	39
16. Major change in financial state (e.g., a lot worse off or a lot better off than usual)	38
17. Death of a close friend	37
18. Changing to a different line of work	36
19. Major change in the number of arguments with spouse (e.g., either a lot more or a lot less than usual regarding child-rearing, personal habits, etc.)	35
20. Taking on a mortgage greater than $10,000 (e.g., purchasing a home, business, etc.)	31
21. Foreclosure on a mortgage or loan	30
22. Major change in responsibilities at work (e.g., promotion, demotion, lateral transfer)	29
23. Son or daughter leaving home (e.g., marriage, attending college, etc.)	29
24. In-law troubles	29
25. Outstanding personal achievement	28
26. Wife beginning or ceasing work outside the home	26
27. Beginning or ceasing formal schooling	26
28. Major change in living conditions (e.g., building a new home, remodeling, deterioration of home or neighborhood)	25
29. Revision of personal habits (dress, manners, associations, etc.)	24
30. Troubles with the boss	23
31. Major change in working hours or conditions	20

Fig. 21. Social Readjustment Rating Scale
A method of cataloging stress and estimating the probability
of stress-related illness within the next two years.
(above and opposite)

Reprinted with permission from T. H. Holmes
and R. H. Rahe, "The Social Readjustment Rating Scale,"
Journal of Psychosomatic Research 11 (1967): 213–18.
Copyright © 1967 Pergamon Press, Ltd.

32. Change in residence	20
33. Changing to a new school	20
34. Major change in usual type and/or amount of recreation	19
35. Major change in church activities (e.g., a lot more or a lot less than usual)	19
36. Major change in social activities (e.g., clubs, dancing, movies, visiting, etc.)	18
37. Taking on a mortgage or loan less than $10,000 (e.g., purchasing a car, TV, freezer, etc.)	17
38. Major change in sleeping habits (a lot more or a lot less sleep, or change in part of day when asleep)	16
39. Major change in number of family get-togethers (e.g., a lot more or a lot less than usual)	15
40. Major change in eating habits (a lot more or a lot less food intake, or very different meal hours or surroundings)	15
41. Vacation	13
42. Christmas	12
43. Minor violations of the law (e.g., traffic tickets, jaywalking, disturbing the peace, etc.)	11

There seems to be a well-documented and clear relationship between life change and physical disease. It is impossible to make accurate predictions on an individual basis, since most of these findings are statistical. In our subjective judgment, we would estimate that you might be able to interpret your life change scores as follows:

LIFE CHANGE SCORE FOR PREVIOUS YEAR	PROBABILITY OF ILLNESS WITHIN NEXT 2 YEARS
Less than 150 (low stress)	Low
150-199 (mild stress)	30%
200-299 (moderate stress)	50%
300 or more (major stress)	80%

tion and try to weed out the cause of your slide, rather than trying to ride it out unexamined.

Keep in mind that even events that are neutral or positive can induce such behavior. So even when things are going smoothly and well, an executive can be under stress.

PHYSICAL AND MENTAL DISTRESS SIGNALS

Dr. Selye has prepared a list of 31 common danger signs. The list is long because it runs the gamut of signs that appear among a great range of individuals. If even a few are turning up regularly in your life, they could mean trouble.

PRIMARY SYMPTOMS

Depression. Depression is best defined as a feeling of dejection about life. It can vary in intensity and is often accompanied by inactivity, feelings of sadness, worthlessness, and futility, and a lack of energy and goals. It is not unusual for people to experience a depression of limited duration as a direct reaction to a marked life change or crisis, such as the illness or death of a loved one or the loss of one's job. But the more debilitating form of depression is a chronic, unrelenting brand that often appears to have no immediate justification. This is the kind of stress that psychiatrist David Viscott describes as "a sadness which has lost its relationship to the logical progression of events."*

Depression is often associated with (or is even a direct cause of) several other stress symptoms, such as changes in appetite and sleep patterns. Many depressed people feel better after raiding the refrigerator; or they eat without pleasure, just to take their minds off their problems. Others lose their appetites completely. Then there are those who can't sleep or who wake up in the middle of the night—and those who are too depressed to face the world, so they stay under the sheets all day long. The sudden appearance of pains, soreness, and aches is also associated with depression.

One estimate puts the number of people with serious depression at 15 percent of the U.S. population.

Anxiety. This feeling of tension, apprehension, and worry certainly needs no description. But anxiety should be distinguished from such feelings as fear and frustration. Fear is a response to a pending or immediate danger; it may save your life someday. Anxiety, on the other hand, is a reaction to *anticipated* danger, and usually this reaction is far out of proportion to the actual threat. Frustration results from your apprehension of an obstacle that prevents, or threatens to prevent, attainment of a goal.

Like depression, chronic or intense anxiety may be associated with changes in appetite and sleep.

SECONDARY SYMPTOMS

Insomnia. This symptom usually goes hand in hand with anxiety or depression, but can occur by itself. Chronic insomnia can be quite a problem on its own. There are many approaches to relief, among them sleep clinics, nutritional and folk remedies, relaxation techniques, and, as a

*Reprinted from *Executive Health*, by Philip Goldberg, Copyright © 1978, by McGraw-Hill, Inc., New York, NY 10020. All rights reserved.

1. General irritability, hyperexcitation, or depression
2. Pounding of the heart, an indicator of high blood pressure
3. Dryness of the throat and mouth
4. Impulsive behavior, emotional instability
5. The overpowering urge to cry or to run and hide
6. Inability to concentrate, flight of thoughts, and general disorientation
7. Feelings of unreality, weakness, or dizziness
8. Predilection to become fatigued, and loss of the "joie de vivre"
9. "Floating anxiety"—that is to say, we are afraid, although we do not know exactly what we are afraid of
10. Emotional tension and alertness, feeling of being "keyed up"
11. Trembling, nervous tics
12. Tendency to be easily startled by small sounds
13. High-pitched, nervous laughter
14. Stuttering and other speech difficulties
15. Bruxism, or grinding of the teeth
16. Insomnia
17. Hypermotility
18. Sweating
19. The frequent need to urinate
20. Diarrhea, indigestion, queasiness in the stomach, and sometimes even vomiting
21. Migraine headaches
22. Premenstrual tension or missed menstrual cycles
23. Pain in the neck or lower back
24. Loss of appetite or compulsive eating
25. Increased smoking
26. Increased use of legally prescribed drugs, such as tranquilizers or amphetamines.
27. Alcohol and drug addiction
28. Nightmares
29. Neurotic behavior
30. Psychoses
31. Proneness to accidents

Fig. 22. Danger signs and symptoms of stress

Reprinted, by permission of the publisher, from *Managing Stress: A Businessperson's Guide*, by Jere E. Yates, © 1979 by AMACOM, a division of the American Management Associations (pp. 82–83). All rights reserved.

last—and, ideally, temporary—resort, drugs. (Many researchers believe that drugs inhibit some therapeutic qualities of sleep.)

Neck or back pain. Many people tend to tense their muscles repeatedly when under stress. The back and neck are often the first areas to tighten up. Some people feel the muscle tension in other areas, such as the jaw and head.

POOR SOLUTIONS
TO STRESS-RELATED PROBLEMS

Sometimes a symptom is nothing more than a poor attempt at a solution. In the case of stress, many of the solutions that we adopt to improve the situation do very little to ameliorate it. In fact they often make it worse.

Eating. Some people stuff themselves just to get some relief. Others hope to accomplish the same thing by starving. Neither approach works. You just get fat or undernourished, or you wind up a junk-food junkie.

Drinking. Excessive drinking is very popular among stress addicts. It can aggravate the symptoms of stress. But usually it works too well and the victim becomes the victim of chronic tranquilization. Thus, the root causes of the stress reaction are never confronted—and the liver and stomach pay the price.

Smoking. Smoking more now to escape the stress? But nicotine acts as a stimulant. Besides, imagine how stressful it must be to know you're increasing your chances of becoming a statistic.

Caffeine. It is not unusual for coffee, tea, and cola drinkers to increase their consumption of these caffeine-bearing beverages during periods of stress in order to get a "lift." But excessive amounts produce symptoms similar to anxiety. And caffeine has been linked to nervousness, insomnia, ulcers, even heart disease.

Drug abuse. Drugs weaken the body in a variety of ways, mentally and physically. They even weaken the immune system, making the user more susceptible to disease. Prescription drugs are used to treat stress only on a short-term basis, and only as a last resort. Needless to say, a doctor's supervision is essential.

One rule of thumb: If the solution can become a stressor, it's probably not a very good solution.

Physical Signs

1. Excess weight for your age and height
2. High blood pressure
3. Lack of appetite
4. A desire to eat as soon as a problem arises
5. Frequent heartburn
6. Chronic diarrhea or constipation
7. An inability to sleep
8. A feeling of constant fatigue
9. Frequent headaches
10. A need for aspirin or some other medication daily
11. Muscle spasms
12. A feeling of fullness although you've not eaten
13. Shortness of breath
14. A liability to fainting or nausea
15. An inability to cry or a tendency to burst into tears easily
16. Persistent sexual problems (frigidity, impotence, fear)
17. Excessive nervous energy which prevents sitting still and relaxing.

Mental Signs

1. A constant feeling of uneasiness
2. Constant irritability with family and work associates
3. Boredom with life
4. A recurring feeling of being unable to cope with life
5. Anxiety about money
6. Morbid fear of disease, especially cancer and heart disease
7. Fear of death—your own and others'
8. A sense of suppressed anger
9. An inability to have a good laugh
10. A feeling of being rejected by your family
11. A sense of despair at being an unsuccessful parent
12. Dread as the weekend approaches
13. Reluctance to take a vacation
14. A feeling you can't discuss your problems with anyone
15. An inability to concentrate for any length of time or to finish one job before beginning another one
16. A terror of heights, enclosed spaces, thunderstorms, or earthquakes

Fig. 23. Physical and mental signs of stress

Jack Tresidder (ed.), *Feel Younger, Live Longer* (Chicago: Rand McNally, 1977). Reprinted, by permission of the publisher, from *Managing Stress: A Businessperson's Guide*, by Jere E. Yates, © 1979 by AMACOM, a division of American Management Associations (pp. 89–90). All rights reserved.

STRESS-RELATED DISEASE
AND DISORDERS

Excessive stress, if unchecked, is certainly a contributing factor in the onset of many diseases. In some cases it may be the most important factor; in others it may simply accelerate the appearance of a disease. Hans Selye believes that although many factors (such as heredity, diet, and environment) may indeed make an individual a candidate for a particular disease, it is excessive stress that causes a potential problem to blossom into a full-fledged disease. By this way of thinking, there are millions of potential heart attack victims who can avoid having one by controlling stress. Many doctors disagree. But it is worth noting which diseases appear closely linked to excessive stress.

Heart disease. Heart attack, stroke, hypertension, and angina have all been linked to excessive stress. In that linkage, stress joins a long list of other factors, including smoking, obesity, and heredity. We do not know to what extent stress plays a role in cardiovascular disease, but there is little doubt that excessive stress can trigger a heart attack in a "high risk" individual. Selye has been able to trigger heart attacks in rats by inducing stress in them.

Stress itself often induces the "fight-or-flight" response that results in an elevation of the blood pressure. If this happens repeatedly, the result can be that the pressure eventually ceases to return to normal. The result is hypertension, or high blood pressure, greatly increasing the risk of stroke.

Angina pectoris, a tightening or pain in the chest area, is caused by temporary blood deprivation in some part of the heart muscle. It is known to occur during periods of physical and emotional stress.

Headache. Excessive stress is a principal cause of both tension headaches and migraines, but for different reasons. Tension headaches are the result of muscular tension in the scalp and neck. Muscle contraction is a common response to stress. The condition tends to be self-aggravating because the muscles may respond to the pain by tightening further.

Migraines are caused by a dilation of blood vessels in the head and neck. The pain can be excruciating and incapacitating. Curiously, migraines tend to come not during, but after the stress has subsided. Dr. Harold Wolff has observed that migraines are common on Sundays, when the contrast between the high stress of the week and the relaxation of the day of rest is greater.

Backache. Many of us have weak back muscles as a direct result of the sedentary life-style that comes with a desk job. Add to that the tightening of these muscles as a result of stress and you've got a backache. While stress is a common factor here, chronic back pain should not be subject to a spot diagnosis. There may be some structural damage. Get thee to a physician.

Ulcers. The relationship between stress and ulcers is part of American folk-lore. The expression "It's giving me an ulcer" is tantamount to saying that something is causing aggravation.

There is wisdom in this assertion. Constant stress prevents the gastrointestinal system from returning to a dormant stage and thereby in-creases the acidity in the stomach and intestine. A single, ultra-high-stress event occasionally results in bleeding in a matter of hours.

According to Dr. I. Mendeloff, "It's what's eating you rather than what you're eating"* that causes ulcers.

Diabetes. It appears that diabetes is to a large extent genetically deter-mined. But many people with the genetic predetermination never develop the disease. Apparently, environmental considerations and the way the body reacts to stress determine whether the disease remains latent or sur-faces. There is no question that high levels of stress can make a diabetic's condition worse.

Cancer. Yes, even cancer appears to have some connection with stress—at least in theory. The reasoning is that stress lowers our resistance to disease by weakening our immune system. Perhaps, say some researchers, the stress-weakened immune system is unable to neutralize malignant cells before they establish themselves in the body.

Other diseases. Many specialists believe that intense stress can bring on allergy attacks in those who suffer from them and can aggravate existing symptoms. Stress has also been linked with arthritis and sexual dysfunction.

---

*From Kenneth Lamott, *Escape from Stress* (New York: Berkeley Medallion, 1975).

Selye's tips on stress reduction

Because we have such a highly developed nervous system, we are quite vulnerable to psychological insults from others. From a lifetime of research and practical experience, Selye offers several tips (paraphrased here) for dealing with these insults:

1. Don't waste your time trying to befriend those who don't want to be recipients of your love and friendship.

2. Don't be a perfectionist; strive to do something that is within your capabilities.

3. Don't underestimate the genuine pleasure that can come from the simple things of life.

4. Carefully assess each situation to see whether a syntoxic or catatoxic response will serve you best. Only fight for that which is really worth it.

5. Concentrate on the pleasant side of life and on the activities which can improve your lot. As the old German proverb says, "Imitate the sundial's ways; count only the pleasant days."

6. When you do experience a setback or defeat, reestablish your self-confidence by remembering all your past accomplishments.

7. Don't procrastinate in tackling the unpleasant yet necessary tasks you have to do. Get them over with quickly.

8. Realize that people are unequal in many ways at birth. All people should have access to equal opportunities, and their progress should be evaluated on the basis of their performance. Leaders are leaders only as long as they have the respect and loyalty of their followers.

9. Live in such a way as to earn your neighbor's love, and your life will be a happy one. Selye believes that this adapted version of the Golden Rule (love your neighbor as yourself) is more in line with the way humans really are, i.e., egotistical. He's not against the Golden Rule; he just believes that almost no one can love his neighbor as much as he loves himself. So for him the important thing is to work on perfecting yourself so that you will have some usefulness in society.

Fig. 24. Dr. Hans Selye's advice on how to reduce stress

Reprinted, by permission of the publisher, from *Managing Stress: A Businessperson's Guide,* by Jere E. Yates, © 1979 by AMACOM, a division of American Management Associations (p. 113).

BURNOUT

This is the ultimate, when you've reached the breaking point. Industrial psychologists Jack Jones and Dennis Joy have identified three stages of burnout:

Confusion. A vague feeling that something is wrong; nonspecific anxiety; dull and/or boring days; minor physical problems, such as headache and nausea

Frustration. An increase in drug or alcohol abuse; more trouble with co-workers; feelings of isolation and powerlessness; frequent talk about negative attitude; resentment and cynicism about life in general.

Despair. Extreme feelings of inadequacy; short-temper; some are openly hostile, others retreat to apathy, as if they "don't give a damn."

COMMON SENSE AND COMMON MYTHS

The concept of stress has been used as a means to sell products and programs that are either ineffective or unnecessary; it's become a tagline, like bad breath or ring around the collar.

The findings are conclusive. Stress can kill you. But everyone is different, and not everyone responds to potential stress situations in the same way.

For one thing, stressors are difficult to identify and quantify. Recent research somewhat discredits the Social Readjustment Rating Scale (see pp. 172–73), by showing that the major life events don't stress people as much as those annoying little moments that occur frequently in everyday life like waiting on a line or finding a fly in your soup.

As far as personality types are concerned, it has proven difficult to classify these types as more or less stress-prone. One high-strung Type A personality may thrive on a hectic pace, while it may prove dangerous for another. It appears that in many cases, the overall effect of stress is to make you unhealthy. And being unhealthy or living in an unhealthy way is what kills you. So if you guard your life-style, eating right, getting enough sleep and exercising regularly, you will be doing a great deal to cope with stress all by yourself.

On the other hand, the mental and physical wear-and-tear of stress can create problems for an otherwise healthy individual. If you are taking good care of yourself, and still feel the anxieties and pressures taking their toll, you should consider a stress reduction program.

Compensation In spite of Madison Avenue's attempts to trivialize stress, using it to sell vitamins and cassette tapes, medicine has acknowledged the problem as anything but trivial. And increasingly, employees have been winning the battle to have insurance companies pay medical costs and workers' compensation in cases of job-related stress. This is a ripe area for abuse, and claim-happy workers could trigger a backlash. But the company and its insurers certainly realize that it makes more sense to cover the cost of treating stress than treating a heart attack. So if you are bothered by stress, seek help. At least go for a consultation. There are many stress management and reduction programs that produce solid benefits. If you treat stress symptoms as a sign of weakness and cover them up, you could be doing yourself and your company a grave injustice.

STRESS REDUCTION
AND RELAXATION TECHNIQUES

Wherever there is a problem, there are people ready to make money by offering solutions. In the stress-control business, the techniques offered as solutions usually involve some form of physical or mental relaxation. What follows is a cataloging of the most popular and successful approaches to relaxation. However, before we begin I'd like to point out that you already know some of the most effective methods of stress reduction: exercise, good nutrition, good living habits, effective management of time and work load.

THE TRANSCENDENTAL
MEDITATION PROGRAM™

The TM Program™ reduces stress by triggering a state of very deep rest during which the body seeks to normalize, or to correct any negative effects of stress. Practitioners report feeling relaxed, yet alert after a typical session. Scores of studies of TM technique done at many independent research facilities have monitored physiological changes and verified the unique state of rest that the Transcendental Meditation Program engenders. Other studies confirm the generally positive effects that regular practice of the TM Program has on the body, mind, and behavior.

Although it is difficult to determine exactly what benefits you will derive from the regular practice of the TM Program, it does appear safe to say that the technique is good for you. And, despite the claims of detractors, there appears to be no conclusive evidence that there is any other mental technique quite like TM, in terms of either the physical and mental state it elicits, or the benefits that result.

In addition to the physiological studies, which indicate a reduction in oxygen consumption, cardiac output, and other signs of deep rest, several studies have been done on the TM Program in the business environment.

Organizational psychologist Dr. David Frew studied the effects of the TM Program on 500 male and female workers. His findings:

- Job satisfaction increased.
- Performance improved.
- There was an improvement in relationships with co-workers and supervisors.
- There was less of a desire to leave the company.

A pilot study done at a General Motors plant in Fremont, California, was even more dramatic:*

Those practicing the TM Program filled out questionnaires after completing the program. They claimed that they:

- required less sleep: 37%
- fell asleep faster: 50%
- drank less hard liquor: 37%
- drank less beer and wine: 23%
- eliminated or reduced the use of tobacco: 55% of the smokers in the study
- used less aspirin: 20%
- drank less coffee: 20%
- felt more confident: 53%
- felt improved emotional stability: 60%
- noticed improvement in organizing ability: 53%

Many enthusiastic executives have gone a step further and made TM instruction available to interested employees. In some cases the courses are conducted on company premises. Overwhelmingly, the results have been positive.

It should be noted, however, that the TM Program is a holistic method of self-development, affecting all aspects of life. Reduction of stress is only a small part of the potential benefits.

Although several unauthorized "how-to" books have appeared in an attempt to capitalize on the popularity of the TM program, there is really only one way to learn—from a trained instructor. There are TM Program centers in every major city where you can take the course.

For more information on the Transcendental Meditation Program, check your local phone directory under "International Meditation Society" or "TM," or contact:

International Meditation Society
World Plan Executive Council
17310 Sunset Boulevard
Pacific Palisades, California 90272

---

*From *TM and Business* by Jay B. Marcus, pp. 164–166, Copyright © 1978 by Jay B. Marcus. Used with permission of McGraw-Hill Book Company.

SUGGESTED READING

TM and Business by J. B. Marcus (New York: McGraw-Hill, 1978)
Management of Stress: Using TM at Work by David R. Frew (Chicago: Nelson-Hall, 1977)
The TM Program: The Way to Fulfillment, by Philip Goldberg (New York: Holt, Rinehart & Winston, 1976)
TM: Discovering Inner Energy and Overcoming Stress, by Harold Bloomfield, Michael Cain, Dennis Jaffe, with Robert Kory (New York: Delacorte Press, 1975)

BIOFEEDBACK

In recent years investigators have demonstrated that we can exert some control over so-called involuntary body functions through the use of an electronic "feedback system." The feedback system allows us to monitor and manipulate body mechanisms once thought to be beyond our voluntary control. One function commonly manipulated is circulation: People have been enabled through conscious effort to lower blood pressure and increase the blood flow to different parts of the body. That's why biofeedback has been effective in relieving certain types of headache pain. In terms of its usefulness as a stress-control method, the results have been mixed.

Essentially, patients are trained to relax by manipulating certain physiological functions. The biofeedback device doesn't do anything but monitor a bodily change, keeping you aware of your progress. If all goes as planned, you eventually are able to associate specific subjective feelings with bodily changes. Eventually you develop the ability to elicit certain responses at will.

Most biofeedback training involves hooking up to a machine that monitors a bodily change associated with relaxation. The most common approaches involve monitoring GSR (skin's resistance to electric current, an indication of perspiration), skin temperature, EEG (brain waves), or EMG (muscle tension). All of these are good indications of the degree of relaxation or tension in the body. And it appears that, to a degree, increase in GSR, increase in skin temperature in extremities, reduction in muscle tension, and the presence of alpha brain waves are all associated with relaxation.* The machine signals you when you have achieved a given objective. Some experts claim that after a while, the feedback machine is no longer necessary.

Does it work? Sometimes, for some people. Feedback involves learning, and where there is learning, variances in native ability will be reflected in results. In order for biofeedback to work, conditions must be optimal: You must thoroughly understand what you are trying to accomplish, and you must be certain that the malady you are trying to alleviate bears some

---

*However, other approaches, most notably the technique used in TM, bring about such changes in concert and without focused effort.

relationship to the function you wish to control. For example, a machine that monitors muscle tension will do little for you if you are suffering from migraines or a cerebrovascular condition, neither of which causally involves the muscles.

You must be on guard against artifacts—false signals generated by "noise" in the feedback system. For example, gritting the teeth or assuming certain facial expressions will often produce "desirable" brain wave patterns. If care is not taken, you could wind up training yourself to grit your teeth.

The best way to get into biofeedback is through a reputable clinic where you will be under the care of trained specialists who use reliable equipment. Always begin with a visit to your doctor. And do not rush out and buy a commercial biofeedback machine without making sure that it is reliable and the proper machine for you.

SELF-HYPNOSIS AND AUTOSUGGESTION

Hypnosis is a trancelike state that results from focusing the attention on a set of suggestions and being receptive to them. We've all seen the more theatrical versions in nightclubs or on television. But a quieter, simpler form can be self-administered. Usually this involves being trained by an expert.

The hypnotic state can produce a feeling of calm. But the rest the body receives is no deeper than that of sitting quietly in a chair. In some cases, breathing becomes shallower. Many people find self-hypnosis relaxing and refreshing. But not everyone can learn it.

A variation, in which we "suggest" to ourselves certain attitudes or behavior changes, is called *autosuggestion.* This technique is often used to facilitate the breaking of habits, such as overeating and smoking. But conventional hypnosis, administered by a hypnotist, is more effective than autosuggestion in controlling habits.

PROGRESSIVE RELAXATION

In some respects, Progressive Relaxation is the granddaddy of biofeedback. In 1929 Edmund Jacobson published this technique, which is based on a very simple theory: Emotional and inner tension manifests itself in muscular tension; by becoming aware of the nature and location of that tension and then relaxing the tensed muscles, we can produce a state of overall relaxation and thus a reduction of tension in the mind as well as the body. Progressive relaxation is a set of sequential physical and awareness exercises to achieve this state.

Since its introduction, many other specialists have modified the basic technique or developed their own versions. But Jacobson's basic approach is still around—and it does work to undo at least some of the effects of stress. You need a good half hour in a quiet place where you can lie down. And while the feeling of relaxation is subjectively quite satisfying, I have found no strongly persuasive evidence that Jacobson's technique is effective in fighting chronic deep-rooted stress.

A good summary of the Progressive Relaxation method appears on pages 204–206 of *Executive Health,* by Philip Goldberg (New York: McGraw-Hill, 1978).

AUTOGENIC TRAINING

This sequence of exercises designed to induce deep relaxation was developed by German psychiatrist Johannes H. Schultz. This technique draws from self-hypnosis, autosuggestion, Jacobson's Progressive Relaxation, and yogic breathing exercises. In many cases it does produce some relaxation. But, as with the Jacobson technique, the scope of its effectiveness is problematic.

It's best to learn Autogenic Training from a knowledgeable psychiatrist or psychologist. But Jere Yates's book *Managing Stress* (New York: AMACOM, 1979) offers a reasonably good do-it-yourself summary.

BREATHING DEEPLY

Most of us breathe in a shallow manner, taking short breaths and never actually filling the lungs with fresh air or emptying them entirely of old air. Breathing deeply from the diaphragm, filling the lungs, will reduce tension and fatigue.

Believe it or not, several books have been written about breathing. *Breathplay* by fitness expert Ian Jackson (Garden City: Doubleday, 1986) provides exercises and "games" to help you use your lungs to your best advantage.

MASSAGE

Massages can be very relaxing and beneficial. If you are seeking a professional massage, make sure the masseur or masseuse is licensed. One who is not properly trained can cause injury.

Rubdowns are generally less effective than Swedish or Shiatsu massage. You can do a lot of good through self-massage. And if you are careful and follow instructions, a massage by a spouse or a friend can be quite effective.

STRETCHING

An imporant part of any exercise program, stretching also greatly encourages relaxation. The most comprehensive and clearly illustrated book on stretching techniques is *Stretching,* by Bob Anderson (Bolinas, CA: Shelter Publications, 1980).

YOGA

Literally, this term means union, and it applies to many systems of mental, physical, and spiritual development. Hatha yoga, the form of yoga most commonly practiced in the West, employs, among other techniques, a series of asanas (poses, or postures) and breathing exercises to achieve a state of physical and mental well-being and an expansion of awareness.

Hatha yoga practiced health-spa style is simply a set of stretching exercises used out of context. They may help you loosen up, but this approach misses the ultimate aim of hatha yoga—enlightenment. And in order for hatha yoga to have any real effect on stress, it must be practiced diligently, with proper sequencing. The discipline is time-consuming and requires the attention of a good teacher; in general, such teachers are few and far between.

For a general, practical manual on Stress, you might get a copy of *Personal Strategies for Managing Stress* by Maya Ollson (New York: American Management Association Extension Institute, 1984). Billed as a self-study course, it could easily be described as a workbook manual on stress, because there are lots of tables, charts and quizzes which will allow you to get a very personalized, if simplistic, view of the stresses in your life and how you are dealing with them. At $94.95, the price is steep, but you do mail in an exam of sorts for evaluation, and receive two Continuing Education Units (CEUs—see Chapter 19).

12

USE IT OR LOSE IT: EXERCISE FOR EXECUTIVES

Being in shape is, of course, a question of life-style. It involves stress control, proper nutrition, and sufficient rest, as well as exercise. But, increasingly, researchers are finding that exercise may be the most important aspect of health maintenance. The effects of regular exercise seem to spill over into other phases of life: Exercise has a profound impact on both weight control and stress control; and it builds self-confidence, an important component of good health.

The sad fact is that while many Americans spend a great deal of money on sports and exercise equipment, and a great deal of time talking about it, most of us are not in good condition. "Soft goods" make up 70 percent of sporting goods sales, *i.e.*, fashion items, sweatsuits and sneakers. A U.S. Public Health Service study found that 80–90 percent of all adults don't do enough vigorous exercise to maintain cardiovascular fitness. And according to the *Wall Street Journal* and NBC News poll taken in 1985, 34 percent of the men and 42 percent of the women surveyed don't exercise at all.

WHAT IS "IN-SHAPE"?

There are many different opinions and parameters. Apart from purely medical concerns, getting in shape is a highly personal matter, dependent on individual goals and needs. If your hobby is mountain climbing, you'll have to train harder than your friend the golfer. But, in general, there are certain minimum standards that must be applied if your exercise program is going to help keep you healthy.

In this sense, the executive—or, indeed, anyone who wants to use exercise effectively—has some things in common with the athlete. The exercise programs that prepare one for sports competition are often those that also lead to health, happiness, longevity, and better job performance; and the basic rules of training and diet apply equally to the executive and the athlete. Further, the primary goals of a soundly structured exercise program are the same for athlete and nonathlete. Each one of these goals should be served in your workouts:

Flexibility. Often neglected, this goal is a must. Even if you are fit in other ways, tightness in the muscles, ligaments, and joints will restrict your movement and make you more susceptible to strains and sprains.

Gaining flexibility is simple. Do stretching exercises before and after strenuous activity and on a regular basis (daily, if possible) as part of your fitness routine. Books for runners, tennis addicts, and even roller skaters usually include some recommended stretches, but most people I know skip over those parts. That's a mistake.

The goal of stretching is not the sort of flexibility required for contortionist tricks. Rather, we stretch to tone our muscles and connective tissue, and to relax our body and increase fluidity of movement. Nor is stretching meant to be painful. A stretching sensation is not the same thing as pain.

A do-it-yourself test of flexibility: Sit on the floor with your legs straight out in front of you. Touch your toes, holding the position for sixty seconds. Next, sit with your legs spread. Bend forward, placing your elbows on the floor between your legs, fists together. Bring your forehead to your fists; hold for sixty seconds. These two positions test the bare minimum in flexibility. If you have difficulty, you should be especially conscientious in your stretching.

Strength. Strength alone is not an important requirement for fitness. But a healthy body is usually a strong one: The muscles are firm and in good tone. In addition, it is important that opposing muscles be well-balanced. If one muscle is very well developed and an opposing muscle is very weak, it could produce instability in the body. Many executives have sufficient strength in their arms and chests, but weak lower-back and abdominal muscles.

One popular method of increasing strength is isotonic exercise. The muscles are pitted against a moving, steady resistance. This brings about a gradual increase in strength. Weights and exercise machines are often used.

Muscle mass. This is perhaps the least important aspect of fitness. Unless, of course, you are vain and want to hold your own at muscle beach or the company picnic. Don't underestimate the power of vanity. According to the director of one of the nation's largest executive health consulting firms, the principal motivation of businessmen to get in shape is vanity. "They aren't as afraid of a coronary as they are of looking bad as they grow older."

You build muscle mass through maximum effort—isometric exercise, in which the muscle works against an unmoving resistance. Weights and machines can be used to build mass.

Enlarged muscles are not necessarily strong. But they are heavy—heavier than fat. So if building muscle is your bag, don't be surprised to see your weight increase rather than decrease.

Endurance. The main event. Endurance depends upon the ability of the muscles to store and burn energy and the ability of the cardiovascular system to deliver large amounts of oxygen. In short, it comes down to how long you can last at a particular activity or sequence of activities.

In a larger sense, endurance is concerned with how long you can last at the activity we call life. Endurance training increases the body's ability to meet the physical and mental demands made on it each day. That is why endurance training is far and away the most important phase of any fitness program.

Endurance is primarily a function of the cardiovascular system (abbreviated CV from now on). CV fitness programs involve pushing the body well beyond its "normal" operating capacity, but still within the limits of health. The idea is to throw the body into high gear for a short time, which is something the typical American rarely does in day-to-day activity.

There are various viewpoints concerning just how hard you should push. They range from 80 percent of maximum attainable heart rate for 12 minutes every day, to 60 percent of maximum for 30 minutes three times a week. One plan calls for reaching a pulse rate of 130 beats per minute and keeping it there for five minutes every other day.

Exercise that brings about this effect is called *aerobic*, because it is designed to increase the maximum amount of oxygen that the body can process in a given time. Aerobic exercise does this by increasing the lungs' ability to suck in large amounts of air, expanding the heart's capacity to deliver large amounts of blood, and improving the vascular system's capability to deliver the increased blood volume to all parts of the body.

Increasing your aerobic capacity delivers an important by-product that can greatly reduce the risk of coronary accident. Regular aerobics actually results in the enlargement of the coronary arteries, which reduces the likelihood of blockage. There is evidence that in some cases, the body grows new vessels to supply the heart; these new vessels could provide an alternate in case of blockage. But such findings are far from conclusive.

Since one uses a great deal of energy during strenuous exercise, the fat concentration in the blood is lowered. So is blood pressure, in many cases, because of the enlargement of the vessels.

No one can say for certain how much protection aerobics provides against heart disease. But judging from studies done on athletes, there is little doubt that it strengthens the heart. The heart of a well-trained athlete is more muscular and therefore pumps the same amount of blood with 50 beats as the average Joe pumps in 75. That's a saving of 13 million beats a year! So the jock heart works less and rests more. All other things being equal (they never are, though), a heart that maintains this efficiency should last longer than the average.

WHAT DOES AEROBIC EXERCISE CONSIST OF? Anything that gets it up—your heart rate, that is. The most accessible aerobic exercise is running, but any vigorous exercise that moves your entire body will probably do the job. Some popular methods are biking, swimming, rowing, cross-country skiing, and machines that simulate these activities. Any exercise shown to be aerobic (and safe) will do. The key is to pick something you like; otherwise, you'll have difficulty staying with it. And, because of a phenomenon known in sports-medicine circles as reversibility, if you don't do the exercise regularly, you won't accrue its benefits.

Reversibility. This is backsliding. The body is constantly adapting, and just as it adapts positively to the increase in physical demands made upon it, it will adapt negatively to inactivity. This negative adaptation takes place a lot faster than you get in shape. A layoff of just a few days produces noticeable backsliding. A few weeks will be serious.

What about weekend workouts? Great fun, but they don't work. Whatever endurance gains you make over the weekend, you give back if you are inactive during the week. Your skill at a particular activity may very well improve, but not your overall fitness.

Another important point: *Light exercise provides no real endurance benefit.* In most cases, it won't even cause you to lose any weight, unless you spend hours at it.

EXERCISE AND WEIGHT CONTROL

Most experts agree that exercise and weight control are the main ingredients of health maintenance. No matter what the diet program involves, the only way to lose weight is to burn more calories than you take in. And this is where exercise comes in.

Exercise burns calories. The amount of fuel you burn is a question of how much weight you move, and the distance you move it. How the weight is moved—what type of exercise you do—doesn't matter. For example, if you move your body 18 inches off the floor with each pushup, you burn the same number of calories as you do when you take an 18-inch stride during running. If it seems tougher to do a pushup than to take a running stride, that's because the pushup (using your arms to lift your body off the ground) is a tougher way to move weight than is running (using your legs—which are longer and more powerful).

If you are interested primarily in burning calories, choose the way that's fastest and/or most congenial for you. If you want endurance benefits too, you may have to modify your plan.

Exercise helps control appetite. Research indicates that the appetite control mechanisms of the body work better in active people. After adopting an exercise regimen, some people eat more than they did before; some eat less. But usually, the result of regular exercise is movement toward a healthier body weight and better eating habits. When active people eat more, it is usually a justifiable increase rather than a case of gluttony.

Exercise helps stabilize the blood-sugar levels. Fat is utilized, so there is less often a need to take sugar out of the bloodstream. Since a drop in blood sugar triggers hunger, it isn't surprising that active people are less hungry than inactive people.

Many people eat out of nervousness or anxiety. The relaxing effects of a swim or a jog can help them cut down on compulsive eating.

Exercise helps you lose the right kind of weight. When you diet, you lose muscle as well as fat. If you don't exercise, about 25 percent of the weight lost will be muscle. If you are active during dieting, you will tend to lose a lower percentage of muscle, because the body needs that tissue. Rather, the loss will come more from the stores of fat in your body. Many executives who convert rapidly from inactives to exercise freaks find that they lose not pounds, but inches. That is, they replace the lost fat with muscle, so there is minimal weight loss. But because what is left is solid, the appearance is trim and healthy.

If you choose not to exercise while dieting, you should do so when you go off the diet. When you start eating normally, you will gain back some weight, and unless you exercise, all of that weight will be fat. So the net result of the diet will be that you lost some fat and some muscle—and replaced it with 100 percent fat. You may weigh a few pounds less, but the percentage of body fat will have increased. Women must be especially careful, because their bodies normally contain a higher percentage of fat than men's bodies do, and that percentage increases with age.

EXERCISE AND MOOD

Undoubtedly, you've heard runners speak of the "natural high" they get. Well, there does appear to be a correlation between exercise and a more positive mood. There are various theories, none proven.

A matter of balance. The upshot of all this is that there is no easy or quick way to stay in shape; you just can't get by on a few minutes a week. However, exercising can be enjoyable. Pick a program you like and a structure that you can live with. A well-balanced workout should include some stretching, some endurance, and, if possible, some strength exercises.

Be sensible. Don't train too hard or too much. Such effort can actually reduce your training time by causing you to slack off early in the workout, or by making too many demands on your schedule, causing you to skip workouts. On the other hand, expect that once in a while a skipped workout and a rich meal will be unavoidable. If you can keep them to a minimum, there's no need to feel guilty.

TIPS FOR A PROPER WORKOUT

Establish your proper training pulse rate. The best way is to visit your physician, but your trainer can help, as can the following table (heart check guide). Take your pulse at the beginning, halfway through, and at the end of the workout. That's the bare minimum. If you're doing strenuous exercises that push the upper limit, monitor your pulse more frequently to make sure you don't overdo it. Eventually, you'll be more in touch with your body and you will know how hard you are working by how you feel.

Warm-up. I'm sure you've been told this many times before. It is very important to assist in avoiding injury. Concentrate on loosening and relaxing the muscles. Move your joints through their full range of motion. Do stretching exercises. An overall stretching is essential, with extra emphasis on the joints and muscles to be favored during the type of workout you perform.

Vigorous exercise should never be stopped abruptly. Cool down, gradually reducing your activity. Walk around or move about. Don't just stand around.

If you miss a few workouts, build back up to your previous level gradually. Don't resume again at your previous level. A layoff of several days is enough to cause you to backslide. Five weeks is all it takes to lose all the accumulated benefits of a regular exercise program.

WHERE TO WORK OUT: CHOOSING AND USING A HEALTH FACILITY

Health spas, health clubs, gyms, and fitness centers all purport get you in shape, help you lose weight, and mold a movie-star figure out of your once-flabby or once-skin-and-bones self, as the case may be. The simple fact is, all of these places are only facilities—that is, rooms with machines, pools, saunas, and whatever the latest wonder-gizmo happens to be. If any molding and shaping is done, it is done by the individual. It's his time. And his sweat. Which brings us to the first rule:

HEART CHECK GUIDE

Age	Heart's Upper Limit (Beats per Minute)	Exercise Heart Range — 70%-85% (Beats per Minute)	
		60-second Count	10-second Count
20 or younger	200	140–170	23–38
25	195	137–166	23–28
30	190	133–162	22–27
35	185	130–157	22–26
40	180	126–153	21–25
45	175	123–149	20–25
50	170	119–145	20–24
55	165	116–140	19–23
60	160	112–136	19–23
65 or older	155	109–132	18–22

Adjust your exercise pace to ensure that your pulse rate, as measured at your wrist or neck, stays within your 10-second exercise heart range for at least 20 consecutive minutes. Lower gives little cardiovascular benefit, higher puts you at risk for heart problems.

Fig. 25. Health Check Guide

Source: Taken from LifeCourse Fitness Trail, New England Memorial Hospital, Stoneham, MA

Choose a facility that is either near home or work. Make it as quick and easy as possible to get there. You are sure to go more often.

Check the hours. The club must be open on the days and times that suit your needs. Some clubs stay open very late to accommodate the singles crowd, but don't open for the day until 7:30 or 8:00. In many large cities, high-powered executives are at their desks by then, and need clubs that are operating at 6 a.m.

Examine the facilities first. A wide range of facilities call themselves health clubs or spas. Some have pools, tennis courts, saunas, and exercise rooms. Others are strictly for exercise. You've got to see for yourself, because the advertising can be misleading. A place may have one tennis court that is poorly kept and always in use, but the ad would have you believe that tennis is a principal feature. Ask yourself if the facility is the kind you want. Does it emphasize training and conditioning, or sports? Does it seem more like an "urban country club" than a serious fitness center? If it isn't what you want, look elsewhere.

Try before you buy. Work out at the club if you can before you join. It is really the only way to know how well the equipment is kept, and how long the lines are.

Visit the club during the hours when you will be using it. At one New York club, the early morning hours are uncrowded and dead-serious. Lunchtime is also no-nonsense, but more chatty as models and entertainment-types mingle with execs who can take two-hour lunches. By evening, the place is packed to the rafters, and every facility is operating at capacity.

Is the staff qualified? Many spas claim to have fitness experts, nutritionists, even physiotherapists who will custom-tailor a program to meet your needs. Experienced, well-trained professionals in these areas cost money to hire. You should be able to get an idea of how qualified such supposed experts really are by talking to them and watching them work. If the facility offers you a trial membership, make sure that you put the staff (as well as the machinery) through its paces.

Beware of joining a club while it's under construction. Artistic renderings are a great form of advertising. But the club may not turn out as promised. It may take longer than projected for completion, and the hours and set-up may not suit you. You are flying blind. Once, I joined a club that was a bit out of the way on the promise that the same firm was opening a sister club in my neighborhood, and that I would have automatic membership there. That was six years ago, and I have yet to see their "sister" club.

The club should have equipment and facilities that provide both strength and cardiovascular workouts, and an adequate warm-up and cool down area. Ideally, there should be several different systems so you don't get bored with the same type of exercise.

Who goes there? This should not be overlooked. A workout should be enjoyable, and it can be more so if you like the crowd. You may lose interest in working out at a club where you feel out of place.

Consider the total cost. Many clubs have one-time initiation fees in addition to annual fees. There are also extra charges, in some cases, for towels, swimming and court time. It pays to compare. Also examine the freeze policy. If you have to be out of town for a month, some clubs will allow you to freeze your membership, suspending it for that month, and tacking an extra month on the back.

A unique approach. When people are left to themselves, they rarely train properly. There is a tendency to work the parts of the body that are already in good condition. One avoids pain and looks vigorous in the gym, but the benefits are minimal.

As for machines, they are only as good as the people who operate them. And if you've got to wait in line to use a particular one, you might tend to skip it.

In the first edition of this book, I expressed the hope that the personal trainer concept would catch on. It has, in a very big way. Health club owners see it as a source of extra revenue as they skim a portion of the trainer fees off the top (in many cases). And entertainers and models have taken to the idea, making celebrities out of some personal trainers.

In general, I still believe a personal trainer can be of great help, especially when getting started on a fitness program or returning after a long layoff. But too often, it has become a kind of crutch; "a shrink with a towel and a stopwatch" encouraging you, flattering (or abusing) you, and interfering with your ability to know your own strengths, weaknesses and limits, and to develop a sense of discipline. *If you can't get through a workout without a trainer, get another trainer.* He or she hasn't done his job.

WORKING OUT WHERE YOU WORK

The American Association for Fitness in Business says that over 700 companies offer comprehensive employee fitness programs that include health profiles, exercise, sports, stress management, weight control and smoking withdrawal. Thousands of others offer less complete fitness programs. As you might guess, the programs seem to pay off in reduced absenteeism, increased loyalty and employee morale, better health (and thus lower insurance premiums), increased productivity and in some cases, tax benefits.

THE HOME GYM

Fitness experts are divided on the benefits of the home gym. On the plus side, you can outfit your own gym for little more than the cost of an annual membership in a good health spa. And you don't have the inconvenience of traveling to and from the club. You can control your own environment, which is important, since some health clubs take on the chatty, circuslike atmosphere of a singles bar, blunting your concentration and slowing your progress through the exercise circuit.

On the negative side, there is no supervision, and you can injure yourself if you don't know what you are doing. Even if you're a pro, an intense workout and the resulting high can affect your judgment, and there might be nobody around to restrain you as you push beyond your limits. For those who need motivation, working out with others helps you toe the line. At home, with nobody watching, its easier to slough off.

Unless you have unlimited funds, you will buy one or several exercise machines, and you will have to live with them. You might tire of them after a few months. At a good health club, if you get bored with an exercise bike, you can switch to the cross-country ski machine, rowing machine, stair climber or aerobics classes.

Pros and cons notwithstanding, home gyms are a rapidly growing business. Equipment sales have already exceeded 1 billion dollars. Bicycles are the most popular piece of equipment, followed by rowing machines.

13
A LEAN COURSE
IN NUTRITION

According to a 1978 survey conducted by ABC News and Louis Harris, eating is the number-one leisure activity of American men and women. We do so much of it, it is amazing that we aren't better at it. And since we're among the best-fed people in the world, good nutrition should be . . . er, a piece of cake.

If you don't maintain a well-balanced diet and good eating habits, sooner or later you will do yourself a lot of damage. Here's what you need to know.

CARBOHYDRATES

These are sugars, starches, and cellulose. Carbohydrates are the chief source of energy, providing the body with fast, cheap fuel. They also help us utilize fat and protein. Snacks high in carbohydrates are good before exercise or other demanding activity, because they are quick energy. The trouble is, many of us tend to include too much carbohydrate in our diet, thus crowding out other important foods. Diets high in carbohydrates tend to be low in vitamins and minerals mostly because they include large amounts of refined foods such as white flour and white sugar.

Once out of favor as a source of relatively empty calories, carbohydrates are now in vogue because they have been found to be an important source of energy in strenuous exercise. A form of pre-exercise diet called "carbohydrate loading" is popular among marathon runners who dine on pasta the night before, and body builders.

PROTEINS

The importance of protein is overrated. By that I mean that since the average American eats twice the protein required, there is little reason to worry about not getting enough. Next to water, protein is the most plentiful substance in the body.

Protein is the major building material of muscles, skin, hair, and internal organs. The body requires about twenty-two amino acids to synthesize protein, and it can make fourteen all by itself. The remaining eight, which must come from the diet, are called "essential amino acids" (looks great on food labels). Foods that contain all eight are called "complete proteins."

Most meat and dairy products are complete proteins. Vegetables and fruit are incomplete.

To clear up a few common misconceptions: Protein needs don't increase with activity—even an athlete needs no more when competing than he does at rest. As an energy food, protein is rather inefficient. Its energy yield is lower than that of both fats and carbohydrates, and it costs more.

Protein-rich animal products also contain lots of fat, so it is wise not to derive all your protein from them. Eat fresh fruits and vegetables, grains, and beans.

FATS

Ounce for ounce, fats furnish more energy than any other major class of food provides. They also serve to carry the fat-soluble vitamins, help maintain body temperature, cushion internal organs, and round out the body contours.

Fats are made up of fatty acids, of which there are two types—saturated and unsaturated. Saturated fats are solid at room temperature and come from animal sources. Unsaturated fats are usually liquid at room temperature and are derived from grains, vegetables, nuts, and seeds. Sometimes they are hardened by a process known as hydrogenation.

Unsaturated fat has become popular in the forms of margarine and cooking oils, because it is cholesterol-free or low in cholesterol. (More about cholesterol later.)

Because of the high caloric content of fats, eating excessive amounts of them will lead to obesity. They can cause poor digestion by slowing it abnormally.

VITAMINS

Vitamins have no energy value, and they are not used in the composition of bodily structures. But without them, the body couldn't convert food into energy or make tissue. Vitamins are vital constituents of enzymes, which regulate almost all bodily biochemical reactions. Vitamins are derived from animal products, fruits, and vegetables; and the human body can synthesize only a few.

The importance of vitamins is one of the most hotly contested topics in nutritional science. What is at issue is not whether we need them or not, but the dosages required. Recommended Dietary Allowances (RDAs) have been established by the National Research Council, and these standards are undoubtedly safe levels, designed to meet the vitamin needs of the "typical American." The trouble is that the "typical American" exists only in statistics. Climatic conditions, amounts of physical activity, eating habits, and the types of food eaten all have an effect on nutritional requirements. And, recently, research has demonstrated that stress can increase vitamin needs.

The fact is, very little is known about vitamins and the proper amounts needed. Most doctors know very little about the subject. In medical school, only minimal time is devoted to nutrition.

Use the RDA figures as a guide, but be sensitive to signals from your body that your diet might be lacking in some way. Excessive fatigue, anxiety, depression, or chronic aches and pains are common signs of vitamin insufficiency. If you can't identify the nature of the problem yourself (see Fig. 26, at the end of this chapter), then it might be wise to consult a nutritionist. Certain chemical analyses performed on blood, urine, and hair have proved helpful in nutritional analysis.

Unfortunately, taking vitamin supplements can be as dangerous as suffering a deficiency, because excessive amounts can be harmful. Some vitamins are actually toxic at high levels, while an excess of others is simply excreted in the urine, rather than stored. And there is no conclusive evidence that vitamin supplements improve performance, strength, or endurance, increase energy, or prevent colds or injury.

Another important point: It's not what you eat that matters most, but what your *assimilate*. Even a vitamin-rich diet can turn out to be deficient if you're a heavy smoker or a heavy user of laxatives or aspirin—substances known to interfere with vitamin absorption.

There are a great many athletes and executives that swear that vitamin supplements have done remarkable things for them. If you feel they are helpful to you, then go right ahead in spite of the smirks of your doctor. Just make certain that you are aware of the maximum safe dosages, the potential side effects, the best time to take the vitamins, and the adjustments you must make in your diet. And try to establish beyond a reasonable doubt that it is the vitamin program that deserves the credit for your improved health, not another positive step, such as an exercise or a diet regimen, that you may have taken around the same time.

There are at least twenty known vitamins, but, lately, people have become the most concerned and excited about:

VITAMIN C   Ascorbic acid is a water-soluble vitamin most commonly found in citrus fruit and fresh vegetables. We've known for years of its importance in maintaining the health of connective tissue and its role in promoting healing.

Any amount of Vitamin C that you can't use immediately passes out of the body within a few hours after you've swallowed it; the excess is eliminated in the urine and perspiration. The controversy over vitamin C concerns the minimum dosage, with estimates ranging from the 45 milligrams RDA, to the 2,300-9,000-milligram range recommended by Linus Pauling.

Another aspect of the controversy focuses on the benefits. Recently, claims have been made that megadosages of C can prevent or cure the common cold, treat drug addiction, fight common viral diseases, or even cure cancer. Once again, there is no conclusive evidence supporting any one of these claims, but no shortage of people willing to step forward and testify to their validity as a result of personal experience.

The most common side effect of vitamin C overdose is diarrhea. But since we pointed out the proposed-but-not-fully-substantiated benefits of the vitamin, we'll do the same for possible negative side effects. Massive doses of C have been linked to kidney stones, decreased fertility, liver damage, miscarriage, bone fractures, destruction of vitamin B_{12}, and iron poisoning. And some studies have revealed the possibility of a vitamin C "drug dependence": There is a tendency for those who get lots of vitamin C to get scurvy more quickly, when deprived of the vitamin, than those who normally got a lot less C. There is little doubt that when vitamin C is taken with a nitrate source it will inhibit the conversion of that source into nitrosamines which can be carcinogenic. If there is a direct relationship between cancer and nitrosamines, vitamin C could well be useful as a cancer preventative.

VITAMIN E   This fat-soluble vitamin appears to have several important functions. Very little is known about vitamin E and the proper dosages of it. Most of the claims made concerning vitamin E therapy are still unsubstantiated.

Vitamin E burst into the American consciousness because of its reputed role in sexual potency. Can vitamin E do anything for your sex life? Probably not. But a serious deficiency of E could possibly result in problems in the reproductive organs. Such deficiencies are rare.

Vitamin E supplements could be toxic. Almost as bad, they could be a waste of money.

VITAMIN B_{12} Deficiency of this vitamin can be quite serious, both physically and mentally. The earliest and most common symptoms are fatigue and weakness.

Vitamin B_{12} deficiency is rare. But since the substance is found almost exclusively in animal protein, pure vegetarians are susceptible to deficiency; those who shy away from animal products may require a supplement. If you eat dairy products, meat, fish, or eggs, you are probably getting all you need.

There is virtually no scientific evidence that large amounts of B_{12} will have any value to someone who is getting enough. But there are a great many people who are hooked on B_{12} injections and make all sorts of claims as to their benefits, especially as an energizer. Since no cases of B_{12} toxicity have been reported, I suppose there's nothing wrong with the shots if you feel that they help you. But I have observed that most people who use them are people who don't eat properly, or don't get enough rest and exercise. They could be suffering from a deficiency that a glass of milk could solve just as easily. But then again, there are a few pro athletes who sing the praises of B_{12}.

MINERALS

The body uses about seventeen minerals in making tissues and regulating biological functions. Even though the body requires only trace amounts, they are vitally important, and often overlooked. The minerals are interrelated in their action, and a shortage of one can seriously inhibit the effectiveness of the others.

The most important minerals are calcium, potassium, sodium, and magnesium. These minerals interact in the body, and often a deficiency in one will occur in tandem with a deficiency in another.

Calcium is the most abundant mineral in the body. A great deal of it is stored in the bones, and the average diet is rich in calcium. So our supplementary requirements are minimal, with the exception of growing children and pregnant or lactating women.

There is some belief that we lose calcium when we exercise. This is untrue.

The treatment of certain diseases with calcium has been attempted, without conclusive results. However, calcium does appear to function well in some people as a natural tranquilizer or sleep-inducer. Excessive amounts of calcium or vitamin D can lead to hypercalcemia, which is the calcification of bones and tissue. Milk, cheese, and other dairy products are the primary sources of calcium. Dark green vegetables, dried legumes, and sardines also contain calcium.

Potassium serves many important functions in the body, including the regulation of activity in the circulatory and nervous system. Potassium helps keep muscles from overheating during exercise. In the process, it is released in the blood and excreted in the urine. As a result, exercise can deplete potassium supplies. So can high intake of alcohol, coffee, and sugar.

Potassium is found in virtually all fruits and vegetables, in fish, eggs, seeds, and nuts.

Magnesium is intimately connected with calcium. Increasing the calcium levels in the body calls for an increase in magnesium, both to counterbalance the effects of potassium and to aid in its absorption. Magnesium has other important roles to play in metabolic activity. Low levels can result in muscle cramps and/or fatigue.

Nuts and green vegetables are excellent sources.

Sodium is a very important mineral, found primarily in the body fluids. It is contained in virtually all foods, especially salt. We get so much of it that the concern is over too much, never over too little. More on that in the section on salt.

The only people who use sodium supplements, in the form of salt tablets, are athletes who sweat a great deal. But this remedy has been shown to be unnecessary, as serious salt depletion rarely occurs outside of deserts.

WATER

Water is by far the most important food substance. It is the primary constituent of tissue, and it helps transport nutrients and waste products and helps control body temperature. You must make sure that you drink plenty of it. Fruits and vegetables are excellent sources of pure water.

With the recent popularity of bottled mineral water, debate has been raised over its value. Some drink it because of the good things (presumably minerals) it contains. Others drink it because of the bad things in tap water (chemicals, carcinogenic agents, bacteria). The jury is still out.

THE BAD BOYS OF NUTRITION

These are the foods that recently have been insulted, maligned, and, in many cases, shunned. It's no fault of theirs, really. Each of these substances is a healthy, wholesome, nutritious food. The problem lies, as usual, in our abuse of these foods and our ignorance concerning their proper use.

SUGAR

Well, it definitely promotes tooth decay. But it has taken the rap for more. The sugar we refer to is white sugar, a refined form that is pure carbohydrate and contains no vitamins or minerals. Some claim that it has no nutritional value. That is not quite fair. It is an excellent source of quick energy, and anyone who has experienced a "sugar rush" knows that in the right circumstances, the lift is welcomed.

We eat a lot of sugar, about a hundred pounds a year. You think you are cutting down by staying away from table sugar? Nice try, but most sugar enters our body through many other foods that we eat. White sugar is probably the most common food additive, next to salt. Besides the obvious, like cake, ice cream, cookies, and candy, white sugar is added to foods like ketchup, canned fruits, and soups. And foods such as spaghetti, white bread, and pancake mixes contain refined starches that quickly turn to sugar once digested.

A large intake of sugar appears to be a negative factor in health. Some nutritionists feel that sugar depletes the body of vitamins, minerals, and other nutrients by upsetting the delicate nutritional balances: Bombarding the body with about two pounds of sugar a week is sort of a nutritional bull-in-the-china-shop.

Many medical experts are skeptical about the extent of the damage caused by high-sugar diets. They maintain that we get so much more than we need in the way of nutrients, that even if sugar does have this depletion effect (and they don't all agree that it does), it causes little if any harm.

Others are not sure. While they eschew the prohibition-era rhetoric of the anti-sugar movement, they have found certain links between sugar intake and several degenerative diseases. The most alarming are a connection with heart disease and the possibility that sugar elevates serum cholesterol levels. Sugar, of course, is bad for people suffering from diabetes and a disease called reactive hypoglycemia (low blood sugar brought on as a reaction to sugar intake), but there is little evidence to suggest that excessive sugar intake causes these diseases.

From what I've been able to discover, it certainly can't hurt to cut down on sugar. If you are average in your sugar intake and then cut your consumption in half, you will still be swallowing fifty pounds per year. That is not what I call depriving yourself of sweets. You should cut out table sugar, or at least cut down. Read food labels, and if sugar is one of the first ingredients mentioned (ingredients are listed in order of amount), try to avoid that food. Rely on foods containing more complex carbohydrates, such as bananas, beans, vegetables, and whole grains. This is especially important, because many people begin to crave sugar when they cut down on it. Satisfy your craving with a carbohydrate source other than refined sugar or starches.

Sugar provides energy. Period. Chances are, you eat plenty of energy foods in the forms of fats and complex carbohydrates; you just don't need that much sugar. It's just that you have developed a fondness for its sweet taste. Cut down. You'll probably feel better, and you just might save some money on dental bills.

SALT

Since we sprinkle salt on food, we tend to overlook it as a major constituent of our diet. Foods like nuts, canned soups, and cold meats, and snack foods like chips and popcorn are loaded with the stuff. Fact: We don't need nearly as much salt as we consume. The average American consumes sixty times the minimum daily requirement.

There is a lot of evidence that high-sodium diets (a major ingredient of salt) do harm. Too much salt can contribute to the onset of hypertension, raise the body's potassium levels, cause blood clotting, and even interfere with the body's ability to *retain* salt.

Most people would do well to cut down on salt. Some dishes might taste a bit bland at first, but the taste buds will adjust rapidly and you will begin to notice subtle flavors in foods that heretofore had been obscured by the presence of lots of salt.

CHOLESTEROL

Some years ago, heart specialists teamed up with certain food manufacturers to blacken the word *cholesterol* until it became synonymous with certain death. Cholesterol is a fat substance that the body uses to make hormones, nerve fiber, bile, and other substances and tissues. It is also a source of very high energy. It is important enough that our bodies are equipped to manufacture it. However, the more we eat, the less we make.

Cholesterol has been linked with heart disease. It travels through the bloodstream as part of substances called lipoproteins. Cholesterol is a major factor in the formation of plaque on the inside walls of blood vessels, which may lead to atherosclerosis, or hardening of the arteries, and eventually to heart attack or stroke.

In this regard, cholesterol is considered the primary dietary culprit in the onset of cardiovascular disease.

After years of debate, recent research results leave little doubt. High cholesterol diets are a major factor in the development of heart disease. A study polished this year in the *Journal of the American Medical Association* showed that certain drugs—when combined with diet modifications—can lower blood cholesterol levels. The implication is that the damage can at least be partially reversed.

Not everyone agrees. Some doctors claim that other findings show that the clogging of arteries by cholesterol cannot be reversed and further, that atherosclerosis is not simply due to dietary cholesterol.

Nevertheless, the evidence to date suggests that everyone should watch their cholesterol levels. Many experts believe that for every 1 percent you lower your blood cholesterol, you lower your chances of a heart attack by 2 percent.

In round numbers, every 100 mg of cholesterol we consume raises the blood levels by 5 mg. The risk of heart disease rises substantially when one's blood cholesterol exceeds 180 milligrams per deciliter. The average American has a level between 210 and 220 milligrams per deciliter, but according to a National Institutes of Health panel, adults over thirty should have serum cholesterol counts under 200. Over half of the population exceeds that amount.

What not to eat: Foods such as egg yolks, organ meats, butter and cheese, cream and those "greasy-spoon" foods often found in animal fats or saturated oil.

What to eat: Monounsaturated or polyunsaturated oils (i.e., most vegetable oils such as soybean and safflower, except palm and coconut).

Fruits, vegetables, and starches are good; among animal products, stick with white-meat chicken and turkey (no skin) and fish.

COMMON SENSE ABOUT NUTRITION

Don't skip breakfast. And eat a healthy one. There are many alternatives to the traditional bacon and eggs, from yogurt and fresh fruit to whole grain cereal.

Don't rely on vitamin supplements. First of all, most supplements are unnecessary and do little to improve health. Second, they are not a substitute for smart eating, and often people rely on them when not following a well-balanced diet.

Watch your snacks. Even if you eat well at your "three-squares," a coffee and donut binge can destroy all the benefits of a healthy diet. Many snack foods are loaded with fat, salt, caffeine and other questionable ingredients.

Treat lunch with respect. Don't skip lunch. Don't rush through. Try to take a short walk before and when you've finished. Don't eat lunch at your desk; give yourself a suitable atmosphere in which to digest it. Eat light and lean, avoiding alcohol, fried and greasy foods.

Don't use sugar as a pick-me-up. Get enough sleep. Eat well, and don't look for an energy boost from sugar. It'll only let you down harder.

If you drink caffeinated beverages, do so in moderation. The effects can last for up to 3½ hours. If you are having more than the equivalent of three cups per day, cut down. Don't forget to include tea and cola drinks, which also have caffeine.

Don't rush nutrition. Don't eat on the run. Don't eat in the car, while walking or driving, or attending to some demanding activity. When you eat, that should be your body's principal activity. Proper digestion requires a great deal of energy.

Don't eat at night. Or if you must, make it a light nourishing low-calorie snack like unadulterated fresh berries or popcorn without the butter.

In general, eat more fibers and starch. Eat less salt, sugar, alcohol and fat, especially cholesterol. And stay within the recommended weight range for your height, body type, and age.

diet analysis

Food Item	Measure	Weight g	Calories	Protein g	Fats g	Carbohy-drates g	Water g	Calcium mg	Iodine mg	Iron mg	Magne-sium mg	Phos-phorus mg	Potas-sium mg
Breakfast egg, fried.	1 med.	50	108	6.2	8.6	0.4	34.0	30.0	—	1.20	50	111.0	70
whole wheat toast	1 slice	19	55	2.4	0.6	11.0	5.6	22.0	—	0.50	18.0	52.0	62
honey	1 tbsp.	21	64	0.1	—	16.0	3.6	1.0	—	0.11	0.6	1.3	11
skim milk	1 cup	246	89	8.9	0.2	13.0	223.0	298.0	—	—	35.0	234.0	357
orange juice	1 med.	180	88	1.8	0.4	20.0	154.0	74.0	—	0.72	19.8	36.0	360
Sub total		516	404	19.4	9.8	60.4	420.2	425.0	—	2.53	78.4	434.3	860.0
Lunch													
Sub total													
Dinner													
Sub total													
Snacks													
Sub total													
Total													
RDA													
+ or −													

Sample

Fig. 26. Diet analysis chart

Enter the foods eaten at each meal, and use a nutrition table
to fill in the basic nutrition information for each food.
Then you can easily compute your total intake of the basic
dietary components and see where you are lacking.

208

Sodium mg	Copper mg	Vitamin A IU	(Thiamine) B₁ mg	(Riboflavin) B₂ mg	Vitamin B₆ mg	Vitamin B₁₂ mcg	Biotin mcg	Choline mg	Folic Acid mg	Inositol g	Niacin mg	Pantothenic Acid mg	Vitamin C mg	Vitamin D IU	Vitamin E mg	Vitamin K mg
169.0	0.03	71.0	0.05	0.15	—	—	—	—	—	—	0.10	—	O	27.0	—	—
119.0	—	—	0.04	0.02	—	—	—	—	0.010	0.01	0.60	—	—	—	—	—
1.1	0.04	O	—	0.01	0.004	O	—	—	0.001	—	0.06	0.04	0.21	—	—	—
118.0	0.01	998	0.10	0.44	0.100	1	—	—	—	—	.25	0.90	2.50	100.0	—	—
1.8	0.14	360	0.18	0.05	0.108	O	—	—	0.010	0.38	0.72	0.45	90.0	—	0.43	0.002
408.9	0.22	2,068	0.37	0.67	0.212	1	—	—	0.021	0.39	1.73	1.34	92.71	127.0	0.43	0.002

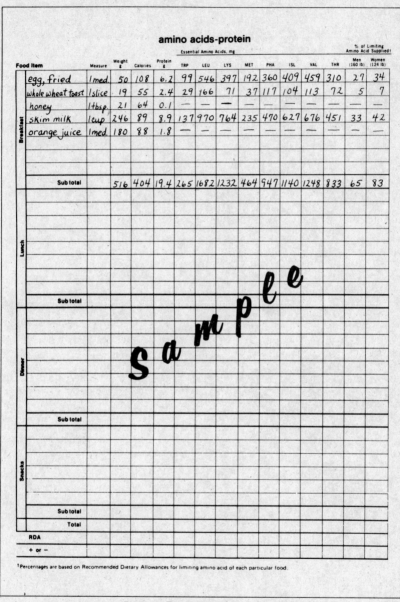

amino acids-protein

Food Item	Measure	Weight g	Calories	Protein g	Essential Amino Acids, mg								% of Limiting Amino Acid Supplied	
					TRP	LEU	LYS	MET	PHA	ISL	VAL	THR	Men (160 lb)	Women (124 lb)
Breakfast														
egg, fried	1 med.	50	108	6.2	99	546	397	192	360	409	459	310	27	34
whole wheat toast	1 slice	19	55	2.4	29	166	71	37	117	104	113	72	5	7
honey	1 tbsp.	21	64	0.1	—	—	—	—	—	—	—	—	—	—
skim milk	1 cup	246	89	8.9	137	970	764	235	470	627	676	451	33	42
orange juice	1 med.	180	88	1.8	—	—	—	—	—	—	—	—	—	—
Sub total		516	404	19.4	265	1682	1232	464	947	1140	1248	833	65	83
Lunch														
Sub total														
Dinner														
Sub total														
Snacks														
Sub total														
Total														
RDA														
+ or −														

†Percentages are based on Recommended Dietary Allowances for limiting amino acid of each particular food.

Fig. 27. Protein analysis chart
Use this chart as you would the diet analysis chart. In this
case, you are tracking your intake of essential amino acids.

From *Nutrition Almanac*, by Nutrition Search Inc., John
D. Kirschmann, Director, © 1979 by John D. Kirschmann.
Used with permission of McGraw-Hill Book Company.

14
THE PHYSIOLOGY OF JOB PERFORMANCE

In a sense, your job is no different from that of an astronaut or a professional athlete. Even if you are in excellent health, your performance will be affected by several external and internal factors that act directly on your nervous system and, consequently, affect your ability to think and act.

LIGHT

Sunlight is a nutrient; it is used by our bodies. Several experts have proposed that we aren't getting enough of it and our health is suffering as a result.

Artificial light is not a poor substitute; it is *no* substitute. "Cool white" fluorescent light is utterly unlike sunlight. Incandescent light, although it offers some benefits, cannot compare to sunlight.

Of the three, only sunlight contains the full light spectrum. There is some evidence that full-spectrum light influences endocrine activity in the body and stimulates the production of vitamin D (in a form superior to any form you can buy as a supplement, and therefore irreplaceable). The lack of sunlight may also retard our immune system, affecting our ability to fight off disease, including cancer.

What can you do? Well, if this makes sense to you and you want to get more sunlight, you can do so without burning yourself to a crisp on some beach. What you really want is natural daylight—you don't need bright sunlight. A fifteen-minute walk each day will help. And you can install a special "full-spectrum" fluorescent bulb in your work areas. Several companies make them. Full-spectrum light affects your brain most directly through your eyes. But the glass in most eyeglass lenses, including contacts, distorts the solar spectrum. You can get full-spectrum lenses through your optometrist.

LIGHT ON THE JOB   Natural daylight is the most useful form of light for the workplace, but it is getting scarce. Artificial light produces more strain and fatigue. If you haven't a choice, make sure that the artificial light is diffused, rather than shining directly onto the page. Bounce it off walls and ceilings, or use good-quality reflectors. The result will be a more even light, with less glare. Avoid spotlights as a source of work light. They force the eyes to readjust constantly as they move from objects illuminated by the spot's beam to those outside it. However, spots are okay if used as part of a general illumination system or as attention getters.

LIGHT AND SLEEP   Recent research indicates that light plays an important role in the regulation of body rhythms. The mechanism appears to date back to the ancient hibernation of primitive mammalian species, which produce sleep-inducing chemicals in winter in response to shorter days. Some people are so sensitive that they get depressed in winter, and light therapy (spending some time each day in front of a full-spectrum light source) has been proven to be effective. For most of us, getting out in the morning light as soon as possible is a good idea, because it will keep your body's biological clock in phase with your wake-up time, and minimize any trouble you might have waking up, especially on cold winter days. If you don't want to venture outside, try turning on a full-spectrum light source for fifteen minutes or so when you wake up. It makes sense to consult a doctor or a sleep clinic before tampering with your body's internal rhythms.

SEATING COMFORT

Offices do not do nice things for the human body. In fact, years of office work eventually take their toll, probably hastening the onset of circulatory diseases and contributing to chronic lower-back problems.

Since you spend a great deal of time sitting, you should spend some time selecting the proper *chair:*

The seat should be high enough so that your lower legs rest comfortably at a right angle to the floor and your feet rest "flat footed." The thighs should then be horizontal, or approximately parallel to the floor.

The seat should not be so high that it puts pressure on your legs and thighs by "lifting" your legs off the ground and placing your thighs on an incline.

The seat should not be so low that your thighs are inclined and body weight is centered on your upper thighs. This is extremely tiring and bad for circulation.

You should sit upright with your back inclined *slightly* forward.

Your desk or table should not be so low as to cause slouching or so high that your arms seem jammed into your shoulders.

HEAT

According to Peter Russell, your brain works best at 65 °F (18 °C). A temperature of 68–70 ° is simply too warm for optimal brain functioning. Wear a sweater and heavier socks if you feel chilled.

CIGARETTE SMOKE

Even if you don't use tobacco, you may be one of millions of "second-hand smokers" due to the environment in which you live or work. In a smoke-filled room the nonsmoker is exposed to about 75.5 milliliters of carbon monoxide gas for each cigarette consumed. If you are sensitive to smoke, you could be running the risk of a health hazard. But even if you fail to notice any immediately adverse reactions, your performance could be affected.

Dr. Steven Thacker has noticed a decrease in attention span and an impairment of psychomotor abilities in people exposed to cigarette smoke. And since many find the smoke annoying, it can be a distraction and cause tension in the office.

Although it is not my intention to get into the controversy of smokers' rights versus nonsmokers' rights, it is worth noting that a resolution of the problem is a positive and significant step in terms of overall office performance. It should not be allowed to fester.

If you are a smoker, don't forget that some people have very strong feelings about cigarettes, and their perception of you will be affected if you light up. If a superior is annoyed by a smoke-filled room and you are sitting there with a lit cigarette, he will consider you the source of his annoyance. Some executives see smoking as a sign of weakness. For the sake of your career as well as your health, it pays to quit. But don't preach or boast or berate others. Being free of a bad habit is a plus; being obnoxious about it is not.

THE AMERICAN CANCER SOCIETY   sponsors clinics, usually run by ex-smokers. The methods used involve an awareness of the behavioral aspects of smoking—what leads us to light up. Gradual withdrawal is aided by a buddy system and by a regimen of such substitutions as chewing on coffee stirrers or gum and keeping the hands busy with rubber bands. The sessions are free.

SMOKENDERS is a private program involving weekly two-hour seminars for two months. The general idea is to motivate you to *want* to stop, and then to help you withdraw. The first five weeks are spent learning about your smoking habits. By the end of that time you have quit, and the remaining weeks are spent in coping with the pangs of withdrawal. SmokEnders claims a 92 percent success rate by the end of the course. A year later, 22 percent of the initially successful group will have gone back to smoking. About 12 percent of beginners never finish the course. Taking backsliders and dropouts into account, about 45 percent of those who begin the program end up ex-smokers.

Contact:
SmokEnders World
Phillipsburg, New Jersey 08865

HYPNOSIS This involves making unpleasant suggestions regarding smoking while the subject is under hypnosis.

BEHAVIOR MODIFICATION The act of smoking is punished by such methods as electric shock.

AVERSION THERAPY Ever smoke three cigarettes at once? Most people get very sick, and the traumatic experience is one you don't forget easily. Not for people who have weak hearts or who are in generally poor health.

ACUPUNCTURE Smoking is treated by acupuncture in many different ways. Some are intended to reduce tension and relieve stress, helping the smoker who lights up out of anxiety. Other methods involve inserting needles in certain areas to alleviate the effects of nicotine withdrawal or to suppress the desire to smoke.

Do all these methods work? Yes. But none of them work for everyone. Some people claim that one or two sessions of hypnotherapy or acupuncture did the job; others required two years. It is important that you investigate the clinic and/or therapist before placing yourself in their hands.

DRUGS

Drugs are a very serious problem among executives. The use of both marijuana and cocaine has increased markedly in recent years. But the real scare comes from the prescribed drugs. And of course, alcohol.

Alcohol is a drug. It also brings out the worst in other drugs. Since it impairs judgment and motor coordination, it lowers efficiency. Drinking at lunch puts you at a disadvantage. Even though a drink or two may relax you, it's better to find another way.

Taking more than two drinks a day can have a negative effect on health. (In this context, a drink equals two ounces of 80 proof liquor, six ounces of wine, or 16 ounces of beer.)

The Drug Abuse Warning Network (DAWN) has compiled a list of the ten most dangerous drugs. Some of them may surprise you:

- Valium
- alcohol in combination with other drugs
- heroin and other morphine derivatives
- aspirin
- flurazepam (tranquilizer)
- Darvon
- Librium
- Elavil
- phenobarbital
- secobarbital

NOISE

Excessive noise levels can be downright harmful; and insistent, irregular sounds can cause distraction and annoyance. You can learn to live with the hum of an air conditioner, but the sequence of buzzers, beeps, hums, and clicks generated by a copier can be annoying if it's very near your desk.

DESK FATIGUE

Doing desk work for prolonged periods can result in a syndrome that consists of mental fatigue, tired eyes, and tense muscles. Take frequent breaks to stretch, rest your eyes, and allow your mind to retreat, if only for five minutes at a time, from the task on which you were working.

"FAR-OUT" FACTORS: DO THEY AFFECT YOUR PERFORMANCE?

BIORHYTHMS

Scientists have known for years that many of our bodily functions operate in a cyclical, or at least rhythmic, fashion. There is ample evidence that bodily rhythms play an important role in the regulation of our physiology, and our understanding of that role is expanding every day. Alertness, sex drive, hunger, even proneness to stroke are all subject to a daily rhythm.

Unfortunately, they have been unable to get data reliable enough to allow us to predict or regulate our performance or bodily functions.

Recently, however, several self-styled experts have advanced the theory of "biorhythms." It is loosely based on the work of Wilhelm Fliess, who formulated a half-baked theory of biological rhythms in 1887. The concept was okay, but the formulas were simplistic and awkward. Fliess probably would have faded into obscurity faster than the Dave Clark Five had he not hung around with Dr. S. Freud. Fliess was a skilled surgeon who operated on Freud's nose and was among the first to use cocaine as an anesthetic. (I wonder what *that* does to biorhythms.)

The theory states that among our many cycles are three biorhythms—physical, emotional, and intellectual. These cycles follow rigid patterns from low to peak: The physical cycle lasts 23 days, the emotional, 28 days, and the intellectual, 33 days. Supposedly, they are triggered at birth. The critical days of each cycle are at the start, the middle, and the end. If all three cycles are at a low point on the same day, stay home and watch soap operas; you are in for a bad time. But if they all reach their peak on the same day, you are in top form; now is the hour to mount your takeover attempt of General Motors. Thus you predict your probable performance.

This theory of biorhythms has attracted a surprising number of adherents, considering there is no conclusive evidence that they function as charted. Lately, however, few seem to care that much about objective studies, or about whether evidence is conclusive or not. If there's a chance, say athletes, airline pilots, and even executives, it's worth a try.

Nevertheless, I call your attention to an article in the April 1978 issue of *Psychology Today*, in which Arthur M. Louis zapped the biorhythm theory but good. He pointed out that the biorhythms of one Reggie Jackson indicated that he would be a "bum," as we say in New York, during the 1977 World Series. Indeed, noted biorhythm expert Bernard Gittleson had gone on record saying that Reggie would find it "very tough to get a hit."

Close. Jackson, you will recall, batted .450 and set a Series record by hitting five home runs. Louis, however, anticipated the rebuttal that one isolated case does not a counter-theory make. So he analyzed 100 no-hit baseball games between 1934 and 1975 and 100 heavyweight title fights between 1899 and 1976. There was no significant correlation between the presumed biorhythms and individual performance.

More studies are being done—on injury patterns of railroad workers and drivers of automobiles, for example. I confess that while I wait for the results, I'll continue to regard biorhythms as bunk.

WEATHER

There is some evidence that the weather may affect your performance. And I don't mean that you might miss a day's work on account of snow.

ARE YOU "WEATHER SENSITIVE"? Many people have adverse reactions to excessive heat, precipitation, winds, high or low pressure fronts. Physicians and psychiatrists have observed a relationship between weather and:

- sleepless nights
- back pain
- upset stomach
- migraine
- depression
- loss of appetite
- irritability
- lack of judgment

Some estimates put the rate of weather sensitivity in its various forms at 33 percent of the population. There is not much you can do about it, except to be aware of the problem—and even that is difficult. There are so many other causes of the above-listed symptoms that it is almost impossible to tie them to the weather. The exception is when you change climates. If you live in Chicago and feel terrible in Miami on a winter trip, it could be that you are sensitive to heat and/or humidity. See how you feel when you return to Chicago—and note whether history repeats itself during any subsequent Miami trip.

If you are fairly certain you have a weather sensitivity, keep it in mind when you must select a location for a business meeting.

Most people are uncomfortable when the THI (temperature-humidity index) is over 73.

STORMY MONDAY   In 1960 *Reader's Digest* published an article on the possible effects of negatively charged oxygen ions in the air. Shortly afterward, GE and Emerson Electric started making ionizers for their air conditioners. The interest died down (GE and Emerson ceased production long ago), but the speculation did not.

The theory: Desert and mountain winds, thunder and lightning (electrical storms), and cigarette smoke are several of the conditions that give air a positive charge. Positive ions are said to be bad for you because they stimulate the thyroid to overproduce adrenaline and cause serotonin to be released in the brain. Serotonin, the theory states, is the real villain, because it causes the usual nonspecific stress symptoms: irritability, uneasiness, headache.

Ever notice how good you feel *after* a thunderstorm? Or in a mountain valley or by the seashore or a waterfall? The reason, believers say, is that these environments have an abundance of negative ions, which suppress the secretion of serotonin and clear viruses and bacteria from the air.

The cities are hotbeds of positively charged air, what with all the smoke, central heating (a big producer of positively charged air), pollution, and winds generated by "skyscraper canyons."

If you believe that there is something to this, get yourself an *ion counter* and/or a *negative ion generator.* Since the above claims have not been officially substantiated, negative-ion generators can be sold only as air cleaners. Indeed, they do take suspended particles out of the air (unfortunately, those particles can wind up on your walls).

Several mail order houses specializing in consumer electronics offer compact, efficient, inexpensive units.

You might want to spend some time in a negative-ion environment—they tend to be attractive places—and observe whether you feel better.

ALTITUDE   There is no doubt that altitude affects our performance. Some acclimate more quickly than others. Be careful not to exert yourself until you get used to the altitude.

POLLEN   Rain and ocean breezes tend to rid the environment of pollen. Forests are not good, because they trap the stuff.

SMOG   Not much you can do about it short of joining the Sierra Club. Listen to the radio for air-quality announcements. On "fair" or "poor" days, don't overexert yourself. When the conditions are more serious, stay indoors, limit activity, or get out of town!

THE ATMOSPHERE AND YOUR BODY

Extreme heat, cold, altitude, or any sudden change in the weather can affect your bones and joints, and your heart.

WAKING UP FRESH

Getting enough sleep is one thing. Awakening feeling fresh and clear is another. Many people have trouble getting out of bed, or wake up feeling drowsy and irritable, even though they do not suffer from insomnia.

Don't oversleep. Only one in ten needs more than nine hours of sleep, and most people need seven or eight. Even if you are up late the night before, sleeping-in can throw your biological clock out of whack.

Try to stick to a consistent sleep schedule, even on the weekends. If you stay out late on the weekends because you don't have to work the next day, you could be screwing up your week. By staying up into the night, and sleeping late in the morning, you will surely be resetting your body's clock in a way that makes little sense come Monday.

Don't use sleeping pills or alcohol. While they may be helpful in falling asleep, they can contribute to a groggy feeling in the morning, and in the case of some medications, forgetfulness.

Get your blood flowing. Morning exercise makes sense for some people. The increase in blood flow and body temperature can increase alertness and energy. Early morning workouts appear to be fine for healthy people, but a word of caution is justified. Research has shown that there is a greater risk of stroke and heart attack in early morning, so you might wish to check with your doctor.

Don't exercise before bedtime. Your body might well react by becoming recharged, as if it were earlier in the day. You want to wind down gradually as you approach your sleep time.

Meditate. Meditation morning and evening is an excellent way to restore a relaxed alert feeling to the mind and body. It is an excellent way to start the day, in preparation for the stresses and strains of daily life. In the pre-dinner hours, it can help prepare one for the evening's activity, and the added rest will help prevent "overtiredness," which leaves one wound up and jittery just when one should be getting drowsy. This writer recommends the Transcendental Meditation Program™ (see Chapter 11).

Get out into the light. A short walk in morning light will help your body respond to activity, as its light-sensitive mechanisms react to daylight. (See section on Light).

BURNING THE CANDLE AT BOTH ENDS

Not a good idea—but sometimes unavoidable. And if you have some discipline and a clear understanding of your own physiology, you can on occasion put out 500 percent without getting caffeine fits, hallucinations from sleep deprivation, malnutrition, or atrophied muscles.

Amid all the recommendations, estimates, and approximations made in this chapter, one fact emerges as irrefutable: Every individual is different from the "average," and requirements for effective health maintenance vary accordingly. We differ from one another in our tolerance of drugs and in our nutritional requirements. The stress symptoms that we display vary from one person to the next. No wonder everyone has an opinion on what is good for you and what is not.

Saying that everyone requires eight hours' sleep is absurd. That everyone requires 2,000 milligrams of vitamin C daily is equally absurd. But the more you can find out about your own needs, the better able you will be to gauge your own limits and live freely within them.

SKIPPING SLEEP

There is no "normal" amount of sleep. Many people quite naturally sleep less than others. Even those who require less than four hours a night are not wildly unusual. It should come as no surprise that lower-than-average sleep requirements are quite common among the very famous or successful. Recent studies of confirmed "workaholics" also show less need for sleep.

Personally, I envy people who need less sleep than I do. It gives them that much more time to work and play. Until recently, I believed that you couldn't push it. But this is not quite true.

First of all, there may be a great deal of difference between what your body actually *needs* and what it is *conditioned* to getting. Years and years of sleeping about the same number of hours each night has its effect: If, now and then, we don't get that amount, the body reacts negatively. It's sort of like a bad habit, such as overeating. When you diet, you feel hungry at first, even though you are getting enough nutrition. If you are disciplined, you will eventually get used to eating less.

According to several researchers, the same thing appears to be true of sleep. You can retrain your body to sleep less, perhaps as much as an hour or so, without harmful effects. You just cut down gradually, about a half hour every two weeks. If you've been getting more sleep than you need, the fatigue and irritability should recede.

You won't lose much in the way of deep sleep. Rather, you will spend less time in a lighter stage of sleep, called REM (for "rapid eye movement"), during which you do most of your dreaming. The loss of some of this REM, or dream time, doesn't appear to be serious. Unfortunately, we don't know that much about the function of dreams: There may in fact be some side effects of dream deprivation yet to be discovered.

If you decide to attempt a sleep-reduction program, remember to keep a daily log and to sleep regular hours. Otherwise, you'll have trouble. Be psychologically prepared for some discomfort, and don't forget that you may require more sleep during times of great stress. (Don't begin this program during such a period.) Most important, don't overdo it. That means that you shouldn't cut down any faster than one-half hour every two weeks: Everyone needs sleep, and it is unlikely that you can get by on less than five hours. If you try to live on less than that and don't adjust after about two weeks, you've passed your limit; sleep a little more. Some scientists believe that sleep requirements may be in part hereditary— and you can't fight your genes.

A few other tips. Make sure that:

- the room is not hot
- your bed is comfortable
- you are not too hungry or too full
- the room isn't noisy
- the room is reasonably dark
- you exercise regularly during the day

FOR ONE OR TWO NIGHTS   Practically anyone can get by for one or two nights on less sleep than usual. Sometimes, just knowing that you'll be okay helps you get through the day without incident. But don't press it. Get a good night's sleep at the first opportunity. Naps can be helpful. Of course, there is a difference between needing less sleep and depriving yourself of what you need. Even a confirmed workaholic couldn't sustain a pace that required him to consistently come up short in the sleep department.

Recent tests conducted on military personnel demonstrate that while lack of sleep usually won't impair your judgment you may be sloppy about details and routine jobs. Your memory, creativity and your temperament may also be affected.

Have little doubt that being well rested is an important ingredient of success. The degree of rest and the degree of alertness are intimately connected. Robbing yourself of sleep will eventually rob you of good health as well. In order to maximize performance, and be able to skip a few hours of sleep when necessary, you must be able to sleep regularly and well. If you are troubled by persistent insomnia, see your doctor.

FORGETTING FOOD

Skipping one meal, or even several, does not present a problem for a healthy person. It can even be a good thing. In our well-fed society, even several days without food won't result in any serious nutritional problems.

You should keep in mind that intense hunger can be quite distracting. And those with weak stomachs or poor digestion should avoid going for long periods with an empty stomach. It is usually wise to pull yourself from your work long enough to have a quick meal—one that is served quickly, not eaten quickly. Wolfing your food down to save ten minutes is unhealthy and absurd.

ELIMINATING EXERCISE

You don't get out of shape overnight, so it's okay to skip a workout here and there. But it's not a good idea to go too long without some form of exercise. If you are putting in ten-hour days at the desk, get up and go for short walks, even if it's only around the room. A little stretching is also a good idea.

STAYING ALERT: AIDS TO CANDLE-BURNING

A cup of strong coffee is still the fastest and most reliable way to stay sharp under siege. As a general rule, avoid drinking too much coffee or tea. However, if you are usually moderate in your consumption, a few heavy-caffeine days won't hurt you, unless you are the type that has an adverse reaction to large doses of the stuff. It can cause irritability, tremors, nervous tension, and insomnia.

Stay away from drugs, including amphetamines. Some of them do stimulate the central nervous system and increase activity levels, but there is little evidence that they improve cognitive ability. And the depression and fatigue that follow, aptly called "crashing," can be disastrous. One other drawback: They can be habit forming.

Partaking of alcohol and cigarettes other than very sparingly will cause your performance to deteriorate rapidly. So will ingesting a very large meal, which tends to make one feel sluggish and dull.

I'm going to share a secret known only to the most successful workaholics. A great invigorator is . . . fresh air. Open the window, breathe deeply. Or get outside. In general, air quality is important. Many people find central heating or air-conditioning very tiring. Negative-ion generators, humidifiers, and air filters all have their proponents.

For more information on sleep and sleep disorders: Most major cities have a hospital or two which operates a sleep clinic for treating serious sleep disorders and dispensing advice on minor problems. Contact the Association of Professional Sleep Societies, 604 2nd Street., S.W. Rochester, MN 55902.

15

HEALTHY HARDWARE

A very large industry manufactures hundreds of devices, each claiming to be the "scientific" or "most effective" or "easiest" or "newest" way to good health. If you want to avoid throwing money away on useless—and sometimes dangerous—equipment, you had better educate yourself before purchasing. Many of the marketing tactics used in the industry are a mixture of hype, myth, pseudoscience and, in some cases, outright exploitation of our insecurites and vanity. Fortunately, the scientific facts are accessible, and the firms that make products with verifiable tangible benefits will always be eager to back up their claims with hard data from a third party.

A GUIDE TO EXERCISE EQUIPMENT

Much of the equipment is worthless, for at least one of several reasons. First, many involve unfamiliar or uncomfortable movements. Second, many lose their effectiveness with repeated use. Third, many are unsafe. Fourth, we easily become bored with them and stop following the routine.

If you are serious about acquiring exercise equipment for your home, you've got to have the available space—and be prepared to spend some money.

Machines are basically of two types. Those that provide aerobic, cardiovascular benefits, and those that slim, tone and build muscles and strength. A wide range of fitness accessories and gadgets are also available.

CARDIOVASCULAR

Exercise Bikes come in different shapes and sizes, but work essentially the same way. You pedal on them and they work your heart by providing resistance to your pedalling motion, delivering an efficient form of aerobic exercise. They differ from ordinary bikes in that they are stationary, and provide variable resistance; outdoors, you can do something of the same thing as you go up and down hill, or change gears.

Stationary bikes are popular because a basic good quality model is relatively cheap, you don't have to be in super shape to use them, and they take up relatively little space. You don't have to be very coordinated, and they are ideal for ex-joggers who want to spare their bodies from the shock and stress of roadwork. Your shins and knees will last longer on a bike.

Newer, more expensive models, such as Bally's Lifecycle, have a small onboard computer which allows you to program a workout which attempts to simulate an outdoor ride, complete with uphill and downhill stretches. These machines are called *ergometers* (from the Greek for "measurement of work"). The resistance varies, and you can see your progress on an LED readout. You can set the level from 1–10, sequentially improving your performance level as you get in better shape. The Lifecycle is not cheap—about $2000, compared to under $200–400 for a top-notch "stupid" bike. But the Lifecycle does work—I've used one for several years—and it is modular, so if a part breaks you just snap it out and replace it.

The Lifecycle and several similar brands also monitor your overall fitness level by keeping track of your heart rate, target zone, calorie consumption, elapsed time and resistance setting in watts. You have to take your own pulse; to be truly automatic, you can attach a pulse monitoring device.

A major complaint about stationary bikes is that they don't exercise your upper body. Schwinn has attempted to meet this objection with its Air-Dyne bicycle. The handles are actually levers which you can pull while you ride, thus working your arms, chest and shoulders. The Air-Dyne lists at $595. Another variation is a bicycle that puts you in a reclining position when you pedal.

Stationary bikes cost about $300; ergometers are at least double.

The Rower is a more legitimate way to work both upper and lower body. While a stationary bike simulates outdoor pedalling, a rowing machine simulates rowing or more accurately sculling on the water.

You strap your feet in and pull and push on levers that simulate the action of the oars, working your arms, chest, back and shoulders. As you do so, you must move forward and back in your seat, which, to simulate the action on the water, is mounted on a movable rail. This forward/back movement is propelled by your legs.

Following the lead of bicycle manufacturers, the rowing machine makers have begun computerizing their models, providing essentially the same fitness-monitoring programs.

Good rowing machines are not much more expensive than stationary bikes, and in many cases, cheaper. They are simple, reliable, and many models fold up for upright storage in a closet. But a rowing machine is more demanding. You need to be in better shape to spend twenty minutes to half an hour on a rower than you do on a bike.

There are two types of rowers: hydraulic, which uses pistons, and cable, which uses a flywheel and cable system. Cable systems are smoother and more like water. Generally, they produce less back strain and greater aerobic benefit, but recent improvements in hydraulic systems have minimized the differences, and many hydraulic systems provide superior upper body workouts.

Rowing machines generally cost between $300 and $600.

Treadmills closely simulate regular running, but they are expensive and take up lots of space. The better models provide elevation to simulate running uphill. Non-motorized models are cheaper, but they require you to move the treadmill by pushing back on them, making you more prone to injury than on a motorized one. Motorized treadmills cost $1500 and up.

Cross-Country Skiers. As the name implies, they mimic cross-country skiing. Some consider them the ultimate aerobic workout. Indeed, a recent study rated them higher than bikes and rowers in cardiovascular benefit. The first and most popular model is the NordicTrack, invented about ten years ago by cross-country skier Ed Pauls.

The skis are mounted set into grooved tracks, and slide freely, as the stride works every major muscle group. You pull alternately on pulleys to similate the action of ski poles, and the overall effect is quite strenuous. The track is portable and fits into a 15 × 17 storage space. Other brands employ moving ski poles instead of cables; most machines cost around $500.

STRENGTH TRAINING

There are scores of home gyms available, proporting to build strength and muscle tone. They all provide resistance to muscle action. Some use cables, some pistons, others use rubber tubes, air, even water; naturally there are many that use weight stacks. And then there are freeweights—good old barbells and dumbbells.

Machines are easier to use than freeweights and generally safer because there are no weights to drop and because the motion of your muscles is isolated and guided along a set path (to an extent).

Multistation gyms are machines which provide the means to perform a wide range of strength exercises, usually working all the major muscle groups. They are expensive.

Recently, companies such as *Nautilus* have adapted their gym equipment for home use, and come out with a home line of dedicated machines: one that works the abdomen, one for the back, etc. If you want to be able to do a complete workout with these machines, you are going to have to put several in your home or basement, *i.e.*, a home fitness circuit.

Multistation gyms employing weight stacks and heavy-duty construction cost in excess of $1000; those using cables run around $500.

Remember: no matter what the salesperson tells you, it is very difficult to get a good cardiovascular workout on a strength machine. It is difficult to keep within your training pulse range, and some studies indicate that this type of activity doesn't improve cardiovascular condition even when the user manages to stay within the training range for more than twenty minutes. So if it's health you're after, and you have to choose between strength and cardiovascular condition, pick a rower, ski machine, bike or a treadmill. Or buy a strength machine and commit yourself to a regular program of jogging or aerobics. There is no substitute.

Jump rope. Cheap. Basic. And once you get good at jumping, one hell of a workout. A twenty-minute interval session of rope skipping will get your heart rate right up there. Leather ropes with ballbearings set into wood handles are best. Some have "jump counters" built into the handle. Most important, make sure the rope is the proper length. It should reach your armpits while standing on it with one foot.

Because there is a burgeoning market, a new high-tech device appears almost every week. Don't be misled by the promise of instant benefits. A lot of brainpower has gone into designing improved machines delivering safe, superior workouts. But some are pure marketing hype. Be careful and do your homework. When in doubt, go with a time-tested basic machine. And don't be surprised if you have to build an extension to your home just to house this stuff.

Accessories. The only accessories you really need are those that provide measurements. The key to a good sound workout program is accurate monitoring and measurement, so that you progress gradually and steadily, and know enough about your own physiology to customize your workout.

The most useful are *pulse monitors* which electronically keep track of your pulse. Some models will beep when you exceed or slip below your training range. Others are programmable to prompt you on pulse rates through warm-up, workout and cool down. Good ones start at about $100.

A good scale. Most home models are simply unreliable. And when you are serious about your health and weight, a scale that is off by a few pounds can be exasperating and misleading. Ordinary household scales are commonly off by as much as three or four pounds. The fancy digital scales look high-tech, but they are not ultra-accurate. A simple scale, well constructed with few moving parts and little springs, is preferable. Sliding balance beam scales such as the *Detecto* are best; high quality spring-loaded scales are second best. Expect to spend $200–300 for a quality scale. Remember, if you are closer to your proper weight, you can work out harder than if you are overweight.

The skin caliper measures body fat by pinching and measuring the amount of flesh between its jaws in millimeters. You take the measurements in several places, and compare your results to a table to determine total body fat as a percentage of overall weight. A computerized version called the Skyndex Electronic Body Fat Calculatro does all the figuring for you and costs around $400. A highly accurate quality model called the Lange Skinfold Caliper costs about $175. But the Ross Adipodometer Skinfold

Caliper, a plastic model costing around $3.00, works just fine, even if you have to do the math to come up with your body fat percentage.

Knowing your body fat is important if you want to customize your diet and exercise program to work on problem areas.

Other less sophisticated but useful workout devices include a *pedometer* to measure the distance walked or jogged, and a stopwatch.

EYEGUARDS

The most common injuries in racket sports involve the eyes. The damage can be extremely serious, and even a minor blow can cause complications. If you get hit, resist the macho urge to shrug it off: Go see an eye doctor.

The growing interst in squash and racquetball has led to the development of impact-resistant eyeguards. Your basic eyeguard is about $7, but eyeguards can run upward of $30 for the flashy, padded, goggle type. If you wear glasses, it's best to have prescription sports glasses made by an optometrist.

Adequate eye protection is also important in skiing, scuba and skin diving, and hunting. You can get prescription ski goggles, scuba masks, and swim goggles. Seeing well is important during these activities.

BRACES

Most of the over-the-counter knee, arm, ankle and back braces are helpful only in the case of a mild strain. Very often, especially in the case of the knee, a $3 brace provides a false sense of security. A good doctor will not only diagnose your injury, but will also prescribe the best brace for your problem. The high-priced professional athletes have subsidized great advances in the design of braces and supports. For example, I wear a knee brace originally designed for Julius Erving! You won't find it in any drugstore.

SUGGESTED READING

A good health maintenance program might well begin with the hefting of a good book. If you want to delve further into topics discussed in Part III of *Executive Essentials*, check out these titles:

Executive Health, by Philip Goldberg (New York: McGraw-Hill, 1978)

Managing Stress, by Jere E. Yates (New York: AMACOM, 1979)

Sportsmedicine, by Gabe Mirkin, M.D., and Marshall Hoffman (Boston: Little, Brown and Co., 1978)

Nutrition Almanac, by Nutrition Search, Inc. (New York: McGraw-Hill, 1979)

Stretching, by Bob Anderson (Bolinas, California: Shelter Publications, 1980)

Sleep Less, Live More, by Everett Mattlin (New York: J. P. Lippincott, 1979)

Running Away from Home, by David Colker (New York: Jove Publications, 1979)

The New Aerobics, by Kenneth Cooper (New York: Evans and Co., 1970)

Royal Canadian Air Force Plans for Physical Fitness (New York: Pocket Books, 1972)

PART IV

WINNING

"Success is simply a matter of luck.
Ask any failure."

Earl Wilson

16

THE SUCCESS SCRIPTURES AND WHAT YOU CAN LEARN FROM THEM

There is considerable overlap in the subject matter of business success books, but that is not surprising when you consider that power, money, happiness, and even sex are intimately interconnected in the minds of the public. It's tough to write about power without writing about money too. And a book about succeeding in company politics can't ignore the concepts of power and negotiation skills.

The primary differences among these books lie not in subject matter, but in perspective: The author perceives the obstacles to success in a certain context. The key is finding a book that reflects a point of view you can identify with.

Therein lies the reason that many bad self-help books become best-sellers. So many readers identify with the *problems and obstacles* set forth by the author that they willingly snap up the book even though solutions may be sorely lacking. For example, if you feel that politics and infighting are holding you back, you'll be drawn to a book on company politics. If you think you've got to become a better leader, you'll find yourself reading much the same information in a book on leadership or power. Sloppy or forgetful? How about a memory book? Disorganized? There are time management books.

Another consideration is the author's personal philosophy. Some people would not welcome advice that they lie in order to accelerate success; others wouldn't think twice before adopting this tactic.

The number of success formulas is unlimited. No seminar speaker, author, or business leader has a lock on "the best method." So if a friend of yours thinks that Robert Ringer is America's greatest living genius, but you feel unreceptive to his message, don't feel obliged to absorb his teachings.

There are several hundred self-help titles on the bookstore shelves. And there will be many more by the time this book appears. What follows is not an extensive review of success books, but, rather, a guide to the major criteria for choosing a success guru.

By the way—there is one principle of financial gain that most (but not all) authors omit: "There will always be people out there looking for a shortcut to success." If the number of success books in print is any indication, there must be plenty of such people around.

WHO'S WRITING THIS STUFF?

Success formulas are based primarily on the author's observation, experience, and point of view. The successful entrepreneur might be quick to point out that you should rely only on yourself, but a corporate man who has built a successful career as part of a team might see it another way. So before you accept any of these books as gospel, consider where the authors are coming from. I've divided the exploding population of success gurus into several types:

SELF-MADE MILLIONAIRES

In the publishing world, being a self-made millionaire appears to be a kind of qualification for writing a success book, as having a PhD in American lit would be for writing a Hemingway study. Why does a millionaire write a book on success? (1) He is not really a millionaire. (2) He is a millionaire, but doesn't feel he's quite rich enough. (3) Making money turns him on, even when he doesn't need it. (4) Pure vanity, plain and simple: He's rich, now he wants to be famous. (5) He really believes that he has something of value to share with the world. (6) His book is an attempt at self-discovery.

The most interesting kinds of "millionaire success books" are those written by those who do so for reasons (5) and (6). Many of this ilk feel somehow "plugged in" to the cosmic order of things. They wish to give expression to those principles, and they believe—in earnest—that they will work for everyone if applied.

Sounds weird? You should take a look at some of these books. Judging by some of the "rules" and "laws" laid down, we can conclude that in America, you needn't be a rational thinker to succeed—just a passionate one.

Personally, I do believe that there are some basic laws of nature that are so primal in form that they escape the awareness and perception of our complex and culturalized minds. And I do believe that some successful people have become so because of the sheer simplicity and basic truthfulness of their approach. Since such people often operate from intuition, their methods are often considered mystical, or just so much armchair motivational psychology.

If you pick up a book by Napoleon Hill, Clement Stone, or Og Mandino, take a second look before dismissing it as nonsense.

INSIDERS

These writers succeed for many of the same reasons that made Hedda Hopper and Walter Winchell so successful. They orbit amid the inner circles of business, where they are surrounded by, if not steeped in, success (stories). This proximity arms them with a store of great anecdotes and rags-to-riches sagas. The problem comes when they attempt to extract useful "tips" and principles of success from their observations and conversations. This is a formidable job for even the most disciplined sociologist, who will at least strive to make his sources varied and well balanced, and will attempt to be objective. But the methods of popular authors appear to be strictly catch-as-catch-can.

Everyone learns by example. And the stories of the rich, famous, and powerful make fun reading. But even the winner himself may not be able to adequately explain why and how he got where he is. Therefore, it may be unwise to model your approach after an author's description of how several of his acquaintances or interviewees "made it."

Glean what you can from the success stories, even if it's only inspiration and a small tip about how to answer a phone. But be aware that many authors shoot from the hip—it saves time and trouble. Sometimes they hit. Sometimes their stories and principles strike a responsive chord, but following their advice on that basis alone can be disastrous.

SCHOOLBOYS

The academics. Academics are hooked on scientific methodology. This means hypotheses, research, and theories. If they are successful, they come up with findings that encourage them to run grey areas into black-and-white. Often, they do so even if they are unsuccessful. I mean, who would spend three years studying "cross-cultural relations within the business community," only to announce that he has emerged with no theories? And, of course, there is the pressure to publish.

On balance, academic studies of the business community are quite useful. Just keep in mind that they often deal in norms, averages, probabilities, and statistical significance. So what they say may—or may not—apply to you, your co-workers, or your company. Studies of success in business can be valuable because they give you a sense of the values and methods of the environment in which you earn your living. They can give you a better view of the total picture.

Since academic studies often make no value judgments, but, rather, emphasize what is, and why it is, you get a "cleaner" feeling about success. An academic may subconsciously try hard to vindicate his theories, but it is less likely that he will be espousing a personal moral (or immoral) ethical philosophy—the stuff of so many how-to books on success.

Many studies are not published in books, but in journals; or they may be available only as limited editions through sponsoring research institutions or foundations or universities. You must peruse business abstracts or some type of business index if you wish to stay informed. Browsing through a bookstore, or even through *Business Week*, will not keep you abreast of the latest intelligence.

TECHNICIANS

These are the authors whose bag is technique. Industrial psychologists. Engineers. Organizational psychologists. Management consultants. Logistics specialists. They will talk to you of procedures, principles, and methods. Organization. Reorganization. Flowcharts. Follow-through. Education. Communication. Evaluation. Backup. Feedback.

These authors can be very redundant, because many of the methods they evolve in seemingly endless variations are reducible to a few tried-and-true approaches to problem solving. But if you don't spend a lot of time reading such books, you won't notice the repetition. Besides, some of them are very inventive.

The basic tenet of the technicians' books is that success is the direct result of a job well done. Improve the workings of the company and your own lot will improve automatically.

One of the reasons, I suspect, that the managerial techniques books don't teach back stabbing, throat cutting, or even the tamer power games is that most of them are written from the point of view that the corporation is paramount; the needs of the individual come second. While this may be a good attitude to cultivate among American executives, a few facts belie it: Most of the people who *started* the companies were rugged individualists, with loyalties rarely extending beyond family and a few trusted friends.

Although many executives live happy, fulfilled lives as company men and women and are rewarded with nice benefits when they retire, most experts believe that the way to the top is not straight, but a zigzag through many companies. The reason: Competence is more important than loyalty, and other firms are less likely to be eager for your skills when you've all but blended into the woodwork as a loyal member of the "team." America is not Japan: U.S. corporations (with few exceptions) simply cannot be counted on to "take care of you." More important is the good old American tradition of striving for a bigger piece of the pie.

236

GUNSLINGERS

These are the authors who are interested in telling you how to survive. To them, the executive's road to success is a matter of guerilla warfare, or kill-or-be-killed. In the unhappy event that you are working in a dog-eat-dog environment, you may need such books. But first you should ask yourself if this is really the kind of job you want to have.

Most gunslingers are erstwhile victims of business treachery who decided to fight fire with fire. It worked for them, they feel, and now they stand at the top of the hill, bloodied but unbowed. Fortunately, they are going to share with you their knowledge of the tactics of corporate combat, so you too can come out a winner. Unfortunately, these guys won't be around to help if you stumble and wind up like General Custer rather than Alexander the Great. Worse, you will probably have trouble getting them on the phone when you need a friend to talk to and you've already lost all the friends you had in your pregunslinger days.

There's nothing wrong with picking up a few secret weapons to protect yourself from the business world's seedier elements; these authors can help. Just remember that a weapon is only a weapon if you know how to use it properly. See such books for what they are—not blueprints for success, but tools of last resort—the lowest road to success.

WHAT THEY PROMISE

POWER

Books on power vary according to the definition of the term. A "power book" could be about getting the things you want, being able to influence, control, or manipulate people, gaining control over your own life, or any combination of the above.

The best-known book on the subject is *Power! How to Get It, How to Use It,* by Michael Korda (New York: Random House, 1975). This book is often interesting, but very uneven. Some of Korda's insights are worthwhile, but in my opinion much of the book is shoddy, offering advice based on questionable values and ethics.

I recommend to you *Power in Management,* by John P. Kotter (New York: AMACOM, 1979) as tops among the "power" books. It is based on a study of over 200 executives in 26 organizations. Kotter, an associate professor of organizational behavior at Harvard Business School, has a great deal to say on power-oriented behavior, the positive functions it serves, and how it operates. The findings ring true. The book is well written and well organized and gives you far more significant

---

information on power than Korda's book, in less than half as many pages.

SUCCESS

Books about success arrive at a definition (or help you define it for yourself) and then give you tips on how to achieve it. Be careful, though: Many of these books attempt to prey on our weaknesses. For example, some books de-emphasize the role of skill and hard work in success. The authors will tell you that appearances and visibility count most; you are as great as anybody around, but you haven't been letting the world know. This explains the emphasis on the trappings of success. Don't be lulled into thinking that the only difference between you and the other guy is a matter of PR. Promoting yourself is fine, but not at the expense of performance.

In the world of publishing, one successful book begets another. Michael Korda followed *Power!* with another popular work, *Success!* (New York: Random House, 1977). Here's a notable quote that's bound to get you in trouble if you swallow it whole: "Ability and talent won't take you very far. You can even succeed through failure if you are calculating enough."

For all its "hard-nosed" observations and unrepresentative examples, *Success!* is not a bad book. Appearances *are* important, and Korda's book will help you maintain them. Just don't be fooled—there is more to success than what lies within its pages.

If ever there were a challenger to Michael Korda for the title of head success guru, it would have to be Robert Ringer. He is at least as good as Korda in devising gut-level book titles, just as fast in following up his first best-seller with another (*Winning through Intimidation* succeeded by *Looking Out for Number 1*), and far better at obscuring questionable ethics.

Ringer believes that successful people are not nice. His message, as I read it, is that there is some conspiracy to deceive people into being good while all the "winners" are out there putting the screws to everyone.

As in the case of Korda, Ringer does provide some specific advice that can be of value to the would-be king of the hill. But in doing so, he mangles and degrades human nature, and preys on the very weaknesses of others that he claims to abhor in himself. I suspect he does it for the shock value.

Where does money fit into all of this? As Korda says, "It's *always* better to be rich."

WEALTH

You would think that if you have success and power, you would probably make money as well. Not necessarily. Some money books are *economic battle plans*. Others take the attitude that all the world is a Las Vegas casino, and you can beat the house. Just because a strategy for making money succeeds for some, it doesn't necessarily follow that it will succeed for you.

There are also "psych" books on money. You know, "the power of the subconscious mind": Dream about a Cadillac (or Mercedes, if you prefer) and you'll soon own one.

The most famous is *Think and Grow Rich*, by Napoleon Hill, originally published in 1937. This is a pretty good book. Hill is a true original. He is practical and thoughtful, and he has done his homework. While his principles may not always get you a million, they will usually help. It takes a special kind of person to lock into Hill's formula and follow his principles to the letter; they leave some people cold. But many have told me that upon reading Hill's book, they realized that they were doing what he suggests all along. His book validated their approach, thus firing them up. For those who can't get into this type of reading (I empathize), try the cassette version of *Think and Grow Rich*, published by the Success Motivation Institute and narrated by Earl Nightinggale, with a special guest pep talk by Napoleon Hill (yes, he's still alive). This tape is great while shaving or driving to work. Some like it before bed in place of the "Tonight Show" or "Starsky and Hutch." It'll give you the gist of what Hill is saying. If you like what you hear, go out and read the books, which are more detailed.

For a discussion of money books see Investment section.

INSPIRATION

Inspiration comes in all packages:

EGO-MASSAGE "I'm okay, you're okay, so why can't we both make it?" Learn to be your own best friend and pull your own strings.

RELIGIOUS Do God's work and you'll get a commission.

MOTIVATIONAL Success is within your grasp if you have the energy, willpower, and determination to go out and get it.

Inspiration and optimism are vital ingredients in everyone's life. Get them any way you can. Sometimes you can inspire yourself with the help of an insight or creative idea. One comment comes to mind, said by a well-known actor: "Talent is commonplace. What is rare is the ability to develop and exploit that talent." Chances are you've got what it takes. Go forth and figure out how to make it work for you. Don't take all this self-help stuff too seriously, but when you do pick up an insight, use it. And if you're uptight about being accused of being part of the "Me Generation," keep your how-to books to yourself.

A few popular inspirational books are *Self Love*, by Robert Schuller (Old Tappan, New Jersey: Fleming H. Revell, 1975), *Psycho-cybernetics*, by Maxwell Maltz, M.D. (Englewood Cliffs, New Jersey: Prentice-Hall, 1960), and *The Power of Positive Thinking*, by Norman Vincent Peale (Englewood Cliffs, New Jersey: Prentice-Hall, 1954).

Motivation expert Zig Ziglar, author of *See You at the Top*, offers a typical example of inspirational fare with a four-step formula:

- *Reverse the way you get out of bed.* Don't attack the alarm clock, Ziglar advises. Get up, clap your hands, and say, "Oh, boy, it's a good day to get up and go get 'em!"
- *Establish some symbols.* Change your vocabulary. Transform "stoplights into golights," "weekends into strongends," and so forth.
- *Set your gyroscope for success.* "If you want to be optimistic . . . you have to act it." Answer the phone with "Hello, it's a great day."
- *Feed your mind.* Listen to motivational tapes. Read inspirational books.

RELIEF FROM FRUSTRATION

Many people are just plain unhappy with their lot. They are frustrated and bitter. Some books take their side, telling their readers that they are justified in feeling that the world stinks. Then the books turn to telling how to dish it out, giving tips on infighting, maneuvering, manipulation, and naked deceit.

Some people claim to have turned their lives around as a result of such a book. But they are the exceptions.

Other books provide relief in a more soothing, constructive manner. The most popular book for relieving pain is the Bible. Other pep talks designed to make you aware of what's wrong and how to set it right include Wayne W. Dyer's *Your Erroneous Zones* (New York: Funk & Wagnalls/T. Y. Crowell, 1976) and *I'm O.K., You're O.K.* by Thomas A. Harris (New York: Harper & Row, 1969).

SPECIFIC SKILLS

These are the original self-help books. There is a wide selection of books on all sorts of business, management, and noncognitive skills. For example, the popular *Memory Book*, by Harry Lorayne and Jerry Lucas (Briarcliff Manor, New York: Stein & Day, 1974). Or *Memory Made Easy*, by Robert L. Montgomery (New York: AMACOM, 1979).

Will these books help? Depends. Some skills can be learned out of a book; some require personal instruction.

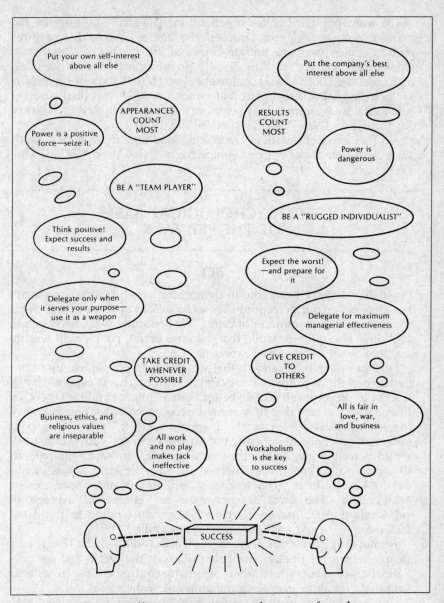

Fig. 28. Different perspectives on the success formula
Often, apparently contradictory viewpoints can be reconciled.
Success, to a large extent, depends on the ability to live with
ambivalent feelings, resolve dichotomies, and selectively
accept and reject values. The bubbles above represent
common points of view on success. As you can see,
many conflicts arise.

The most popular books on general management skills are by the manager's manager, Peter Drucker. His books have sold over three million copies (over one million copies of *The Practice of Management* [New York: Harper & Row, 1954]). To be effective, says Drucker, managers need both a basic competence and the will to perform. Profits are not the goal of a company, but rather a need. A vast distillation of his ideas and opinions appears in *Management: Tasks, Practices, Responsibilities* (New York: Harper & Row, 1974).

Another excellent work is *Leadership: What Effective Managers Really Do ... And How They Do It*, by Leonard Sayles (New York: McGraw-Hill, 1979).

THE PSYCHOLOGICAL BASIS
OF THE PEP TALK

SET

Psychologists have been able to demonstrate that expectation clearly has an effect on our perception. The expectations are called "set." Set is the basis for the common criticism, "He sees only what he wants to see." It is also quite possible that, because of set, people will tend to overlook what they are not expecting.

Further research has shown that we may help people live up to our own expectations of them. For example, a group that is expected by its teacher to do very well will do better than a group of children identical in every way except that they are not expected to excel. This is known in psychological circles as the Pygmalion effect,* and it has been observed not only in schools, but in the business and professional world as well. It may be that the teacher or other authority figure tends to notice and encourage success in the "smart" group, while overlooking failures. The teacher's "set" is toward above-average achievement. The same teacher may be set toward average or substandard performance in the other group, tending to point out lackluster work and pass over displays of ability.

Set not only affects our perceptions; it affects our beliefs. That is why people with strong beliefs are able to look at the world and see only validation of them, while others see many contradictions. It has been said that "religious people see religion everywhere."

This may be a news flash for you, but it comes as no surprise to the success gurus who preach "positive thinking" and other variations on the same theme: By creating a positive set—expectation—of success for ourselves and a positive self-image, we increase the likelihood of

---

*From Peter Russell, *The Brain Book* (New York: Hawthorn, 1979), p. 213.

---

fulfillment of our goals. Set programs our minds to lock into elements or events in our environment that support our activities.

Call it what you will—"psyching yourself up," "mind over matter," "positive thinking"—it does work, to varying degrees, in everybody. A problem may arise when you pick up a "pep talk" book that aims at creating a positive mental set: To begin with, you need to have the kind of set that leads you to expect that the book will work. And so it goes. That's why a book that comes highly recommended by a friend or relative you admire and respect is more likely to work for you. You are more favorably disposed toward it, and therefore it is more likely that the author's words will elicit a positive response in you.

There is an inspirational, pep-talk book for every "set" and every taste. Don't sell them short. Find one that you like. Better yet, don't sell yourself short. Many people don't need to be told how to create a positive set about themselves. And besides the books, there are other ways—like religious faith, warm family relationships, a pat on the back.

IMAGINATION

It has also been shown that imagining or visualizing a situation helps to create a mental set in which the fulfillment of that "vision" is more likely.

Several psychotherapists have been able to help patients who don't interview well by showing them how to imagine themselves doing well at the interview, visualizing each step.

This may be related to hypnosis or autosuggestion. Napoleon Hill often speaks of visualizing the specific amount of money you wish to have. Just wanting to be rich is not enough, because it is too abstract. The greater the detail, the greater the ease and effectiveness of imagining and visualizing.

A good time to imagine or visualize is at bedtime, as you are drifting off, or when you awake in the morning. Any "quiet time" is suitable. But please, not at a staff meeting.

WOMEN'S SUCCESS MATERIALS

Books and seminars on success in business directed at women are very much in vogue. Everyone is out to make a buck here, and because job discrimination has held women back, there is a shortage of genuine experts.

There are no real "rules" of success. And very little can be learned in a one-day seminar. Books for women contain essentially the same material included in those written for either sex, except that they usually give some attention to problems like sexual harassment, affirmative action, and the home/career conflict. But if you want only the basic facts about investments, skills, or general management, pick what you like without regard for the sex of the author or for whether the word *women* is in the title.

COMMON ERRORS OF SUCCESS BOOKS

- Generalizing from the specific
- Assuming that survival-oriented behavior is premeditated
- Assuming that, for most people, power, money, and success are their own rewards
- Assuming that getting people to do what you want them to do requires deceit or coercion
- Appealing to, rather than debunking, the myth that acquiring power, influence, and success is for the hard-boiled who do nothing out of sheer altruism
- Assuming that the contents of their books can change the readers' behavior
- Believing that *admitting* that you are doing something purely for money or power places you above reproach
- Assuming that a quotation or two from a highly respected, definitive work constitutes a validation or approval of the author's point, just because the author being quoted may appear to be saying a similar thing

17

WHAT EVERY BUSINESS PERSON OUGHT TO KNOW SOMETHING ABOUT

This chapter looks at important skills and concepts as though they were independent entities, for the sake of convenience and because we vary in our needs, strengths, and knowledge. But, in the final analysis, it's how you put them all together that counts.

WHAT IT TAKES: A THUMBNAIL SKETCH OF THE SUCCESSFUL EXECUTIVE PERSONALITY

Psychologist Roger Birkman has compiled a list of major personality traits that set successful executives apart from their peers:*

A need for power. The successful executive appears to need power to accomplish his goals. For him, though, power is a *tool*, not an end in itself. Power must not become an addiction, and it shouldn't be exercised needlessly.

A need for challenge. All executives thrive on challenges; it's just that the more successful ones are better at selecting and managing them. When faced with a challenge, they are better at calculating risks. They don't create or accept challenges they can't meet.

The successful executive appears to have a need to put himself to the test, and a great deal of his satisfaction is derived from overcoming challenges.

---

*Adapted from Roger Birkman, "What Sets an Executive Apart from His Peers?", *S.A.M.*, *Advanced Management Journal,* Summer 1978 (New York: S.A.M., a division of American Management Associations, 1978), pp. 59–63.

Ability to delegate. Effective delegation is very difficult to master. It involves a fair amount of risk. Often poor delegation is really not delegation at all. Rather, it is an attempt to impose one's methods or to pass the buck. The less successful executive may attempt to derive satisfaction by applying his own skills and getting things done his way. The more successful executive derives satisfaction from motivating, inspiring, influencing, and guiding others into turning in a superior performance. An executive who can effectively lead several subordinates is obviously worth more than an executive whose contribution is limited to his own output.

There should, however, be no misunderstanding: The executive himself must make the hard decisions and take responsibility for results.

Ability to balance empathy and objectivity. A successful manager can understand and empathize with the predicaments of subordinates, but at the same time view the situation in an objective light. This gift of balance is important, because the best interests of a worker and the firm are often at odds. And the worker's own view of what's best often differs from the manager's.

Less successful executives are often insensitive to the needs and feelings of others—or blinded by them to the extent that they lack objectivity.

It is emotionally easier to take a simple stand—either a confirmed disinterest in co-worker feelings and problems or a confirmed feeling of empathy. But the successful executive is the one who steps up and confronts the ambivalence, often making a decision that proves agonizingly difficult, precisely because he can see both sides.

Some years ago, psychologist Abraham Maslow noted that one sign of a healthy personality was the ability to accept and integrate ambivalent or ambiguous feelings and values.

A need for competition. This is common to most executives. But the more successful ones appear to have an expanded view of the process of competition and the joy of winning. They want to win, but in a manner consistent with their own methods and ethics. They are interested in long-range results—the war, not the battle. Effectively, they superimpose a code of honor upon the concept of "survival of the fittest."

In order to be successful, one has to stay on top. Those that do stay there know that honor and consistency—playing by the rules—make one less susceptible to treachery.

Independence. Successful executives tend to avoid group-dependence. That is to stay, they *do not require* group approval, reinforcement, or risk sharing. On the other hand, such executives *don't object* to working in groups when appropriate—and when they get results. Because their source of self-esteem and confidence comes from within, they see groups as vehicles for problem solving, idea and information sharing, and (as a sometime bonus) enjoyment of camaraderie.

A need for change. Birkman's analysis reveals that successful executives are more restless than the average. They prefer to achieve a broad perspective or overview and then move on, rather than to spend a great deal of time intensely probing a single subject.

Of course, this may be because, as successful executives, this is the nature of their jobs: They have larger responsibilities and cannot afford to dwell on one subject when they have subordinates on staff to do follow-up work. However, it is possible that it takes a special type—one who likes to "shift gears" often—to be successful in top management. Such a person must be able to quickly grasp the essence of a situation or problem and integrate the parts into a whole. Such minds are not content to stay with one thing for very long.

The successful executive is far from being a stereotype composed of the traits summarized above.

Birkman points out that although most top executives will have many of these traits, very few have them all.

Besides personality differences, other factors influence success. There are genetic factors, specific skills learned on the job and in our social environment, and several other factors, identified by Birkman:

Opportunity. The sociopolitical-economic structure of our society makes opportunity more elusive for some, more readily available for others. Race, sex, educational background, parental income, and where you spent your childhood all play a role in determining the opportunities available to you.

For more information on these factors, see my own discussion and the book *Who Gets Ahead?*, by Christopher Jencks (New York: Basic Books, 1979), which is discussed further in Chapter 19.

Motivation. This takes the form of a desire to achieve goals, accomplish objectives, and get to the top.

Insight. Defined for our purposes as the ability to size up a situation and acutely perceive the actions, motives, and feelings of others, insight also involves *self-awareness*—the ability to see yourself as you really are, accurately assessing your own needs, strong and weak points, and other special traits.

A drive to action. This is where you put it all together, translating motivation and insight into concrete, realistic, effective action, taking advantage of the opportunities afforded and transcending the obstacles. All successful individuals are doers.

If you wish to read more on Birkman's findings, get a copy of the Summer, 1978, issue of the *S.A.M. Management Journal*, and read the article "What Sets an Executive Apart from His Peers?" by Roger Birkman

(S.A.M. stands for Society for Advancement of Management, a division of American Management Associations). Any good business library will have it.

DELEGATING

Good management is terribly difficult without effective delegation. Delegation enables you to control your workload; to communicate with and evaluate your subordinates, to bring them along; and, in general, to make life easier.

HOW NOT TO DELEGATE

- planning poorly
- issuing too many orders and directives
- overcontrolling
- undercontrolling
- overworking subordinates
- applying pressure
- criticizing too much
- imposing too many rules
- imposing too few rules
- being indecisive
- lacking objectives and priorities
- passing the buck
- exemplifying disorganization

HOW TO DELEGATE

THE ONE THING YOU NEVER DELEGATE IS ACCOUNTABILITY You are still on the line. If you have delegated well and effectively, you'll come out well. But if the situation doesn't pan out, *do not blame the delegate involved.* You'll lose the respect of your superiors and the loyalty of your subordinates. Never delegate blame.

THE OTHER THING YOU DON'T DELEGATE IS A JOB THAT HAS YOUR NAME ON IT You are where you are because you do something well—even if it's only delegating.

CHOOSE CAREFULLY Don't delegate a task to someone because he's there, but because he's right for the job. If there is no such person available on your staff, try to find someone in another part of the organization. Or do it yourself.

MAKE SURE YOUR DELEGATES UNDERSTAND THE OBJECTIVES *You* set the objectives, perhaps with the input of others. *They* must carry

---

them out. So first you must have well-defined goals; then you'd better make sure they are understood.

STATE THE LIMITATIONS UP FRONT   Budget? Authority? Deadlines? Let your helpers know the rules of the game.

DELEGATE RESPONSIBILITY, NOT JUST JOBS   You've got to keep accountability. But you can—and should—give a degree of free rein. If you can't do that, at least engender a sense of responsibility in your delegates.

DELEGATE AUTHORITY, NOT JUST RESPONSIBILITY   Authority is part of what your subordinates need to get the job done. But define the limits of that authority; and make sure that they check with you at even the slightest question of overstepping it.

YOU MAKE THE BIG DECISIONS. THEY ADVISE, RECOMMEND, AND ANALYZE

ANALYZE THE RISKS   Delegation is a form of risk taking.

LET THEM DO IT THEIR WAY   You are interested in the "what." How your delegates do it should be left to them as long as they understand the limits. You can offer help, but don't push your methods on them.

KEEP YOUR EAR TO THE GROUND   Establish checks and balances, building your delegates into the process. Request progress reports concerned with spending, time periods, or fulfillment of certain tasks or needs—or a combination of these considerations—any method that allows you to monitor the situation.

ESTABLISH STANDARDS OF PERFORMANCE   Whatever your subordinates do reflects on you. Make sure their work is up to snuff. The best way is to set the standards in advance.

ENCOURAGE INDEPENDENCE   If delegates must check with you before every move, you might as well do it yourself—but then how will you ever develop a competent support staff that you can rely on?

BE SUPPORTIVE   As a superior, you should be more like a coach to your team than a dictator. Be firm, stern, and tough. But you will all benefit if your team has a high morale. You've got to be supportive.

GIVE CREDIT WHERE IT IS DUE   If a job has been done well, say so. And not just to them. Allow at least some of the praise to filter upstairs. If a subordinate feels that you have his best interests at heart and want him to succeed, you've won his dedication. (There are exceptions.)

IF THINGS GO AMISS, MOVE!   Don't sit by while the job gets plagued by crisis after crisis. Step in and set it back on track. Or use a subtle guiding hand. This is not meddling. You step in if it's a critical situation, not something minor.

BUILD TRUST You may have to take a few chances. But mutual trust is a very potent weapon in the business world, precisely because there is so little of it in circulation.

DELEGATE THE GOOD AND BAD Don't just pass along what's distasteful. We all know how that feels.

DON'T RUSH THE JOB It takes time to build an atmosphere of trust, respect, cooperation, and proper communication.

DELEGATE IN STAGES First delegate small tasks. Don't dump the whole work load on subordinates. Many managers are quick to do that when they get their first assistant, or a new one. Even if it means that you must do more than your share of the work at the beginning, remember that training is a gradual, steady process. Don't burn out your staff.

IF POSSIBLE, DELEGATE IN ADVANCE Results tend to be better when a staff member knows in advance that a problem or task is his "department."

MAKE THE DELEGATED TASK "COMPLETE" Give your delegates the whole story—background and desired results. Too often, they just get the tip of the iceberg and never fully understand what they are doing, or why. If possible, give them a whole job, not just a part—and *specific results to achieve*.

DON'T DELEGATE JOBS THAT ARE "OVER THE HEADS" OF THE DELEGATES It's okay to give them a challenge, or tax their limits. But if the goal is way out of their range, the results could be disastrous—a botched job, mistrust, poor morale, and a bad career move for you.

BE CONSISTENT If your subordinates don't know what to expect from you, they will be either too timid (fearing your wrath) or too bold (expecting no response)—or both.

WHEN YOU ARE THE DELEGATE

SEIZE THE OPPORTUNITY! Someone is giving you a chance to show your stuff. If it's a crummy job, you can still profit by building a relationship.

DON'T ACCEPT BLINDLY If you feel the job is not right for you, say so. If it could be done simpler elsewhere, say so.

IS THE WORK BEING DELEGATED CONSISTENT WITH YOUR GOALS? If you see the delegated tasks and responsibilities moving you into an area where you don't want to go you might want to decline the job. Don't be afraid to say as much.

GET YOUR SUPERIORS TO TELL YOU WHAT YOU NEED TO KNOW

MAKE SURE THAT THEIR FEEDBACK IS VALUABLE "Good" or

"Could be better" doesn't tell you much. You want to learn how your superiors think and what their standards are. Draw it out of them. Will they think you a pest? That's a risk you take.

INSIDERS' TRICKS

The delegation game can be played dirty. For the most part, you don't need me to tell you how. But here—in case of need—are a couple of delegation strategies that management experts don't like to talk about.

NEGATIVE DELEGATION   If you've got a subordinate who is after your job or threatens you in some other way, freeze him out by delegating only the most mundane tasks. Never ask for his opinion, and never comment on his good work. He'll ask for a transfer; or he'll be "broken" and continue, in harness, with considerably less initiative. But there's one other thing he might do—turn the subtle power battle into an all-out war.

VOLUNTEER FOR EVERYTHING   This takes the pressure off the boss when he's got things that nobody wants to handle. This kind of eagerness is so rare that you will become famous. But, you ask, how do I avoid becoming overcommitted? Simple. Make sure that you know how to delegate effectively, so that you do the volunteering and somebody else does the work. Devilish.

MODIFYING BEHAVIOR: B. F. SKINNER AND THE BUSINESS WORLD

Thomas Bonoma and Dennis Slevin have applied the basic principles of behavior modification to the manager's job. These principles are based on research that was first conducted at Harvard by B. F. Skinner using pigeons. Now behavior modification is used to help people stop smoking and cure phobias—and to get them to do what you want.

THE BASIC CONCEPTS

1. *If you reward a certain behavior, it is more likely to be repeated than is unrewarded behavior.* Reward for behavior is called reinforcement.
2. *Reward behavior intermittently rather than continuously.* This is called partial reinforcement. The idea is to keep 'em guessing. Sometimes you give the reward; sometimes not. Studies have shown that this uncertainty is a more effective inducement to effort than is certainty of reward.
3. *Complex behavior patterns are made up of simple behavior patterns linked together.* To reinforce complex behavior, you merely reinforce the simple behaviors and link them together.

There you have it: an approach for improving compliance by systematically reinforcing certain behaviors. For any given behavior, you can provide either a reward or a punishment—or you can simply ignore it.

HOW TO MAKE BEHAVIOR MODIFICATION WORK

(A) Look for and isolate the behavior you want to change. (B) Decide on the desired behavior pattern. (C) Set up a feedback system so you can keep track of the degree of change from the undesirable to the desirable behavior. (D) Determine the rewards, or consequences, if the behavior is, or is not, changed. (E) Reinforce the desired behavior by doling out the reward or punishment at a time when the relationship between the reinforcement and behavior will be clear.

Sounds a bit scary, doesn't it? This kind of conscious manipulation reeks of *1984.* But most of us do it to some degree without ever seeing it in these terms. And although you may not wish to establish a specific behavior-and-reward pattern for every task in the office, awareness of these principles can help you avoid some of the more destructive patterns.

AVOID CRITICISM OF A GENERAL NATURE It is destructive, because it tends to attack the more general attributes of a person, rather than a specific behavior. In essence, you are telling someone that he is no good, rather than that you did not like the way he did this or that.

IF YOU ARE GOING TO REWARD SOMEONE, DON'T WAIT TOO LONG Annual bonuses work because they are perceived as a kind of profit sharing for a good job or a profitable year. But they are not linked to specific behaviors. If you want to reward somebody for something, do it soon after the accomplishment so that the relationship is established.

WHEN SIZING UP SOMEONE'S WORK, TRY TO DO IT FREQUENT-LY, SPECIFICALLY, AND IN SMALL DOSES The longer you wait, the more nonspecific the appraisal becomes and the smaller the opportunity to reward or punish an isolated, specific behavior. This is why *coaching*, a frequent appraisal and pep talk (the this-is-right/this-is-not approach) works better than a formalized, judgmental performance appraisal.

IS BEHAVIOR MOD BEING USED ON YOU?

What incentives does your boss create for you? How does he try to influence your behavior? A common managerial mistake is choosing the wrong kind of punishment or reward. If you detect that your superiors are attempting to encourage a certain kind of behavior, you have several options:

If you feel comfortable "doing it their way," do so. But make sure that you get a meaningful reward. Suppose they want to give you money, but you want power. Let them know.

IF YOU CONSIDER THE BEHAVIOR YOUR BOSS IS TRYING TO ELICIT IN YOU TO BE UNACCEPTABLE, TURN THE TABLES It is possible for subordinates to reward management by getting desired results, assuming responsibility, and providing desired information. Establish a link between "doing it your way" and the reward. Chances are the bosses will chuckle about how you've got a mind of your own, but as long as you do your job, it's okay. Such behavior turns to defiance only when you fail to provide suitable rewards to your superiors.

WHEN USING BEHAVIOR MOD TO MANAGE YOUR BOSS, MAKE SURE THAT YOU DON'T FORGET PARTIAL REINFORCEMENT It's great to be loyal and trustworthy. But it's very easy to be taken for granted. Don't salivate every time the bell is rung. Throw a few curves. Let superiors know that a simple pat on the back doesn't always work, nor does increased responsibility or a bonus. Contrary to popular belief, the rewards will not cease. Rather, your unpredictability will keep them on their toes. On the flip side, don't reward them every time they behave to your liking.

More than an attempt at manipulation, partial reinforcement is a defense against being regarded simplistically. You've heard people say the equivalent of "Oh, Jones'll do anything if he thinks there's a few extra bucks in it. Let's call him." Jones may get a bit richer, but probably never very powerful.

METHODS OF LEADERSHIP

Nobody leads in quite the same way. Some leadership roles call for vastly different approaches from others. And the specific needs and requirements of the individual play a role in determining how one approaches a leadership position.

Professors Thomas Bonoma and Dennis Slevin, of the University of Pittsburgh, have identified four basic types of leadership in their book *Executive Survival Manual* (Belmont, California: Wadsworth Publishing, 1978):

- *Autocrat.* The autocrat makes decisions alone, requesting little or no information from subordinates.
- *Consultative autocrat.* This leader gets as much data as possible from his staff, but then makes the key decisions alone.
- *Consensus manager.* This manager encourages not only group input, but also group decision making.
- *Shareholder manager.* The manager does not encourage input or information exchange, but allows the group to make the decision.

Essentially, the differences in these approaches are purely in terms of (a) where the information comes from and (b) who makes the decisions:

- *Autocrat.* Relies on self for information—maintains authority.
- *Consultative autocrat.* Subordinates get increased access to information and increase input, but the boss still calls the shots.
- *Consensus manager.* The group gets more involved in exchanging information and in making the actual decisions.

These three approaches are all valid, given the conditions propitious to them. Bonoma and Slevin deride the "shareholder" approach as bad management—an unjustified delegation of authority without foundation.

It is worthwhile to determine which leadership style you and your boss each display:

- *Where do you get your information?* Peers? Superiors? Subordinates? The conventional information sources (libraries, books, computers)? Anywhere you can?
- *Who decides?* You alone? Your staff? Who above you?

Now ask yourself if this is your preferred modus operandi. If not, what can you do to change it? Every style of leadership has its own unique set of problems and advantages. And not all styles suit every situation. Manage as an autocrat and run the risk of making a decision without benefit of crucial information and other points of view. Manage by consensus and run the risk of the problems that come from group pressures and conflict. Take a look at the kinds of decisions you have to make, the kinds of people you work for, the kinds that work for you, and your company in general. Then take into account the kind of person you are and decide on an approach to leadership.

Your approach need not fit neatly into one of the three categories. It could be your own hybrid of two or more approaches. Sometimes different responsibilities call for different methods.

RISK TAKING

Explaining the obstacles to innovation, many Westerners cite peculiarities of the Soviet economic system. At its most basic, there is a disinclination to take chances. "There is a constant fear among bureaucrats," says a U.S. metals executive, "that if an unproven technology doesn't work, they will end up in Siberia." But to a U.S. manager, one Western economist comments, "risk is an opportunity, because that's where the pay-offs are."

—"Russian Know-How,"
The Wall Street Journal,
March 21, 1980, page 1.

Having "potential" won't get you much further than getting hired for your first job. You've got to bring that potential out. In the competitive business environment, you can rise to the challenge and display your talent openly. Or you can freeze up, "choke," or just turn in an average, lackluster performance.

Often, what determines how well you put out, and whether you get noticed, is the way you take chances. To get ahead, you must put yourself on the line. That's how individuals succeed, and that's how companies succeed. With the increasing rate of change, "the status quo" is almost nonexistent—you are constantly at risk.

WHAT DOES RISK TAKING MEAN?

In the final analysis, risk taking comes down to either betting on yourself (and influencing the outcome) or betting on chance (the probability that things will go in your favor). Even when you bet on others, you are betting, to an extent, on yourself—on *your judgment* of the ability of others.

Risk taking means going from a situation of some security to another, less secure, situation. Every executive must place himself at risk in order to advance.

HOW FAR ARE YOU WILLING TO GO?   This is the critical issue. And it differs according to the individual. Some people are willing to take greater risks than others. They perceive situations differently. They differ in personality and intellect. It may even be a matter of genes. Each person sizes up the situation—gauges odds, risks, and rewards in a different way. *A great many people are unwilling to take risks that directly involve themselves.* Often, this is the critical difference between the executive who goes places and the one who marks time.

WIN OR LOSE, YOU'VE GOT TO PLAY THE GAME IF YOU WANT TO GET GOOD AT IT   If you play it safe for an extended period, you may begin to lose your touch. Keep trying, even in the face of failure. You will learn how to assess risks and rewards more accurately and can then formulate a set of rules that work for you.

THERE ARE TWO BASIC TYPES OF RISKS IN BUSINESS: ECONOMIC AND INTERPERSONAL   You take economic risks to make money. For your company and for yourself.

In the interpersonal area, you take a risk every time you decide to hold on to or let go of power. In this sense, you are taking a risk when you delegate, but also if you do the job yourself. Another kind of personal risk involves the decision to open up to someone—let someone know what you *really* think or feel. The flip side is to play your cards close to your chest. If your boss asks you how you feel about his pet project, you might want to assess the risks of telling him the truth—it stinks—possibly saving the company megabucks—versus the risks of stroking him while he goes ahead to disaster.

RISKS CAN BE ACTIVE OR PASSIVE Some risks involve inaction—an attempt to avoid risks (to avoid losses). But an active, dynamic risk is one in which one "goes for it"—an attempt to make gains.

CREATIVITY AND RISK TAKING ARE INTIMATELY CONNECTED There are lots of creative ideas, but few creative achievers. Creative ideas are often unusual; unconventional. Fighting for them almost invariably involves risks.

YOU CAN HEDGE AGAINST RISK BY MAKING IT A GROUP DECISION But, you say, the group will want to play it safe, talk you out of it. Not so. Research has shown that groups usually influence individual decision making toward higher risks. If it's your idea and the group decides to go ahead, you'll probably get the credit for proposing it. But you've spread the risk around, as a safeguard against failure.

HOW TO TAKE RISKS

NEVER RISK MORE THAN YOU CAN AFFORD TO LOSE An old gambling rule. The tough part is determining how much you can afford to lose and the degree of risk to that money or thing.

Make sure that the risks are justified. Don't risk a lot for a little. It's very tough to follow this rule. But it may help to remember and heed it when you are about to expose yourself to considerable risk just for a little satisfaction, face-saving, or a "matter of principle" that is less than fundamental. And remember, revenge may be sweet, but not in the corporation.

DON'T DISCOUNT INTUITION The risk should "feel" right.

CONFRONT THE FEARS THAT MAY BE HOLDING YOU BACK Fear of failure, fear of uncertainty, fear of disapproval, to name a few.

KNOW YOUR LIMITATIONS It is to your credit that you are willing to step up and bet on yourself. But don't let that satisfaction lull you into making a bad bet. There will be times when you will be outclassed, outranked, or outfoxed. Don't be foolhardy. A long shot is one thing. An impossible or no-win situation is quite another.

ALWAYS HAVE A CLEAR IDEA OF HOW MUCH AUTHORITY YOU HAVE AND HOW MUCH POWER YOU YIELD Authority is officially sanctioned control. Power can and often does go beyond this sanction. If you have a "power base" among your peers and key superiors, you can take the risk of exceeding your authority, but you must appraise the situation *before* acting.

KNOW THE RULES There are virtually no rules—everything is subject to change; but the idea is to be an observer of human and organizational behavior. See if you can isolate the favored modus operandi of your peers, supervisors, and subordinates. You can then venture a guess as to how they will react to any move you make. And that will help you assess the risks.

HAVE A CONTINGENCY PLAN Suppose your risk doesn't pay off. Are you ready to cut your losses? Perhaps you can save face, or even make a small gain. Seasoned risk takers prepare with a variety of alternatives or contingencies. They are better equipped to compromise, cooperate, and negotiate. One executive told me, "I like to go in feeling 'heads I win, tails I win.' " Of course, if that were really the case, where would be the risk? But it's an ideal worth striving for.

PAY ATTENTION TO TIME AND PLACE Be tactful. Don't use social situations for tactical moves. Don't make your move at a time or place in which someone will be unnecessarily degraded or embarrassed. Most people understand that risk taking is part of the game. But your insensitivity and your victim's humiliation won't be forgotten. Behave that way often and you'll have lots of people gunning for you.

Rather, try to orchestrate any risk-taking move involving others so that it's kept "in the family."

GAUGE IN ADVANCE JUST HOW FAR YOU CAN GO Never (well, almost never) exceed these limits. There are times when the spoils go to the risk taker who goes where wise men never tread. But you should know when you are stepping over the line.

GO FOR MAXIMUM IMPACT Lawyers know that it isn't just the strength of the argument, but how it is argued that counts. When you take a risk, be dramatic. Do it orally, with style. A memo or other "paper risk" cools it off and leaves you vulnerable to behind-the-scenes moves and varying interpretations. Avoid any risk-taking methods that blunt your momentum.

GIVE 'EM SOME SPACE Don't push too hard. When you take a risk, it's okay to apply pressure to help things along. But if you push too hard, you may bust your hand.

KNOW WHEN TO QUIT Ever notice how one risk leads to another? And another? At the time you take the first risk, you should already know how far to go. When you reach that point and you're not ahead, cash in your chips. Maybe.

JUDGE YOUR WINNINGS AND LOSSES OVER THE LONG TERM Unless it's a winner-take-all situation (which should be avoided, if possible), you shouldn't be discouraged if you lose. The important thing is where you stand over the long haul.

FOUR MAJOR RISKS

According to Richard Byrd, author of *A Guide to Personal Risk Taking* (New York: AMACOM, 1974), these are the rough ones:

THREATENING TO QUIT This is an all-out risk unless you've got a better job already lined up. Do so only when your most basic rights and principles are being violated.

SEEKING A CONFRONTATION   Leveling with someone about your opposition to his apparent interests or his position on an issue is a risk to you, because you are threatening him, thereby prompting retaliation. However, the risk is even greater to the other side, because he must frame a response: mount an offense or a defense, or neutralize by agreeing with you. Confrontation can be a healthy risk if those in your work environment can deal with emotionalism.

GOING OVER OR AROUND THE BOSS   This is akin to threatening to quit, because it is also a high-stakes risk, and you may lose your job if it backfires. Even if it doesn't, you'll lose your boss's trust. Do the rewards justify it? Well, if you stand to gain enough, you might not need his trust. Maybe you'll even wind up *his* boss.

STICKING TO YOUR GUNS   If you firmly believe you are right, holding out against all odds may be the only thing to do. Just make sure you do it with class, without acrimony and bitterness. And make sure that the issue is important enough to be obstinate about.

NEGOTIATING

Negotiation is called for in any situation involving incompatible goals between parties.

IS THIS NEGOTIABLE?

ARE YOU IN A POSITION TO DEAL?   First, consider whether there is an insurmountable power gulf. If you carry much more weight than the opposition, you won't need to negotiate. If the other party carries much more power than you, he will take what he wants. So the time to negotiate is when there are no gross power differences.

HAS HE GOT SOMETHING YOU WANT?   Or: Have you got something he wants?

ARE THERE ANY PHYSICAL, TEMPORAL, OR LEGAL OBSTACLES?

HAVE A PLAN

WHAT ARE YOU LOOKING FOR?   What is your best deal? You must have a clear notion of your best deal if you hope to move the other party in that direction.

WHAT WILL YOU ACCEPT?   Besides knowing what the best deal is, you must know what the worst deal consists of. The bottom line represents the minimum acceptable offer, beyond which you will not go.

WHAT IS YOUR OPPONENT AFTER?   The idea is to find out what

---

the other party's bottom line is while keeping him from finding out yours. Then you want to move his bottom line in a direction more favorable to you: Get him to give ground without relinquishing much of your own.

DECIDE WHO WILL DO THE NEGOTIATING   You are not in this for ego massage; you are in it to win. Sometimes that means delegating the negotiation to someone else. Or bringing in a team. Team negotiation has the advantage of sheer numbers, and your case may be buttressed by several different points of view and areas of expertise. Just make sure everyone understands the strategy and agrees on tactics and the chain of command.

   Going it alone has advantages, too. You call the shots and don't have to worry about someone else screwing things up.

DECIDE ON YOUR APPROACH   Tackle the tough issues first? Or last? Take up points one at a time or in blocks? Negotiate each point as separate, or use Kissinger-type "linkage"? What are your basic assumptions? Does your opponent share them, or does he have a set of his own? How will you get him to see it your way?

DECIDE HOW TOUGH YOU WILL BE   Will you compromise, and to what extent? Are you prepared to come away empty-handed, or must you strike some kind of deal? What can you afford to give away?

TIME AND PLACE   This is more important than it might seem. Always go for the home-court advantage. If not, seek a "neutral" site.

   Keep time on your side. The best time to negotiate is when your adversary is feeling the pressure of time and you are not. If he is in from out of town, try to find out how long he is planning to stay. If you are from out of town, you might want to conceal that information.

REHEARSE   Not only might this prepare you for the unexpected, but it will also provide some valuable insights. Do some role playing.

BRAINSTORM   Throw out ideas, tactics, strategies. The key rule in brainstorming is that "no idea is too stupid to be mentioned." One never knows.

CONTINGENCIES   You should now be equipped to develop a few contingencies in case the opponent has a few curves of his own (which he undoubtedly will).

AT THE BARGAINING TABLE

Use all the tactics, as needed, against your opponent:

- *Wait him out;* show patience.
- *Surprise him.*
- *Back off* for no apparent reason.
- *Table an issue.* Bring it up later when conditions are optimal for you.

- *About-face.* He is following your reasoning and direction; then you go the opposite way.
- *Fake-out.* Make it seem like you are going one way. All the while, you are setting up your opposite number, surreptitiously moving in another direction.
- *Use endorsements.* Break out statements of support by experts or prominent people. Better yet, get them there in person.
- *Bracket.* Try to flush out the truth by shooting left, right, center, high, low, middle—and watching what happens.
- *Use questions for several approaches.* They can get attention, be provocative, and give direction: "Have you given any thought to doing it *this* way?" "What would you say if I told you . . . ?"

    Questions can bring things to an end—get to the bottom line: "So, do we have the job?" "Where do we go from here?"

    Then there are the more conventional uses of questions—to gain information, or to give it: "What is . . . ?" "Did you know that . . . ?" "Why is . . . ?"

DON'T MERELY LISTEN; WATCH!   Everyone displays a wide variety of nonverbal cues. Is your adversary clenching his fists? Scratching his head? Leaning forward across the table? Are his arms folded? These things tell you a great deal about how he is feeling at the time—tense; puzzled; aggressive; defensive.

Be aware of your own nonverbal cues. A nimble negotiator may actually use them to create a false impression; he may, for example, look nervous or fidgety to give the impression he's on the ropes. The adversary, smelling blood, moves in for the kill, only to be met by an effective counter-punch.

IT'S NOT JUST WHAT HE SAYS, BUT HOW HE SAYS IT   Listen to the tone of voice. Watch for gestures. And be aware of exactly how the point is made. "Off the top of my head" is meant to imply a spontaneous remark, an estimate, a ball-park figure. Is it really? Or does he merely want you to think so? How about this one: "By the way. . ." implies that what follows is an aside, a minor or secondary point. In fact, it may be *the* point he's been working on all meeting long. Or this one: "This is strictly confidential" tells you that you are privileged to be let in on a secret, and that he wants you to share it with him alone. Well, who else has been told this "confidential" information? And does he really expect you to keep it to yourself? Or does he hope you'll spread it around? Similar expressions: "Between you and me . . ." and "Off the record . . ."

PUT THE OTHER PARTY AT EASE   Pay attention to his needs, physical and psychological. It is understood that you are bargaining in your best self-interest, but negotiation sessions shouldn't be attempts to beat each other's brains in. If everyone is relaxed and functioning well, you will do business. When someone feels that he's lost control, he often freezes and refuses to budge. So you get nothing done and must have another meeting.

(Of course, if he's under the pressure of a deadline, you can really put the screws to him by forcing him to deal under duress. But he'll remember that for a long time.)

Putting someone at ease can mean accommodating the nonsmoker. And it can mean displaying some empathy—letting your opponent know that you see his side of it.

IF YOU REACH AN AGREEMENT

Often, unfortunately, the game is not over now that it's contract time. It's amazing how many deals break down or get delayed at this stage. Usually, the disagreement involves one or more of three basic issues:

- the amount of legal protection afforded the principal parties
- the duration of the agreement
- how much of the specifics gets written into the contract—and how much remains a gentlemen's agreement, subject to interpretation

The first question you should consider is whether you need a formal contract. Often, a person's word or good faith means more. People with their integrity and honor on the line will comply with the spirit of an agreement, especially if they've committed themselves in front of others.

Legal contracts are, of course, easier to enforce, but many clauses will prove subject to interpretation. Besides, they are far from black-and-white. People tend to look to the paper, rather than to themselves, for guidance on how to comply.

If you go with a formal contract, you then have to decide how specific to get. If it is a deal to distribute a product, will it specify a set sales volume that must be reached, or will it be "best efforts"? Many deals have been killed because lawyers crowded them with clauses and subclauses. Sometimes, a compromise can be reached in which the conditions are neither set nor open-ended; rather, they are tied to changing conditions in the company, marketplace, etc. This way, neither party is locked into a static agreement, and each can share in the profits or losses in a manner that reflects the environment and performance.

IF YOU FAIL TO REACH AN AGREEMENT

Besides the obvious approaches like backing off or going elsewhere to get what you want, there's always mediation and arbitration. You can use a nonaligned consultant, industry expert, or attorney to help fashion an agreement. Many trade and professional organizations will arbitrate. Arbitration is a binding judgment, so both parties must first agree to accept the decision.

A FEW FINAL WORDS ON NEGOTIATION

WALKING AWAY SATISFIED DOESN'T ALWAYS MEAN THAT YOU'VE DONE WELL   When they finally reach an agreement, people tend to feel reduced tension and, therefore, are usually happy. Research shows that, in most cases, both sides are satisfied when they come to terms. But this has little to do with the terms of the deal. What did you gain? What did you give up? These are the questions that your superiors and colleagues will be interested in, not the smile on your face.

DON'T PROJECT   Most people, in trying to analyze the opponent's point of view, project their own attitudes, perceptions, and assumptions. There is an excellent chance that your adversary does not see the issues, the goals, and the world the way you see them.

AIM HIGH—BUT NOT TOO HIGH   Always shoot for the maximum deal you can reasonably expect. Chances are, you'll have to come down. But it's better to come down from a top offer than from a mediocre one. However, remember that if you are too high, you can bring about a dead-lock, because people will react negatively to your goal and think that you don't really want to negotiate.

HONESTY REALLY WORKS SOMETIMES   I've heard many executives say, "He knows what I'll accept, and I know what it's really worth, so why can't we cut the bull and quit wasting time?" In reply, many salesmen say that just one slip—that one time in a dozen that he gets the better of you—makes all those extra hours worthwhile.

   However, when you are dealing with a principled executive who is *well prepared* and each of you knows exactly where the other stands, being up front can be exhilarating. You won't be able to do it with everyone, because your honesty will often be met with deception. But there will be a few who you can deal with without guile. These people usually turn out to be lifelong friends.

PUBLIC SPEAKING

Any talk should:
- get audience attention and keep it
- be interesting
- be delivered in clear, simple language
- summarize key points
- motivate people

HOW TO PREPARE

WRITE A SHORT "PLAN OF ATTACK"   State your purpose and how you propose to go about fulfilling it.

NOTE THE KEY POINTS ON INDEX CARDS AND SPREAD THEM

OUT IN FRONT OF YOU   You may also wish to use the "mind map method" (*see* Chapter 7).

STRUCTURE THE TALK   First, you want to arouse your listeners' interest. Get them interested in you, the subject, a problem you are addressing, or a specific, provocative issue. *The opening* will depend on the overall structure. Some common approaches are: (1) stating the problem, the solution, and the rewards; (2) itemizing the causes of something, and pointing out the effects; (3) bringing out your theme in a historical perspective by offering details in chronological order.
   Always end with a summary.

PREPARE VISUALS   Photos, diagrams, charts, important words or numbers are all helpful, where appropriate. If a visual doesn't add anything or aid in comprehension, don't use it.

KNOW YOUR AUDIENCE

- How much do they know about your subject? Does everyone know about the same amount, or is there a large gulf in knowledge?
- How much background and introductory material is needed?
- Will they be interested? Why?
- What are their attitudes? Opinions and other background?
- What do they know about you? Your authority and expertise?
- In terms of status or power, are you speaking "up" or "down"? (Is this the board of directors of your company? Or a group of prospective job applicants?)
- Learn what you can about past speeches given to this group: speeches and topics its members liked and disliked; the kind of delivery they prefer.
- Anything objectionable? Is an off-color joke okay? Any subject touchy?
- Now, taking all this into account, formulate the style, content, and delivery of the speech. And try to anticipate the reception the audience will give you—hostile? friendly? questioning? skeptical?

REHEARSE   Get familiar with the material, both the words to be spoken and the visuals to be shown. Time your run-through and make sure it fits the allotted period, leaving ample time for questions. If poor transitions or poor logic become apparent in rehearsal, eliminate them and then rehearse again. Several rehearsals will help you to look and feel more comfortable.

IF IT'S A NEW SPEAKING ENVIRONMENT, ARRIVE EARLY   Get the feel of the surroundings. Perhaps you can place the chair, blackboard, or other props in a way that's more to your liking. If there are cables, wires, or other obstacles, you can get rid of them or at least be forewarned. It's also good for your attitude—a feeling of familiarity helps delivery.

MAKE SURE THAT YOUR EQUIPMENT IS SET UP AND OPERA-TIONAL   Is the film or slide projector set up and plugged in? Film threaded? Are slides loaded? Projectors prefocused? Tapes cued? Can everyone see?

GIVING THE TALK

BE WELL GROOMED AND MAINTAIN GOOD POSTURE   Look smart; sound smart.

BE CLEAR   Use short sentences and short words. Simplify complex ideas.

BE LOGICAL   Good, crisp, graceful transitions.

KEEP THE INTENDED PACE   The talk should not be markedly longer—or shorter—than planned.

BE AWARE OF AUDIENCE RESPONSE   Are they bored? If they are yawning, dozing, doodling, reading, giggling, or cleaning fingernails, it's time to try to recapture their attention.

TAKE BREAKS   One or a few, depending on how long you speak and on the format of your speech. Presentations that have variety—films, etc.—require fewer breaks than "all-talk" speeches.

SPEAK AT A NATURAL VOLUME AND IN A NATURAL TONE   Do not read; it will create a monotone. You may raise your voice to gain attention.

SPEAK CLEARLY   Don't slur or mumble. Think before and as you speak. *Listen* to yourself. How do you sound?

BREATHE NATURALLY

CHOOSE YOUR PHRASES CAREFULLY   Try to avoid "um," "uh," and "you know."

DON'T BE NERVOUS ABOUT BEING NERVOUS   Most audiences expect some unease in all speakers but the professional. They tend not to notice excessive nervousness; just ignore it.

WATCH WHAT YOU DO WITH YOUR HANDS   When standing, never let your hands drop below your waist. You can hold something; index cards, pencil, pen, eyeglasses, papers, a pointer. You may also gesture with your hands or fold them. When you sit, it's okay to rest one hand in your lap.

LET YOUR ENTHUSIASM SHINE THROUGH   If you are not enthusiastic, you haven't prepared well enough. You should be able to get "up" for even the most uncongenial subject.

MAKE EYE CONTACT WITH PEOPLE IN THE AUDIENCE   Shift your attention about the room to different people, but always look at the audience.

USE FACIAL EXPRESSIONS AND GESTURES   They help you communicate. You use them in everyday conversation. Why not now?

WHEN A QUESTION IS ASKED, MAKE SURE YOU ANSWER IT   It's usually a mistake to use a question as a lead-in to another point. But if you should do that, make sure you answer the question along the way; or say, "I'll answer your question, but with your permission, I'd like to first . . ." Don't go off on tangents.

AFTERWARD

- Ask yourself how it went. Did the audience enjoy it? Did they respond? Were they persuaded? Motivated?
- Ask others who were there what they thought.
- Is there any way to measure the outcome?

IF YOU ANTICIPATE SPENDING MUCH TIME BEFORE THE BROADCAST MEDIA, GET PROFESSIONAL ADVICE

Perhaps you are called upon to be a company spokesperson. You've got to defend the firm against the charges of a consumer advocate on a local talk show, or testify at a Senate or EPA hearing on environmental impact.

There are several firms that will, in several days, put you through the paces—a simulated TV studio setup, complete with interviewer and antagonistic questions. You'll analyze the videotapes and learn how to look and act on TV, and how to handle yourself better in the hot seat.

Among the best-known media training companies are:

JACK HILTON, INC.   Hilton runs the two-day TeleCounsel program limited to eight participants. It consists of interview situations and videotape replays of them, with constructive criticism from "faculty" members. Hilton believes in as much realism as possible in order to get participants away from the "it's not for real" psychology, so he uses a fully equipped TV studio and professional interviewers. Past courses have featured such luminaries as Edwin Newman, Sander Vanocur, and George Reedy. The cost is over $10,000.

Contact:
Jack Hilton, Inc.
60 East 42nd Street
New York, New York 10017

SPEECH DYNAMICS   is the brainchild of former actress and talk-show personality Dorothy Sarnoff. Ms. Sarnoff has written several books and numerous articles on speech and personality training. It is a wholly owned subsidiary of the Ogilvy and Mather ad agency. The Speech Dynamics program is flexible: Depending on the needs of the clients, it can consist of a two-day seminar, provide studio sessions, even large group meetings.

The program includes media training, but also concentrates on speeches and presentations.

Contact:
Speech Dynamics and Communications Service, Inc.
111 West 57th Street
New York, New York 10020

HOW TO ARGUE*

Ever since we were kids, we've been told not to argue. We argue all the time. And there is nothing inherently wrong with arguing. It's a legitimate method of resolving a disagreement and ends in your (a) convincing the other party that you are right, (b) becoming convinced that your opponent is right, (c) arriving at a compromise, or (d) arriving at an impasse. It needn't degenerate into a brawl, although it frequently does.

Verbal brawling, like the physical kind, demonstrates a lack of control and an inability to persuade peacefully. And it often brings out the darker side of your personality—the part that's best left below the surface, or expressed, if need be, at more appropriate times.

Since an argument is something you want to win—and it is usually in your best interests to do so—keep the basic tactical points in mind:

TRY TO SIZE UP THE ARGUMENT AS IT TAKES SHAPE, BUT BEFORE IT GETS GOING   Are you going to be on the defensive, or on the offensive? Is the subject or position really worth arguing about? By the way, exactly what *will* you be arguing about?

AVOID ARGUING WITH FANATICS

BE NICE

UNTIL SHOWN OTHERWISE, ASSUME THAT THE OTHER PARTY HAS SOME REASONABLY GOOD REASONS FOR THE POSITION HE IS TAKING   Most people are rational. If they aren't, you won't be able to convince them anyway.

LISTEN CAREFULLY AT ALL TIMES   Speed of reply counts for very little in an argument. Therefore, it is not necessary to formulate a reply while the other person is talking. Listen to what he has to say, retaining just a vague idea of your reply. Acute listening allows you to spit back precisely what the opposer has said. This makes any attack on him more credible. Besides, how are you going to compose an effective reply if you don't know what has been said?

---

*Some material adapted from *How to Win an Argument*, by Michael A. Gilbert, Copyright © 1979 by McGraw-Hill. Used by permission of McGraw-Hill Book Company.

IF THE OTHER PERSON IS NOT LISTENING TO YOU, DON'T LOSE YOUR COOL

PATIENTLY REPEAT

CONCENTRATE   Not only will you make a better argument, but you will generate more intensity: Brain power can be "felt."

RELAX   Thanks to Clint Eastwood spaghetti westerns, we have all learned that we can be quite deadly when we are relaxed. We also demonstrate that we can't be intimidated—and this can be quite unnerving to an opponent who tries to win by getting under your skin.

WHENEVER YOU ARE UNSURE OF WHAT YOU ARE ARGUING ABOUT, SEEK A CLARIFICATION   You may have already reached agreement on the important issues and are now just debating a minor or procedural question. Having a point explained to you also serves as a break in case you need time to think. If the opponent has "pulled a switch," compel him to come back.

DON'T ATTACK THE CONCLUSIONS OF YOUR OPPONENT; ATTACK THE REASONING THAT GOT HIM THERE   Disagreeing with a conclusion does not produce any movement: He thinks one way, and you another—impasse. To get him to move, you've got to erode the foundations upon which his conclusions are built.

IF YOUR OPPONENT USES ANALOGIES OR EXAMPLES, TRY TO BREAK THEM DOWN BY SHOWING THAT THEY ARE NOT REALLY ANALOGOUS OR SIMILAR TO THE SITUATION IN QUESTION
   Most people love to fall back on examples or shoddy analogies. Don't let them get away with it. On the other hand, if you think you can drive a point home with an analogy or example and (a) feel you can get away with it, or (b) can defend it, by all means use it.

ESTABLISH THE BASIC PRINCIPLES THAT UNDERLIE YOUR ARGUMENT AND THAT OF YOUR OPPONENT   The idea is to defend yours and attack his. The main principles are the lifeline of your argument. Or they can be its Achilles' heel.

DEFEND YOUR PRINCIPLES, EVEN IF IT MEANS CONCEDING A NEGATIVE OR UNCOMFORTABLE CONSEQUENCE   If you are willing to desert your basic position just to avoid the heat generated by an unpleasant situation, you are on shaky ground.

WATCH OUT FOR CIRCULAR REASONING   This is the name of the game when an argument assumes something it's supposed to be proving—as, for example, in saying that if you want to win an argument, you should follow these rules, because without them, you will certainly lose. Unless you are dealing with a dummy, never use circular reasoning. Even if you get away with it, onlookers will think that you are a sloppy thinker. When you see circular reasoning in others, attack! Point it out, but not derisively. Make sure that others are aware of the fallacious argument.

DON'T ARGUE OVER LABELS There are umpteen definitions of a communist, a good Christian, a capitalist, etc. It's too subjective. Find out what is meant and argue at that level.

DEMAND THAT THE OPPONENT JUSTIFY ONE-WORD, GLIB CONCLUSIONS "Nonsense!" "Absurd!" "Ridiculous!" do not constitute part of an argument; they are conclusions. Demand to know precisely why your opponent feels this way.

THE WILL OF THE MAJORITY HAS LITTLE TO DO WITH RIGHT OR WRONG Just because "most people use this" or "think that," it doesn't automatically follow that such behavior or opinions are valid. And if your opponent says that "everyone knows this" or "does that," and you or someone you know does not, then he is wrong.

BE CAREFUL WHEN INVOKING THE EXPERTS An expert is only an expert if he is one on the subject you are discussing. Dr. Spock had strong opinions on the Vietnam War, but his expertise is in child care, not international affairs. Therefore his Vietnam stand didn't carry much weight as expert opinion. *A posture becomes flawed if it relies on the opinions of an expert inappropriate to the subject.*

WHEN AN EXPERT IS INVOKED, BE SURE TO DISTINGUISH BETWEEN HIS PROFFERED FACTS AND HIS EXPERT OPINION Opinions, even from experts, can always be challenged. But when an expert is able to supply crucial facts, he strengthens one side or another of the argument.

Examine the character of the expert. Is he given to making rash statements? Outlandish predictions? For example, relying on the views of Nobel laureate William Shockley could get you in trouble, because he has been associated with the view that certain races are genetically inferior. This view is so unpopular, that even the most erudite and innocuous statements of the man are often suspect.

IF THE EXPERT HAS GONE OVER YOUR HEAD, DON'T TRY TO FAKE IT Never agree with him if you don't know what he is saying. Make him explain—and back up—his statements.

ATTACKS ON A PERSON'S CHARACTER ARE USUALLY OUT OF BOUNDS Name-calling and character assassination are common. Deal with them by demanding that your opponent justify any slur or allegation and explain why he feels it is relevant to the argument.

KEEP TRACK OF ASSUMPTIONS You may want to attack a basic assumption of your opponent. Or retract one of yours.

THAT SOMETHING SEEMS LOGICAL, PROBABLY TRUE, OR APPARENTLY ELEMENTAL IN A CAUSE-AND-EFFECT RELATIONSHIP

DOES NOT MEAN THAT IT IS TRUE Be skeptical. Question everything. Believe nothing. If you point out that there is even one other explanation for the cause of a problem or situation, you have cast doubt on the validity of the opponent's claim that his explanation is *the* explanation.

JUST ONE EXCEPTION IS SUFFICIENT TO FALSIFY GENERALIZATION It is unwise to shoot for eternal truths or universal conclusions; you are very vulnerable to even a minor exception. Don't generalize any more than you have to. Generalizations are a common trap, because they often sound learned and authoritative.

WHEN YOU ARE OFFERED AN EITHER-OR CHOICE, BE ON YOUR GUARD Some opponents make a conscious attempt to limit your choices artificially. Philosopher Michael A. Gilbert cites the example "America— Love It or Leave It."

An excellent book on the art of arguing is one from which much of this material was drawn: *How to Win an Argument*, by Michael A. Gilbert (New York: McGraw-Hill, 1979).

A GUIDE TO MANAGEMENT THEORIES
AND CURRENT FADS

Most management theories are packed into books, seminars, speeches and tapes. Indeed, they are big business, and the market seems insatiable as managers struggle to stay ahead of the pack and produce results in the companies. The Japanese miracle has caused American managers to reevaluate their way of doing things. A general preference for the short-term results over the long-term view has left Americans vulnerable to the quick fix.

I would take pride in providing the reader with a guide to the new management theories that appear to work. But most haven't been adequately tested. And by the time they are, they will be out of vogue anyway. So here—just so you won't feel out of touch—is a guide to the most popular management trends, theories and terms to date, plus sourcebooks in case a theory strikes your fancy and you want to know more.

Back to Basics In the view of authors Thomas Peters and Robert Waterman, *In Search of Excellence* is where every company ought to go. "Far too many managers have lost sight of the basics, in our opinion: quick action, service to customers, practical innovation and the fact that you can't get any of these without virtually everyone's commitment." In *A Passion for Excellence*, written by Tom Peters and Nancy Austin, the authors claim that a "back-to-basics revolution" is sweeping corporate America.

Corporate Culture   A term popularized by Allan A. Kennedy in his book *Corporate Cultures*. Kennedy, a former McKinsey consultant, based his 1982 book on much the same research used in *In Search of Excellence*. But his book concentrates on the values, goals, games, rituals and heroes that form a company's style and atmosphere. Kennedy believes that shared values, rituals, beliefs and ideals exert a strong influence on a firm's success or failure.

Competitive Advantage   Strategic planning is still important, and is being neglected. In *Competitive Advantage*, Harvard Business School strategic-planning expert Michael E. Porter states his case.

In the past, mistakes were made by leaving the planning to line managers and planners and having them reviewed by senior management. *Bottom-up planning is a no-no.* Porter advocates a stronger relationship between senior management and subordinates, with seniors initiating top-down planning.

Quality is currently being neglected. Quality is not simply a matter of satisfying certain internal requirements. Relative quality, *i.e.*, how consumers view the quality of your product in relation to those of your competitors, is critical.

Product differentiation is critical. Products must be cleverly designed and manipulated so that they are perceived as different by the public. Managers must track changes in consumer tastes and behavior.

A competitive edge must be sustained, or it will be lost. Planning must take customers, suppliers, and distributors into account in planning and implementing a strategy.

Basic problem.   For this to work, a company and its senior management must be willing to devote considerable time and money to research and strategy formulation. And so far, Porter hasn't told us how to implement these strategic plans once they are formulated.

Demassing   Sounds so much better than saying that you are firing people, slimming down the work force and even demoting managers. Just say you are demassing.

Peter F. Drucker   The grandaddy of management theorists. Still going strong at 75, Drucker is the Spencer Tracy of the management field, hardworking, streetwise, and with a sense of history. Most of all, he has wisdom.

It is impossible to read a Drucker book without learning a great deal. The depth of his knowledge is staggering, and his insights are usually valuable, even if he leaves you wondering how he came to his conclusions. After fifty years of experience and twenty-two books, the reader gets the benefit of his scope and historical perspective. He was an acute observer of the business and management scene long before it was fashionable and profitable.

In his latest book, *Innovation and Entrepreneurship: Principles and Practices* (New York: Harper & Row, 1985), Peter Drucker states his views on a topical subject. His basic theme is that innovation is not intangible, but something that can be achieved through discipline and careful practice. He also champions "creative imitation," citing the IBM-PC as an example, and "entrepreneurial judo," as in how low-cost smaller Japanese producers of copiers dropped Xerox to its knees. Being first, he notes, is not always best. Drucker addresses himself to the reasons why managers fail to perceive opportunities for innovation, and suggests, contrary to a popular view, that the start-up entrepreneur should stay in charge, even when the company has grown into a large corporation.

Entrepreneurs   Could be the movie stars of the eighties and nineties, in that it is what everyone wants to be. Connotes young, brilliant, independent, and very, very rich, very, very fast. In practice, entrepreneurs play an important role in the American economy and society, as hard-working, hard-driven, businesspeople willing to take risks and seek fortune. In terms of numbers, very few are involved in high-tech or anything innovative for that matter. But they are very competitive.

Entrepreneurship has its place. But we are finding out what we already knew. Starting a business is very different from stabilizing it, managing it and overseeing its sustained growth. Business does not live on entrepreneurship alone.

If the Japanese have their *samurai* to revere, warriors who have pledged fealty to their lords and to the common good, we Americans have our John Waynes and Lone Rangers, rugged individualists winning battles in their own ways, remaining on the outskirts of the mainstream. It is easy to see why entrepreneurs have been the objects of hero worship in the world economy that increasingly resembles a war game.

Just like the movies, not everyone can be a star. Don't be dazzled. In fact, as a recent study by *Inc.* Magazine and *USA Today* revealed, "Forget rebel. Forget misfit. Forget poor boy makes good. As a group, the creators of the new economy come straight from the mainstream, upwardly mobile Anglo-Saxon inheritors of the traditional American dream. Eighty-five percent are married, 7 out of 10 to their first spouse. They have 1.4 children and take two weeks off each year. They play golf, vote Republican, and prefer *Time* to *Newsweek* . . . Only their success seems unconventional." Oh, and only 12 percent have an MBA.

They may be rugged, but they aren't so individualistic. The entrepreneurial business is very much a family affair, with the entrepreneur relying on spouse, friends and relatives for financial support, cheap labor, advice and moral support.

Before you go thinking that the successful entrepreneur is everyman, think again. Maybe the demographics reveal him to be part of the mainstream, but the psychological profiles do not. Entrepreneurs are far more intuitive; they gravitate toward risks; they are charismatic, charming and socially adroit; they are willing and able to gather information from many sources; they are open-minded and their curiosity is immense. On the downside, entrepreneurs can be very insecure, stubborn, intolerant of others' opinions, and distrustful. They sometimes see the world simplistically, critical issues as matters of black or white; they may see themselves as infallible, and be suspicious of authority. So in spite of the positive qualities, an entrepreneur may be saddled with enough negative traits to ensure his downfall.

In Search of Excellence   Merely the title of the bestselling management book of all time. But its contents have taken on the status of a new theory, or at least come to symbolize an approach. It is popular enough to deserve a section all its own (see below). You should know something of its ideas and message.

Intrapreneurship   Gifford Pinchot III's argument for entrepreneurial activity on the inside, and the title of his book on the subject (New York: Harper & Row, 1985). Pinchot believes that the structure, size, management style and culture of large companies impede innovation. In his view, "The large corporation will become an umbrella under which numerous small intrapreneurial groups interact in voluntary patterns too complex and synergistic to be planned from above . . . Finding a way to motivate and keep entrepreneurs is the most important strategic issue of our times."

   Much of what is said in his book echoes the work of Peters and Waterman, in that managers are advised to provide a more flexible environment which supports the innovators and innovation, and keeps them clear of bureaucracy.

Intuitive Manager   The title of a book by Roy Rowan, *The Intuitive Manager* relies on his intuition as well as logic in decision-making. However, Rowan doesn't see intuition as simple rumblings from the Great Beyond. Rather, as a kind internal gut feeling resulting from an interaction between inner faculties and collective personal experience. But Rowan goes on to say that even lack of experience can be a plus because "inexperience may make us more daring." This sounds to me as if he is saying that pure intuition untempered by experience is good, intuition plus experience is also good, and too much time spent with facts and figures is not so good. One danger: confusing intuition with fantasy.

   Every hot business book needs a scapegoat; there must be a problem in order for there to be a solution. In the case of *The Intuitive Manager*, it is "analysis paralysis," or a condition in which there is a large scale accumulation of data, so that the mind is overwhelmed with the task of analyzing it and there is little opportunity for it to mull things over and come to a conclusion. Another book providing more insight and speculations about what intuition is and does is *The Intuitive Edge* by Phillip Goldberg (J.P. Tarcher).

One-Minute Managing   A simplistic rehash of behavior modification principles. In other words, learning to reward your employees with one-minute praise and give one-minute reprimands. In the words of *BusinessWeek,* "the executive equivalent of paper-training your dog." It isn't so much that the ideas, er, idea of *The One Minute Manager* is so wrong, but that it is so limited. There is so much to the practice of good management that this skinny little book seems to insult the profession by its very existence. Still, the material must be fresh and useful for some managers, as it has sold well. Other simplistic One-Minute rehashes are out now; I hope they write a One-Minute Promoter to teach us how to turn simple books into bestsellers.

Quality Circles   Once upon a time, in the years following World War II, the Japanese had a reputation for shoddy products. Believe it or not. In 1962, as a response to this problem, Japanese manufacturers introduced quality circles. Generally, quality circles are small groups of volunteers from the same work areas, usually eight to ten, who meet regularly to identify, analyze and solve quality-related problems in their fields. Often, some training in quality control and problem-solving techniques are involved. Many Japanese credit quality circles with correcting problems and boosting the reputation of Japanese products in world markets.

Many experts believe that the quality circle as practiced in Japan is not the best method for ensuring quality control in the United States. Indeed, the Japanese have modified their approach to quality control in their U.S. factories to suit the American worker. For more on Quality Circles read *Quality Circles: Changing Images of People at Work* by William L. Mohr and Harriet Mohr (Addison-Wesley, 1983). Another viewpoint on quality control can be found in *Quality Without Tears* by Philip E. Crosby (New York: McGraw-Hill, 1984).

Quick Fix   Joseph Kilmann's term for a highly promoted, trendy management theory purporting to be the solution to every company's problems. In his book, *Beyond the Quick Fix: Managing Five Tracks to Organizational Success*, Kilmann may have intentionally capitalized on the backlash. He advocates a slow fix, and argues against simplistic solutions. There are no easy answers, and the real solutions involve developing an integrated approach. He postulates that there are five "tracks" that can be managed and controlled: culture, management skills, team-building, strategy-structure, and the reward system. With this notion, he swallows every hot new concept, from corporate cultures to one-minute managing. He doesn't so much disagree with the ideals and vision of the latest corporate gurus, but rather in how, and how long it will take to achieve the goal. Kilmann compares the management system to a hologram, using it as a basis for arguing for participatory management and against strict managing by the numbers. Problem-solving is complex, and must be solved on his five tracks at once rather than on a single track by a quick fix. He also argues for the use of outside consultants and the paycheck as a motivator.

Research   As used in management theory, a very broad term, mixing case studies, subjective observations, value judgments and interviews to come up with a new conceptual model or absolutely seminal list of key ingredients for success, usually culminating in a book aimed at the business and management population. In several rare cases, the scientific method and quantitative techniques have also been used.

Strategic Planning   Once popular, emphasis on long-term planning strategy fell out of favor until popularized again in books by Michael E. Porter.

Strategic planning is essentially an American invention, and it has not worked very well so far. Advocates blame the implementation not the concept, for its failure. Most firms, they say, are not really committed to it. Planning is a ritual, delegated to planners, who are isolated from the key executives who should be involved in formulating and implementing the plan, and taking it seriously.

Another complaint is that corporations aren't going about it in the right way, which is "ends-ways-means." That is, you establish corporate objectives (ends), develop at strategy for meeting those objectives (ways), and deploy the necessary resources to carry out the strategy (means). Many companies seek innovation, acquisitions, and grand product redesigns as if they were ends in themselves rather than strategies to achieve formulated objectives.

A third complaint is that firms don't give planning the time to work. They are too short-term.

Skunk   A terrific buzz word coined by Tom Peters (*In Search of Excellence*) after Lockheed Corporation's famous "Skunk Works," a slightly cloak-and-dagger R & D unit that Peters considers a model of innovation, an area of "controlled chaos." In *A Passion for Excellence*, Peters and co-author Nancy Austin describe the skunk's work as "highly innovative, fast-moving and slightly eccentric activity operating at the edges of the corporate world." The skunk then, is the new corporate hero. Anyway, it makes a great logo for Peter's seminar business, called Skunk Camp, and it decorates tee-shirts, totebags, coffee mugs and the like. Maybe there's a Saturday morning kids show in the works. Look out, Bugs Bunny.

Theory Z   A term coined by management professor William G. Ouchi, and the title of a very popular book published in 1981. Along with *The Art of Japanese Management* by Athos and Pascale, it got everyone talking about the Japanese way of doing things. Theory Z is still around, but in disguise. Some are saying that it is an American invention, and that the Japanese took it from us and refined it, just like the transister radio. Peters and Waterman have co-opted the issue by claiming that Theory

Z is neither Japanese nor American, but part of a set of characteristics that are universal to all successful companies, wherever they may be.

There is an overlap between Theory Z and the more recent notions, but the basic principles aren't identical. They are long-term employment, relatively slow evaluation and promotion, broad career paths, consensus decision-making, built-in controls with objective measurement, high levels of trust and egalitarianism, and a holistic approach to people.

Keep in mind the following facts: Japanese firms following Japanese management principles are not always more successful than American firms running things in a more homegrown manner. The great success of Japanese companies is not solely the result of their management styles. Many factors have played a role. As we have pointed out, Japanese management techniques are not unique to Japan. Clearly, most Japanese methods can be adapted for domestic use. And finally, allowing for the caveats, there is much to be learned from the Japanese about running companies. Wisdom has a universal quality to it. If you can help your firm with a solid concept, don't worry whether it comes from Japan, China, Germany or the U.S.A.

Value chain   A term coined by Michael E. Porter for a graphic model of the link between a firm's individual activities and effect on quality, costs, product differentiation and margin of the product line.

Wellness   A new-age buzz word co-opted by the corporate types, wellness appears to go beyond the concept of being healthy, to describe a state in which you are fit and feel good. You can get the lowdown in *The One Minute Manager Gets Fit.* No kidding.

IN SEARCH OF EXCELLENCE

With over five million copies sold and still going, the profits from *In Search of Excellence* are at least as impressive as its contents. Clearly, the book is worthwhile, but it is not as ground-breaking as its sales figures might indicate. Indeed, its pouplarity might be in part due to the fact that it celebrates the notion that American companies possess the means and potential for excellence, after scores of other books told us that we should be worshiping at the feet of the Japanese.

The messages of *In Search of Excellence*, and its sequel, *A Passion for Excellence* (written by Tom Peters and Nancy Austin; Waterman has since gone solo) are that there are many examples of managerial excellence, and they are alive and well in the United States.

The authors did extensive research, selecting six industry categories and then using six financial measures to identify the best performing companies in each category. (The six are high technology, consumer goods, general industrial, service, project management and resource-based. The financial measures are compounded asset growth, compound equity growth, average ratio of market-to-book value, average return on total capital, average return on equity and average return on sales.) They came up with seventy-five companies which they later pared down to thirty-six which truly passed their "excellence" test. By studying these companies, they were able to draw eight basic tenets of excellence: a bias for action, close to the customer, autonomy and entrepreneurship, hands-on, value driven, productivity through people, stick to the knitting, simple form, lean staff, and simultaneous loose-tight properties. *Whew.*

The authors were consultants at McKinsey and Company, where they did much of the basic work on the book's contents. They put forth the McKinsey 7-S Framework which ties together seven key characteristics of excellence: Structure, Strategy, Skills, Staff, Style, Systems and Shared Values.

If they sound familiar, you might have encountered these characteristics in *The Art of Japanese Management* by Athos and Pascale. That's okay, because Athos and Pascale both worked with Peters and Waterman on the development of the McKinsey model. Indeed, *In Search* concludes that successful Japanese and American companies are more similar to each other than they are to less successful companies in their respective countries. *The message: there is a common thread running through successful companies, and it crosses international borders.*

Peters and Waterman also concluded that excellent companies were very good at the basics of business. They insist on quality, treat their customers as number one, listen to their employees and treat them with respect, and encourage innovation and experimentation.

While the method of culling the excellent companies relied somewhat on quantifiable indicators, the eight attributes appear to be the result of the authors' observations.

This would be fine if the authors were simply providing food for thought, and a grab bag of ideas. But they seem to be advancing a new theory of management, and at the same time discrediting others. To rely solely on anecdotes, observations, and secondary sources is an inadequate way to justify conclusions. So read, be challenged and inspired, but beware of generalizations and rash conclusions. Like many other management theories, this one could be here today and gone tomorrow.

OTHER NOTABLE BOOKS

The Change Masters by Rosabeth Moss Kanter (New York: Simon and Schuster, 1983)   There is no better book about people who innovate and the conditions in which they thrive than *The Change Masters*. Ms. Kanter goes after some familiar demons like lack of vertical communication, a segmented organization, and indifference. But she clearly knows her territory, and gives us rich detail instead of fluffy anecdotes. Kanter blends theory and practice well, providing an excellent perspective on a complex set of problems. Best of all, she doesn't ignore the fact that implementing mechanisms such as improved teamwork, participatory management and the like is very challenging and difficult. For an overview of managing change and innovation, this book has few peers.

Leaders: The Strategies for Taking Charge, by Warren Bennis and Burt Nanus (New York: Harper & Row, 1985)   This is a provocative book on what makes leaders. It isn't about general skills, or even about personal qualities that set men apart from the pack. Leaders, say the authors, are people who can construct and communicate a vision, and rally the organization around it. To stay on top, they must nurture and maintain this vision as they lead the troops into action.

Although based on interviews, this is not an academic book, and the authors don't make much of an attempt to prove their leadership model. Nor is it a how-to book. They don't oversell their ideas and they don't apologize.

I think their arguments have merit. This is a fresh and interesting book.

What They Don't Teach You at Harvard Business School, by Mark McCormack (New York: Bantam, 1984)   So what if there is nothing new here? The advice of former lawyer and founder of International Management Group, a multimillion-dollar sports managing and marketing firm, is succinct and sensible. Best of all, it's very accessible, and not overblown with too many gratuitous examples. He is a success, and if you don't agree with him, fine. What I find most valuable about this book is the state of mind that is conveyed. Here is advice borne of a man who is obviously very observant, tactful, patient, and intelligent. He's a student of human nature as well as business.

MBO

If ever there was a term that was self-explanatory, MBO—Management by Objectives—has got to be it. There is more to it than just three letters, but not so much that you have to go to business school to understand what it's all about. The basic structure of the MBO process is exceedingly simple. It's the application of the process to your management functions that is difficult.

A Definition: "A management process whereby the supervisor and the subordinate, operating under a clear definition of the common goals and priorities of the organization established by top management, jointly identify the individual's major areas of responsibility in terms of the results expected of him or her, and use these measures as guides for operating the unit and assessing the contributions of each of its members."*

---

*From George S. Odiorne, *Management by Objectives*. Copyright © 1965. Reprinted by permission of Pitman Learning, Inc., Belmont, CA, pp. 55–56.

THE MBO PROCESS

SETTING OBJECTIVES This is the strategic planning phase. Objectives should be clear, specific, well-defined, and mutually understood. There are several types:

Organizational Objectives are set for the entire company.

Unit Objectives are those of a specific division.

Individual Objectives are usually formulated as a complement to the larger-scale objectives. This is important because the individual is the key work unit and, therefore, must know exactly what his part in this process is all about.

Personal Objectives are those that an individual sets on his own—his objectives for accomplishment, achievement, promotion, etc.

Objectives can be set for virtually any kind of job, from the routine through the most innovative, problem-solving variety.

IMPLEMENTATION Objectives are one thing; deciding how to attain them is quite another. The action plan should be detailed and thorough, but also flexible. It should include contingencies.

Going back over the plan is one way of insuring that it is valid. Flaws often show up. Better to catch them here than after you've embarked on your course.

REVIEW OF PERFORMANCE At this stage, review the situation to see where you stand. Appraise the results and, if necessary, modify your objectives or add new ones. You, as an individual, should do this frequently—on a daily or weekly basis. More formally, on a quarterly basis, meet with your boss for a review. This should not be a traditional appraisal by a superior of a subordinate: Because you both have objectives to work with, the review should be a cooperative venture intended to *improve* performance, not place blame. Of course, how and when you review the situation depends on the objectives involved and the timetable you are laboring under.

REPORT AND FEEDBACK It's a good idea to prepare periodic reports that cover points of progress vis-à-vis the action plan, discuss performance, and reevaluate the objectives.

Then use the report to readjust objectives and actions. Formulate any additional actions needed to remove obstacles. One of the biggest advantages of MBO is that it treats management as a continual *process:* ongoing, always in a state of flux. If conditions change, objectives change, and it's likely the kind of action will change. Maybe even the personnel. MBO encourages input to facilitate this ability to "feed back" into the system so that it can readjust. Encourage input from everyone involved.

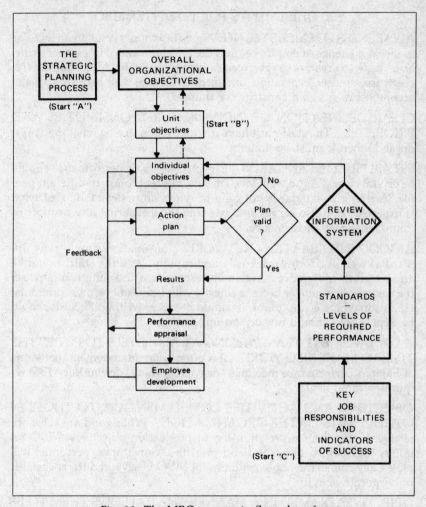

Fig. 29. The MBO process in flow chart form

Reprinted from *Strategic Planning and the MBO Process*,
by William C. Giegold. Copyright © 1978 by McGraw-Hill.
Used with permission of McGraw-Hill Book Company.

REQUIREMENTS FOR EFFECTIVE MBO

AWARENESS OF EMPLOYEE NEEDS MBO should result in an increase in the competence of employees and the development of important skills. You've got to create a supportive atmosphere in which they view the frequent assessments, evaluation, and measurement of their performance and accomplishments as a constructive thing.

CLEAR DELINEATION OF INDIVIDUAL RESPONSIBILITIES AND PRIORITIES The staff must have no doubts concerning what they must do and when it must be done.

ESTABLISHED STANDARDS Expected levels of performance should be crystal clear. "A job well done" means different things to different people. Arriving at standards not only provides an understanding of what is expected, but also serves as a baseline for measuring any dropoff or improvement in performance.

A GOOD INFORMATION NETWORK Information should flow upward as well as downward, easily and rapidly. And the staff should be able to tell the difference between important data and clutter; otherwise, the network will rapidly become clogged with irrelevant memos, printouts, etc. If something is important, it should be put in writing. Records should be kept. MBO should not be too informal.

A MANAGEMENT TEAM WILLING AT ALL LEVELS TO PUT IN THE TIME TO MAKE MBO WORK It is often upper management that scoffs at having "performance meetings" or writing things down. But MBO requires commitment.

OBJECTIVES AND ACTIVITIES COMPLEMENTARY TO THOSE IN OTHER PARTS OF THE ORGANIZATION What good are sales objectives if they bear no relationship to production objectives? MBO requires interlocking objectives and priorities. Sometimes, personnel will play a key role in the implementation of MBO in several different phases of corporate activity.

OBJECTIVES FRAMED IN A MANNER THAT ALLOWS THEM TO BE MEASURED It may not be possible to measure quality or quantity in a strictly numerical way. But some systematic method can always be worked out.

DEADLINES Most of us need the discipline of a time limit.

REALISTIC OBJECTIVES AND A PLAN OF ATTACK ACCEPTABLE AND CHALLENGING TO ALL Involve subordinates in the setting of the objectives and creation of the action plan. *All parties involved must be given the authority needed to get their jobs done.* If this means delegating, so be it.

Are the objectives within the capabilities of the individuals involved? Are they technically feasible? The very asking of these questions explains why the process of arriving at an objective is so important. Goals that are out of reach just result in frustration.

MBO is not just another gimmick. Nor is it a panacea. You've got to go into it carefully, because employees can easily mistake it for a punitive approach meant to keep tabs on them—a sign of suspicion and distrust. It is also important to follow through once you've started on MBO. Many executives simply get tired of it.

If implemented with conviction, MBO will produce many benefits, including greater efficiency and communication, better planning, a more informed, committed work force, greater trust, fairer evaluation, and even personal growth.

WHERE TO LEARN MORE ABOUT MBO

Most of the principal business schools and university adult education programs offer courses in MBO. You might also try one of these good books:

- *Management: Tasks, Responsibilities, Practices*, by Peter E. Drucker (New York: Harper & Row, 1973)
- *Management by Objectives*, by William C. Giegold (New York: McGraw-Hill, 1978)

"IF THE CUCKOO WON'T SING, LET'S WAIT UNTIL IT DOES": THE JAPANESE WAY*

The advice about the cuckoo is translated from a traditional Japanese short poem, or *haiku*. According to management expert Mitz Noda, this haiku characterizes the modern Japanese management system.

No manager can afford to be ignorant of Japanese methods. He may choose not to incorporate any of the practices, but he's got to know how his competition operates.

The Japanese prefer to encourage achievement by setting goals, stimulating motivation, and attempting to make work pleasant. They avoid intimidation and threats.

At one level, the approach is similar to the positive-reinforcement aspect of behavior modification. But there are differences, too. First, the Japanese methods are institutionalized; they are, in effect, modern applications of ancient tradition. Second, Japanese managers begin with certain basic assumptions about their workers: They enjoy being productive; working

---

*Adapted in part from "Business Management in Japan," by Mitz Noda, *Technology Review*, June/July 1979, pp. 20-29. Used with permission from *Technology Review*, Copyright © 1979 by the Alumni Association of the Massachusetts Institute of Technology.

is a natural part of life for them; they take pride in their work and will conduct themselves with honor and self-control.

The Japanese are expert delegators. In many companies, lower level management makes major decisions.

In Japan, the company's interest in the worker extends beyond the workday. Management provides recreational facilities and sponsors social gatherings in addition to granting such benefits as company-built residences and retreats, job retraining, and the financing of weddings.

They put great emphasis on face-to-face communications. The Japanese manager tries to avoid communication via memo. He will seek out his superiors or subordinates, and be welcomed.

Top management personnel move around. They are shifted to different markets and divisions so that they can get a feel for different marketing and distribution approaches and the forces at play in different world markets.

The Japanese rely on the "ringi" system of decision making. Put simply, it's the middle management that makes decisions and choices. Top management reviews the decisions, discussing them with middle management and making certain that everyone is satisfied.

The government is presumed to operate in the best interests of business. In the United States, government often acts as an antagonist of the corporation—protecting businesses from each other; protecting workers. While the relationship between Japanese government and business has justifiably come under fire, it should be noted that most people do not fear that companies will exploit them; therefore, relatively few of them feel a need for the government to function as an advocate of workers' rights.

Sushin koyo. Perhaps the most famous aspect of the Japanese system, because it differs so markedly from ours, sushin koyo is employment for life.

How it works. Management tends to hire fresh out of school. This makes for a generally younger work force. Executives come up through the ranks—never from the outside.

Mandatory retirement is strictly enforced at 55–60 for most males, but at older ages for top level management. Senior directors often remain active into their seventies, but mostly in an advisory capacity.

Retirement always brings financial reward. Employees who put in 35 years of service get, in addition to pension, a lump sum that equals a multiple of their average annual pay. The bonus is tax-free. If an employee resigns, he is considered "retired" and receives retirement pay based on length of service.

Does it work? "The employees I raised are never dismissed," says Saizo Idemitsu, founder of Idemitsu Kosan Co. "We are one big family and have no need for such things as time sheets and labor unions."

The facts appear to bear Mr. Idemitsu out: Unemployment in Japan runs about 1 or 2 percent; per capita personal savings are more than double American levels; Japan loses only one-eighth as many days to strikes as the U.S.; and, currently, capital investment in new equipment is double the American figure.

Sushin koyo may also explain the remarkable Japanese gift of innovation: Job security means that employees are not afraid to take risks—or even make suggestions that could eliminate their jobs. They know that the company will find a place for them.

Japanese promotion and pay practices. Except at the highest levels, promotion is based on age and length of service. Therefore, employees are confident that if they work hard, promotion to a managerial position is inevitable. And they needn't fear being bypassed for a position in favor of an outsider.

As time passes, the worker's age and length of service naturally increase. So does his salary. Education is also taken into account in establishing pay levels. But efficiency and performance just don't play a very large role. There are allowances made for hardship, exemplary attendance records, and job rank.

In top management ranks, promotion and pay are more directly a function of performance and position.

What all this means to American managers. To some extent, absolutely nothing. We are a nation of diverse cultures, rugged individualists, highly suspect of authority. We are excellent team players, but we'll work on that basis only as long as it suits us.

In Japan, employees often must wait 16 years, or until they are about 37, before they are eligible for a management position. We are a nation of impatient people, and expect quick rewards for performance.

This is not to say that the United States does not have the kind of employees who are willing to trade loyalty and dedication for security and fair and consistent increases in pay and position. But few of its citizens would welcome such a situation as the only established method of getting ahead.

Nevertheless, as a lesson for Westerners the Japanese ideal of the company in a "parental" role is valuable, if not for what it provides, then for the feeling generated—a sense of community, cooperation, and trust.

Matsushita, one of the world's leading electronics firms, has set these principles for all employees to follow:

- Seek progress through hard work.
- Make contributions to world harmony.
- Display the true form of a human being in national society.
- Be fair about responsibilities to owners and employees.
- Be successful in business by achieving these goals.
- Understand that profits are merely the reward of good service.

There are a few signs that the traditional Japanese approach is coming apart. It is essentially the method that was built on a feudal system, in which the business replaced the fiefdom. But now, many individuals have increased influence and independence. Some experts predict that ringi, sushin koyo, and other pillars of the Japanese system will have to be modified.

SUGGESTED READING

Theory Z: How American Business Can Meet the Japanese Challenge, by William Ouchi (Reading, Massachusetts: Addison-Wesley Publishing Company, 1981; reprint paperback ed., New York: Avon Books, 1982).

The Art of Japanese Management: Applications for American Executives, by Richard Tanner Pascale and Anthony G. Athos (New York: Simon and Schuster, 1981).

COMPETITION IS FOR THE COMPETENT: THE ABSOLUTE THEORY OF MANAGEMENT (ATOM)

This expanded vision of management is that of Maharishi Mahesh Yogi, who gave us the Transcendental Meditation program.

The Absolute Theory of Management looks at management in terms of natural law, drawing on principles from physics, mathematics, chemistry, biology, and philosophy, among other disciplines. The result is really quite practical.

The ATOM is systematically presented in a series of videotapes moderated and with commentary by Maharishi. One of the central themes of the course is that nature itself knows best how to organize and manage. By undertaking a systematic, interdisciplinary study of natural laws, we can uncover the basic principles of management. A few examples:

FROM PHYSICS

1. Thermodynamics explains that nonliving systems increase in entropy, or disorder, over time. That's why a file cabinet eventually becomes

---

disorganized, and why a paper clip winds up in the container that holds rubber bands. Inherently, this condition is irreversible: The odds are overwhelmingly against order spontaneously reasserting itself over disorder.

2. Thermodynamics also tells us that by creating a state of least excitation—by quieting things down—we can increase orderliness.

3. This doesn't mean that, in the name of increased orderliness, we cease all business activity. It does suggest that we should *periodically* reduce the activity or excitation in the workplace and in the nervous systems of the people in it. By doing so, we reduce the entropy, counter its buildup, and therefore reduce mistakes. Physicists have observed that in super-fluid states, when the entropy is virtually at zero, the molecules of substances are elegantly organized. An overall reduction in activity could very well introduce that basic organizational intelligence into the human management system.

Maharishi teaches that a technique that produces a state of least excitation in the human nervous system—a state of profound rest—should be incorporated into the management system. Such a technique is the Transcendental Meditation Program.™ Some of the results of regular daily practice of the TM technique in the workplace have already been measured, largely through the work of Dr. David Frew.* (See Chapter 11.)

FROM BIOLOGY

Life is elegantly organized. The simple cell is "managed" by its nucleus, and the DNA within the nucleus possesses all the vital information to be tapped as needed. Other portions of the cell pursue their specialized functions, as directed by the "manager."

This principle operates on more gross levels as well:

The reticular formation in the brain "manages" the human nervous system, directing "data" to its various parts.

Study the function of the enzyme: It behaves as a catalyst, reducing the barriers, the time and energy necessary for a reaction to take place, but remaining unchanged. Many occasions call for this kind of behavior on the part of the manager—not actually taking part in the performance of a task, but helping it along.

For more information on the Absolute Theory of Management and the Transcendental Meditation program, contact:

World Plan Executive Council
17310 Sunset Boulevard
Pacific Palisades, California 90272

Department of Business Administration
Maharishi International University
Fairfield, Iowa 52556

---

*See David R. Frew, *Using TM at Work* (Chicago: Nelson-Hall, 1977).

STATISTICS

"There are two realities simultaneously playing themselves out before our eyes: the way we feel and the way we are told the data show we feel. It is a very insecure society that won't credit its own experience." So said Meg Greenfield in the September 10, 1979, issue of *Newsweek*.

No modern executive can avoid playing the numbers game.

Will the product sell? The numbers say, Probably not. But your gut feeling is, Yes, in a big way.

The conflict exists between numerical data and our own feeling about the reliability of our intuition.

Often you will use research and data, not as a primary method of making decisions, but as a means of backing up decisions you've already arrived at. You do this to put everyone at ease. Then, if the project doesn't fly, they can always say, "The numbers looked good."

So it's no surprise that a perennial best-seller among researchers is the book *How to Lie with Statistics* by Darrell Huff and Irving Geis (New York: Norton, 1954).

The executive who is interested in results must be equally wary of statistics, on the one hand, and his own logic, judgment, and intuitive feelings, on the other.

18

POWER: OUT OF
THE CLOSET

Power, put simply, is the ability to get people to do what you want them to—and the ability to resist being forced to do what you don't want to do.

You cannot get ahead without acquiring some power and learning to use it. Not only is power both a prerequisite and an attribute of one's success as an individual; it is necessary for good, effective management.

Colleges, universities, even business schools don't teach you about power. Perhaps it's because they are unable to do so. More likely it's because of some moral trepidation. Power and sex used to be treated in a similar manner: Everybody needs it, but won't talk about it, and society regards it as slightly immoral. The difference is that sex is out of the closet—now considered a healthy, natural part of life—while power, on the other hand, is still a dirty word.

Power is healthy. It is the *misuse* of power that is not. And there is entirely too much worry over its abuses. Everyone has power to some degree—as a parent, supervisor, organization member, buyer, or seller. Most people handle it well. But it's the abuses that make headlines. As George Bernard Shaw once said, "Power does not corrupt men; but fools, if they get into a position of power, corrupt power."

POWER AND JOB-RELATED
DEPENDENCE ON OTHERS

Professor John P. Kotter of Harvard Business School has made a study of power in business organizations. According to his findings, an important component of managerial work is the manager's dependence on the activities of other people. This dependence leaves one very vulnerable and, indeed, is quite contrary to the dynamics of power, because it restricts the control you have over your own job and limits your ability to assert control over others. Unfortunately, as one rises in

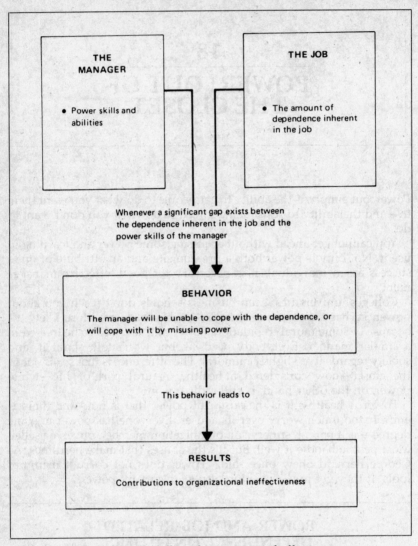

Fig. 30. Power skills and organizational effectiveness
This chart summarizes what happens when there is a gap
between the abilities of the manager and the amount of
dependence on others required by his job. He wants to break
out and grab for power, but the job structure holds him back.
The result is misuse of power and organizational
ineffectiveness.

Reprinted, by permission of the publisher, from
*Power in Management: How to Understand, Acquire,
and Use It,* by John P. Kotter, © 1979 by AMACOM,
a division of American Management Associations (p. 78).

the corporate hierarchy, the problem gets worse, not better. You have a wider range of responsibility, and although you may exert authority over more people, you are also more dependent on them. Add to that dependency the increasing complexity of dealing with greater numbers of subordinates.

Power derived from authority is inadequate. You are dependent upon the performance of some people over whom you have no authority. Besides, very few subordinates "blindly obey" anymore just because you are in charge. They often have recourse, and they know it. And they can follow your orders in a variety of different ways, depending on how they regard themselves, and you.

Professor Kotter's central theme is that power dynamics are not the result of a lust for power, or even of a burning desire to succeed. Rather, they are *the result of a disequilibrium in which the degree of on-the-job dependence on others far exceeds the power or control given the individual.* In other words, you have only a limited control over your own destiny, and there are a great many people who might act to reduce that measure of control.

Everyone needs some power. And every manager will attempt to gain enough power so that he feels comfortable.

The greater the job-related dependence, the greater the time and energy spent playing power games. The manager copes with job dependence by trying to expand and increase his control in the work environment.

As this job-related dependence increases, the manager gets more desperate, and his tendency toward the more risky, negative, and disruptive power tactics increases.

Job dependence is related to four internal factors:

- *responsibilities.* The greater your responsibilities, the more you need to rely on the help and cooperation of others.
- *span of control.* The more people under you, the more difficult it is to keep tabs on them, on how they do their jobs, and on whether to replace them.
- *degree of interdependence.* If a job involves interacting with other departments and personnel, it is more dependent than a job that involves self-contained tasks you handle alone.
- *bosses.* The greater the number of bosses, the more answerable you are.

With the exception of the number of bosses, all these factors increase as you move up the corporate ladder. That is why you have to be a better player near the top. Most can't handle it and make a desperate, clumsy attempt to consolidate power because they can't cope with their increased dependence on others. That's tough on the "rugged individualist." No wonder they're a dying breed.

Other factors related to job dependence can come from the outside. For example, you can be dependent on suppliers if you are in production, or on technology if you are in product design, or on a few people at an ad agency if you are in marketing.

THE TACTICS OF POWER

This section will tell you, in the most basic terms, *what* people do to acquire and perpetuate power. What it will *not* tell you is *how* you go about doing these things. Every situation is different.

Build relationships. Let's look at some of the methods of forming binding relationships.

Get other people to feel obligated to you in some way. Good managers make this happen automatically. They don't do a favor or make a gesture just to "hook" someone; they do such things because they make sense, and because they enjoy doing them. Usually the result is the company benefits, the people directly involved benefit, and gratitude is a natural outgrowth.

If you can't create a situation in which people are dependent on you, make them feel that they are. This is an area where you can be perfectly justified in creating an "illusion." First convince the people in question that they need someone or something. Then convince them that you can deliver.

People don't have time to probe deeply into the true nature of things—or of people. Often, the first impression is the only impression they ever have time to form. They keep dredging it up every time they see the person. "Bill Hawkins . . . gold Rolex watch." "Steve Fischer . . . corner office with that beautiful ship in a bottle; very rich, I think." And so on.

Creating the illusion of power goes beyond how you look, dress, and decorate your office. The company you keep is also an indication. So if one of your high-school buddies is now famous, exploit it. This, by the way, is one of the themes of *Smart People*, by John Spooner (Boston: Little, Brown and Co., 1979).

Establish credibility. Back up your work and your word. That's how you build trust and, eventually, dependence.

Develop a reputation. Establish yourself as an expert and people tend to rely on you and defer to your judgment. The best way to earn a good

---

reputation is to perform. But you've also got to make sure your performance is noticed.

Control as much information as possible. Data control is a power weapon, because people rely on access to data to do their jobs. The intelligent use of data is also the best defense against attack. Privileged information is, of course, an even greater power tool.

The easiest method of controlling data is controlling its flow—the information channels. This is not merely a question of power for your own selfish ends. In large part, the modern corporation lives or dies by the way it handles information. (Look at the different ways automakers responded to the news that gas was going up in price.) The more information you have, the greater your ability to analyze and solve problems. With that kind of advantage, you probably won't need to manipulate the flow of information.

Control resources. This is the oldest of the power-grabbing methods; I can picture two roving bands of Neanderthals fighting for control of their mutual water supply. Money; equipment; employees; space; transportation—these are just a few of the resources worth winning.

Become a Willie Stargell. If you speak and act in a manner that expresses the "spirit" and sentiments of others, they tend to identify with you and elevate you. They will almost always bestow a greater amount of power on you than you deserve.

Civilization is full of examples. What did Che Guevara mean to Latin American radicals? The '69 Amazin' Mets to a faltering NYC? The 1980 U.S. Olympic Hockey Team to a frustrated nation?

This is no easy quality to culture; you are asking people to develop an idealized view of you. But it can be done. You must win respect; be visible; keep your ear to the ground so you know how people feel about important issues.

Most important, be sincere. Phonies do not last in this land of power play. You've got to develop understanding, a deep insight into the people around you. It's a matter of feelings as well as intellect.

Sometimes a particularly skilled politician will come on like the JFK of the corporation, and pull it off. But if he's not the genuine article, don't bet on his lasting long.

People need to look up to someone. Why not you?

Locate the sources of power in your organization. Don't rely solely on organization charts.

Take risks with the power you have in order to build more. In order to make a grab for something greater, sometimes you'll have to "use up" some of the power you've built.

Stay away from activities and projects that could result in decreasing your power. (Here is where risk analysis bears most directly on the attainment of power.)

Don't overstep the acceptable limits of fair play. Even the less-than-lily-white game of power has its code of behavior. Outfox and outmaneuver. But don't lie, cheat, or break your word. Not if you can help it.

Count the ways you can influence people. Go at 'em face to face and/or use more indirect methods, such as controlling schedules, meetings, agendas, memos, etc.

Remember that playing the power game may begin in the genes. Or at least in early childhood experiences. There is undoubtedly some intuitive ability involved in all this. Either you have a lot of intuition or you have a little. Make the best of it.

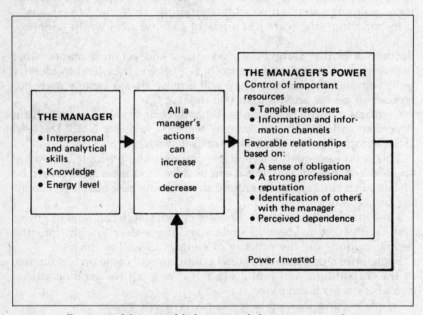

Figure 31. Managerial behavior and the acquisition of power
How the manager acquires power by using his personal
skills, knowledge, and energy to attain control
of resources and form strong relationships.

Reprinted, by permission of the publisher, from
*Power in Management: How to Understand, Acquire,
and Use It*, by John P. Kotter, © 1979 by AMACOM,
a division of American Management Associations (p. 37).

Make sure that the energy and time you put in trying to get people to do something your way is justified by the importance of the situation. The more important it is, the more intolerant and inflexible you'll want to be. Don't play power games over unimportant matters.

ABUSES OF POWER

Lack of integrity. If we learned anything from Watergate, it was that driving ambition that ignores the greater good is potentially self-destructive. Effective managers are able to balance their individual goals with those of their colleagues and the company. Ideally, better service to the institution fosters personal power, which in turn leads to increased service, which leads to greater consolidation of personal power, and so on. Often it doesn't work that way, but that's not a reason to abandon goals outside the personal sphere. Besides, the psychologists tell us that we are a species with strong altruistic tendencies, for whom doing good things for others is a primary source of satisfaction.

The power-dependence mismatch. Professor Kotter found that power is often abused by those who feel there is too much dependence in their jobs, and not enough power.

Bad examples. Misuse of power in upper levels not only sets a bad example; often it also forces the abuses downward, thus institutionalizing them.

GETTING READY TO PLAY THE POWER GAME

How well equipped are you to play? Do you possess the abilities necessary to use the strategies and tactics needed to acquire power? What are your strengths? Weaknesses?

Always be aware of how your actions are seen by others. This is one way to avoid committing costly errors, making crude attempts to attain power, and misusing the power you have.

Analyze your own power/dependence situation. Whom are you dependent on? How are you dealing with these dependencies? What have you been doing to accumulate power to offset them?

Are you in a job in which there is too much dependence and not enough power? You are in trouble if the answer is yes. Redefine your job (power and dependence), or get a new one.

LETTING 'EM KNOW YOU'RE THERE: COMPANY POLITICS

Assume that every company has some politics. No matter *what* they tell you. It's in every company.

Locate the political factors (political climate):

- what gets people promoted
- who's got the *real* power
- who's in the "in" crowd
- who's on the "outs"

Give the "power people" what they want. Aim to please.

Run with the "in" crowd.

Know your job, know your company, know the business.

Work your butt off. Some books say that hard work alone will get you nowhere. That may well be true. But politics or power games will also get you nowhere if you can't justify your claim to power. People who can't perform or deliver have to resort to treachery—pass the buck, or look good by making others look bad. Sooner or later it catches up to them. And until it does, they're always looking over their shoulders.

Seek out and go after opportunities. Be aggressive.

On the other hand, don't take risks that aren't justified.

Learn how the game is played. Cliques; alliances; double-crosses; tactics—and who uses them against whom.

Always know what you want before you act.

Size up the competition. Age? Experience? Background? Ability? Attitudes? Do they have what it takes? More important, do they possess the qualities that people in power will like?

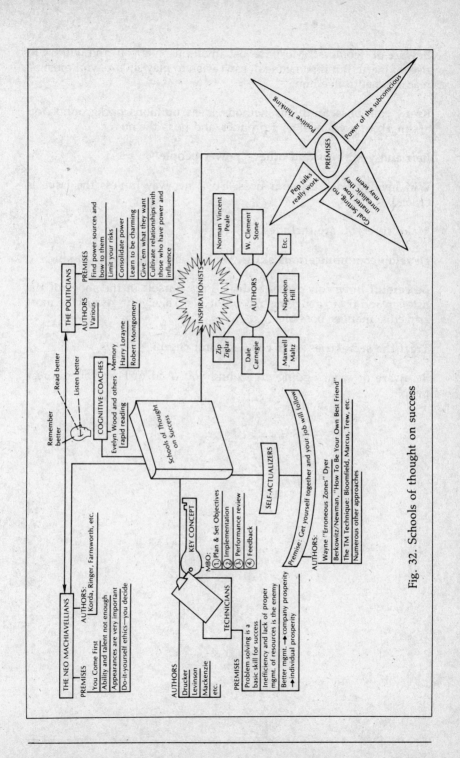

Fig. 32. Schools of thought on success

295

Beware of "comers." Most are just ambitious, like you, and will try to rise on merit. But if someone doesn't wish to play square, you must be ready to neutralize him.

Know your boss. Study his methods, ideas, opinions, background. You are marketing yourself as a product, and he is the buyer.

Befriend your boss and other "power people."

Win loyalty. Back up your boss: Do it his way (unless the issue is crucial).

Make sure you are included.

Develop communications skills. Writing, listening, and speaking.

Be careful how you present ideas. Put yourself in the shoes of the listener, and try to gauge his receptivity. Package your idea in the most attractive manner possible.

Treat the secretaries with courtesy and charm.

Be aware of what's going on around you. And of how you impress people.

19
LEARN AND EARN: EXECUTIVE EDUCATION

The flow of technical knowledge is so rapid that your education may be obsolete before you graduate. Some experts predict that in the future, employees will earn top dollar fresh out of school, when they have the latest skills and technical know-how. Later on in their careers, when their knowledge is less current, they become less valuable and are therefore worth less. Knowledge appears to be taking on more importance than experience.

Frankly, you can't afford to stay out of school. You must protect yourself against lagging behind by taking advantage of the many educational options available to you. You do not have to quit your job. You probably won't even have to pay for your continuing education. Most companies will subsidize job-related education, if not completely cover its cost.

There are many alternatives, from one-day seminars to degree programs lasting several years.

SEMINARS

WHO GIVES THEM?

Almost anyone with enough cash to hire a meeting room and mailing list can hold a seminar. And practically everyone is doing it. The reason, of course, is that it is big business. The old-timers in the field include the American Management Associations, university adult education divisions of institutions such as Wharton (University of Pennsylvania) and New York University. But anybody who thinks he can pass himself off as an expert, speaks somewhat dynamically, and can write good direct-mail copy has jumped on board.

The independents tend to carve out a niche for themselves by concentrating on the soft areas that are less academic and more motivational, marrying business and self-help psychology. Examples include time management, negotiating skills, salesmanship, positive thinking, getting rich in real estate.

Seminars and conferences are a major source of education, training, and development for the U.S. business community. Anthony Whyte of AMR International, a leading seminar firm, estimates that American firms spend about $1.2 billion annually on employee seminars—57 percent (about $700 million) on in-house training and 43 percent (about $500 million) on external programs. There are over 1,000 organizations, trade associations, and educational institutions offering these courses. There are also countless one- and two-man operations.

WHY ARE THEY POPULAR?

Although some seminars last a day or two, they can be a very efficient use of time, because the eight or so hours involved are often less time than it takes to read a tedious book on the same subject; and seminars can be fun. You tend to retain more, you can ask questions, and you are usually provided a workbook or manual that you can review as needed. And you can make worthwhile contacts. I'd rather hear about the arts of negotiation or tax shelters than read about them, any day. True, books are cheaper, and you can read them on your own time. But they are less up to date.

SELECTING A SEMINAR

"It is becoming extremely difficult for individuals to delineate [sic] between the programs which are not going to be any good, many of them very trendy, versus programs that really cover some meaty topics and give them three or five or ten ideas which can be implemented when they get back to work," says Heidi Kaplan of the New York Management Center. Here are a few suggestions from Kaplan and others:

PICK A COURSE OR SEMINAR BASED ON YOUR ACTUAL NEEDS   Don't go to a seminar because it's in New Orleans and that's where your brother lives. Or even because it sounds interesting. The important question to consider is, Will this seminar prove useful in my current position or future career plans? Many training experts have discovered that negative experiences with seminars are often attributable to casual selection. Don't wait for a brochure to cross your desk and then fill out the coupon. Actively seek out the most valuable seminars.

SCRUTINIZE   The seminar field is so crowded with so many types of firms that no one is quite sure just how large the industry is. There are universities, publishing firms, consulting firms, individuals—anybody who thinks he can say something meaningful—all giving seminars. It's becoming more and more difficult to make a decision. Here are a few basic considerations:

- What are the credentials of the person leading the seminar? Does he have adequate experience?
- Is this his first seminar? (Can he teach?)
- Who is sponsoring it?
- Does the brochure provide a detailed analysis of what will be covered?
- Is it accredited by an educational institution?
- Is it tax deductible?
- What is the quality of the advertising? Is this a shoestring deal? Beware if the instructor solicits you directly.
- Has there been coverage of the seminar or its central figure by the news media?
- Has the person conducting the seminar published anything on the subject? Look at his book or his magazine articles.
- How does he demand payment?
- Is there really enough material on the subject to merit a seminar?
- Guarantees?
- Endorsements?
- Can the sponsor provide you with data on the students in past seminars? If reputable, the sponsor should have records of who has been attending the seminar and, possibly, would refer you to people in your industry.
- Is this a "promotional" seminar, meant to push a product or service?

OBTAINING COMPANY APPROVAL

Seminar choices are usually left to the individual, but most companies will foot the bill. It is therefore important to keep your superiors abreast of the reasoning behind your use of their dollars spent on courses. In addition, without feedback afterward, firms have no way of evaluating the quality, content, and effectiveness of a course or seminar. Consulting with the people in your firm who oversee educational programs is a sure sign that you take the subject seriously. Educational expenditures are investments made by the company in its executives and, consequently, in its future. They should be respected as such.

HAVE A GOOD IDEA OF WHAT YOU WANT TO LEARN   Do your goals and ideas about your development and future responsibilities agree with those of your superiors? Don't assume that certain skills will be helpful later on. Explain the reasoning behind your decision to attend a seminar.

BE SURE A SEMINAR IS THE BEST APPROACH   Some of us hate school and see seminars as an easy way to get knowledge. They are short, little is expected of us, and the work isn't graded. But, often, seminars are simply insufficient. In other cases, a firm's training staff can provide a program in-house. And then there's the learn-on-the-job approach, which can work quite well. If, after you've examined the alternatives, the seminar still seems like the way to go, you should have little trouble getting approval.

COME PREPARED   Presumably, you've done some research on the seminar in question. You should have the course outline, brochures, and other pertinent information with you to support your case.

MAKE A "NO-FRILLS" REQUEST   An increasing number of seminars are being given in vacation spots so that attendees can come for a seminar and get a deductible vacation; your boss probably won't be interested in sending you to one of these. Since many of the seminars are "road shows" given in various cities, find the location nearest you. The exception: You have business to attend to in a distant city and the seminar can be combined with the business trip.

ATTENDING THE SEMINAR

PREPARE   If you receive seminar materials in advance, read through them, or at least skim them.

Remember that the time before the seminar is critical. If you do not delegate effectively and clear your schedule, you are headed for trouble. You could well be spending seminar time on the phone, or on ducking out for appointments. Be ready to give the seminar your full attention.

GET INVOLVED   Question; list; outline. If there's something you want to know and it isn't covered in the seminar, catch the instructor during lunch or coffee break.

WHEN YOU GET BACK

USE IT OR LOSE IT   If the seminar is worthwhile, you will come away full of new ideas and procedures. You should take some time to put into practice what you've learned. If you don't do it soon after returning, you probably never will.

FEEDBACK TO OTHERS   If your organization has a training department, provide its personnel with a detailed evaluation. If not, write up a memo about the seminar and send it to someone in the personnel department who would be interested; keep a copy for your files. If the program is so valuable that you think the entire staff should attend, you can arrange to have the seminar given on company premises. It's cheaper that way, and will probably be more effective.

HAVE REALISTIC EXPECTATIONS   More training is not always the sole answer. Personality or environmental problems may make it difficult for you to utilize what you've learned. And if you are an underpaid or underutilized employee, you will probably gain little from a "motivational" seminar; it doesn't address what is, for you, the real problem.

SOURCES OF SEMINAR AND COURSE INFORMATION

TRADE ASSOCIATIONS   Many associations sponsor seminars and keep members up to date (usually by newsletter) on relevant seminars held by various firms. Organizations such as the National Association of Accountants have made a major commitment to providing continuing education to their membership.

TRADE MAGAZINES   Such magazines usually have calendar sections that include information on seminars. Sometimes they even sponsor a few of their own. Also watch for advertisements by seminar givers.

COMPANY TRAINING OFFICES   Training-office staff will be familiar with many of the seminars and their sponsors. They will also have the brochures on file, and perhaps some evaluations from others. There is also a good chance that they can get the lowdown on an unfamiliar seminar by calling their counterparts in other companies.

UNIVERSITIES   Most major universities and many smaller colleges offer some form of continuing education programs. They are very eager to tell you about their offerings.

DIRECT MAIL   Seminar givers rely on direct mail to reach you. They often get their lists from business magazines, so you're probably receiving at least a few brochures. If you aren't, call several of the larger seminar sponsors; they'll be glad to put you on their mailing lists.

EVALUATION FORM

You recently attended a program on the subject of _____
_____ which was put on by
_____

Will you please take about ten minutes to complete this form. This will help us in our continuing analysis of the effectiveness of the management training education and development programs that we use. Please be open and candid in answering all the applicable questions in PART I. If you wish, use PART II for any additional information that you feel would be helpful to us. Please return to me by _____ if possible.
                              (date)

If our identification of the program title and sponsor stated above is incorrect or incomplete, will you please show it correctly on the attached.

_____
Coordinator of Evaluation Program

Fig. 33. Evaluation form for seminars,
prepared by Mantread Inc.
(*through page 305*)
Reprinted by permission.

PART I – BASIC EVALUATION

Name of Program:

Sponsoring Agency or Resource Used:

Approx. Dates of Participation:

Month: Year:

Where Attended:

Place an "X" on the line which denotes your evaluation of each of the following questions which are applicable:

	POOR	FAIR	GOOD	EXCELLENT	For Office Use ONLY
1. How were the physical facilities?	—	—	—	—	
2. How well was program run, as for example in scheduling, administration and creating a learning atmosphere, etc.?	—	—	—	—	
3. How well did the subject matter fulfill the stated objectives of the program?	—	—	—	—	
4. How effective did you think the leaders and other resources were considering purpose of the program?	—	—	—	—	
5. List the names of the leaders and key staff people and then evaluate their effectiveness.					
_____	—	—	—	—	
_____	—	—	—	—	
_____	—	—	—	—	
_____	—	—	—	—	
_____	—	—	—	—	
6. Was there group participation? YES_____ NO_____ If yes, how useful and constructive was it?	—	—	—	—	
7. What is your overall evaluation of this program?	—	—	—	—	
8. Indicate how well each of the following contributed to the program. Cross out items that don't apply.					
– Reading materials	—	—	—	—	
– Bull sessions outside meeting	—	—	—	—	
– Ideas explored and studied	—	—	—	—	
– Visual aids	—	—	—	—	
– Contacts with others in program	—	—	—	—	
– Others (describe please)					
_____	—	—	—	—	
_____	—	—	—	—	
_____	—	—	—	—	

9. Would you recommend this program for others in your organization?   YES _____ NO _____
   If yes, what type of person (or job title) would you recommend?

10. Please give an example as briefly as possible of something you gained from this program which may help you on your job. (If more space is needed, continue into PART II, pp 4).

11. Please state as briefly as possible what caused you to attend this program.

12. (Personal information so that your reactions can be most effectively used in our summary.) PLEASE CHECK APPROPRIATE BOXES.

	Less than 1	1 3	4 10	Over 10
• Years with present employer?	☐	☐	☐	☐
• Years in present position?	☐	☐	☐	☐

	20 29	30 39	40 49	Over 49
• Age?	☐	☐	☐	☐

	HS Grad or Less	Some College	College Grad	Graduate Degree
• Years of Formal Education:	☐	☐	☐	☐

	None	1 2	3 4	Over 5
• How many other off the job programs taken in last 3 years?	☐	☐	☐	☐

Please place check mark in front of the key words which come closest to generally describing your position:

Level of Position: Top & Upper   Middle   Supervisory   Non
                _____ Management   _____ Management _____ Management   _____ Supervisory

Primary Duties:

_____ Executive (Manages enterprise, department, or subdivision)
_____ Administrative (Assists executives or higher level administrators on policy interpretation or works in a specialized staff area)
_____ Professional (Position requires advanced knowledge in a field of science or learning)
_____ Outside Sales (Makes sales at customer's place of business)

NOTE: If you think additional information is needed to generally describe your position, place check here _____ and add information at end of PART II.

304

PART II – ADDITIONAL INFORMATION (OPTIONAL)

To conserve your time, questions in PART I were purposely very brief. However, if you can take the time, your completion of as many of the following items as possible would give us a more in-depth understanding of the program.

A. About how many people were enrolled in the group? _____

B. About what percentages of them fell into each category:

   Foreman, first line supervisors, staff assistants   _____ %

   Middle management and mid-level staff   _____ %

   Upper management – division heads, officers, etc.   _____ %

C. About what percentage of the program was:

   Theoretical? _____ %   Practical? _____ %

D. About what percentage of the material presented was:

   New? _____ %   Refresher?_____%

E. Were there handout materials to take home? YES _____ NO _____ If yes, how likely that you will find use for them?

   Likely _____   Unlikely_____   Don't Know _____

F. Were there handout assignments to do before the program? YES _____ NO _____ If yes, how much did they add to the value of the program?

   Much _____   Little _____   Doubtful _____

G. What was the length of the program in days?_____

   Was the length of the program:

   Too long?_____   Too short?_____   About right? _____

H. Please use this space to add any additional feelings or opinions you have that may not have been adequately covered above or in PART I:

═══════════════ FOR EVALUATION COORDINATOR USE ONLY ═══════════════

305

THE BIG NAMES IN BUSINESS SEMINARS

THE AMERICAN MANAGEMENT ASSOCIATIONS (AMA) is the largest seminar giver in the nation. AMA is a nonprofit organization that boasts 70,000 members, and giving seminars is consistent with its goal of encouraging dialogue among its members, keeping them informed and facilitating contact with leading management thinkers.

The AMA's Center for Management Development offers over 2,000 courses a year, from 12 divisions:

- Finance
- General Management
- Marketing
- Research and Development
- Packaging
- Purchasing
- Insurance and Employee Benefits
- Manufacturing
- Management Systems
- Human Resources
- International Management
- General and Administrative Services

The Center maintains a full-time staff of coordinators and program directors who monitor course quality, recruit instructors, and develop new courses. They draw from a "faculty" of over 800 guest speakers.

In addition, there are 13 major "councils"—committees of top executives who examine seminar quality, content, and delivery and assess postseminar evaluations by attendees.

There are indications that AMA has been working very hard to maintain and upgrade the quality of its courses. In 1977, postseminar surveys revealed that 66 percent thought the seminars "excellent"—up 37 percent from 1973; 30 percent rated them "good," and only 4 percent thought them "fair," an 8 percent decrease from '73.

AMA officials claim that they have been able to get 100 percent of the managers to take part in postseminar evaluation. As for the 1/2—1 percent that consistently rates the seminars "poor," AMA officials are reluctant to take the blame. They say the response may be the result of a negative attitude on the part of employees pressured or even ordered to take the course; or the attendee made a poor choice in attending a seminar that was ill suited to his needs.

Contact:
American Management Associations
Center for Management Development
135 West 50th Street
New York, New York 10020

AMR INTERNATIONAL is a New York-based, profit-making educational firm that offers about 700 seminars a year on approximately 60 topics.

AMR, clearly at a disadvantage because of AMA's nonprofit status, goes in for more topical, freewheeling courses. The company doesn't have the same kind of accountability as AMA, so perhaps it can be a little more controversial and innovative: There are no advisory councils to please.

AMR has no in-house instructional staff. It draws instructors from the business community, and many approach AMR, rather than the other way around.

With over 250,000 past customers, AMR strives for repeat business. It claims a renewal rate of almost 100 percent from its clients—about 20,000 private and governmental organizations.

> Contact:
> AMR International, Inc.
> 1370 Avenue of the Americas
> New York, New York 10019

THE CONFERENCE BOARD, INC. is a prestigious nonprofit organization that conducts a great deal of business and economic research.

The Conference Board's approach to seminars is markedly different from that of either AMA or AMR. It holds three basic types of meetings that tend not to overlap or compete with others in the industry:

Large "theme" conferences. Attendance ranges from about 300 to 1,500. These conferences are open to both members and nonmembers and usually deal with basic issues: antitrust, exporting, new-product development, etc.

Private, invitational meetings. These are very prestigious and are aimed at the members that really make the Conference Board work—the chief executive officers. There are usually about 50 in attendance.

Usually held in a retreat or conference center over a weekend, these meetings are exchanges among an elite from top corporations worldwide. The speakers usually come from their own ranks—and they are always heavyweights. On occasion they'll bring in an outsider to discuss a new idea, if none of the conferees has gained the necessary expertise in the field in question. In such cases they always go with a well-known name. And they try to avoid people with strong biases.

One-day seminars. These are open to all. Since the Conference Board deals in research, it sends resident experts and authorities on tour to give seminars on important topics. This is as close as the board comes to conventional seminars, but they are treated as methods of disseminating research findings and other information resulting from the board's other activities. In that sense, they are not really "products" for the training marketplace; i.e., not developed to meet specific training needs.

The Conference Board can operate this way because it gets plenty of cash from its prestigious membership—enough so that it could make ends meet without seminars.

In 1979 the Board conducted about 20 open conferences, 15 CEO invitational meetings, and 32 briefing seminars.

      Contact:
          The Conference Board, Inc.
          845 Third Avenue
          New York, New York 10016

OTHERS IN THE FIELD

PROFESSIONAL ASSOCIATIONS AND FIRMS In fields such as accounting, many states require Continuing Education Units for the professional who wishes to retain his license. Nonprofit associations such as the National Association of Accountants and profit companies such as the prestigious accounting firm of Peat, Marwick, Mitchell & Co. fulfill this need by giving seminars.

MAGAZINE PUBLISHERS In the case of industries that are poorly organized, trade magazines often act as de facto professional organizations, organizing forums, and seminars. Recently, business magazines with a more general readership have jumped in. Among them: *BusinessWeek, Forbes,* and *Dun's Review.*

PACKAGERS These are companies that administer and market seminars conducted by institutions with little experience in running the business end of the seminars themselves, or little inclined to do so. One of the largest and best known is the New York Management Center, Inc.

New York Management Center, Inc. NYMC coordinates programs primarily for prestige universities like Wharton School of Business (University of Pennsylvania), New York University, and the University of Chicago.

Generally, NYMC leaves the planning and content of the seminars to its clients and concentrates on the marketing and finance end. An important part of their effort is the direct-mail campaign; but billing, evaluation, facilities management, and the printing of course materials are also included.

NYMC has helped a great many schools compete successfully in the seminar marketplace. And since the schools are in it for prestige and donations as well as tuition profits, they are generally sticklers for quality. They want to to create a positive image in the public and private sector. You'd probably think twice before sending your son or daughter to a school that offered bush-league seminars. And there are alumni, individual and corporate supporters to please.

Contact NYMC for information about the seminars being offered by their client schools:

New York Management Center, Inc.
360 Lexington Avenue
New York, New York 10017

THE CEU: WHAT'S IT WORTH?

The CEU, or Continuing Education Unit, is a halfhearted attempt to give legitimacy to noncredit courses. In some professions the units are required for relicensing or recertification, but they are little more than records of attendance. CEUs are also popular because they make the courses more attractive—the promise of credentials, no matter how ludicrous, lures people to the courses.

Serious-minded students interested in education for personal enrichment couldn't care less about CEUs. And those who feel the need for a substantial increase in education or the acquirement of additional skills would be wise to go for a degree or, at least, credit courses. When credit is offered, the instructor evaluates your performance and proficiency as well as your attendance. But there will always be those who spend their time, and the company's money, attending noncredit courses. They lack the need, motivation, time, or interest in additional formal schooling. The CEUs stand as the business world's equivalent to the Good Housekeeping Seal of Approval—CEUs mean the course actually did exist, one actually attended it, and the records are there to prove it. The value? Perhaps the course can go on your résumé without embarrassment, and it may have a certain promotional value—such as in a curriculum vitae or a company brochure.

Wisely, organizations such as the American Management Associations grant CEUs for all their courses.

HOW TO SELECT A SCHOOL AND PROGRAM

If you've been to college, you already have some idea about what is involved: You pick the school and the program, the teachers, and the classes.

THE SCHOOL

If you intend to keep your job, you obviously must choose a local school. Get all the catalogs and bulletins and read them. Look for evidence that the school is keeping pace with the changes in the business environment and is abreast of the latest techniques. The best way to tell is by the courses the school offers. Any school that claims to be in touch should have courses on computer applications in business, international business, systems analysis, information systems, and macro- and micro-economics. Few schools will have them all; if the school you're considering has none, or even very few, it is suspect.

Once you've established that the school has what you want in the way of courses and degree programs, you should find out something about its reputation. Ask around; people in personnel or training and development departments should know. Check with friends who faced a similar choice. And, by all means, ask school officials for placement records, starting salary levels of graduates, and any form of independent rankings. Ask about the intellectual caliber, academic achievement, and business experience of the students; you want to construct a profile of the typical student. If you do not fit the profile, you might find that the school would not meet your needs.

Ask the American Assembly of Collegiate Schools of Business for information on the school's accreditation status. Or consult *The AACSB Membership Directory.*
Contact:

American Assembly of Collegiate Schools of Business
11500 Olive Street Road
Suite 142
St. Louis, Missouri 63141

THE TEACHERS

The best way to find out about a teacher is by asking current and former students. If you have an idea that you may be taking a particular instructor's course next semester, try sitting in on a class or two this semester. Don't be shy about arranging a meeting with the instructor. Talk about your needs and how his course may fit into your educational and professional plans. And size him up in terms of sincerity, ability to articulate, clarity of thinking, knowledge, and experience. Credentials can be deceptive. Not every instructor with an illustrious background in academia is a good teacher, nor is every highly successful businessperson.

PLANNING YOUR COURSES

What exactly do you wish to learn? More important, how, if at all, do you expect this education to help you? If you attend classes because you enjoy learning, fine. But if you are interested in career advancement, your courses must have a focus. You can't afford to be a dilettante. Pick a goal—a degree, a certificate, or a level of proficiency in an important specialty. Companies are sometimes more willing to pick up the tab if you work at developing a skill in which the company is sorely lacking.

You might want to start your planning by consulting *Graduate Study in Management,* a complete guide to business degree programs. You'll find it in college and major bookstores. Or contact:

Admission Council for Graduate Study (ACGS)
Box 966
Princeton, New Jersey 08540

YOUR DEGREE OPTIONS

THE MBA   Generally, the MBA requires 60 semester hours over two full-time years, or three to four years part-time (two or three hours, two nights a week). People who make job and promotion decisions are familiar with MBAs; they know what you have to learn to get one. The vast majority of graduate business degrees are MBAs. In 1980 approximately 52,000 MBAs were awarded—up from 21,000 in 1970. This glut, combined with economic uncertainties, means that the degree is no longer a ticket to a job.

MBAs typically come with a higher price tag, and they are generally hired into training positions where they don't at first contribute much to the company. In periods of recession or slow growth, companies simply hire fewer. Don't be surprised to see MBA programs scrapped at some schools.

If you have prior business experience along with your MBA, you are in a much better position. Most top companies prefer at least two years of work experience.

Now let's assume that you have a job, but not an MBA. You may feel that, in a poor business climate, the extra degree won't make a difference in terms of promotions or pay raises. But consider a part-time MBA. You don't give up your job. And when things rebound, you might find yourself sitting pretty. Another option: If you've got the smarts to get yourself accepted to one of the top B-schools—like Harvard, Stanford, M.I.T., Yale, Wharton—and you think that you'll do reasonably well, you needn't worry about getting a job. There are always openings for the cream of the crop.

The part-time MBA. This can mean the slow and steady route of three or four years of night school one day a week, or an occasional semester-long "educational leave of absence." It depends on your desire, on your work load, and, of course, on your company. Recently many schools have begun "early bird" and lunchtime classes.

The MBA is still the degree most in demand, but you do have other options: You can get an MS in business with less effort, in less time; or a PhD in business with more effort and a lot more time.

THE MS IN BUSINESS requires only about 30 semester hours. You can get it in as little as one year, part-time. This program is a maverick, invented by Columbia University. The MS program cuts down on class time by de-emphasizing general business training and concentrating on a specialized area—accounting; personnel; computers. It has caught on at other schools, primarily because of its lower costs, fewer hours, and emphasis on a specialty. New York University, the University of Massachusetts, Florida State, Northwestern, San Diego State, Ohio State, Georgia Tech, and University of Southern California are among the schools that offer it.

THE PhD Doctoral programs in business shouldn't be undertaken without considerable forethought; they do not give you much more general business training than you get with the MBA. The PhD in business is a prestige degree that will help you establish credentials as an authority, spokesperson, teacher, journal editor, or consultant. But in terms of its value to a manager, it hardly justifies the time and effort—unless, of course, you enjoy the quest for knowledge.

Doctorates are offered in economics, computer science, finance, and marketing. Part-time, it will take between five and eight years and will set you or your company back as much as $12,000.

THE EMBA or executive MBA, was devised to appeal to older executives in middle to upper management. The emphasis is on top-level management skills, with less time spent on specialties. Only 45 semester hours are required. One of the main attractions of an EMBA program is the scheduling. It usually consists of one full day per week (Friday or Saturday), or two days every other week.

EMBA students like learning with their peers, rather than being mixed in with younger students in the MBA program. For this reason, it is generally unwise to enroll in an EMBA program if you are relatively young or hold a lower-level management position.

GLAMOUR COURSES These are the blue chips—the prestige non-degree management programs intended for key executives. If your company sends you to one of these courses, it's a pretty good indication that you are being groomed for a promotion. If that doesn't pan out, you'll be in a better position by virtue of the contacts made at the course.

It's difficult to measure what one gets out of such courses; there are no grades. And the fact that most graduates succeed begs the question, since the very fact that you are chosen by your firm to attend is a sure sign you're on your way up. In most cases, such courses will broaden your perspective on problem solving and give you an opportunity to learn about areas outside your own field.

Stanford offers an eight-week program intended for those who have more than ten years of managerial experience or who hold a senior management post.

There are seven courses of instruction: Financial Management and Control; Management of Marketing Strategy; Management of Human Resources; Economics, Public Policy and Business; Management Science and Computers; Management of the Total Enterprise; The International Economy.

In 1978 the class had a median age of 43.

Contact:
Stanford Executive Program
Graduate School of Business
Stanford University
Stanford, California 94305

Harvard's Advanced Management Program is perhaps the best known and most respected. It lasts thirteen weeks. You live on campus. The program is very structured, with six hours of lectures and seminars each day. But you can't just sit in the back of the room and coast through it: The Harvard B-School "casebook" method is used. You must prepare for class and be ready to participate. The curriculum includes Operations Strategy and Structure, Business Policy, Business and the World Society, Management Control, Human Behavior in Organizations, Financial Management, Marketing Management, Management Control, and a few electives.

If you get an opportunity to attend this course, do not turn it down. It is a sure sign that you are headed for bigger things.

Contact:
Advanced Management Program
George Pierce Baker Hall
Harvard Business School
Boston, Massachusetts 02163

Columbia's executive program takes a different approach. For one thing, it is conducted not on Columbia's New York City campus, but 50 miles upstate, at Arden House. The program is less structured, and there is more emphasis on the exchange of ideas than on classroom learning. Topics taken up include the relationship between the planning and implementation functions, and the impact of the environment on business. The session lasts six weeks.

Contact:
Executive Program in Business Administration
Columbia Graduate School of Business
Columbia University
New York, New York 10027

MIT The Massachusetts Institute of Technology likes numbers. True to form, the cost of its Senior Executive Program is exceptionally high but includes a field trip to Washington, D.C. The approach is quantitative, with courses covering finance and accounting, electronic data processing, computer technology, control techniques, information systems, and quantitative analysis.

Contact:
MIT Program for Senior Executives
Room E-52-456
Sloan School of Management
Massachusetts Institute of Technology
Cambridge, Massachusetts 02139

Other good glamour programs are offered by Wharton (University of Pennsylvania), University of Chicago, University of Virginia, University of North Carolina, Carnegie-Mellon, Berkeley, and Northwestern.

Harvard has an additional course—the Program for Management Development (PMD)—designed for middle management—that lasts 14 weeks.

WHERE TO GET INFORMATION ABOUT MANAGEMENT PROGRAMS

The best sources are:

- *Bricker's Directory of Management Enhancement Programs*
- *American Management Associations Directory of Management Education Programs*, an excellent source, contains over 1,100 primary program entries in all major management fields. It includes a comprehensive listing of the important data on each course.

Both of these directories are available in most public and university libraries.

TEACHING YOUR WAY TO THE TOP

Power is built on influence. And influence is, in part, built on knowledge, reputation, and visibility. More and more, career-minded executives are viewing teaching as a success strategy, rather than a refuge for those who can't cut it in the business world.

The surge in demand for MBAs has created a need for good teachers with practical business experience. And long gone is the antagonism that existed between academia and the business world in the sixties.

More professional teachers have accepted off-campus work as consultants, and this trend has made it easier for executives to accept part-time teaching posts. The interchange between business and universities is out in the open.

Teaching is not easy. You don't stand in front of a class and tell them tales of your exploits. You've got to prepare, stick to a curriculum, and maintain strict academic standards. You'll be spending a fair amount of out-of-class time preparing for class and reading students' work.

For a good teacher, the rewards are numerous. As your course becomes more refined, you may develop an approach and a body of knowledge worthy of being published. Teaching and publishing form a symbiotic relationship: One helps the other.

When you teach, you come in contact with dozens of students who will be entering the working world (if they are not already working). They'll know who you are, and you will get to know many of them. So you will be forming the nucleus of a reputation, at least on a local level.

A good teacher usually learns a great deal from the teaching process. Your own understanding of the subject will deepen and your communications skills will improve. This will undoubtedly help you on your job in the business world.

Last, but not least, is the joy of teaching—sharing knowledge and helping others succeed.

If you are unsure about making a commitment, you might start by giving or participating in a seminar. Then move on to night school. Contact the school or sponsoring agency and offer your services and credentials. The need for knowledgeable teaching executives is greater than you might imagine.

WHAT YOU SHOULD KNOW: OPINIONS FROM BUSINESS AND ACADEMIA

The American Assembly of Collegiate Schools of Business (AACSB), in an effort to upgrade and standardize the curricula of accredited business schools, has undertaken a major study. The first phase involved scanning business-school catalogs and consulting with faculty and administrators to come up with a list of "major knowledge areas." The result was a list of thirteen major knowledge areas, or "modules" (*see* Fig. 34).

This list was used as a basis for surveying over a thousand business people, students, alumni, and the general public in order to determine just how much time should be spent on each of these areas while in B-school.

Since this work will eventually form the basis of a standardized B-school curriculum and, maybe, an accreditation exam, the list is a useful indicator of what B-school students will be learning—and the kinds of things you should know within the knowledge areas most closely associated with your job.

ACCOUNTING

Module No. 1—Managerial & Financial Accounting
  Nature & uses of accounting; accounting as measurements of managerial performance; structure & analysis of financial statements.
Module No. 2—Financial Accounting (Mod. No. 1—prerequisite)
  Capital structure; long-term debt; stockholders equity; capital budgeting and cost of capital.
Module No. 3—Accntng. Systems & Internal Control (Mods. 1 & 2—prerequisites)
  Flexible budgeting; standard costs; break-even analysis & pricing for profit planning; accounting systems & planning.

ECONOMICS

Module No. 1—Microeconomics I
  Theory of demand & individual utility functions; measures & determinants of demand elasticity; cost & production theory.
Module No. 2—Microeconomics II (Mod. No. 1—prerequisite)
  Theories of firm; price & output decisions under varying market structures & environments; role of prices & profits in a decentralized economic system; impact of government policy on firm behavior.
Module No. 3—Macroeconomics
  Theory of national income determination; economic fluctuations, growth, inflation; monetary & fiscal policies & the role of government; economic forecasting.

FINANCE

Module No. 1—Financial Structure (Econ. & Accntg. are prerequisites)
  Financial institutions; sources of financing; role of financial management & financial analysis.
Module No. 2—Financial Management (Mod. No. 1—prerequisite)
  Financial forecasting & budgeting; management of working capital; management of current assets.

HUMAN BEHAVIOR & ORGANIZATION THEORY

Module No. 1—Individual Behavior
  Personality & individual differences; perception & cognition; theories of motivation; learning & development; styles of problem solving & decision making.

Fig. 34. Major business knowledge areas
These categories emerged from a study conducted by the
American Assembly of Collegiate Schools of Business (AACSB)
and involving B-school professors and business executives.
(through page 318)
From AACSB Accreditation Research Committee.
Reprinted by permission.

Module No. 2—Small group dynamics (Mod. No. 1—prerequisite)
  Group process & dynamics; group effectiveness; leadership & influence; interpersonal conflict; inter- and intra-group conflict.
Module No. 3—Organizational Theory
  Alternative organization models; approaches to organization design; organization development & change; organization effectiveness.

INFORMATION SYSTEMS

Module No. 1—Management and MIS
  Systems approach; systems design concepts in management; data base management systems.
Module No. 2—Mgmt. Information Systems (Mod. No. 1—prerequisite)
  Design & implementation; general knowledge of computer; use of computer in management.

INTERNATIONAL BUSINESS

Module No. 1—International Economics
  Foreign exchange market; balance of payments & adjustment process; national & international monetary policy; international trade; national & international trade policy.
Module No. 2—Foreign Investment
  Methods of pursuing international business; characteristics of direct foreign investment; impact of host state, parent state, & international policies on business strategies.

LEGAL AND SOCIAL ENVIRONMENT

Module No. 1—The Systems Nature of the Bus. Environment
  Linkages between bus. & society; social system, process, and structure; political system, process, and structure; government system, process, & structure; relationship with business.
Module No. 2—Legal & Regulatory Subsystems (Mod. No. 1—prerequisite)
  Characteristics of these subsystems; political nature of these subsystems; impact on business; points of influence.
Module No. 3—Law & Business (Mods. 1 & 2—prerequisites)
  Antitrust; uniform commercial code; law as an expression of social values.

MANAGEMENT OF HUMAN RESOURCES

Module No. 1—Management of Human Resources
  Human resource policy in organizational context; manpower planning for the organization; recruitment & selection including affirmative action factors; training & development; performance appraisal, compensation, & reward systems.
Module No. 2—Labor Relations
  Historical evolution of union-management relations; legal framework; collective bargaining; mediation & arbitration; grievance systems.

MANAGEMENT POLICY & STRATEGY

Module No. 1—Development of a Strategic Plan
  Relationship to general management; analysis for strategic decisions; corporate structure, development & strategy; acquisition analysis; developing a strategic plan.
Module No. 2—Implementation of Strategy (Mod. No. 1—prerequisite)
  Corporate structure; environmental context for strategy; personal values & strategy; managing the implementation process; integration of functional strategies.
Module No. 3—Planning & Control (Mods. 1 & 2—prerequisites)
  Development of goals for planning & control; budgeting as a control mechanism; sources, costs, & uses of information for planning & control; computer-based planning systems; PPBS.

MARKETING

Module No. 1—Principles of Marketing
  Marketing concept; competition & demand models; product, price, promotion, & place issues & strategies; contemporary social, ethical, & governmental issues in marketing.
Module No. 2—Marketing Management (Mod. No. 1—prerequisite)
  Consumer behavior models; industrial marketing; marketing research strategies.

QUANTITATIVE ANALYSIS

Module No. 1—Probability & Sampling
  Probability theory; sampling distributions & theory; measures of central tendency & dispersion.
Module No. 2—Estimation & Hypothesis Testing (Mod. No. 1—prerequisite)
  Analysis of variance; multiple regression; covariance analysis.
Module No. 3—Decision Theory & Analysis
  Decision & Utility theory; Bayes' Theorem; prior & posterior analysis.

OPERATIONS RESEARCH

Module No. 1—Use of Ops. Res. (Quantitative Analysis courses are prerequisites)
  Operations research & problem solving; model design; linear programming; dynamic programming.
Module No. 2—Ops. Res. Techniques (Mod. No. 1—prerequisite)
  Inventory models; queuing theory; game theory; simulations.

PRODUCTION (OPERATIONS) MANAGEMENT

Module No. 1—Production
  Design of production function & physical system; job design; measurement of output.
Module No. 2—Quantitative Techniques & Production (Mod. No. 1—prerequisite)
  Inventory systems & problems; quality control systems & problems; production scheduling (PERT, etc.); simulation models.

NONCOGNITIVE SKILLS

There is some question whether noncognitive skills can be taught: Unlike cognitive or empirical skills, they do not involve set bodies of knowledge. They are primarily a matter of innate aptitude and abilities, personal attributes, character traits, and attitudes. But since everyone agrees that such skills are critical to business success, the AACSB decided to go ahead in an attempt to identify and define various noncognitive skills, or traits.

Using an extensive search of literature and lists compiled by academic and corporate experts, the AACSB research team arrived at a list of 89 traits (see Fig. 35).

The list was reduced to six basic "noncognitive characteristics groups" (see Fig. 36).

There is no question that you should become familiar with the noncognitive characteristics noted here; they are vitally important for success. The sooner you assess your strength and weaknesses, the better.

Although the list is a good one, it is interesting that it makes little mention of the kind of skills that may be necessary to insure personal career advancement and survival, such as power tactics, politics, and delegation skills. The skills mentioned in the AACSB are certainly those that make for a good and effective manager—but not necessarily a successful one.

For more information on this research project, contact:

American Assembly of Collegiate Schools of Business
11500 Olive Street Road
Suite 142
St. Louis, Missouri 63141

Your request for information should refer to the AACSB Accreditation Research Project.

SKILLS AND ABILITIES

1. Quantitative Ability
2. Analytical/Problem Definition & Analysis
3. Resources Management
4. Interpersonal Relations
5. Communications
    a. Oral
    b. Written
6. Listening
7. Reading
8. Decisiveness
9. Learning Ability
10. Imagination/Innovation
11. Risk Tolerance
12. Judgment
13. Ability to Generalize
14. Leadership
15. Application of Knowledge
16. Ability to Identify Alternatives
17. Questioning Skills
18. Creativity
19. Implementation Skills
20. Objectivity
21. Organizational Skills (Administrative)
22. Persuasiveness
23. Memory
24. Reasoning Ability
25. Problem Solving Ability
26. Ability to Synthesize
27. Assessment of Reasonableness
28. Ability to Set Priorities
29. Mental Ability
    a. Organization of Thinking
    b. Discriminatory Thinking
    c. Decision Making Skills
    d. Concentration
30. Negotiation Skills
31. Ability to Exercise Authority
32. Ability to Deal with Government Regulations

ATTITUDES AND VALUES

33. Respect for Authority
34. Motivation
    a. Desire to Work
    b. Willingness to Work

Fig. 35. Results of AACSB survey of noncognitive trails
Findings where grouped by skills, attitudes, and personal
characteristics of B-school graduates.
(above and opposite)

From AACSB Accreditation Research Committee.
Reprinted by permission.

35. Realism
36. Entrepreneurial vs. Organizational Ambitions
37. Level of Expectation
38. Functional vs. General Management Orientation
39. Balance of Rights and Responsibilities
40. Appreciation for
    a. Economic Values
    b. Private Enterprise
41. Global Perspective
42. Meritocracy Awareness
43. Risk/Benefit Sensitivity
44. Goal Orientation
45. Citizenship
    a. Social Responsibilities
    b. Loyalty/Commitment
46. Belief in Human Worth
47. Appreciation for Legislative Process
48. Optimism/Positivism
49. Sense of Tradition
50. Contribution vs. Exploitation Ethic
51. Desire to Expand Personal Influence/Power
52. Need Achievement
53. Compatibility of Personal & Corporate Ethics
54. Career Orientation
55. Competitiveness
56. Positive Understanding of Corporate Goals and Responsibilities
57. Tolerance
58. Commitment to Results
59. Long Range Viewpoint
60. Personal/Career Values (Balance)
61. Profit Motive/Value
62. Sense of Responsibility

PERSONAL CHARACTERISTICS

63. Honesty
64. Maturity
65. Grooming
66. Mental Alertness
67. Inquisitiveness
68. Manners
69. Emotional Stability
70. Sincerity
71. Social Skills
72. Objectivity (Integrity)
73. Sense of Humor
74. Perceptiveness
75. Self-Discipline
76. Sensitivity
77. Humility
78. Self-Respect
79. Self-Starter
80. Empathy
81. Toughness
82. Flexibility/Adaptation to Change
83. Intelligence
84. Common Sense
85. Competitiveness
86. Energy
87. Self-Confidence/Esteem/Ego
88. Perseverance
89. Resiliency

1. Administrative Skills
   a. Organizing and Planning
   b. Decision Making
   c. Creativity
2. Interpersonal Skills
   a. Behavior Flexibility
   b. Personal Impact
   c. Social Objectivity
   d. Perception of Threshold Social Cues
   e. Oral Communication Skills
   f. Leadership
3. Intellectual Ability
   a. Range of Interests
   b. General Mental Ability
   c. Written Communication Skills
4. Stability of Performance
   a. Tolerance of Uncertainty
   b. Resistance to Stress
5. Work Motivation
   a. Primacy of Work
   b. Inner Work Standards
   c. Energy
   d. Self-Objectivity
6. Values of Business

Fig. 36. Important noncognitive skills

From AACSB Accreditation Research Committee.
Reprinted by permission.

WHO GETS AHEAD?

In *Who Gets Ahead? The Determinants of Economic Success in America* (New York: Basic Books, Inc., 1979), Christopher Jencks, a Harvard sociology professor, along with a team of researchers, analyzes the question. In a study of American males between the ages of 25 and 64, based on the statistical analysis of 11 different surveys conducted over the course of a decade, Jencks et al examine the relationship between a worker's personal characteristics (measured in terms of family background, cognitive skills, personality traits, and education) and his economic success (measured in terms of occupational status and level of earnings).

If you have Horatio Alger—like illusions about who makes it in America, you may be surprised to read some of the study results.*

FAMILY BACKGROUND: HAVE PEDIGREE, WILL TRAVEL

EFFECT ON OCCUPATIONAL STATUS

- *The Silver Spoon Syndrome:* Being born into the "right" family pays. For instance, a doctor owes 48 percent of his occupational advantage directly to his family background and 52 percent to factors that differentiate him from his own brother.
- *Like Father, Like Son:* Father's occupational status is the single most significant effect on his son's status. Even after Jencks controlled for variables such as educational attainment, this factor yielded a "modest" influence. The implication of this finding is "that we are not necessarily dealing with general effects of privileged upbringing, but with something specific to occupations." Jencks suggests that the explanation may lie in the "direct transmission of specific jobs."
- Race, ethnicity, religion, and farm background exert a consistently strong effect on occupational status, independent of educational attainment.

EFFECT ON EARNINGS

- Again, having the "right" family pays—a lot. As the study concluded, if a family's sole concern "were to increase their sons' earnings, the most 'successful' fifth of all families could expect their sons to earn" 45 to 80 percent "more than the average man."
- Race substantially affects level of earnings.

---

*Adapted from Christopher Jencks, *Who Gets Ahead?* (New York: Basic Books, Inc., 1979).

- Father's occupational status affects sons' earnings only insofar as it affects occupational status.
- Religion: Catholics and Jews have greater incomes than Protestants with similar demographic backgrounds and schooling.

COGNITIVE SKILLS:
AMERICAN "MERITOCRACY" — A MYTH?

If test performance is a measure of ability (a dubious assumption, Jencks notes), then the findings of this study would indicate that America is *not* a "meritocratic" society: Ability, per se, is not a determinant of success.

EFFECT ON OCCUPATIONAL STATUS

- An adolescent's cognitive skills seem to have only an indirect effect on occupational status. Such skills affect educational attainment, which in turn affects entry into initial occupation and may later influence career mobility.

EFFECT ON EARNINGS

- A "modest" association. To achieve a high level of earnings, "high scores are neither necessary nor sufficient. They are merely helpful."

PERSONALITY TRAITS:
MOST LIKELY TO SUCCEED?

EFFECT ON BOTH OCCUPATIONAL STATUS AND EARNINGS

- The traits associated with occupational status are quite different from those identified with level of earnings. Industriousness seems associated indirectly with occupational status, in that that quality influences educational attainment, which in turn affects occupational status. Measures of leadership are to some degree particularly associated with earnings. However:
- "No single, well-defined trait emerged as a decisive determinant," but the combined impact of various traits was comparatively strong.

SCHOOLING

Educational attainment was measured in terms of the last year of formal schooling completed. Jencks and his team offer no definitive explanation for the positive correlation established between completed schooling and subsequent economic success. They do conclude, however, that evidence suggests "only part of the association between schooling and success can be due to what students actually learn from year to year in school."*

EFFECT ON OCCUPATIONAL STATUS

- Of all measurements taken, the single most significant indicator of adult occupational status is the highest school or college grade completed upon entry into the labor market.
- The completion of last year of high school, first year of college, or last year of college has a particularly strong impact—more so than any of the intervening years.
- "Differences in college quality [ranked according to selectivity] had no impact on occupational status" in subjects of equivalent educational attainment.

EFFECT ON EARNINGS

- Of all measurements taken, the single most significant indicator of level of earnings is the highest school or college grade completed upon entry into the labor market.
- Each successive year of schooling completed raises level of earnings to some extent. Certification, per se, does not carry extra weight.
- Attendance at any selective college (not necessarily the most selective) increased earnings by 28 percent over men with similar backgrounds who attended unselective schools.
- Good grades are linked to high earnings only because they are associated with completion of school rather than with dropping out.
- Higher education increases earnings by helping people enter high-status occupations, which may have licensing and other devices that exclude those with less education. In that sense, it is not what college teaches the student, but rather the doors that it opens in the high-status job market that render it valuable.

*Christopher Jencks, *Who Gets Ahead?* (New York: Basic Books, 1979), p. 266.

PART V

MOVING THROUGH THE JOB JUNGLE

"Without work
all life goes rotten."
Albert Camus

20

DO YOU SINCERELY WANT TO BE A CORPORATE EXECUTIVE?

Wanting to be an executive, say the experts in career counseling, is a matter of desire. There is no room at the top for the fainthearted or the wishy-washy. Commitment is crucial.

To get *there* from *here*, first find your bearings: That is, make an intelligent, clear-sighted evaluation of where you are now; then set the goal. Without a sense of direction, you are bound, at best, to proceed hesitantly; at worst, to travel aimlessly.

What *is* a corporate career? Before you sign your life away, you'd better find out.

Management consultant David J. McLaughlin writes, in *The Executive Money Map* (New York: McGraw-Hill, 1975), "When one's current position is a way station to greater things, we speak of having a career instead of a job." In the corporate world, those "greater things" to which one aspires are the executive positions—preferably the upper echelon of executive positions. But if you're not already privy to the inner sanctum of the executive suite, you still may be in the dark as to what executives do there day to day.

191 WAYS AN EXECUTIVE FILLS HIS DAYS

In 1959, the Educational Testing Service of Princeton, New Jersey, asked 93 executives at five major corporations just what it is they do. For the purposes of the study, an executive position was defined as one that "entails responsibility for supervising someone who is also a supervisor." That is, a management position above the "second line." The study, conducted by John K. Hemphill, identified ten major types of work performed by executives:

- providing a staff service in nonoperational areas
- supervision of work
- business control

- technical-product and markets
- human, commodity, and social affairs
- long-range planning
- exercise of broad power and authority
- business reputation
- personal demands
- preservation of assets

The study concluded that:

- Executive positions are complex (any *one* position encompassing three to five different types of work without apparent pattern).
- Work type is not informed by job title.
- What work an executive performs is only in small part dependent upon his place in the organizational hierarchy, his area of function, or the company characteristics.*

In other words, it's not easy to pin down the nature of the executive animal. For that very reason, the ETS researchers compiled a questionnaire. Based on the original responses of the participating executives, "The Executive Position Description" contains 191 statements of position elements. By rating each element on a 7-to-0 scale in terms of the part it plays (ranging from "most significant" through "substantial" and "minor" to "none at all") in the executive's position, the executive can arrive at a practical description of the job.

So take a look at the questionnaire (*see* Chapter 26) and learn the 191 ways an executive fills his day. It is a useful standard against which to measure your own skills, interests, and experience, and it will provide a handy reference when you are ready to put together a *personal* executive description, your résumé (Chapter 25).

CHARTING A COURSE

Okay. You're committed. You have a *sense* of direction. To insure your arrival at the top, however, some career planning is essential. Though good luck may play a part in its achievement, success is rarely gained through serendipity alone. Particularly in these times of increased career mobility, an advancement strategy is required. Chart a course. You will want to consult your plan, perhaps revise it, at critical points along the way. Current thinking on the subject of career planning, as popularized by such people as Richard Bolles, in his widely acclaimed book *What Color is Your Parachute?* (Berkeley: Ten Speed Press, 1979), emphasizes the first

---

*From John K. Hemphill, "Dimensions of Executive Positions" (Princeton, NJ: Educational Testing Service, 1959). Reprinted by permission of the author.

---

important step: taking a self-inventory. The theory is that what you have in the future is in large measure determined by what you have now. If you have begun to "find your bearings" as suggested, you have already begun this crucial process of taking stock of your personal (not financial) assets and liabilities.

SELF-ANALYSIS

What are your aptitudes? Also known as a cognitive skill, an aptitude is a natural or acquired ability, a capacity as well as an inclination to do a given thing. Commonly called intelligence, aptitude reflects *potential*, or readiness, in learning and understanding. If you aren't aware of what your aptitudes are, do some psychological testing.

What are your talents? A talent is defined as a skill for which you have demonstrated an aptitude. Typically, a talent is an activity you perform well and joyfully.

What are your interests? hobbies? What places, people, activities, ideas, or things arouse your curiosity? What fascinates you? What absorbs your attention? What do you *love* to do? What might you *like* to do? Also, what do you *hate* to do?

What experience do you have? This question requires specific answers: "I do bookkeeping, accounts payable and receivable," or "I supervised an office staff of seven people." Experience does not have to be on-the-job. ("I directed the fund-raising campaign for my church.") Of your actual experience, what have you enjoyed the most? the least?

What are your personal priorities? This is probably the most critical and most difficult question you will have to answer—and ask again and again—in the course of your career. To assess your priorities, consider the principles by which you guide your life. It is an emotional process as well as an intellectual one: What are the *feelings* that inform your actions? What do you value above all else? *In order to answer some practical questions, you must often first ask philosophical ones.* What are you willing to do to get ahead? What and how much are you willing to sacrifice? Your leisure time? Time with your family? Is that time for sale? What is the price tag?

For many people, work does have its own rewards. Through working, people gain a sense of self-respect, a sense of usefulness, a sense of purpose, a sense of accomplishment. For some people, a job offers a genuine challenge, an opportunity to demonstrate abilities, an opportunity to grow and develop. The corporate arena provides ample opportunities for those seeking power or status. But, for most people, the bottom line is this: When you work, you effect a trade-off; you exchange a degree of personal autonomy for a degree of financial security with the hope that financial security brings its own brand of freedom.

So be prepared to make some choices—practical ones. Would you exchange your present life-style—say, a house in the country, fresh air and open spaces for your kids—for a better position in a big city, or even in a different country?

Some of your choices will be simpler, a question of personal style: Do you prefer big corporations to smaller ones? The nonmanufacturing industries over manufacturing ones? Or a service-oriented company over both? Are you more interested in working with people or figures, personnel or finance? The point is, in establishing your career strategy, you must begin to narrow the vast field of opportunity around you.

THE GOOD LIFE

The American business environment offers so many options, that an aspiring manager should take a few moments to consider whether the executive life-style will provide fulfillment and happiness to himself and family.

How do American managers feel about their jobs, and what of the executive life-style? The Quality of Employment Survey conducted at the University of Michigan sheds some light on the issue.

As a rule, managers rate their jobs as "good jobs," agreeing that they get to do a number of different things and that their work is significant. Most executives say they have freedom to make decisions, receive timely feedback, and that they know where and how they make a contribution to the company's business.

An overwhelming majority—92 percent—say they are satisfied with their jobs, and contrary to a popular view, there appears to be no difference in the degree of stress felt by managers as compared with non-managers. In fact, 89 percent said they were free of physical and nervous problems.

By a margin of 96 to 88 percent, a greater number of managers than non-managers described themselves as happy. And more than 90 percent described themselves as generally happy with their lives and jobs.

21
NARROWING THE FIELD

The first step to planning a career is to look inward. The second step is to look up and around. When you embark on your career, you enter what is known as the labor force. The labor force competes in what is known as the job market. What chance you have in succeeding in your career depends in some part upon the kind and number in the labor force as compared to the kind and number of jobs on the market. To translate that into personal terms, to maximize your career opportunities, locate your place in the labor force by identifying your particular skills and experience, then locate that sector of the job market that has a high demand for people with your abilities. If you can't locate a market that calls for your brand of expertise, then go back to square one and develop some new expertise. It's a simple principle, not unlike the one upon which certain intelligence tests are based: Only the mentally deficient try to fit large square pegs into small round holes.

FITTING IN: THE JOB OUTLOOK OF THE EIGHTIES

The factors that affect the availability of jobs are economic, social, and political.

GNP

The economic growth of this country is traditionally measured in terms of the Gross National Product (GNP), or the total goods and services produced per year. Judging by that index alone, the American economy has generally been thriving.

In the coming decade, corporations will seek to cut costs while maintaining productivity and increasing the volume of sales. Industry will focus on those areas that directly affect productivity and profitability: data processing and information systems, research and development, manufacturing, marketing and sales.

GOVERNMENT CUTBACKS

Government may be making some budget cuts as well. Depending on which services are cut and which government projects are suspended, certain industries will feel the blow directly.

TIGHTER REGULATIONS

In addition to possible cutbacks in government projects, experts foresee more government regulation, particularly with regard to retirement, job safety, environmental protection, and equal employment opportunity. Such regulation would have some direct impact on the distribution of jobs within the labor force.

EXPANDING LABOR FORCE

While government and industry may be tightening their belts, the labor force is suffering middle-age bulge: The baby-boom generation has come of age. During this decade workers between the ages of 25 and 44 will expand the work force by 21 million; they will fill 70 percent of the jobs. And although the Labor Department predicts that new jobs will continue to be created, their growth will be at a reduced rate. Only 23 million newly created positions are expected to open up between 1980 and 1990. In other words, there will be more workers vying for (possibly) fewer jobs, and those who will have it toughest are those who are already counted within the present ranks of the work force, not those who will be entering into it.*

CONSUMER TRENDS

Unlike the sun, however, which is said to shine on all things equally, the factors that affect business conditions do not cast light, or even shadows, in quite so democratic a fashion. Even while some industries will suffer in the coming decade, others will thrive. Certain kinds of businesses are more susceptible than others to economic swings. For instance, those businesses, such as travel and advertising, that do not produce essential goods or services are likely to feel a pinch in a downswing.

Also, the factor known as "consumer tastes" is likely to exercise its fickle finger upon the future of certain businesses.

---

*From supplement of *The New York Times;* articles by David E. Rosenbaum and Thomas C. Hayes.

PROSPECTS FOR THE EXECUTIVE

Different experts manage to draw differing conclusions from the same data. There are, of course, always those who, given a donut, will contemplate the hole. Those who prefer to regard the sweeter side of things predict that although the job outlook for the eighties is less than rosy, at least it promises to be better overall than the dismal picture that developed in the seventies. For the executive, in particular, the future holds some promise. The key to maintaining steady employment and a chance for growth is to come up with the right mixture of skills and experience, industry, and location.

More than half the new job openings in the eighties will be filled by white-collar workers, who also happen to constitute half the present-day labor force. What is particularly promising about that statistic is that white-collar jobs are expected to continue growing at an accelerated rate compared to blue-collar jobs. Thirty years ago, professionals and managers filled one in every 12 jobs. Today, they occupy 25 percent of all positions.

EXPERTISE

The toughest executive positions to fill in the coming years, according to a survey conducted by the search firm of Haskell & Stern Associates, New York, will be "general management" openings. Apparently, the lack of qualified generalists is due to the fact that lower management these days tends to produce specialists. The same survey observed, however, that after general managers, qualified technical specialists, computer specialists, and engineers will be hardest to find. Although Haskell & Stern cited the financial function as one that will be easy to fill, an article in *Esquire* magazine named management accounting as an area that *needs* qualified candidates and is an open field especially for women.* To a lesser degree, a need is identified for personnel managers, particularly in industrial relations, and for puchasing managers whose job will be to cut down company costs.

INDUSTRY

The consensus seems to be that *service industries* will offer the most job opportunities in the eighties, particularly:

- *business services*, including insurance and banking. Barring major economic disaster, banking remains one of the most stable pro-

---

*Myra Friedman, "Is This Any Way to Make a Living?" (*Esquire*, July, 1977), p.66.

335

fessions and, as it continues to expand its services, is currently thriving. Although banks tend to offer good benefits, they are also very paternalistic and *very* selective. They can afford to be. Beyond the ground floor, however, it is not easy to get a foot in the door.

- *information gathering and data processing*, considered *the* business technology of the future
- *computers and related industries, including electronics.* For those with the special or technical backgrounds, these fields continue to yield a bumper crop of opportunities, particularly in the fertile "sunbelt" region.
- *communications*, including radio and TV broadcasting, especially cable TV
- *entertainment and leisure industries*
- *medical services*, including health care and hospitals
- *transportation services*

Other growth industries:

- *energy*, petroleum and petrochemicals
- *synthetic fibers*
- *copper-ore mining*
- *retailing*, particularly department stores and restaurants. The retail sector, according to a 1979 report in *The New York Times*, is the nation's largest employer and is expected to generate the greatest number of new jobs in the coming decade. In the past ten years, the major chains, such as Sears, Roebuck, K Mart Corporation, Saks Fifth Avenue, and Neiman Marcus, experienced an average growth of 10 percent per year. A need is predicted in retailing for middle and upper management personnel, particularly in merchandising, real estate (investments in store property), and marketing and promotion.

RECENT TRENDS

Loyalty is out   In a recent *BusinessWeek*/Harris Poll of middle managers, 65 percent of the respondents said salaried employees were less loyal than they were ten years ago. Aggressive cutting of management staffs and the recent wave of mergers and acquisitions have victimized middle managers, leaving them wary of planning careers around long-term commitments to a firm. Company and executive alike view the relationship as a short-term contract that can be terminated by either side on short notice. Undoubtedly, corporate loyalty has helped shape American business, but in the years to come American business will have to learn how to do without it.

Cutbacks have become acceptable   In the past, corporations were willing to reduce costs by eliminating jobs, but usually not on the middle, upper and professional levels. All that has changed as automation, reorganization, mergers and gains in productivity reduce the demand for managers.

More will manage by contract   As companies cut permanent staff, they have become more willing to assign projects which were once reserved for managers to freelancers. Increasingly, contract workers are performing financial analysis, marketing, strategic planning, project management and human resource management, as well as the more customary jobs such as computer software design and programming and product engineering.

Does this make sense? It makes senior management look good, because fewer heads show up on the payroll. And although wages are generally higher, there are large savings on employee benefits and Social Security.

For the worker, there are benefits ranging from greater freedom, greater control and greater variety to tax benefits. On the downside, there is the uncertainty of a lack of steady income and the expense of paying for benefits and insurance.

Older managers are choosing early retirement over reassignment   Increasingly, top management has been seeking to reduce the work force by eliminating older managers through an attractive early retirement package. The alternative is often a dead-end job or a kick downstairs to a lower-paying or less responsible position. More and more managers are opting to take the early retirement package.

The demise of U.S. manufacturing has been greatly exaggerated   It appears that economists confused a cyclical downturn with a long-term trend. The recent recession, intense foreign competition, and the increase in military spending have made American manufacturing tougher and more likely to prosper. Workers are more dedicated, organizations are leaner, and government is more cooperative.

Most takeovers are not hostile   From January 1984 to mid–1985, 400 of the 850 largest firms on *Fortune*'s list underwent restructuring. But only 52 were the result of hostile takeover threats. Most mergers and acquisitions are reactions to the needs of the competitive marketplace rather than profiteering. As the going gets tough, m & a's will keep on going.

Middle managers are not an endangered species   Out of 2,780 firms surveyed by Management Recruiters International, 35 percent planned to expand middle management and/or professional staffs, while 51 percent said they would keep all they now employ. Only 12 percent planned cuts. The most hiring will come from the mid-Atlantic region.

BW/HARRIS EXECUTIVE POLL:
NO JOB IS FOREVER

Employee loyalty toward corporations has dropped dramatically, according to a special survey of middle managers. And they believe the wave of layoffs and buyouts of salaried staff is not about to end. Though most middle managers think top management comes out best in a cutback, they still think employees are usually treated fairly.

Q When you started work for your current employer, did you assume that as long as you did a good job, you could keep it as long as you liked?

A Did assume 56%
Did not assume 43%
Not sure 1%

Q Now, please think of your current job situation. Do you think that as long as you do a good job, you can stay with your current employer for as long as you like?

A Can stay 44%
May not be able to.......44%
Not sure 12%

Q Has your employer cut back its salaried work force or not in the past five years?

A Has cut back 55%
Has not 43%
Not sure 2%

Q How likely is it that your employer will cut back its salaried work force in the next few years?

A Likely 46%
Not likely 52%
Not sure 2%

Q From what you know about companies that have reduced salaried employment over the past few years, is it your impression that those who lost their jobs or gave them up voluntarily were treated fairly by their employers or not?

A Were treated fairly 72%
Were not treated fairly ...14%
Not sure 14%

Q When a company lays off or buys out salaried employees, which group of workers do you think has the most trouble adjusting?

A Those in their 30s 2%
Those in their 40s 17%
Those in their 50s or older 78%
Not sure 3%

Fig. 37. Poll of middle managers at 600 corporations drawn from the BUSINESS WEEK 1000.
The survey was conducted July 15-21 by Louis Harris & Associates for BUSINESS WEEK.

BW/HARRIS EXECUTIVE POLL:
NO JOB IS FOREVER

Q In the layoffs and buyouts that have taken place, which group do you think gets the best treatment?

A
Top management	79%
Middle management	5%
Junior management	2%
Clerical employees	3%
All about the same	5%
Not sure	7%

Q If you were laid off by your current employer or accepted a packaged deal to leave voluntarily, which of the following do you think you would do?

A
Retire	5%
Get a better job	37%
Get an equivalent job	44%
Get a lesser job	7%
Become unemployed	3%
Start your own business	3%
Not sure	1%

Q I'd like to read you some statements about the effects of reducing white-collar employment in companies. Do you agree or disagree?

A
	Agree	Disagree	Not sure
Cutting back on salaried employees can get rid of a lot of dead wood	81%	15%	4%
If cutbacks are made, those with less seniority should be the first to go	29%	67%	4%
A corporation that is fored to reduce its salaried work force probably hasn't been very well managed	47%	49%	4%

Q Finally, let me ask you about the loyalty of most salaried employees to the companies they work for. Compared with 10 years ago, do you feel that salaried employees are more loyal, less loyal, or about as loyal as they were back then?

A
More loyal	5%
Less loyal	65%
About as loyal	29%
Not sure	2%

Edited by Stuart Jackson

Reprinted from August 4, 1986 issue of *Business Week*
by special permission; © 1986 by McGraw-Hill, Inc.

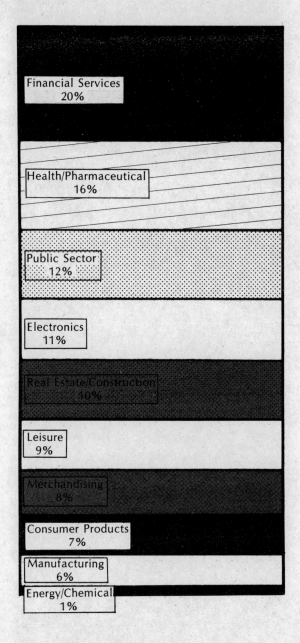

Fig. 38. Where the Jobs Are for Senior Executives—
Positions paying more than $100,000
Source: Korn/Ferry International

22

A LOOK AT YOUR ENTIRE CAREER

A useful aid in charting your own executive career is studying the careers of those who already have made it to the top. However, each person's career is unique, just as each person is unique. Apparently, the path to the top is not necessarily the most predictable or the most logical.

In the course of a thirty-year, perhaps forty-year, career, your direction may take many turns, and the particulars cannot be predetermined. Nevertheless, management consultant David McLaughlin has described four basic phases through which most executives might well pass while traversing the corporate countryside, and he has sighted specific guideposts and milestones that mark the way. On the following pages is an "atlas" compiled primarily on the basis of McLaughlin's overview. Insofar as it helps to delineate the choices, it is a handy travel guide for anyone planning to embark upon a corporate career.

THE CORPORATE CAREER ATLAS

KEY:

The fully achieved corporate career is divided into four periods: the preparatory; the formative; the critical stage, or watershed; negotiating the heights. Each period is described according to the following classifications:

TIME FRAMEWORK: approximate duration of phase and/or approximate age of "traveler"

COMPENSATION: expected salary range and projected net worth

CHARACTERISTICS: includes noteworthy sights and things to do

OPTIONS: major crossroads commonly encountered at that particular stage of career

ALERT: a guide to possible pitfalls and high-risk options

TIPS: helpful hints on how to insure a first-class route to your destination (practical principles to guide your career choices)

MILESTONES: your objective for that phase of journey, the achievement of which marks passage into the next

PREPARATORY STAGE

TIME FRAMEWORK: the school years: undergraduate as well as graduate training; usually ages 18–25

COMPENSATION: usually no substantial income

CHARACTERISTICS:

• Acquire a broad-based formal education. Focus on preparing for career by taking at least supplemental business courses.

(continued)

- Teachers, parents, friends offer career guidance. Begin to investigate career options and job market.
- Develop good work habits, character, and personality.

OPTIONS:

- Get broad liberal arts background as an undergraduate. Worry about particulars later, or take heavy course load in mathematics, economics, or business. Go right into job market with undergraduate degree.
- Specialize in a highly technical field. Go for advanced academic degree.
- Go on to MBA program.
- Work/study. Through an internship or part-time work, begin to get some field experience while attending school.

ALERT:

- Specializing in a very narrow field too early could limit future options.
- Companies are sometimes wary of corporate "converts"— people with advanced academic degrees who are trying to break into industry. Beware of appearing overqualified.
- Higher education, including the MBA degree, may buy you a first-class ticket to only the first stop on your career itinerary. Statistics show that amount of schooling does not influence level of earnings much beyond the initial entry into the job market.

TIPS:

- A degree has little intrinsic value to a prospective employer. Perceived potential is what the employer is willing to pay for.
- Therefore, the value of "good" academic credentials is judged in terms of those skills and personal qualities that one hopes are developed in the course of earning a degree: character, personality, creativity, energy, focus, motivation.

MILESTONE:

- Aim to be in a position at the end of your schooling that maximizes the number and quality of potential job offers.

(continued)

FORMATIVE STAGE

TIME FRAMEWORK: first 10–15 year postpreparatory period; ages 25–35

COMPENSATION: $20,000–$50,000 annual salary (no perquisites)

CHARACTERISTICS:

- Greatest number of options in this period and, therefore, greatest mobility and fastest growth.
- Promotions and compensation will be rewarded increasingly on the basis of on-the-job experience and demonstrated abilities vis-à-vis educational background and perceived potential.

OPTIONS:

- Options are almost unlimited: Almost every size and type of industry and company has entry-level positions in the $20,000–$50,000 range.
- The formative years are usually spent within one of three specific functional areas—personnel, marketing, and accounting. Therefore, your choice of functional area is, at this stage, more crucial than choice of industry or size of company.
- Join a "career" corporation within the first five postgraduate years. The bastions of the corporate world, such as General Motors, generally recruit for entry-level positions *only*. Barring unusual circumstances, this early phase in your career is the only chance you will have to join these ranks.
- Typically a period of much movement, through promotions within a company or through a new job in a new company.
- Make a lateral shift from one area of responsibility to another.

ALERT:

- The advantage of opting for a "career" organization is that you gain excellent experience. On the other hand, these granddaddies of the business world tend to offer a conservative pay scale to newcomers that doesn't make any great jumps for as long as 15 years; they tend to give little autonomy; and, unless it is a big company that has managed to stay young and keep small by developing new products and by diversifying, it may tend to be entrenched in its ways—a stifling environment for an eager young executive.

(continued)

- Beware of too-early industry specialization. Five to eight years of one-industry experience is a salable commodity, but could lock you in. Beyond a point, breaking into a new industry is difficult.
- Beware of the lure of fast-track promotions or job-hopping that increase the value of your paycheck only. Look for meaningful growth in experience: A lateral shift is justified only if the move increases your level of responsibility, results in a new kind of responsibility, or seems to broaden the possible channels for growth.

TIPS:

- Make frequent and *meaningful* job changes, once every two or three years at first; then, every three or four years.
- Look for the companies that offer the greatest growth potential.
- At this stage of the game, it is acceptable to sacrifice substantial financial gain to opt for new and greater responsibility. However, a truly better job usually means better pay.

MILESTONES:

- Acquire in-depth experience while increasing visibility through job performance. This should land you in the most advantageous position with maximized future options.
- Your goal in the organizational hierarchy should be, generally, an upper-middle management position.
- Your salary objective: approximately $1,500–$2,000 per year of your age; i.e., 35 years old/$52,000–$70,000 a year.

CRITICAL STAGE OR WATERSHED

TIME FRAMEWORK: second 10-year postpreparatory period; ages 34–45

COMPENSATION: salary range $50,000–$125,000, plus some stock options. Net worth is beginning to accumulate.

(continued)

CHARACTERISTICS:

- Pivotal mid-life period. Time to take new self-inventory and make major reassessment of priorities and goals as measured against actual accomplishments and unactualized potential.
- Typically a period of increased financial growth, but also of increased financial responsibilities; home, family, children's education.
- Time to make major career commitment or change of course.
- Size of compensation package becomes increasingly dependent on job performance.

OPTIONS:

- Change course and try something completely new: Become an entrepreneur or take over a small, but growing establishment.
- Scale down. Take a position of less responsibility in a less high-powered organization.
- Commit your career to your present corporation or to a new one that offers equal or better opportunities for growth.

ALERT:

- To become an entrepreneur is to fulfill a great American dream. It is probably the only means still available to amass a truly great fortune—if you possess the right combination of talent, know-how, and luck. Nevertheless, the early years of any new business are likely to be characterized by hard work, long hours, and short cash. A new business is a risky business. Success in the long term makes all the risk seem worthwhile. But are you willing and able in the short term to make the necessary sacrifices? Moreover, do you possess the qualities of self-confidence, courage, ingenuity, and business acuity that make a successful entrepreneur?
- You always have the option to step backward or *out*, if that is in tune with your personal desires. But if you do make such a career decision, it's always wise to maximize future options and not to burn bridges behind you unnecessarily.
- Keep an eye on the changing scene and avoid a commitment to a career position that is bound for obsolescence.

(continued)

TIPS:

- Weigh the demands of your professional life against the requirements of your private life and determine what personal needs you are willing to sacrifice to your career ambitions. Make the necessary adjustments.
- When you do settle upon a career commitment, look for a situation within a company that suits your tastes in terms of overall style and function and that is willing and able to meet your financial requirements. Compensation packages vary from industry to industry; find a company that offers the kind of package you want. Also, fittingly, statistics show a correlation between a company's performance and executive pay potential. Look for a strong company with sound prospects.

MILESTONES:

- Have a practical program to meet your financial needs as well as your net-worth goals.
- Take a reading of the real progress made in your career. Measure realized potential against unrealized aims. Reconcile the difference and adjust your course accordingly.

NEGOTIATING THE HEIGHTS

TIME FRAMEWORK: the final lap of the journey; age 45+

COMPENSATION: big bucks

CHARACTERISTICS:

- More expanded responsibility and more challenging opportunity.
- Increased opportunity for higher earnings through negotiation of incentive plans, stock options, etc.
- Very substantial growth in personal net worth.
- Achievement of full professional potential.

OPTIONS:

- Move up as high as you can go within your present

(continued)

corporation. Then hope for a corporate merger or acquisition, or the departure of a key executive, or some other act of fate to make room at the top available to you.

- If waiting your turn doesn't suit you, take over a young company looking for a new leadership, become the professional manager of a family-held business needing new blood and your expertise, or take the helm of an established enterprise in troubled waters and turn it around.
- If you don't have what it takes to make it to the peak, keep out of trouble, keep busy, and hope the corporation doesn't outgrow its need for your talents.

ALERT:

- This is high stakes. Protect your share with an employment contract, if you can negotiate one.
- When you walk fresh from the outside into the top spot in an established business, you risk the cold-shoulder treatment due an outsider. This can make your job unpleasant, at best; impossible, at worst.

MILESTONES:

- Top Dog.
- Top Dollar.
- A bundle put aside for your old age.

CHANGING TIMES

If you recall singing that refrain along with Bob Dylan in the sixties, you may be pleased to note that even in the corporate sector, some windows have been shaken and walls rattled. The old guard still thrives in the likes of IBM, 3M, and AT&T, of course, and, thank goodness, the demise of the capitalistic system is in no way imminent. (After all, you do have a vested interest now.) Nevertheless, the changing social trends of the past few decades are reflected today by changing corporate trends as characterized by executives' career patterns. The one-corporation career man, though not quite an endangered species, is, however, a declining phenomenon. His territory is being usurped by a new breed of executive called the "mobile managers," so named by Dr. Eugene Jennings of Michigan State University, who first observed their unique habits in the mid-sixties.

YESTERDAY

Traditionally, the prudent aspiring executive valued job security and stability: He found himself a "good" company, applied himself to his work, and maintained his faith in the paternalistic corporate system, which, if he did his job well and with enthusiasm, would reward him regularly with promotions and increased pay. If you were loyal to the company and excelled in your work, you could hope one day, with time (maybe 30 or 40 years) and some luck, to be president, CEO, or even chairman of the board. It was sort of like believing in America: Anyone could "grow up" to be president.

TODAY

A recent survey of 1,700 executives showed that if you began your career in marketing, finance, or a professional or technical field, there is a 66–75 percent chance (in personnel, a 48 percent chance; and in manufacturing, a 30 percent chance) you will continue your career within that *industry*. However, other studies show that although many stick to one industry, an estimated 17–20 million Americans change *jobs* each year. The average American changes jobs once every five years. In 1977, 11.5 percent, or more than one-tenth of the *entire* employed work force, made a job switch.

Particularly in the corporate world, there is no progress without change. A recent report by the National Personnel Association on mid-level managers (incomes of $14–75,000) stated that at any given time, approximately 29 percent of all managers have their résumés in circulation, and other experts estimate that another 40 percent are *considering* sending theirs out. Of people holding managerial positions, according to one survey, 75 percent who make the move *choose* to leave secure positions to take new ones. The high value once attached to "company loyalty" is to a great extent inappropriate to today's corporate executive. Mobility characterizes the current trend in building a corporate career.

THE TREND: MOVING ON, MOVING UP

What is the official attitude toward all this change? Judging by the proliferation of mobile managers, corporations today take a favorable view toward job mobility—that is, of course, when the change is made with obvious forethought and purpose. Although only 19 percent of people moving into new jobs actually accept the same or reduced salaries, studies indicate that most people do not choose to make a change primarily for financial reasons, but for reasons related to their work. In fact, of the 9 percent of would-be switchers who end up staying in their old jobs because the employer made a good counter-offer, most switch jobs within a year anyway. Experts cite the following motivations behind an employee's decision to seek a new position:

- He feels a lack of autonomy or responsibility in his present job.
- He is impatient because he feels his progress is hampered by a slow-

moving superior, or by the lack of corporate growth or creativity.
- He feels there is a conflict of philosophy or personality between himself and his superiors and/or the company.
- He feels a lack of attention from, support by, or access to top management.
- He feels stuck in a dead-end job, unfairly passed over for promotion, or "lost" in a too large organization.

In other words, the quest for personal fulfillment, rather than for financial gain, has become the major force behind the current trend favoring career mobility.

A NEW ETHIC

This shift in emphasis from the material rewards of work to the nonmaterial is rooted in some fundamental changes in both the economic fabric and the social fabric of society. We are an affluent society to a degree unprecedented in history. For most American executives, this means we already possess those essentials—and quite a few extras—that money can buy. We have secured for ourselves a relatively high degree of material comfort and as a result, the traditional work ethic is called into question: We have worked hard and earned our daily bread, and stomachs comfortably full, have sat back in our chairs and begun to realize that indeed man does not live by bread alone. Less concerned with the size of their paychecks, many people have become more concerned with the quality of their lives, and this shift in concern has begun to alter long-held attitudes about work.

WOMEN IN THE WORK FORCE

Causing another wave of social economic change, women are entering the labor force in increasing numbers. Two-paycheck households decrease the financial demands made on the traditional breadwinner in two ways: First, such households tend to have fewer children; second, the burden of bringing home the bacon is redistributed between two earners, and, therefore, neither is so strictly bound to make career choices on the basis of financial motivation.

COMPACT CAREERS

Not only are more workers making more and more changes during the course of their careers, they are making them in less and less time. This is particularly true in the corporate world. First of all, executives tend to take on more responsibility at an earlier stage in their careers. In 1950, 57 was the average age of a corporate president; twenty years later the average age had dropped to 49.

Also, the average length of time executives hold a given office has markedly decreased. In the ten years between 1962 and 1972, the number of company presidents (in a study including 500 major industrial companies) in office over five years dropped from 45 percent to 25 percent.

Finally, with the lowering of the mandatory retirement age and the increase in the number of attractive retirement packages, more executives are simply calling it quits sooner than they used to. The overall result: a compressed career span.*

THE AGE OF SPECIALIZATION

Concurrent with the rise of affluence has been the accelerated growth of technology, and the two forces together have reshaped the course of many careers. Advanced technology has created an age of specialization: In terms of the labor market, that means more job opportunities as more new jobs are created in highly specialized fields. America remains a land of opportunity for those with the right credentials.

What does all this mean for *you?* With the accelerated pace of change, the multiplication of choices, and the stiff competition for promotions, the necessity of career planning is more important than ever before.

OTHER CAREER TRENDS

It is becoming acceptable to return to the old firm. With management turnover at an all-time high as ownership changes, many have been lured back—or even *asked* to return—to their old firms. While there is interest in the return of a "prodigal son" from both sides of the table, the phenomenon is still exceedingly rare. Only about 5 percent actually do so, and most in that group were asked to come back.

Corporations are turning to outsiders to fill key jobs. Recent research by the Hay Group has shown that companies that put outsiders in upper level management have performed better than ones that don't. Coming in at a higher level in a new firm is not easy on the newcomer or the old-timers, and often the newcomer doesn't last long. But a fresh perspective on problems and opportunities has been shown to be useful to a firm.

Downward movement is becoming more common. Are you ready for a trip *down* the corporate ladder? It is happening with increasing frequency for a variety of reasons.

---

*From David J. McLaughlin, *The Executive Money Map* (New York: McGraw-Hill, 1975), pp. 14–15.

Under what conditions would you accept a downward move?			
	Total by %	Established by %	Nonestablished by %
1. Under no conditions	24	21	27
2. If it were part of a formal career plan	21	14	23
3. If it involved a salary increase	28	20	32
4. If it were seen as career enhancing	31	24	33
5. If people I respect had made similar moves	8	8	7
6. If the only other alternative was to leave	56	67	41
7. Other	12	15	8

Note: Numbers represent percentages of individuals who checked a given response.

Fig. 39. Reactions of Employees to a Downward Move

Reprinted by permission of the publisher, from "Downward Movement and Career Development," by Douglas T. Hall and Lynn A. Isabella, p. 17, *Organizational Dynamics,* Summer 1985, © 1985 American Management Association, New York. All rights reserved.

Generally, downward movement is defined as a reduced level of responsibility and authority. In some cases, a promotion can be "downward," as the executive gets increased rank and salary, but less responsibility. While most commonly imposed because of poor performance, a demotion may be acceptable for a variety of reasons. It might be part of a larger plan: the executive takes the demotion to help the company fill a gap, or to get in the front lines, only to be rewarded later with a big promotion. Sometimes, a downward move is an alternative to termination or a move away from the "front lines" as a way of gradually phasing out an executive nearing retirement. If handled carefully, with respect and compassion, the downward move might make more sense than terminating the relationship.

More executives are opting for "second-careers." However, the experts tell us that it usually doesn't work out. A change of career is often a response to midlife crisis, but is usually an inappropriate one. Starting a second career is often a deeper commitment than going into business for yourself in your original field of accomplishment.

23

ROADBLOCKS

The necessity of career planning is clear, but, as the poet said, even the best-laid schemes go oft astray. You follow the rules. You plan your career step by step. You get a good job. You make all the right moves. Then all of a sudden you are out on the street again, unemployed and looking for a job. *That* was not in the plan.

An unexpected roadblock, a detour, can set you off your path temporarily. Once it happens, stay steady and clear and you will find your way back.

GETTING FIRED

THE FACTS

Twenty thousand middle and upper level managers changed jobs in 1979. Of those, 8,500, or almost 43 percent, were given their walking papers. The turnover rate of executives doubled in the period from 1960 to 1970, and experts warn that the number of executives fired each year will continue to grow.

In most fields, the higher you go, the greater are the chances for dismissal. And if you are forty years old or over, there is only one chance in five you won't be forced to take a step backward and/or accept a lower salary in your next job.

Furthermore, a currently unemployed person faces unusually stiff competition in the job market.

Seventy-two percent of all job applicants are already employed in secure positions, and they get 81 percent of the available jobs. They also receive, on the average, a compensation package 18 percent higher than an equally qualified but unemployed candidate. Being fired can be a depressing experience, and, unfortunately, the foregoing hard facts don't help to make things brighter.

WHO GETS FIRED?

- *The Problem Personality:* Personality conflicts between employee and supervisor, often over operating style, account for 33 percent of all terminations. That means *most people are not fired for personal reasons.*

- *The Fifth Wheel:* Company mergers and acquisitions, the numbers of which are on the rise, often create overstaffing problems.
- *The Lame Duck:* Office politics: The new boss decides to bring in his "own team."
- *The Obsolete Veep:* The company recognizes or takes a new direction and no longer needs your particular skills.
- *The Cut Corner:* In these inflationary times, financial cutbacks are, unfortunately, a growing phenomenon.

THE NOT-SO-SURPRISED PARTY

You know how difficult it is to give a surprise party at which the guest of honor is actually caught by surprise. When people are conspiring around you, for whatever purpose, their behavior is usually quite transparent—at least to the alert eye.

Why should you be the last to know you are getting fired? Don't be caught by surprise. Keep a lookout for telltale signs:

- Old friends in the office seem to be unusually *un*friendly.
- Old enemies in the office seem to be unusually friendly.
- Conversations stop cold when you enter a room unexpectedly.
- You are given a new office. It has no window or carpet. Your old one had both.
- You are asked if you wouldn't mind sharing your secretary with the new exec in the next office.
- The new exec in the next office seems to know a lot about your work.
- Everyone in the office gets new name plaques. Yours, however, is "not ready yet."

THE TERMINATION INTERVIEW, OR
WHAT TO DO WHEN THE GUILLOTINE FALLS

You have been asked into the boss's office for what seemed like a friendly chat. Somewhere into the conversation you hear your boss tell you that you are being dismissed, terminated, laid off, let go, severed, asked to leave, or told to leave. No matter what euphemism your boss has used to blunt his instrument, at some point you will register the impact of the blow, and it will hit hard: *You are fired. You have lost your job.* What do you do?

FIRST OF ALL, DON'T PANIC   At least not in front of your executioner. This is easier to do when you realize that, unless he has a reputation for sending heads rolling, what he is doing is probably as hard on him as it is on you. Remember, the odds are 2 to 1 that your "termination" is really nothing personal. The person delivering the message just pulled the short straw in the "who's-gonna-be-the-one-to-tell-him" office lottery. Most people are decent enough and truly hope they will never have to conduct a termination interview; therefore they have not made a career of learning *how*. Your interviewer may seem overly harsh or overly solicitous. In either case, he is probably just trying his best to get through an unpleasant and awkward task.

PULL YOURSELF TOGETHER   Again, this is not easy to do when you have just been axed. It's not a nice feeling under any circumstances to lose a job, but you will have nothing to gain by indulging your emotions. Self-pity will not pay the rent or get you another job. The interview is the time to begin to take action.

NEGOTIATE FOR SEVERANCE COMPENSATION   Severance compensation is not a game-show booby prize and should not be doled out in that fashion. Most terminated employees have played a fair game, and when circumstances "disqualify" a worker from continuing on his job, the company has a real responsibility to see he doesn't suffer unduly. If you are terminated, recognize three things:

1. You have a right to be fairly compensated and to negotiate for the best severance arrangement to suit your needs.
2. Your terminating interviewer may not be fully aware of the company's severance policies.
3. Your interviewer, at the moment he drops the ax, may appear:
   - remote and stingy, in which case he is probably just uncomfortable, and you should politely decline his current offer and suggest you discuss the severance package at a later date (when you've both had time to think it over), or with a personnel person, or both; or
   - sweet and generous, in which case he probably feels uncomfortable and guilty, and you should hit him hard for all you can get.

THE TYPICAL SEVERANCE
COMPENSATION PACKAGE

As executive turnover becomes more commonplace due to an increasing number of mergers, company cutbacks, and reorganizations, corporations generally are developing more responsible and liberal attitudes toward severance compensation. The principal parts of a typical severance package are:

THE FINANCIAL PACKAGE   Severance pay is usually a percentage of your yearly salary—anywhere from 50 percent to 100 percent, depending on your status in the hierarchy. You should be sure to get the maximum due you, because this may be your only rent money for as long as six months to a year. Insurance and medical benefits are fairly standard parts of the pay package. Depending on what other forms of compensation you received or had coming to you (stock options, deferred compensation, etc.), find out what your rights are to such monies.

OFFICE SUPPORT SYSTEM   You should negotiate for use of office space, including a desk, a telephone, and secretarial assistance. A reasonable employer will usually agree to have the switchboard take calls and messages for you. When you are unemployed and hunting for work, this support is a practical necessity.

COUNSELING OR OUTPLACEMENT   This is a recent, but growing development in severance compensation. Outplacement counseling, the domain of a rising number of specialized consulting firms, has a double-edged function. Under contract to a particular corporation, the outplacement counselors provide their clients with advice and strategies for use in terminating both individuals and groups of employees. Then, in turn, the counselors are commissioned to provide employment counseling as well as moral support to dismissed personnel for the duration of their job search. The purpose of outplacement is to re-place the terminated employee.

Mixed reviews for outplacement: Reviews are mixed as to the effectiveness of these outplacement professionals. They claim excellent results—in some instances, 80 percent of their cases employed within four to six months, 60 percent of those in better jobs. Many newly placed executives happily confirm this track record. However, outplacement counseling, although it represents a relatively minor cost to the corporation— maybe $3,000 to $5,000 per terminated employee who receives counseling—is a hefty portion of the entire severance package. Some severed employees have noted ruefully that they might have spent that better had they received it direct from the employer.

Some major outplacement firms: Fuchs, Cuthrell and Company, New York; Drake-Beam and Associates, New York; the TH Inc. Consulting Group, New York; Challenger, Gray, and Christmas, Chicago; and Eaton-Swain Associates, New York.

A FINAL WORD ON THE FINAL WORD

The reality of termination is simply this: A job hunt is a job hunt no matter what the cause behind it. Granted, being fired and unemployed makes it tough on the ego, but that is all the more reason to attack the job market with a vengeance. Develop your search plan and follow through!

MERGERS AND ACQUISITIONS: CAREERS TURNED UPSIDE DOWN

SOME HARD FACTS ABOUT MERGERS AND ACQUISITIONS

On the average, an acquiring firm is four to five times larger than the firm it absorbs.

To the victors go the spoils. All things being equal, you stand a better chance of keeping your job if you are part of the firm doing the acquiring, or in the case of a merger, the management team that is going to run the new firm.

The financially healthy firm you once worked for may be substantially weakened. Many takeovers are accompanied by dramatic increases in debt.

Most managers are more concerned with the survival of the corporation and the growth of its assets—financial, human and line-related. Managers may be unprepared when they find out that stockholders may be willing to cash in and put an end to the company as they know it, in exchange for a one-shot buyout offer.

There is no scientific evidence that merged companies are more efficient.

In the current climate, it can take you 25 percent to 50 percent longer to find a job. Six months or more is not unusual.

The human factor is critical to the success of a merger. Consider this: Researcher J.R. Boland asked 50 CEOs involved in merger plans to rate the importance of 26 factors to consider when investigating a possible merger or acquisition. When surveyed prior to a merger, only three of the top twelve factors chosen were related to human resources; after the mergers went through, the same CEOs chose human resource issues in seven out of the top twelve factors.

Changing a name, a logo or a corporate headquarters is easy. Dealing with your staff is the real challenge.

To some degree, a takeover is the result of weakness. Many experts believe that the best way to avoid a takeover is to maximize performance and sell your strategy to the shareholders. Takeover artists rarely go after the strong, vibrant healthy companies. They look for unrealized potential, usually not reflected in the stock price.

If your management team is not fully exploiting the revenue potential of the firm's assets, if profits could be increased through more efficient management, reorganization or divestiture, your company might be vulnerable to a raid. Well-managed firms aren't immune, but they do make tougher targets.

Revolving-door ownership is here to stay. Even the scandals and ill-conceived deals have yet to reduce the merger and acquisition activity.

Perhaps even more significant is the wave of leveraged buyouts that occurred in the early '80s. Many are now being prepared for resale, bringing a large group of companies onto the auction block. Don't count on much relief from the chaos.

QUESTIONS TO ASK AT THE FIRST SIGN OF A MERGER

1. What are the reasons for this merger; why is the change necessary?
2. How will we conduct business during the transition?
3. Which departments will stay, which will be eliminated? What changes are contemplated? Outline the proposed structure of the merged firm.
4. What are the differences and similarities between departments, jobs and their counterparts in the other company?
5. What about the chain of command?
6. Who will be on the top management team?
7. What are the proposed changes in management?
8. Which functions will be expanded? Which will be cut?
9. What policy changes are contemplated?
10. What about changes in wages and salaries?
11. How will the merger affect opportunities for promotion?
12. Will there be performance appraisals used to determine who remains with the new firm and at what position?
13. Will there be career counseling available?
14. Will I keep my present title?
15. How will my benefit package be affected?
16. Who will be my immediate supervisor?

Fig. 40. This list is based on one compiled by Arlyne Imberman
for an article in *Management Review*.

Reprinted, by permission of the publisher, from
"The Human Element of Mergers," by Arlyne J. Imberman,
p. 36, *Management Review*, June 1985
© American Management Association, New York.
All rights reserved.

What to do when a takeover comes

Situation	Your response
A merger is probable but not definite	Keep cool, don't take sides on the merger, and stay out of the office rumor mill. If you are in line for a job contract or have one that is expiring, try for three years' coverage.
A merger is definite, and you are nervous	Research the aggressor company's history in past takeovers. Learn all you can about your boss —and your counterpart—in the new company. Make no overt job-hunting moves, but use business friends discreetly for a line on new jobs. Stay close to the scene, avoiding extended travel if you can.
The merger date is close, and you fear being frozen out	Use a low-key campaign to find a new job. Contact friends and several executive recruiters known to be reliable. If your salary is less than $40,000, see top-rate employment agencies as well. Don't discuss the merger, but concentrate on selling your own experience and strong points.
The merger date is close, and you want to stay on	Make your feelings known to your old boss, and— if possible—to your expected new boss. Talk candidly about what you want. Then concentrate on work.
The merger is set, and you own stock in your old company acquired via a stock option	Don't make a hasty sale. Sit tight and be guided by the advice of the board of directors. Selling out will make you look bad to both sides.
You hold an unexercised stock option	Don't buy the shares hastily. Seek advice from your boss and your company's top financial officer. Remember that your option—and any premium growing out of the merger—will probably carry over to the merged operation.
The merger has happened, and you feel your job is in danger	Work hard, but make a strong new-job effort. Be candid about the merger in job interviews, but avoid any impression that you are fleeing a tough situation. If fired, fight for the best severance settlement you can get—such as 50% to 100% of a year's pay, which is common. Pay $150 for a consultation with a good lawyer who, if necessary, will represent you in severance negotiations.
Same as above, but you're over 50	The same advice holds, but also review all fringe and retirement benefits. If eligible, figure out your income under early retirement. You may be eligible for a lump-sum payout under a qualified pension or profit-sharing plan. This is true even if you retire from your company and take a new job.
You have survived six months since the merger	Do your best work. If no added rewards come within a year, consider starting a discreet job search.

Fig. 41. Merger advice from *Business Week*

Reprinted from the September 17, 1979, issue of *Business Week*
by special permission, © 1979 by McGraw-Hill, Inc., New York,
NY 10020. All rights reserved.

THE BRIGHT SIDE OF MERGERS

Generally speaking, the merger and acquisition wave has been bad for managers, especially middle managers. We have cited employment statistics, the time it takes to find another job, etc. But you are not a statistic. Adroit, talented executives have made the changing climate work for them. Here are some positive results to keep in mind:

You may find yourself the object of affection. Since many mergers and acquisitions involve firms in unrelated industries and fields, the top management of the dominant company may know very little about the business. They may go out of their way to entice you to stay.

There is often an increase in senior management positions. Sure, a merger produces lots of overlap, and the need to trim staff. But it also makes things more complicated, and more difficult to coordinate activities and strategy at the top.

Be aware of the "job creep" brought about by a merger. While executives are being let go, the firm could quietly be staffing up with strategic planners, assistants to CEOs and other types of overseers. You might wish to target a merging firm as a place with an emerging opportunity for someone of your skills. Consider a discreet inquiry to a firm that is part of a merger, even if the newspapers report cutbacks.

The demand for general managers is stronger than ever. Again, with the odd combinations of enterprises that wind up under the same umbrella as a result of mergers, general managers are important.

The demand for financial executives is stronger than ever. It used to be that top management got to the top because they knew the industry and knew how to run a company. Nowadays, somebody upstairs had better understand how to fend off a hostile merger, how to deal with greenmail, leveraged buyouts and junk bonds.

The decline in middle management ranks has been slowing. A lot of the cutbacks were not due to mergers, but to the effects of the recession in the early eighties. That trend has moderated. Besides, drastic cutbacks are most likely at companies in trouble, and in some cases (but not all), the efficiencies and cash infusions brought about by a healthy merger can actually make one's job more secure.

Consultants are in. Companies undergoing restructuring need experienced people to work on short-term projects. In the past, few seasoned executives went into the consulting field, which tended to draw from more academic and professional areas. Today more executives are willing to be guns for hire, no doubt because golden parachutes have helped them get through the touch-and-go period of financial uncertainty associated with starting a consulting business.

THE TRANSFER NOTICE

WHO GETS IT?

Experts have estimated that corporations transfer 250,000 to 500,000 employees a year, and the number seems to be swelling. There are three different circumstances under which an executive may receive a transfer notice:

- as a prerequisite condition of being offered a job in a new corporation
- as a prerequisite condition of being offered a promotion within the present corporation
- as a result of a corporate relocation in which the plant or head-quarters are moved and the employees are asked to move along with it.

According to an Atlas Van Lines "Survey of Corporate Moving Practices," cited in a 1979 issue of *D&B Reports*, "The typical employee being relocated by the companies [surveyed] is male between the ages of 31 and 40 years old [62.4 percent] . . .with 53.2 percent in the sales/marketing field. The salary range with the greatest frequency of employee transfers is in the $21,000-30,000 range [64 percent]." In another survey, conducted by Merrill Lynch Relocation Management, Inc., an estimated 62 percent of the transferred employees owned homes that they would be required to give up as a result of relocation.

WHAT DO YOU DO WITH IT?

You can take it or leave it, of course. But if you refuse to accept a transfer, your refusal could cost you your job: The Merrill Lynch study noted that "45% of companies don't hold it against employees when they refuse to be transferred. About 20% said they didn't mind refusals as long as the reason is 'valid.' But 8% definitely said refusal was looked upon unfavorably and could harm an employee's career." So consider the following questions and determine for yourself if you stand to gain more than you lose by making the move:

WHAT WOULD THE MOVE COST YOU OUT-OF-POCKET? Moving your home and family, particularly if you are a home owner, can be a costly affair. Consider the following types of expenses, named in *D&B Reports*, you might incur in the process:

- travel expenses
- house-hunting expenses
- interim living expenses (for executive and dependents)
- moving costs (including insurance, storage, automobile)
- lease cancellation or mortgage-rate differentials

- income-tax consequences
- real estate expenses (costs of selling old home and buying new home)

WHAT IS THE RELOCATION POLICY OF THE COMPANY?   More and more corporations are formalizing policy on relocation as well as expanding the coverage offered to transferred employees. According to one estimate, a transferring employee spends an average of four months (not full time) organizing a move. *The Wall Street Journal* reported that the number of relocated employees reporting difficulty selling homes rose from 16 percent to 28 percent as a result of "tight money markets and a dearth of buyers."* The costs of making a transfer should be covered by the company. Be sure you won't be left holding a hefty bill.

IS THIS TRANSFER REALLY A PROMOTION?   Or just a fast track to nowhere? Are you being offered more responsibility or just a bit more money? Is the money alone worth the disruption in your life? Beware of some companies who put their young executives on a fast-track transfer circuit that is long on cash but short on real job growth.

IS YOUR SPOUSE CURRENTLY EMPLOYED?   The Merrill Lynch study revealed that of the 686 corporations surveyed, only 30 percent offered to help employed spouses of transferred workers in finding new positions, although this figure is almost doubled over the previous year's. Of those employees who declined to accept a transfer, 17 percent of them so chose in order to protect a spouse's career. Of all transferred employees in the U.S. in 1978, only 3 percent were female executives.

WHAT WOULD THE TRANSFER COST YOU—AND YOUR FAMILY—EMOTIONALLY, PSYCHOLOGICALLY, AND PHYSICAL-LY?   The psychic costs of moving can be devastating to a family. Children must leave their schools and their friends; everyone in the family gives up the security and comfort of a familiar community for the problems confronted as a stranger in a new one. Of course, many families adjust to change well or go through the difficulty of the move to find themselves enjoying their new life. Relocation can be a stressful operation and carries no guarantee that it will result in a change for the better.

DO YOU WANT TO MOVE YOUR FAMILY FROM BIG SUR TO THE BIG APPLE?   From Los Angeles, California, to Columbus, Indiana? From Houston, Texas, to Fairbanks, Alaska? From Boston, Massachusetts, to Montgomery, Alabama? A change of location can mean a drastic change of life-style as well as a change in the quality of your life. Are you giving up the good life for a better one?

---

*"Relocation Blues," *The Wall Street Journal*, September 25, 1979, p. 1.

WHERE THE GRASS IS GREENER

You may recall a social studies lesson back in your school days in which your teacher instructed that America had (and the term would be chalked on the blackboard) the *highest per capita income* of any nation. This meant, the teacher explained, the average American earned more money that the average person in any other country. The teacher concluded, remarking, no doubt, with pride: "Americans enjoy the highest standard of living of any people in the world." Hearing this news then, do you remember sighing just a little, feeling somehow relieved and reassured to know that life in America was so *good?*

Thus many Americans grew up with the belief that life in America *is* good and will remain so as long as all *capita* earn an average income. In the final analysis, however, the pursuit of a good wage does not seem to insure the enjoyment of a "good" life. Despite their high *standard* of living, some Americans have become concerned about the lack of *quality* in their lives.

A STUDY ON THE QUALITY OF LIFE

In 1970 the Midwest Research Institute, questioning the moral of that long-ago lesson, conducted a study to measure and compare the "quality of life" (QOL) in the 50 United States. (Later the study was revised to assess the U.S. metropolitan areas particularly.) The researchers believed that standard measures such as per capita income and GNP are not accurate indicators of the quality of life. If "quality" were strictly a function of "quantity," or material wealth, then why were so many substantially well-to-do people feeling discontent with their lot?

Unfortunately, the MRI studies, summarized in the first edition of this book, were never updated. Nevertheless, much of the data remains valuable. In 1987, the trends revealed in the MRI studies no longer appear valid, as explosive growth in the Northeast, reindustrialization of the Midwest, and the oil and real-estate bust in the Southwest has devalued the overall quality of life in the Sun Belt relative to the rest of the nation. Many of the cities once considered "substandard" have become models of excellence, such as Pittsburgh, while Houston has clearly slipped.

Many "best place to live" studies have been compiled since MRI's work, but the methodology is not as tight and many of the conclusions ultimately rest with the subjective judgments of the researchers. In one recent report, Nashua, New Hampshire was Number One on the list, while in another, it failed to make the top twenty.

THE COMPONENTS OF QUALITY   In the introduction to the study, the Institute suggests that such by-products of economic growth as changes in institutional structures and the allocation of resources are sometimes so costly to the quality of life as to more than offset the gains made by

```
                                               YES OR NO
1. REAL ESTATE
   a. Purchase old home ....................  _____
   b. Pay expenses incidental to sale ........  _____
   c. Pay loss on sale of real estate..........  _____
   d. Pay lease breaking expenses............  _____
   e. Loan for purchase of new home ........  _____
   f. Mortgage interest differential ...........  _____
   g. Other real estate assistance ............  _____

2. PERSONAL EXPENSE
   Pre-move visit by spouse: ................  _____
   a. One trip ..........................  _____
   b. More than one trip ...................  _____
   c. No trips............................  _____
   d. Children or baby-sitting included........  _____

   Family travel at time of transfer...........  _____
   a. Actual expenses (including meals, motels,
      etc.)...............................  _____
   b. Daily allowance .....................  _____
   c. Limited expenses .....................  _____

   Temporary living expenses................  _____
   a. Temporary quarters..................  _____
   b. Meals and incidental expenses..........  _____

3. SELECTION OF CARRIER
   a. Traffic Manager selection ..............  _____
   b. Traffic Manager-employee preference ....  _____
   c. Employee make selection ..............  _____

4. PACKING
   a. Full pack authorized...................  _____
   b. Pack breakables only ..................  _____
   c. Maximum limitation...................  _____
   d. Mobile homes ......................  _____

5. TRANSPORTATION
   Normal household goods: ................  _____
   a. Unlimited weight ....................  _____
   b. Limited weight ......................  _____
   c. Limited weight, new employees only ....  _____
```

Fig. 42. Moving Policy Check List
(*above and opposite*)

From "Corporate Moving Policy Manual," (Evansville, IN:
Atlas Van Lines, 1979), pp. 33-34. Reprinted by permission
of Atlas Van Lines.

    d. Automobiles........................... _____
    e. Second Automobiles.................. _____

Unusual items:........................... _____

    a. Limitation on items such as boats, trailers,
       statuary, etc........................... _____
    b. Air express frozen foods............... _____
    c. Air express pets...................... _____

6. **APPLIANCE SERVICE**
    a. All appliance service.................. _____
    b. Origin service only .... _____
    c. No appliance service.................. _____

7. **SPECIAL SERVICES**
    a. Housecleaning or maid service.......... _____
    b. Carpet removal....................... _____
    c. Disassembly of unusual items such as
       playhouses, swimming pools, regulation
       pool tables, etc .... _____
    d. Altering rugs and drapes............... _____

8. **VALUATION**
    a. Release of 60 cents per pound per article _____
    b. Release at $1.25 per pound............ _____
    c. Lump sum value in excess of $1.25 per
       pound................................ _____
    d. Additional insurance for items of unusual
       value................................ _____
    e. Claims handling assistance............. _____

9. **STORAGE**
    a. Unlimited storage-in-transit .... _____
    b. Limited (time) storage-in-transit......... _____
    c. Limited (dollars) storage-in-transit .... _____
    d. No storage-in-transit .... _____
    e. Extra pickups and deliveries .... _____
    f. Permanent storage.................... _____

10. **PERFORMANCE REPORT**
    a. Required on all moves................. _____

raising our standard of living. The researchers therefore developed five separate components by which to measure *overall* national well-being:

- economic • political • environmental
- health and education • social

Altogether, the five indicators comprised 120 variables, including, for example, quantitative measures of income inequality; level of informed citizenry; levels of air, visual, and noise pollution; available means to promote maximum development of individual capabilities; and the availability of sports and cultural events in each Standard Metropolitan Statistical Area (SMSA). The SMSAs were divided into three groups according to size of population:

- large (500,000 or more)
- medium (200,000 to 500,000)
- small (200,000 or less)

and the SMSAs in each population group were separately rated:

A: outstanding
B: excellent
C: good
D: adequate
E: substandard

for each of the 120 components. The ratings were based on the QOL index values relative only to the respective group means. Therefore, comparisons between SMSAs can only be made within the same-size population group.

THE BEST LIFE   On the basis of collected data, the study concluded:

- "QOL is not necessarily a direct function of income and material wealth, at least beyond a certain level of subsistence." In other words, "an outstanding rating in the economic component did not simultaneously have outstanding ratings in social, political, environmental, health, and education components."
- The *major* disparities in QOL among SMSAs are *not* economic and political, but have to do with social, health, educational, and to a lesser degree, environmental considerations.
- Data suggested that those geographical regions with the greatest relative number of SMSAs of outstanding and excellent ratings are:
  The West Coast
  East North Central states
  Mountain states
  New England

The conclusions of the research in the long term will have far-reaching implications for our policymakers who continue to measure the quality of our lives solely in terms of output and income.

In the short term, the study yields immediately useful information to

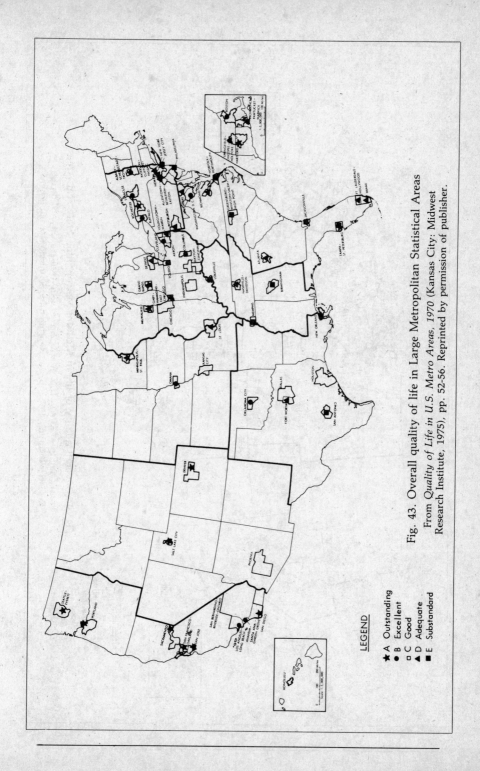

Fig. 43. Overall quality of life in Large Metropolitan Statistical Areas

From *Quality of Life in U.S. Metro Areas, 1970* (Kansas City: Midwest Research Institute, 1975), pp. 52-56. Reprinted by permission of publisher.

LEGEND

★ A Outstanding
● B Excellent
□ C Good
▲ D Adequate
■ E Substandard

369

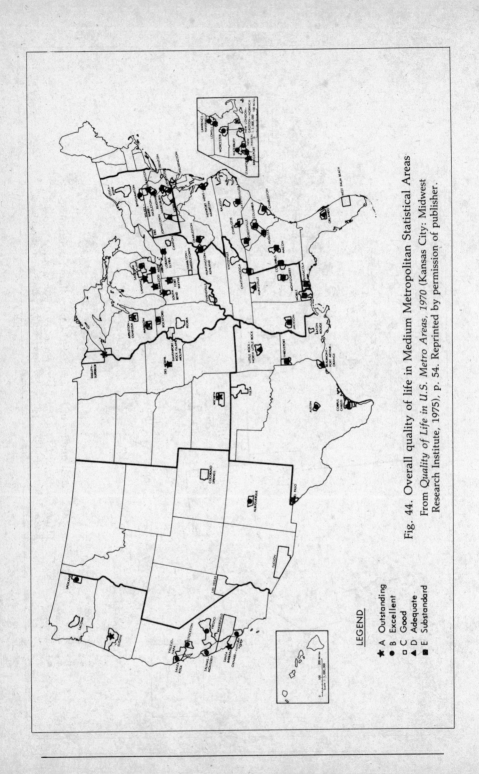

Fig. 44. Overall quality of life in Medium Metropolitan Statistical Areas

From *Quality of Life in U.S. Metro Areas, 1970* (Kansas City: Midwest Research Institute, 1975), p. 54. Reprinted by permission of publisher.

LEGEND

★ A Outstanding
● B Excellent
□ C Good
▲ D Adequate
■ E Substandard

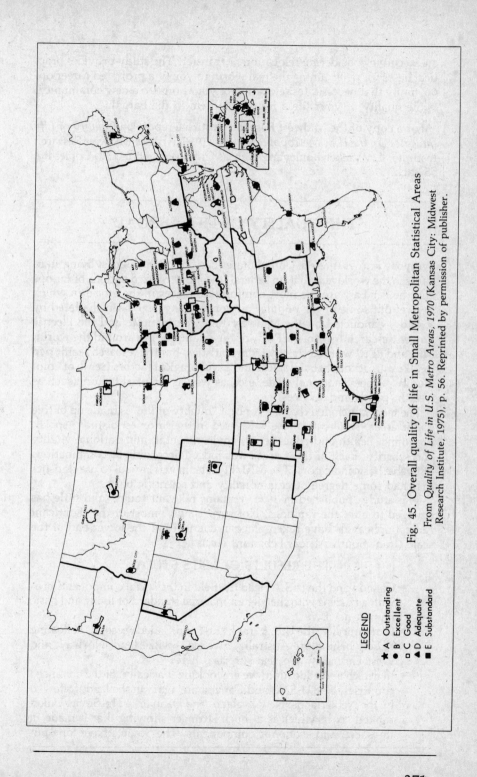

Fig. 45. Overall quality of life in Small Metropolitan Statistical Areas

From *Quality of Life in U.S. Metro Areas, 1970* (Kansas City: Midwest Research Institute, 1975), p. 56. Reprinted by permission of publisher.

LEGEND

★ A Outstanding
● B Excellent
□ C Good
▲ D Adequate
■ E Substandard

an executive considering relocation or transfer. The study provides practical bases for determining the real worth to you of a proffered career opportunity that necessitates relocation of your home to a new community. Is the quality of your life a negotiable item in the bargain?

For a copy of the Midwest Research Institute report on *Quality of Life Indicators in the U.S. Metropolitan Areas, 1970,* write to Midwest Research Institute, 425 Volker Boulevard, Kansas City, Missouri 64110. Copies are $5 each.

THE QUALITY OF LIFE ABROAD

Everyone knows that the United States has one of the highest living standards in the world and that, in general, the industrialized nations of Europe and the Far East are the most comfortable places in the world in which to live. But some of the popular misconceptions have been shattered by a study, conducted by the Midwest Research Institute and the Electric Power Research Institute (EPRI), of the quality of life around the world. MRI and EPRI worked strictly from statistics, but the research team tried to take into account sociological and psychological factors (sense of community, esteem, national pride, etc.) as well as material factors (such as wealth, goods and services).

The team concluded that the concept "quality of life" is made up of five major areas, similar to those MRI used in their domestic study: social, economic, health and educational, environmental, and national vitality and security. Each of these areas was judged according to combinations of twelve basic indicators. The MRI/EPRI team was careful to use statistics that had some degree of commonality and scientific basis.

This study, published in 1975, remains relevant today, and little has changed to alter the rankings. Not surprisingly, most of the significant radical upheavals have taken place in countries at the lower end of the scale (Iran, South Africa, Lebanon, etc.).

THE RESULTS OF MRI'S STUDY

- Canada and the U.S.A. lead the field in the social component, providing citizens with the highest material standard of living and basic human needs.
- Economically, the U.S.A. ranks first and Canada second. Following closely behind are Australia, Sweden, Switzerland, Norway, and West Germany. No real surprises here.
- In health and education, we are looking, basically, at the advanced countries. The U.S.A. and Canada are again in the lead, followed by the Netherlands, New Zealand, and Denmark. The Soviet Union ranked sixth, which is a much stronger showing that it made in the social and economic components. The Soviets have long put

special emphasis on education and medical care, and that emphasis shows up in the study.

- The environmental component suffers from a dearth of statistics. Australia, Argentina, and the U.S.A. were the high scorers, due largely to their relatively even population distribution and vast amounts of arable green land. Japan and West Germany were relatively low scorers. This result, when compared with the other components, reveals the extent of the trade-off that these two countries have made: environmental deterioration in exchange for incredible growth in industrialization.
- National security? No punches pulled here. Israel and the U.S.S.R. top the list. Not surprising when you consider that both countries have undergone a massive military buildup. Next come Taiwan, the U.S.A., Australia, Czechoslovakia, Bulgaria, and Poland. This component also measures the national vitality—the overall stability of a nation and its relative economic self-sufficiency. In this regard, many of the advanced nations are much more vulnerable than those with totalitarian regimes and limited foreign trade.

When the figures were compiled to produce an overall QOL (quality of life) ranking, the list that resulted could set the State Department back twenty years:

- Oil-rich nations like Saudi Arabia, Kuwait, Libya, and Venezuela did very poorly. It takes more than money.
- The Soviet Union held its own. And several "iron curtain" countries outscored western nations such as France and Italy.
- In general, Latin American nations, along with the Africans, brought up the rear (South Africa being no exception).

This study was based on 1975 figures and, therefore, doesn't reflect the incredible political, social, and economic changes that have taken place since then. Scientists at both MRI and EPRI refuse to speculate on how the rankings may have changed since then. But a close look at the data used in this ranking suggests that the Arab countries won't improve much, because economic gains will probably be offset by increasing unrest and dependence on foreign trade. Runaway inflation might serve to drop some countries, such as Israel, while giving a boost to other countries, such as Switzerland, that have kept inflation under control. With so many variables, one can see why MRI is unwilling to venture a guess.

If you would like a detailed summary of the MRI/EPRI study, you can write to the Electric Power Research Institute, requesting a copy of "Income, Energy Requirements, and the Quality of Life Indicators: An International Comparison, 1975." There is no charge.

Contact:

Electric Power Research Institute
3412 Hillview Avenue
Palo Alto, California 94304

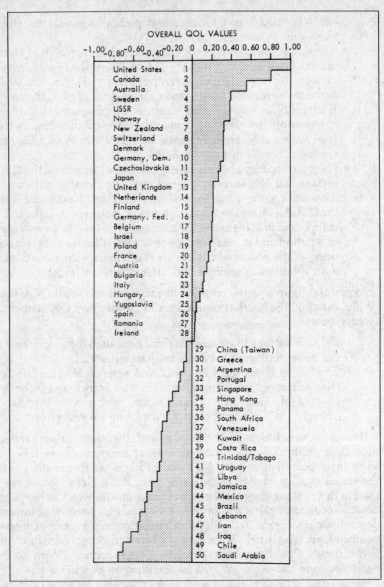

Fig. 46. Overall quality of life values, per Midwest
Research Institute Study. The values are based on an
index with the United States equal to 1.

From *Income, Energy Requirements and Quality of Life Indicators*: An
International Comparison by Ben-chien Liu, PhD, Claude E.
Anderson, PhD (Kansas City: Midwest Research Institute, 1979),
p. 12. Reprinted by permission of sponsor, Electric Power Research
Institute, Palo Alto, California.

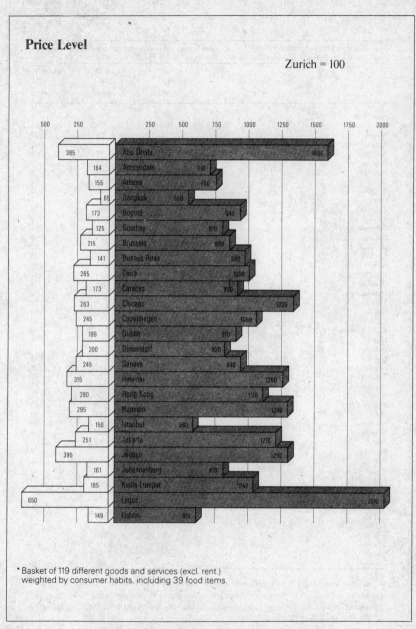

Price Level

Zurich = 100

Abu Dhabi 385 / 1680
Amsterdam 164 / 710
Athens 155 / 750
Bangkok 65 / 550
Bogotá 173 / 940
Bombay 125 / 610
Brussels 215 / 880
Buenos Aires 141 / 980
Cairo 265 / 1000
Caracas 173 / 920
Chicago 263 / 1330
Copenhagen 245 / 1060
Dublin 199 / 810
Düsseldorf 200 / 820
Geneva 245 / 940
Helsinki 315 / 1280
Hong Kong 280 / 1110
Houston 295 / 1290
Istanbul 150 / 560
Jakarta 251 / 1210
Jedden 395 / 1290
Johannesburg 161 / 810
Kuala Lumpur 185 / 1040
Lagos 650 / 2040
Lisbon 149 / 510

* Basket of 119 different goods and services (excl. rent.)
weighted by consumer habits, including 39 food items.

Fig. 47. Price levels of major international cities,
indexed to Zurich

From "Prices and Earnings Around the Globe," by R. Enz and
E. Mäder (Zurich: Union Bank of Switzerland Economic
Research Department, 1985), pp. 6–7. Reprinted by permission.

The Table shows the percentage by which price, salary (wage) and purchasing power levels in the various cities are above or below those of Zurich. For all indices, Zurich = 100

City	Price level[1]	Salary (Wage) level gross[2]	Salary (Wage) level net[3]
Abu Dhabi	385	61	78
Amsterdam	164	70	61
Athens	155	36	37
Bahrain (Manama)	383	42	52
Bangkok	65	12	14
Bogota	173	19	22
Bombay	125	6	8
Brussels	215	69	63
Buenos Aires	141	20	22
Cairo	265	11	11
Caracas	173	46	56
Chicago	263	129	126
Copenhagen	245	98	66
Dublin	199	53	48
Dusseldorf	200	74	63
Geneva	245	103	96
Helsinki	315	74	57
Hong Kong	280	36	42
Houston	295	113	119
Istanbul	150	15	13
Jakarta	251	9	12
Jeddah	395	67	80
Johannesburg	161	46	45
Kuala Lumpur	185	26	28
Lagos	650	23	28
Lisbon	149	17	17
London	191	57	51
Los Angeles	281	136	128
Luxemborg	180	71	67
Madrid	224	41	41
Manila	210	8	9
Mexico City	196	17	19
Milan	198	53	52
Montreal	237	109	99
New York	362	142	126
Oslo	324	92	80
Panama	246	33	37
Paris	181	56	56
Rio de Janeiro	132	18	20
Sao Paulo	124	23	25
Seoul	395	31	36
Singapore	275	31	29
Stockholm	265	70	59
Sydney	219	85	77
Tel Aviv	146	38	32
Tokyo	624	100	104
Toronto	289	106	102
Vienna	191	61	56
Zurich	261	100	100

[1]A basket of more than 119 different goods and services weighted by consumer habits

[2]Calculated on the basis of the gross average hourly earnings in 12 different occupations

[3]Calculated on the basis of the net average hourly earnings after deducting taxes and social insurance contributions in 12 different occupations

Fig. 48. Price, salary and purchasing power
in 45 international cities

From "Prices and Earnings Around the Globe," by R. Enz and
E. Mäder (Zurich: Union Bank of Switzerland, Economic
Research Department, 1985), pp. 6–7. Reprinted by permission.

24

THE HUNT

A career strategy is concerned with long-range, broad objectives. The job hunt is conducted within the context of an overall career plan for the purpose of accomplishing a specific and immediate goal: getting employed.

A PHILOSOPHY OF JOB HUNTING: DON'T BE RULED BY PROJECTIONS AND STATISTICS

In the previous few chapters I've offered lots of projections, replete with statistics, about the job market for the eighties.

The prophets of boom and bust do not have access to crystal balls. They make informed predictions, well-educated guesses; but they don't have a hotline to the future. Don't discount the economic projections altogether; but don't let them scare you into passivity, either. Appraise them. Digest them. Then move on. The point is, have a "take charge" attitude toward your job hunt. Go after the job you *want*, not the one that's most likely to be available five years from now. If you truly enjoy the work you do, you will excel. If you excel, there will always be jobs to choose from. As long as one job is available, believe that you can have it. *That* is the key to a successful career.

WHO ARE THE HEADHUNTERS AND WHY ARE THEY AFTER YOU?

Not every unexpected detour in your career path will be unwelcome. In 1977, according to *Fortune* magazine, 16,000 executives were snared by professional "headhunters" and lured into new corporate habitats. In fact, of all executives in the $30,000–$50,000 income bracket, 60 percent of those who exchange their present positions for new and often better ones are "searched out," as are 75–80 percent of executives in the $50,000-plus bracket.

Recent estimates indicate that there are approximately 10,000 recruiters or search consultants, generating about $1.5 billion in fees annually in the U.S. Each year, they successfully recruit over 100,000 executives.

Once a low-profile field dominated by a handful of old-line firms, the business has grown much more volatile and competitive. As a result, standards, practices and pricing can vary significantly.

Headhunters, who are not terribly fond of that appellation and prefer to be known as management consultants, are specialized recruiters who are employed by businesses to "search out" top executive talent for hire in new jobs. Executive search firms (to use another preferred term) generally work strictly for the corporation (vis-à-vis the individual executive), and the corporation pays the search firm a very substantial fee—as much as 30 percent of the new recruit's annual salary—for its services. Other compensation methods include *per diem* fees and fixed fees. Firms may work on contingency, getting paid only if the search results in success, or on retainer. The headhunter offers the corporation know-how, access to the crème de la crème of executive talent, objectivity, and anonymity in the recruitment process. Before the recruiter begins his search, he conducts a comprehensive interview with the client company in order to determine the job specifications and the kind of talent the corporation wants for the job. Armed with this information, the headhunter sets to work.

WHO IS FAIR GAME FOR THE HEADHUNTER?

Any resident of the executive suite. Headhunters stalk their prey in current business directories, through data banks, by word of mouth, by keeping files of press clippings and dossiers on any newsworthy executive, and by keeping close tabs on all other industry sources that might turn up the name of a likely candidate. The one most "likely" is almost invariably an already employed executive. The *best* candidate is an executive who is not only employed, but happily employed and not even looking to leave.

WHAT LURES THE HAPPY EXECUTIVE AWAY?

Usually it's the opportunity to gain additional "psychic" income such as expanded territory of influence, greater power and status, and, of course, extra cash benefits and noncash rewards.

HOW TO TALK TO A HEADHUNTER

KNOW THE NOMENCLATURE   If the voice on the telephone identifies its owner as a "recruiter," the company pays the fee and this is a voice worth listening to. On the other hand, if the voice says "job counselor," cut it off; otherwise, the call may cost *you* money in the long run.

BE OPEN AND DIRECT WITH THE RECRUITER   He makes a living on that phone and has already heard every cute remark in the book. That recruiter is in a position to turn you on to possibly the best career opportunity in your life. Don't turn *him* off. Save your biting wit for another occasion.

ON THE INITIAL CONTACT, THE RECRUITER WILL WANT SPECIFIC INFORMATION:

- Your present salary. On this point you don't have to be too specific. A ball-park figure will do: high thirties, low fifties, etc. However, don't try to fool the recruiter. He has his ways of finding out the truth without your help.
- Your willingness to relocate. The recruiter will want to put a price tag on this: How much would it take to convince you to move? Again, be nonspecific. Leave the point open for negotiation.

ASK QUESTIONS OF YOUR OWN   At this time it's fair game for you to find out:

- a basic job description
- what the position pays
- why the position is available and how long it's been available
- how long your predecessor held the position and why he vacated it

On the other hand:

- DO NOT push for the name of the company.
- DO NOT pursue an interview if you are not really interested in the job opportunity. It wastes the recruiter's time—and yours—and it won't endear you to him. Maybe this position isn't for you, but a more attractive offer might come in the future.

If you do choose to pursue the current opportunity, be sure you feel confident the recruiter has your best interests at heart as well as those of the client corporation. Once the matchmaking begins, a good recruiter has the concerns of both parties in mind and, in pursuit of a happy union, should be willing to educate you about the prospective employer.

WHAT TO DO WHEN THE
HEADHUNTER DOESN'T CALL

Courtships are lovely, and everyone likes to feel pursued. But it's possible you'll have a long and unproductive wait if you spend your professional life sitting by a telephone waiting for Mr. Right to call.

Taking it as it comes is a useful attitude in coping with the unexpected obstacle and even the unexpected opportunity. If you want to advance your career, however, you are usually going to have to take a more active approach to your future than waiting in fear of a pink slip or in hope of a telephone call. So take charge. Go out and get the job you want.

A headhunter conducts a particular search with a pretty clear idea in mind of the credentials of the ideal candidate. If he has a large square vacant hole, he wants a large square peg to fit it. Generally, he has no use for carrying a lot of extra large round pegs in his back pocket. He works almost exclusively for corporate clients and isn't equipped to serve the individual executive looking to make a career change.

One day, however, the headhunter may be looking around for a peg just about your size. In that case, *you want to make yourself as visible as possible*. When trying to attract the attention of a headhunter, the trick is *don't* be coy. If you expect to lure him with your extraordinary qualities, first he has to notice you.

- *Publish* in professional journals or even in popular periodicals.
- *Make speeches* at your trade or professional associations.
- *Be newsworthy*. Be active in social and civil affairs. Make a good name for yourself.
- *Cultivate professional contacts*. Headhunters are plugged into the corporate grapevine.

THE LAST RESORT:
APPROACH A HEADHUNTER DIRECTLY

Still no phone call? It's possible, of course, that you may never turn the head of a hunter and the only way to get his attention is, finally, to introduce yourself to him. Collectively, recruiters represent thousands of job opportunities a year, and they usually have exclusive knowledge of the positions they fill; so you don't want to give up on them too easily.

To approach a headhunter directly is a delicate affair, and experts suggest the following etiquette be applied in making your contact:

- Never walk in cold to a recruiter's office expecting an interview.
- Send a résumé. Wait one week and call for an interview.
- If you don't get an interview, wait a month and resubmit your résumé.
- If you do get an interview, keep it very brief: 30 minutes or less; unless the recruiter keeps it going.
- Follow up the interview with a thank-you note and a *short* reiteration of your present situation. Do *not* follow up with a phone call.
- Keep in mind that recruiters work for client corporations and not for you. They generally do not have the office systems to keep efficiently maintained files of inactive résumés, and they generally do not give any interviews unless they have a job in mind for you. Don't let that stop you, however; you could be lucky, time it right, and get an instant response.

BEFORE YOU APPROACH A RECRUITER

Ask yourself: Have I evaluated all my past and present achievements? Have I taken stock of all my strengths and weaknesses? Do I have a clear understanding of my immediate, short- and long-term objectives? Am I willing to relocate? Am I willing to travel?

Compensating Factors

Look before you leap. That's excellent advice for the senior executive who has a good position now and is considering a job offer. Don't allow yourself to be swayed by hyperbole and hollow promises; instead, negotiate for a full compensation package, with attention to the following factors.

Salary: An increase of 20–30% is warranted for a new position with increased responsibilities in a high-risk company. These percentages could vary, depending upon the total pay package (the salary/bonus mix) and the employer's financial status.

Incentives: The incentive should be linked to performance, and should be large enough to motivate you. Target and maximum incentive amounts and associated performance requirements should be specified. A guaranteed bonus for the first year of employment is appropriate in a turnaround (or high-risk) situation.

Long-term incentives/capital accumulation plans: Calculate the value of any equity or long-term cash incentives promised by the new employer. Be certain that what you receive provides a meaningful estate-building opportunity and makes up for what you will forfeit by leaving your current position.

Deferred compensation: The tax advantages of a deferred compensation plan can be attractive to a senior executive. Inquire whether the new employer is amenable to such an arrangement.

Replacement income: Don't disregard the value of any current and projected retirement benefits you may forfeit in a job switch; ask the new employer to provide equal benefits. This can be achieved through a nonqualified or supplemental retirement program.

Insurance coverage: Ascertain whether the new employer offers adequate life, health, short- and long-term disability, and spouse survivor insurance coverage.

Perquisites: Don't forget to ask what perks come with your new position. Among the most popular are company cars and club memberships.

Impact of Five Compensation Elements on Executives

Compensation elements	Impact on individual executive		
	Attract	Retain	Motivate
Salary	High	High	Moderate
Employee benefits	Low	Moderate	Low
Perquisites	Low	Moderate	Low
Short-term incentives	High	Moderate	High
Long-term incentives	Moderate	High	Moderate

Fig. 49. Compensating factors and
impact of five compensation
elements on executives.
© Peat Marwick Main & Co.,
Reprinted by permission.

SIZING UP THE HEADHUNTER

Try to find out a bit about the search firm you are working with. Word of mouth is the best way. Ask colleagues, other professionals in your industry and bosses (if you can).

Ask the recruiter to assess the search assignment. Is it a difficult position to fill? Are there any unique difficulties associated with the job description?

WHERE TO FIND A HEADHUNTER

Consultant News publishes a national directory of executive search firms. You can write direct to the publisher to obtain a copy. The address is Templeton Road, Fitzwilliam, New Hampshire 03447. Copies are $10 each, $15 for the international edition.

Some management consulting firms also do executive searches. Many of the large accounting firms have executive search departments as well. Fig. 50 is a list of names (with home offices) of major recruiters. Most of them have branch offices in other cities.

EVALUATING A JOB OFFER

According to J. Larry Tyler, President of Coker, Tyler, a returned search consultant firm, there are only three major considerations in evaluating a job offer: money, opportunity, and location.

Generally speaking, a job change for purely monetary reasons alone should be considered only if the increase in compensation exceeds 15 percent. When comparing your compensation, don't just compare salary, but the entire package.

Consider the opportunity being offered with the new job. Will it provide you with a chance to grow and expand your authority and responsibilities? Will this growth mean greater financial reward and more power? Will the new job provide you with a chance for greater job satisfaction and more challenges? Naturally, the definition of opportunity is a personal thing, so it makes sense to form your own definition of opportunity before assessing the situation.

Many experts consider location the most critical factor in a job change because it has such an impact on the quality of life and work for you and your family.

Involve your spouse and consider the opinions of your family very carefully. And remember that if you are part of a two-career marriage, sooner or later, someone will have to compromise.

Bacci, Bennett, Gould & McCoy, Inc.
375 Park Avenue
New York, NY 10022
(212) 688-8671

600 Montgomery Street
San Francisco, CA 94111
(415) 989-8212

Bartholdi & Company, Inc.
65 William Street
Wellesley Hills, MA 02181
(617) 237-3710

1415 West 22nd Street
Oak Brook, IL 60521
(312) 325-8474

610 Fifth Avenue
New York, NY 10020
(212) 489-7280

Battalia, Lotz & Associates, Inc.
342 Madison Avenue
New York, NY 10017
(212) 986-4380

J. W. Bauder Associates, Inc.
5580 LBJ Freeway/Suite 550
Dallas, TX 75240
(214) 386-0481

Billington, Fox & Ellis, Inc.
20 North Wacker Drive
Chicago, IL 60606
(312) 236-5000

Atlanta Center/Suite 1420
250 Piedmont Avenue, N. E.
Atlanta, GA 30308
(404) 659-8300

1100 Superior Avenue, N. E.
Cleveland, OH 44114
(216) 781-1000

One Main Place/Suite 920
Dallas, TX 75250
(214) 744-4900

3701 Wilshire Boulevard
Los Angeles, CA 90010
(213) 661-2500

529 Fifth Avenue
New York, NY 10017
(212) 661-2500

Billington, Fox & Ellis International
529 Fifth Avenue
New York, NY 10017
(212) 661-2500

*Australia, Belgium, Brazil, Canada, England, France, Germany, Italy, Japan, Netherlands, New Zealand, South Africa, Sweden

Booz Allen & Hamilton Inc.
245 Park Avenue
New York, NY 10017
(212) 697-1900

229 Peachtree St., N.E.
Atlanta, GA 30303
(404) 659-3600

135 South La Salle Street
Chicago, IL 60603
(312) 346-1900

1100 Chester Avenue
Cleveland, OH 44115
(216) 696-1900

Suite 550
523 West Sixth Street
Los Angeles, CA 90014
(213) 620-1900

2210 Republic Bank Tower
325 North St. Paul Street
Dallas, TX 75201
(214) 741-5011

*Belgium, Brazil, England, France, Germany, Iran, Japan, Venezuela

Boyden Associates, Inc.
Suite 2000
260 Madison Avenue
New York, NY 10016
(212) 949-7600

Suite 1738
Lenox Towers
3390 Peachtree Road, N.E.
Atlanta, GA 30326
(404) 261-6532

Suite 1650
10 South Riverside Plaza
Chicago, IL 60606
(312) 782-1581

*Denotes Foreign Offices or Affiliates

Fig. 50. Association of Executive Recruiting
Consultants, Inc., Member Firms (New York).
(*through page 388*)
Used by permission.

Suite 706
River Oaks Bank & Trust Bldg.
2001 Kirby Drive
Houston, TX 77019
(713) 526-9913

5670 Wilshire Boulevard
Los Angeles, CA 90036
(213) 933-5563

Allegheny Tower
625 Stanwix Street
Pittsburgh, PA 15222
(412) 391-3020

Suite 1760
One Maritime Plaza
San Francisco, CA 94111
(415) 981-7900

Suite 433
606 Madison Avenue
Toledo, OH 43604
(419) 255-1160

Suite 803
815 Connecticut Avenue, N. W.
Washington, DC 20006
(202) 296-6705
*Australia, Belgium, Brazil, Canada, England,
France, Hong Kong, Italy, Japan, Mexico, New
Zealand, South Africa, Spain, Switzerland,
Venezuela

The Brand Company, Inc
12740 North River Road
Mequon, WI 53092
(414) 242-6203

Thomas A. Buffum Associates
Two Center Plaza
Boston, MA 02108
(617) 227-4350

La Societe Caldwell
Suite 2201
1115 Sherbrooke Street West
Montreal, Quebec H3A IH3
Canada
(514) 849-5357

The Caldwell Partners International, Inc.
Suite 610
Two Houston Center
Houston, TX 77002
(713) 757-1958

Suite 103
50 Prince Arthur Avenue
Toronto, Ontario M5R 1B5
Canada
(416) 920-7702

Suite 1918
500 Fourth Avenue, S.W.
Calgary, Alberta TZP ZVG
Canada
(403) 265-8780

William H. Clark Associates, Inc.
330 Madison Avenue
New York, NY 10017
(212) 661-8760

Suite 7912
200 East Randolph Drive
Chicago, IL 60601
(312) 565-1300

555 South Flower Street
Los Angeles, CA 90071
(213) 489-2240

One Embarcadero Center
San Francisco, CA 90071
(415) 489-2240

David W. Cogswell & Associates
Suite 609
400 Montgomery Street
San Francisco, CA 94104
(415) 788-1070

Thorndike Deland Associates
1440 Broadway
New York, NY 10018
(212) 840-8100

Devine, Baldwin & Peters, Inc.
250 Park Avenue
New York, NY 10017
(212) 867-5235

Statler Office Building
Boston, MA 02116
(617) 423-1682
*England

DeVoto & Berry Partners, Ltd.
120 South Riverside Plaza
Chicago, IL 60606
(312) 346-8278

Eastman & Beaudine, Incorporated
Suite 2150
111 West Monroe Street
Chicago, IL 60603
(312) 726-8195

Suite 2005
437 Madison Avenue

*Denotes Foreign Offices or Affiliates

New York, NY 10022
(212) 486-9655

Suite 940
Two Century Plaza
2049 Century Park East
Los Angeles, CA 90067
(213) 552-6005

Suite 4152
44 Montgomery Street
San Francisco, CA 94104
(415) 788-1666
*Belgium, England, France, Hawaii, Holland,
Japan, Germany, Mexico

Leon A. Farley Associates
Steuart Street Tower
Suite 1001
One Market Plaza
San Francisco, CA 94105
(415) 777-2888

Suite 1001-E
7315 Wisconsin Avenue
Bethesda, MD 20014
(301) 654-9090

Foster & Associates, Inc.
Steuart Street Tower
Suite 1115
One Market Plaza
San Francisco, CA 94105
(414) 777-0330

1700 Pacific Building
Seattle, WA 98104
(206) 624-8943

Haley Associates, Inc.
375 Park Avenue
New York, NY 10022
(212) 421-7860

Harris & U'Ren, Inc.
1976 Arizona Bank Building
101 North First Avenue
Phoenix, AZ 85003
(602) 257-1072

Haskell & Stern Associates, Inc.
230 Park Avenue
New York, NY 10017
(212) 687-7292
*England

Hayman, Hardison & Fowler, Inc.
Suite 1311
8150 N. Central Expressway
Dallas, TX 75206
(214) 696-4000

Heidrick & Struggles, Inc.
Suite 2800
125 South Wacker Drive
Chicago, IL 60606
(312) 372-8811

100 Federal Street
Boston, MA 02110
(617) 423-1140

1100 Superior Avenue
Cleveland, OH 44114
(216) 241-7410

2728 Republic National Bank Tower
Dallas, TX 75201
(214) 741-9121

2650 Pennzoil Place
South Tower
Houston, TX 77002
(713) 237-9000

Union Bank Square
Los Angeles, CA 90071
(213) 624-8891

245 Park Avenue
New York, NY 10017
(212) 876-9876

600 Montgomery Street
San Francisco, CA 94111
(415) 981-2854
*Belgium, England, France, Germany, Mexico,
Switzerland

Helmich, Miller & Pasek, Inc.
Suite 280
5725 East River Road
Chicago, IL 60631
(312) 693-6270

1100 Quail Street/Suite 103
Newport Beach, CA 92660
(714) 752-7447

P. O. Box 1448
Green Valley, AZ 85614
(602) 625-6232

Hodge-Cronin and Associates, Inc.
Suite 904
9575 West Higgins Road
Rosemont, IL 60018
(312) 692-2041

The Ward Howell/Consulting Partners/TASA Group Ward Howell Associates, Inc. (U.S.)
99 Park Avenue
New York, NY 10016
(212) 697-3730

*Denotes Foreign Offices or Affliates

One East Putnam Avenue
Greenwich, CT 06830
(203) 629-2994

John Hancock Center
Suite 3350
875 North Michigan Avenue
Chicago, IL 60611
(312) 266-9431

10100 Santa Monica Boulevard
Los Angeles, CA 90067
(213) 553-6638

Three Embarcadero Center
Suite 2680
San Francisco, CA 94111
(415) 398-3900

*TASA Inc.—Latin America:
Douglas Centre, Suite 1001
2600 Douglas Road
Coral Gables, FL 33134
(305) 448-0100
Argentina, Brazil, Colombia, Mexico,
Venezuela

*Consulting Partners:
Europe—Middle East—Africa
Belgium, England, France,
Germany, Italy, South Africa
Switzerland

**International Management
Advisors, Inc.**
485 Lexington Avenue
New York, NY 10017
(212) 490-3858

Charles Irish Company, Inc.
420 Lexington Avenue
New York, NY 10017
(212) 490-0040

**Kearney: Executive Search
Division of A. T. Kearney, Inc.**
100 South Wacker Drive
Chicago, IL 60606
(312) 782-2868

29425 Chagrin Boulevard
Pepper Pike, OH 44122
(216) 292-3770

One Wilshire Building
Los Angeles, CA 90017
(213) 627-0721

437 Madison Avenue
New York, NY 10022
(212) 751-7040
*Belgium, Canada, England

Kremple & Meade
1900 Avenue of the Stars
Los Angeles, CA 90067
(213) 456-6451

Lamalie Associates, Inc.
13920 North Dale Mabry
Tampa, FL 33618
(813) 961-7494

Tower Place
3340 Peachtree Road, N.E.
Atlanta, GA 30326
(404) 237-6324

120 South Riverside Plaza
Chicago, IL 60606
(312) 454-0525

Central National Bank Building
Cleveland, OH 44114
(216) 522-1650

Olympic Tower
645 Fifth Avenue
New York, NY 10022
(212) 688-0545

First International Building
1201 Elm Street
Dallas, TX 75270
(214) 747-1994

Lauer, Sbarbaro & Associates, Inc.
135 South LaSalle Street
Chicago, IL 60603
(312) 372-7050
*England

Locke & Associates
Suite 3145
One NCNB Plaza
Charlotte, NC 28280
(704) 372-6600

The John Lucht Consultancy, Inc.
The Olympic Tower
645 Fifth Avenue
New York, NY 10022
(212) 935-4660

MWS Executive Search
55 East Monroe Street
Chicago, IL 60603
(312) 726-8730

12860 Hillcrest Road
Suite 105
Dallas, TX 75230
(214) 387-4838

*Denotes Foreign Offices or Affiliates

1900 M Street, N. W.
Washington, DC 20036
(202) 833-1866

Management Woman, Inc.
The Galleria—14th Floor
115 East 57th Street
New York, NY 10022
(212) 888-8100

McFeely, Wackerle Associates
20 North Wacker Drive
Chicago, IL 60606
(312) 641-2977

Moriarty/Fox, Inc.
20 North Wacker Drive
Chicago, IL 60606
(312) 332-4600

Oliver & Rozner Associates, Inc.
598 Madison Avenue—11th Floor
New York, NY 10022
(212) 688-1850

Parenti & Jacobs, Inc.
Harris Bank Building
Suite 2525
115 South LaSalle Street
Chicago, IL 60603
(312) 782-9844

Parker, Eldridge, Sholl & Gordon, Inc.
440 Totten Pond Road
Waltham, MA 02154
(617) 890-0340

Pinsker and Shattuck, Inc.
Suite 501
100 Bush Street
San Francisco, CA 94104
(415) 421-6264

Suite 101
1333 Lawrence Expressway
Santa Clara, CA 95051
(408) 247-5050

Paul R. Ray & Company, Inc.
1208 Ridglea State Bank Building
Fort Worth, TX 76116
(817) 731-4111

Suite 1718
400 Colony Square
1201 Peachtree Street, N.E.
Atlanta, GA 30361
(404) 892-2727

Suite 600
1900 Avenue of the Stars
Los Angeles, CA 90067
(213) 557-2828

277 Park Avenue
New York, NY 10017
(212) 371-3431

Suite 1925
100 South Wacker Drive
Chicago, IL 60606
(312) 876-0730

First International Building
Suite 5383
Dallas, TX 75270
(214) 651-9812

3612 Dresser Towers
601 Jefferson Street
Houston, TX 77002
(713) 757-1985
*England

Robison, Sockwell & McAulay
3100 NCNB Plaza
Charlotte, NC 28280
(704) 376-0059

Russell Reynolds Associates, Inc.
245 Park Avenue
New York, NY 10017
(212) 682-8622

230 West Monroe Street
Chicago, IL 60606
(312) 782-9862

1200 Smith Street
Suite 3350
Two Allen Center
Houston, TX 77002
(713) 658-1776

555 South Flower Street
Suite 3220
Los Angeles, CA 90071
(213) 489-1520

3 Landmark Square
Stamford, CT 06901
(203) 356-1940
*England, France

Ryan/Smith & Associates
P.O. Box 253
Westfield, NJ 07090
(201) 232-5720

*Denotes Foreign Offices or Affliates

Sadovsky, West & Associates
12700 Park Central Place
Suite 1300
Dallas, TX 75251
(214) 387-8580

John W. Siler & Associates, Inc.
5261 N. Port Washington Road
Milwaukee, WI 53217
(414) 962-9400

Spriggs & Company, Inc.
John Hancock Center
Suite 4015
875 North Michigan Avenue
Chicago, IL 60611
(312) 751-1200

Paul Stafford Associates, Ltd.
45 Rockefeller Plaza
New York, NY 10020
(212) 765-7700

222 South Riverside Plaza
Chicago, IL 60606
(312) 454-0942

888 17th Street, N.W.
Washington, DC 20006
(202) 331-0090

Staub, Warmbold & Associates, Inc.
655 Third Avenue
New York, NY 10017
(212) 599-4100

7275 Wynhill Drive
Atlanta, GA 30328
(404) 394-9177

200 East Randolph Drive
Chicago, IL 60601
(312) 861-0900

California First Bank Building
350 California Street
San Francisco, CA 94101
(415) 781-1196
*Belgium

S. K. Stewart & Associates
The Executive Building
P.O. Box 40110
Cincinnati, OH 45240
(513) 771-2250

Governour's Square
1193 Lyons Road
Dayton, OH 45459
(513) 434-4311

Spencer Stuart & Associates, Inc.
Suite 300
500 North Michigan Avenue
Chicago, IL 60611
(312) 822-0080

2626 Republic National Bank Tower
Dallas, TX 75201
(214) 748-1990

555 South Flower Street
Los Angeles, CA 90071
(213) 620-0814

437 Madison Avenue
New York, NY 10022
(212) 754-1400

Three Landmark Square
Stamford, CT 06901
(203) 324-6333

3773 Redwood Circle
Palo Alto, CA 94306
(415) 493-0340
*Amsterdam, Brussels, Dusseldorf, Frankfurt, Hong Kong, London, Madrid, Manchester, Melbourne, Paris, Sao Paulo, Singapore, Sydney, Toronto, Zurich

George Sullivan Associates, Inc.
Rumson Road
Rumson, NJ 07760
(201) 741-4544
*England

William H. Willis, Inc.
445 Park Avenue
New York, NY 10022
(212) 752-3456
*Australia, England, France

Witt & Dolan Associates, Inc.**
1415 West 22nd Street
Oak Brook, IL 60521
(312) 325-5070

Yelverton & Mace, Inc.
350 California Street
Suite 1680
San Francisco, CA 94104
(415) 981-6060

*Denotes Foreign Offices or Affiliates
**This firm specializes in the health care field.

TACTICS FOR GETTING
THROUGH THE JOB JUNGLE

Don't quit. If you have managed to keep your job this long, don't quit before you have secured a new one. As bad as your present position may seem, being unemployed with no immediate prospects for work won't be any better. The statistics show that an employed candidate is more attractive to a prospective employer and will be compensated, on the average, 18 percent more than an equally qualified out-of-work candidate.

Have a base of operations. Preferably, your base shouldn't be your home. If you feel comfortable telling your present employer that you are in the market for a new job, then do so and carry out your hunting activities from your own office if it's possible. If not, perhaps you can make arrangements with a friend to borrow the resources of his office.

Protect your position. Obviously, the job hunt will be easier if you do not have to be concerned with conducting all related business undercover. If confidentiality is crucial to your current job security, however, be very cautious and discriminating while making your contacts. Even a casual reference to your job-hunting activity dropped at some cocktail party may get back to your office the next day.

Gear up for a long haul. Be prepared to put in some time looking for the job. Hunting for big game, you can expect to take three to six months—or much longer. Usually, the bigger the stakes, the more time it takes.

Have a hunting strategy. Planning your job-hunting strategy is a process fundamentally like planning a career strategy. An employment campaign is a career plan in miniature and should reflect the same kind of thinking given career planning.

- Update your self-inventory. Each time you change jobs, you will have new experience, new "stock" of which to take account.
- Update your goals. At each stage of your career, your employment goals will be different. Establish your pay objective, your choice of functional area and industry, and your general preferences and priorities.
- Design a strategy for systematically targeting job opportunities.

ZEROING IN ON THE OPPORTUNITIES

THE WANT ADS

Want ads are the most obvious source of job leads. Or are they? The experts seem to disagree, as usual. According to an item in *The Wall Street Journal*, a 188-company survey conducted by the Bureau of National Affairs revealed that 80 percent of the surveyed firms used classified advertisements to recruit professional and managerial people. In another article, also in the *WSJ*, Betsy Jaffe, director of programs for employers at Catalyst, a nonprofit career information clearinghouse based in New York, was quoted as saying that 80 percent of available job openings are not advertised. The source of her statistic is not noted. In any event, *some* executive positions are recruited through the classified ads, and you should not discount any available source of jobs:

- Major newspapers, such as *The Wall Street Journal, The New York Times* (the Sunday business and finance section), etc., business magazines, and, especially, trade journals in your field all carry classified advertising.
- Some experts recommend that you follow up any ad that advertises heavily for any kind of executive position, even though there is no specific mention of a need for people in your functional area.
- Performance Dynamics International (PDI), a personnel marketing firm, puts out a national weekly directory of classified ads. You can subscribe to the *National Reporter of Job Openings* through PDI, 400 Lanidex Plaza, Parsippany, New Jersey 07054. Subscriptions are $90 per quarter.

Robert Gerberg, president of PDI, claims that "success in job hunting depends 70 percent on personal marketing skills and 30 percent on a person's background and abilities."* For $15 you can read up on PDI's self-marketing techniques in a widely read book called *The Professional Job Changing System.* For a larger investment, about $500—950, you can buy from PDI a how-to-sell-yourself miniprogram to work on at home. Contact PDI at the address noted immediately above (see inset, last paragraph).

PERSONNEL AGENCIES AND JOB COUNSELORS

WHAT AN AGENCY CAN DO FOR YOU   Unlike executive search firms, personnel agencies and job counselors are easily approached and geared to serve the individual executive looking for new employment. For this service the executive sometimes pays the fee (as much as 25 percent

---

*Quotation from William Flanagan, "The Job-Changing Game" (*Esquire*, August, 1979), p. 7.

of a year's salary), although many positions available through these agencies are company paid even at the management level. An agency can offer you:

Expertise. A good counselor makes his living by knowing how to conduct a thorough and selective job search. He can save you time, although some experts warn that dealing with go-betweens in a job hunt can also end up wasting your time. Those experts advise that the time you spend looking for a *good* agency might be better spent looking for a job direct.

Job opportunities out of town. National Personnel Associates is an international network of 226 independently owned agencies located in 130 cities. These agencies, many of which specialize in management jobs, exchange over 1,600,000 résumés and job listings a year. If you wish to relocate to a specific locale, a member agency can link you with an affiliate in that area, saving you the time and expense of making a blind job-hunting trip out of town. For the National Personnel Associates office near you, look in the local white pages. If no listing appears, call the main office in Grand Rapids, Michigan, toll free, at (800) 253-2578.

Coaching and insight. A skilled counselor can help prepare you for an interview by coaching you in general interviewing techniques and by providing information and insight into a prospective employer.

HOW TO PICK AN AGENCY   The same survey that revealed that four out of five companies recruit executives through classified ads also showed that three out of four companies recruit through employment agencies.

Stick to the employment agencies that specialize in recruiting for executive positions. For the most part, agencies recruit only for lower or middle level positions. Don't waste a lot of time filing applications with several agencies. Pick one or two of the top agencies and let them do the footwork for you.

Agencies advertise positions in the classified sections. Look through the ads for the names of those agencies that seem to specialize in jobs for your field.

Speak to personnel people or business associates who may be able to direct you to a reputable or outstanding agency.

HOW TO APPROACH AN AGENCY   After you have selected a handful of agencies, send a résumé to each one along with a brief cover letter. Follow up with a telephone call and make an appointment for an interview.

Keep the interview short. Prepare to state your case in about 15 minutes. Agencies do a volume business.

If no appropriate job openings turn up immediately, you may be called later on when something comes up that is in your field. Agencies do keep extensive and up-to-date files. It could pay to keep your résumé on file with an agency even if you have no real immediate desire to move on. Filing with an agency may give you the first shot at the best opportunities.

If you are concerned with maintaining the confidentiality of your search, give clear instructions to any agency you contact. A good agent knows how to be discreet, and counselors claim that in instances of information leakage, the client's own carelessness is often to blame. Nevertheless, make your position clear to your counselor.

CREATIVE JOB-HUNTING:
HOW TO INVENT A JOB

Classified ads and personnel agencies are by no means the only sources of job leads. They are merely the most obvious and the most easily accessible. Professionals in the field of job hunting claim a vast number of other job openings can be found if you know how and where to look for them.

Conduct your job hunt the way Sherlock Holmes conducts a criminal investigation. Only a lesser sleuth is satisfied with the obvious (e.g., the butler did it) and lets it go at that. Ads and agencies are the butlers of the job market: At first glance, they are the most likely job sources, and they can save you work. However, a more creative approach to your investigation may yield more exciting, creative results—a position tailor-fit to your specifications, for instance. Here are some experts' suggestions on how to best piece together the perfect job solution:

CULTIVATE CONTACTS

Most experts agree that contacts can produce leads to jobs that otherwise would be inaccessible to you. Your best contacts are your business colleagues and associates—the people you work with, the people you do business with, the people who do business with the people *you* do business with. Build up a network of *meaningful* contacts. Trade association meetings, trade fairs, even cocktail parties can produce a number of good contacts. Beware, however, people don't like to be put on the spot, especially in social situations. So drop only discreet words, if any at all, that you are actually in the market for a job. Keep your inquiries casual at first. A recommended approach: Ask for *advice*, not a job. Pursue any substantial leads.

BE PERSISTENT

John C. Crystal, a professional noted for his innovative ideas on job-hunting, suggests that you save any formal rejections, wait a month or two, and then recontact the employer with an enthusiastic letter reiterating your interest in working for him or his company.

WATCH THE NEWS MEDIA

Creative job hunting calls for creative detective work. Learn to anticipate opportunity by learning how to scan the media for clues to *potential* job openings. The newswatchers often monitor and report on the internal affairs of corporations. Keep an eye open for news of corporate mergers, acquisitions, even purges—mass firings and the like. Such reorganization often means jobs open up; make inquiries. Read trade papers to keep on top of the current developments in your field in particular.

TARGET COMPANIES

Go through the Yellow Pages. Go through any directory that lists corporations according to industry and target the names of any business in which you think your experience might fit. Go back to the trade papers; learn all you can about these key companies. Check *Standard and Poor's Register* for the names of the current top officers. Send a résumé addressed to the appropriate executive (i.e., the one with the power to hire) along with a cover letter stating your great desire to work for that person in that organization and stating your qualifications to do so. Mention in the letter that you will follow up with a phone call on a specific day; then do it.

START A CORRESPONDENCE

Write to the key person in the one corporation for which you would like to work. Study the corporation and its service or product, do some original thinking, and submit your ideas in a personal letter to the chief executive officer, president, or chairman of the board. This is a creative, but somewhat indirect approach. One expert suggests that you back up your interest in the company by becoming a shareholder, if you can.

TARGET THE TOP BANANA

This is the principle of the highest first, propounded by maverick thinkers such as Crystal. Find out everything you can about the one executive in your field who is considered to be the most eminent/creative/powerful. Call him. Tell him how much and *exactly why* you admire him. Ask him if you can speak to him in person to get his expert advice about your career. DO NOT mention you are looking for employment. The idea is that if he grants you an interview, you then have the opportunity to impress *him* with your credentials, your enthusiasm, and your drive. Follow up the interview with a thank-you note so he has your name and address on paper for the record.

You get the general idea: If you cannot get the job you want through the obvious channels, then use your ingenuity to create new channels, even new opportunities. For the person who demonstrates ambition and enthusiasm—and the intelligence to use these qualities in unusually creative ways—a top executive with both smarts and authority can *make* an opening where none existed before.

25

THE ONE-TWO PUNCH: RÉSUMÉS AND INTERVIEWS

A market is an arena for exchange of particular goods and services between buyers and sellers. In the job market, as an executive looking for work you are like a salesperson looking for a customer. Your experience and capabilities are the products you proffer for sale to buyers in the corporate hierarchies.

As marketing and sales professionals will tell you, how well you package and present the product is crucial to closing a sale.

GETTING THROUGH THE DOOR IN AN ENVELOPE: THE RÉSUMÉ

Before you can deliver a sales pitch, however, you do need the proverbial foot-in-the-door. In the job market, your résumé is, as Jill Smolowe wrote on the subject in *The New York Times*, "the calling card that brings job candidates to the attention of employers." A résumé is an advertisement for yourself. Like any advertisement, it should entice the customer to want to know more about the product.

Books have been written on the philosophy and practice of writing the proper résumé. As John C. Crystal expressed it, some experts claim that "the résumé is the soul of the job-application process." Other experts, like Crystal himself, maintain that this is a myth—that most résumés end up in the circular file. Experts aside, it is fair to say that at some point in your working life you will probably have call for a résumé, and you will want to compose one intelligently.

COPY AND LAYOUT

The form and content of a résumé are for the most part dictated by plain common sense. As to form, you want to use standard paper (white, 8½ by 11 inches). The finished product should be neat and carefully

Name
Address

JOB OBJECTIVE

A simple statement that indicates the specific type of work you're interested in and the type of business for which you would like to work. Example: "General-assignment reporting for a metropolitan newspaper." This should take only one sentence and be tailored to meet a particular opening.

WORK EXPERIENCE

1975-present: Job title, place of employment, city, state.

A one-sentence statement of job responsibilities that avoids use of the personal pronoun. Example: "Covered city politics with an emphasis on budgetary matters."

Brief summaries of successful projects initiated, accomplishments that benefited the company and awards or commendations received. Example: "Broke the scandal on kickbacks in City Hall that led to indictments of nine officials."

1972-75: **Note that the list is offered with work experience listed in reverse chronological order.** If you have limited work experience, you might want to take a functional, rather than a chronological, approach. Here you would divide your qualifications into categories which stress skills you have acquired in school, organizational activities or part-time jobs that relate to your job objective. Example: "Writing: Wrote publicity releases for the local theatre," or "Gathered and analyzed information for college poll." If you do a functional listing, then list educational experience before work experience.

1970-72: **Never apologize for time spent out of work; turn it to your advantage.** Example: "Spent these years in independent enterprise," "Personal needs dictated spending time away from career — will explain at interview," or "independent consultant."

EDUCATION

B.A. Journalism, college, year of graduation, grade-point average.
This list should be in reverse chronological order with all degrees since high school. If you are just out of school, include academic honors and scholarships received. If you paid for a significant portion of your education, say so; it indicates industriousness. Recent graduates can include information about courses, papers written (that might pertain to the job), and any offices or memberships held in school organizations. If you are willing to travel and relocate, say so. List military training, on-the-job training, and results of college-equivalency tests.

PERSONAL

Brief statements that include any honors received, and a concise listing of outside interests that might pertain to the job. Example: "Edited community-group newsletter. Outside interests: photography, reading." You are not required to include the following: age, sex, marital status, and health status. You should not include past salaries or salary desired.

REFERENCES

A simple statement, such as "references available on request." This saves space, and a résumé should never be more than two pages long. Career counselors often stress that "the more you've done, the less you write"; meaning that your job history will speak for itself. If you are just out of school or have been absent from the job market for a long time, you might need more room to explain the skills you've picked up in volunteer jobs and extracurricular activities.

Fig. 51. Sample résumé

From *The New York Times* National Recruitment
Survey, October 14, 1979.
©1979 by *The New York Times* Company.
Reprinted by permission.

proofread—without errors of any kind—just as advertising copy would be. It should be professionally duplicated; photo offset is the recommended method. The résumé should be concise: Two pages is absolute maximum length; one page is preferred. Below, reprinted from Smolowe's article, is an example of a standard résumé format, including generally accepted guidelines for résumé content.

Though most résumés conform in principle to the one shown in Fig. 51, expert opinion differs as to the kind of details you should include in your description. Smolowe maintains that you need not include information about your sex, age, etc.; other professionals point out that any company that would eliminate you on the basis of such data in your résumé would not be any more likely to hire you after an interview for the very same reasons. You might save yourself the frustration of the interview by being candid in your résumé.

Likewise, excluding a statement of salary range or your flexibility regarding relocation, especially in answering "blind" job ads, could result in many pointless interviews. Let your own judgment tell you when it helps or harms to be frank about these issues in your résumé.

GENERAL POINTERS

Sell your experience. Titles in and of themselves are generally meaningless. Industries and individual corporations devise titles for different purposes. Besides, a title provides no in-depth information about the actual responsibilities of a particular executive job.

Describe your achievements. Don't just list duties; talk in terms of facts and figures: "Increased departmental profits by 10 percent in eight months."

Be selective. Play up the good and learn to obscure the gray areas in your work experience.

Think like an advertising copywriter. Use action verbs and eschew use of the first person singular pronoun. "Promoted to vice-president"; not "I was made." "Responsible for"; not "I was given." Don't make up stories; just find the most appealing angle on the truth.

THE RESUME VS. THE LETTER

Currently, the letter is touted by some experts as the sensible alternative to the résumé. If résumés are commonly disposed of without ceremony, letters, say these experts, at least have some chance of being read. The other side of that argument is that the pertinent information gets lost in the verbiage of a letter and that the résumé makes the point more clearly and simply. Most experts do agree, however, that a cover letter is an essential supplement to any résumé. In a cover letter you can address yourself more specifically to the particular requirements of a position or corporation. Of course, if you are following through on a contact, mention in your letter the name of the person who referred you—if it is a meaningful contact. Make certain that you convey that you are interested in working for the company. Be clear about this, but be subtle.

CLOSING THE SALE: THE INTERVIEW

The résumé may get you through the door, but the interview is the forum in which the salesperson gets to show his stuff. If you don't hook your customer at the interview, you have absolutely lost the sale.

SALESMANSHIP:
THE DYNAMICS OF AN INTERVIEW

As any good salesperson knows, selling requires a subtle understanding of human psychology. In a sense, you cannot *sell* anything. What you can do is demonstrate in a convincing manner that you have just the item your customer is looking to *buy*. In an interview situation, you begin with a decided advantage from a salesperson's point of view: In most instances, there is no question that the employer is in the market to buy. He has an organizational need, and he is shopping for the particular product that best fills the specified need. As salesperson, your job is to convince him that your product *is* the best of all products of its kind on the market.

In that case, however, it is still a buyer's market, with many salespeople competing for a single customer. Well aware that any salesperson worth his name is going to pitch his goods in superlatives, the wise consumer will use his own techniques to scrutinize the product and the pitch. These are the dynamics at work in a job interview. While you, as applicant, are selling the employer on your assets, the employer, as interviewer, will be listening to pick out your liabilities: Your customer is not interested in buying a defective product and is wary of smooth-talking salespeople.

BEHIND THE LINES

The best survival handbook for the interviewing applicant is the textbook written for the person on the other side of the desk. In the interest of self-protection, *know thy adversary* and *know what thy adversary knows.* For a definitive look into the minds of personnel professionals, read a classic, *The Evaluation Interview*, by Richard A. Fear (New York: McGraw-Hill, 1978).

This technique for conducting a "patterned" interview is known in the business as the Fear Method. The irony of this name is fully apparent only when one reads Fear's advice to would-be interviewers. On facial expressions: "Raising of the eyebrows, in particular, should take place whenever important questions are posed and . . . . a half-smile [should] be permitted to play about the lips, particularly when asking somewhat personal or delicate questions. The edge is taken off a delicate or personal question when it is posed with a half-smile and with the eyebrows raised."*

The Fear Method may seem more comical than fearful, but the point to be learned is this: While the interviewer may seem to exercise the hand of fate over the future of your career, he is, nevertheless, a human being, and, like you, subject to his own foibles, professional as well as personal. Learn the ins and outs of a professional interviewing technique. Knowing a good technique will help you spot the poor one as well; no doubt many a job has been lost by a well-qualified candidate who fell victim to an interviewer unskilled in his art.

THE BIG TEN QUESTIONS
INTERVIEWERS LOVE TO ASK

Below is your crib sheet.

Never go into an interview without knowing clearly your answers to these questions. Study them, read the rest of this section on how to protect yourself in the interview, and then prepare your answers to the questions.

1. *The icebreaker question:* So, what do you think of this weather we're having? *Alternative:* I see from your application you enjoy dogsledding. It sounds fascinating. Tell me, how did you become involved in such a unique sport?
2. What was your last job? Why did you leave?
3. What did you like about your past jobs? What did you hate?
4. Those were your duties. What were your *achievements?*
5. Tell me about yourself. *(Watch for raised eyebrows.)*
6. Now I know your best points. What about your shortcomings?
7. If you could describe your ideal job, what would it be right now?
8. What would be your ideal job five years from now? Ten years from now? What are your career goals?
9. Why do you think you are the ideal candidate for *this* job?
10. And how much money did you say you wanted?

OTHER PROBING QUESTIONS

Tell me about your boss. What is his title, and what is his function?

If you had to choose just one, what would be the single most significant achievement of your career?

When you are under pressure, how do you go about getting your staff and colleagues to help?

Of the people you hired at your last job, how long did they stay and how did your selections work out?

In your last job, what sort of things did you do to improve your performance?

---

*From *The Evaluation Interview,* by Richard A. Fear, p. 63. Copyright ©1978 by McGraw-Hill. Used with permission of McGraw-Hill Book Company.

How do you go about making critical decisions?

What does it take to be successful in your profession?

Tell me about any failures you might have had, and how they came about.

What were the risks you took in your last job, and what were the outcomes?

Tell me about your present company. Its strengths, weaknesses, methods and positions in the marketplace.

How might your present (or former) company be more successful?

If I were to phone the people you work for at your current (or former) job, what would they say about you?

PREPARE. BE CLEAR. BEWARE.

PREPARE The interviewer's task at the outset is to get as much information as possible *from* you while giving up as little information *to* you as he can. If you are blessed with an experienced, well-intentioned interviewer, he will try to accomplish this goal in an amiable manner. Even so, since he is not likely to *supply* you with information, you are best prepared to come to the interview well equipped with your own. Likewise, be ready to supply information about yourself. *What* information you choose to supply will depend on your educated assessment of what is in your best interest to tell. *Knowledge is your best protection against the unknown.* Therefore, arm yourself beforehand with any and all information you can gather.

Know thyself. Just as you did when mapping out your career strategy, take an unsentimental look at yourself before the interview. Take stock of your achievements. Recognize your failures. Take an emotional inventory, too: How do you *feel* about your successes and, particularly, your failures?

Know the position for which you are applying. Tap every available source. If the interview was set up through a friend or a professional intermediary, don't be shy about questioning him. Your predecessor on the job, if he is accessible, is a good source of information. But be discreet. It's possible he may be unaware of his lame-duck status. If it is inappropriate or impossible to contact your predecessor, try someone close to him within the company. When possible and proper, try to find out from insiders what the job is about and what happened to the one whose shoes you may be filling. If you can't get the inside scoop on the job specs, get in touch with people who hold similar positions in similar firms. Use your contacts.

Know the corporation. Read the company's annual report or prospectus, if there is one. This could provide vital statistics about your prospective supervisor as well as about the company itself. It may even give you a clue to company compensation policies. Ask around the industry for any information you can get about the company, its reputation, its relationship with its customers, its suppliers, its competitors. Research the industry itself. Go to trade shows. Read the trade journals. Scan the financial papers for any fact, big or small, that may be valuable for you to know. The more you know, the more you will have to talk about. *If you are interested, you will be interesting.*

Know the interviewer, particularly if he will be your boss when the job is yours. Use all available resources to find out his professional reputation, how he relates to his associates, what his personal likes and dislikes are. On the other hand, don't pay too much heed to gossip. Keep an open mind when you go into the interview and establish an unprejudiced relationship with the interviewer.

BE CLEAR

Sleep right. Eat right. Be fresh and rested. Don't be hungry, but don't be overstuffed, either. You'll want to feel comfortable.

Dress right. If you don't know what that means in your particular situation, conservative dress is always safe. If you don't know what *that* means, read one of the many books on the subject of proper dress for the executive. These reminders may seem obvious, but in a preinterview bout with nerves, you may overlook the obvious. (See The Executive Wardrobe section in Chapter 40)

Establish your priorities. What do you want in a job? Match your job expectations to your talents. It is not to anyone's advantage, least of all your own, to accept a job for which you are ill-suited. A position that puts too much stress on your weak spots may not be the one you want. Represent yourself accordingly. That the job *could* be yours doesn't make it right for you.

Be articulate. You may be truly capable, eager, and right for the job. The trick, however, is to be able to communicate your self-confidence and enthusiasm to the interviewer. Don't just protect yourself. *Sell* yourself.

Be specific. Did you mention a preference for performing managerial duties over accounting details? Don't be too casual. Be clear: "It's not that I *hate* accounting work. I'm actually quite skilled at it. I simply *prefer* hands-on management."

Pay attention. This is easier said than done when nerves have the better of you:

- Answer the question you've been asked. Answer all parts of the question. On the other hand, be selective. Don't give answers you haven't been asked for.
- Listen for the giveaway word or phrase that may uncover the employer's bias.

- Recognize the calculated pause. It's okay to fill the gap, but don't run on at the mouth.
- Observe your interviewer—discreetly. Bodies have a way of speaking without words. What is his body communicating? Of more importance, what is *yours* communicating?

BEWARE   Your store of knowledge is your protection against being caught unaware at an interview. *Beware* means *be aware;* be neither defensive nor off-guard. Be steady and alert.

The first five minutes of your interview are probably as important as all the rest of the time. If you find that your interviewer is asking about the weather or some other seemingly irrelevant topic, don't be paranoid. These are probably not trick questions, but simply techniques for generating small talk, commonly believed to be an effective tool to open a relaxed, yet directed interview. But be prepared for a more pointed approach as well. Your interviewer may prefer the prosecuting attorney's method, or the rapid-fire line of questioning. On the other hand, he may take an "unpatterned" approach, which may seem to you like no approach at all. In this case, you take control. This is probably the response he is looking for.

In a good interview, both sides come prepared. The skilled interviewer will ask his questions with a purpose in mind. Don't be unnerved if he makes notes while you do most of the talking.

The interview is your chance to look over the company. You too are entitled to ask questions.

Don't assume the interviewer knows what is best for you. Don't even assume he knows how to do his job. Your interviewer may not have a clear idea in mind of what he wants or needs to learn from you. It's entirely possible he isn't even quite sure what the open position is all about.

Your interviewer is not your confessor. Though *you* may recognize your shortcomings, it is not incumbent upon you to reveal them to *him.* As Madeleine Swain, a career consultant with Eaton-Swain Associates (New York), has said, "Whoever said honesty was next to godliness, probably never had to interview for a job."*

An interview that discloses no unfavorable information regarding the applicant is an unsuccessful interview—at least according to Fear tactics. In the interest of getting to "the real you," the interviewer will couch his comments in euphemisms and phrase his questions in such a way that, as one critic wrote, "the applicant self-destructs without realizing it." Don't be unnerved. If you prepare properly, no question should throw you off-balance.

---

*From Madeleine Swain, "Fired! Recoup, Recover and Re-enter!" (*The Executive Female Digest*, May/June 1979).

Your interviewer's manner of conducting himself may give you some insight into the company that keeps him on its payroll. The interview is usually your first direct personal contact with the company, and at that time the interviewer is expected to represent to you the corporate image. It is a matter of style. If your style doesn't jibe with his, will it jibe with the corporate image? Perhaps a union here is, after all, not a marriage made in heaven.

When all else fails: Is the interview deteriorating rapidly? Have you nothing else to lose? Then, as John Berendt suggested in an article in *Esquire* magazine, you may be interested to know that federal and certain state regulations limit the line of questioning that an employer may take at a job interview. Questions concerning race, religion, ethnic background, age, or history of arrest (not *conviction*) are deemed unlawful by the federal government. In addition, New York State, for example, prohibits questions asking for maiden name, place of birth, number of children, social club memberships, and other such facts not directly pertinent to the job. If your rights are being violated, go ahead—stand up for them.

THE CHEMISTRY TEST

The following anecdotes are based upon real incidents reported in various newspaper and magazine articles. For each interview situation, respond "yes" if you think you get the job, "no" if you think you don't. Compare your answers to the actual outcomes given below.

1. The interviewer takes a cigarette and offers one to you. You refuse politely, but ask if he minds if you smoke a pipe. He says he doesn't mind.

2. You have been flown to town and put up in a good hotel, where your prospective employer meets you for an interview over lunch. It goes very well, and at the end, as he is about to leave, you realize it has unexpectedly begun to rain. You happen to have an extra raincoat in your room and offer to lend the man your spare. Although it is a bit small on him, he accepts the offer.

3. During the interview the fact emerges that you have just moved your family into a new home—a large Victorian house in an exclusive neighborhood. As it turns out, your interviewer shares your fondness for Victorian houses and also has a pretty accurate idea of what such houses sell for. He remarks that, considering your current salary, you must have borrowed to the hilt to buy the house. You frankly admit you did, but add that you didn't feel a moment's hesitation about the decision; you felt it was an excellent investment and, given the inflation rate, decided it was cheaper to get what you wanted today, on credit, than to buy tomorrow with cash.

4. You are a steak-and-potatoes man from way back, but on the interview, your prospective employer takes you to lunch at a

continental restaurant where a very limited menu of haute cuisine is served. You allow your interviewer to order for you. The first course is whole artichoke. You are embarrassed to say you have never eaten one before, but you pick up your knife and fork and do your best.

5. You are asked by the interviewer about your family. You tell him enthusiastically about your nine-year-old son's little league team, which you enjoy coaching.

6. You are being interviewed for a job as a personnel executive specializing in industrial relations. Your prospective boss is telling you about his proposal for a change in a particular corporate policy. You tell him frankly that you disagree with his idea and give him your reasons for taking odds.

ACTUAL RESULTS

1. *No.* This interviewer didn't mind pipes per se. However, he associated pipe smoking with the laid-back atmosphere of a university faculty lounge and not with the high-pressured, high-paced life of an executive. He felt someone who smoked a pipe would not fit into his organization.

2. *No.* This interview *had* gone well until the employer put on the raincoat and realized just how *short* the applicant actually was. He himself was a tall man and believed that to be respected in business, you literally had to be looked up to by other people. He did not want a short person representing the corporation.

3. *Yes.* This is a composite of two actual situations. One interviewer admitted favoring a particular candidate who shared his interest in Victorian houses. He felt this reflected a compatibility of styles. In the second interview situation, the employer wanted to hire someone who had personally borrowed to the limit because he thought this act was characteristic of one who was self-confident, aggressive, and unafraid to take risks. This was the kind of executive he needed for the job.

4. *No.* In this situation the interviewer refused to hire someone who didn't know how to eat an artichoke properly. He was appalled at the candidate's lack of what he considered basic etiquette.

5. *No.* The interviewer was turned off by the applicant's animated description of his little-league coaching efforts. He perceived a possible conflict of loyalties between home and office, and he wanted an executive who clearly placed the company above all else.

6. *Yes.* This interviewer was looking to hire a tough negotiator who would not be intimidated easily. The applicant showed the right kind of spunk when he openly disagreed with the interviewer's ideas.

ANALYZING THE CHEMISTRY TEST   If you scored poorly on the test,

don't be discouraged. Despite the results of the actual interviews, there are no "right" answers. In each illustration, your answer could have been yes or no with equally sound reasoning. If the "chemistry test" seemed unfair, it *is* unfair. You did not have the benefit of the whole picture—the candidates' overall qualifications or the job specifications—but the fact is that *the employer did not consider the whole picture in making his choice.* That, of course, is the point of the chemistry test. In the final analysis, the reasons by which hiring decisions are made defy common sense and logic.

There are *sensible* reasons why a particular candidate is turned down for a job, such as refusal or reluctance to relocate, inappropriate personality, and high required salary. According to a survey conducted by researchers at Northwestern University, of the 14 reasons given for rejecting job applicants, seven are interview related. The most common of these is the inability to demonstrate self-assurance, enthusiasm, or clearly defined career goals.

According to some experts, however, in more than 50 percent of all cases, the best-qualified applicant *does not get the job.* This is where the "X" factor—personal chemistry—comes into play. It is a variable in the hiring process whose effect is totally unpredictable; yet it is a crucial catalyst in the employer's decision-making.

There have been many attempts to explain the chemistry factor, but the evidence is contradictory. One popular theory holds that like attracts like. In other words, a chief executive officer tends to hire in his own image. This, according to the National Personnel Associates, would explain discriminatory hiring practices against racial and ethnic groups and against women: Most chief executives are white males. Proponents of this theory maintain that a hiring decision may also be made on the basis of perceived shared values and interests—the Victorian house, for example. The applicant who shares such values with the prospective employer will more likely be chosen over the candidate who does not share such values, even though the latter candidate may be equally or even better qualified in other respects.

A 1979 survey conducted by the New York–based search firm of C. Stewart Baeder Associates would seem to refute that theory, however. According to the survey, less than half of the CEOs interviewed expected their successors to have backgrounds similar to their own. The consensus was that in order to meet new corporate challenges, the top executives looked for candidates who offered an operating style different from their own.

The only flat statement most experts are willing to agree upon is that the "X" factor is more than ever a major consideration in the hiring process. The job applicant may be called back for four or five evaluation interviews to meet not only with prospective supervisors, but with prospective peers and subordinates as well. With the growing corporate trend toward participatory management, in which staff is consulted with rather than

simply dictated to from above, a compatible "chemistry" among co-workers is vital to operations.

THE CORPORATE SNOOP:
PRIVACY AND THE JOB HUNT

HIS MODUS OPERANDI

Somewhere in Gotham, the details of your life history may be locked into a computer memory bank and available to anyone at the press of a recall button. So warns Robert Ellis Smith in his book *Privacy: How to Protect What's Left of It* (New York: Doubleday & Co., Inc., 1980).

Think back to all the positions for which you have applied and all the jobs you have actually had—and all the forms you filled in to apply for them, to secure them, and to get compensated for them. Think of all the information you have voluntarily supplied to your employers or prospective employers: the psychological tests you may have taken, the forms you filled in disclosing your job history, personal background, medical history, credit record, arrest history. Imagine all the data your employers could have collected on you *without your knowledge:* from information provided about you by people who know you, by people to whom *you gave* formal authorization to disclose as well as to collect information you yourself disclosed in previous questionnaires. You should assume, says Smith, that the record you have provided of your life "will become part of a computerized network and that it will take on a life of its own beyond your control." So the corporate snoop collects the information that goes into your dossier. You have probably done your share to make his job a very easy one.

YOUR LEGAL RIGHTS

While our laws protect our individual liberty from abuses by the government, the individual has almost no protection at all under law from abuses of these same rights by private business. According to Smith, there are almost no legal restrictions, for example, on information gathering by employers, nor on the disclosure of that information to others, nor on the system of storage and dissemination of that information. In forty-five states there is not even a legal requirement that an employee be allowed to inspect his dossier, and only in Michigan is the employee given the right to amend inaccuracies or unfair statements on the record.

HOW TO BE A VIGILANTE

The corporate snoop is a serious threat to your right to privacy. The present legal codes offer you inadequate protection against such invasion. However, Smith offers some practical suggestions on how you personally can combat the effect of past abuses as well as protect yourself against the occurrence of future ones:

- As previously mentioned, the law *does* give you the right to withhold certain information from an employer. You can refuse to disclose your race, color, national origin, age, sex, handicaps, possession of a driver's license, or other facts not directly relevant to the job you will perform. Exercise your rights.

- When completing questionnaires, fill in the blanks but learn to "fog" your answers. Use abbreviations such as "N/A" for "not available" or "not applicable," or more obscure abbreviations such as "WBSUE" for "will be supplied upon employment," or "UOQ" for "unsure of question." Where you are asked to provide age, for example, you can be truthful, but vague: "eighteen plus." Most clerks handling the forms will be too embarrassed to admit that they don't understand the abbreviations, or too lazy to pursue the answers any further.

- Proposals have been made to Congress to draft laws giving an employee the right to inspect his records, and many companies, wary of future repercussions, are in some instances voluntarily beginning to comply with individual requests to do so. Take advantage of this option and demand to look at your own files as well as to correct or delete out-of-date or inaccurate information. Also, demand to be notified if any information from these records leaves the company. You have nothing to lose by asking to exercise these yet unprotected rights.

- You do have a right under the federal Fair Credit Reporting Act to request to be given notice of any investigation into your personal life, character, or reputation. The employer has five days to comply with your request by reporting to you both the intent and extent of any such inquiry. In addition, the employer must disclose any adverse action taken pursuant to the findings of the inquiry. If such action has been taken, the employer is required also to disclose the name and address of the investigating firm. You then have a right to learn from the consumer investigation company the matter of information contained on you in their records and also the names of those employers who have been given access to these records in the past two years. If you challenge any of the data in your file, you may request a new investigation or demand inclusion of your version of the story in the record.

REFERENCES ON REQUEST: THE RISKS AND REWARDS

As the competition for jobs heats up, more and more exaggerated resumes have been appearing on the desks of headhunters and employers. As a result, verification by checking references has become more widespread.

Fearing repercussions, many employers are reluctant to furnish more than straight facts and figures. However, employees of the firm seem more willing to talk. Besides, some prospective employers are asking for written permission to look into an interviewee's past.

Reference checking over the telephone can last over an hour and involve as many as seventy-five or a hundred questions. One of the main concerns is that the job-seeking, when listing accomplishments, will take credit for achievements that he wasn't really responsible for, even if he was there at the time, or played a minor role.

A bad reference can sandbag your career. The simplest, most common reason for an unjustified bad reference is bad blood. There are a few things you can do:

First, canvas your references. Let them know you will be giving their names and try to get a feel for what they will say about you. Remind them of your achievements. Hopefully, any animosity will surface at that time.

Be alert. If you are missing jobs that you think you should have gotten, it may be a sign that your references aren't holding up. Ask the recruiter or interviewer if this is the case. And if you are a victim of a poor reference, confront the situation.

Don't panic. Savvy employers and recruiters tend to throw out comments by references that are extreme—either too positive or too negative. Usually they can tell when a job prospect is the victim of a vendetta.

Perform. The toughest bad reference to shake is one that is well-deserved. Most executives take references seriously, and they will not give a glowing one if it is undeserved, even if they like you and were your good buddies on the job.

26

APPENDIX TO PART V: ACTIVITIES AND RESPONSIBILITIES OF THE EXECUTIVE

The following questionnaire, designed by John K. Hemphill for his study of executive positions, serves as a useful self-test in defining your own job. There is a total of 191 questions in the four-part questionnaire. Follow the instructions at the beginning of each part.

From John K. Hemphill, "Dimensions of Executive Positions"
(Princeton, N.J.: Educational Testing Service, 1959), pp. 27-37.
Reprinted by permission of the author.

PART I   POSITION ACTIVITIES

Consider each of the following statements which may describe something that
would be done by an individual in your position. If the statement describes
something that does not apply to, or is not true for your position because it
describes something that is delegated by you to a subordinate, it is not a part of
your position. Enter a number between 0 and 7 in the blank before each statement
according to the following scheme.

0.   Definitely not a part of the position, does not apply, or is not true.

1.   Under unusual circumstances may be a minor part of the position.
2.
3.
4.   A substantial part of the position.
5.
6.
7.   A most significant part of the position.

AN INDIVIDUAL IN THIS POSITION WOULD:

_____   1. Plan the analysis of quantitative data.
_____   2. Forecast the volume of work to be done in the near future.
_____   3. Maintain personal contact with heads of union groups.
_____   4. Schedule work so that it flows evenly and steadily.
_____   5. See representatives of institutional investors.
_____   6. Assist salesmen in securing important accounts.
_____   7. Nominate key personnel in the organization for promotion.
_____   8. Make assignments of jobs to subordinates.
_____   9. Submit regular reports concerning accomplishment of groups
               ofemeloyees.
_____ 10. Visit each of the company's major units at least once a year.
_____ 11. Write or dictate at least 25 letters per week.
_____ 12. Verify important facts before they become part of a record.
_____ 13. Edit drafts of special reports.
_____ 14. Make speeches at public gatherings.
_____ 15. Sign documents that obligate the company to the extent of at least
               $1,000.
_____ 16. Travel at least 30 days each year as a representative of the
               company.
_____ 17. On the average spend at least one hour per day completing routine
               paper work.
_____ 18. Approve transfers of workers from one job to another.
_____ 19. Keep detailed and accurate records.
_____ 20. Make recommendations on matters at least as important as the
               construction of a new plant.

_____ 21. Advise junior persons on technical matters related to the business.
_____ 22. Make analyses of statistical reports.
_____ 23. Approve the introduction of new products or services.
_____ 24. Have a public speaking engagement at least as often as once every six months.
_____ 25. Be involved in establishing sales objectives for the company.
_____ 26. Approve labor contracts.
_____ 27. Set profit objectives.
_____ 28. Justify capital expenditures.
_____ 29. Make suggestions for improvements in company products and/or services.
_____ 30. Appraise the results of operations.
_____ 31. Anticipate new and/or changed demands for products and/or services.
_____ 32. Serve on a committee concerned with appraisal of performance.
_____ 33. Compute the costs of producing products and/or rendering services.
_____ 34. Set profit objectives for operating groups.
_____ 35. Bargain with union representatives.
_____ 36. Review reports on inventory.
_____ 37. Analyze expense items involving a gross of at least $5,000.
_____ 38. Furnish guidance to others in the preparation of budgets.
_____ 39. Assist sales representatives on large projects.
_____ 40. Analyze regularly the effectiveness of operations.
_____ 41. Review budgets for operations.
_____ 42. Establish effective expense controls.
_____ 43. Supervise a team of specialists.
_____ 44. Represent the president outside the company.
_____ 45. Analyze operating performance reports.
_____ 46. Devise procedures to properly reflect the results of operation.
_____ 47. Trouble-shoot special problems as they arise.
_____ 48. Plan the best use of available facilities.
_____ 49. Explain divergence between budget and actual expenditures.
_____ 50. Make use of staff people.
_____ 51. Consolidate estimates from various sources.
_____ 52. Evaluate records of production.
_____ 53. Analyze sales techniques.
_____ 54. Secure facts and information for others.
_____ 55. Serve as a member of one or more committees concerned with company policy.
_____ 56. Set goals for future performance.
_____ 57. Serve as a consultant in work with branches of the company.
_____ 58. Brief others on the contents of reports, letters, etc.
_____ 59. Appraise the results of operations.
_____ 60. Define areas of responsibility for supervisory personnel.
_____ 61. Make recommendations for salary increases.
_____ 62. Serve as a consultant in the interpretation of data and/or other information.
_____ 63. Keep a constant check upon the activities of subordinates.

PART II   POSITION RESPONSIBILITIES

Consider each of the following statements which may describe something with which an individual in your position must be concerned. If your position requires that you be attentive to, worry about, be responsible for, or oversee the matter described in the statement, you are to consider it a part of your position, regardless of how much time you devote to it personally. However, if the statement describes something which is strictly the concern of a superior or of a subordinate you should not consider it a part of your position. Enter a number between 0 and 7 in the blank before each statement according to the following schema.

0. Definitely not a part of the position, does not apply, or is not true.

1. Under unusual circumstances may be a minor part of the position.
2.
3.
4. A substantial part of the position.
5.
6.
7. A most significant part of the position.

AN INDIVIDUAL IN MY POSITION MUST BE CONCERNED WITH:

_____ 64. Long-range objectives of the organization.
_____ 65. Preparation of an annual budget of at least $200,000.
_____ 66. Optimum return on investments of the organization.
_____ 67. Preservation of capital assets.
_____ 68. Capital expenditures.
_____ 69. Payment of salary and/or wages.
_____ 70. Expenditure of sums exceeding $10,000 in routine operations.
_____ 71. Selection of new employees.
_____ 72. Labor contracts.
_____ 73. Definition of areas of responsibility of supervisory personnel.
_____ 74. Payment of company obligations.
_____ 75. Forecasting future trends or events.
_____ 76. Preparation and circulation of bulletins and reports.
_____ 77. Development of new business.
_____ 78. Enforcement of rules and regulations.
_____ 79. Control of inventories.
_____ 80. Improvements in product design.
_____ 81. Protection of company property.
_____ 82. Employee benefit plans.
_____ 83. Preparation of standards and/or specifications.
_____ 84. Reduction of costs.
_____ 85. Pricing company products and/or services.
_____ 86. Promotion of the company's products or services.
_____ 87. Proper handling of other than personal monies.
_____ 88. Compliance of practices with state and federal laws.
_____ 89. Relationships with unions.

_____ 90. Insurance programs and/or policies.
_____ 91. Delivery schedules.
_____ 92. Coordination of certain activities of many subdivisions of the company.
_____ 93. Loss of the company's money and/or property.
_____ 94. Acceptance of the company in the community.
_____ 95. Price trends.
_____ 96. Promises of delivery that are difficult to meet.
_____ 97. Product specifications.
_____ 98. Sales quotas.
_____ 99. Merchandising policies.
_____ 100. Activities of competitors.
_____ 101. Market records five to ten years in the future.
_____ 102. Long-range solvency of the company.
_____ 103. Employee attitude surveys.
_____ 104. Employee vacation and benefit plans.
_____ 105. Interpretation of details of a collective bargaining agreement.
_____ 106. What business activities the company is to be engaged in.
_____ 107. Long-range trends in management thinking.
_____ 108. Taxes (other than personal).
_____ 109. Control of product quality.
_____ 110. Industrial relations.
_____ 111. Opportunities to promote the company before the public.
_____ 112. New competitive products.
_____ 113. Union activities within the company.
_____ 114. Over-or-under staffing of jobs.
_____ 115. Maintenance of proper inventories.
_____ 116. New markets for the company's products.
_____ 117. Engineering standards.
_____ 118. Details of a collective bargaining agreement.
_____ 119. The long-range potentialities of the business.
_____ 120. The effectiveness of a force of 100 or more employees.
_____ 121. Proposed legislation that might affect the company.
_____ 122. Pilot projects.
_____ 123. Sizing up people.
_____ 124. Evaluating new ideas.
_____ 125. Responsibility for products having a value of at least $100,000.
_____ 126. Redesign of products to reduce costs.
_____ 127. Quality control.
_____ 128. Good will of the company in the community.
_____ 129. New markets for future products.
_____ 130. Market conditions affecting the users of the company's products and/or services.
_____ 131. Efficiency of operations.
_____ 132. Preparation of quarterly (or more frequent) reports on operations.
_____ 133. Development of management trainees.
_____ 134. Human relations practices.
_____ 135. Consolidation of data and/or information from numerous sources.

PART III   POSITION DEMANDS AND RESTRICTIONS

Consider each of the following statements which may describe a restriction, limitation, control or demand upon an individual in your position. Consider that the statement describes a part of your position if it is true when applied to your position and it is likely that failure to observe the matter described would cause others to think you inadequate or unqualified for your position. Do not consider that a statement describes part of your position if it is not true or does not apply or because it agrees with your personal view about what is proper. Enter a number between 0 and 7 in the blank before each statement according to the following schema.

0.   Definitely not a part of the position, does not apply, or is not true.

1.   Under unusual circumstances may be a minor part of the position.

2.

3.

4.   A substantial part of the position.

5.

6.

7.   A most significant part of the position.

MY POSITION REQUIRES THAT I:

_____ 136.   Refrain from activities that might imply sympathy for unions.

_____ 137.   Be active in community affairs.

_____ 138.   Avoid identification with political elements that others consider radical.

_____ 139.   Even during most relaxed social occasions avoid deviations from generally accepted behavior.

_____ 140.   Maintain membership in one or more clubs.

_____ 141.   Keep informed about the latest technical developments in a professional area.

_____ 142.   Avoid any public comment critical of good customer and/or supplier.

_____ 143.   Avoid the use of any kind of profanity.

_____ 144.   Be very careful to avoid inadvertent disclosure of confidential information.

_____ 145.   Spend as much as 50 hours per week on the job.

_____ 146.   Take a leading part in local community projects.

_____ 147.   Work with persons whose interests conflict with the demands of my position.

_____ 148.   Sit at a desk at least 20 hours per week.

_____ 149.   Be capable of performing the jobs of all subordinates.

_____ 150.   Participate in outside activities to increase the prestige of the company.

_____ 151.   Gain the respect of very important persons.

_____ 152.   Work with information of questionable reliability.

_____ 153.   Maintain membership in two or more business organizations.

_____ 154. Present the company to the public in its best light.
_____ 155. Avoid publicity associated with personal difficulties.
_____ 156. Refrain from being seen at a place (bar, club, etc.) having other than the highest repute.
_____ 157. Maintain active membership in two or more professional organizations.
_____ 158. Get to know each person under me.
_____ 159. Be an active member of at least one civic organization.
_____ 160. Refrain from public criticism of the company's operations.
_____ 161. Make decisions without consulting others.

PART IV   POSITION CHARACTERISTICS (Miscellaneous)

Consider each of the following statements which may be either true or false if applied to your position. If the statement is true only because of your particular relationship to your position and would not be true of another incumbent, do not consider it a part of the position. However, if the statement would be true regardless of who holds the position, then the statement describes a part of the position. In this case your task is to decide how substantial a part of the job it is. Enter a number between 0 and 7 in the blank before each statement according to the following schema.

0.   Definitely not a part of the position, does not apply, or is not true.

1.   Under unusual circumstances may be a minor part of the position.
2.
3.
4.   A substantial part of the position.
5.
6.
7.   A most significant part of the position.

MY POSITION:

_____ 162. Signifies membership in top or middle management.
_____ 163. Offers an opportunity to utilize professional training.
_____ 164. Permits access to information regarding executive salaries.
_____ 165. Involves dealing with persons within the company of substantially higher rank.
_____ 166. Involves first-hand contact with customers of the company.
_____ 167. Assures that the incumbent will be noticed by top management.
_____ 168. Is within the normal path of promotion to higher levels.
_____ 169. Offers an opportunity to work with the more influential people within the community.
_____ 170. Allows great freedom of action.
_____ 171. Involves very frequent contact with the public.
_____ 172. Involves maintaining the highest respect of a few important persons.

0. Definitely not a part of the position, does not apply, or is not true.

1. Under unusual circumstances may be a minor part of the position.
2.
3.
4. A substantial part of the position.
5.
6.
7. A most significant part of the position.

_____ 173. Involves first-hand contact with machines and their operations.
_____ 174. Offers an opportunity to gain experience in management.
_____ 175. Involves the "good will" of the company.
_____ 176. Involves meeting problems produced by factors over which I have no control.
_____ 177. Allows me to make decisions that are not subject to review.
_____ 178. Provides an opportunity for actually managing an important part of the business.
_____ 179. Provides a company automobile for my use.
_____ 180. Entitles me to my own secretary.
_____ 181. Involves sharing in a bonus or profit-sharing plan.
_____ 182. Involves close association with women employees.
_____ 183. Involves many regularly assigned duties.
_____ 184. Carries a personal expense allowance.
_____ 185. Directly affects the quality of the company's products or services.
_____ 186. Involves spending at least 10 hours per week in direct association with superiors.
_____ 187. Involves very few routine activities.
_____ 188. Involves activities that are not closely supervised or controlled.
_____ 189. Provides an office that is located in one of the more desirable areas.
_____ 190. Is considered a staff rather than line position.
_____ 191. Involves working under constant pressure to meet deadlines.

PART VI

GETTING YOUR SHARE: EXECUTIVE COMPENSATION

"When a fellow says, 'It ain't
the money, but the principle
of the thing,' it's the money."
Frank McKinney Hubbard

27

WHAT EVERYBODY WANTS

Remember when earned income meant strictly salary, and ordinary income meant interest on your savings? Well, no more. The question of executive compensation has become very complex, and as you advance up the corporate ladder, you will be carrying a more mixed and increasingly hefty bag of compensation benefits.

Compensation packages are largely a reflection of the times. Changes in the work ethnic and social values have caused most executives to view compensation not strictly in terms of money but, rather, as an amalgam of alternative compensation forms to accommodate changed priorities. To meet these demands as well as to keep up with corporate needs and the ever-changing rules and regulations of the IRS, executive compensation planners have created a smorgasbord of goodies so abundant and exotic that many an executive has stood before it wondering where to dig in.

To get your share of the compensation smorgasbord, you need to approach the negotiating table with the discriminating taste of a connoisseur, but the appetite of a glutton.

To begin to develop a fine appreciation for what goes into an executive compensation package, ponder the following questions:

- *What are you after?* What are your short-range cash income needs and long-term net worth objectives?
- *What is the company after?*
- *What does Uncle Sam want?*
- *What goes on the table?*

WHAT ARE YOU AFTER?

When it comes to compensation, every executive wants *more*. That is not the question. The question is what is the real dollar value of your current income and assets, and how much more cash do you actually need to support yourself and your family in the next year; the next ten years? And, in the long term, how much capital accumulation do you require to maintain your present life-style through your retirement years? The break-even point between your projected family needs and your projected family income and assets will determine your bottom line in compensation negotiation. Any compensation above the break-even amount is gravy—and you will undoubtedly want a hearty portion of that on top of your steak and potatoes.

How to determine your current cash value and near-term cash needs: As David McLaughlin suggests in *The Executive Money Map*,*

- you can gather together all your personal financial records and deliver them to a financial consultant, accountant, or other professional and pay a substantial fee to receive a "base cash projection," i.e., a ten-year forecast of your annual income based on current data; or
- you can gather together your records, a calculator, and a textbook on the fundamentals of accounting and using work sheets such as McLaughlin has devised (*see* my Chapter 30, Fig. 63), do the forecast for yourself.

How to determine your net worth goals: Achieving ultimate financial independence and security requires practical planning. Here again, doing a base case projection is the recommended approach to determine projected net worth goals and a capital accumulation strategy. Also, begin to look over the smorgasbord of compensation alternatives to determine which ones will best fulfill your particular net worth goals. For purposes of capital accumulation, the basic compensation forms available to the executive are pensions, profit sharing plans, deferred compensation, and future value incentive plans.

WHAT IS THE COMPANY AFTER?

In determining executive compensation policy, the corporation's objectives are:

- to attract you and keep you
- to reduce or eliminate financial strain to the executive
- to stimulate and increase your interest in company growth and well-being by increasing your financial stake in it, i.e., tieing compensation to performance
- to minimize outflow of corporate cash and minimize cost to stockholders

*David McLaughlin, *The Executive Money Map*, edited by Jonathan Rinehart (New York: McGraw-Hill, 1975).

- to keep a lid on company stock holdings by executives
- to minimize dependence of compensation value on stock market prices
- to maximize tax benefit and minimize tax liability to both you and the corporation

Where your interests and the corporate interests coincide, you and your employer can come to easy terms. Where your interests conflict, *you* will have to drive a hard bargain.

The view from the other side: If you want to gain added insight into how compensation decisions are made, you might take a look at *How to Compensate Executives,* by James E. Cheeks and Gordon D. Wolf (Homewood, Illinois: Dow Jones-Irwin, 1979). This is an evenhanded look at the executive compensation issue, although the book is intended for the employer. It emphasizes the true costs of the programs to the employer, and the tax benefits to both employer and employee of the various plans. This straightforward volume will give you insight into how compensation programs are structured and why the employer seems more flexible on some points than on others.

WHAT DOES UNCLE SAM WANT?

Uncle Sam wants something from everybody. What Uncle Sam wants, of course, is money—money out of the money you make and out of the money your employer makes. He sends around the tax man to collect. The tax man has a guidebook over 40,000 pages long telling him *what* he can collect from whom.

The Tax Reform Act of 1986 has altered tax treatment of stock options, capital gains, and other aspects of individual and business taxation. Such provisions may affect your compensation plan. It is wise to consult an accountant.

Playing favorites: Uncle Sam's preferences are built into the tax structure. The design of tax provisions "favors" certain forms of compensation and investment income and thereby determines the popularity of particular compensation plans.

Playing the tax man's game: The complicated tax structure makes it difficult for an executive to evaluate the true dollar worth of a compensation offer and to compare offers made by various companies. However, the greatest difficulty faced by executives and compensation planners alike in playing the tax man's game is keeping up with the tax man's changing rules. A compensation policy that looked rosy under last year's provisions may pale in the light of new and current regulations.

Don't cheat the system, beat the system: McLaughlin points out that tax *avoidance, not* tax evasion, is a legitimate means of beating the tax system—or, at least, of making the best of it. The government leaves to the individual the responsibility of formulating a strategy to minimize taxes. You are expected to use established policies to your personal financial advantage: Give yourself every break permitted by law.

Whether or not you actually can *beat* the tax man at his game is a moot question. You do have to keep up with it, though; so unless you yourself are a tax consultant or accountant, you will in the long run do best to seek the advice of a professional when structuring your pay package.

28

HOW MUCH?
SHORT-TERM COMPENSATION

In the current economic environment, a buck in the hand is worth two on the books. Salary, delivered *now* in cold hard cash, is still the most coveted prize. The size of the paycheck is predetermined and guaranteed. There is no risk; no cost; no restriction. You can spend it, save it, invest it as you please. From your viewpoint, it's "take the money and run." From the corporate viewpont, "cash motivates," and that looks good, too.

Even so, when it comes down to the negotiating table, many executives do not know how to determine their fair share of the boodle or how to bargain for what they are worth. The corporate cashier is regarded by the executive with some distrust: his motives are suspect; his decisions arbitrary.

The truth of the matter is that compensation decisions should be, and usually are, quite reasonable, and corporate pay policies are not only accessible, if you know where to find them, but also quite understandable from the corporate point of view. Salary levels are carefully determined by corporate personnel who have to defend their judgments not only to you, the executive, but also to the chairman of the board, company stockholders, and Uncle Sam.

WHAT REALLY COUNTS:
SALARY FACTORS

In certain instances, especially those involving top management at large corporations, perks such as stock options and pension plans can be even more important than salary. But in the vast majority of cases, the real bargaining takes place over salary and bonus.

Some careful studies have been made of compensation patterns, and several key factors have emerged:

Industry. Some industries tend to pay more than others, across the board. Salary levels tend to be set by intraindustry competition, rather than by the broader corporate environment.

423

Company size within an industry is also a factor to consider. Some surveys show that larger companies, on the average, tend to pay higher salaries. In cross-industry comparisons, however, there are notable exceptions to this rule.

Region. According to studies published by Financial Executives Institute, the highest-paid top executives in 1978 were in the West, followed by executives in the Northeast, Rocky Mountains, Midwest, Mideast, Southwest, and Southeast. However, the study notes, these statistics are "general in nature. Actual regional differences can vary greatly depending upon size of company and industry."

Top Executives:
Average percentage increase in total compensation by industry *(1985–1986)*

	Bonus Companies	All Companies
MANUFACTURING GROUP		
Durable Goods		
Basic Materials	11%	11%
Computers and Related Office Equipment	13	11
Electrical and Electronic Equipment/Instruments	9	9
Machinery	9	8
Metals Processing and Fabricating	10	9
Nondurable Goods		
Chemicals	12	12
Food Products and Tobacco	13	13
Nondurable Consumer Goods	17	16
Paper Products	7	8
Petroleum	3	3
Publishing	12	11
NONMANUFACTURING GROUP		
Business and Professional Services	13	11
Communications	10	10
Construction and Contracting	14	12
Mining and Energy Extraction	19	13
Retail Sales	13	11
Transportation	17	13
Utilities	6	7
Wholesale Trade	13	11
FINANCIAL SERVICES GROUP		
Banking (Commercial)	12	12
Banking (Thrift Institutions)	16	13
Diversified Finacial Services	17	15
Insurance (Life)	7	7
Insurance (Property and Casualty)	20	17

Fig. 52. Percentage increase in top executives compensation by industry.

Copyright © 1987 Arthur Young and Company.
Reprinted by permission.

Tax provisions. Corporations, like individual executives, are concerned with juggling their compensation plans to minimize costs and maximize tax advantages. The corporation, unlike the executive, faces the additional considerations and restrictions imposed by IRS standards of "reasonableness." Corporations must be able to show to stockholders, as well as to the IRS, that an executive's compensation level is justified in terms of services rendered. As reported by compensation experts James E. Cheeks and Gordon D. Wolf in *How to Compensate Executives* (Homewood, Illinois: Dow Jones-Irwin, 1979), reasonableness is determined by:

- what other executives earn in similar positions in the same industry
- the level of experience and credentials of the executive

All Executives:
Average percentage increase in compensation *(1985–1986)*

	CEO and Top Executives	Senior Other Management	All Executives
ANALYSIS OF BONUS AND ALL COMPANIES			
Bonus Companies (Total Compensation)	12%	10%	12%
Base Salary	9	8	9
Bonus	45	44	45
All Companies	11	9	11
INDUSTRY GROUP ANALYSIS			
Manufacturing—Durable Goods	9	8	9
Manufacturing—Nondurable Goods	12	8	10
Nonmanufacturing	11	9	10
Financial Service	14	12	13
REGIONAL ANALYSIS			
Northeast	11	10	10
Southeast	12	10	12
North Central	12	9	11
South Central	11	9	11
West	11	10	11

Fig. 53. Percentage increase in executive compensation 1985–1986.

Chief Executive Officer		
Comparison of average 1986 compensation		
	RANK	INDEX
		(All CEO's = 100)
Diversified Financial Services	1	1.43
Transportation	2	1.42
Petroleum	3	1.39
Retail Sales	4	1.19
Food Products and Tobacco	5	1.18
Insurance (Property and Casualty)	6	1.18
Chemicals	7	1.17
Publishing	8	1.16
Nondurable Consumer Goods	9	1.13
Communications	10	1.11
Computers and Related Office Equipment	11	1.10
Business and Professional Services	12	1.08
Electrical and Electronic Equipment	13	0.96
Mining and Energy Extraction	14	0.95
Construction and Contracting	15	0.93
Paper Products	16	0.90
Banking (Commercial)	17	0.90
Utilities	18	0.88
Basic Materials	19	0.88
Insurance (Life)	20	0.85
Metals Processing and Fabricating	21	0.84
Machinery	22	0.81
Wholesale Trade	23	0.80
Banking (Thrift Institutions)	24	0.67

Fig. 54. Comparison of average 1986 compensation
by industry. Figures expressed are for chief executives.

Copyright © 1987 Arthur Young and Company.
Reprinted by permission.

- the current income level of the executive
- the level of responsibility of the job
- corporate size and organization
- company earnings
- general corporate compensation policy
- size of dividend payouts to stockholders
- prevailing business conditions

To conform to standards of reasonableness, an executive's salary need not
be justified by each and every one of these determinants, but only a few.

Average percentage increase in total compensation by industry *(1985–1986)*

	Bonus Companies	All Companies
MANUFACTURING GROUP		
Durable Goods		
Basic Materials	12%	12%
Computers and Related Office Equipment	4	4
Electrical and Electronic Equipment/Instruments	10	9
Machinery	13	10
Metals Processing and Fabricating	13	11
Nondurable Goods		
Chemicals	17	16
Food Products and Tobacco	8	8
Nondurable Consumer Goods	23	20
Paper Products	0	2
Petroleum	5	5
Publishing	16	16
NONMANUFACTURING GROUP		
Business and Professional Services	12	11
Communications	15	14
Construction and Contracting	10	7
Mining and Energy Extraction	*	5
Retail Sales	14	12
Transportation	21	16
Utilities	6	9
Wholesale Trade	14	11
FINANCIAL SERVICES GROUP		
Banking (Commercial)	17	17
Banking (Thrift Institutions)	21	18
Diversified Financial Services	18	16
Insurance (Life)	11	10
Insurance (Property and Casualty)	25	22

Fig. 55. Average percentage increase in
total compensation by industry. Figures expressed
are for chief executives.

Copyright © 1987 Arthur Young and Company.
Reprinted by permission.

By IRS standards, reasonableness applies to the compensation package as a whole, not to individual elements of the package. Therefore, as Cheeks and Wolf note, "if a salary of $90,000 and a bonus of $10,000 is reasonable for a job, then a salary of $10,000 and a bonus of $90,000 is equally reasonable for that job."*

*From James E. Cheeks and Gordon D. Wolf, *How to Compensate Executives* (Homewood, IL: Dow Jones-Irwin, 1979), p. 26, copyright ©1979 by James E. Cheeks and Gordon D. Wolf.

Corporate power structure. Top executives play a role in determining their own salary and in influencing board members who create compensation policy.

Character of top executives. Their personal philosophy and views on the work ethic contribute to policy.

Bargaining factor. Successful executives are shrewd and tough negotiators with political savvy and innovative, creative techniques. They know how to get what they want.

Gender. There are more and more women in the workplace than ever before. Indeed, one third of American managers are female. But they still earn an average of 42 percent less than their male counterparts at the same managerial level.

Job security. In the uncertain environment created by the merger/acquisition wave, few companies are in a position to guarantee employment, much less permit you to take it for granted. Generally, the greater the

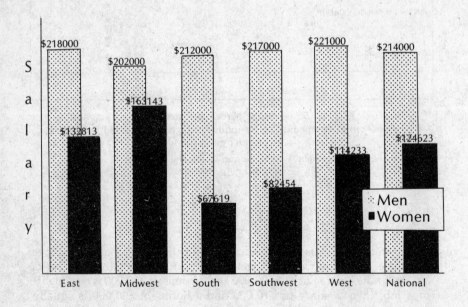

Fig. 56. Women's salaries
Source: Heldrick & Struggles

428

risk of a sale or merger, the higher the compensation package. This is especially true in the case of a turnaround, in which the board of directors tries to make a last ditch attempt to save a firm from the specter of a sale or bankruptcy. In such cases, executives have come to view such cases as episodes of Mission: Impossible. Since chance of failure is high, even if they are talented, they want to be able to walk away with enough money to tide them over.

COMPUTING YOUR COMPENSATION

Wouldn't it be great if there were a simple mathematical formula for determining what a job is worth? Well, there isn't, but not for lack of trying. Every so often, one of these attempts reveals some numerical relation-

Chief Executive Officer:
Bonus eligibility/payments

	Percentage Bonus-Eligible CEOs	Bonus (where paid) as a Percentage of Base Salary	Percentage of CEOs Eligible But Not Receiving a Bonus
MANUFACTURING GROUP			
Durable Goods			
Basic Materials	96%	50%	17%
Computers and Related Office Equipment	94	51	27
Electrical and Electronic Equipment/Instruments	96	55	44
Machinery	72	51	29
Metals Processing and Fabricating	91	53	32
Nondurable Goods			
Chemicals	95	58	11
Food Products and Tobacco	97	62	15
Nondurable Consumer Goods	87	62	15
Paper Products	89	39	13
Petroleum	100	63	44
Publishing	100	84	7
NONMANUFACTURING GROUP			
Business and Professional Services	90	59	20
Communications	85	50	19
Construction and Contracting	94	72	21
Mining and Energy Extraction	67	51	25
Retail Sales	88	93	17
Transportation	83	63	21
Utilities	51	38	23
Wholesale Trade	84	57	31
FINANCIAL SERVICES GROUP			
Banking (Commercial)	84	45	17
Banking (Thrift Institutions)	82	37	13
Diversified Financial Services	88	83	12
Insurance (Life)	84	30	25
Insurance (Property and Casualty)	81	52	0

Fig. 57. Percentage of bonus eligibility/payments of chief executives, by industry

ships that help our understanding of the factors involved, even if it is a less than foolproof indicator of dollar value.

Eugene Finkin, writing in *Personnel Journal*, observed that salary is most closely related not to corporate profit, not to division profits or sales, but to *the salary of the CEO* (which is related to corporate sales) and *your level in the hierarchy.*

Top Executives:
Bonus as a percentage of base salary by industry
(Bonus-paying companies only)

	1986
MANUFACTURING GROUP	
Durable Goods	
Basic Materials	33%
Computers and Related Office Equipment	29
Electrical and Electronic Equipment/Instruments	30
Machinery	32
Metals Processing and Fabricating	34
Nondurable Goods	
Chemicals	34
Food Products and Tobacco	43
Nondurable Consumer Goods	42
Paper Products	34
Petroleum	37
Publishing	31
NONMANUFACTURING GROUP	
Business and Professional Services	35
Communications	34
Construction and Contracting	31
Mining and Energy Extraction	30
Retail Sales	36
Transportation	51
Utilities	24
Wholesale Trade	34
FINANCIAL SERVICES GROUP	
Banking (Commercial)	25
Banking (Thrift Institutions)	20
Diversified Financial Services	49
Insurance (Life)	15
Insurance (Property and Casualty)	32

Fig. 58. Bonus as a percentage of base salary
for top executives, by industry.

If you know the sales figure and how many people get paid more than you, you should, says Finkin, be able to arrive at a reasonable approximation of compensation in dollar. He has even proposed a formula for CEO compensation:

$$c = Ax^{B*}$$

wherein c = compensation in dollars, x = sales, and A and B are appropriate constants.

Once the CEO compensation is determined, the senior management salaries are determined as a percentage of that. Finkin found that in 1976 the second-highest-paid executives of Fortune 500 companies received, on the average, 72 percent of the CEO salary. Senior and executive VPs positioned third to fifth in the company got between 52 percent and 54 percent. The next level was in the 35–37 percent range.

The results seem to indicate that it would be better to hold a senior management position in a billion-dollar company than in a 100 million dollar company, and that a promotion in a larger company may be worth much more in terms of dollars than a switch to a smaller company where you would have more potential for advancement. But this is far from a hard and fast rule: It may not apply to closely held or private companies. It doesn't take the dollar value of perks into account. And the value of these figures is questionable due to the effects of inflation and energy costs on profits, sales, and living cost since 1976. In addition, the constants, A & B, may be affected by such factors.

The formula is based on power laws. If you are interested in the math behind all this, see "How to Figure Out Executive Compensation" by Eugene F. Finkin, in the July, 1978, issue of *Personnel Journal*, pp. 371–375.

Comparison shop. A general method to estimate a reasonable salary level for a particular position is to determine the "going rate" for someone of your qualifications holding a similar position within the same industry. Good sources for salary information are:

- trade associations
- trade papers and journals, particularly publications for personnel professionals
- classified advertisements
- personnel agencies and executive recruiters
- company proxy statements (an excellent source of information on entire compensation policy, not just salary)

---

*Reprinted with permission from *Personnel Journal*, Copyright © July, 1978.

THE CASH OR INCENTIVE BONUS

The lure of more cash (even if it is paid out in stock, a bonus is taxed like cash) makes this dish an especially appealing and popular one to the executive. From the corporation's perspective an incentive bonus is a means to tie an executive's compensation to corporate performance and thereby motivate the executive to further the company's career as well as his own.

In the past, the cash bonus has been a staple in manufacturing industries, but in recent years, service companies, especially banks and insurance firms, have begun to join the bonus plan bandwagon. Since 1972, 25 percent more major corporations have begun to offer executive bonuses. Oddly enough, those corporations that offer a bonus plan very often also offer a higher pay scale.

The bonus formula. The formula, which varies from situaton to situation, identifies a specifically defined corporate or divisional performance goal (commonly related to sales, profits, return on investments, or dividends) as well as the bonus amount (usually a percentage of base salary or profits) to be received by the executive once the goal is met. A divisional plan is preferable, particularly for a division executive, because it is possible for a division to perform well even though overall corporate performance is poor.

Whether the corporate philosophy is to reward the "team" across the board or to reward the "stars," the particular formula applied reflects the corporation's attitude toward its executives on performance standards. If everyone gets the bonus, you may want either your salary level or your bonus formula percentage to reflect your individual performance and visibility.

How the bonus is structured and administered, how performance is to be judged, the timing and form of the payout, and especially how the company bonus plan has worked in practice (not just how it appears on paper) are issues that should be studied carefully when you appraise the value of a bonus offer.

Discretionary bonuses. Not linked to a predetermined performance goal, these bonuses may be awarded in recognition of some noteworthy accomplishment by an executive.

1. 12½ percent of consolidated net income less 6 percent of the average common stock equity less the amount of current dividends for the year
2. 10 percent of net income after deducting 5 percent of average capital in business
3. 6 percent of profits after taxes that are in excess of 6 percent of capital
4. 8 percent of the first $5 million net income plus 10 percent of the next $5 million plus 1 percent of the remainder after net income has been reduced by the larger of: (a) 6 percent of average net capital, (b) dividends on preferred stock plus $2.50 per share of common stock
5. 6 percent of net earnings before taxes and percentage compensation or 8 percent of earnings after taxes and percentage compensation
6. 6 percent of net earnings before taxes, after deducting 10 percent of capital employed
7. 10 percent of the excess after dividend requirements of preferred stock plus 5½ percent of the total stated value of common stock plus 5½ percent of the surplus.
8. 12½ percent of the amount by which net income exceeds 6 percent of stockholders' equity
9. 15 percent of net income (plus minority interest in net income less variable compensation and interest on long-term debt) less 7 percent of invested capital
10. 20 percent of bonus net income (net income less 6 percent of capital stock and surplus for current and preceding years plus provision for B bonus fund)
11. The amount by which net earnings before taxes plus 10 percent of invested capital exceed $10 million
12. 12 percent of net earnings after deducting 6 percent of net capital
13. 3 percent of the amount by which net income exceeds 6 percent of capital investment
14. 2½ percent of the total combined salaries of plan participants multiplied by the percentage points that consolidated income exceeds 35 percent of capital employed—to a maximum of 35 percent of total combined salaries of plan participants
15. 3 percent of the first $15 million net income plus 5 percent of net income exceeding $15 million
16. 6 percent of net income, maximum equal to 25 percent of aggregate paid dividends on common stock
17. 6 percent of the amount by which consolidated pretax earnings exceed 10 percent of shareholder's equity

Fig. 59. Short-Term Incentive Fund Formulas

From Ellig. Bruce, *Executive Compensation—A Total Pay Perspective* (New York: McGraw-Hill, 1982), p. 189.

PUT UP OR SHUT UP—
PAY-FOR-PERFORMANCE POLICIES

While it might be difficult to determine exactly how much Michael Jackson is worth to Pepsi, it is often just as tough to determine what a CEO is worth in leadership, expertise and contribution to the bottom line.

A recent Conference Board study revealed that 92 percent of American manufacturers have annual incentive plans for their managers and executives, ranging from an average of 57 percent of annual salary for CEOs to about 20–25 percent for low level managers. Obviously, in such cases, the annual bonus is a major part of the compensation package. Merit increases in salary averaged only 7 or 8 percent.

Research on the relationship between compensation and performance has yielded contradictory results. Whether or not top executives are earning their keep depends largely on how you measure their performance.

A common problem. Often, management incentive plans are merely clever ways to deliver predetermined compensation. It may appear as if the bonus is linked to performance, but in reality it is tied to a measure that is fairly easy to predict so employee and firm know precisely what it will come to. In this case, a bonus is not an incentive at all, but simply a different way to draw fixed income, or satisfy a bookkeeping or personal financial need.

In light of the increasing competitiveness of American firms, the notion of pay-for-performance has become more important than ever. And recently, efforts have been made to make compensation a direct reflection of actual performance.

Are there objective criteria to judge an executive's performance? Maybe. Most incentive programs are "formula-driven," relying on one or several financial measurements.

In most cases, these financial measures are applied to an overall bonus or award plan, where a group of key managers who are collectively most responsible for the firm's performance are compensated accordingly to that performance. If you become part of such a plan, take a hard look at the appraisal methods used, with an eye toward fairness. Does this plan make sense to you? Do you believe it is an accurate reflection of performance? This could well become a critical factor in choosing between several job offers.

What is the fairest financial measure upon which to base an incentive program? Simple sales figures are inadequate because they don't reflect profit, which is of course, a better measure of success (see Fig. 59).

While profits are a better benchmark, it doesn't take into account mismanagement and other moves which might have weakened the long-term prospects of the firm and/or its stock price.

434

How about the stock price, then? Is it a more accurate reflection of the state of the company? Of course not. Over the short-term stock prices have more to do with market expectations than performance. Besides, stock-related performance compensation can make for a bizarre turn of events.

For example, if an executive's mismanagement contributes to the firm's desirability as a takeover target, which in turn drives up the stock price, he may be rewarded with a higher bonus for doing a lousy job. The shareholders may get a one-time windfall, but due to the ineptness of the executive, they are probably losing out on a better return over the long run had he kept the firm strong.

Return on equity (ROE) appears to be the most accurate financial method of gauging performance, according to a 1985 analysis by Louis Brindisi of Booz, Allen and Hamilton. For over a decade, he says, management compensation has been tied to earnings per share (EPS)—85 percent of short term plans and 75 percent of long term plans were tied to EPS. But this approach penalizes executives for implementing strategic programs such as divestitures and asset redeployment which may lower EPS but in the end increase the return on equity (ROE).

A company's overall performance is usually the result of a team effort, and as in sports, the team might not fare well, while one or two stars stand out. How can I get my just desserts, even if the company hasn't done as well?

Needless to say, incentive plans are inherently unfair because the gap in the incentive between the best performer on the team and the worst performer is likely to be very narrow or nonexistent, because they are part of the group compensated under the same formula.

What about performance appraisals? There are all sorts of methods, and they are generally used to evaluate lower level management, and in cases where the job has less of a direct impact on profits. But performance appraisals are either too subjective or provide inaccurate evaluation methods.

Many firms have some kind of individualized performance-based incentive program. The trouble is, that it comprises a very small percentage of overall compensation.

Split the difference. A fresh concept has emerged marrying the incentive plan approach to the performance approach. The incentive plan uses its formulae to determine a benchmark "total bonus." Then, each individual member covered by the plan is evaluated individually, and the bonus he is given is determined according to his performance "score" in relation to the grade of others. This is not too different from the curving of test scores in college, where your overall score—along with how well you did relative to the rest of the class—determined your grade.

If you are in a position to have a direct impact on your company's overall profitability and competitive position, you will want to tie your compensation to performance.

THE GOLDEN PARACHUTE

So-called "golden parachutes" are now the most lucrative form of executive compensation package for top executives.

What is a "golden parachute"? Basically, its a provision in a management contract that guarantees a cash settlement if the company changes hands. Hence the sexy term which implies that being tossed out—or bailing out—of the firm can be profitable.

Why do companies agree to them? Two reasons: first, in order to remain competitive in attracting qualified top management. Today, this kind of protection against the onslaught of mergers and acquisitions is considered necessary by top-notch executives.

Second, as an anti-takeover provision. Golden parachutes can be so rich that the costs serve to deter all but the most determined takeover artists.

Bendix   William Agee, chairman   **$4 million**
Agee resigned in wake of takeover by Allied, February 1983.

Esmark   Donald Kelly, chairman   **$2.7 million**
Kelly resigned after takeover by Beatrice, May 1984.

Revlon   Michel Bergerac, chairman   **$36 million**
Bergerac resigned after hostile takeover by Pantry Pride, November 1985.

Beatrice   Six top executives   **Exceeded by $15 million**
The six were displaced by a leveraged buyout by Kohlberg, Kravis, Roberts & Co.

Pabst   Seven top executives   **Total of $2 million**
The seven resigned (2) or were fired (5) after takeover by S&P Co., early 1985. S&P sued to block payments, settled out of court in February 1986.

International Harvester Archie McCardell, chairman   **$600,000**
McCardell resigned in May 1982.

Fig. 60. A few golden payouts.
ARTHUR EVES/INSIGHT

436

How widespread are they? Very. A 1982 study by Ward and Howell International showed that 40 percent of the Fortune 1000 protect their top officers. The golden parachute payouts range from several hundred thousand dollars to more than $5 million. In 70 percent of the companies, the payout exceeds $1 million and in 63 percent, covers two or more executives.

Pros. It is tough to get the best top management without protecting him or her, especially if the firm is perceived as vulnerable to a takeover.

Indeed, most believe a good manager is entitled to some protection in that case.

Managers, free from the worry and panic that a takeover attempt brings, can analyze the situation on its merits rather than in terms of their own financial security.

Cons. The job of the top manager is to protect the interests of his company and its shareholders. He shouldn't need added inducements to do just that.

Many critics believe that the executive with a golden parachute sees himself in a "no-lose" situation, and in some cases may be better served by allowing the company to change hands and cashing out, even though it is not in the best interests of the shareholders. *In short: if, upon losing the takeover fight you get a multimillion-dollar payout, you might be tempted to skip the battle and take the money and run.*

Who gets them? At the beginning, golden parachutes went to the CEO, period. No longer. More companies are extending them to lower ranking executives. Some large companies cover over 200 key executives, and parachutes for fifty or sixty are no longer unusual.

Must the executive leave or be forced out for a golden parachute to be activated? Not necessarily. In some cases they are in effect even if the executive quits voluntarily at the point of takeover or a later date. In some parachute clauses, an executive is entitled to a payout even if he remains as a consultant or interim manager. And some even permit an executive to receive a payout if he finds another job at another firm before he leaves his current one; this is called "double dipping."

Must the firm be taken over for the golden parachute to be activated? Here again, the answer is "not necessarily." Some contracts provide for activation if an acquirer purchases a certain percentage of the stock or if the majority of the board of directors change.

When are they enacted? Increasingly, they are put in place as part of the initial compensation negotiation with the executive. But many are enacted only in response to a takeover attempt.

Is the government stepping in? Yes. Congress got into the act by attempting to limit the size of the payouts. An excessive payment to an exec displaced by a merger or aquisition is defined by Congress as three or more times the average annual salary over his last past five years of employment. If the parachute exceeds that limit, the executive is taxed 20 percent on the excess. Of course, by formulating limits, Congress has legitimized golden parachutes that fall within the guidelines. As for "excessive" parachutes, some superstar executives have compelled their companies to fit the bill for the extra tax.

The SEC is recommending that golden parachutes be prohibited once a tender offer begins, and that they be described in detail in proxy statements to shareholders, and voted on at shareholders meetings.

Are they likely to continue? Yes, as long as they work. On the other hand, they have triggered a string of lawsuits by shareholders and acquiring companies alike. It appears likely that court rulings will clarify their legal status, although to date most parties have settled out of court. (In many such settlements the golden payouts are reduced.)

Depending on the outcome, golden parachutes will either proliferate even faster, or slowly diminish.

Should a golden parachute be on your negotiation agenda? Executive recruiters are reporting that upper level executives are increasingly reluctant to take a job without a golden parachute. And it should at least be food for thought when negotiating your next employment contract.

29
FILLING OUT THE PACKAGE: BENEFITS AND PERKS

The combination of a rapidly changing business environment and tax reform have resulted in an overall shrinkage in employee benefits and perks. However, the more important ones have survived, along with some interesting innovations and new benefits more suited to the current lifestyle.

According to a recent survey conducted by the U.S. Chamber of Commerce, the average firm reporting figures pays benefits which equal 36.6 percent of the payroll, or an average of $7,582 per employee. The figures varied with the firm, ranging from 18 percent to more than 65 percent of the payroll.

At the same time, slower economic growth has resulted in the curtailment of the more extravagant and wasteful fringe benefits enjoyed by top executives during the booming sixties. The important ones have survived, and they are described in this chapter. You should be familiar with them, because perks are often as important a part of a compensation package as salary and bonus.

COMPANY INSURANCE PLANS

Since almost everyone gets company insurance, no one seems very excited about it. As David McLaughlin points out, insurance is bad news, it's boring, and everyone assumes big daddy is looking after it. Nevertheless, properly planned company-paid insurance coverage can represent a hefty "extra" to the executive. Generally the company contribution to executive insurance is not taxable income to the executive and is tax deductible to the corporation, making insurance a tax-favored compensation alternative all around.

From the point of view of the individual executive, however, company insurance plans are often inadequate, because they are usually geared to the group and directed to the needs of the average employee. In addition, group policies are often designed and revised in piecemeal fashion and, as a result, tend to be outdated or to offer poor coverage. Due to the tax-

What an ideal compensation package might include for a senior executive making $200,000 a year and a junior executive making $100,000 after the new tax law takes effect*:

	SENIOR EXECUTIVE	JUNIOR EXECUTIVE
Long-term Incentives		
Type of awards	Restricted stock, options, bonus shares	Restricted stock, options, bonus shares
Annualized value of awards (as percentage of salary)	45%	30%
Retirement Income		
As percentage of final 3-year average of total cash compensation	60%	50%
Supplemental retirement plan	Yes	No
Health and Welfare		
Supplemental medical coverage	Comprehensive	Some
Supplemental life insurance	$500,000	$300,000
Annual physical	Yes	Yes
Business-travel accident insurance	$200,000	$100,000
Supplemental disability insurance	$175,000	$60,000
Executive Perks		
Company car	Yes	Yes
Investment, tax counseling	Yes	Yes
Club memberships	Yes	Yes
Paid travel for spouse	Yes	No
Employment Contract Provisions		
Salary continuance	3 years	1 to 2 years
Bonus guarantee	3 years	1 year
"Golden parachute"	Yes	Yes

Fig. 61. An Executive Wish List for Benefits

Source: A.S. Hansen, Inc. Reprinted by permission of *The Wall Street Journal,*
© Dow Jones & Company, Inc. (1986).

*The tax reform law is being phased in over several years. These figures may not accurately reflect the actual rates for the current year.

favored status of insurance, however, many corporations are willing to negotiate individual policies geared to meet the needs of key executives. If you cannot negotiate a policy that is suited to your needs, you may be wise to see if you can do better by securing coverage on your own.

The value of any particular company policy is its "replacement" cost to you, i.e., what you yourself would have to pay out-of-pocket for equal coverage. A typical plan for an executive can run several thousand dollars. Of course, if the company coverage is company paid, by all means take it. But if the coverage is insufficient, supplement it with a private plan.

LIFE INSURANCE

Life insurance is intended to protect your family by providing for its financial needs in the event of your death. For a young executive, especially one with a family and with little opportunity so far to have built up net worth, life insurance is most essential as well as very costly.

The value of the coverage you require will be determined by the number and age of your children, by your spouse's age and by projected future family income needs, including cost of education for your children and the repayment of outstanding debts. Don't accept the company plan blindly. Beware, not all plans can be taken with you if you leave the firm. Consult an expert. Most of them recommend you carry private protection and that you update your coverage periodically.

MEDICAL INSURANCE

The great majority of corporations provide medical insurance to most of their employees, and the typical executive is usually covered under the group plan. The problem is that many executives find upon examining the corporate plan that, although the company often pays a high percentage (if not all) of the total premium, coverage is inadequate.

Basic medical coverage should survive the Tax Reform Act of 1986 intact.

In addition to basic medical plans, many companies have opted for a HMO plan (Health Maintenance Organization) which provides complete medical care for a fixed monthly fee. Because there is no further charge, such plans do encourage more regular visits and thereby enable physicans to practice more preventive medicine, reducing the chances—and costs—of serious illness. However, many executives resent the fact they may only be treated by physicians who are part of the plan. Some plans are experimenting with "linking up" so they can expand the options of members and also provide coverage for the traveling employee.

HMOs have grown fast. In 1982, there were 267 in the United States covering 11 million people, and the figure is certainly much higher today.

Ironically, there has been a general shrinkage in medical benefits due to rising costs. While some employers have curtailed benefits, others have increased the employee contribution to premiums or increased the deductible.

It is essential that you get all the details about a company's medical plan when negotiating your compensation package. For many executives, basic coverage is simply inadequate, and the time to negotiate for excess coverage or a supplemental plan is when you are bargaining for a package. If you are part of a two-career marriage, you must take your spouse's coverage into account. Sometimes, it pays to drop one or the other; sometimes one can supplement the other. Remember: if you opt to refuse or drop a medical plan, it may be tough to get back in.

DISABILITY INSURANCE

Disability insurance may be paid as sick-leave pay, short-term disability, or long-term disability, depending on the length of illness. Social Security benefits and workmen's compensation are collectible in the event of extended sick leave. Company coverage, however, is usually limited, and you should study plans to determine if sufficient protection is provided. Avail yourself of maximum coverage offered, but if it is limited and your salary is high, consider subscribing to a policy on your own. Amounts earned as sick pay from the company are considered fully taxable income to the executive. However, payouts on a private policy are not subject to tax.

THE COMPANY PENSION PLAN

Compensation provisions for retirement are clearly an important part of the pay package. The value to the executive in terms of replacement cost is extremely high, because the coverage provided by most company plans would be a substantial expense if the individual were to carry it alone. In any case, many qualified plans are actually company paid. Nevertheless, you can expect that the company pension plan, which, unlike other compensation forms, cannot by law discriminate in favor of the executive, will be inadequate to meet your retirement needs (usually calculated as some percentage of preretirement income).

THE STRUCTURE OF A PENSION PLAN

The pension plan is a very complicated arrangement, and even compensation planners are advised not to construct a program without the advice of specialists. Its complexities notwithstanding, you are well advised to carefully scrutinize the provisions of the corporate pension plan long before your retirement is due, and plan ahead if the coverage is inadequate. When reviewing the plan, consider the following points:

ELIGIBILITY REQUIREMENTS How do you qualify to take part in the plan? Usually there is some minimum employment period before you can participate.

THE FORMULA Is your payout a percentage of annual earnings, a career average, or some final average (say, total pay over the last three to five years)? Does it take the number of years of service into account? Is there a maximum payout? Beginning in 1987, companies won't be able to consider annual salary that exceeds $120,000 in their qualified plan calculation of final average salary.

COVERED EARNINGS Do bonuses count as earnings? IRS guidelines discourage the inclusion of the bonus as part of earnings for the purposes of a pension plan (as this would unfairly discriminate in favor of an executive), but some companies are able to argue the point effectively and include at least a portion of bonus payments as earnings.

CREDITED SERVICE What periods of your employment are considered "credited" in terms of the pension? Your total years with the company, or only those years in which you actually participated in the company plan? What about leaves of absence? What if there is a company merger? Is there an upper limit on the number of years that can be counted as credited service?

WHO PAYS? Is the plan contributory or company paid? If you are required to contribute, how much will it cost you? If employee contributions are voluntary, how much can you contribute?

VESTING You are not automatically entitled to the monies in your pension fund. Depending on your years of credited service, you are entitled to none, a percentage, or all of your pension. In some circumstances, you can lose all or part of your right to the funds if you leave the company.

RETIREMENT AGE If you want to retire before 65, what provisions are there for an earlier retirement age?

PAYOUT Is it guaranteed for life, or at least for a minimum period? What if you become disabled before retirement? If you die before retirement or after retirement, are there special provisions governing the payment of your pension to beneficiaries?

NON-QUALIFIED PENSIONS Because of the latest tax limitations on qualified plans, many executives are supplementing them with other pension arrangements. However, qualified pensions must be pre-funded by law; the company segregates those funds. Supplemental plans don't come with that kind of protection and in some cases are no more than a promise to pay out the benefits when the time comes. To secure these extra pension benefits, try to make a trust arrangement, locking in the nestegg.

PROFIT SHARING PLANS

As the name implies, profit sharing plans relate employee compensation to company profitability. In most plans, the employee receives a share of profits determined by a certain percentage of his base salary. There are three common plans:

- *cash profit sharing plans*, commonly used in banking establishments, in which some annual payout is made to the employee
- *profit sharing retirement plans*, commonly used in younger corporations in place of a pension plan, in which payout is deferred to provide retirement income
- *thrift or savings plans*, commonly used as a supplemental pension plan, in which payout is deferred much the same as in a profit sharing retirement plan

EVALUATING A PROFIT SHARING PLAN

To evaluate a particular plan, consider the following:

CONTRIBUTIONS TO THE PLAN   Who makes them? When? What is the rate of contribution? Are contributions based on straight salary, or salary plus bonus? Are employee contributions voluntary or mandatory? Is there an earnings maximum? What is the choice of investment vehicles?

VESTING AND SETTLEMENT PROVISIONS   When are you vested in the plan? Do you stand to lose the monies if you lose your job? How is payout made? What will be the tax consequences of payout timing?

VALUE OF THE PLAN   Depending upon the contribution rate, the profitability of the investment vehicle, the period of participation, and the rate of growth of the executive's compensation, a profit sharing plan can be an important factor in net worth growth. As McLaughlin puts it, "profit sharing is a big compounded earnings game. The trick is to get as much money as possible into the tax-sheltered trust in your early years."*

THE INVESTMENT VEHICLE   Should you keep your money in a fixed-income trust fund, a conservative mutual fund, a riskier stock fund, or some combination thereof? One common option is to invest in the corporate stock. The investment results will in large measure determine the real value of your settlement.

WITHDRAWAL PRIVILEGES   The advantage of profit sharing plans over any pension fund is that *some* profit sharing plans grant withdrawal

---

*From David J. McLaughlin, *The Executive Money Map* (New York: McGraw-Hill, 1975), p. 11.

privileges, usually under restricted conditions. Also, since most pension funds allow withdrawal only of contributions made by the corporation, any personal contributions to such a fund must be considered forced savings.

DEFERRED COMPENSATION PLANS

WHY?

Deferring payment of *currently* earned compensation is a means of timing income gains to minimize tax liability. According to the tax principle of "constructive receipt," you are not liable to the IRS until payment is actually made, even though the money was earned at some earlier date. In the typical plan, the payout, usually in cash, stocks, or a combination of both, is made at intervals over a period of years or deferred until retirement, when the executive anticipates a substantial reduction in income and, therefore, in taxes. The latter type of deferred compensation plan is a valuable alternative to the executive who has had to forfeit pension benefits when changing jobs.

WHY NOT?

For obvious reasons, deferred compensation plans, particularly those that do not invest deferred earnings, have received some mixed reviews from financial advisors.

THE BUCK-IN-THE-HAND THEORY PREVAILS   Deferred compensation is *current* income intentionally held back for future payout. If double-digit inflation returns, postponement of payment cannot be justified *unless* the deferred income is invested wisely for the deferral period. If not, you lose not only a pecentage of the current dollar value of that income due to inflation, but also potential interest or investment income.

THE TAX SITUATION IS UNRELIABLE   The tax laws have been changing virtually every year. With tax policy so closely tied to the economic climate and national politics, you cannot count on the regulations remaining the same over time.

YOU RISK PARTIAL OR TOTAL LOSS OF THE DEFERRED INCOME Corporations are not obliged to put aside actual funds equal to your deferred earnings. Usually their commitment amounts to no more than an entry on a ledger sheet. If the company should go bankrupt, your monies are not guaranteed.

FUTURE VALUE INCENTIVE PLANS:
TAKING STOCK

Stock ownership programs fall generally into the category of long-term incentives as opposed to short-term incentives like cash, because they are intended to build net worth rather than support an executive's immediate living costs and needs.

Herein lie the executive's best opportunities for substantial capital accumulation and net worth growth. Most of these plans have two things in common:

The executive is given an option to purchase shares of company stock at a set price over a period of time, usually five to ten years.

Remember, a stock ownership plan always has an investment component. Even if you do not contribute any of your own funds, the value of your *holdings* will be tied to a measure subject to fluctuation. Indeed, if the award involves real stock or special stock (which mimics the performance of actual stock), you are playing the Wall Street game, like it or not. So when you are considering such a plan, don't just ask yourself, "Is this a good compensation deal," but also "Is this a good investment?" Many an executive has walked away from the bargaining table with a fabulous stock plan, only to have the stock price suffer a sharp decline in value, taking his net worth down with it.

Qualified stock options was so named because the difference between the option price and the sale price was taxed at capital gains rates. Certain regulations have to be met, including holding the stock for at least a year.

However, under the Tax Reform Act of 1986, capital gains treatment are taxed like ordinary income, so the major benefit over non-qualified plans has been eliminated.

One important advantage does remain: under the qualified plan, you pay tax only when the stock is sold; you pay nothing when you exercise the option.

Nonqualified stock option (a.k.a. unqualified stock option). This plan follows the basic theme of the qualified option, except the terms are changed: The price is set at current market value *or* at a discount from market price, and the option can be exercised over a ten-year period.

Under the new tax law, nonqualified options are taxed twice; when the options are exercised and again when the stock is sold. *The Wall Street Journal* advises that the best way to participate in a nonqualified stock option plan involves tying in to a "cash offset" which provides the executive with the cash needed to pay the tax when the option is exercised. Such offsets are usually formula-driven.

Performance option. Rights to purchase stock can be exercised only when the executive has met predetermined performance goals.

Variable-priced options. Depending on certain conditions, such as market appreciation or corporate performance, the option price may drop below the price set at date of grant.

Tax-offset options. When the executive exercises his option, the tax liability, incurred as a result of profits made on the appreciation in value of the option since date of grant, is offset by a cash payment made to the executive.

Tax-offset options are especially important in light of the Tax Reform Act which affects nonqualified incentive plans and eliminates favorable capital gains treatment.

Formula value option. The award price is set not at market price, but according to some formula (for example, book value). The company has the right to repurchase shares at the same rates determined by the formula.

FVS is often used when top management believes that a formula can more effectively tie executive stock awards to performance than publicly traded stock can.

Stock appreciation rights (SARs). A modified version of the nonqualified stock option plan, SARs entitle the executive to choose to receive the appreciation in market value of the option in cash *or* in stock, or both, in lieu of exercising the option. There is no investment cost to the executive, and gains are charged to corporate earnings.

Phantom stock (a.k.a. fictional stock units). This plan is commonly a simulated option. The executive is granted fictional stock units valued at the actual market price of a company share, and he receives the appreciation in market value over the term of the plan and, in some cases, also and/or the accrued dividend equivalents or in some cases, the total market price. Profits can be received in cash, real stock, or both. The unit value is taxed to the executive upon payout.

Book units (a.k.a. formula value grants). This plan is like the phantom stock option, but the stock units are granted at book value, not market value, and appreciation is paid on book value as well. The advantage of this plan over phantom stock is that value of the units is independent of market fluctuations, yet the executive benefits from actual gains in profits.

Stock purchases. Stock purchase plans grant the executive the opportunity to purchase over a period of time actual shares of corporate stock, usually at a discount from market price and/or with a loan arranged by the corporation.

A stock purchase plan differs from a stock option in that the latter plan extends over a longer term. Purchase plans usually involve purchases over regular intervals, with price determined at the time of purchase. By contrast, stock options involve a set price and can be exercised at any time before expiration.

Book purchases (a.k.a. formula value purchases). The executive has the right to purchase stock at book value, not market value, and the stock is subject to repurchase by the corporation at the same formula value.

Performance shares. The executive receives a grant of stock units that convert to actual stock contingent upon the achievement of specific and predetermined performance goals to be accomplished over a set time period, typically three to six years. Performance is measured by appreciation in book value, earnings per share, or return on investments. The employee may elect to receive the award in actual stock, cash, or both. This is a popular version of combination-type incentive plans in which both the amount of the award and the value of the award are variable depending upon corporate performance and stock market appreciation. Such arrangements are popular with corporations, because if goals are met, the executive, the shareholders, and chief officers alike are apt to be pleased with results.

Performance units. Unlike performance shares, performance units are granted at an assigned dollar value not related to current market price, and if performance objectives are met, the executive earns the value of the award in cash or equivalent shares of stock.

Restricted Stock Plans. A conditional transfer of stock. A restricted stock plan is an arrangement whereby the executive receives an outright grant of stock at no cost, but contingent upon his continued employment. The restriction: The stock is nontransferable and subject to forfeiture for a set period of time. Restricted stock plans are especially useful as an up-front bonus or as part of a "golden handcuff" program. Restricted stock can be a way of giving a retired executive something of value, while giving him a disincentive to help the competition or harm his old company in any way.

PERKS: THE PRIVILEGES OF POWER

Perquisites are those little extras that can add up to a lot—or to nothing. In many instances, the true value of a particular perk is measurable in status rather than in dollars and cents, but in the hierarchical corporate world, power and prestige are both valuable tools and valued rewards that come with the upper territory.

Executive perks have been on the decline since the Deficit Reduction Act of 1984 limited depreciation and tax credits on company cars. The Tax Reform Act of 1986 goes further because it reduces deductibility of travel and entertainment, and makes direct compensation more attractive by lowering personal tax rates.

According to a survey by Growth Resources, the value of chief executive perks declined 20 percent from 1984 to 1985. Seventy-eight percent of CEOs still drive company cars; half have company club memberships; and 75 percent have supplemental insurance. Twenty-five percent can get a favorable loan through the company and legal and financial counseling.

THE PERQUISITE PREREQUISITE

To determine what a perk is really worth to you, consider whether it can be converted to a cash benefit and whether it provides you with something that you would purchase for yourself, at greater cost.

TOP-OF-THE-LINE PERKS

Usually reserved for the top corporate ranks, these perks are particularly valuable in that they are designed to stimulate the growth of net worth.

COMPANY LOANS   A timely low-interest, or even no-interest, long-term loan can give the executive the leverage he needs to make an investment that can in turn yield substantial amounts of capital. The loan may be arranged by the company and financed through a third party, or may be funded directly by the corporation. In either case, be clear on the terms of the loan. It *does* have to be paid back *whether or not* your investment is lucrative.

PERSONAL ESTATE PLANNING AND FINANCIAL COUNSELING
The personal financial concerns of a successful, busy executive can themselves be quite time-consuming. Recognizing that fact, corporations have begun to provide company-paid financial counseling to those executives whose already sizable incomes and net worth warrant such attention. Of course, the real value of such counseling depends to a large extent upon the quality of the advice—and much of it is less than "expert." Nevertheless, *good* advice can be invaluable, and this particular perk, which is low-cost to the company, is one whose popularity is growing.

THE COMPANY CAR   The number-one transportation perk provides convenience and, if properly packaged—in the body of Cadillac, for instance—a symbol of status as well. Especially for the executive who might

In this example, participants in the FVS plan are top executives in a venture business unit of a large, diversified public company. The venture has just become profitable.

The measure chosen for the formula to value the FVS is return on investment (ROI), since the parent is evaluating the venture's success on the basis of its return relative to alternative investments. An ROI of 15% or more is desired by the end of 5 years.

The initial value of the stock to be issued is $1 for every percentage point of ROI. The stock will appreciate or depreciate according to this formula:

Years 1 & 2   5 percentage points up or down for every point of ROI above or below 5%.

Years 3 & 4   4 percentage points up or down for every point of ROI above or below 10%.

Years 5–10   4 percentage points up or down for every point of ROI above or below 15%

When the stock is issued, ROI is at 2% and produces an initial stock value of $2.00. ROI and resulting stock values for the 10-year period are as follows:

					End of Year					
	1	2	3	4	5	6	7	8	9	10
ROI	6%	9%	9%	15%	19%	21%	24%	22%	25%	25%
Stock growth	5%	20%	(4)%	20%	16%	24%	36%	28%	40%	40%
Stock value	$2.10	$2.52	$2.42	$2.90	$3.37	$4.18	$5.68	$7.27	$10.18	$14.25

On the basis of these facts, an executive who bought a share of stock for $2 at the plan's outset would have a $12.25 gain on that share after 10 years—an average annual increase of 21.7%. After the first 5 years, the annual increase would be 11.0%, followed by average growth of 33.4% over the next 5 years.

So the return on the stock would parallel the parent's results from the business unit relative to the parent's expectations. During the first 5 years, when the unit produces a steady rise in ROI toward the company's goal of 15%, the stock experiences moderate growth (11% a year). During the next 5 years, when the unit begins to realize its potential, the executive is rewarded at a rate (33.4%—the growth in stock) that would be difficult to achieve from alternative investments.

Now suppose that after 5 years the FVS may be sold back to the company or converted to the company's publicly traded stock at the ratio of their prices when the FVS was transferred. At transfer, the FVS was worth $2 while the publicly traded stock was priced at $20; thus the conversion ratio becomes 10 shares of FVS for 1 share of public stock. At the end of 5 years, the common stock is trading at $38.50, while the FVS has a value of $3.37 (see table above).

If the executive chooses to convert at that point, he swaps 10 shares of FVS worth $33.70 for 1 share of common stock worth $38.50. The common stock is worth more than the FVS because its price has risen faster. If the executive wishes to cash out the stock, it makes sense for him to convert the FVS into common stock first and then sell it on the open market.

However, if the executive expects his business unit to grow at a faster rate than it has grown thus far (due to strong market position, cost efficiencies, and so forth), he or she may choose to hold onto the stock to realize the appreciation that is unlikely to occur in the parent's more mature stock.

Another example of how formula value stock works is an incentive stock option granted for business-unit stock. Again, begin with the set of facts outlined above and the granting of an option when the stock's fair market value is $2.00. The option has a 10-year term and can be exercised either when a 15% ROI is achieved or 5 years have passed, whichever comes first.

Since the fourth year ROI is 15%, the option can be exercised at the end of the fourth year. If the executive exercises the option any time after that but before the end of the ninth year and if he or she sells the stock at the end of the tenth year, the executive will realize $11.80 per share after tax ($14.25 minus a capital-gains tax of $2.45) on a $2 investment.

Fig. 62. Illustration of Formula Value Stock Plan

Reprinted, by permission of the publisher, from "Executive Compensation: Taking Long-Term Incentives Out of the Ivory Tower," by Claudia Zeitz Poster, p. 24, *Compensation Review*, Second Quarter 1985, © 1985 American Management Association, New York. All rights reserved.

otherwise be unable to afford a second car, it can be an attractive part of a pay package. There is no cash outlay for the executive, and any later costs tend to be lower due to the quantity discount rates charged to a corporation on purchase and service. The true value to you of the company car is commonly calculated at 25 percent of what it would cost you to purchase and support a privately owned car.

THE EXECUTIVE DINING ROOM: ALL YOU CAN EAT—TAX FREE
The executive dining room, intended as a place to conduct business over lunch, is another low- or no-cost convenience perk. The true value of such services will depend largely upon your personal eating habits. A fine company dining room whose basic fare is prime ribs and potatoes is not worth very much to a vegetarian executive. If you are not a fussy eater, but you do enjoy a good meal, you can probably save yourself as much as $10 a day, or about $2,000 a year by lunching in corporate facilities.

HOUSING   For the commuting executive who often works late into the evening, or for the executive who makes frequent business trips to a particular regional office, the executive apartment or hotel suite is a perk that makes sense. Otherwise, executive housing is not worth much, unless, of course, it can be utilized as a getaway or resort—in which case it is a high-status item.

CLUB MEMBERSHIPS   In suburban areas, the country club usually offers the best facilities for business entertaining, and corporations will pay membership fees for some ranking officers. In urban environments, membership in the "luncheon" club—university clubs, athletic clubs, or exclusive social clubs—is a popular perk. The higher your status, of course, the more prestigious the club. Here again, the company will foot the bill for the initiation fee and monthly dues, although day-to-day expenses are usually limited. These clubs offer a variety of facilities—dining rooms, libraries, various athletic facilities, exercise rooms, and the like.

EXCESS MAJOR MEDICAL INSURANCE AND HEALTH CARE With rising costs of medical care, this perk is increasingly popular. The company directly reimburses the executive for all medical (and often dental) expenses not already covered by his existing insurance policy—and there is nothing deductible. Many corporations are also offering free medical checkups, vaccinations, and the like. Depending upon the executive's status, the checkups can be very thorough and elaborate, sometimes conducted by private physicians at posh health facilities.

PRODUCT PERKS

Most companies offer all their employees some privileged access to the corporate product or service. Depending upon the nature of the business—be it discounts on company merchandise to employees of a major retailer, or special traveling privileges to employees of an airline—these perks can be of some genuine value even to the executive.

THE NEW PERKS

HEALTH PROGRAMS

The work force has become more health and fitness conscious, and is growing progressively older. To insure that aging executives remain healthy ones, several new perks have been instituted:

Fitness facilities   While exercise programs have been around for some time, the facilities have become more elaborate, with many large firms providing full workout facilities on the premises, or nearby.

Diet programs   Among the fastest growing perks, top management is convinced that employee morale and productivity can be improved, and medical costs lowered through proper diet and nutrition.

Disturbance bonuses   One-time benefits to assist the executive with job relocation and other difficulties caused by taking the job.

452

"DOMESTIC PARTNERS"

Some firms have been experimenting with offering coverage to domestic partners. The employee must sign an affidavit that the two are unmarried but "share the common necessities of life." Given the divorce rate and the pain many associate with marriage (especially when children are involved), it is not uncommon for mature consenting adults to live together unmarried. Corporations used to discourage this, and certainly, it is still considered less-than-ideal behavior for a senior executive. But good management is nothing if not realistic, and they know that executives perform better when things are good at home. If this cohabitation situation applies to you, and your "partner" has inadequate coverage, make a discreet inquiry.

CHILD CARE

Child care has become a very important perk for two reasons. First, "the baby boom echo": the large number of children born after World War II have grown and are now having families of their own, producing a bulge in the birth rate. Second, the rise of the two-career couple has meant that there is no parent at home during working hours to be with these children. Child care facilities on employee premises help relieve families of the burden of guilt as well as financial strains, and can be a major consideration in choice of job.

KIDNAP AND EXTORTION INSURANCE

Unfortunately, terrorism has become commonplace, and every executive traveling abroad on business should give the problem some thought. Many of the larger U.S. firms and multinationals insure their executives against terrorist acts. These policies usually provide funds should a ransom payment be demanded, as well as direct benefits to the family of a victim. Under such plans, insurance companies also provide anti-terrorism training and risk analysis for business trips abroad.

Companies are very discreet about such policies so as to not encourage terrorists to go after large ransoms by seizing employees. But the largest extortion-loss underwriter, Cassidy and Davis, claims 9,000 corporate clients covering millions of employers.

VACATIONS

THE VANISHING VACATION

In the life of a busy executive, the vacation seems to be a dying benefit: Fewer and fewer executives are exercising their option to take time off. A survey by Rene Plessner Associates of 210 executives earning between $50,000 and $75,000 per year revealed that almost 50 percent of them had not taken their allotted two- or three-week vacation time last year. Yet, judging by the high suicide rate among their peers, these middle managers, more than anyone else, probably need to take time off.

NEW TRENDS

Without a doubt, many executives are suffering from a syndrome that impairs peak performance. Known to the medical community as dysponesis, it's known to most of the rest of us as being burned-out. The traditionally prescribed antidote to the strain of too much activity has been rest, usually taken in the form of a vacation. But in recent times the traditional work schedule—50 weeks on/2 weeks off—has come under scrutiny, and ideas for alternative schedules have emerged:

THE FOUR-DAY WEEK   A number of corporations, particularly in the publishing and advertising fields, have already instituted some form of a four-day work week, an alternative recommended by some experts as a way to provide relief from the increasing stress of daily corporate life. The four-day week generally does not reduce the number of working hours, but redistributes the same hours over a four- or four-and-a-half-day week, thus extending the weekend to two and a half or three full days. Some companies juggle the hours so schedules alternate: five days one week, four days the next. Such extended-weekend scheduling is particularly popular during the summer months, which in some businesses tend to be comparatively slow anyway.

LESS PAY, MORE LEISURE   In February, 1979, *Psychology Today* magazine reported a study in which workers were given the hypothetical choice of receiving a 2 percent pay hike or a reduction in work time (10 minutes less per day, 50 minutes less per week, 5 extra days off per year, *or* 1 week earlier retirement per each year worked). Eighty-five percent surveyed chose shorter work time over increased pay; more than half of those opted for the additional 5 days off per year. When the figures were raised from 2 percent to 10 percent more pay and to 10 percent more time, 41 percent still chose to have more time.*

---

*Fred Best, "Preferences on worklife scheduling and work leisure tradeoffs" (U.S. Department of Labor: *Monthly Labor Review*, June, 1978), pp. 31–37.

SABBATICALS   An increasing number of executives are opting to take extended periods of time off (one month; six months; even a year or longer) from work for doing their own thing. In a provocative book by Bernard Lefkowitz, *Breaktime: Living without Work in a Nine to Five World* (New York: Hawthorn, 1979), the author looks into the lives of 100 people who have opted to stop working altogether. While these people do not represent a major shift in social trends, their increasing presence in our society is a further indication of the move toward a new work ethic. For the majority of executives, a permanent vacation is not a desirable option, but for a growing number, the mid-career sabbatical is an important time of rejuvenation and reevaluation.

WHEN CAN A VACATION BE HARMFUL?

- When it is poorly organized and disappointing as a result
- When it generates a sense of idleness and concomitant feelings of guilt
- When it forces too much unwanted contact with friends and/or relatives
- When it eliminates much-yearned-for privacy

Some psychologists maintain that a vacation under such conditions can actually create, rather than eliminate, stress. A remedy, of course, is to plan a vacation carefully to suit your real needs for rest. At least one writer on the subject maintains that for the genuine workaholic, even a planned vacation is likely to generate dis-ease and discomfort.

YOU AND YOUR VACATION

If you happen to cherish your vacation time either as a period of rest and relaxation for yourself or as an important opportunity to be with your family, then be aware of what the corporate vacation policy is—not just on paper, but in actual practice. Find out how many executives are actually taking allotted vacation time off, and if they are not, whether they are at least receiving their vacation pay for their overtime, or whether unused time is accrued in following years.

FLEXIBLE COMPENSATION

Flexible benefit programs allow employees to customize their compensation packages by permitting them to trade off between a number of benefit options like insurance benefits, cash payouts and vacation time.

Such plans have been around for over a decade, but they have entered the spotlight recently largely because of rising insurance costs. Cutting insurance costs usually means cutting benefits across the board.

Time off with pay
  Employment contract
  Liberalized vacation
  Work at home
  Disability
  Sabbatical
  Severance pay
  Outplacement assistance

Employee services
  Company product samples
  Automobile
  Chauffeured limousine
  Security system
  Parking—company premises
  Parking—other
  Aircraft
  Yacht
  Dining room
  Physical fitness
  Apartment/hotel
  Legal service
  Tax assistance
  Financial counseling

Healthcare
  Medical examinations
  Supplemental health care

Nonperformance awards
  Title
  Office
  Washroom
  Liberalized expense account
  Club membership
  Season tickets
  Credit cards
  Home entertainment
  Domestic staff
  Conventions
  First-class travel
  Personal escort
  Spouse travel expenses
  Business liability insurance
  Personal liability insurance
  Education for children
  Loan
Retirement
  ERISA supplement
  Full supplement
  Short-service supplement
  Deferral of pay
Survivor protection
  Business travel
  Assignment protection
  Key employee insurance
  Kidnap and ransom
  Term/permanent
  Split dollar
  Retired lives reserve

From *Executive Compensation—
A Total Pay Perspective* by
Bruce Ellig. Copyright © 1982 by
McGraw-Hill Book Company.
Reprinted by permission of the publisher.

In essence, the company is saying, "we can afford to spend x dollars on your benefits. *You* decide how you want us to use it." It is a clever way to induce employees to pay for all or a portion of base coverage, which they might have gotten for free under more conventional plans. But it also allows a healthy, young executive who might not require as much coverage to trade off for other benefits that are more useful. If anything, it has forced participants to think carefully about which benefits they truly need or want.

For companies, the reasoning is, "why should healthy and health-conscious employees have health insurance benefits as extensive as those who are older or in only fair health?"

The flexible benefit idea is catching on. According to a survey of 1,000 employers conducted by Peat Marwick and Mitchell in 1983, 39 percent of all respondents indicated that they had already implemented—or were in the process of implementing—a flexible benefit program. Another 50 percent said they were actively investigating the program.

TRENDS IN EMPLOYEE BENEFITS

Compensation specialists Jon Sutcliffe and Jay Schuster have identified many emerging trends. Among them:

- Employees are paying for more of their benefits.
- Benefits programs are being streamlined and simplified.
- Retirement plans are being examined for ways to cut costs.
- Cash compensation is becoming more important.
- Legitimate pay-for-performance methods are on the rise.
- Cost-of-living increases are out-of-favor.
- Bureaucratic expensive job evaluation programs are on the decline.
- Employees are trying to correct inequities in compensation among executives.
- Men still earn more than women.
- Strategic planners are getting involved in the structuring of long-term incentive programs.

FUTURE TRENDS

- Social Security benefits will be reduced.
- Fixed benefit retirement plans will diminish.
- Executives will be asked to pay a larger share of benefits.
- Profit-sharing will assume some of the burden now carried by retirement programs.
- Incentive programs will become the heart and soul of compensation programs, and evaluation methods will become more accurate and fairer.

30

MAKING YOUR BEST DEAL: THE BARGAINING TABLE

Now that you have a taste for what's on the table, go after your desires with a robust appetite.

WHEN?

Negotiate a new pay package when:

- you accept a new job
- you accept or decline a promotion
- you accept a division transfer
- you are called for a performance review

YOUR BARGAINING POSITION

The strength or weakness of your position depends upon:

- the uniqueness of your skills and qualifications
- your past performance and visibility
- supply and demand—how much the company needs you
- who sought out whom
- your current employment status
- the condition of the company

PREPARE BEFORE YOU BARGAIN

- Establish your income and net worth goals.
- Study company policy.

- Investigate the financial health of the company.
- Investigate existing compensation plans and policies of the corporation.
- Know the corporate operating style and philosophy.
- Investigate the going rate of executive pay for like positions.
- Investigate the company's record of meeting its bonus and incentive program payouts.

BARGAINING PROTOCOL

Timing is an important factor in successful bargaining. Know *when* to bring up compensation issue.

- Establish parameters early, but don't make compensation the big issue. Or:
- Don't bring it up at all, and when the question arises, turn it around: "Now that you mention it, what *is* the salary range for this job?"

Know when to drive a hard bargain.

- When you are sure the company wants you, i.e., when the employer has made a commitment, *push*.
- Don't put off for tomorrow what you can negotiate today: Get 'em while they are still smiling.
- Don't accept an offer on the spot: Think it over and push some more tomorrow.

Once bargaining begins, take an active role.

Be a glutton. Have confidence and shoot for the most. If you doubt you deserve what you want, you won't get it.

Never demand a plan that is not already part of the corporate compensation policy. Unless the circumstances are quite unique or unusual.

The higher the stakes, the more room to negotiate.

Compensation planners are, by training, sticklers for detail and tight-fisted. If they appear stingy, don't mind. They are only doing their job.

In compensation terms, an executive is defined not by title, but by his perceived value to the company. What counts is his net effect on corporate success and prosperity.

POINTS WORTH BARGAINING
FOR IN A NEW JOB

Salary. If they recruited you, you are worth a 25–50 percent cash increase; if you approached them, you are worth 10–15 percent more; if you are unemployed, you are not worth much more than your last salary, if that.

Long-term income plans. The *key* bargaining issues are capital accumulation plans. Salary range of a position is often predetermined, and beyond a certain latitude salary alone is not a negotiable point.

Pension and stock options. If a prospective employer has sought you, and if by leaving your present job you would sacrifice stock option or pension benefits, negotiate to replace them with comparable plans.

Severance. Ask for a severance package (one year's salary) *just in case*, especially if the financial future of the company is shaky or if a merger is imminent.

Company-paid relocation costs. A must item when negotiating a transfer.

Employment contract. A rule of thumb: If you make $40,000 plus, negotiate for a contract. Many experts advise, however, that if you are still in the formative years of your career, you will not want to tie yourself down to any one corporation too long. A two- or three-year contract would be maximum in that case. If a merger is looming on the horizon, then bargain for some formal commitment if that is what you want.

Company executive bonus plans. Request *at least* minimum participation for first year of new employment. Review carefully the precise details of the bonus formula, noting how it is applied and how rewards are administered in practice as well as in principle.

Promotions. If you are on a fast track, agree now upon a time schedule for your next promotion as well as upon the terms of compensation increase.

Perks. Inquire about company policy on perquisites, but *do not push* on this point.

MAXIMIZE YOUR TAX ADVANTAGE

Having a basic understanding of general tax principles helps to provide some framework within which to evaluate various compensation plans. Considering the complex tax consequences, you will want to plan your pay package to maximize your tax advantage. McLaughlin suggests you can do this in three ways:

Combine plans for maximum profit and minimum tax. Certain fringe benefits are virtually tax free or taxed at lower rates.

Time payout. Deferred compensation and stock option plans are two available modes that allow you to time receipt of gains to minimize tax liability on large sums of income.

Maximize allowable deductions. You are allowed deductions for charitable donations and medical expenses and the like, but you can also "shelter" additional income through investments designed for that purpose. The opportunities for sheltering income were drastically reduced under the Tax Reform Act of 1986, but there are still a few options worth exploring.

Most important: Get relevant tax advice from a competent professional.

EYE ON THE BOTTOM LINE

What is the true value of the award? What is the size of the award? What does it cost you in direct contributions, cash outlay, or financing?

What are the potential risks? Does payout depend upon company performance? Are earnings tied to the fluctuations of the stock market? What are the terms of the plan? When are you vested? Do you lose the right to any benefits if you lose or leave your job?
   You should know at least enough to ask the important questions by the time you are ready to bargain.

FOR MORE ON COMPENSATION

For a comprehensive, comprehensible tour of executive compensationland, read David J. McLaughlin's *The Executive Money Map* (New York: McGraw-Hill, 1975). Due to recent tax reforms, a few facts are dated, but, overall, McLaughlin provides valuable information and perspective on executive compensation as an aspect of both personal financial and career planning. I hope that Mr. McLaughlin will revise his book to reflect the tax revisions. The book is currently out of print. I hope that McLaughlin will offer a revised edition of this excellent volume.

Another excellent, more technical work is *Executive Compensation— A Total Pay Perspective* by Bruce R. Ellig (New York: McGraw-Hill, 1982).

Form 1

TOTAL COMPENSATION SUMMARY FORM

FOR _____

CURRENT INCOME _____

HISTORY

Year	Salary	Bonus Award Dollars	Bonus Award Percentage of Salary	Cash Profit Sharing Dollars	Cash Profit Sharing Percentage of Salary	Total Cash Compensation	Percentage Change	Comment
_____	$_____	$_____	_____%	$_____	_____%	$_____	_____%	_____
_____	_____	_____	_____	_____	_____	_____	_____	_____
_____	_____	_____	_____	_____	_____	_____	_____	_____
_____	_____	_____	_____	_____	_____	_____	_____	_____
_____	_____	_____	_____	_____	_____	_____	_____	_____

PROJECTIONS

_____	$_____	$_____	_____%	$_____	_____%	$_____	_____%	_____
_____	_____	_____	_____	_____	_____	_____	_____	_____
_____	_____	_____	_____	_____	_____	_____	_____	_____

SALARY RANGE   Minimum $_____   Midpoint $_____   Maximum $_____

SALARY INCREASE POLICIES

Merit increases   Size range_____% to _____%   Time guidelines_____

Promotion increases   Size range_____% to _____%   _____

BONUS AWARDS

Payout options   ☐ Current   ☐ Over _____ years   ☐ Deferred _____

Comments _____

Projected Bonus	Size		Assumptions/Requirements
	Dollars	Percentage of Salary	
Minimum	$ _____	_____ %	_____
Most likely	_____	_____	_____
High	_____	_____	_____

PERQUISITES/INCOME EQUIVALENTS _____

Type	Estimated Value	Imputed Income	Comment
Company car	$ _____	$ _____	_____
Parking	_____	_____	_____
Personal financial counseling	_____	_____	_____
Tax preparation assistance	_____	_____	_____
Excess medical	_____	_____	_____
Luncheon club	_____	_____	_____
....	_____	_____	_____
Country club	_____	_____	_____
....	_____	_____	_____
Executive physical	_____	_____	_____
Company dining facilities	_____	_____	_____
Housing benefit	_____	_____	_____
Spouse travel	_____	_____	_____
Tuition reimbursement	_____	_____	_____

PROTECTION _____

Type	Coverage	Personal Contribution Required	Imputed Income
Basic group life	_____	$ _____	$ _____
Supplemental life	_____	_____	_____
Accidental death and dismemberment	_____	_____	_____
All-risk accident	_____	_____	_____
Travel accident	_____	_____	_____
Comprehensive personal liability	_____	_____	_____
Long-term disability	_____	_____	_____
Hospital/surgical	_____	_____	_____
Major medical	_____	_____	_____
Dental	_____	_____	_____

Fig. 63. Compensation planning form

From *The Executive Money Map* by David J. McLaughlin.
Copyright © 1975 by McGraw-Hill. Used with the permission of
McGraw-Hill Book Company.

PART VII

THE OFFICE ARSENAL

"Civilization advances by
extending the number of important
operations which we can perform
without thinking about them."
Alfred North Whitehead

31

THE OFFICE OF
THE FUTURE

One of the hottest buzz words in managerial circles these days is "the office of the future." Trouble is, the office in question is here—if not in your work space, perhaps in that of your competitor. Office automation has fallen prey to a paradox that is common in our technological society: The technology is often available before there is sufficient market for it—before people are ready to accept it, or are even aware of it.

Almost every office function can be improved through the use of some form of machine or computer. And almost every one of these machines involves microprocessors, microcircuitry, or some other form of electronic wizardry such as "laser printing" and fiber optics. In the last decade, industrial productivity was up 90 percent, while office productivity rose only 4 percent. The office remains a holdout to space age technology.

WHAT IT IS

An office is essentially a work site where people go to interact with each other and the information network. Productivity involves the use of analytic, creative, intellectual, and communication skills.

The office of the future is a *concept* that involves the introduction of sophisticated new technologies to improve office communications, increase productivity, and motivate workers by increasing job satisfaction.

The office of the future is also a *tactic*. Used properly, it can provide a means for a company to get the jump on its competition.

Unfortunately, your first contact with "the office of the future" is not likely to include the above considerations. The term is most commonly used to describe a confusing and ill-defined collection of high-tech office machines currently being hyped by their vendors as every office worker's dream come true. In other words, "the office of the future" lives, in our minds and in the brochures, primarily as a *sales pitch*.

CAN YOU AFFORD TO IGNORE IT?

No way. All the hype aside, the introduction of automation in the office environment is an extremely significant development that will affect your job in several different ways, ranging from your specific responsibilities to methods and procedures—and, ultimately, to your overall performance and its relationship to the company's profits.

For those who can see through the fog generated by the hardware/software hard sell, the office of the future is a concept of major importance in modern management techniques. It doesn't take much technical training or vision to see the potential value of the new technologies, especially since we have been using them already in our homes, at the bank, etc. The question is when and how to implement these advances.

You'd better get with it. Sooner or later, everybody else will. There is no doubt that a well-planned and well-implemented move to office automation can give a firm a clear competitive edge over the nonautomated firms. And *the manager that spearheads such a move will probably score a few extra points when the office begins to hum with the sound of automatic printers and glow in the pale green light of video display terminals.* If the thought of that ambiance doesn't motivate you, then visions of reduced paperwork, fewer errors, lower costs, and swifter communications certainly should.

WHAT'S BEHIND THE RAPID GROWTH OF OFFICE AUTOMATION?

The lag in office productivity.

Technological innovation. Recently, competition for a share of the booming office equipment market has led to an astounding level of sophistication in design of such products.

Mounting economic and competitive pressures. Rising costs of goods, services, and labor have forced managers to look to previously unexplored regions for ways of cutting costs and staying competitive. The office, with its poor productivity, is prime territory for reducing costs.

The American love affair with gadgetry. If it beeps, buzzes, talks back, or makes pictures on the TV screen, it's simply irresistible. For many of us, price and cost-effectiveness just don't matter when we are faced with the chance to make our desks look like the flight deck of *Starship Enterprise.*

WHY IT'S NEEDED

Although the office of the future will initially cost companies a lot of money, it makes good sense, for several reasons.

The bulk of a manager's time is spent communicating. Phone calls, conferences, and originating and receiving correspondence eat up over 70 percent of the typical manager's day. Many of the executive timewasters are related in some way to the communication function. For example, the majority of phone calls are essentially one-way conversations made to convey information, requiring no immediate interaction with the person on the other end; still, many executives engage in chitchat. And about 70 percent of all business calls are not completed on the first try. Then there is the time it takes to travel to and from a meeting. The rapid, efficient management of information and communication strikes at the heart of what the office of the future is really about.

Offices are not very productive. The office is the last holdout to automation. Automated machinery is common in manufacturing plants. And kitchens across the nation are equipped with microprocessor-controlled microwave ovens. So how come you are still using that old adding machine and that awful file cabinet?

The office productivity situation has become very serious as a result of rising costs. An average business letter costs over five dollars to dictate, transcribe, and send. Reaching a business executive by phone during business hours will set your company back between $3.50 and $6.00. Filing (including misfiling) is a multimillion-dollar business. The average misfile costs $75. The misfile rate? One estimate is 3 percent and some experts put the rate as high as 20 percent. American business and governmental organizations are currently being drained by a "productivity leak" that is estimated to cost hundreds of millions of dollars each year.

Office equipment salespeople love to fire these numbers at you, then whip out their pocket calculators and show you how their gizmos will save you money by increasing productivity. In most cases they are on solid ground. Automated equipment can contribute significantly toward an improvement in office productivity.

Many white-collar workers don't like their jobs. Can you blame them? So much of the work is tedious. Repetitive. Routine. Dull. Rather than stimulating the workers, it creates sluggishness. And little time is left for the challenging and idea-oriented tasks that provide success and satisfaction.

With computers to take over a good deal of the tedium, much of the white-collar legion will be able to play it a bit more fast and loose. And to show more initiative.

This will work out fine, provided upper management cooperates and workers don't feel threatened by computers that do what *they* once did. The jury is still out on this one.

Office automation can be used as a tactical weapon. With gloves-off competition in the marketplace coming not only from other domestic firms, but from Asia and Europe as well, it's kill or be killed. And the battles are being fought in the fields of marketing, price cutting, and distribution. Managers are scrambling to force even a slight advantage. One way we can do that is to exploit the slight lead in computer technology enjoyed by American business. Here are a few strategies:

Accelerate new-product development. Automation allows such projects to be tightly coordinated between engineers, factory personnel, marketing and sales; everyone has instantaneous access to pertinent information.

Increase the return. An automated office can more accurately and rapidly monitor the marketplace and better estimate demand, competition, and the economic and regulatory environment.

Use heavy equipment more efficiently. "Smart" information systems can monitor and control machinery 24 hours a day so that it runs more efficiently.

Improve inventory controls and investment. With computer monitored inventory, you always know what you've got, what you need, what you will need, and where to find it.

Improve control of sales and service costs. For example, the sales force can use the information system to zero in on the most profitable customers and be prepared to discuss the most appropriate product. Order entry and paperwork, as well as service histories, can be handled more efficiently.

Market for less. If your office is automated, you stand on the threshold of the next revolution in sales and marketing: The customer will be able to view, order, and pay for products and services—all electronically, by conversing through his own terminal with the vendor's computer. In some areas, it's already possible. Many of the nation's largest banks offer electronic banking services which allow the customer to pay bills, transfer funds, buy CDs and securities and do financial planning, all through a personal computer without leaving home or office.

Serve new markets. Information management allows you to isolate specialized potential markets, opening opportunities that didn't exist before.

Build loyalty. If you make it easier for your customers to receive information, order and receive goods and services, they will enjoy doing business with you.

Open new distribution channels. Increasingly, goods and services are being sold via computer technology through systems such as on-line services and computerized telephone ordering systems.

Distribute faster, more accurately, and less expensively. You do it with computer-assisted dispatching, delivery mode selection, cost computation, etc.

Control cash better. Institute computerized cash flows, forecasts, and linkups with banks and customers.

Improve compliance with rules and regulations. Getting through the maze of government rules and regulations is a colossal task. And if you are challenged by a government agency, you had better be ready with records, test results, quality control data, and other documentation. Automation is a godsend in this area: you can order up this data faster than you can get a BLT from the corner deli.

WHAT YOU NEED TO KNOW ABOUT OFFICE AUTOMATION

Dealing with the changes brought on by the office of the future will soon be a critical part of your job. *If you get involved in the design and implementation of an automated system,* it could be a major career coup— or a nightmare. The office revolves around people, and *concern for the staff's feelings and needs is vital.* Equipment should fill needs, and one must be on guard against pushing solutions that don't address problems—office equipment overkill.

The flip side—learning to adjust to a job redefined by automation—is an even greater challenge. Managers and executives are especially threatened, since they regard computers and the like as tools used by clerks, secretaries, and the data processing people—not by the "decision makers," or "strategists," or managers. *However, if you know your way around, you can learn to exploit the equipment that's been laid before you* in order to free your mind to do the kinds of things that will place you on the cutting edge—to think, create, plan, and innovate.

That's why you must learn the basics regarding the *structure, function,* and *hardware* of the office of the future.

OFFICE AUTOMATION EQUIPMENT MAKES USE OF FIVE BASIC CAPABILITIES:

PROGRAMMABILITY   The set of instructions that tell the machines what to do and how to do it. Programs or sets of programs are usually referred to as software, i.e., a computer product other than hardware.

PROCESSING   Manipulation of the information the machine receives. Examples: mathematical computations, sorting, alphabetizing.

STORAGE   The capability of a computer to retain information in its memory, or to read information stored outside the machine (usually on tape or magnetic disc).

INPUT/OUTPUT   The capability of the machine to receive and send instructions and information. This is the phase that involves converting human logic and language into instructions understood by a computer, and vice versa.

ELECTRONIC TRANSPORT   The transmission of data by electronic methods. The form of the data may be impulses understood only by computers; or it may be the human voice, still images, or video. Means of transport include cable, telephone lines, microwaves, fiber optics; even satellite hookups may be involved.

HOW AUTOMATED OFFICE EQUIPMENT
USES THESE CAPABILITIES
TO SOLVE BUSINESS PROBLEMS

ELECTRONIC CONFERENCING   There are already several viable electronic alternatives to the face-to-face meeting. In addition to the telephone conference call, which is already commonplace, *closed circuit video conferences* are within reach. The simple telephone call can be electronically enhanced through the *simultaneous transmission of documents, graphics, photos, and other data*. Microwave and satellite transmission makes it possible to conduct such conferences involving a large number of people in many different locations worldwide.

DATA TRANSMISSION   We've come a long way from the pony express. In the late 1980s virtually all information will be transferred at the speed of light. But speed is only one aspect of effective information transfer. Computers have made the process more reliable than ever before. Miniaturization has brought input/output capabilities to the desk top. And since the entire transmission process saves labor through reduced time and errors, it can actually cut costs.

INFORMATION RETRIEVAL   Retrieval of important documents and data relating directly to productivity is now potentially a push-button affair. Managers need not spend hours tracking down problems and tracing errors, clarifying policies and regulations. Computerized external data bases make it possible for executives to access a wide range of specialized and general information from journals, news services, and statistical publications.

TRANSACTIONS   You are part of this process every time you use a charge card. The purchase or sale of goods and services is processed electronically and recorded in the appropriate place, with the appropriate parties receiving notification. Automation is rapidly becoming the modus operandi for virtually all types of consumer-related business transactions. It has resulted in a reduction in the paper flow that clerical workers are required to handle, and thus has increased their potential and their accuracy. It's no secret that because a credit card can input to a computer, plastic money is rapidly replacing paper.

PERSONAL COMPUTING The manager's primary work is not of a procedural or transactional nature. But the manager can use the automation at his disposal to aid in analysis, problem solving, research, and even decision making, planning, and implementation. With the advent of portable computers, salespersons, too, have been able to utilize the electronic resources of the home office by simple access over the phone. Even such routine managerial functions as dictation and editing of correspondence have benefited from automation through the introduction of advanced dictation and word processing equipment.

WORK AND ACTIVITY MANAGEMENT One of the most difficult managerial functions involves monitoring the progress of employees and projects. Office automation expands this capability in several ways:

Time management. Time management software can be very helpful in organizing tasks and reducing stress caused by unnecessary time pressures.

Monitoring of projects. The manager can assess the relevant data to see how the project is proceeding on a step-by-step, or even a daily, basis. The manager can then help solve problems and even input pertinent comments, information, and reminders.

Monitoring of facilities. Energy. Security. Machinery. And more.

WHAT WILL YOUR OFFICE NEED?

Unfortunately, most executives have little or no say as to how their offices will be equipped. Large corporations utilize purchasing agents and productivity experts to determine what kind of equipment to acquire. In smaller firms the situation is often worse, because this area is easily neglected. Often, the boss will buy a computer because the competition has a computer. Or because his buddies at the country club have computers for their businesses.

Then there are the old-timers, who believe that modern office technology is an elaborate hoax, designed primarily to separate the hard-working entrepreneur from his money. After listening to some of the salespeople in this business, I've come to believe that the old-timers are not totally wrong.

The key to intelligent purchasing is to determine just how much technology you really need, and how much is cost-justified. Using seven low-paid file clerks and an adding machine, instead of a computer, could be costing you dearly. But so will an office full of gadgets that are rarely, if ever, used. There are many firms out there eager to sell you everything but the electronic kitchen sink.

What follows is a very basic guide to the state of the art in office equipment and gizmos. We have reached the point in our civilization where it often takes longer for words to go from the writer's hand to the bookstore shelf than it does for a new product to go from designer to retail store. This means that practically all of the information regarding prices and models that I have before me will be severely out of date by the time you read this. For this reason I have decided not to review the specific makes and models. Instead, I have listed and described the major categories, all the while keeping an eye toward the future so you will know what to expect in the way of innovation.

32

THE COMPUTER

"By 1990, as much as 90 percent of all managers as well as clerical/administrative personnel in large organizations will be using computers and/or computerized devices." Or so predicts The Diebold Group, Inc.

The computer is the foundation of the office of the future. Saying that a piece of office equipment has been automated is almost always just another way of saying that it has been computerized. Computers, besides being able to accept, store, manipulate, and output information that you provide, can control other devices.

In many cases, the computer circuitry is built into the machine. For example, several new copiers have their own microcomputers to tell them when to stop or start, and whether to lighten or darken the copies. In other cases, computers control from the outside, as with heat and lighting systems that are kept at certain levels by a central computer. Virtually every modern office will have a computer lurking somewhere.

With the possible exception of several specialized executive positions in a small number of industries, it is not necessary for the average manager to become so intimate with a computer that he can pull it apart and put it back together. In most cases it is not even necessary to learn how to program one. But since most of us will be using computers (if we aren't already), there are a few things about them that it wouldn't hurt to know.

THE PERSONAL COMPUTER

Electronic, computerized office equipment has been around for years. But it was the advent of the personal computer (PC) that spurred the evolution of the automated office.

The PC is all things to all white collar workers: it is powerful, fast, inexpensive, incredibly versatile and increasingly user-friendly (*i.e.*, easier to use). But the real revolution in office automation is just beginning. In the past, automation equipment was intended for operators, subordinates who managed records, processed words, ran graphics departments. No longer. *If you are a manager, expect to be spending more and more time with your PC.* And expect to work more efficiently.

Secretaries account for only 6 percent of the total white collar wage bill; executives and professionals for 76 percent. An improvement in management productivity would have a significant impact on the bottom line.

But, you say, I'm a manager and a decision-maker. I don't do letters or crunch numbers. So what do I need a PC for?

Consider a 1980 study by Booz Allen Hamilton which showed that executives spend 67 percent of their time communicating. When you read on, you will see that improving communication efficiency is one of the strongest arguments for a PC. Take the average dictated letter; it cost $8.10 in 1984. After a little training, you could compose your own on your PC, leaving only the editing and the one- or two-minute printing to your secretary, or do the entire job for yourself, probably in around the same time as it takes to dictate.

THE BASIC ADVANTAGES OF COMPUTERS

More speed. Computers can calculate, sort, search, compile, and print out at blinding speeds.

Accuracy. All the jokes aside, computers rarely make errors. In many systems, millions of calculations are executed without a single mistake.

Reduced costs. Any device that can reduce labor costs and save time has the potential to save money. In the case of computers, though, this cost reduction can be offset by an increased dependence on the system—overutilization—not to save money, but to produce more accurate work and a less tedious day for the staff.

Reliability. Modern computers are solid state, and the CPUs have no moving parts. Again, the fact is contrary to popular myth: Computers rarely break down.

Size. Computers used to require entire rooms. Now a desk top or table will do in many cases.

Self-guidance. Unlike most of us, computers don't have to be told twice. They remember instructions. And names, dates, and figures. If you program them properly, you can input the data and walk away leaving the computer to process the data. You don't have to look over its shoulder.

THE COMPONENTS

Virtually any computer can be divided into five basic sections, which are described in terms of the functions they perform.

Input. Information from a variety of sources—such as letters, numbers, voice, magnetized ink, and sounds—is "translated" into patterns of electronic pulses that the computer is capable of understanding and utilizing.

The most prevalent input devices include *keyboards* which allow you to manually input letters and numbers, *modems*, which accept electronic data from phone lines, and *optical scanners* which convert printed images directly to electronic data that the computer can process.

Memory. This is the section that stores the information until needed. There are two basic types of memory facilities: *Primary storage* is an essential section of the computer that uses ferrite metal cores or semiconductor devices to hold programmed instructions, data to be processed, the results of intermediate calculations, and data to be "output."

Semiconductor memory chips are used in virtually every personal computer. The most common measure of memory capacity is referred to by the number of kilobytes (a byte being essentially the smallest unit of information that can be processed). In the beginning, PC's typically came with 256k (256,000 bytes) of RAM (for Random Access Memory); today the standard is 512k and 640k, with more advanced models coming equipped with 1 mb, or one million bytes.

Secondary storage is located outside the basic computer. Information is often stored on magnetic disks, magnetic tapes, or paper tapes. Secondary storage media hold data not immediately required by the computer. When it is needed, the data from secondary storage is inserted into the primary storage for use.

Arithmetic and logic. This is where the actual electronic manipulations, which allow the computer to add two numbers or compare several quantities, takes place. This activity is often referred to as "number crunching" and data manipulation.

Control. The control unit regulates the activities of the system. It regulates the flow of information to and from the memory and arithmetic/logic sections, interprets and executes each step of the programmed instruction, and keeps track of the current status of the system and its components.

Taken together, the *primary storage, arithmetic/logic,* and *control* sections comprise the central processing unit, or CPU, of the computer.

Output. Here the processed data is converted to electrical impulses capable of controlling many different devices. Thus the output can be used to operate other machinery, or even to feed information to another computer. Most commonly, output refers to the process of converting those impulses into information understood by humans: words and numbers on a video screen, printed out on paper by a printer, or "spoken" by an artificial voice.

THE SOFTWARE PROGRAM

The program is simply a series of instructions that the computer stores for future use. Programs are designed to solve problems and control procedures and processes, and fall under the heading "software." Software comes in two basic types:

Operating Systems Software. Operating systems control the computer's basic functions, issuing instructions which allow the machine to run a wide variety of programs for specific applications. Operating systems are often compared to "traffic cops," but I prefer the analogy used by office automation expert Walter A. Kleinschrod, who compares the operating system to a waiter placing an order, serving the food, and clearing the table. Operating systems function like the waiter; the various software applications (word processing, financial analysis) are like the courses. Operating systems prepare the computer to use the applications software, assist in its utilization, and then clear the machine, making it ready for the next job. Obviously, this is very simplistic, but most managers needn't concern themselves with precisely how operating systems function, only with how to use them.

Currently, there are four dominant operating systems for PCs or microcomputers as they are often called. A fifth has been announced and, as of this printing, is due out in 1988.

Generally speaking (this is an area of innovation), applications software written for one operating system will not work on another. To get around this limitation, custom circuit boards and special software can be used in certain circumstances to allow a computer using one operating system to use that of another. Currently, the biggest market for such devices concerns compatibility of the IBM PC standard and the Apple line of PCs.

CP/M (Control Program/Microprocessor) pioneered by Digital Research was one of the first and the most popular operating system for the early generations of microcomputers. As a result, there is a lot of software written for it. It is rarely used in the design of newer machines in the United States.

MS/DOS (Microsoft Disk Operating System) has become the *de facto* standard operating system for business software, primarily because IBM chose it as the operating system to use in its personal computers. Since IBM's machines quickly became the standard in offices, so did its operating system.

MS/DOS has grown more powerful over the years, and frankly, with all the software out there that runs on MS/DOS, and all the installed computers that use it, you can't go wrong. Machines termed IBM compatibles or "clones" must conform to the MS/DOS standards.

Unix is a very powerful operating system, developed by Bell Laboratories and available by a licensing agreement from other vendors. The strength of Unix is most evident when it is running several tasks at once on several different machines. Unix is likely to become more popular as more PCs are linked together, and as new machines appear that can harness its power.

Recognizing that many users already know MS/DOS, which is just fine for single-user applications, expect the new machines that run Unix to be designed to run MS/DOS as well, so there is no either-or choice to be made.

OS/2 or Operating System/2. A new operating system introduced by IBM to accompany its Personal System/2 line of new personal computers. Among its most significant features is the elimination of the 640k memory barrier which keeps MS-DOS from taking advantage on new microprocessors and complex software programs. MS-DOS can only work with 640k at a time, but OS/2 can support up to 16mb of RAM, over twenty times more memory. This will enable OS/2 users to perform many tasks at the same time, called *multitasking.*

IBM has gone even further. In contrast to MS-DOS, which was only an operating system, OS/2, in its full configuration, includes communications, a database and a "windowing" (multitasking) applications program.

Fortunately, as in earlier cases, IBM released its own version of the OS/2, while its developer—Microsoft—released a generic version, which runs on many existing clones.

Macintosh Operating System is unique to this elegant machine from Apple. The library of programs designed to run on the Macintosh keeps expanding, as are the ways in which *Macs* can be linked to the omnipresent IBM PC. There was a time when *Mac* users were deprived of the most popular and powerful business software, and couldn't utilize files created in offices running MS-DOS. No longer. Besides software programs that link *Macs* to PCs, there are a few add-on boards available to allow Macintosh and Macintosh IIs to run MS-DOS. Increasingly, we are seeing Macintoshes crop up in IBM bastions like "big eight" accounting firms.

Applications software programs are written to solve specific problems or perform specialized tasks for the user. Common examples include text editing or word processing, and mathematical computation/projections programs called spreadsheets.

You should know that special programs exist, called *assemblers, compilers,* and *interpreters*, which employ a variety of methods to convert the source language (the language the computer understands). This allows the user to operate the computer with a single language that resembles English.

EXECUTIVE GUIDE TO APPLICATIONS SOFTWARE

As of this writing, the technological innovations in PC hardware have slowed. Manufacturers have built so much speed and power into the machines, that the line between *microcomputers* and their "bigger" cousins, *minicomputers* is blurring.

The software, however, has lagged behind. The situation is akin to having a slew of very fast, roomy and efficient high performance automobiles, in a world with poor roads and no place to go.

But the software makers are catching up. After five years of astounding developments in personal computer hardware, *the software years are about to begin.*

Essentially, the act of writing applications software is a creative activity. Computers can do lots of things. Often it is just a matter of a creative software designer thinking up an idea or *application*, and setting to work writing the *program* or set of instructions. So you can expect to see hundreds—perhaps thousands of application software packages in the next few years. Unfortunately, the lag time in publishing makes books a poor way to keep up with new developments. You should rely on computer periodicals to track the innovations.

Fortunately, several basic categories have emerged, largely in response to basic needs of the marketplace.

The basic applications programs used by business are *word processing, spreadsheets, data or file management and communications software.*

Popular, but deemed less essential are *word processing add-ons, desk management programs, graphics, DOS shell* and other *utilities, macro, and project management.*

WORD PROCESSING

Interestingly, while more businesses own spreadsheet software than word processing programs, it is word processing which ranks first in application. Ninety-one percent of Fortune 1000 firms use their micros for word processing.

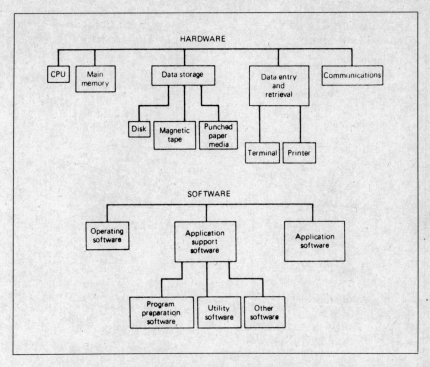

Fig. 64. Basic elements of computer hardware and software.
A simplified schematic representation.

From Robert Allen Bonelli, *The Executive's Handbook to Minicomputers* (New York: Petrocelli Books, 1978), p. 14. Reprinted by permission of Petrocelli Books.

Basically, word processors manipulate text, taking the tedium out of the process of writing and revising. There is no longer a need to manually retype an entire document when you wish to change it. Once input (by a keyboard or scanner), the document can be manipulated and printed out at a very high speed.

The benefits range from the simple correction of typos to moving large blocks of text around (what we used to call "cutting and pasting"), to compiling indexes and tables of contents.

Formats can be changed in seconds. A misspelled word or name appearing in a document can be corrected everywhere it appears with one or two keystrokes. A form letter can be merged with a list of names and addresses, and the computer will do a mass mailing, filling in the blanks where appropriate.

With the addition of word processing utility programs, you can check spelling, grammatical style, get synonyms at a touch of a key from an electronic thesaurus, even compare two very similar drafts, with the pro-

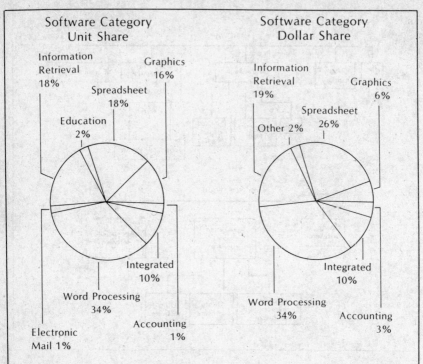

Software Category
Unit Share

Information Retrieval 18%
Graphics 16%
Spreadsheet 18%
Education 2%
Integrated 10%
Word Processing 34%
Electronic Mail 1%
Accounting 1%

Software Category
Dollar Share

Information Retrieval 19%
Graphics 6%
Spreadsheet 26%
Other 2%
Integrated 10%
Word Processing 34%
Accounting 3%

A survey of retail outlets for microcomputer software, conducted in October by Infocorp, showed word processing to be the primary application being sold in terms of units and dollars. Spreadsheet and information retrieval products were equal in terms of units sold, but the spreadsheet products accounted for a higher dollar volume.

Fig. 65. Word Processing
Remains the Top Best Seller

Infoworld, volume 9, issue 3,
January 19, 1987

gram highlighting all the differences in the text. If you are working with a document in a way that requires you to repeat a series of keystrokes or phrases over and over, you can further streamline the operation using a macro utility which combines a series of keystrokes into just one or two.

Indeed, word processing programs have grown so powerful that a personal computer equipped with a good word processing program can perform as well as or better than a "dedicated word processor," (specialized machines designed to do only word processing tasks).

IBM has discontinued its *DisplayWriter* line because it simply does not pay to buy a dedicated word processor when you can get all the power and features on a more versatile personal computer which can also do your books and manage your customer files.

As word processors have grown more powerful, the market has segmented. There are those in technical fields that want programs that can handle scientific notation. Authors and academics who want superior footnote and index capabilities. Business and legal users who want powerful all-purpose programs. And home users and executives who may prefer a simple program for tapping out a quick letter or memo. All of these markets are currently being served.

Usually, the greater the number of features, the slower the speed.

In the near future, look for screens large enough to display a full page of text, the ability to input by writing longhand or speaking directly into a microphone, and keyboards that will allow you to place proofreading marks on the document.

THE CASE FOR WORD PROCESSING

Word processors do lots of things well. Ultimately, the decision whether or not to purchase one depends on the office procedures and needs of your operation. But it's also a matter of deciding whether the implementation of a WP is worth *altering* your office procedures to come up with an overall improvement. Here's a list of some of the things WPs can facilitate:

FASTER DOCUMENT ORIGINATION   The average secretary can type 60 wpm, but mistakes resulting in "whiteouts" and retyping can bring the real average down to 3–4 wpm. With WP, trained operators average 15–30 wpm, including setup, referencing, and other button-pushing time.

FORMATTING   Legal documents, marketing and sales letters, thank-you notes, and letters to your mother-in-law are filled with standard "boilerplate" paragraphs that get used over and over. With WP, these paragraphs (and "boilerplate" sentences, phrases, and words as well) can be stored in memory. They can be retrieved at will and merged or linked to create new documents or letters.

"CUSTOMIZED" CORRESPONDENCE   A standardized document can be customized by inserting new text in any location, and by changing names, dates, and personal pronouns as needed.

PRODUCTION OF FINAL DRAFTS   Under the old system, every time there is a revision, even a minor one, the document has to be retyped. With WP, the corrections can be made on the display, proofed and reproofed before the final draft is automatically printed—in as many copies as you desire. And the final draft can be stored electronically for later use and/or printout of additional copies.

PRODUCTION OF FORM LETTERS   Form letters sent to a large number of clients can be cumbersome. Offset printing has an impersonal feel, and you may wish to avoid that. This means that, lacking WP, the typist has to type the same letter over and over. And then there's the address: Gummed labels shout "junk mail," but the alternative is typing them by hand.

Some WP printers give a "billing statement" look that can be worse than offset—little dots (matrix printers) and no curved lines.

A WP equipped with a special typewriter printer can turn out individually typed, personalized letters quickly and efficiently.

MAILING LIST HANDLING   Form letters and mailing lists can be stored in the WP memory. The WP will merge any mailing list with any form letter, so you can pull a number like, "Send our overdue payment letter to every company on our aerospace client list, but hold back a week before sending the 'we must take legal action' letter to our automotive clients."

SORTING   In order to get bulk rates from the post office, you've got to sort the mail by ZIP codes. The WP will play virtually any sorting game you like, from alphabetizing to ZIP coding to alphabetizing *under* each ZIP code.

FILING   One of the biggest problems with filing is the decision of what heading to file under. Should you classify the record by client name? By subject? By industry? By geographic area? By numerical code? Once you decide, will other members of the staff be on your wavelength and be able to retrieve the file? As we have seen, the cost of locating a missing file is quite high, as is the cost of duplicating files.

All the relevant information can be stored in "digest" form in a WP's memory. But the real WP edge comes in retrievability. You can classify a single file in many different ways and retrieve it instantly, *without removing the information from the file.* This means that, unless the floppy disk or storage medium itself is lost, the information in the file cannot be misplaced. The user never takes it with him or her, but makes a hard copy if it's needed.

The user also has some control over format of the file output. For example, a file of customers in New York State could be displayed either alphabetically or in order of annual sales (if that information is available to the WP).

UPDATING   Everyone hates the chore of going through files and updating them. With WP, it's easy. Call the record up from memory and review and edit selectively, making additions, deletions, corrections; altering formats. In some machines, a file can be transferred from the WP's "active" memory, where it stays for continuous access, to the "archival memory," usually on tape or floppy disk or diskette, which can be removed or stored until needed.

COMPILING OF LISTS AND DIRECTORIES   Store and sort lists of hundreds of names for easy access. Be able to create and compile an "instant directory" custom made to specifications.

COPY PRODUCTION   Take the load off the reprographics department. The WP can produce hard copy as needed and also allow instant access, thereby, in many cases, eliminating the need for extra copies, since any authorized colleague at any terminal can have a look.

SCHEDULING   Suppose there are several terminals, or, ideally, one for each key staff member. If everyone were to enter his schedule into the WP, it could be checked by anyone with authorization. That means you can always be up to date on meetings, conferences, cancellations, rescheduling, etc. In addition, one is less likely to forget a given meeting or task, since it can be placed on the itinerary for a future date and will appear when that schedule is examined. Some executives program their WPs to remind them a day or a week beforehand of an upcoming important meeting, so they can prepare.

PHOTOTYPESETTING   WPs can interface with phototypesetting equipment, providing several advantages. The reduction of time and costs is often one of them, depending on the volume of type your firm uses. You will save time because you can typeset at will, as opposed to what often happens when you send work out for setting. More important, you have more control, because the operation is totally in-house and the material can be stored in memory for future use and revision.

INCREASED FLEXIBILITY

Personnel. How many times have you passed up a real go-getter? Bright. Aggressive. One who would be loyal and efficient. The problem? He can't type, and the job calls for some typing. Enter the WP. Now the person with other redeeming characteristics, presumably intelligent, will master a WP in no time and can use it to compensate for slow or poor typing.

Productivity. In an article in the April, 1978, issue of *Administrative Management*, findings from a survey by consultant Robert Schiff were reported: Fifty-three non-WP secretaries said they spent 14 percent of their time waiting for work; the rest of the day was divided between essentially "go-for" and clerical duties. These secretaries are not as efficient as they should be because their attention is too diffused among many small jobs. They are unable to concentrate on any one job for very long.

WP is changing all this, because it allows for a difference in job organization. There's the typist or WP specialist who handles typing and related skills, and the administrative assistant who functions more in support of the superior's special needs.

"HIDDEN" BENEFITS   Finally, there are those benefits of WP that cannot be measured, but are nevertheless quite real. If a firm uses its WP equipment properly, it should produce neater, more detailed and thought-out correspondence, reports, and other printed material—and produce it more promptly. The bottom line is that the image of the company, as it is viewed from the outside, will be enhanced. And how can you put a dollar value on that?

WHO NEEDS WORD PROCESSING?

FAST-GROWING COMPANIES   WP means people can work faster—in some cases, two to three times faster.

COMPANIES WITH A HEAVY CORRESPONDENCE LOAD   You can personalize those form letters. WPs are three times faster than mag card and more than four times faster than a 100 percent accurate typist.

THOSE THAT REQUIRE 100 PERCENT ACCURACY, AND RAPID-CHANGE CAPABILITY   For example, law firms, insurance firms; anyone with a lot of contract work, advertising production, etc.

THE OTHER SIDE OF THE STORY

Word processors are clearly part of an irreversible trend, but don't necessarily rush right down and buy one. The timing may not be right. Take it from one that knows—the U.S. government. David Larkin of the Office of Administrative Services and Procurement, U.S. Department of Commerce, says that few federal agencies have been able to recover their investment costs on WPs. Some of the blame goes to the equipment, and some to the users:

DOES A WORD PROCESSING PROGRAM OR ELECTRONIC TYPE-WRITER REALLY SAVE MONEY?   The added costs of an automatic typewriter or WP may not be justified by the reduction of typing time. Since the typist must type the original material, the only real savings comes if there is a large volume of "auto typing" of previously keyboarded material. In actuality, claims Larkin, some automatic typewriters *increase* the time required to type an original.

More important is the way word processing typing time is measured—words per minute. The vendors claim that a typist will type such-and-such a percentage, or hard numbers, of words per minute. However, office personnel aren't paid by piecework—5 cents per word, or something like that; they are paid by the hour or week. And it is very tough to accumulate enough saved time in "words per minute" to eliminate even a part-time helper, or give a secretary a significant amount of additional work.

LET'S ASSUME THAT WORD PROCESSING DOES SAVE REAL TIME—DOES THIS RESULT IN INCREASED PRODUCTIVITY?   That depends. Is the typing work load a limiting factor in your office productivity? If you freed the typists to some degree from such chores, would they be able to do other significant work, such as follow up phone calls, inventory, etc.? What good is saved time if that time cannot be converted to productive work? Chances are that if a typist finishes an hour typing job in forty-five minutes, the time won't get filled with an additional fifteen minutes of typing. It might even mean an extra personal phone call to a friend.

More food for thought. Early word processing vendors, recognizing this problem, reintroduced the concept of typists and machines clustered in work pools, thereby producing the "WP center," which benefited from the so-called "economy of scale." Multiply these fragmented bits of saved time and increased efficiency and you will get savings in terms of hours rather than minutes. But many feel that the real benefits come from the concept of the pool, not from word processing. In any event, if you don't have enough personnel or volume to justify such an approach, the "economics of scale" notion is out of reach.

COMPUTERPHOBIA Many first rate office workers are intimidated by computers and sophisticated electronic typewriters. If the work scores high in other areas, does it really make sense to compel him or her to work with word processing hardware and software? The resulting anxiety could hurt productivity and morale.

Sure, there are thousands of young workers with no such fears, but will they measure up in other areas, such as knowledge, reliability, trustworthiness, loyalty, and basic writing skills?

THE GLAMOUR BIT Even in our austere and dedicated federal agencies, PCs have been acquired as status symbols or morale boosters for execs and their secretaries. Image-conscious managers who want to project a "state of the art" appearance in the marketplace may wind up with lots of expensive machines gathering dust.

SPREADSHEETS

The advent of the spreadsheet is one of the principal reasons for the growth of the personal computer. Anyone who has worked with rows and columns of numbers, often linked by a maze of formulas, knows how tedious calculating and recalculating can be. A single change can result in an entirely new spreadsheet; if you want to work with hypotheticals, to see how the numbers look under a different set of assumptions, you've got to start all over again.

Spreadsheet programs essentially turn hours of manual calculation into seconds of computer time. Raw number-crunching speed and power— along with clever design—has turned budgeting, forecasting, and financial analysis into a smoother, quicker job, and eased some of the fear of numbers common in many business people.

By end of 1987, some 7 million copies of spreadsheet programs will be on the desks of users.

Dramatic improvements in spreadsheet programs have made them more accessible to non-financial types. They are no longer just for accountants or statisticians. Over the years, they have not only grown more powerful (the amount of data they can crunch), but they have become faster and easier to use.

An innovative new program, *Lotus HAL* from Lotus Development, allows the user to request sophisticated financial calculations in plain English, eliminating much of the need to use mathematical notation.

Office automation expert Amy Wohl estimates that there is a 400 to 700 percent increase in productivity when one shifts from an electronic calculator to a spreadsheet. Financial analysts have derived the most benefit.

Most important, spreadsheets have made financial analysis, and numbers in general, more of a tool, and easier to conceptualize. More and more middle managers are using spreadsheets to get a snapshot of where the business is and where it is going. Spreadsheets are changing the way we look at numbers.

DATA MANAGEMENT

It is unlikely that data management programs will overtake spreadsheets or word processing in popularity, but they appear to hold a lock on third position in the business applications scoreboard.

Data management software can be helpful to all businesses, but is clearly better suited to some more than others. Growth has been hampered in part because these programs are more difficult to master.

Database software begins by helping you create a database, or a collection of information organized into files consisting of categories or fields. Then you can add, delete, sort or manipulate the data in a wide variety of ways. For example, you can ask for all the clients with the same zip code or same salary range, and the database manager will produce a report in minutes, if not seconds.

Newer, more powerful databases simplify the tasks of entering the data, setting up the search and report parameters, and performing statistical analysis and graphing.

With a database management program, a business can create an information bank all its own, providing storage, and immediate access, search and retrieval of data.

COMMUNICATIONS SOFTWARE

While the capability for telecommunications through a PC is built-in, most personal computers don't come with the necessary hardware or software. The required hardware is a device called a modem, which we will discuss in another section. Communications software essentially tells the modem what to do.

488

Communications software performs a number of practical useful functions. It dials the phone number of the on-line database or other computer. It sets the modem to conform with the technical specifications needed to send and receive messages with a specific party. It allows you to keep files of text prepared in advance so you don't waste time composing your message while you are "on-line"; it simply empties the file, quickly and accurately. Inversely, it will receive and save "downloaded messages, storing them for later use after you are done communicating.

In addition, your most commonly used communication numbers and protocols are saved and "remembered" by the software so you don't have to keep entering them. And most offer some form of "error-checking" procedure to catch—and correct—garbled messages and data.

GRAPHICS SOFTWARE

Presentation graphics programs plot data, creating an exciting array of visual charts and graphs in color or black-and-white, on the monitor or with the proper peripherals, on printers, plotters or slides, even videotape.

Until now, such programs were rarely used outside of art departments and engineering. But now that PCs have more memory and graphics capabilities, and higher resolution monitors, they are becoming more commonplace in general business applications, whenever a business is seeking more clarity and impact through a visual presentation. The powerful graphics programs can integrate charts, text and a library of images and figures for incredibly sophisticated and dramatic visuals.

PROJECT MANAGEMENT SOFTWARE

Project management software is designed to assist you in keeping track of projects with a large number of tasks over a set period of time, involving great coordination. It could be a marketing campaign or a construction project. Such software generally makes use of the *PERT* and *Gantt* systems of project management, only the tracking is done automatically and displayed graphically. You can also ask "what if?" questions concerning schedule changes.

UTILITIES PROGRAMS

Utilities is a catch-all term that is loosely applied to software that supports the principal applications done on a PC. For example, some utility disks feature a grab-bag of programs that allow you to recover lost files, get a look at exactly what is on a disk, or check the internal workings of the computer. Others, like those called DOS shells, let you simplify the syntax of MS/DOS into a customized set of commands that suit you, eliminating the need to remember complicated MS/DOS commands.

Another group of utilities manages your printer, ordering it to print sideways, in customized fancy fonts, or in some other method of improving the print quality.

Word processing utilities add dictionary, thesaurus or style checkers.

Another category might be called desk management utilities because they are meant to eliminate desktop clutter and organize a series of small tasks. The most common features enable you to do quick calculations, jot notes, keep track of tasks and appointments, keep a current phone directory and dial automatically. In addition to these basic tasks, the intense competition has created a wide array of special features added to these desktop utilities. These vary with the manufacturer.

Desktop programs are primarily intended to be RAM resident, meaning that they are loaded into the computer's main memory and stay there, in the background, while you run other *primary* applications. A few keystrokes activates the utility program and it appears on the screen. So if you are in the middle of a spreadsheet, and you just want to look up a telephone number or make a reminder note, you can do it without having to exit the spreadsheet program or use a scrap of paper that you might misplace.

DOS SHELLS

Originally, this group of software was designed to simplify the use of MS-DOS by eliminating the need to remember the syntax of DOS commands. The DOS "shell" provides a menu with commands spelled out in English. When a menu selection is made, the program translates it to DOS syntax and executes it for you. This is especially helpful to the executive or occasional user who hasn't committed "chkdsk," "dir," or "diskcomp" to memory.

The desire of software designers to differentiate their products and gain a competitive edge has resulted in the addition of a great many extra features including file viewers and editors, security and encryption functions, file labeling, and hard disk organization.

A GRAB BAG OF USEFUL SOFTWARE FOR EXECUTIVES

The following is a collection of personal favorites that don't quite fit the major categories, but nevertheless are extremely useful to the computing executive:

TIME MANAGEMENT

Prime Time is a first-rate time management program for the IBM PC and compatibles. It can be used alone or in a RAM resident mode, loaded and standing by while you take on other jobs. What makes Prime Time so good is that it allows you to prioritize tasks and keep your "to-do" list up-to-date; no more looking back at old calendar pages for reminders, or tediously recopying notes. Prime Time is also a project manager which keeps track of tasks delegated to others, maintaining a file on the person assigned to the task, as well as the task itself. Deadlines and due dates are noted. It also contains the customary alarm clock, phone directory and auto dialer. Prime Time, Wiseware, Inc., 3176 Pullman At., Costa Mesa, CA 92626

Control Center is a time management and organizer developed for use with the award-winning Time Design paper planner. It has many capabilities, including project management. It has a free-form style which allows you to input notes and data as you see fit. Control Center is comparatively expensive, as is Time Design.

Traveling Sidekick is the road version of Sidekick, the most popular desk organizer. Basically, it allows you to print the contents of Sidekick—phone directory, appointment calendar, files, etc., in sheets that are cut and inserted into a binder, giving you a customized planning system. Traveling Sidekick must be used with Sidekick. Borland International, 4585 Scotts Valley Drive, Scotts Valley, CA 95066

Tornado Notes is an excellent free-form note-taker, information manager that is designed to keep those small bits of paper from cluttering up your desk. Essentially, it's a computerized pile of notes that are stored in a "stack" that can be sorted and manipulated, popping on or off the screen at will. Very worthwhile. Micro Logic Corp., P.O. Box 174, 100 2nd Street, Hackensack, NJ 07602

FINANCIAL

101 Macros for Lotus 1-2-3 (Macropac International, 19855 Stevens Creek Blvd., Cupertino, CA) is a toolbox for users of the popular spreadsheet. It provides the user with a collection of "macros," a pre-programmed series of keystrokes that increases the power and convenience of Lotus. The *101* macros include a pop-up calculator, a "Go-To Key" that remembers where you've been, a macro to add a fancy border to your spreadsheet, and one to make a graphics "slideshow." The company also makes *101 Macros* for *Symphony* and *Excel*.

Forecasting can be a valuable tool for executives, but often involves sophisticated statistical techniques beyond the firm's comptrollers. *WISARD Forecaster* (SHADE Information Systems, Green Bay, WI) is a well-conceived program that creates a forecast, using an award-winning technique. You can input data directly into the program or import a lotus spreadsheet.

UTILITIES

Bookmark electronically marks the place in a file where you stopped working so you don't have to go searching around when you resume. Since most programs take you back to the beginning when you restart, this is quite useful. Bookmark also saves your work automatically, reducing the possibility of lost data. Intellisoft, 70 Digital Drive, P.O. Box 1972, Novato, CA 94948

Norton Utilities. Peter Norton was among the first to market a disk of essential utilities, and his is still among the best, with programs allowing you to recover lost files and see hidden information, among others.

Peter Norton Computing, Inc., 2210 Wilshire Blvd., Santa Monica, CA 90403

Cruise Control (Revolution Software, Inc., 715 Route 10 East, Randolph, NJ) is a RAM-resident program that improves the performance of cursor keys on IBM PCs and compatibles. It increases the speed of the cursor, and adds an anti-skid device, making the task of moving around large spreadsheets and documents much easier. The program also contains a number of other features, like an automatic screen dimmer to preserve the life of your monitor. This little program is one of the best values on the market. It works with most popular application software and other RAM-resident programs.

Sooner or later, you are going to wind up with scores of files, containing contracts, reports, correspondence, memos, etc. You will have a list of files by name and description, but chances are, you won't be able to remember what is in them. That is where *ZyIndex* (ZyLab Corp., 233 East Erie Street, Chicago, IL 60611) comes in. ZyIndex creates an index of your files; then the program allows you to search for a word or phrase, telling which file(s) include the data. It goes even further, displaying the file(s) and highlighting the exact location of the searched word or phrase.

ZyIndex has been around for years, but recent improvements have made it lightning fast and compatible with most popular word processors. It comes in three versions, Standard, Professional and Plus.

In my evaluation of this program, I created an index of files containing the chapters of this book. Finding any word takes only seconds. Take my advice: get a copy of ZyIndex and index all your valuable text files. Before the inevitable happens.

WORD PROCESSING ACCESSORIES

CompareWrite is an ingenious program that compares two documents by creating a third one which shows exactly how and where the two differ. It is a fast and simple way to take note of additions and deletions made to an original document, such as a contract, report or letter. Jurisoft, Inc., 6 Story Street, Cambridge, MA 02138

ForComment (Broderbund Software, 17 Paul Drive, San Rafael, CA 94903) is an ingenious program that is best described as a word-processing utility. As the name implies, it allows users to make comments and revisions on a document. But unlike a word processor, the revisions made by ForComment are recorded without altering the original document. Up to sixteen users can put their two cents in, and ForComment neatly keeps track of who said what. Even more amazing is the fact that the "reviewers" of the document can use their own word-processing program, even if it differs from the one which created the original document. So you can use *Word Perfect* to make comments about a contract prepared by your lawyer on *Multimate*, then send it to your accountant who can use his copy of *Microsoft Word*.

RightWriter (Rightsoft, 2033 Wood Street, Sarasota, FL 33577) is essentially an electronic editor that proofreads a document, evaluating grammar, punctuation, style and usage. The program is based on the tried-and-true Flesch-Kincaid standard for writing clarity. Frankly, I was astounded at the speed of the program and the quality of the advice. Although Rightwriter might be inappropriate for stylized writing such as advertising copy or fiction, it is ideally suited for business communications. Frankly, I wish I owned a copy before writing this book.

MISCELLANEOUS

Interactive Easyflow is a simple but elegant program for making flowcharts and organizational charts. A flow chart is often the best way to clearly depict a decision-making or production process; uses are virtually unlimited, from business plans to employee training. Easyflow is written for IBM and compatibles. It produces crisp, attractive flowcharts on most printers. I find myself reaching for it whenever I fear that I might have trouble getting my point across. From Haventree Software, Kingston, Ontario.

GRAPHICS

Inset (APG Software, 12 Mill Plain Road, Danbury, CT 06811). Once you've created graphics or flowcharts, you might want to include them in a written presentation. But rather than put a full page chart in, you might wish to include the chart in the text portion, so it can be used to reinforce the written word. Inset allows you to do just that. It lets you "capture" graphic images from your computer screen, and "paste" them onto your document while using your word processor.

Graph-In-The-Box (New England Software, Greenwich Office Park #3, Greenwich, CT 06830) is an intriguing program that might be considered the opposite of Inset. It lies in wait in your computer's memory while you run other applications software. Should you be working with data that you would like to convert to graphics, simply summon Graph-In-The-Box, and it will "capture" data from a document, spreadsheet, database, or virtually any other program, and produce a graph to accompany the document or report.

DATABASE

Notebook II (Pro/Tem Software, 814 Tolman Drive, Stanford, CA 95405) is an easy-to-use, excellent database program designed to manage large lists or records containing large amounts of text. It is especially useful for managing client lists, cataloging contracts and other legal documents, and important research material. It is also excellent for creating a bibliography, which can be done automatically with the addition of Pro/Tem's *Bibliography* program. This software package is excellent for managing information especially if you—like me—keep your own little database of reference articles, books, assorted data and statistics.

PROJECT MANAGEMENT

InstaPlan (InstaPlan Corporation, 655 Redwood Highway, Mill Valley, CA) is a planning program designed specifically for the executive. It allows you to organize projects in a simple "top down" form similar to an outline. After you input the information, InstaPlan converts it to a standard GANTT or PERT project management chart. It also can output a variety of useful charts, including calendar, workflow, activity (to-be-done) list, and a listing of your "project team." Since InstaPlan is not intended for those building a Space Shuttle, it is not as powerful as some project management programs that track thousands of tasks. But it is much less expensive, easier to use, and a lot more "relevant" to the responsibilities of the typical executive.

Power Up! Not a program, but the name of a catalog that represents a much-needed approach to the marketing of personal computer software.

The basic applications programs (word processing, spreadsheet, etc.) are widely available, often at discount prices. But the wealth of accessory software—much of it quite useful—consists of products designed by small companies with little money or marketing clout. As a result, such programs are often hard to find.

Channelmark Corporation (2929 Campus Drive, San Mateo, CA 94403) is seeking to fill this niche by marketing and distributing high-quality accessory software through the *PowerUp!* catalog.

Several are products of other firms. (An example is *Graph-In-The Box*, also reviewed in this section.) More significantly, Channelmark has developed and published its own exclusive line of accessory software. Channelmark products share some basic features. First, they are simple, usually because each program has been designed to perform a single function. Second, they come with free technical support via a toll-free number. Third, they are packaged without the frills. In many cases, the instructions are built into the program, and you are "prompted" through it, so you don't need a manual. In other cases, the manual is on the disk itself. An inconvenience, yes, but considering the low cost of Channelmark programs, understandable.

Channelmark programs come packaged in little gray boxes not much larger than a disk. Usually, there's only a disk and registration card inside. My only criticism is that several are copy-protected (virtually extinct in the industry), and in a rare case or two, the how-to documentation is a bit sparse. Among my favorite programs, all available through the *PowerUp!* catalog:

Financial Reporter takes the drudgery out of producing financial documents that require columns. Quicker and easier than setting up a table with a word-processor, or using a spreadsheet and then reformatting it. My favorite Channelmark product.

Pocket Address Book. Organizes and prints your name/address/phone list onto Rolodex cards, or into a *Day-Timer* pocket binder (provided, along with computer paper designed to fit right in).

Quick Schedule is a lean, mean project manager. In go the tasks, dates, allotted times, out comes the schedule, quickly and clearly. You can track your progress and modify the schedule. The least expensive project manager widely available; *Calendar Creator*, makes calendars of every conceivable kind for every conceivable purpose.

Off-the-Record, a file encryption program to secure sensitive files; *Computer Checkup*, a very complete diagnostic disk to test the performance of your PC; *Disk Quick*, a hard-disk utility program; *Retriever*, an index and retrieval program similar to *ZyIndex*; *File Clerk*, a file organizer that creates "file cabinets" which list files and a long descriptive note for each one.

Letters On-Line, a library of 800 letters and standard business documents for much less than the cost of one hour of legal time; *Labels Unlimited* prints a label for every purpose.

The Deciding Factor, an inexpensive expert system program which lets you apply AI principles in building a model to assist you in decision-making.

DOS SHELLS

Pathminder (Westlake Data, Austin, TX) is widely regarded as one of the finest and most complete DOS shell programs. It is logical, easy to use, allows you to create your own custom "menus" and offers file management, a data protection (security) system, editor, usage-logging system, and systems to manage your hard disk and files.

Norton Commander (Peter Norton Computing, Santa Monica, CA). A convenient, no-frills program that is among the easiest to learn, from Peter Norton, author of the indispensable Norton Utilities and one of the gurus of the personal computer revolution.

Q-Dos II (Gazelle Systems, Provo, UT) is noted for its speed, simplicity and Lotuslike horizontal menu. Use it only if you can afford its hefty memory requirements (100k).

KeepTrack Plus (The Finot Group, Palo Alto, CA) is a comprehensive program with many features, but its ability to back-up and restore files from hard disk to floppy is what sets it apart.

1 Dir+ (Bourbaki Inc., Boise, ID) offers a password protection security system, restricting access to your files. This is useful if you share your computer with many other users. 1 Dir+ is extremely flexible and may be customized in a variety of ways.

Xtree (Executive Systems, Inc., Sherman Oaks, CA) allows user to work with files in all directories because it works across the entire hard disk. It has a simple, easy-to-follow display and command structure.

PCEasy (Transec Systems, Delray Beach, FL) is a shell that distinguishes itself by allowing the user to name files with as many as 32 characters. (Because of the limitations of DOS, file names are restricted to eight characters and a three character suffix. Usually, the file names are cryptic, filled with abbreviations instead of descriptive phrases.)

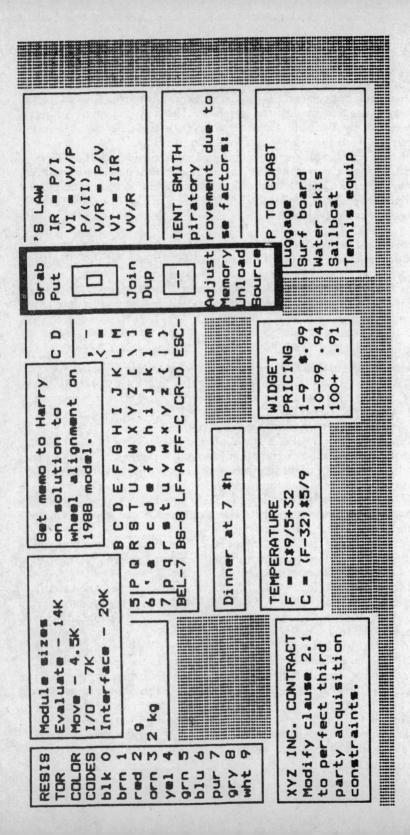

Fig. 66. Simulated photo of Tornado Notes screen

FORM GENERATORS

There are several programs on the market which allow you to select and print from a large library of forms, saving time and money. You can also customize them.

Formworx (Analytx International, Arlington, MA) is a powerful program that is amazingly flexible and works with over 100 printers. Once you get the hang of it, the possibilities are unlimited. Fast, flexible, powerful and simple.

Polaris Forms (Polaris Software, Escondido, CA) is an excellent form generator for the Hewlett Packard Laser Printer and compatibles.

Forms File (PowerUp!, San Mateo, CA) is an easy-to-use program that lacks the ability to build custom files, but instead provides you with a library of 100 ready-made business forms. And while you can't draw lines or adjust columns, you can personalize the forms by adding text.

Grid Designer (PowerUp!, San Mateo, CA) another simple program from this innovative firm does only one thing: generates grids of all kinds. Get ruled paper, 12 ledger formats, graph paper—all from your printer—in minutes.

SKILLS

The Art of Negotiating is a program designed to assist and prepare you for a negotiation session. Can it get you a better deal? Perhaps. If nothing else, it will provide you with a better understanding of the negotiation process. The same firm also markets a program called the Idea Generator designed to stimulate creative solutions. Experience in Software, Inc., 2039 Shattuck Avenue, Suite 401, Berkeley, CA 94704

Subliminal Suggestions and Self-Hypnosis Programs. How about a program that flashes a message of your choice on the computer display, at a rate so fast that you hardly see or notice it? The premise is that such suggestions will be noted by your subconscious mind, helping you to break habits, change attitudes, etc. The New Life Institute believes that it works, and they've designed this program. New Life Institute, P.O. Box 2390, Santa Cruz, CA 95063

TRAVEL

Bonus Wizard is a positively ingenious program from MicroSmart that assists you in keeping track of your frequent flier mileage and bonuses. It is simple, accurate, up-to-date, and it works. With free trips and upgrades at stake, and most of us forgetting to submit mileage or double-check the airlines' figures, this program is very cost-effective. MicroSmart, P.O. Box 15543, Stamford, CT, 06901–0543

INSIDE THE PC

THE BASIC COMPONENTS OF A PERSONAL COMPUTER

The system box contains the main circuitry including the main or mother-board, the CPU, memory chips, interfaces for peripherals, and one or several storage devices.

IBM PC compatibles are "open" systems, meaning users can open the box and insert or remove some of the circuitry, which is printed on cards that fit neatly into slots inside.

The keyboard The primary input device, and it is similar to a typewriter keyboard, although there are additional keys.

Keyboards are either part of the system box or connected by a cord (some are infrared wireless) so you can move them without having to move the box. Independent vendors make several variations on the basic IBM keyboards.

The video monitor The primary output device comes in three basic types. In order of price, a simple monochrome or single color; an enhanced graphic monochrome monitor for graphics and generally higher resolution, and a color monitor for both color and high resolution.

The storage media In addition to the data stored in the computer's memory, data must be stored in a *non-volatile* medium, *i.e.*, in a permanent form of storage that holds the data until you and your computer are ready to use it, even while the power is off.

The internal memory Used for computing power, to manipulate data while the computer is in use. *Storage media* holds very large amounts until needed. Internal memory is usually expressed in k's for *kilobytes* of RAM (Random Access Memory), with the current crop of personal computers weighing in with between 512k and 1 mb (1000k) of RAM.

Magnetic storage media is the most popular form. Information is stored magnetically, similar to audio or video tape.

The floppy disk is the most popular magnetic medium. The data is stored on magnetic wafers which are read by *floppy disk drives*. One or more disk drives are standard on most personal computers.

The most popular standard is 5¼", but the 3.5" standard is gaining in popularity. Even though smaller, the 3.5" is more advanced and holds more data.

Floppy disk drives are mounted in the system box near the front so you can place disks in and out through a slot. External floppy drives are also available in their own chassis that sit outside the computer.

Fixed or *hard disks* are magnetic disks that are constructed differently, allowing them to hold much more data (30 to over 100 times as much as a 5¼ ") and access it more quickly. Once a high-priced luxury, most PCs are now purchased with a hard disk, usually 10–40 mb (one megabyte equals one million bytes). The drawback is that, except for a few exotic expensive cartridge types, hard disks cannot be removed, and they require more electric power.

Hard disks can be mounted into the system box. Another type is also internal, but simply fits into one or two of the slots allotted for circuit boards. External hard disks have their own case and sit outside the computer, taking up more desk space.

Streaming Tape Backups are primarily used to back up hard disks in case of data loss. As the name implies, they use magnetic tape.

CD/ROM for *Compact Disk/Read Only Memory* is a bit different from all the rest in that for the near future, these disks will be used to *deliver* rather than *record* a large amount of stored information.

CD/ROMs can hold entire encyclopedias. These optical disks are related to compact audio disks, and as such they are light, cheap and sturdy.

The principal drawback to widespread acceptance is that special devices are needed to access the data on CD/ROMs, and there are very few disk readers out there. Currently, PCs don't come with CD/ROM drives, and the market is very new. Besides, you can't write on a CD/ROM—it is "read-only" so you can't store your own data or modify the disk.

"Write-once" systems are beginning to appear, allowing the user to record a tremendous amount of data onto a blank CD, but one time only. This is akin to a phonograph record. You cut a record and that is that. If you want to do it again at a later date, you make another record. You can't alter the first version.

THE COMPATIBILITY ISSUE

In spite of the *de facto* standard set by IBM personal computer and office products, compatibility still remains a problem. For one thing, many designers are justified in believing that IBM's products leave room for improvement, and that at least a segment of the market would welcome innovation. For another, not every attempt to make a machine "IBM compatible" succeeds. In technologies where there is no dominant specifications from IBM or any other leading vendor, the situation is often worse. The areas of concern:

Storage disks   Can one machine read the disks written by another?

Microprocessors   Often, microprocessors that are functionally identical do vary slightly, just enough to cause problems.

Circuit boards   Cards made for IBM compatibles don't work in every make or model.

Display Different display standards can create hardware and software interface problems.

Character and keyboard sets Is the keystroking of one machine compatible with another?

Printers There are hundreds of models available, and software designers can't design instructions or *drivers* for every one. Often, you must experiment, using trial and error until you find the driver that works with your printer, even if not perfectly.

System box Machines advertised as compatible with IBM or another brand should run any and all software designed for that machine. The situation here has been improving rapidly, and most IBM compatible computers on the market today perform with little difficulty. Experts usually select a demanding software program to put a compatible to the test. For the IBM PC, *Microsoft Flight Simulator*, a small plane simulation game, was used to test for compatibility. If the machine couldn't run Flight Simulator, it wasn't compatible. If it did, it probably was.

IBM PERSONAL SYSTEM/2

Recently, IBM introduced its Personal System/2 line, which differs from its original PCs—and thus from its clones—in several ways. It uses smaller, higher capacity 3.5" floppy diskettes instead of the older 5.25" version. It employs a new graphics mode and video display, which is incompatible with monitors built for the old standard. And except for the lowest-end model, the PS/2 line will not accept add-on circuit boards designed for the old PCs and clones.

The good news is that the new models (except the low-end Model 30) were designed to take advantage of a powerful new operating system, OS/2. The graphics are simply incredible, with the potential of approaching or even exceeding those of the vaunted Macintosh.

Most experts agree that the machines are well-engineered, if not revolutionary, and that IBM will eventually succeed in establishing a new standard, although it will take time.

As for clone-makers, IBM has made it tougher for them to legally copy IBM's system architecture, but it is likely they will discover other ways to deliver the same performance. It will take longer, however.

PITFALLS

Failure to match the right computer system with your needs. Do you have too much power, or too little? The right hardware for the software you need most? Most important, is the cost of your system justified by the gains? Computers are not ends in themselves. Always weigh the benefits and potential benefits against the acquisition costs.

Lack of training. You had better consider the time and expense required to adequately train those whom you expect to use the computers.

A bad mix of software. You should aim for software compatibility among users in the office, and if possible, identical programs. If the same data must be entered by two different users, there is room for improvement; the data, once entered, should ideally be accessible by others.

Getting hooked. Many people find computers fascinating, and you can eat up large blocks of time tinkering, game-playing, problem-solving and experimenting. Your productivity may go down rather than up if you or your staff spends too much time at the keyboard.

COMPUTER PERIODICALS

Personal Computing	*PC Magazine*
PC Week	*Compute!*
PC	*MacWorld*
Infoworld	*Run*
PC World	*A*^{s}
PC Tech Journal	*Compute!'s Gazette*
Byte	*Family Computing*

GLOSSARY

Bit: The smallest form of information, represented by a "0" or a "1."

Boot: The initial starting-up of a PC. The operating system is brought into main memory and takes over control.

Byte: Eight bits. One element of memory. A kilobyte (KB or Kbyte) equals 1,000 bytes, and a megabyte (MB or Mbyte) equals one million bytes.

Compatibility: The ability to run the same software programs and connect the same peripherals and add-on equipment (e.g., boards, printers, modems) as another PC. When a machine is said to be "compatible," it is more often than not compatible with the IBM PC. Compatible PCs are also referred to as "clones."

Command: An issue to the PC to execute a function, such as print, file, erase or send a document.

Header/footer: A word or series of words, and/or page numbers that appear consistently at the top or bottom of all pages of a document. This could include copyright notices, company logos or names, etc.

Icon: A pictorial representation of a command to the PC. An example would be a picture of a garbage can to ask the computer to erase a file.

Memory: A place where information is stored. There are various types including RAM, ROM and permanent storage. Usually referred to in kilobytes. For example, a PC with 64 kilobytes of memory.

Menu: A type of user interface that lists the possible commands that the user can perform on the PC. This type of user interface is much easier to understand than command-driven interfaces that require the user to remember complex strings of characters.

Microprocessor: The heart or brains of a PC.

Modem: A device used to send data from one computer to another using the telephone lines.

Mouse: A small box with a large button on it, attached to the PC with a cord. The user pushes ("clicks") the button to issue commands to the PC.

Off-the-Shelf: Standard software package that is not customized for any particular vertical, or industry, market (such as medical, legal). Off-

the-shelf packages include Multimate, Lotus 1-2-3, MicroSoft Word).

Operating System: The set of rules which control the computer. PC DOS is the most common operating system found on PCs, although there are many others as well.

PC network: Provides storage and printer sharing between PCs, allowing PC users to "talk to" each other through connecting cables. Also called local-area network.

Printers:

• *Dot matrix printer:* Prints a series of dots formed together to create a character or graphic.

• *Fully formed character printer:* Characters are fully formed and located on a wheel or thimble. Much like the printer portion of an electronic or electric typewriter. These printers have alphanumeric output of the highest quality, but cannot print quality graphics.

• *Non-impact page printer:* Prints without a hammer or character wheel striking the page. For this reason, it is called non-impact. There are several different technologies of non-impact printers, but the most predominant for the PC is the laser printer, whose technology is similar to the copier.

• *Thermal printer:* Like a dot matrix printer, the thermal printer produces characters by connecting a series of dots. Those dots are often generated by heating up specially treated paper and burning a hole through this paper to form the character.

RAM: Stands for random-access memory. The information in RAM is lost when power is removed.

ROM: Stands for read-only memory. The information stored in ROM is permanent (wired-in) and will not be lost if power is removed.

Storage: The amount of space allotted for storing information on the PC. Information from word processing, spreadsheet, database, and any other files. Storage capacity can be as small as a few hundred kilobytes to over 20 megabytes.

WYSIWYG: Stands for "what you see is what you get." The ability to view on a PC screen exactly what will be printed. This includes different typefaces, the placement of graphics and scanned images, column layouts and headers/footers. ∎

"Glossary" from "A Guide to the Personal Computer, *The New York Times* (advertising supplement of June 1, 1986).

33

PERIPHERALS

As the personal computer industry came to be dominated by IBM, Apple, Compaq and a small group of "clone" makers, many entrepreneurial geniuses saw a road to riches in manufacturing a wide array of attachments and add-ons, allowing the user to make his computer much more versatile, powerful, faster and smarter.

These attachments, or *peripherals*, take many forms. Devices exist to enhance or replace virtually every basic component of the PC, from add-on boards that are placed inside the system box to input devices such as alternate keyboards, bar-code readers, joysticks and "mice," to a large number of output devices such as high resolution monitors, printers, modems, and plotters.

OUTPUT DEVICES

Monitors   Simply, is a video screen that displays the text, charts, or other graphic material that you are working with. It allows you to see what you are doing, and what the material looks like as you manipulate it. Another advantage is that the display enables you to verify the data and commands as you enter them on the keyboard; it visually represents them on the screen. Therefore, you can catch errors before the material is transmitted or printed or stored in an electronic memory. Documents that are displayed before being printed can be corrected without the need for new page generation (starting over) or other mechanical correcting measures like "whiting out."

Although part of the basic PC system, the buyer can choose from many different types of video displays. In many cases, monitors are sold "bundled" with the computer itself, but almost any vendor will sell you the screen of your choice. The type of monitor you buy depends on what kind of computing you will be doing.

Monitors are either *monochrome* or *color*. Monochrome monitors usually have a black background, with green or amber characters. There are several that offer white-on-black or black-on-white. The color you choose is largely a matter of personal preference.

505

The resolution may also differ. That is, the density of the visuals. Resolution may be a function of the monitor itself, or the video circuit card that drives the display (located inside the computer), or both.

Color monitors, often called RGB (for Red, Green, Blue), are similar to color televisions, but they have a higher resolution and no tuner to receive TV signals. The resolution can vary widely between makes and models, and the range of colors can be quite dazzling.

Generally, color monitors are more expensive, and the cost is only justified if you are using your system with graphic applications, where several colors will enhance clarity and readability. However, many users find that color is helpful for word processing and spreadsheets, especially when there is more than one software program on the screen at one time.

Whatever your needs, it is a good idea to spend ten or fifteen minutes in front of a display to see if it suits you. Make sure that the lighting, height, and distance of the monitor are basically the same as the conditions in your work place.

Printers   There are five basic types of printers used with personal computers. All do essentially the same thing: output by printing on paper, thereby creating a "hard copy," of a document, spreadsheet or graphic.

Printers receive instructions from computers; unlike typewriters, they do not have keyboards, although IBM makes several models with optional keyboards that plug in, allowing them to be used as typewriters.

Impact printers, as the name implies, print by making direct, mechanical contact with the paper. Dot matrix printers do so with a series of pins, forming characters and graphics with a series of dots. The closer the dots, the better the print quality. In general, printers with a greater number of pins produce denser, higher quality letters.

Dot matrix printers are the workhorses of the personal computer industry. They are reliable, fast, relatively inexpensive, and can print both text and graphics. Recent improvements have resulted in crisp, clear text that comes close to the "letter quality" look of a typewriter.

Another type of impact printer produces fully formed letters and numbers when a printing element strikes the page. The characters are molded on a plastic disk, called a *daisywheel*, a "thimble," or in some cases, the old IBM-style "golfball" element made famous by the *Selectric*.

Such printers produce characters like that of a typewriter, enabling the output to look "hand-typed." These printers are noisy, relatively slow and cannot print graphics. But they are popular because of the personal "feel" conveyed by documents printed on them.

Non-impact printers form images and text, but the ink or toner is the only thing that touches the page. They fit into three categories: ink-jet, thermal, and laser.

Thermal printers are the least expensive. They "burn" the images into specially treated paper, or use heat to "melt" special ribbons onto the page.

Most use pins to form characters, so the image and capabilities is similar to that of dot matrix, although the print quality is different. Several thermal printers work in colors.

Ink-jet printers shoot a stream of electrostatically charged ink droplets at the page. These printers are very quiet and very fast, and many can print in color.

The laser printers are currently the Rolls Royces of office printers. It's easy to see why: using a technology similar to copiers, these machines employ a laser beam to "write" on drums which transfer the image to paper. Laser printers are quiet, ultra-fast (ranging from five to two hundered pages per minute), and produce very high quality text and graphics.

Less expensive models emulate daisywheel printers and as such, don't do graphics. At the high end, laser printers are suitable for some types of publishing. And recently, several manufacturers have introduced a machine that combines a laser printer and copier in one box, thus saving space.

MODEMS

A modem is a communications device and as such, performs both input and output function. Essentially, it receives the electrical impulses that are processed and stored by the computer and converts them to sound that is transmitted over telephone lines. As a receiver, it processes the sounds coming in over the telephone line and converts them to electrical impulses which can be understood by the computer. In this way, modems allow your computer to communicate with other computers by telephone. The machine at the other end may be a bank's computer, an on-line database, or a computer at a branch office.

The old-fashioned modems were *accoustically coupled*; they were cradles designed to accept ordinary phone receivers and communicated through them. Newer modems are *direct-connect*; they plug directly into the phone line through a jack. These modems can be internal, *i.e.*, in the system box, or external, as a separate unit.

Modems come in several speeds, measuring in bauds per second (bps), currently widely available in ranges from about 300 to 2400, which transmit at rates approximating 30 to 240 characters per second.

Modems work in conjunction with communications software packages, which program them with specific sets of instructions (see communications software). For a discussion of potential uses, see the section on databases.

INPUT DEVICES

Keyboards The basic input device, virtually every computer comes with its own keyboard. Again, IBM set the standard. But while millions purchased IBM PCs, there were many who were less than happy with the keyboard design. So several manufacturers offered alternative keyboards which could be purchased separately and plugged into the IBM PC line as a replacement.

Some of these keyboards offer different layouts or more keys; a few offer extras like "beep" tones, LED indicator lights and built-in *track balls* (input devices similar to the mouse).

Mice The mouse is simply a hand-held input device that rolls around the desk, either on its surface or a special pad. It does not replace the keyboard in most applications, as it does not input letters or numbers. Rather, it moves the cursor to any point on the screen smoothly and rapidly. One, two or three buttons on the top of the mouse (depending on the make and model) allow you to execute certain commands after you position the cursor. With software specially designed to accommodate the mouse, you can save time by executing a series of "point-and-click" commands instead of using keystrokes to move the cursor and input.

A mouse is also useful in graphics applications, because it enables you to draw free-form lines as you move it across your desk, up and down, back and forth.

Some ridicule the mouse as a toy; don't listen. Spend the short amount of time it takes to master the mouse, and it will increase your computing speed significantly.

Variations on the basic desktop mouse have begun to appear, including the *foot mouse*, a similar device which you operate with your foot, leaving your hands free.

Touchpads are stationary; you move a pointing device on the pad, and the cursor moves on the screen. *Light pens* work by holding them directly to the screen. And recently, a device appeared which attaches to your head, allowing you to move the cursor by tilting it from side to side and forward and back.

Joysticks are used primarily for playing computer games.

Scanners transfer a printed document to the computer's memory without the need for keystroking (typing it in). Scanners, also called OCRs for Optical Character Recognition, scan the page, "seeing" the characters, recognizing the letters and numbers, and converting them to electrical impulses to be read and stored by the computer.

The value of such machines comes from the fact that they can input the document faster and more accurately than a typist entering it manually. As they become even faster, more accurate (they sometimes misread letters, and can't recognize all typefaces) and cheaper, they will proliferate.

ADD-ON BOARDS

As noted earlier, IBM PCs and most "compatibles" are "open architecture" designs; you can open up the system box, and add and/or replace circuit boards.

The central microprocessor and some memory sit on the *motherboard*, which is the source of the primary circuitry and therefore indispensible. While some manufacturers offer options allowing a user to make changes on the motherboard, most add-ons involve additional circuitry printed to "cards." These cards fit into slots inside the system box; to replace them, you simply slide them in and out.

The sheer number and variety of add-on boards is too numerous to cover here, but let's consider several basic families of cards:

Memory expansion boards add more RAM to the computer, increasing its processing capacity, allowing it to handle more information more quickly.

Accelerator boards generally employ a faster microprocessor chip, or one adapted to run at a faster "clock speed." Such cards can increase the raw speed of a computer by as much as three times.

Graphics cards run the video display. Depending on the graphics card you choose, your display may be capable of text, text and graphics, high resolution graphics, special application and/or color. Certain software packages employ sophisticated graphics that will only work with the proper graphics card. Once again, IBM provides the standard, with the specs made popular by the Hercules line a runner-up. The graphics standard employed by Apple's MacIntosh, while not available on the other computers, is dazzling. In fact, many people choose the MacIntosh solely because of its superior graphics interface.

Multifunction boards are just what the name implies. Almost every combination of the above three categories is available, but many multifunction cards include useful extras that don't require an entire board of their own:

Clocks keep running while the computer is off, automatically resetting to the correct date and time when you power up.

Print spoolers assign some memory to hold a document (or a portion of one) while it waits its turn to be sent to the printer, allowing the user to move on to another task. In other words, you don't have to sit there and wait for a fifty-page report to be printed. The report is loaded into the spooler, which automatically feeds it to the printer, while you use the rest of the computer to crunch numbers or begin another report.

Game ports provide a place for you to attach a joystick, trackball or other device for playing computer games.

Additional ports   Many cards provide extral serial and/or parallel ports which make it easier to connect other peripherals. Especially useful if you are using two printers or two monitors, or an extra disk drive.

OTHER IMPORTANT DEVELOPMENTS
IN OFFICE AUTOMATION

Laptops and transportables   Miniaturization has given rise to a family of smaller personal computers.

Laptops are small enough to fit into an attaché case, or on a lap, which is how they got their name. The screens are flat and usually inferior to a CRT display, except at the high end. Most are battery-powered, running for just a few hours. But they are more powerful than the original IBM PCs and are quite useful when you need to do some computing on a trip or simply away from the office. Screen quality has been improving steadily, and many models now accommodate a hard disk.

The older, larger cousin of the laptop is the *transportable*, which is compact and light enough to be carried home or taken on a trip, but is still considered a desktop model.

Transportables are convenient for home use because they run on AC power and can be stored out of the way in the closet when not in use. Transportables or luggables as they are sometimes called, are generally cheaper than laptops, and have better screen visibility for the money.

Laptops have sex appeal, so look for them to become dominant among the computer elite.

LAN (Local Area Networks)   Several hardware and software manufacturers have designed products that allow personal computers to link up, sharing peripherals, storage and memory, software and commands. Unlike modems, PC networks don't use ordinary phone lines to communicate, but rather employ their own cables.

LAN networking will create efficiencies in computing speed and costs. With LANs, the need for a full-fledged computer at every desk can often be reduced or eliminated, because *workstations*—display/keyboard combinations with no storage (disk drives) and stripped-down or specialized circuitry—will serve just as well, as long as they can network into a powerful PC.

Artificial Intelligence (AI)   Advanced software programs have begun to utilize artificial intelligence. Essentially, the earliest versions of AI software will be able to respond to commands in plain English. They will also be capable of some rudimentary "learning"; that is, if you customarily

---

perform a task in a set way, the software will "learn" that way, "remember" it, and incorporate it into its operating procedure.

In the not-so-distant future, AI word processing programs will be able to compose business letters based on previous ones you have written.

A simple but very useful AI program is *Lotus HAL*, which allows you to use *Lotus 1-2-3* spreadsheet software by issuing commands in plain English instead of complicated strings of numbers and letters.

Voice Output and Recognition   Computers are now able to generate and, in limited circumstances, understand human voice commands. Devices that allow you to phone a computer and leave a voice message for its owner are already available on the retail level.

Faster, more powerful machines   New microprocessors such as the INTEL 80386 are ushering in a new era of brute power and blinding speed for personal computers. The popular MS/DOS, Unix and Xenix operating systems are being revamped to take advantage of the machines' potential. The new OS/2 will also be capable of exploiting much of the 80386 chip's high performance.

User friendliness   The icon-based graphic environment pioneered by *Apple Computer* in its *MacIntosh* line is becoming more widely available in other makes. In general, computers are becoming smarter and easier to use.

Desktop Publishing   Simultaneous advances in graphics, laser printers, software and computer hardware have made it possible to produce typeset quality newsletters with a PC, laser printer and special software.

Many manufacturers are bundling the components into so-called "desktop publishing systems." Since such systems save money, they amortize quickly, so sales have been brisk among those who put out newsletters and mass mailings.

THE ELECTRONIC TYPEWRITER

The Resurgence of the Typewriter. When it became clear that personal computers equipped with word processing software could outperform even expensive electronic typewriters, they went into a sales decline. But the market has returned in a big way for several reasons.

First, there are some jobs that are quicker and easier on a typewriter, like an envelope, Rolodex card, or carbon copies.

Second, electronic typewriters have replaced electrics, and the new models are cheaper and more reliable, with fewer moving parts, and are much quieter.

Third, the manufacturers have responded with clever redesigns. By transplanting some PC technology, vendors created a line of electronic typewriters that are intended for light word processing, offering all or most of the WP conveniences like error correction, spell-checking, and storage, in a simpler, smaller package. When the primary use is word processing of correspondence and short documents, an inexpensive electronic is often a better alternative to the PC with its cables, monitors and printers.

Some electronic typewriters offer video displays; most offer some kind of screen to display a few words or a sentence. A few models can switch between word processing and typewriter mode.

The following is a list of features commonly found in electronic typewriters. Keep in mind that most PC word processing software can do all and more of what is listed below:

ONE-LINE MEMORY   The built-in electronic memory retains all the material on the line as you type it. This function aids in correcting errors and formatting the typing on the page.

AUTOMATIC ERROR CORRECTION   Since the machine can remember what you typed, a single keystroke will send it back over the material on that line, the memory guiding the typing element so that you can erase anything up to one line.

FORMAT STORAGE   Frequently used formats can be stored and accessed so that there is less fiddling and lining things up.

AUTOMATIC CENTERING   The intelligence is smart enough to calculate the center and send the typing element to that point.

ELECTRONIC MARGINS AND TAB STORAGE   Margins for business letters, columns for financial work, special settings for scripts can be stored so that the operator can get the right settings for the job in seconds.

NUMBER ALIGNMENT   This feature is a great help when you've got rows of figures, because the machine will automatically align on the decimal point.

AUTOMATIC INDENTING   This could increase typing speed a bit by eliminating the need to count out spaces for indenting. But so can a conventional tab setting.

PHRASE STORAGE   Conjure up your favorite greetings and/or salutations, closings, and routine wordings in seconds. Hit the code for "As per our conversation" and the machine spits it out.

AUTOMATIC CARRIER RETURN   This is one of my favorite features. When the carrier enters a "hot zone" (usually 5–7 characters before the right margin), it automatically hyphenates the word and heads for the next line.

CHARACTER PITCH/TYPE STYLE   You don't need to go electronic to have the advantage of the changeable pitch and type styles. Nevertheless, all the electronics have this feature. The most common typing elements are the "golf ball," pioneered by IBM, and the "daisy wheel," which is used by Olivetti and several other vendors.

AUTOMATIC UNDERLINING

PROPORTIONAL SPACING   Will adjust the pitch to fill the page.

RELOCATE   The carrier returns to where the typist left off before he stopped to correct something.

THE MEMORY TYPEWRITER

MEMORY   Some units have internal "sealed memories"; others have unlimited storage capacity through the use of separate storage media such as cassettes or diskettes, which can be removed and filed away. These units are at the high end of the category. Some units have memories that can be boosted by adding additional accessories.

TEXT EDITING   One can move type in memory, by word, sentence, paragraph, line, or character. So you can add something new (a word, a sentence, a paragraph, etc.); or you can delete.

SAVE/RECALL   Save a segment of type, and recall it at will without retyping it manually.

CHARACTER STRING SEARCH   What's a character string? A sequence of characters—high-tech lingo for a word or part of a word. If you're looking for a word or series of characters (abbreviations, numbers, initials) and it's in the machine's memory, it will be found.

FILE   These machines have two kinds of memory: storage memory, which holds information for future use; and working memory, which is the memory that can be manipulated—what you're working with. When you've finished with a document, you can "file" it, i.e., transfer it from the working memory to storage. Automatically, the machine will assign it a file number, making the document easy to call forth again when needed.

RIGHT-HAND MARGIN JUSTIFICATION   This feature really makes a difference. The visual impact is very professional, especially if you type newsletters and material that will ultimately be printed.

GLOBAL SEARCH AND REPLACE   Global search is just like character string search, except that after it finds the string in its memory, it continues searching the whole document automatically for that string. Suppose you typed a report on Ronald Reagen and, later on, discovered the misspelling. This feature allows you to find all the *Reagens* in the document and change them to *Reagans*. Some machines will correct every *Reagen* automatically once you enter the right spelling.

SWITCH/MERGE   This is the switching or merging of two memories (two tracks, diskettes, etc.). Suppose one contains a standard letter, and the other a list of names and addresses. Merge the two so you can get that letter automatically typed with each of the names and addresses on the list.

WHO BUYS SMART TYPEWRITERS?

It's hard to say. But we do know who the vendors are *after*: the small office, which can't afford the larger scale commitment to word processing, or which doesn't have the volume to justify it. And the reluctant executive, who wants to hold on to a personal secretary, not give letters to a "word processing operator." The electronic typewriter is a good compromise, because it makes the secretary faster and more efficient without having the effect of replacing or radically altering the job. The secretary remains loyal to the boss, doing the work on a futuristic new machine that looks and feels much like the old one.

34

ELECTRONIC DUPLICATION AND STORAGE

COPIERS

Copiers generate 100 billion pieces per year. Funny how simple they seemed when they first came out: Place original face down, press button, out comes copy. And, of course, in the beginning there was only Xerox. Today there are over 200 models with many features and complex controls so that many firms employ "reprographics" managers—copy experts. In lieu of that, here's this:

Fiber optics. This is the major new advance in copier technology. It replaces the standard lens/mirror optical system with light-conducting fiber. What this means to you is a reduction in production costs, resulting in also a reduction in price over comparable lens/mirror machines. Fiber optic machines are more compact, weigh less, and deliver sharper, more consistent copies.

Toners. The type of toner was once a critical factor in the quality of the copy. However, the choices have narrowed as almost all copiers use dry or powdered toner. Liquid or wet toner copiers are generally inferior, and there are few currently available.

Toner replacement. Replacing the toner should be easy so you don't have to call a repairperson or company maintenance to do it. It can be messy, since some machines require you to pour the toner into a hopper, or turn a bottle face down. Toner cartridges are the simplest, but some models are easier than others. *Try before you buy.*

Copy process. The toner is bonded to the copy paper with heat or cold pressure. Heat is now the preferred method, and it does yield a better copy. But while cold pressure produces copies with a shiny finish, the machines don't require a lengthy warm-up period when first turned on.

Speed. The smaller machines designed for light copying and low volume can do 6–12 copies per minute (cpm), while the fastest obtain speeds of 50 cpm.

There are other factors to consider in determining the overall speed of copying: the "first copy time," or the time it takes to make the first or a single copy. Since most machines take 5–6 seconds to do so, picking up speed on repeats, "first copy time," could be important if you usually make single copies instead of large-scale duplication runs. Also consider "pre-select capacity," *i.e.*, the number of copies you can program the copier to make. Most machines will go up to 99; the largest ones go to 999. If you are making 200 copies on a machine that pre-selects to 50, you will have to put it through four separate (time-consuming) cycles.

Reduction/enlargement is becoming a standard feature. There are two basic types: *fixed ratio*, which reduce or enlarge according to pre-set proportions such as enlarge by 2x, 3x, etc., reduce by 1/2, 1/4, etc., and *zoom scales,* which reduce or enlarge continuously over a range, allowing you to select any reproduction ratio you wish. The range is generally from 60 percent to 150 percent. With zoom, you can, for example, take an odd-shaped piece of paper and program a ratio that will give you an image that fills an 8½ × 11 page.

Most models equipped with zoom also come with several fixed ratio settings for convenience.

Edge to edge copying. Some machines copy right up to the edges; many do not. If you copy many borderless or narrow-margin materials, edge to edge may be an important feature.

Platen. The part of the copier on which you place the original. The primary issue is whether the platen moves or remains stationary. Less expensive desktops usually have moving platens; they make noise and take up more room as they move back and forth. In addition, the original might slip as the platen moves.

Paper size is an important determinant in selecting a copier. Most copiers will do letter and legal size to size copying. Some offer smaller "statement" size and ledger size, and a few go even larger for specialty uses. Be careful here: many machines will accept large originals, but will only produce a reduced copy. So you must consider the size of the copy that the machine can handle as well as the maximum size of the original.

Paper weight. Most machines can copy on the most commonly used weights, but some perform better than others on a specific type of paper. It is a good idea to test the papers you will be using. Also, check the kind of papers the manufacturer recommends; that is a good indication of which will yield optimal results.

Dual paper trays. Many copiers store the paper sheets on cassettes or trays. The newer ones have two, so that two sizes and/or types of paper are available to you while you operate the machine, eliminating the need to change and/or empty cassettes or trays while you are in the middle of a copying job.

An interesting new feature is **automatic selection:** the copier recognizes the size of the original and automatically selects the paper tray best suited to making a copy, taking any reduction or enlargement into account. Some machines can do it in reverse: you select the paper tray, and the copier automatically computes the proper reproduction ratio needed to match the paper size.

The state of the art in paper tray gadgetry is something called "limitless copying," which connotes several new ideas that do the same thing—make sure you don't run out of paper. One way is to automatically switch from one paper tray to another when the first is empty; while the machine is taking paper from the second tray, you can reload the first, eliminating the need to stop. Other methods include ultra-large paper trays.

By-pass is a very sensible feature: Suppose you want to make just one copy, say, on your letterhead, but your machine's paper trays are filled with blank white copier paper. By-pass allows you to feed the single sheet of letterhead in manually, by-passing the paper tray. This feature is also useful when copying onto very light or heavy paper.

Image editing. Found only on state-of-the-art copiers, basically it is the capacity of a machine to make a copy that differs from the original image, either by deleting or selecting only a portion of it. It is a form of electronic cutting and pasting.

The most advanced image editing is on machines equipped with electronic scanning devices that digitalize the original image, and use several techniques to alter it. Text or pictures can be eliminated, or moved about on the page, or expanded or reduced. For example, you can take a original newsphoto and eliminate the caption on the copies.

Laser copiers (see section). Best suited for image editing, but even some inexpensive basic models offer trim and mask features, which are primitive forms of image editing.

Book copying. Sometimes called serial copying, is a feature that allows you to place the entire double page spread of a book face down on the platen; the machine first exposes one page, then the other, eliminating the need to reposition the book.

Margin shift. A form of image editing, allows you to make a clear margin on copies intended for binding or hole punching.

Automatic duplexing. Duplexing means copying on both sides of the same sheet, and it is feasible on most machines. But in manual form it means flipping the paper over and putting it back into the paper tray, and running it through a second time. Automatic duplexing eliminates this task, although on all but a few machines, the operator must turn over the originals.

Auto duplexing operates at slower speeds than simple single-side copying.

Color. Full-color copying on plain paper is now a reality, using either a four-color toner process or photographic process. These machines are very expensive.

A more common form of color reproduction is single color imaging, which is akin to printing with a colored ink. You substitute a single color toner for black; in some cases you can switch toners and re-copy to produce blended colors.

This type of color copying is widespread, especially on low-end models because it has become a marketing gimmick, an easy option to design into a machine. This feature makes sense only if you don't mind changing toner colors any more than you do changing ink colors in your ballpoint pen.

User friendly. Many machines come with electronic keypads, simplify the task of controlling image density (which can usually be set to automatic), paper size, etc. In addition, many machines have electronic message displays to prompt you through the copy sequence and inform you of errors or trouble.

Automatic document feed. This is a real plus, a real time-saver. The document is fed automatically and, through the automatic registration feature, aligned for a perfect copy. It works so well that it will handle even paper that has been wrinkled or crumpled. (Of course, you've got to straighten it out somewhat—the machine that will take a ball of paper has not been invented yet.)

There are two types of automated document feeders. Semi-automatic (SADF) involves manually feeding paper into a slot, as into a mailbox, while the machine takes the original aligns it, copies it and ejects it. Automatic document feeders (ADF) allow you to stack up your originals, freeing you from the process entirely. The machine takes the sheet off the top and then moves on to the next.

Sorters. Attached to the receiving end of copiers, they sort or collate the output. Most mid and high volume machines accept them, as well as several low volume models.

Sorters are useful when making a large number of multi-page documents.

Recirculating Document Handlers (RDH). Eliminates the need for ADF and sorters by performing the functions of both. Suppose you have a ten-page document and you want to make twenty sets. With an ADF and a sorter, the machine makes twenty copies of page one, placing each in a sorting bin, and moves on to page two, makes twenty copies, etc. With RDH, the machine feeds the document into itself, makes one copy of the document (very quickly), recycles the original, feeds it in again, makes another copy. As you can see, to make twenty copies, the original goes into the machine twenty times. In doing so, wear-and-tear on the original is increased, but you don't need a sorter.

Laser copiers. Quite similar to laser printers in their reproduction technology. They turn the image into digital electronic signals, essentially computerizing it. The information is then used to drive a laser beam which "writes" the image onto a drum which then uses conventional copier technology to reproduce the image. Laser printers work the same way, except that they don't start with a hard copy.

Because the machines are so similar, manufacturers have begun combining the machines. Laser printer/copiers print using the same method, but can receive originals in electronic (from a computer or word processor) or hard copy (a document placed on the platen) form.

Besides speed and clarity, laser copiers offer excellent image editing capabilities. Technically, once a hard copy has been digitalized by placing on the platen, the electronic image could be sent by cable or phone line to another laser copier somewhere else.

Electronic copy control systems. Arose to fight the copyholism epidemic. At least 20 percent of all copies made are unnecessary. About 30 percent are made on the wrong machine for the job. These two sins can cost a firm 50 percent or more of its total copy expense in unnecessary copy charges. Copy control software simply keeps a record of who is making the copies and how many they are making, broken down by client, job, etc.

THE ECONOMICS OF COPIERS

Added Costs

Toner. Like ink, toner must be replenished. Naturally, if you copy lots of items with dense or solid black sections, you will use more toner than if you copy documents with lots of white space. Toner costs, expressed in terms of cost per copy, range from 0.4 cents to 0.6 cents.

The drum, or photoreceptor as it is sometimes called, wears out with use. Usually, they last for between 50,000 and 200,000 copies, with the new amorphous silicon drums going for 500,000 copies before replacement. Costs per copy average between 0.2 cents and 0.4 cents.

Miscellaneous parts like rubber rollers do need occasional replacement, but are not major cost factors.

Service. An important cost component in the operation of a copier is service. You can pay "on-call" at the going hourly rate for labor and for parts.

Another approach involves purchasing a "copy kit"; you buy toner, drums (and sometimes the paper) needed to run off a set number of copies, and the price includes parts and labor while you use the copy kit.

Many firms opt for a service contract which usually covers all or some parts and labor over a given period specified by time (usually twelve months) or usage (number of copies), whichever comes first. Some service contracts offer unlimited copies yearly.

In order to make the best decision with regard to service, you will need to have a clear understanding of how your copier will be used. How much volume? Can you afford an out-of-order machine for a few days? A few hours? More important than service is the proper selection of the best make and model for your needs.

Models. Models are designed to handle light, medium or heavy-duty needs as measured by copies per month. The manufacturers assume that the greater the volume requirements the more likely the user will welcome extras such as high speeds, reduction/enlargement, larger size document-handling and ADF.

Generally, the larger the monthly volume, the lower the average cost. The copy costs mentioned below include the cost of toner and replacement drums, parts and labor (except in the case of mini-copiers).

Hand-held. A recent innovation, miniature copiers don't replace conventional ones. Rather, they are useful for library-bound students, traveling executives, engineers and others who feel the need to capture a portion of a document while on the go. At present, these machines work by passing one end, equipped with a rolling copy head, over the document. The result is a strip several inches wide.

Mini-copiers. Also called personal copiers, are low-volume machines which are intended for less than 1,000 copies for month and copy at speeds from 8–10 cpm. Several can copy legal as well as letter-size, and a few offer reduction/enlargement. *Operating costs average between two cents and 3.5 cents per copy.*

Low volume copiers. Best for between 1,000 and 5,000 copies per month. Their speeds range from 10–12 cpm, and some can copy documents larger than legal. *Average costs per copy on these machines is about 1.7 cents (5,000 copies per month) to two cents (1,000 per month).*

Lower mid-volume copiers. All such machines can copy ledger size documents and run at speeds from 15–20 + cpm. If you are making 5,000–10,000 copies per month, such machines are ideal. *Expect to average a little under 1.6 cents per copy, to a high of a little under two cents if your volume is at the lower end of the range.*

Mid-volume copiers. Intended for between 15,000 and 20,000 copies per month, these machines run between 20–30 cpm and nearly all offer reduction/enlargement. *Copy costs should average 1.5 cents or less.*

Upper mid-volume copiers. Will serve needs up to 30,000 copies a month at 35–40 cpm; many have automatic duplexing and special document handling features. Costs per copy run less than 1.5 cents, with the cost falling with increased volume.

High volume machines. Justifiable if you are making 35,000/50,000 copies per month; speeds range from 40 to 60 cpm. *Above 40,000 copies per month, expect to pay about 1.1 cents per copy.*

Copiers are sold at a discount to list price; expect around twenty-five percent.

What to look for in a copier. According to a recent survey conducted by *Administrative Management* magazine, users of large copiers rated high reliability and good service the number-one desirable features of copiers, followed by reasonable costs. For users of smaller machines, reliability and service also finished at the top, but copy quality was next on the list. This difference is easy to explain. All copiers have their share of downtime in which they chew, smudge, and otherwise destroy paper—but among the larger machines, which are more expensive, copy quality is almost always good; with smaller ones, it's catch-as-catch-can, especially when dealing with coated paper.

Here are the results of the survey in a nutshell:

USERS OF LOW-END COPIERS

most wanted features

1. prompt response to service calls
2. reduced frequency of paper jams
3. service with expertise
4. reduction of downtime
5. frequent scheduled service calls
6. consistent copy quality
7. smudgeproofness of copy image
8. uniform quality across page
9. minimum quality fall-off between scheduled maintenance calls
10. copy counter that clears to zero after run

least wanted features

1. mobility, portability of unit
2. erasability on copy
3. sheet bypass
4. service code display cards
5. stream-feeding of originals
6. copying on offset master stock
7. copying on colored paper
8. duplexing
9. trade-in allowance

USERS OF HIGH-END COPIERS

most wanted features

1. servicemen's expertise
2. prompt response to service calls
3. net uptime
4. reduced frequency of jams
5. reasonable out-of-pocket costs
6. frequently scheduled service calls
7. reduced job turn-around— time in to time out
8. replacement parts availability
9. reasonable consumable supply costs
10. automatic document handler (ADH)

least wanted features

1. feeding unburst computer printout
2. copies on offset master stock
3. enlargement capability
4. dedicated electric line
5. machine resale value
6. trade or rental credit allowance
7. ADH for 11" × 17" originals
8. copies of film transparencies
9. reproduction of colored images
10. no image edge skip

If you are puzzled by the wide range of machines and features, take a careful look at this list before you make your final decision. If you are going to look at equipment, take the survey with you. If you don't want to carry this book, you can always . . . well . . . make a photocopy of the survey.

A COPIER CHECKLIST

This checklist* is designed to help evaluate your office reproduction system, to assess its needs and special problems. It will be useful in deciding what equipment is best.

1. How long have we had our present copier(s)?
2. If leased or rented, what kind of lease or rental agreement is involved? How long does it run? When does it expire? What are renewal arrangements? What are the penalties, if any?
3. How many copiers do we have? What type of copiers are they? Are they centralized or decentralized?
4. What type of copier do we have—plain paper or other? Dry toner or liquid toner?
5. Are different supplies—papers, toners, developers—used for each, or are special supplies needed?
6. Can we copy onto all types of material: letterheads, self-adhesive labeles, transparencies, offset masters?
7. Do we have any policy to control length of runs on each unit and/or to prevent unauthorized copying?
8. Do we have any other duplicating machines?
9. What is the monthly volume of copies for each machine we have? What is the manufacturer's recommended usage for each model?
10. What is our cost per copy? In the case of rental equipment, does this cost include all supplies?
11. What kinds and sizes of documents are we copying on a regular basis?
12. Do we get consistently good copy quality, with solid black tones in both text and artwork?
13. What is our experience with misfeeds and breakdowns?
14. Is our principal copier rated as high-speed or medium-speed? Do we have any other copiers available?
15. How fast a copying speed do we need for our copy volume?
16. What is the average number of copies run per original?
17. What special copier requirements do we have, for example, two-sided copying; transparencies; book copying; reduction; ability to copy from a wide range of different types of originals?

---

*Reprinted by permission of Toshiba America, Business Equipment Division, Wayne, New Jersey.

---

18. Are disadvantages to our having high-speed copiers inherent in the electrical requirements; the question of centralized vs. decentralized copying; size; reliability (the higher the speed the greater the possibility of jam); availability of backup equipment in case of downtime?

19. Are we using our copier for reproduction that would be substantially cheaper if it were done on a printing press or a duplicator?

20. In computing our indirect copying costs, do we figure in such factors as supervision, personnel time (waiting, walking, operation), waste, and downtime?

21. Are major multipage documents being reproduced unnecessarily when a few routing or file copies would be sufficient?

22. Are the reasons we selected centralized or decentralized copying still relevant to today's requirements?

23. Are there budget benefits in departmentalizing copiers for accurate allocation of costs?

24. Is there a benefit in having more than one copier available for use in case of breakdowns, elimination of travel time, queuing time, etc.?

FOR MORE INFORMATION For a detailed report of the results of this survey, contact:

Richard Hanson & Associates
Box 353
Setauket, New York 11733

Richard E. Hanson is a recognized authority in the field of copying and duplicating. His user-oriented report, "Hanson's Guidelines . . . Best Copier Buys for the Small User," discusses prices, user experience, and new models and features. It is updated quarterly. Another helpful publication from Hanson is his book *A Manager's Guide to Copying and Duplicating.*

For more detailed information on copiers, The Buyer's Laboratory puts out "Copier Review," which includes a monthly newsletter on the industry, test reports on copiers, dry toners, and duplicating systems, a 28-page guide to copiers, and information on controlling copier costs. This mateial is obviously intended for purchasing agents in large companies, but you can obtain the reports on a one-time basis, as opposed to a subscription. The reports are Consumers Union style, unbiased and bench-tested.

Contact:

Buyer's Laboratory, Inc.
20 Railroad Avenue
Hackensack, New Jersey 07601
(201) 488-0404

What to Buy for Business is a monthly publication that bills itself as a "consumer report for business," and it devotes frequent, considerable attention to copiers. Its editorial, research and buyers' guides are all first-rate, providing more than you probably want to know about evaluating, selecting, purchasing and maintaining copiers.

Contact:

What to Buy for Business
350 Theodore Fremd Avenue
Rye, New York 10580

MICROGRAPHICS

A product of nineteenth-century technology, micrographics has survived and quietly prospered throughout the years because of several distinct advantages.

Micrographics takes several forms. But basically, it is an inexpensive, compact, efficient, unalterable method of duplication, storage and retrieval of records and archives.

Recently, however, the computer revolution has seriously eroded the competitive advantage of micrographics. First, micrographics is a photographic medium in an increasingly electronic world. If a record or image is in digital electronic form, it can be sent across the room or around the world, altered, stored, retrieved. To overcome the obvious shortcomings, micrographics manufacturers have designed ways to link up with computers. But because it is photographic technology, micrography can never really be directly connected with computers.

For example, computers can now be instructed to locate a particular roll or microfilm or microfiche, even to the extent of operating a mechanical device that will retrieve it from a file. But with the use of a hard disk, a computer can call up a stored record and display it in seconds, ready to be altered, amended, print out or sent elsewhere.

Recent advances have produced machines that can digitalize micrographics, electronically process them with computers, and then transfer the material to a new microfilm or paper. These innovations will prove most helpful to institutions which already have a large number of micrographic files, but will hardly attract new users.

One of the shortcomings has emerged as a strength: *permanency.* Electronic storage (disks, etc.) can easily be altered or erased. Micrographics records cannot be changed, so they are the better choice for archives, especially when the records are kept for posterity and rarely retrieved.

For "active" files, electronic storage is preferable. And the advent of CD/ROM technology threatens micrographics's advantage in archives because optical disks can be permanent and unalterable, like the compact audio disks currently popular in home stereo systems.

TYPES OF MICROFORMS

Micrographics involves the use of microforms, a generic term for any microphotographically produced printed matter. Microforms cannot be read without the aid of a reader that magnifies the microform and usually projects it onto a screen. There are several formats:

MICROFILM   Microform in 16mm or 35mm roll format, microfilm is the granddaddy of microforms, developed as a space saver for copying newspapers and magazines.

MICROFICHE   The format is a 4" × 6" film card that carries reduced images, assembled in rows. Fiches may be either black-and-white or color, and the conventional fiche can hold up to 98 pages of text.

MICROBOOK FICHE   The microbook holds page reproductions that have been greatly reduced (between 55 and 90 times), allowing them to hold up to 1,000 pages.

Other forms include microprints and microcards, which are gradually being replaced by microfiche.

PRINCIPAL USES OF MICROGRAPHICS

1. as protection against information loss
2. as insurance against the deterioration commonly associated with paper
3. as a rapid, inexpensive means of duplication
4. as an efficient means of storage and retrieval

The microforms used in the modern office are almost always *microfilm* or *microfiche.*

WHAT MICROFILM CAN DO

Microfilm can file information in as little as 10 percent of the space required by paper. Microfilm storage can be extremely cost-effective. Some experts have estimated that even with the cost of converting to microfilm, the first year's expense would be half that of maintaining an equivalent amount of paper files.

WHAT MICROFICHE CAN DO

It occupies less than 1 percent of the space required by paper. It is cheaper than paper. A microfiche report costs between 7 percent and 30 percent less than a copy of the same report on paper. A new fiche system utilizes fiches that can be added to, erased, and even written on.

COM (COMPUTER OUTPUT MICROFILM)

COM is the fastest-growing segment of the micrographics industry. Simply stated, data from a computer is converted to an image which is reduced by a lens system and recorded on film or fiche. The next step is processing and, if necessary, duplication of the film.

COM TRENDS

- *CAR* (computer assisted retrieval). The biggest complaint about micrographics is that retrieving it can be a big hassle. CAR solves this problem, with a computerized index to help locate a microform.
- *CIM* (computer input microfilm). One such system uses OCR (optical character recognition) to scan a microform, convert it to bits, and put it on a screen or even transmit it. Thus, in CIM, the computer "sees" the microfilm and, therefore, accepts it as input.

35
TELEPHONES

I don't have to tell you that there is a major telecommunications revolution taking place. The kinds of equipment and services that are offered are so extensive, so diverse, and so individualized that all I can offer are some basic guidelines.

THE PRINCIPAL DEVICES

Automatic dialers. They do just what you'd expect. You program the most frequent used numbers into the dialer's memory and label a series of buttons with the parties' names. Push a button, and the number is dialed almost instantly, with nary a misdial. Purpose? Well, it saves money on misdials and may save you a little time in looking up the numbers. But so would a card that holds the same numbers and sits on your desk next to the phone. Will it save you time in dialing?

For most executives, the benefits are negligible, although dialers are so widespread and so inexpensive, you probably have one at your disposal, so you might as well use it. If you have poor vision, it can be of significant value, or if there are several numbers which you might need to dial in time-of-the-essence situations. Stockbrokers and bankers swear by them.

The major difference in machines is in the number of phone numbers they can store. Some of the flashy features include a "last number dialed" redialing feature, so you can keep trying if you get a "busy" the first time. I suppose that any machine that saves you the trouble of redialing a busy number is worth the price in saved aggravation when calling a government agency, a movie theater for times, or any teenager.

Telephone answering devices. These machines are unquestionably the most popular of the accessories on the market, and if you haven't made contact with one yet, pinch yourself—you're probably dead. They are everywhere, and as much as we dislike them, they are often more reliable than human answering services. And they don't talk back. However, a calling party will rarely hang up on reaching a service, but many, many people hang up the minute they hear the wow and flutter of your voice on tape.

Originally these machines were very simple. After a number of rings, they would greet your caller with a taped message and signal him to leave a message on the machine, usually on a special message tape for recording these messages (the two-tape system is better and more costly than a single-tape).

Lately, these machines have become much more sophisticated, with an eye toward the business market. Several models can carry on a simulated conversation with callers, allowing it to take orders and the like. Several can be programmed to take a survey by asking the caller a series of questions and pausing for a reply. Voice activation allows the machines to "know" when the caller is through speaking and stop the message tape and reset.

Most answer-and-record units allow you to vary the number of rings required to trigger the answering machine, to limit or allow for unlimited message lengths, and to retrieve your messages from an outside phone. Other advances include automatic call diversion, which diverts your call to the number where you can be reached, and machines that can handle up to 12 lines simultaneously. Most units allow you to monitor the caller's voice and decide if you want to pick up the call as it comes in or tend to the matter later.

Some problems exist with these machines. They are dependent on voltage levels and other electronic cues from the telephone system, and little glitches in the phone lines may cause them to malfunction. The endless loop tapes stretch easily, thus, after a time, the voice on the message will be distorted. Many of the machines do not incorporate high-quality play or record heads, so you get fuzzy reproduction, poor tape quality, and even some static.

Commercial units offer better tape mechanisms and recording quality, but most of the same features are also found in the better consumer models.

Speaker phones. These devices enable you to hear phone calls without putting your ear to the phone's receiver. Duplex devices allow two-way conversation. How they work: They employ small speakers and condenser microphones, and the circuit amplifies the phone signal and throws it into the room via the speaker. The condenser microphone, similar to the one in your portable cassette recorder, picks up speech in the area and transmits it to the phone unit. Thus, you can walk, pace, organize your desk, take notes, or make love while talking on the phone. No hands needed (at least not for the phone). Many standard business phone consoles have speaker-phones built in, as well as a few home units.

Timing devices. Timing devices are added features that can be found on anything from auto phone dialers to amplifiers to answering machines, since they are not central to the function of the device, but are just clocks, built in as an add-on.

Telephone security devices. There are three basic types: *locks,* which prevent dialing and/or summoning the operator; *code devices,* which require the phone system to respond to codes before allowing calls to go through—all calls, if you prefer, or only calls to a specific party; and *"debugging"* devices, which let you know when someone is listening in, or (so goes the manufacturers' claim) prevent bugging from taking place.

Cordless phones. Consist of a wireless telephone handset, equipped with an antenna, and base station and antenna which plugs into the telephone jack. Voice and dial tones are transmitted between the phone and base station by radio waves.

   Business applications appear very limited in this case, although I know of one retailer who has chosen to equip his premises with one base station and several phones near the registers, rather than to wire the store for regular phone extensions.

Cellular phones. Due to some recent advances in telecommunications technology, and cooperation by the FCC, cellular phones have proliferated across the country. All you need to know is that you can place clear, reliable telephone calls from a phone in a car or a portable cellular carried in a briefcase. The phones are expensive but affordable for most business users. However, the cost per minute is several times that of ordinary toll charges, and cellular phone calls have a way of adding up quickly.

   In cities like Los Angeles, where a great deal of valuable business time is lost in commuting, cellular phones can be invaluable. Indeed, the largest number of phones in service is in California and Texas.

Souped-up phones. Since the FCC and court rulings have sanctioned competition in the phone equipment market and the specifications have been standardized, you can walk into a "phone store," and buy any phone you like. And all the laws of the marketplace prevail.

   Telephone units now come equipped with all sorts of options such as LCD indicator lights, one-touch auto dialing, speakerphones with mute buttons, paging and electronic hold, to name a few.

THE EXECUTIVE WORKSTATION

The latest in telephone technology is something known as the IVDT, for integrated voice/data terminal. Since executives increasingly are using telephone lines for more than just phone calls, manufacturers have begun to integrate the major telecommunications functions in one unit.

531

The most important elements of such units allow the user to place phone calls and send and receive data through electronic mail and on-line databases, as well as teleconferencing and facsimile transmission.

The units include video display terminals, phone units, microprocessor and circuit boards and keyboards.

Other extras include electronic phone directories and autodialing, built-in modems, automatic redial, electronic messaging, electronic appointment calendar, clock, alarm, calculator, programmable "soft" keys, and message logging and billing features.

THINGS TO REMEMBER
ABOUT TELEPHONE SERVICE

Check your bills carefully. Look for calls improperly charged to you each month. Every six months, check your monthly statements for service and miscellaneous charges.

Talk telephone with your accountant. Equipment rental is tax deductible. Purchase gives you investment tax credit plus accelerated depreciation.

Remember WATS lines are not free. And long conversations defeat their purpose and cost effectiveness.

Analyze your service deal and configuration. You often have more service than you need, or the wrong kind of service. You'll pay dearly for it.

If you have a switchboard, consider the computerized option. Such devices can perform faster and better than an operator. By one estimate, you'll enjoy up to a 30 percent return on investment per year through use of such equipment.

Use credit cards only when you can't dial without operator help. They are often used simply because they provide you with a record of calls made from the outside. But credit-card calls are operator-assisted and, therefore, very expensive. There are better and cheaper ways to record your phone calls and costs. Try a little phone log or the expense section of your pocket diary. Or use direct dial long distance services such as MCI or Sprint.

When you're in a hotel or motel, however, the telephone charge may be less if you use a credit card than if you use the hotel switchboard services for intrastate calls.

Do not ignore abuse and misuse of telephones. The amount of time and money devoured by employees on the phone is incredible. Executives have a number of options. Obtrusive methods involve asking people to cut down, log their own calls, etc. There are also unobtrusive computerized devices that will restrict and/or log calls automatically. The return on investment on these is very rapid. Don't supply company phone credit cards. Rather, reimburse employees for personal credit card use; this method protects the company if an employee quits or is fired.

Reassess your equipment periodically. There are many new options and suppliers to consider. Besides, inappropriate or outdated equipment often wastes money. Take a good look at least every two years—more often if your company is growing very fast. And keep an open mind toward alternatives.

Learn how to work with consultants. As in the computer business, telephone system options get so complicated that, often, you must rely on consultants to lead you through the maze. Ideally, consultants will make a thorough study of your office and then recommend ways to cut costs and improve service. If they suggest new equipment, they should provide several options.

Be careful when you choose a consultant. Many "consultants" are simply former salesmen who've gone out on their own, but maintain ties to their old company. Others may receive a kickback under the table. How to protect yourself: Ask for the names of the last ten jobs and check to see who the vendors were. If it's the same in all or most of the cases, you just might have a problem.

Ask for a statement in writing that the consultant is in no way affiliated with any vendor and that he receives no sales commissions on any equipment purchased.

Don't pay on the basis of percentage of savings in phone equipment or service costs. Any fool can save you money by buying inexpensive equipment or downgrading your service. Pay a per diem or a fee for the entire job.

OCCS

OCC is shortened for other Common Carriers, or any telephone service other than AT&T, such as Spring or MCI. Should you use one, and if so, which one?

The question boils down to costs per minute. Which service, AT&T or one of the alternatives, provides *your* business with the lowest overall toll costs per minute? The comparisons in ads don't count; only the cost comparison based on the phone patterns of your particular firm.

A few other issues to consider:

Billing. Some of the OCCs provide detailed billings which break down charges according to accounting codes, making it easier for you to assess charge and control costs.

Voice clarity. If the phone calls are filled with static and frequently interrupted, the long distance service may not be worth the savings. Try to arrange a trial or at least get references from other users.

Data transmission. Some OCCs offer telephone lines for data transmission only at special savings.

Multiple usage. Unlike WATS lines, which involve dedicating a specific number of lines to the service, OCCs offer low-cost long distance on virtually every line in your system (unless you wish to limit the usable lines); this eliminates unnecessary waiting for long distance lines.

SUGGESTED READING

How to Cut Costs and Improve Service of Your Telephone, Telex, TWX and Other Telecommunications, by Frank K. Griesinger (New York: McGraw-Hill, 1974).

This is an excellent book, written by one of the true authorities in the field. It is very thorough and will undoubtedly save you some money in the long run. It is a bit outdated, though, with respect to rates and the latest equipment, and currently out of print.

36

COMMUNICATIONS AND ELECTRONIC MAIL

Another one of those fancy marketing buzzwords, *electronic mail* can mean one specific service or an entire field, depending on who you're talking to. The safe way is to take the broad approach and use the term to apply to any electronic means of transmitting data or messages. Here are the principal ones:

- communicating computers
- communicating text editors
- telex and TWX
- facsimile
- mailgrams
- telegrams
- message switching
- teleconferencing
- video teleconferencing

Electronic mail is emerging rapidly, and undoubtedly becoming a very important part of the modern business workplace. The speed and efficiency of the new devices make information gathering, sharing and communications virtually instantaneous, and places it under the pinpoint control of the users. In some businesses, the information gateway is open twenty-four hours a day, seven days a week.

Electronic mail comes in many forms. Basically the systems are either *outside networks,* such as those run by Western Union and MCI; *internal networks,* such as those run by Texas Instruments and Citibank; and *local networks (Lans)* for use with an office.

According to the U.S. Congress Office of Technology Assessment, more than 40 billion messages will be transmitted electronically by 1995; the number is projected to pass 60 billion by the turn of the century.

The technology has been available for years. But recently, it has improved in speed and reliability, and equipment and transmittal costs have come down, making it more economical to use "E-mail." As the business community overcomes its computerphobia and recognizes the potential of E-mail, use will grow rapidly. Most important is the fact that there are now so many terminals in use; a user inclined to send a message stands

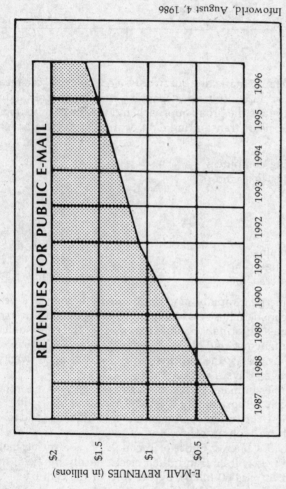

Fig. 67. Suppliers of public-access electronic mail services will see their revenues grow more than five times within a decade, according to a recent report.

SOURCE: INTERNATIONAL RESOURCE DEVELOPMENT INC.
Infoworld, August 4, 1986

a better chance that the addressee will be suitably equipped to receive it. Every terminal is a potential electronic mail box.

Keep in mind, however, that electronic mail must still be considered an emerging technology; it has a long way to go before it becomes commonplace. While the arguments for rapid growth appear logical, especially if business readily embraces the most cost effective communications technology, the rate of acceptance is difficult to predict.

At present, about 900,000 people use "public" E-mail networks, while about 1.5 million use internal networks.

For simplicity's sake, we will divide our discussion of electronic mail into two parts: systems that require a computer or computer terminal, (LAN, voicemail, EMS) and systems that generally require other types of equipment or none at all (Teletype, Facsimile, Teleconferencing, Videoconferencing).

TELETYPE SERVICES

These are the primary "wire services." Technological first cousins of the telephone, they use teletypewriters instead of phones to send printed messages. Both are owned and operated by Western Union, and although telegrams are obsolete for business uses, telex and TWX are certainly not. These systems are fast, and they are *cheaper than phone.*

TELEX/TWX/TELETEX

TELEX (for Teleprinter Exchange Service) uses technology that dates from the '50s. However, it has one important advantage over more modern systems: it is already in widespread use here and abroad.

Low-end TELEX terminals are very basic; more advanced units have some storage capacity. It is now possible to access the TELEX network with a personal computer through an on-line data service (see section on databases).

TELEX transmits at about 10 characters per second. A newer system called TELETEX, in limited use, transmits at about 300 characters per second.

Like TELEX and TELETEX, TWX is owned by Western Union. But TWX started out as a system that competed with TELEX, originally owned by AT&T and Telcos. Western Union acquired it in 1971 and found itself with two incompatible, overlapping systems. TWX differs little from TELEX, and is not as common.

FACSIMILE

The most typical facsimile machines use a light-sensing device to scan the page and transmit the pattern via telephone lines to another transceiver, where it's reproduced. Such systems have actually been around for years; they have been in use since the 1920s in the weather bureaus, news services, and law enforcement agencies. But it wasn't until 1966 that the "fax" entered the business market.

Facsimile machines are booming. 125,000 units were purchased in the United States in 1985. Computer technology has made them more reliable and much easier to operate.

There are four basic classes of business fax equipment:

- Group I, the low-speed models, transmitting at 4-6 minutes per page. Few of these machines are sold today, but there is a large installed base.
- Group II units can send or receive a letter-size page in three minutes. These machines can be programmed to send and receive overnight when phone rates are lower.
- Group III uses digital technology to transmit a page of text in under one minute. They produce higher quality copies with greater number of dots per inch. Group III machines are "smart"; they can store telephone numbers and documents, and automatically transmit to a number of locations at the same time; they can "poll" other devices to see if there are documents waiting to be received or sent.
- Group IV units require a high-speed digital telephone line, and come in three different classes, based on the resolution or quality of the copies, ranging from 200 to 400 lines per inch. These machines use "packet-switching" technology, which moves blocks or "packets" of data around rather than individual bits, to increase speed.
- Facsimile/computer interfaces are integrated products that allow faxed material to go directly to and from the personal computer in digital form. A document received on a fax could then be displayed on a PC, altered or edited, and sent directly back to the fax for transmission. There is no need to rekey the document, as is the case when it is received as a hard copy only. In addition, the fascimile could be stored on a desk and/or sent to a printer for higher speed or multiple copy output.

ADVANTAGES

- *exact copy.* What you see is what they'll get: words, numbers, and pictures exactly as they are on your in-house copy of the fax. Useful for transmitting charts, graphs, ads, etc.

- *speed.* Transmission is immediate, and reasonably fast.
- *virtual error-free transmission*
- *no "rekeyboarding"*
- *no special training needed to operate*
- *easy to install*
- *sender keeps original*

DISADVANTAGES

- *cost.* You've got to rent the equipment and pay for phone lines. When you talk fax, you talk phone charges. And when you are sending a three-page report on a low-speed machine, that's a phone call of around fifteen minutes. Compare that to the cost of mailing the report and, well, it's expensive. A few insiders say that the phone companies make more on the fax systems than the fax manufacturers make. The economics become more favorable with Group II, and especially Group III and IV machines.
- *two machines required for each message.* You can't send a message to someone who isn't equipped to receive. Many companies arrive at a decision jointly with a client or associated company to install a telecopier; for example, a Madison Avenue ad agency and a midwestern food processor may agree that "faxing" ad and other promotional material for approval and revision will be cheaper than overnight package services and other methods of meeting deadlines.
- *incompatibility.* Most low-speed Group I machines cannot communicate with units of other manufacturers.

IN THE FUTURE   The vendors are working on ways to reduce the scanning process so fewer "spots" are required. More speed should mean lower cost. Future users of faxes will tend to be smaller firms, or smaller offices of larger firms. Communicating WPs and other computer-based message systems (CBMS) will replace them in larger firms, where more sophisticated equipment makes sense economically.

TELECONFERENCING

Most of us have taken part in a simple telephone conference call; even many home telephones now come equipped with that option. But teleconferencing can involve dozens of people at locations scattered around the world. Teleconferences may employ a firm's own telecommunications equipment, or be arranged through AT&T or other networks.

Video was once the sole property of television networks. Then came the cable systems. Now comes the business community. Many of the electronic transmission networks are now able to set up a conference in which people interact via voice, video, or pure data, without the necessity of shared physical proximity.

Video teleconferencing (named as such to distinguish from voice-only conferences) allow two or more people to communicate face-to-face across great distances, and includes the transmission of graphics and documents. Typically, they are held in rooms that are permanently equipped for video conferences, the firm or firms having decided to make the investment. In larger cities, such facilities may be rented.

Recently, a special report in *Fortune* magazine cited an SRI report done for the National Science Foundation. It found that about 50 percent of all business travel could be obviated by electronic alternatives. The same *Fortune* report also quotes George Gantz, of the New England Energy Congress, who claims that even by the year 2000, this replacement of travel with electronic communication will conserve only about 1 percent of the total American energy bill.

That's a problem, because energy savings could have provided a great incentive to switch to the teleconferencing. Things will move slowly, because it will take time for the facilities to become widespread and for executives to alter old patterns and get used to newer means of doing business. Nevertheless, we're more familiar with teleconferencing than we probably think. For years now, news programming has resorted to interviews via video transmission. Watching Rather in New York interviewing Chirac in France live no longer seems strange. So when the time comes for you to have a teleconference with a J.B. who's a thousand miles away, you shouldn't be too rattled.

VOICE MAIL

Voice mail is a vague term that covers several different technologies and methods; it can even be taken to imply the simple telephone answering machine. Basically, the difference between voice mail and a simple telephone call is that voice mail means you can leave a "human speech" message to be retrieved later by one or several receivers.

This kind of service is more important than it sounds. The fact is, nearly half of all business calls do not reach the intended party on the first attempt. And studies show that beyond the "hello's," and "how-are-you's," most calls convey information in *one* direction, with one person doing most of the talking.

With voice mail technology, the caller always gets through with the first call, and the person doing the listening can do so at his convenience, rather than in a "real time" one-way conversation.

Executives are less likely to lose messages when on the road. And the savings in avoiding repeated phone calls and time spent on "hold" is obvious.

Another feature is the *voice memo*. Instead of having one typed, copied and distributed, you speak it once, and it is sent to the *voice mail boxes* of all relevant parties.

Unfortunately, voice mail systems are currently expensive, the cheapest ones running about fifty thousand dollars, and the top of the line about half a million. But manufacturers are beginning to incorporate voice mail features into PABX office telephone systems. They will allow you to reach voice mail boxes, automatic re-routing of a message to a "message desk" unit if you are out, and/or "message waiting" indicators on all telephone units (similar to those on hotel phones).

COMPUTER-BASED MESSAGE SYSTEMS (CBMS)

This special form of electronic mail allows the user to be alert to the flow of messages—and to control the flow. For example, you can access incoming messages at your convenience. Once received, a message can be disposed of (erased) electronically, filed, or passed along. CBMS leave tracks—they can be traced back to the source or forward to the last person to see the message. Obviously, such a system reduces filing tremendously. The biggest disadvantage is that the system usually requires executives to be near the terminal and operate the keyboard. Do not be shy about learning to use the terminal. A computer is not a piece of secretarial support equipment. It can be, and often is, a strategic device that aids in decision making. Status should come with the introduction of a terminal to your desk territory. This is one area where you shouldn't be afraid to buck the system. Be the first one on your block to have a cathode ray tube on your desk top. It's the wave of the future.

CBMS are operated for public access by on-line networks such as Western Union, MCI and CompuServe. They can also be internal, company owned and operated, or local, served by Local Area Networks or LANs.

Communicating computers. In its simplest form, CBMS may just be a "my-screen-to-your-screen" form of sending and receiving text and data, through the use of an inexpensive modem, or a LAN network. Even at this level, the process can grow complex and very high-tech. Witness the use of CBMS in newspaper offices, where reporters file stories via computer, either with a modem from the field, or on a terminal at the desk. The editors can then perform sophisticated text editing, and the material can then be processed further and prepped for typesetting.

Indeed, the potential applications for CBMS are tremendous, now that LAN technology has arrived. As software designers catch up, users on the network will be able to share applications software and data, making communication and problem solving more efficient. Of course, this will create several problems as well: if there is an error, its effect could be multiplied; also, new procedures must be developed for delegating and assessing work, and making decisions.

While millions of personal computers will be linked together with LANs, most will not. Lotus Development puts the figure for networked computers at about 25 percent of all corporate PCs. But keep in mind that public E-mail networks and LANs are becoming compatible, and the combination of the two will greatly enhance the potential of CBMS.

Message switching. Originally developed for facsimile machines, message switching technology allows the user to send messages to a station which holds the transmission to be released at an optimal moment. Such systems can also transmit the same message to several locations at once.

CBMS ADVANTAGES

SPEED AND EFFICIENCY

NONSIMULTANEOUS TIME   Use your time the way you want to. Solve problems when you want to. In the case of a completed phone connection, both you and the other party must be "tied up" at the same time. Chances are that one of you is being pulled away from another high-priority task. With CBMS the sender can lay down the message at his convenience, and you can receive it at yours.

PRIORITIZING   The beauty of this system is that you do not have to deal with messages on a chronological basis. The first message of the day may be the last one you actually read. The computer provides a list of the messages on tap; you pick and choose. Some systems even allow a high-priority signal, which lets you know that an important message is coming in.

INTERRUPTIONS   Really cuts them down, especially those that are phone related.

TRENDS IN ELECTRONIC MAIL

Important trends in electronic mail involve innovation in delivery systems, *i.e.*, methods of sending and receiving messages. Recently, engineers from nations around the world have begun to take action to eliminate the "electronic Tower of Babel" by agreeing on standards for various types of data transmission. It is all very political, with many nations seeking to favor homegrown technologies, but there is every reason to be optimistic. After years of negotiation, facsimile standards were agreed upon. Agreements on Integrated Services Digital Network (ISDN) standards may someday eliminate the need for a modem, as most phone transmission goes digital.

Problems still exist in the Local Area Network field, with many manufacturers offering incompatible systems. But standardization makes economic sense. Markets for advanced technology historically do not expand until a standard emerges so that the consumer can purchase without fear.

Satellites. With so many satellites in geosynchronous orbit, there is a large supply of "transponders" and channels, and the cost of satellite direct-broadcast is dropping. Personal computers will communicate via satellite links using small dishes equipped with demodulators. You may recall that computers currently receive information through their modems at between 300 and 2400 bps; satellites can send at speeds from 9600 to 19,200 bps.

Wireless modems. LANs are fine, but they always involve some kind of cabling. Larger networks often utilize telephone lines. And satellite technology is often a case of overkill. For two company buildings say across the street, or on opposite sides of the Mexican border, "wireless modems" may be just the thing. They work like phone modems, except they use advance antennae rather than phone lines or cable. Some systems can link over 200 computers and transmit over a distance of thirty miles using a VHF FM channel. You will see more of this kind of networking as prices drop, especially in situations where cabling is difficult and/or local telephone service is poor.

Subcarrier radio transmission (SCA). Employs unused portions of a common FM radio signal; ordinary receivers can't pick up such transmissions, but the conventional signal can be used to "carry" the subcarrier information.

Vertical blanking interval (VBI). Utilizes the unused portions of ordinary television signals to transmit data and video. This will enable you to pick up video images through your personal computer. The first applications will likely be financial information and news.

LARGE-SCALE DOWNLOADING

Much of the time spent "on-line" involves searching the database for information or a message. As the cost of computer memory continues to drop, and transmission speeds increase, it may well make economic sense for an on-line network to "dump" part or an entire database into the personal computer's memory and sign-off. The PC would then proceed to search and retrieve the needed data under its own power, eliminating the need for costly on-line searching.

ADVANCED PRODUCT TESTING TECHNIQUES

With electronic mail, companies will be able to gather information about their goods and services from test markets and analyze them much more rapidly. Thus, products will fly—and die—at a much faster pace. This eventuality will also mean further market fragmentation, with vendors appealing to more specific and numerous market segments—resulting, in turn, in more choice for consumers and more alternatives for vendors. And this should (with heavy emphasis on the "should") be a very positive development for the free market system, since smaller companies can thrive by zeroing in on a small, but specific market. On the other hand, the huge corporations, usually slow as elephants in capitalizing on small markets, will have the equipment and facilities to move more rapidly. For example, will the large appliance manufacturers be able to generate millions of "one of a kind" models and cut into the market of the prestige manufacturers that are selling to the small numbers of people who are willing to pay for something different?

IN DEFENSE OF PAPER: A PERSONAL TRIBUTE

I have used them all . . . CRT terminals to edit and retrieve vital information, facsimile machines to transmit a brilliant ad to a client's home office for approval; I have searched out little-known articles in obscure journals by scanning microfilm and microfiche; I have sent telexes, TWXes and Mailgrams, and stored manuscripts in the memory of standalone WPs. In every case, one is working with electrons, magnetic charges, bits of celluloid, or sophisticated optical manipulation of characters. But there is no question—and the experts in the industry bear me out on this—that plain old paper is here to stay.

Perhaps I'm sentimental; I don't think so. Paper is personal, and it has purpose. It may be the only medium that we will be able to command better than computers in the years to come. More important, a close examination will reveal that it is not as primitive as the tech boys and girls would have you believe. In fact, it'll probably take decades for the new office technology to catch up to ordinary paper.

You can do things with paper that are far beyond the capabilities of primitive information tools like CRTs, microfiche, and microfilm. You can fold it and stick it in your pocket. You can get it copied "on the street," in thousands of copy centers, or at a coin-op in any library. You can curl it, or curl up with it—in bed, in the sauna, by the pool, on a plane. No terminal is necessary. You can write on it. And it costs very little. It will not erase during a power failure. You can doodle, draw diagrams and little pictures. You can show it to your spouse, your kids, and your parents, so they can swell with pride over your work. And they can show it to their friends.

- FACT: Approximately 82 percent of all correspondence is still originated by some writer, somewhere, putting pen or pencil to a piece of paper.
- FACT: Office paper sales are still growing, currently at a respectable 7 percent.
- FACT: The reading or recording of information on cathode ray terminal displays has been shown to be significantly more fatiguing than reading or writing on paper. And some rumblings about unsafe radiation emitted by CRTs are heard now, too!
- FACT: When was the last time you received a perfume-scented computer-originated letter?

37

OFFICE SECURITY

Before we enter the world of vibration sensors, vaults, and hidden microphones, let's consider a few basic points:

There is no such thing as a totally secure office. A security system can reduce vulnerability, but not eliminate it. The difference in the type of protection is measured in the extent of vulnerability of the office. As you learned on "Mission Impossible" and "It Takes a Thief," there is no such thing as an impregnable office.

Security is not an industry with a large discount market. Bargains are few and far between. And there are even fewer exceptional values. A good security system that is also cheap is a contradiction in terms; such systems don't exist.

A security system is a system. What isn't a system these days? Each piece of equipment must be viewed as part of the whole.

Once installed, the stuff must be used. Professional burglars know that security systems are often not turned on. And these guys are great at playing the odds, picking the office with the switch box that hasn't been opened in weeks.

EQUIPMENT

Locks and keys. Locks have been used for over 4,000 years. And for 4,000 years, the bad guys have been trying to pick them. It's a little tougher nowadays. Some of the newer locks, such as those by Medeco, Illinois Duo, Sargent, Keso, Eagle Three Star, Mela, Fichet, and Miracle Magnetic are highly pick resistant, because they use special keyways and keys. A good lock will insure that it takes a long time for the intruder to gain entry by breaking the lock through mechanical means. If he decides to blow the door, how long it'll take depends on how tough the door frame is. Many locks have a registered key system that prevents duplication by unauthorized personnel. This is a good idea, but it can be quite a nuisance. Some locks have a built-in alarm, which sounds when tampered with.

Glazing. Glass doors, windows, and showcases have always been a problem, because it's one thing to prevent them from being opened, quite another to prevent them from being smashed or broken. One way to deal with that problem is to tape *foil strips* to the window. They conduct electricity and act as a continuous circuit. Presumably, when the glass is broken, the tape and, simultaneously, the circuit are broken, and this triggers the alarm. However, if the burglar has a simple glass cutter, he can cut a hole without breaking the tape, stick his hand in, and release the latch. Or wriggle through the hole. A better solution is the *vibration sensor*, now being touted by Honeywell and others. This, as the name implies, is triggered by excess vibration. Laura Payerlee, of Honeywell, told me that even the slightest pressure on the glass will trigger the sensor, so that no tampering is possible. I hope that birds can't trigger it, or moths flying toward the light. Certainly, if you work in a neighborhood where lots of baseball and football is played, a four-bagger or an incomplete pass could have the whole PD down on the backs of the kids.

Another modern form of glazing protection is surprisingly unelectronic—*tougher glazing material.* Unbreakable, polycarbonate transparent materials have been developed. They look like glass, but are difficult to break, because, among other things, they are less brittle. Plexiglas has been eclipsed by GE's Lexan, which is guaranteed unbreakable. It costs two to three times as much as glass and scratches very easily. Lexan MR-400 is still more expensive, but it won't scratch as easily. The container of my food processor is made of Lexan, and it is certainly tough. Another tough glazing product is similar to auto safety glass. It consists of two pieces of glass bonded together by a layer of tough, transparent vinyl. It can be broken, but the effort takes quite a while and creates lots of noise.

Lighting. Lighting should be sufficient to heighten the chance of detection of an intruder. You don't have to light the entire office, just key points of possible entry so the security personnel can have a clear view. Lighting must be able to operate for an extended period of time in a blackout, brownout, or emergency.

Safes. There are two types of safes, and both, like door locks, are intended to *resist* burglary, not prevent a determined, expert assault.

Money chests. For cash, jewels, and other valuables. These chests will resist burglary tools for one hour or more. Most are suitable for mounting, or anchoring, in a concrete floor. They won't protect against heat or severe temperature change.

TYPES OF SECURITY SYSTEMS

Access control systems. These systems use cards or special keys inserted into a slot, allowing access by electronically releasing the locks, unlatching doors, or activating elevators. Such a system can be a real science fiction gadget: Some of the newer ones will respond to identification of a profile of the hand, fingerprints, signatures, even eye retinas, the patterns of which are stored in the computer for recognition. Texas Instruments has developed a voice-activated device that is now in use at the Department of Defense. (It is rumored that beeps sound in a guardhouse when the device detects a Russian accent.) Some systems keep a record of who entered, at what entry point, and at what time.

However, these security access systems are only as good as the lock and alarm system they are built around. If the access is wired to some cheapo lock that can be picked with a paper clip or a Visa card, it won't keep an intruder out just because he doesn't have a special entry card, a key, or an authorized set of fingerprints.

Surveillance/intrusion systems. These systems will detect the presence of an intruder. The critical element is what the system does when the intruder is discovered. Some merely sound a built-in alarm. The assumption is that it will frighten off the intruders, or that someone, upon hearing it, will phone or otherwise summon the police. Not a good idea. We buy security systems to protect us from, alas! human nature. What good is an intrusion system that relies on that very element? Too often, no good at all. Any good system should be connected to a remote monitoring site, such as the police station or a private security service.

Intrusion detection methods. *Contact devices* act as mechanical switches, breaking a circuit when disturbed. The foil trips mentioned in the glazing section are one type. Another is the *common contact plate*—one element on the door or window, the other on the frame. The device is triggered when the plates are separated. A *string-pull alarm* does the same thing with a string—for example, one stretched across an air conditioner. If an intruder tries to push the air conditioner back into the building from the outside (so he can enter through the hole), he will push against the string, which will be pulled and go off. The key issue: How reliable are the contact switches, and how sensitive? Will they stick, rust, break, crack? Can a burglar outfox them with a light touch? *Pressure-sensitive pads* or mats can be placed under carpets or mats and will go off when triggered by the weight of the intruder.

More sophisticated intrusion detection systems may use:

- *microphones* that detect noise
- *microwaves* or *ultrasonic waves* to detect movement
- *infrared heat sensors* to detect body heat radiation
- *vibration sensors* to detect vibrations
- *intelligent closed circuit TV* specially equipped to digitalize image and detect changes in the grey scale. In other words, this system senses the presence of an intruder by the change in light value. The cameras are of the low-light type, and a time-lapse videotape recorder can be added that will record any incident.

Again, it is worth noting that these systems *detect* the intruder. They don't capture him, or, necessarily, even scare him off. So it is up to people to respond. If your premises are monitored, make certain that the security service or local police are prompt and professional. Go to great pains to avoid false alarms: Never rule out the "boy who cried wolf" syndrome. Some systems use a recorded tape and phone line system, which, when triggered, dials the police number and plays a tape providing the location of the intrusion.

Integrated security systems. Larger corporations and office complexes increasingly are linking security systems together so they can be coordinated from a single security command post, or "war room." The integrated systems can provide controlled access, fire detection and suppression, intrusion sensing, closed circuit TV monitoring, communication with security guards walking a beat and with sentries.

"Bug" detection. There are firms that will periodically "sweep" the premises to uncover any hidden microphones or recording devices. Bug detectors can be useful if you are in an industry rife with corporate espionage or attempts to uncover "blind bids." You can purchase a portable model of your own use.

Shredders. This is a simple (but final) security device that protects against privileged documents falling into the wrong hands. Shredders do exactly what the name tells you—they shred paper sheets so that they come out in a form reminiscent of shredded wheat cereal. Nobody can read or photograph or reassemble a document or computer printout that has been through this process.

Shredders come in several sizes, depending on capacity and power. Many are designed like wastebaskets, so shredding and disposing are accomplished in one motion.

Electric Wastebasket, of New York, makes models that can take two or three sheets at a time and shred up to 2,500 pounds an hour. Many will shred plastic cards, blueprints, and even light metals, and most will take staples and clips. Shredded paper can be sold for recycling.

Intrusion Detectors

Device	Operational Mode	Pattern	Approximate Range	Comments
Acoustic	Listens to sounds	Omnidirectional	25-foot radius	Basically open microphones placed in the protected area. Filters out extreme high- and low-frequency noises; discriminators cancel some sounds. These sensors work best in protected areas with background noises low and continuous. Systems can have listening monitor and two-way communication (talk-back) capabilities.
Sonic	4,000-8,000 cycles transmitted and reflected Doppler signals	Omnidirectional	25-foot radius	Sensor triggered by object moving toward or away from the sensor. May be set off by moving objects such as curtains, doors, etc.
Ultrasonic	18-45 kHz. Transmitted and reflected Doppler signal	Omnidirectional	15-30 foot radius	Does not go through walls or building materials. Best used indoors because of extreme sensitivity to motion.
Microwave	2.5 to 10.5 gHz. Transmitted and reflected Doppler frequency shift principle	Fan-shaped, sausage, and cigar-shaped beams.	Varies with antenna configuration. May cover up to 10,000 sq. ft.	Goes through many building materials; can be set off by moving objects and interfering radar systems.
Infrared	Passive detector senses change in radiated heat	Omnidirectional, fan or cone shaped	20-foot radius	Will not go through walls or other construction materials. May be set off by hot objects such as radiators, heaters, incandescent lights, and the sun.
Infrared/ laser	Electro-optical Pulsed beam	Line of sight	up to 10,000 ft.	More advanced laser systems are not troubled by adverse weather conditions. "Fence" capability with stacked transmitter/receiver set up.
Capacitance	Electrical capacitator creates protective field, change in capacity signals alarm	Omnidirectional	Inches-10 feet	Unaffected by noise; good short range protection. Often difficult to tune or set up. Self-tuning, self-adjusting devices best.
Vibration	Vibration conduction	Omnidirectional	30-foot radius	A specialized type of contact microphone attached to walls, floors, ceilings, or protected object and senses attempts to penetrate the protected surfaces by force.
Photoelectric	Light beam-photocell	Straight line	Up to 1000 ft.	Beam can be pulsed and modulated. Use of mirrors can create angled and criss-cross patterns.
Video	Change within detection of motion zone	Omnidirectional	Varies with camera and lens	Not affected by noise, heat, etc. Senses change in existing static pattern, such as brightness. Needs lighted area.
Seismic	Low frequency vibration in the ground	Omnidirectional	25-50 ft.	Disturbances on the surface, when they exceed a preset amplitude, are sensed by a geophone and an alarm signal is activated. Subject to triggering by ground tremors caused by trucks, noise, etc.
Stress	Flexing in structural members cause changes in resistance of sensor.	Omnidirectional	15-ft. radius	Sensor is affixed to structural beam which flexes. Unaffected by noise, heat, outside signals.
Electro-mechanical	Shorting or opening of a continuous circuit	According to device	Determined by protected surface	A simple system of a continuous circuit around walls, ceilings, doors, and windoes. Includes metal foil, switches, and pressure mats. Simplest and cheapest of all alarm systems.

Fig. 68. Intrusion detection systems

From Jan Reber and Paul Shaw, *Executive Protection Manual*
(Northbrook, IL: MTI Teleprograms Inc., 1976), p. 122.
Reprinted by permission.

Access Control Systems

Type	Description	Features
ID cards	Usually a laminated card with the name of the individual plus signature and photograph	Basic cards use photographs and signature plus data on ordinary paper; the card is sealed by lamination. More advanced cards provide security and forgery resistance in the following ways: use of watermarked papers; photograph printed on special paper; fine line, two color overprinting from engraved plates; fluorescent overcoating detectable by black light; optically readable codes; hidden data printing; magnetic stripe coding; and backside two-color overprinting from continuous fine line patterns not registered on the front of the card. Purposes, or classes or card holders, can be distinguished by graphic design or use of different colored coding bars, letters, etc.
Card/card-key	Electronic access readers: system employ various coding elements including lettering, mechanical hole position, optical or magnetic tape, radio frequency signals. Card must be inserted into a compatible reader; the reader will examine the card and validation will activate the access controlling mechanism.	Access is limited to a "valid" card. Some systems have multiple-mastering features, enabling a quick change of access control codes.
Coded units (for electric door strikes and door operators)	A keyless, coded push button control device which supplies the proper voltage to the locking (electronic) mechanism.	Code must be in the proper sequence to open access control mechanism.
Cards/codes	These are combinations of card readers and coded units. Both the card and a memorized code are needed to gain access. The card is inserted in the reader and a "password" code is entered on a touch key-board.	Since two elements are involved, a greater degree of security is provided. "Passwords" or codes are usually a four-digit memorized series of numbers which must be tapped on the touch keyboard.
Hand geometry/card reader	Verification using an individual's hand geometry characteristics which are measured and compared by a machine; these measurements are compared against data previously encoded on the individual's card — also read by the machine.	This technique is based on a computerized statistical analysis of glove measurements for Air Force pilots. The study concluded: — Hand geometry is a distinct human, measurable characteristic that can be related to individuals. — Tolerances can be established so that the probability of a particular individual cross-identifying can be reduced to one out of thousands.
Signature verification	A measure with respect to time of the pressure applied to a writing instrument when one signs his own name.	Statistics show that each person's "pressure pattern" is unique to the individual and remarkably constant from one signature to the next. Since the technique is only indirectly related to signature appearance, the "pressure pattern" of a forgery is totally different from the genuine signature. Each "pressure pattern" is a distinct personal characteristic which is virtually impossible to duplicate and relatively easy to measure. To enroll in the system a person taps out an assigned identification number on a keyboard and then signs his name several times with a special ball point pen. Signature data are transmitted to a central processing computer which develops a signature "standard" data base for the individual. The standard is then stored in the system's memory.

Fig. 69. Access control systems

From Jan Reber and Paul Shaw, *Executive Protection Manual*
(Northbrook, IL: MTI Teleprograms Inc., 1976), p. 128.
Reprinted by permission.

COMPUTER SECURITY

The advent of the computer has brought many problems, the most critical being that of security. Controlling access to incredible computer-power and databases of sensitive information has become a serious issue for business and government alike. The best and most prevalent methods are described below:

Encryption. The data is coded or scrambled so it can't be read by an outsider. This method provides security not only at the computer site, but when the data leaves via cable or telephone line or satellite.

Encryption devices usually sit between the computer and modem, and slow the transmission of the data. In addition, the codes should be changed often, but this practice often creates confusion.

Several encryption devices are software-based.

Call-back systems. You dial into a computer; the call-back system intercepts the call, requests an access code, and disconnects the line. If you are an authorized user the system phones you back.

Such systems can provide double security by calling you back at an authorized location only. So even if an intruder got by the access code, he would have to be at the right location to log on. If he got into the system, the authorized user would know because he would receive a call.

Call-back systems offer several variations on the theme, providing various levels of security, but the main purpose is always to prevent unauthorized entry and/or access to a computer system.

Identification devices. Similar to the access control systems described earlier. The basic difference is that access control systems use magnetic cards, voice recognition, fingerprints, etc., to control entry to the premises; identification devices for computers use these methods to control use of the computer system. Some access methods will lock you out of the computer if you input the wrong access code more than two or three times. A new ingenious method requires the user to wear a small radio transmitter which broadcasts a signal allowing the computer to be used; when the user moves out of radio range, the system locks up.

Physical restraint systems. Literally, nuts and bolts. Heavy-gauge steel clamps, encasements, bars and locking plates make it difficult, if not impossible to remove computer equipment. Those that cover the machines also prevent access.

An unusual new device triggers an alarm or activates a camera when a computer or other piece of equipment is unplugged.

FIRE DETECTION/SUPPRESSION

Sprinklers. Sprinklers are the most common; the valve melts under heat and the water sprinkles out. They can also be connected to an audible alarm.

Smoke alarms. These are becoming very popular because they provide an early warning: Often, smoke forms before blazing heat and fire. Besides, they avoid the water damage caused by sprinkler systems. They use photocells to detect particles in the air. Beware, however: These alarms are sensitive. A very prestigious Wall Street brokerage firm hired a young whiz-kid analyst. This guy turned out to be the office guru, who spent his idle time meditating. He had a habit of lighting incense, and since his desk was directly under a smoke detector (he said he didn't smoke), he started a minor panic (brokers are used to panic) when he lit up a stick of Mysore sandalwood.

Portable extinguishers. Good investments. Keep them charged. Also good for office Christmas parties, when someone always makes a jackass of himself by squirting someone.

Record cabinets. More accurately described as insulated filing cabinets, protect records against prolonged exposure to heat. They are not burglar resistant, so they are not for cash. There are two types of cabinets, one for paper and one for magnetic records. *Paper* cabinets will keep their contents unscathed in temperatures up to 350° F. *Magnetic media* cabinets will protect up to 1700° F for several hours, and are also good for film and fiche records.

BUYING SECURITY EQUIPMENT

Watch out for the "Watch Mr. Wizard" syndrome, in which you might be led down the garden path by a deep-rooted fascination with gadgets, gizmos, mojos, any metal box with a black matte finish, LEDs, LCDs, and alarm noise that sounds like it's notifying you of a reactor malfunction on the Battlestar Galactica. The Mr. Wizard syndrome attacks the part of the brain known as common sense and twists it until you've made a foolhardy purchase in which you've overpaid, gotten more than you need, or worse, gotten something that is not adequate to your needs.

Play Show and Tell. Make sure that the salesperson shows you the equipment in operation, on an actual site if possible. The "tell" part alone is not enough.

Conform to Underwriters Laboratories standards? More important than you might think.

Do a little research. Get the names of some of the users. Talk to them about the equipment and find out how they feel about it. See if you can arrive at an estimate of the average time between failures and average downtime, or time it takes to repair.

Check out the vendor. Word travels fast; it is not that tough to find out about a vendor. Has he got a reputation for reliability? Competence? How well are the technicians trained? Does he stock a ready supply of spare parts? And—very important—does he offer 24-hour maintenance service? "I'll send someone over in the morning" may be too late.

SECURITY AND SECURITY-RELATED ORGANIZATIONS

Airport Security Council, Box 30705, JFK International Airport, Jamaica, NY 11430; 718-328-2990.

American Polygraph Association (APA), Suite 408, Osborne Office Center, Chattanooga, TN 37411; 615-892-3992; 800-APA-8037.

American Society for Industrial Security (ASIS), 1655 N. Ft. Myer Dr., Arlington, VA 22209; 703-522-5800.

Armored Transportation Institute, 7675 Canton Center Dr., Baltimore, MD 21224; 301-285-7000.

Association of Commercial Record Centers (ACRC), 9715 James Ave. South, Minneapolis, MN 55431; 612-888-4090.

Association of Former Intelligence Officers, 6723 Whittier Ave., Suite 303A, McLean, VA 22101; 703-790-0320.

Association of Former Agents of the U.S. Secret Service, Box 31073, Temple Hills, MD 20748; 301-894-2115.

Association of Political Risk Analysts, 1133 15th St., NW, Suite 620, Washington, DC 20005; 202-293-5913.

Aviation Crime Prevention Institute, Box 3443, Frederick, MD 21701; 301-694-5444.

Committee of National Security Companies, Inc. (CONSCO), 2760 Union Ave. Extended, Suite 514, Memphis, TN 38112; 901-323-0173.

Communications Security Association (CSA), 655 15th St., Suite 320, Washington DC 20005; 202-639-4620.

Computer Security Institute, 360 Church St., Northboro, MA 01532; 617-393-2600.

Fire Equipment Manufacturers Association, 1230 Keith Bldg., Cleveland, OH 44115-2180; 216-241-7333.

Independent Armored Car Operators Association, Security Armored Car Service, 1022 S. 9th St., St. Louis, MO 63104; 314-231-4030.

Information Systems Security Association, Box 71927, Los Angeles, CA 90071.

Internal Security Association/Financial Firms, c/o Salomon Bros., Inc. Internal Security Dept., 1 New York Plaza, New York, NY 10004; 212-747-4004.

International Association for Hospital Security (IAHS), Box 637, Lombard, IL 60148; 312-953-0990.

International Association for Identification, Box 90259, Columbia, SC 29290; 803-776-2001.

International Association for Shopping Center Security (IASCS), Suite 300, 2830 Clearview Place, NE, Atlanta, GA 30340-2117; 404-457-3575.

International Association of Arson Investigators, 25 Newton St., Box 600, Marlboro, MA 01752; 617-481-5977.

International Association of Bomb Technicians and Investigators, Box 6609, Colorado Springs, CO 80934; 303-636-2596.

International Association of Campus Law Enforcement Administrators (IACLEA), 638 Prospect Ave., Hartford, CT 06105; 203-279-3498.

International Association of Chiefs of Police (IACP), 13 Firstfield Rd., Gaithersburg, MD 20878; 301-948-0922.

International Association Credit Card Investigators, 1620 Grant Ave., Novato, CA 94947; 415-897-8800.

International Association of Professional Security Consultants (IAPSC), 2 Sunrise Place, Armonk, NY 10504; 914-273-8590.

International Association of Security Services, Box 8202, Northfield, IL 60093; 312-973-7712.

International Security Management Association (ISMA), 400 Atlantic Ave., Boston, MA 02110.

National Association of Chiefs of Police (NACP), 1100 NE 125th St., N. Miami, FL 33161; 305-891-1700.

National Association of Private Security Vaults, 3562 N. Ocean Blvd., Ft. Lauderdale, FL 33308; 305-565-7233.

National Burglar and Fire Alarm Association (NBFAA), 1120 Nineteenth St., NW, Suite LL20, Washington, DC 20036; 202-296-9595.

National Cargo Security Council (NCSC), 810 18th St., NW, Room 501, Washington, DC 20006; 202-638-5244.

National Coordinating Council on Emergency Management, 7297 Lee Hwy., Suite N, Falls Church, VA 22042; 703-533-7672.

National Crime Prevention Institute (NCPI), University of Louisville, Shelby Campus, Louisville, KY 40292; 502-588-6987.

National Fire Protection Association, Batterymarch Park, Quincy, MA 02269; 617-770-3000.

National Forensic Center, 17 Temple Terrace, Lawrenceville, NJ 08648; 609-883-0550; 800-526-5177.

National Independent Bank Equipment and Systems Association (NIBESA), 1411 Peterson, Park Ridge, IL 60068; 312-825-8419.

Risk and Insurance Management Society (RIMS), 205 E. 42nd St., New York, NY 10017; 212-286-9292.

Security Equipment Industry Association (SEIA), 2800 28th St., Suite 124, Santa Monica, CA 90405; 213-450-4141.

Society of Former Special Agents of the FBI, 2416 Queens Plaza S., Suite 312, Long Island City, NY 11101; 718-361-0051.

United Security Professionals Association (USPA), 3512 W. Beltline Highway, Middleton, WI 53562; 608-831-0003.

Vehicle Security Association, 5100 Forbes Blvd., Lanham, MD 20706; 301-459-9110.

World Association of Detectives (WAD), Box 1177, Long Beach, NY 11561; 516-889-6087.

World Association of Document Examiners (WADE), 111 N. Canal St., Chicago, IL 60606; 312-930-9446.

CANADA

Canadian Alarm and Security Association (CANASA), 2175 Sheppard Ave. East, Suite 110, Willowdale, Ontario M2J 1W8; 416-491-2621.

Canadian Association of Chiefs of Police, 112 Kent St., Suite 1908, Place de Ville, Tower B, Ottawa, Ontario K1P 5P2; 613-233-1106.

Canadian Society for Industrial Security, Inc. (CSIS); La Societe Canadienne de la Surete Industrielle Inc (Quebec Region), Box 4117, Westmount, Quebec H3Z 2X3; 514-870-4243; 514-656-4044.

Commercial Security Association, Inc., 233 St. Marks Rd., Toronto, Ontario M6S 2J1; 416-249-7401.

Fig. 70. Guide to security and security-related organizations

38

THE OFFICE ENVIRONMENT

As an occupant of an office, and as a person who may one day have to take on the responsibility of "office planning," you should know at least something about the raging debate that has polarized people and resulted in factions being formed on both sides of the partition—or the office door, as the case may be.

OFFICE SPACE PLANS

THE CONVENTIONAL OFFICE

This is the kind you played in when you visited Dad fifteen years ago, and the kind you probably fidget in when you visit your accountant or lawyer today. This is an office with a strict quadrangular configuration. The outer offices run along the periphery, and that means they have windows. These are sometimes called "perimeter offices." Then comes some hall space, and an inner row of offices parallel to the window offices. In the center is an open area, often called the "bull pen."

THE CONVENTIONAL OFFICE PECKING ORDER

- *The perimeter offices are for the honchos.* And if you've got *two* windows, you're really special. This is the senior executive turf. A corner office with windows on two walls is usually claimed by a chief executive officer or a partner.
- *The inner offices are for the junior executives.* No windows, but at least there's a door, and an area you can call your own.
- *The bull pen is for the lower echelon and support personnel.* It's like having your desk in the hallway. No privacy. It's tough to swear or sulk out here, because you are utterly visible.

THE OPEN PLAN

The open plan, or OP, is a catchall term for several approaches. The oldest and most radical of these is often called the office landscape. Here it is, in theme and variations:

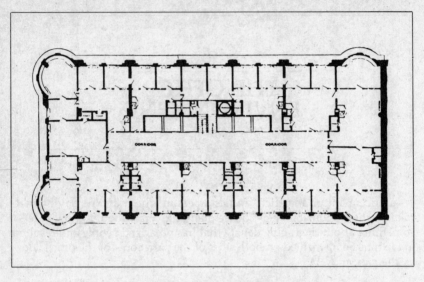

Fig. 71. Conventional office layout
This floor plan shows the design prevalent in older office
buildings with individual offices constructed as part of
the building. This plan is of a floor of the Old
Colony Building in Chicago, built in the 1890s.

Reprinted in John Pile, *Open Office Planning* (New York:
Watson-Guptil, 1978), p. 15.

OFFICE LANDSCAPE   This plan was formulated in Germany in the late
1950s and, thanks to some well-staged seminars and support from
designers, found its way to the United States in 1968, probably on the
heels of the hula hoop of furniture styles, Danish Modern furniture. Instead of enclosed offices, there are free-form groupings, or work clusters.
(In their brochures the vendors use lots of terms that sound like they were
lifted from a scientific monograph on beehives.) These clusters are not
arranged in rows, but, rather, fill the space in a way that is optimal for
the work flow and the flow of human traffic. To avoid a surfeit of eye
contact, the clusters are bounded by free-standing screens, partitions, or
plants (sometimes they're real). The furniture units are the epitome of sleek:
no "desks"; rather, simple drawerless tables. Some of the units are so sterile,
they could double as operating rooms.

The thinking behind the landscape concept seemed sound. Research has
shown that employees work better when there is more sunlight, a feeling
of contact with the outside environment, and some feeling of territoriali-
ty. The office landscape delivers these conditions, along with flexibility
that allows the office to be designed according to flow and function.
Besides, it seems to fit in with our thinking about the American way of

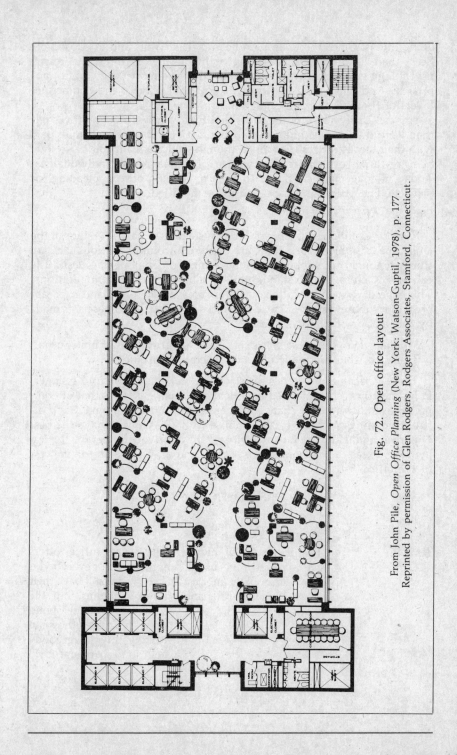

Fig. 72. Open office layout

From John Pile, *Open Office Planning* (New York: Watson-Guptil, 1978), p. 177.
Reprinted by permission of Glen Rodgers, Rodgers Associates, Stamford, Connecticut.

doing things. Since the open plan has no fixed walls and no closed offices, there is no imposing feeling of hierarchy or status. A "team" psychology is fostered by this environment. It's a more "democratic" approach. And what are Americans, if not team players and democrats, lovers of football and the Constitution?

You can easily see why the firms that first went with open offices felt they were doing something special. But the officers couldn't quite part with their status offices. For much though we love team spirit, we love being rewarded even more. And we are, of course, rugged individualists. Today, management continues to cling to its own offices, pleading for privacy: The office landscape had to be modified.

DESIGN APPROACHES

Panel or Component Systems. These systems are "hard" versions of the landscape, in which work areas are clustered around partitions that are sturdy enough to support various hanging *components*—desk, file cabinets, shelves, phone stand, etc.—in almost limitless configurations. This type of system has almost totally replaced the pure landscape approach. It's more system oriented and locks you into the components made by the vendor of the partitions.

Modular (Work Station) Systems. These are groupings of units, usually L-shaped, that are made of wood, metal, or plastic.

The American Plan. Here's the stroke of real genius. Henry Kissinger, in his memoirs, characterized American diplomatic style as that of compromise. And where the changed imperatives of office diplomacy and office formatting converged, compromise we did. Why not have the best of conventional and open plan? Why not have private offices for the upper level execs, a few conference rooms, and an open plan for the rest of the office?

THE OPEN OFFICE DEBATE

	Con	Pro
Personal Offices	The people in the middle get screwed, as usual. They lose their modest 9′ × 12′ with walls and a door.	The open office offers something for everybody. The biggies still have their inner sanctums, but the support personnel wind up with an area they can call their own. Everybody gets some personal turf.

562

| Privacy | In a conventional office, you have the option of closing your door. Many experts feel that the open office may actually impair the performance of high-powered, tough, shrewd employees. Without an office to shut them in, they feel inhibited and less likely to take risks or to "do it their way." | In a conventional office, privacy is just another way of saying that the door closes. Most people either don't want that closed-in feeling or don't want to seem standoffish, so they keep the door open most of the time, and this practice encourages socializing. In this situation the only way to counter interruptions is to position your desk so your back is toward the door. This is creepy and uncomfortable. With an open plan, you can create an L-shape, which gives you a side opening: People don't approach you head-on when they walk by, but will face you if they walk in. Such entrances are difficult and costly to design in a conventional office. |
| Noise | The conventional office insures quiet working environment, free of distracting outside noise. When someone is in your office, he hears you, rather than the person in the next work station. In the open office, sounds and speech travel over the panels. | An open office has many "personal privacy zones," which actually provide greater opportunity for quiet, clear communication. The noise problem can be solved with careful placement of panels to deflect the path of noise. And the newer sound panels are very sound absorbent. |

	Some people hate "white noise"—they find it distracting.	Artificial white noise can also be used. It blocks out sound without interfering with work. Portable units can be set up as needed.
Psychological Aspects	The closed office system sets you apart from the rest of the office. It is conducive to concentration. Closing the door says to others, and to you yourself, that you mean business. It's a great tonic for turmoil. When you have no door, you feel powerless against the raging storm outside your cubicle.	We are an adaptable lot. Before long we will look upon our work stations in much the same way as we look upon our closed offices. Ensconced in them, we will feel removed from the turmoil and very private.
Productivity	Improvement in productivity isn't really attributable to the open office. It's merely a concidence: Open office plans are usually implemented in conjunction with a new office or location, which in itself usually boosts morale and generates a "start-fresh" feeling. New offices also mean better lighting, better color, and more sensible layouts.	The open plan improves productivity.
The future?	The jury is still out. Many of the innovators are going back to basics.	According to a Harris Survey of office environments, conducted in 1978 and polling over 1,000 workers, 87 percent of the business executives and 91 percent of the architects in the sample believe that the open office concept will continue to grow.

This, in a nutshell, is the state of the current controversy. The proponents of "OP" are gaining. About ten thousand offices have gone to open plan in the past five years, with predictions that put American business at about 45 percent open as of this printing. Why? The atmosphere is democratic, humane, and individualized for the majority of office personnel. There are increases in communication, flexibility, and, some say, in productivity and efficiency.

Studying extensive surveys and arguing the pros and cons rarely convince anyone to enjoy the OP environment. If you like it and feel that it works for you, it does. Some find it quieter to work behind partitions and feel that they function more efficiently in the open system. Some of the support workers feel that the system is designed to discourage their talking to each other while they work. But it doesn't seem to work that way. A typist employed in a newly converted office in Manhattan's McGraw-Hill building told me, "It used to be that I could talk to my friend while we both typed, or opened and sorted mail. Now, we go around the partition to deliver something and wind up talking just the same. The only difference is that we can't work *while* we talk."

REASONS FOR THE GROWTH OF THE OPEN PLAN   As usual, it all comes down to dollars and cents. The top-of-the-list advantages of open office cited by the Harris survey respondents were:

The flexibility factor. Office layout can be changed quickly and cheaply, so office "downtime" is reduced. Changes can be made in layout over a weekend; it used to take months. True, but such changes aren't made often, and since office physical plant costs are such a small part of overhead and labor is such a large part, shouldn't the worker preference carry a higher priority? That depends. . . .

Greater adaptability of office space to individual job functions. Very true. If you get a CRT for your desk, your area can be redesigned around it in a jiffy. Got a word processor or a centralized dictation unit coming in? You can make a WP or dictation center and have it waiting for your new gizmo.

And then there are these other possible cost savings under the open plan:

Installation. Although many claim OP units cost less to install than drywall, it has proven difficult to generalize. No clear pattern has emerged.

Space. There are claims of savings at 20–25 percent of floor space. Such claims are hard to evaluate, because open office usually coincides with office reorganization—which almost invariably means better use of space and sometimes also means a reduction in the work force. There is no doubt that OP increases the utilizable *vertical* space: The sheer number of partitions increases the possibility for shelves, cabinets, and other add-ons.

Energy. Open office allows for "task lighting" instead of inefficient overhead. The general illumination in the office can be lower, with individual lighting requirements attended to as needed. A CRT reader may want lower light or indirect light so that the screen is easier to read. Someone who handles lots of paper may wish more light. The task lighting is fixtured to the partition of the component system. At present such lighting equipment is rather costly and a bit too weighty to move around.

HOW TO SET YOURSELF UP IN AN OPEN OFFICE   In your office, OP may be a fait accompli. If so:

Try to get a spot near the back. All considerations of work flow aside, you don't want a visitor to see you peering out from behind your screen just as he gets off the elevator. You want an insulated feeling that conveys status.

Keep your area absolutely immaculate. Work spaces are designed to facilitate work. They have lots of shelves and drawers and desk area spaces that are meant to be used. But since such work stations are not offices, people don't treat them with the same care that they would afford a room. Shelves tend to get untidy, and papers are left on the desk. This is okay for sleeves-up kind of work. But you want to impress upon your visitor (and your boss) that you are a decision maker, not a paper pusher. So an aesthetically stark look—clean, empty desk, neat notebooks and binders arranged artfully on the shelves, pen-and-pencil sets, pictures of the family—will make your spot stand out.

Try for a good space allocation. The current average is 125 square feet per worker. That's not bad. It's a little larger than that 9×12 area rug at home. But the hitch is that, as with all averages, some workers get more, others less. Make sure you get more—maybe even enough for a bric-a-brac shelf or a coffee unit or something totally useless.

IF THERE IS NO OPEN PLAN, BUT ONE MIGHT BE COMING

As soon as you hear the news, begin building a case for getting one of the perimeter offices that will be left. One junior executive I know at an ad agency started having lots of meetings with clients at the agency rather than at the client's office. He tried everything: ordering up breakfast for the client; showing him particularly scrofulous video cassettes on the office machine. Soon he had the client hooked; he loved to come there, and the exec always told his secretary to hold all calls during the client's visits. Now, I might add that this fellow was first-rate—he did a bang-up job. When the office went OP, it was decided that the juniors would get partition space, but would have several conference rooms to use as needed. Our friend very graciously pointed out to upper management that he had a very heavy meeting schedule (he even submitted his daily record for the past several months) and suggested that he didn't want to hold back his co-workers by monopolizing conference space to meet with a single (but very important) client. The brass decided that it made more sense to give the guy his own fixed-wall office. The idea was that whoever had that account would get the office, so no favoritism would be shown. But the junior exec has an even larger office now. He is a senior exec.

If they ask for office-renouncing volunteers, don't do it. You might be tempted because you'd like a change. Or because you want to show that you are "with it" and very adaptable. But once you give up your office, there is usually no going back. Possession is nine-tenths, and all that. If you want a taste of OP, there are other ways of getting it. If you are curious, spend a few hours in your secretary's cubicle when she is out sick.

Don't get uptight. OP may be an irreversible trend that will put everyone in the same boat. Thus, a fixed-wall office, if you've got one, will be a real status symbol, because they're so rare, but the lack of one won't be a negative. And with the current trend in freewheeling, "hands-on" management, maybe even the CEOs, in a fit of team spirit, will abandon their corner offices, just as some answer their own phones or open their own mail.

The current "final word" on OP is the Louis Harris survey on the office environment, commissioned by Steelcase, the world's largest manufacturer of open office systems. Steelcase obviously hopes that the results of this survey will help gain acceptance of its products. In any case the firm should be commended, because the study is well balanced and fair, and although the suggestions are somewhat bland, the findings are not. To obtain a copy, write:

> Steelcase
> 1120 36th Street S.E.
> Grand Rapids, Michigan 49501

Ask for "The Steelcase National Study of Office Environments."

YOUR NEEDS VS. THE COMPANY'S The office environment is another case of balancing your own needs and desires with those of the corporation. If you are too selfless, you will quickly become part of the furniture . . . a component. If you assert yourself too much, you'll become known as the person who is only out for himself. The power-tripper philosophers, like Michael Korda, while accurately pointing out the potential pitfalls of the open office plan and how it can impede your rise to the top, are a bit aristocratic in perspective.

A bad spot in the office is like a sand trap in a golf course. Tricky, and tough to get out of, but how big an obstacle it is depends on how well you play the game.

TO LEARN ABOUT OPEN OFFICE PLANNING The very best book on the subject is *Open Office Planning*, by John Pile (New York: Whitney Publications, Watson-Guptill, 1986). Intended for interior designers and architects, this extremely readable and profusely illustrated book examines the various approaches to OP. It is plainly biased against the conventional office, but attempts to examine the various types of open offices with an open mind.

Contact:
Watson-Guptill
1515 Broadway
New York, New York 10036

THE OFFICE LANDSCAPE AND OFFICE AUTOMATION

Today, the best solution is no longer the open plan, even for companies that pride themselves on being modern. Office automation has wrought changes that open office designers did not anticipate. And since the technology is moving so fast, it is often difficult to keep up. For one thing, the automated office reduces face-to-face contact by rendering much of it unnecessary with advanced communication and retrieval systems. As a result, people feel even more isolated in workstations. In addition, printers, keyboards and electronic typewriters have increased the noise level, making open systems more distracting than before.

If you are about to move or redesign your office, consider the special problems created by office automation:

Cabling. Once upon a time, the only wires you had to cope with were telephone lines and power cords. Today, there are so many wires and cables going in and out of electronic equipment, that *wire management* has become a specialty; offices must take into account the routing of wires and cables in placement of offices, personnel and workstations. Yes, there are wire management consultants.

Desktop space. Desks have been cluttered since the beginning of time. But when it was mostly paper, it could be cleared off and used as workspace. Today, in addition to telephones, a desk might accommodate a computer or terminal, a modem or extra disk drive, a speakerphone, a dialer. So where does the employee spread out his papers and go to work? Carefully consider who needs what equipment and make sure you provide adequate desk space.

Noise levels. Some printers are literally as noisy as power saws. Placement of printers is therefore critical. An acoustic absorption hood will dampen the sound when placed over a printer, but since they block air circulation, the printer underneath tends to heat up. Use a hood that comes equipped with a fan (another noise problem).

Other solutions include acoustic ceiling tiles and wall covering and free-standing partitions.

Heat. In spite of the mostly solid-state technology of modern office equipment, these machines do generate a lot of heat. Personal computers, printers, copiers can collectively produce enough heat to warrant additional air conditioning. Humidity can compound the problem further, affecting the performance of the equipment.

Fortunately, this problem has been with us for a long time, as many offices equipped with sensitive electronic equipment have had to maintain controlled-temperature environments. You should have little trouble getting expert advice on how to maintain optimal temperature for man and machine. This is not an area to skimp on costs.

Static electricity. Once it was only a nuisance. In the automated office, static electricity can damage, even destroy expensive electronic components. Take precautions. They are simple and inexpensive.

Power management. Power surges can destroy data. Power failures can erase data. There are many ways to protect your office, from proper wiring for your needs to power surge protection devices and automatic back-up systems. Make sure you have many outlet options in case you want to move your equipment at a later date.

Lighting and ergonomics. Working with electronic equipment produces a unique set of problems. Proper seating and desk design is more important than before. Lighting for computing situations requires more planning, since glare and eye fatigue is often a problem with video displays. Again, try to build in some mobility, in case you wish to move your equipment.

THE BUSINESS LIFE OF PLANTS: OFFICE GREENERY

Indoor plants are all the rage these days—and the dead and dying are in evidence everywhere. Plants require care and attention. As a result of the plant boom, a new vocation has been created: the plant doctor, who, for a fee, will make house calls, either to heal the sick ones or to administer routine physicals or preventative care, which usually consists of examining the underside of leaves for plant acne or some such thing, making sure the soil is not too wet or too dry, checking on the location of the plants vis-à-vis sunlight, trimming, cutting, replanting, root untangling, etc.

Plants are still selling healthily. And although it is not crucial for any reason whatever to have plants in your office, there are many good reasons to have a few around:

- *Plants fight sterility.* Many offices lack sufficient windows, fresh air, and/or warmth of design, and plants add color, character, and

---

a touch of nature to the environment. If the effect on your mood is positive, then why not go ahead?

- *They can serve a design function.* Well placed and arranged plants can serve as visual screens that can be employed to obscure the view of the executive's desk when the door is open, or to divide an office or work space into two separate areas with two separate functions, for example, work area and meeting area.
- *They enliven the air.* Some will tell you straight out that their plants make the air in the office fresher, cleaner, more "lively" and humid. Such benefits have yet to be proved. And there aren't enough plants in most offices to have any significant effect on the air.

CHOOSING PLANTS FOR THE OFFICE

- *Light.* Where is it? How much have you got to work with? Include both window and electric light. Fluorescents can actually benefit certain plants.
- *Temperature.* Consider the overall temperature levels and, more important, the levels in the places you've singled out for the plants. Placing them near ducts is usually a no-no, because blasts of warm or cold air or sudden changes in temperature will harm most plants. High-heat areas will naturally be better for succulents, which like it hot and dry.
- *Humidity.* Central heating usually means dry air, which is bad for most tropical plants. If the air in your office is dry, get a humidifier or go with the old tray-of-water-under-the-pot approach.

Once you've considered the three variables mentioned above, find a knowledgeable person to recommend plants for your office conditions. Several books are very helpful, but so are the proprietors of reputable plant nurseries and stores accustomed to dealing with office gardening.

Buy from a reputable source. Stay away from florists; they know less about plants than specialists, and they often charge much more, because they are gift-oriented. Find sources that offer advice free of charge, and see if you can get a guarantee. Some sources will give cash credit if a plant dies before the guarantee elapses. If you must have a specific plant that is less than ideal for your growing environment, be prepared to make the necessary adjustments, using humidifiers, grow lamps, etc.

Your first plants should be of the smaller, green foliage variety (examples are philodendrons, dracaena, and ivy). These are the most hardy, and they are less likely to die from your mistakes. The spider plant and cast iron plant do especially well under fluorescent light. Once you have the hang of it, you can go on to trees, shrubs, and even flowers.

THE CARE AND FEEDING OF PLANTS

USE TEPID WATER   Water from the office cooler is often too cold, or, if from the red spigot (perish the thought), much too hot. Go to the john, where you can regulate the water temperature, or to the kitchen if you have one.

ROTATE PLANTS FOR EVEN GROWTH   Especially if a plant is by the window. Since plants grow toward the source of light, a plant kept in one position will lean.

WASH YOUR PLANTS   Using warm water and a damp cloth, wash the leaves carefully. Do this several times a year, or have someone else do it several times a year.

USE FERTILIZER WITH CARE   "The more, the better" is a myth. Your goal is a healthy plant, not a dress rehearsal for "Jack and the Beanstalk." Too much fertilizer can harm a plant, or weaken it with too rapid growth. Keep fertilization down in winter.

GROW LIGHTS   Office light is often sufficient for sustaining plants. When there appears to be a problem, it's often the result not of insufficient light, but of poor positioning. Sometimes a grow light with a timer is necessary. Get some advice on this.

DON'T SPOIL THE PLANTS   Some businesspeople tend to treat plants like neglected kids—give them lots of anything but care. Don't overwater, overfeed, or overcrowd plants. They have different requirements and should be fed and watered accordingly. Don't crowd them together; it's unhealthy. If it's too much trouble to keep up a consistent watering schedule, get fewer plants, or get someone else to help.

PLANTS AND APPEARANCES

A few attractive, well-positioned plants will spruce up your office and enhance its appearance. But don't overdo it. An office that looks like the Amazon or Tarzan's digs won't do. And forget growing herbs or tomatoes in your office. You do not want to come across as Farmer Grey.

An overabundance of plants signals that you are trying too hard to be with it. Or that you have a certain revulsion for the work space and are trying to bury the business environment with some kind of "Garden of Eden" overkill.

Even worse is allowing sickly plants to remain untended in your office. This signals neglect; better to have no plants at all.

39

THE AUTOMATED OFFICE: SURVIVING IN STYLE

Offices are automating so rapidly that most of you will already have had some contact with much of the equipment mentioned. The methods of introducing office automation are as diverse as the number of firms involved, and the same holds true for the executives involved. This chapter is an attempt to help you meet the challenge of the office of the future, and to anticipate some of the problems you may encounter.

CONVINCING YOUR BOSS: WHAT YOU MAY BE UP AGAINST

Bosses always like people who have new ideas, who keep pace with the times. As long as those new ideas don't cost them too much money. The key to convincing your boss to automate or to purchase some otherwise wonderful piece of office hardware is not to show that it won't cost much, but that *it won't cost anything!*

Know your stuff. Find out everything there is to know about the equipment in question. Get some price quotes and comparisons. Check out competitive models and service.

Compute the costs. Not just the costs of the equipment, but of the current situation. Include the cost of equipment, supplies, space, manpower. The idea is to demonstrate that this is the new approach, a sound investment that will enhance the company's competitiveness and general economic well-being. Only you can judge how far and how detailed you'll have to go in your analysis. Maybe you'll have to run time/motion studies. Evaluate work procedures and show how they can be improved. Remember: The biggest attraction of office automation is reduced manpower. This doesn't necessarily spell layoffs. It can mean *fewer people* doing the same work done at the same level of service; or it can mean *more work*, increased level of service with the same people. If it's not one of these two, you're going to have problems. *For the only way to cut costs* *significantly in a modern office is by saving employee time, which saves money.* (One exception—a file system that goes micro can save a good deal in square footage; but unless the office has tens of thousands of files, the saving is not significant.)

Make the presentation. Remember those numbers about industrial productivity (up 90 percent in the last decade) vs. office productivity (up 4 percent). Now, the only way to effectively increase office productivity is to (1) eliminate jobs and nonproductive work and/or (2) make workers more efficient and effective.

Give the boss a complete economic evaluation, covering, essentially:

- *the cost of the present system.* How it works.
- *the cost of the new system.* How it will work.
- *the value of time to be saved by the new system*
- *the expected rate of return on investment.* Example:

$$\frac{\text{total investment}}{\text{daily savings}} = \text{days required}$$

Convert to months and apply a rule of thumb: It should pay out in 12–18 months, unless it's a giant computer or something of that magnitude.

After you get the go-ahead, you'd better make it work. The boss goes on the line for the money allocated from the budget on the strength of your argument. If your theory does not transfer to reality, it'll look bad for him—and for you. So if you are in doubt, hold back. Or if you think it can't wait, but you aren't 100 percent certain, say so, thus transferring at least part of the risk to the person upstairs.

A BASIC PLAN FOR
INTRODUCING OFFICE AUTOMATION

Generate some paper. Prepare a report that discusses the purpose and objectives of your program. Include a schedule for your plan and a sample questionnaire for an evaluation survey. Surveys and polls are "hot." They are often used as a basis for an office automation plan.

Arrange a trial run for equipment. If you can pretest the equipment, so much the better. In some cases, you might wish to hold off on introducing any equipment until you've made a strong case "in theory," based on your survey.

Spill the beans. Tell everyone what you are going to do. Use a memo or meeting to describe the survey and smooth out a few feathers before they get ruffled. You want as many of your colleagues as possible on your side. Fear of office automation can usually be equated with fear of the unknown.

Take your poll. Give out the survey; collect the survey. You can also use work sampling techniques—for example, look at workers' logs with an eye toward production, or the number and types of documents generated. Personal interviews are valuable too. You'll get some juicy quotes and a more "grass roots" idea about how things are going.

Vendors can be very helpful in structuring surveys and helping your personnel understand the machines. But be wary. They can structure your survey in a way that skews the results in favor of their own objectives.

Perform data reduction and analysis. Collate results and prepare a statistical analysis.

Generate some more paper. Summarize the results of the survey, and draw conclusions from your findings. But please: Make your summary short, to the point, succinct, comprehensive.

Your big moment: Present the results. Don't sell so hard that it looks like you are being greased by the vendors. Just present the facts, projections, advantages, cost analysis, cost effectiveness, return on investment; etc.

ADJUSTING TO THE OFFICE OF THE FUTURE

We've all known for quite some time that technology is accelerating change at a rate that is just barely tolerable by human consciousness. The problem is, no executive wants to flip out his staff with a "Buck Rogers" desk and filing cabinet, but no executive wants to be left behind, either. As a manager, your job is to balance the two concerns—human and technological—to produce the optimum effects.

The modern executive himself has to do a bit of adjusting. Office machines are no longer just for the underlings. The notion of having a desk top so sleek and so empty of working tools that it resembles the top of a coffin is going by the wayside. Instead, your desk might look like mission control at the Houston Space Center or something off the set of *Dr. Strangelove*. But what is required is more a cognitive change than a change in personal habits or methods. We must be able to package information so it can be utilized by machines with electronic intelligence. Even more important, we must learn to accept and use whatever data the machines spit back, converting it into the kind of information our brains can use. Personnel changes mean making certain adjustments, so why not look at learning to interact with automated office equipment as learning to adjust to—and exploit—a particularly weird set of friends and co-workers?

TRENDS TO WATCH IN
OFFICE AUTOMATION

There are three primary factors affecting the future development and availability of office technology:

Advances in technology. Each year, improvements in manufacturing techniques and new breakthroughs *drive costs down.* According to recent estimates, the cost of communications is shrinking at a yearly rate of 10 percent, computer logic at a rate of 25 percent, and electronic memory at an astounding 40 percent.

The cost of data processing will be cut by more than a factor of ten during the eighties. The price of storage will decline 80–90 percent. The cost of transfer will shrink with the advent of satellites, fiber optics, microwave and other technologies. Now, more efficient forms of input/output, such as ultra-high-speed printing, are cutting costs.

Everything in the industry has succumbed to the "small is beautiful" psychology, and increased miniaturization is making each generation of PCs and other equipment more intelligent without making them larger.

As electronic parts replace mechanical ones, maintenance becomes easier and cheaper and the fabrication costs go down.

All this adds up to lower prices, or, at least, more for your money. But this advantage is offset by another factor. (No, it's not greed this time, although that was a good guess.)

Marketing costs. The gremlin here is marketing costs. They remain high. This is a very tough, ultracompetitive marketplace, with every guy more than three years out of M.I.T. going into business with his wedding stash or his rich friend's trust fund.

The companies that get ahead must do it one of three ways: by advertising a lot (difficult for companies on limited budget) or by price cutting (which reduces profit margin) or by designing in some unique feature. Quality in this industry is generally quite high, so it's difficult to rely simply on building a superior product.

Another cost problem is operator training. When you sell a machine, you've got to train the staff how to use it. That means instructional manpower and materials. And they cost money.

In the future, look for an increasing trend toward user-engineered items, programmed so the training costs can be reduced substantially. Firms will also take a more sophisticated look at "positioning" and designing products for a segment of the market, rather than the market in general, thereby reducing competition to a manageable amount. This will work only if office automation spreads across the board. If it remains heavily concentrated (within communications, banking and finance, and mail order industries), positioning won't work. You can't design for a market segment that isn't interested in buying your stuff.

User awareness. A product is more difficult to sell when the potential buyer is more sophisticated. The managers who buy office equipment are much hipper today than five years ago. Managers should know at least the basics about what a machine is supposed to do, and what their own needs are. Vendor salespeople can no longer do a "quickie survey" in the office or try some demo-and-fast-talk roadshow and expect to sell. No one is interested in gimmicks. Everyone wants features that they can use, not the option of playing computer battleship during the coffee break, and having the office lights blink and the dictaphones playing "Rule Britannia" every time a ship is sunk.

Salespeople realize this and are changing their approaches, so you can expect a bit more straight talk in the future. Nevertheless, keep your guard up.

Another thing. More data processing people are getting involved in office automation designs and purchase. They see that a marriage is inevitable, so they want to have a hand in choosing the best equipment for their purposes. Unlike the average manager, the data processing people understand how these gizmos work.

WHAT IT WILL ALL MEAN

The best study of the implications has been done by The Diebold Group, a New York–based consulting firm. Some of the more important conclusions:

We will be able to "pick and choose" our work. What Diebold calls "the entrepreneurial work force" will become a reality. With highly advanced methods of telecommunication, electronic mail, data storage and computation, executives can be more selective, doing the kinds of things they want to do and having other work parceled out to others or to a machine.

Since the automated office can serve to interface the work of one executive with the work of others, it will be less crucial that the executive be in the office often, or simultaneously with other members of the staff. Imagine that a car could be designed by a team of designers, draftsmen, and engineers in different parts of the country. Each member of the team could assess all or any blueprints, sketches, or specifications and send an inquiry or a suggestion from a terminal. Obviously, a few brainstorming sessions would be in order. But that's just the point: *The executive, freed from the tedium, will have more time to devote to creative activity.*

Years ago, executives could get ahead on the strength of things like "reliability," accuracy, and long hours worked. In the future, wits will count more, because the computer will be a great equalizer in the area of office routine—everyone will be more accurate and thorough. You'll need more than that to earn a promotion.

The "knowledge workers" of the future will be more independent and, therefore, more able to keep up with their own specialties. They will have more time to devote to maintaining a "state of the art" expertise.

The executive work space will become a communications center. You'll be equipped to assess information from computers, construct models, even engage in teleconferencing. You will be able to do things that only a few years ago were the domain of NASA and its billion-dollar budget—such as communicate via satellite.

The real estate broker will take on another function—that of information broker. All this automation requires very sophisticated and complicated hookups and access and configurations. Office buildings will be equipped with a variety of services, such as advanced phone circuitry with a computerized exchange and switching that will serve the entire building, connection to major info networks and electronic mail, and even a dish antenna on the roof to assess the satellite-based services. Thus, the real estate agent will be a retailer offering a wide variety of information services. It is very likely that such an approach will allow the realtor to purchase the services at wholesale rates and/or commissions and then mark up the costs to the individual tenants.

"Smart" buildings are already here. But so far, tenants seem unwilling to pay for the privilege, preferring to install their own networks.

Workers will be more flexible and independent. Especially in the white-collar area, automation will bring an increase in flexibility in hours, compensation plans, job descriptions, and salaries. Although this will make payroll much more complicated than it already is, the computer will make that job easy to manage.

The home office will probably be commonplace. With all this talk about independence and remoteness from the workplace, it is natural to conclude that you could place a terminal in your home and work from there. Many executives have already done so, if only to supplement their office activity or to provide themselves with a way of staying in touch if their preferred residence is in a rural area or in a city other than the one in which their office is located.

Almost every piece of equipment mentioned in this chapter can be assessed, communicated with, or otherwise instructed from your home, assuming the proper equipment is in place. Lots of experts, including The Diebold Group, believe that the advent of the home-office configuration is just a matter of time. But a few disagree. Success in business, they say, demands a creative and dynamic environment, with the constant interaction that is provided only by continuous presence in the workplace. Company politics, power games, one-upmanship, and all the subtler aspects of the business success game would be hard to play on a computer terminal. Thus, some pundits go halfway and predict that the remote offices will be set up wherever businessmen tend to gather—and that could mean a country club, corporate "club," etc.—anyplace but the home, which is the one environment that the executive wants to keep relatively off-limits from the demands of his job.

Personally, I tend to agree that a "change of scene" is psychologically essential for effective work. But I don't think that we know for certain how that will be accomplished in the future. Some experts have suggested that there will be "office rooms" in dwellings, designed specifically as such by home and apartment builders. Others believe that shared offices will spring up—several friends will pool their resources and take an office to their liking, even though they all work for different corporations.

At present, the growth of the work-at-home phenomenon has fallen short of expectations.

RECOMMENDED READING

Critical Issues in Office Automation by Walter A. Kleinschrod (New York: McGraw-Hill, 1986) is a clear, well-reasoned examination of the modern office in transition. Kleinschrod goes beyond a simple discussion of the technology to examine the forces at work in the modern office, and the factors that affect the process of choosing between the many available options in office automation.

Administrative Management is among the best periodicals covering the modern office. It keeps a close watch on emerging technologies, trends and efficiency methods. It is published by Dalton Communications, Inc., New York.

IN A "CLASS" OFFICE...

Whether in the office of the past or the future, some values remain constant:

- Coffee is served with milk instead of "nondairy creamer."
- The magazines in the waiting room are up to date.
- There's a place to hang your coat apart from the hook on the inside of someone's door.
- You don't have to be an electronics expert to get an outside line on the phone.
- When you need a photocopy, you don't get the same reaction as you would if you wanted access to the company safe.
- Last year's calendar isn't left on the wall until May.
- When you call, they don't play Muzak while you are on hold, so at least you can speak to someone in your *own* office without hearing a plastic version of "Yesterday" going in the background.
- You can obtain entry to their bathroom without having to call an impromptu general staff meeting to find the key.
- You are served tea in a real (nonplastic) cup, and you are given a place to put the teabag.
- Care has been taken not to hire a receptionist who tells you that Mr. Jones's office is the last door on the left when it's last door on the right.
- There are always enough chairs.

40

PERSONAL ACCESSORIES AND APPOINTMENTS: EXECUTIVE STYLE

Ever since primitive man picked up a rock and a stick, tools have been vitally important. Modern man has perhaps added a new dimension: No longer is the usefulness of the tool the only thing that counts. The *look* and *feel* of one's possessions can convey a great deal about who one is and how one thinks. Let's look at a few personal items that every executive should own, paying careful attention to form, function, and the image conveyed.

THE FIRST IMPRESSION: STATIONERY

In many cases, your initial business contacts are made by mail. Stationery can say a great deal about you and your company.

Paper. The *composition* of paper is wood pulp and cotton—the more cotton, the better. So the cheapest paper is all wood pulp, the most costly all cotton; and in the middle are various wood/cotton blends. Invest in all-cotton paper, or something very close to it.

The *weight* of the paper is also important. The rating in pounds is the weight of 2,000 8½ " × 11" sheets of that paper. The higher the weight, the thicker the paper. Go with paper in the 20-24-pound range.

A translucent symbol impressed during manufacture, the *watermark* is usually the name or logo of the paper company. All fine papers have watermarks.

Letterhead size. *Letter size* (8½ " × 11") is the most commonly used format in business. But there is also *monarch* (7½ " × 10½ "), usually reserved for the personal letterheads of upper level executives. Monarch carries prestige. But if you have some monarch made up before your time, don't send it to people who know your status. You'll just look silly.

Printing. There are several methods:

- *offset*. Cheap, and looks it. Avoid.
- *thermography*. Glossy letters with a raised feel. Thermography produces an engraved look for less money than true engraving. It's acceptable in most cases.
- *engraving*. The cleanest, sharpest, and best. Your stationery will impress, provided the recipient can tell the difference. Expensive.

Color. White or off-white—go no further. You can jazz it up with tasteful colored inks—blues, browns, greys.

Logo. This requires a great deal of thought. While you needn't spend hundreds of thousands, as many Fortune 500s do, it pays to hire a designer. Whenever I see an inappropriate or unattractive logo, I ask who is responsible. The results of my survey to date: 75 percent of those logos were done by the spouse of a key executive. The logo should convey something about your company. If you don't want to commit the time or the funds, go with your name and address only, set in a simple type style.

THE BUSINESS CASE

The function of a business case is to transport important papers and small items from one place to another. But in the current climate of first impressions, the case you carry your papers in says as much about you as what's inside. Well, almost.

If the contract is a good one, you should be able to bring it over in a knapsack and still make the deal. But since every executive chooses a business case at least once every couple of years (if not more often), you should consider what goes into making the right choice:

Try to stay thin and light. You should not carry lots of work around with you. The successful executive is not snowed under by paperwork. He's a decision maker. And final decisions don't take up reams of paper. The one exception is a lawyer. But even lawyers are succumbing to the "thin" look. For trips to and from home, many lawyers use a briefcase with capacity for several law books and large briefs; but they carry a thin portfolio or attaché to client meetings during business hours.

Portfolios have become very popular in recent years, because they are light and elegant. They hold about as much as a large manila envelope. But you can't very well carry a fifty-cent manila envelope around; you'll look like a messenger. You can spend over a hundred bucks on a deluxe leather portfolio, and everyone will know that you can afford to spend that kind of dough to carry five sheets of paper.

There are underarm cases that are larger than portfolios, but they are in no-man's land—too bulky to have the status of a portfolio and not as elegant as a good attaché.

If you're buying an attaché, listen to the locks. A nice clean sound indicates a well-made lock. Also, it makes for high drama when you enter the room, place your attaché on the table, and "click" into action. (Just make sure that you don't open your case upside down.)

An insider's tip: The snap of the locks closing is a sign that you are about to leave. You can use this as a negotiation tool. One lock snapped shut says "I'm ready to leave." Two locks shut says "I'm leaving." You can always open the locks again should your adversary change his mind or his offer. Or if you back off on a bluff.

If you use an ID tag on the outside, it should be tasteful.

The handle should be comfortable.

Initials should be very discreet. Initials on a business case are like initials on a shirt; you don't want to advertise. If initials can't be embossed or otherwise affixed in a tasteful, expensive-looking manner, forget them. Stick-on metallic letters are out.

Choose leather if you can afford it. High-quality vinyl looks okay for a while. But it doesn't age gracefully, as leather does. Recently, other natural fabrics have become acceptable in certain situations. Wood such as rosewood or teak attachés and linen or high-quality canvas envelopes are becoming more common.

Consider your business case to be part of your wardrobe. You can ruin the look of an expensive suit with a cheap or tasteless case. Embossed designs—eagles, stars, etc.—are out. Tacky.

Stitching should be unobtrusive. Thread should match the case color. Contrasting stitching is a no-no.

WHAT TO LOOK FOR

IN ATTACHÉS   They all have hard sides and a frame, or they achieve the same effect through molded sides.

- *Good quality leather*
- *Sound overall construction*
- *Hardware* (locks, handles, snaps, etc.). Metal should be brass with a brushed or satin finish. This includes the lid stays, which hold the top open.
- *Lining.* A "status" case is lined with leather, suede, or linen.

- *Interior features.* Two or three organizing file compartments.
- *Lock.* If you are concerned about security, a combination lock is preferable.
- *Color.* Men should choose black or brown. Avoid grey and other neutral colors. Women are safe with the same rules, but can also go with a burgundy or a tan. Stay away from blues, reds, greens, etc. They are not for business.
- *Price.* Expect to spend $200-plus for a good one.
- *Width.* The two-inch model is okay for women, but men should use a portfolio instead if a slim case is what they want. The 3½ inch model is best. Five-inch models can hold a great deal, but they are short on status. After that, the attaché becomes a sample case.

IN PORTFOLIOS Portfolios are made like handbags. Their leather is softer, and they are lighter in weight than either attachés or briefcases.

- *Handles.* You have a choice of fixed handles, retractable handles, or none at all.
- *Hardware.* Brass.
- *Lining.* Suede, smooth leather, or high-quality fabric.
- *Pockets.* Some portfolios have outside pockets for quick access to items such as a folding umbrella or newspaper.
- *Zipper.* Should be brass, very high quality and heavy duty.
- *Price.* $85 and up.

IN ENVELOPE PORTFOLIOS   Very thin and simple, envelopes have a flap closure or top zipper. The emphasis should be on the quality of leather and the construction. The stitching will be very conspicuous, so it should be of high quality.

Because of the popularity of envelope portfolios, many of the better attachés come equipped with a snap-out envelope.

IN BRIEFCASES   Briefcases have the advantage of expandable sides and top loading. They are also very rugged.

- *Compartments.* You'll find up to four compartments inside.
- *Lining.* Usually, none. If the manufacturer does bother to put in a lining, it's of high-quality fabric.
- *Price.* $100 and up.

CALCULATORS

SELECTING A CALCULATOR

Choosing the right calculator for your needs has become almost as complicated as the calculators themselves have become. There are hundreds of models available in a wide range of sizes, shapes, displays, weights,

---

and power sources. And the combinations of functions and features are endless. Tough competition and price cutting practices have led manufacturers to concentrate on specialized calculators, their features designed for specific life-styles and occupations. Executives usually select calculators from one of three basic categories:

GENERAL PURPOSE   If most of your computations involve only simple arithmetic, you need go no further than a general purpose calculator. These models emphasize the four basic arithmetic functions—add, subtract, multiply, and divide. Most of them come with a simple memory, which will store a figure for later use while you continue with another computation. Many have percent keys. Some compute square roots and/or minus numbers.

Besides the advantages of simplicity and a generally lower price, general purpose calculators offer the greatest choice in models. They range in size from "office printing" to ultrathin, "credit card" size. Some come with special add-ons, such as clocks, stopwatches, alarms, and radios. General purpose calculators are built into pens, cigarette lighters, wristwatches, portable cassette recorders, and other devices. Since the basic calculator circuitry is so inexpensive, this trend is likely to continue if the addition of a calculator helps move the product. You'll be seeing them built into attaché cases and appointment books.

Keep in mind that a job change, a new responsibility, or a new investment strategy can render a general purpose calculator obsolete. You might find yourself in need of a more advanced or specialized calculator. But many executives own two—a general purpose for home or travel use and an advanced model for office or den.

SCIENTIFIC   Intended primarily for engineers, technicians, chemists, and others in the sciences, these calculators feature a large number of advanced scientific operations, such as trigonometric functions, logarithms, and metric conversions, and statistical functions such as standard deviation and correlation coefficient. In general, a scientific calculator is not ideal for most business calculations unless (1) it is programmable, allowing you to use business and financial programs, or (2) it is one of the few higher priced, advanced models that feature both financial *and* scientific functions. However, the statistical section of most scientific calculators can be used to solve problems in business statistics. And in cases where business and engineering go hand in hand, a scientific calculator may actually be required to figure costs and profits and perform other business-related calculations.

FINANCIAL   Financial calculators are designed specifically for business executives, financial analysts, and managers. If you often prepare figures, compute interest rates, salary analysis, or projections, or employ technical analysis for investments, a financial calculator can save you lots of time and minimize the possibility of errors. You can also do sophisticated figuring on short notice, which can be a godsend when quick decisions are required. A financial calculator can be especially useful in real estate, insurance, securities, and tax accounting.

The range of available financial calculators is much more limited in size, functions, and design. The manufacturers make models that are quite similar to one another in each price range. But in my calculator survey, Texas Instruments and Hewlett-Packard were singled out by executives who owned financial calculators. "The Hewlett-Packard," says Anthony Candido, of Manhattan Office Products, "is considered the 'Cadillac' of calculators among businessmen," because of its rugged construction and sophisticated features. Both TI and HP claim to have surveyed businessmen for their preferences and incorporated these preferences into the design of their calculators. As the HP and TI (especially HP) lines have grown increasingly complex and powerful, university business departments have begun offering courses in their use.

PROGRAMMABILITY

PREPROGRAMMED   Selected, commonly used programs involving complex calculations are permanently built into the calculator. For example, most financial calculators are preprogrammed to compute *compound interest:* All you need to do is press the appropriate keys and the computer automatically determines the interest rate, present or future value, or time period. Preprogrammed calculators are less expensive than those you can program yourself, but they are also less flexible. However, if your work involves only standard financial and business computations, you may find a preprogrammed calculator with programs that suit your needs.

KEYSTROKE PROGRAMMABLE   This calculator allows you to "command" it to carry out a specific sequence of functions in a specific order; you program the calculator to do so by pushing keys. Then you enter the numerical values and the calculator runs through the sequence, performing the step-by-step operation as indicated in your "program." This feature is a tremendous aid in performing complex and repetitive calculations, and it prevents human error caused by fatigue and the confusion that can result from repetition. However, until you get the hang of it, programming the calculator, in itself, can be tedious, time consuming, and somewhat confusing. Some models are keystroke programmable, but feature preprogrammed computation formulas for the commonly used formulas. Such models are ideal, since most of the time you can get along with preprograms, but you can always write your own when the going gets tough.

FEATURES WORTH LOOKING FOR

- *Automatic shut-off.* The calculator cuts off its own power after a few minutes of nonuse. This saves the batteries.

- *Continuous, constant, or storage memory.* Three different ways to say the same thing—that the calculator will hold a number in its memory even while the power is off. Most calculators erase themselves when turned off. But this feature means that you can store a number as long as the batteries remain good. It's a help if you have a checkbook balance in the memory, or a figure that you know you'll be using later in the day. Some will even store whole programs for later use.
- *Solar power.* Small photocell panels mounted on the calculator convert light to electricity, eliminating the need for battery replacement. *A chronographic feature* (alarms, timers, stopwatches, clocks) will be helpful if you are a clock watcher, or should be.
- *"Memo."* With the flick of a switch, the numbers become letters, and you can spell out simple messages on the display. Hit your memory, and they are stored. Useful? Perhaps, if you dislike making notes or tend to lose those little pieces of paper.

PRICE

A calculator's price may remain fixed for a while, especially if it is unique. But as competition hits the market and the manufacturers recover the initial tooling costs, *they tend to bring the price down.* The cost of materials is not high, so prices can fall pretty far. There are some general purpose calculators available at under $10. Shop around. Some stores do break list prices; some have models that are being phased out at fantastic savings. Even the more exclusive stores will run manufacturer authorized "sales." In general, timing is the key. Buy a calculator that's new on the market and you'll pay the highest price. A model that's been around for some time costs less. Prices for calculators sold through the mail, such as airlines gift catalogs, mail-order ads, etc., are generally full list price. Ordering from them may save you time, but not money. Occasionally, mail-order ads, such as those run by JSA in *The Wall Street Journal* and other publications, will feature a calculator yet unavailable in stores. These mail-order houses have made fortunes catering to the gadget buffs who want to be "the first on the block to own . . ."

HOW TO CHOOSE A PEN

Feel. Never buy a pen without trying it first. It should be well balanced, of the right size and weight for you, and comfortable to write with. The pen should write smoothly at the angle you are accustomed to.

The nib. If you're buying a fountain pen, the nib, or point, is the most important part to consider. First decide on a nib size. They are typed according to the writing line they produce, usually double broad, broad, medium, fine, or extra fine. This is largely a matter of taste. With the possible exception of those who require a fine line for ledger entries, men tend to prefer a broader stroke for general writing purposes, and women a finer line.

Most better pens have gold nibs, as opposed to steel. Some experts claim that a gold point provides freer and smoother writing and ink flow. Gold nibs retain their shape and point longer. Practically speaking, though, the chances of wearing out a nib—either gold or steel—are relatively slim. Most people lose their pens or drop them on their points long before they wear out. And once the point is bent, it almost always has to be replaced.

Eye appeal. Pen designs range from the old-fashioned, bulky pens to modern, sleek, understated designs. They come in a number of metallic finishes—gold or chrome, and the now popular "high tech" black matte finish. Plastic cases, of course, come in a wide variety of colors. And recently, Chinese lacquer-coated pens have been introduced in blue, brown, green, and black.

A pen is a personal item, and its appearance should please you above all others. However, since it is also a piece of jewelry, you might consider how it looks on you. Try it on. See how it fits and looks under your jacket. If you tend toward traditional clothing or deal with conservative clients, you might wish to shy away from the avant garde. On the other hand, an advertising agency or engineer might find an innovative design to be just the thing. Indeed, Isabelle Flax, of Sam Flax, Inc., one of New York's largest pen dealers, reports large sales in a pen that is almost completely flat and, therefore, hard to hold and difficult to write with. But, so many executives like the way it looks that they are willing to put up with the discomfort. One such flat pen can be found in the Museum of Modern Art in New York.

Status. "Under no circumstances should a man use a cheap pen or pencil in the presence of other men," says John Molloy, author of *Dress for Success.* Your pen is part of your wardrobe. Why wear an expensive suit to an important closing and then take a 29-cent Bic pen out of your inside pocket to sign a million-dollar contract? Gold or sterling silver pens are always somewhat impressive, although gold has become a strong favorite.

There are many "prestige" pens on the market, but experts agree that the Mont Blanc Diplomat (about $185) or its smaller brother, the Classic (about $20 cheaper than the Diplomat), is *the* pen to be seen with. Both are great favorites of professional people. The Mont Blanc comes with a lifetime guarantee and a hand-crafted nib of white and yellow gold that makes it one of the smoothest-writing pens made. The jumbo design is unmistakable, and few will fail to notice it.

Other "status" pens include the Dupont de Paris Chinese lacquer coated pens. The imported Chinese lacquer is applied in France, by hand, in 13 coats (100 hours of drying time between coats), onto a sterling silver casing. The finish is hand rubbed. This pen costs over $200, the exact price varying with the color. Warren Brown notes that the Duponts have become so popular that Sheaffer and Parker have followed suit, offering their own Chinese lacquers. They are less expensive—about $150 for the Sheaffer and $100 for the smaller Parker. Incidentally, Dupont de Paris also makes matching Chinese lacquer cigarette lighters.

Price. The price range in pens is enormous. You get what you pay for, up to a point. Gold ballpoints start at $25. Good fountain pens range from $50 to $135. You can't get a fountain pen with a gold point for less than $30. Beyond that you are paying almost strictly for the precious metals in the casing and for unusual design. But if it isn't important to you to have a pen of solid gold or silver, you can get a fine instrument in stainless steel for much less. And there is little difference in the inner workings.

Use. Obviously, if you are going to use your fountain pen only to sign your name, you can afford to be less concerned about its "feel." But if you like to write a lot of personal notes, comfort will be important. So the manner and amount of use will affect your choice. If you must sign many carbon forms, you will need a good ballpoint or rolling marker, because you simply can't bear down upon a fountain pen.

BALLPOINT, FOUNTAIN PEN, OR ROLLING MARKER? The ballpoint has certain advantages over the fountain pen. Its paste ink dries faster; it's retractable; it rarely leaks; and, as just mentioned, it can write through several carbon sheets.

The fountain pen is back in style. In 1986, sales were up 30 percent over the previous year. They have character, both in design and in the way they write. Because the ink flows smoothly without pressure, writing is more comfortable. As the nib wears, it conforms to the unique writing angle and grip of your hand, so it becomes a distinctly personal item. It gives your penmanship a distinctive look, and your signature becomes truly personal. Thus, in signing a contract, a check, or other important document, a fountain pen carries more prestige. A fountain pen will write at any angle. A ballpoint is much more limited. Usually you must hold it closer to the vertical than you would have to hold a fountain pen. As a result, many people find fountain pens more comfortable. Improvements in design have all but eliminated the problem of leakage.

Rolling markers are really just another type of ball pen, utilizing a ball that "floats" on a cushion of liquid ink. Conventional ball pens use paste ink. But the thinner liquid ink flows more freely, approximating the feel of a fountain pen. It's something of a cross between a ballpoint and a fountain pen. Rolling markers are good for people who write a great deal, because you don't have to exert as much pressure. Hence, you can write faster and with less effort. And rolling markers will make clear carbon copies. The ink has a slower drying time than that of a ballpoint, but it's faster than fountain pen ink.

Recently, some manufacturers have introduced convertible models. The pen casing will accept both ordinary ballpoint refills and rolling-marker refills, as well as soft-tip refills (the artsy, artificial-fiber tips, like those found in Flair and Bic Banana pens, more suited to doodling or note taking than to business communication). These convertible systems are very popular, their versatility and well-designed outer cases being the primary reasons.

TIPS FOR LEFT-HANDERS   Writing for left-handers is often difficult, and this minority has invented countless methods for holding a pen in order to get the letters to slant toward the right, as our schoolteachers all taught us they should. In order to write in a conventional manner, lefties have to adopt uncomfortable ways of holding a pen.

An *oblique point* is cut on an angle that makes it easier for the left-hander to write smoothly. Parker makes one for its "75" series. Most other pen makers do not supply them. But check some of the older pen shops; many still have some in stock.

Warren Brown, of Arthur Brown & Bros., New York's largest pen shop, has a suggestion for left-handers: If you've already decided on a make or model, ask to try a few pens in the model of your choice. They look identical, of course, but since most better quality fountain pens have a gold nib that is hand finished, the nibs will vary slightly from pen to pen. Keep trying until you find the one that is comfortable. Mr. Brown says that his salespeople will let left-handers try as many as they need to find satisfaction. Most other better stores also adhere to this practice.

PENS AS COLLECTIBLES

Save Grandma's old fountain pen. It has value as a collectible, and it is likely to increase in value. If it no longer works, repair it soon: Parts are no longer made for older pens, and they are becoming more and more scarce. It might take quite a while to locate the proper part.

One of the nation's leading pen experts is Cecil (a.k.a. "Dr.") Brown, at M. C. Flynn Stationers, in New York. By his count, he is one of the 14 remaining experts in the United States. Manufacturers refer customers to him when they are unable to fix a pen. He keeps a collection of parts on hand and, often, can make a part if it isn't available. Brown has been repairing pens for over 40 years, and he receives them from as far away as Africa (he will service pens through the mail). Says Brown of his passion for pens, "If you cut me, you'd find ink coming out instead of blood."

Contact:
    M. C. Flynn, Inc.
    43 East 59 Street
    New York, New York 10022

THE EXECUTIVE WARDROBE

Who should you listen to when it comes to selecting business clothing? Two arbiters have something meaningful and original to say on the subject and understand the unwritten rules of the business community: John Molloy, who has approached the subject as if he were preparing a PhD dissertation; and Michael Korda, who has brought his typically heavy but experienced hand to bear.

Korda and Molloy differ very little from one another in their advice, except that Molloy is interested mainly in what will gain acceptance and avoid negative reactions, while Korda tells you what successful people wear. In both cases, the message is the same: Stay with a conventional look that will not offend other people, but will make them notice your good taste, your understated elegance, and your appreciation of fine quality. Both implore you to save the Beau Brummel act for after-hours activity. Korda adds that an objective of the "success look" is to look as good at five as you do at nine; to appear unaffected by the elements that may tend to ruffle and undo ordinary folk.

There is virtually unanimous agreement among experts that dress codes do exist, and that they usually filter down from the top of the firm. Most executives needn't be reminded as they pick up their codes through observation and word-of-mouth.

To some extent, dress codes vary with the industry. "Creative" businesses such as film, television, music and advertising allow for more high fashion clothing. Bankers tend to be ultra-conservative.

Beyond industry, many consider it a good idea to fine-tune your choice of clothing to the client or associates you are working with on any given day. One real estate broker told me that she dresses very diffferently when showing an apartment to an investment banker than when accompanying a rock star.

In general, it is a good idea to err on the side of caution. You never know who you might meet unexpectedly. Besides, it is better to appear conventional than risk looking the dandy or eccentric.

Keep in mind that business clothing has been modified to keep pace with the times. Increasingly, men wish to express a personal style, to set themselves apart without standing out. More variety is permitted, and the cut of suits has been modified slightly to give men more choices. You are free to select suits, shirts and ties that will flatter your build and make a personal statement, yet remain well within the bounds of good taste.

WARDROBE COORDINATORS

Wardrobe consultants are a recent development. Sometimes independent, but usually attached to a department store, they assist the executive shopper in selecting a wardrobe. They are especially helpful for those without the time, or fashion-sense to pick a smart wardrobe for themselves. The service works better as time goes on, because the wardrobe consultant will get to know you better, and you are likely to become a bit more open-minded. Eventually, the consultant will be able to put aside several different suits, ties, and shirts when they arrive at the store. All you need do is show up and choose from the selection. No wandering aimlessly from room to room, floor to floor.

Some consultants charge an annual fee. Others expect you to spend a reasonable amount of money. Don't call if all you need is a pair of socks.

Below you will find a distillation of the advice of Molloy and Korda. If you follow their guidelines, you will have little room to maneuver, but it is unlikely that you will ever wear the wrong thing for business. Still, you should not forget that, in the final analysis, you are the best judge of what to wear. Give your choice of clothes some time and thought: Good taste usually requires some education. In general, if you feel comfortable in a particular style and it is well made and suits you physically, you will look good, no matter the fashion. But remember: Clothes are a statement, a means of expression. If you wear the latest Italian fashions on Wall Street or in the Midwest, you will certainly stand out. If that is your intention, fine; many do this with good results. However, if you feel that a flamboyant or flashy appearance is a risk you'd rather not take, stick to the guidelines.

THE EXECUTIVE WARDROBE FOR MEN

	Molloy	*Korda*
HATS	Generally unnecessary. If you must wear one, make sure it's conservative.	Don't wear them. Buy an umbrella.
HAIR	Pick a cut that flatters your face. Make sure that your hair is neat at all times. If your ears are big, wear your hair long enough at the sides to cover them a bit.	Get it styled. Try to tone down big ears. You are after the natural look: Avoid too much spray or creams. If you are bald, better to flaunt your immaculate pate than to use any hair replacement method that has even the slightest chance of detection.
FACE	Most men should avoid growing facial hair. However, in some cases a	Your face should project vigor, health, and energy. Shave carefully and of-

	Molloy	Korda
	beard can convey power or authority. If you decide to wear a beard, make sure it's a full one—no goatees. Keep it well trimmed and shaped, never heavy. Do not wear handlebar mustaches.	ten, even at the office if you have a heavy beard. Get enough rest; and to help eliminate bags under the eyes, bloodshot eyes, and a puffy face, avoid alcohol.
GLASSES	Wire rims look better on younger men; plastic or horn rims make you look older. Pick a frame color that complements your hair color. Frames should be heavier if you have a large jaw and facial structure, lighter if jaw and cheekbones are less prominent.	Keep the frames simple. Avoid decorations. Korda likes gold metal frames.
SUITS	*Style:* Avoid European styling and very fitted suits for business. Never buy a new style the first year it appears; see if it catches on. Do not wear suits with any ornamentation. If you have a large rear end, suits with double vents are preferable. Heavy men should avoid double-breasted suits.	Avoid suppressed waists. Left lapel should have a buttonhole, and there should be 3-4 buttons on the sleeve. Do not wear suits with flared-bottom trousers. Since the object is to appear unruffled at all times, it is wise to avoid sweating unnecessarily—don't wear heavy fabrics, even in winter. Inside, you won't need the extra insulation, and you can wear a heavy overcoat over a lightweight suit to keep warm out-of-doors. Double knit fabrics are acceptable for travel, if in dark colors. Avoid textured patterns, contrasting stitching or piping, or pockets with buttons.

Color: You are safe with blues, greys, and beiges, but browns and blacks are not always acceptable.

You can't go wrong with dark blues or dark greys.

Fit: Remember that ready-to-wear suits are proportioned for the average man. If you are not "average," the waist, seat, or shoulders might not fit properly. If the fit can't be corrected, don't buy the suit. Measurements should be marked with pins, not merely chalked, unless the alteration is a simple hemline. It is wise to tip the tailor five to ten dollars—it'll help you get some extra attention and care.

Custom made suits always fit better, but few will notice unless they wear customs too. Alterations are very important: Don't pay in full until they are done to your satisfaction.

Patterns: Solids are always acceptable, as are pinstripes, chalkstripes, and subtle plaids. Stay away from gaudy stripes and wide or loud plaids. Donegal tweeds and herringbones, common in fine English suits, are also acceptable.

Sport jackets and blazers: Sport jackets and blazers are not a good choice for business. If you wear one, make sure that it is a classic or "status" jacket—for example, a camel's hair jacket paired with simple blue trousers.

Sport coats are acceptable in some businesses, but choose a subdued pattern, such as a lightweight tweed or a small check. Do not wear blazers with badges or coats of arms.

Miscellaneous: Keep a

fresh, pressed suit in your office for emergencies. Have a sufficient number of suits so that you needn't wear one after the pants have lost their crease.

SHIRTS

Fit: Make sure that the shirttail is long enough and that the shirt has a six- or seven-button front so that it will stay tucked neatly in the pants. The waist should fit; fabric shouldn't bunch around the waist. The collar should not be so tight that it wrinkles, and it should have removable stays unless it is a button-down. The height of the collar should be right for the length of your neck— higher for longer necks, lower for shorter ones. Custom shirts are clearly the best; semi-customs are next best.

Fabrics: Cotton is the fabric of choice. Cotton/ polyester blends have their advantages: They are more wrinkle resis- tant, and they will look better after a day's wear. However, they don't "breathe" as well and aren't as absorbent. Silks, see-through fabrics, and knits are all unacceptable for business. Avoid shiny fabrics of any kind.

One hundred percent cot- ton is best.

Colors: White is still the

Whites are best. Blue is

	Molloy	Korda
	safest and the best. Light blues and beiges are also good. The shirt color should always be lighter than the suit you are wearing, and the tie should always be darker than the shirt.	also worn by successful men.
	Patterns: Besides solids, crisp thin stripe patterns are desirable; so are subtle plaids. Ginghams, glen plaids, ribbons, florals, etc. are not.	Narrow, muted stripes.
	Pockets: Shirts without pockets are better. If the shirt does have one, it should be a simple patch style without button or flaps.	Do not put anything in your shirt pockets. *Miscellaneous:* Short sleeves are out.
TIES	*Length:* Usually, a better quality tie is longer. When tied, the tie should fall to the belt buckle— no longer, no shorter. When buying a tie, always keep in mind the kind of knot you prefer, and your height. These factors will affect the length of the knotted tie.	
	Fabrics: Silk is without question the fabric of choice in ties. However, one should avoid cheap or shiny silks. Polyesters are acceptable if they look like silk. Cotton is permissible in the summer and year round in the South. Wools are not good for men with large	

necks, because the knots are large. Whatever the fabric, you should be able to tie a knot easily, and they should look well with the shirt collar you prefer.

Patterns: Solids, small polka dots, diagonal stripes, small repeating shapes, subtle plaids and paisleys are all acceptable. Never wear gaudy ties, picture patterns, or unusual patterns that are trying to look upon. You *can* go all-solid—shirt, suit, and tie.

The less conspicuous or flashy, the better. Stripes, checks, polka dots, and paisleys are fine. Stay with quiet patterns—no geometrics or sunbursts.

Colors: Beiges, blues, maroons, and greys. Pastels for summer. Never wear purples or blacks, except as a small part of a paisley.

Miscellaneous: Tie clips are no longer needed. Tie should be middle-of-the-road in width—not too wide or too narrow.

BELTS

Belts are rarely the problem—usually, it's the buckle. Large, bulky, heavy, or ornate buckles are not good. Stick with traditional, smaller buckles with squared lines.

Belts should be plain, unless you are a real Western style dresser à la J. R. Ewing. In such cases, a belt design is okay. Suspenders are acceptable, especially on lawyers, but wearing a belt and suspenders at the same time is not.

SOCKS

Avoid ankle-length or droopy socks. Socks should be dark in color.

No skin should show when you sit down. Over-the-calf socks do the trick. Black is always a safe color.

SHOES

Gucci loafers and tasseled shoes are acceptable only

Wear elegant, finely crafted shoes. This shows

in ultra-sophisticated cities. Avoid shoes with too much metal. Wingtips are always safe. Plain laced shoes and simple slip-ons are acceptable. Colors for business are black, brown, and cordovan. Patent leather only works in glamor businesses.

others that you never have to "rough it," i.e., slosh through the rain and mud to get to work. If necessary, wear hiking boots and change in the office. Shoes should be free of ornamentation or fancy stitching, and they should be shaped like your foot—not too pointy or too rounded. Black is the most useful color, because it goes acceptably with everything.

THE EXECUTIVE WARDROBE FOR WOMEN

Women have much more flexibility than men when it comes to business dress. Perhaps this is because they are relative newcomers to the executive ranks and are therefore not constrained by so many conventions. However, women should keep in mind that there is a distinct difference between what is worn at the office and what is worn in the evening or in casual situations.

The most important rule is to dress in a tasteful, understated manner that acknowledges your femininity, but does not exploit it. Many men rather like alluring outfits on their secretaries and female support personnel: It enhances the feeling of male dominance and makes it easier to avoid taking these women seriously. But who wants to take orders from a gal in a low-cut sweater and tight pants? In the long run, men react negatively to overtly sexual outfits at the workplace. They set the wearer apart and make it difficult for her to compete and be treated equally.

Simple shirtdresses, suits, and blazer and skirt combinations are usually safe. Don't wear short skirts, blue jeans, or low-cut outfits. With many women entering the work force, magazines catering to this audience have appeared. They can be helpful in guiding you on what the well-dressed executive woman is wearing. Among them, *Working Woman* and *Savvy* are particularly good.

Having stated "the official line," I wish to point out that the ranks of dissenting executive women are growing. First, after ten years or so of generally restrictive, male look-alike man-tailored clothing, women are bored with playing it safe. Second, many women are now in upper middle management and having made it, feel they've earned the right to wear what they want rather than conform to some unwritten standard. Men are being encouraged to incorporate personal business style. But how are women supposed to manage it when confined to charcoal and blue skirts and blazers, with man-tailored shirts and ribbon ties?

It's not that these bolder fashions are meant to ignore business conventions. Clearly, these women wish to convey that they know the difference between business and personal life. They aren't wearing clinging jersey dresses or mini-skirts or cocktail dresses. Rather they are moving away from the uniformlike business suits to more relaxed, unconstructed suits, perhaps with slightly padded shoulders, and tastefully cut dresses in brilliant colors. Skirts and dresses usually remain tastefully below the knee.

Women in lower-level jobs often feel more secure sticking with "the uniform," but increasingly are trying to accessorize with an unusual scarf or tie.

The warnings have been sounded, most notably by traditionalists such as Molloy: women who dress out of the corporate uniform will pay the price. He calls it "fluffing out," and essentially proclaims that the day you do it is the day you stop advancing up the corporate ladder. More interesting than the choice of skirt is the notion that the success of the American woman executive is so inextricably linked to her choice of wardrobe. Clearly, many women aren't buying it and neither do I.

PART VIII

ON THE ROAD: WHAT THE TRAVEL GUIDES DON'T TELL YOU

"People who develop the habit
of thinking of themselves as world
citizens are fulfilling the first
requirement of sanity in our time."
Norman Cousins

41

GETTING THERE BY AIR

Business travel is often one of the most exasperating aspects of executive life. But it needn't be, if you take the time to understand how the travel industry operates, and how you can use the system to meet your own needs.

IS THE TRIP REALLY NECESSARY?

True, the world is shrinking. Jets ply the air corridors, and Concordes whisk us to London in under three hours. At first glance, jet aviation seems like a big boost to business, because you can attend a conference or clinch a sale in Chicago and be in New York for the evening. But more often than not, you find yourself in an orbit of bad coffee, jet lag, wrinkled suits and ripe T-shirts, too much booze and too little sleep. Yes, the world is getting smaller; but in the 1980s, telecommunications will be the main shrinking agent. So before you plan that Marco Polo itinerary, consider the many ways you can get the job done without leaving home and hearth—or office.

Conference calls. Commonly accepted in business today, this approach can actually enhance your status. If handled with finesse, a reluctance to travel can be a sign of a very busy executive whose time is at a premium. Naturally, it's easier to take part in conference calls with people you already know well.

Maybe you're the type that makes a dynamite impression when you appear in the flesh. Obviously, you'll want to use that personal charisma to your advantage. But don't *overuse* it. Always be aware that you have other options besides "the next flight out."

Electronic conferences. Some of the megafirms already have the capability of staging electronic conferences. Get used to them. They save time and money, so they are bound to become more popular as the cost of air travel rises with the cost of fuel inflation (see Chapter 36).

Electronic mail. Take advantage of the wide variety of alternative ways to communicate. There is bound to be a form of electronic mail to suit your needs (*see* Chapter 36).

Caution: In some companies, business travel is the mode of the executive who is not afraid to get his hands dirty—like the field commander, as opposed to the desk captain, in the army. Don't allow yourself to be confused with those who eschew travel because they don't want to be away from their families or don't want to miss their golf game. Keep everything on the cost-effective, business-wise level.

What to do when they start cutting down on business trips, and wield the knife on your travel budget. *Don't fight it.* Those who resist the demise of shuttle capitalism will be tagged as people with weak egos who *fear the loss of status* because they were discouraged from making the trip to Dallas. They'll take this as an indication that their bosses think they haven't been doing a good job, or just aren't needed in those crucial field meetings. *Do not see business travel as a form of ego boost. It either helps you do business or it doesn't. That's the bottom line.*

Some people get lonely on the road. But many others see travel as an opportunity for renewed freedom: Nobody knows you; there are big gaps of time that needn't be accounted for. Whether those hours are spent reading, at a pool hall or at the opera, many members of the business community cherish this time. Enjoy it when you can. But remember—*the company is not obliged to help you live a double life.* And if you fight for more business trips with the lust for going incognito as your primary motive, you'll be on shaky ground. You know when a trip is called for. And when it's a sham.

Jump on the bandwagon. Eliminate wasteful trips on your own initiative. Learn how to be effective in a conference-call situation. You'll be under less pressure and will gain time. Let those factors work for you. And *when you feel you must take a trip, don't be nonchalant about it—make a good case for going.*

PLANNING A BUSINESS TRIP

WORK WITH A TRAVEL AGENT

A good one will save you time, money, and headaches. A bad one is the quickest way to an ulcer. In many cases, you'll have no choice in the matter—the firm has already gotten very cozy with a travel agency. In other cases, the large firms have a convenient in-house setup. This approach is dying out, because it is expensive.

If you don't have a choice, *get close to one or two of the agents* so that they will pay special attention to your needs. When they bend over backward to help you, or act very promptly, show your appreciation (how you do it is up to you).

Be patient, even if it is in the face of utter incompetence; if the relationship is a lengthy one, it is unlikely that the boss will switch agencies on your say-so. Don't allow yourself to be pushed around, and don't be afraid to take an agent to task. But be polite and respectful.

Listen. The travel biz is so confusing, almost nobody gets it right the first time anymore. But if you listen carefully, you will finally figure out where you are going, when you are leaving, where you are staying, and how much it will cost.

HOW TO CHOOSE A TRAVEL AGENCY

Decide whether to go with a generalist or a specialist. This depends on how you travel. And where you go. Some agencies service primarily businesses. This can be a plus. They don't deal with Grand Canyon Tours and the like, but they can get you a seat on the morning flight to St. Louis and reserve a car 30 minutes before flight time. Some specialize in certain locations, so if you do lots of business in the developing nations, the Third World, or the communist bloc, it may be wise to use a specialist. Some agencies specialize in a particular mode of travel. This is not really an issue for business, since you will almost always be taking a plane rather than going by boat or rail. Stay away from agencies that deal primarily with tour packages.

Case the joint. If the agency looks like a dentist's office or a bookie joint, beware. It should be somewhere in between: not excessively neat, since any successful travel agency generates a lot of paper; but not sloppy, either. That piece of paper serving as a coaster for some guy's coffee cup could be your ticket. The agents should have within easy reach such tools of the trade as the *Official Airlines Guide (OAG)* and the *Hotel and Travel Index.* A computer terminal is also a good sign.

ASTA member? The American Society of Travel Agents is the largest industry trade organization. You have to be in business at least three years to join. It doesn't really mean that much, except that ASTA will act as a mediator in the case of a dispute between an agency and its customers. ASTA also offers seminars and conferences to keep its members up to date on changes within the industry. All this might make you feel better if you are going in cold, without a referral.

Certified Travel Counselor? The PhD of the travel biz. You need five years' experience and an 18-month course. The CTC should know considerably more than your average ticket pusher. On the other hand, there are many very good agents who don't bother with things like "certification."

What is the agency willing to do for you? Will its personnel assist you with visas and passport renewals? Are they able to respond quickly? Does the agency have corrrespondent agencies in other countries and cities to serve you when you are away? Are its billing and credit terms favorable? A good agency is one that is looking to build its business on a repeat basis, not a one-shot fleecing. Agents that want you to come back again and again will try to accommodate you.

Learn to speak their language. When you want a reservation or a quote, give agents the info they need—where, when, class of service, room size, class of hotel, type of car, etc.; and method of payment if the costs are not to be charged to your account. If you want a special meal or specific seat location, or if you plan to take along a pet or some weird baggage, say so. The more they know, the more they can help you. If you get familiar with terms like "wait-list," "standby," "CTO" (city ticket office), "ETA" (estimated time of arrival), so much the better.

Don't be afraid to shop around, even if you have a regular agency.

Get the lowdown on the charges before you book. Fees? Service charges? Telex and/or long distance phone charges? Policies on out-of-pocket expenses vary from agency to agency.

KNOW THE GROUND RULES FOR AIR TRAVELERS

FARES

Pay as far in advance as possible. This almost always *can* mean cheaper fares. But make sure you find out all the options. You may qualify for a cheaper fare, but the reservation agent doesn't always make you aware of it.

Shop around. Fares are no longer set by an industry cartel. So one airline's fare may be much more than another's.

Don't trust anybody. Reservation agents—whether by intention, by mistake, or by their inability to unravel fare structures that do often seem more complex than the special theory of relativity—are notorious for their inability to provide you with the same fare quote twice in a row. Some people, including yours truly, have been known to keep calling the airline for quotes, rebooking when they get an agent who comes forth with a lower quote; think of it as a kind of airfare auction. Even travel experts who write for national magazines have been quoted several different fares for the same trip.

It's cheaper to fly midweek than on weekends. The exception is the "business run," such as New York to Chicago and New York-D.C. They can be cheaper on weekends, when airlines want to increase ridership on a route that is more profitable weekdays.

It's cheaper to fly at night than during the day. This doesn't always apply to transatlantic flights, because scheduling demands determine what time the flight leaves. A great many peak-traffic transatlantic flights are evening departures.

Bargain rates usually take a vacation during holiday periods. Bargain rates and discounts are essentially off-season sales. When the demand is high, so are the fares. If you are looking to save money, don't travel around Christmas. Some "super savers" or other discount fares are relatively cheap because one pays well in advance and will have some difficulty canceling. While these are sometimes available for holiday periods, there are far fewer seats allocated for these special fares.

Package deals can be cheaper, but there are almost always strings. Package deals include airfares, lodging, meals, even car rentals. But they often require advance purchase and have minimum and maximum stays.

- Limited seats are available.
- Often, no changes in itinerary are allowed without a penalty. However, for a nominal fee you can get trip cancellation insurance that will cover the penalty on an involuntary cancellation.

What to ask the airline or travel agent

1. *When are the fares lowest?* Get specifics—days, times, dates.
2. *What about stopovers?* Are they permitted? In one direction? In both directions? How many? Extra costs?
3. *Which fare is cheaper, a round-trip ticket or two one-ways?*
4. *Are there special rate structures?* Such as family plans, take-along-your-spouse-for-half-fare, etc.?

RESERVATIONS

Make them ASAP. You'll avoid the businessperson's trap: book last minute, pay full fare. And don't forget to get your seat assignment and line up special meals, etc.

Reconfirm. This is important, because mistakes are often made. If an agent pushes one wrong key on the computer, you could wind up with a special Stillman water diet meal, or something else you didn't want. Or, more commonly, you'll be seated next to a chain-smoker when you're just beginning to think you've kicked the habit.

FLY BY THE BOOK

THE OFFICIAL AIRLINES GUIDE (OAG)   This is the industry bible. Published in two volumes (North American and international), it lists all the flights on every airline and specifies type of equipment, meal service, flight time, fares, airports, and connecting flights. The *OAG* is available as either a bi-weekly or a monthly and is a bit too detailed and cumbersome for you. Also, it's $62 per year for the monthly North American edition alone, $85 for the bi-weekly. But the *OAG* people (they are owned by Dun & Bradstreet) got hip to the fact that jet-set executives were going nuts trying to get through to understaffed airline reservations offices and lethargic travel agents. So they put out the—

NORTH AMERICAN OAG POCKET FLIGHT GUIDE   *Pocket* is the key word here; this is a mini version of the regular *OAG*, containing information on the most frequently flown flights (about 27,000 are listed). The listings, by destination city, provide you with information about stops en route, meals, airline phone numbers for every city shown, and other useful information. This book is a godsend when your entire itinerary falls apart, whether because of a snowstorm or because of a snow job by a client, or when your car or business negotiations break down unexpectedly. The *OAG Pocket Guide* makes it easy to see all the alternatives at a glance. Even though every airline agent has virtually the same information in the computer on the desk, he may be reluctant to tell you about every single flight to Des Moines from 2:00 P.M. on. So you'll get just one or two alternatives—or get put on hold while the agent checks. Besides, sometimes there are exotic ways of reaching a destination that wouldn't even occur to an agent with several calls waiting. Sometimes you can go via another city that you have business in, and catch Des Moines on the way back home. If you travel a great deal, this book is worth the $30 per year for 12 monthly issues. Curiously, mail delivery is extra.

FOR MORE INFORMATION
Contact:
OAG Publications
2000 Clearwater Drive
Oak Brook, IL 60521

A recent innovation is the on-line travel service, which allows the user to access travel information—and even make reservations—through a personal computer. See the following table for a listing of such services. For more on how they work, see the section on databases in Chapter 8.

THINGS THAT GO BUMP
ON THE FLIGHT

THE GLAMOUR IS GONE

The facts are undeniable: deregulation and cutthroat competition not only reduced fares, but caused an overall decline in the level of service. The cabins are crowded with more seats and less leg room. Meals are simpler, cheaper and served less frequently. Citing a desire to reduce weight and conserve fuel, airlines have even replaced the glass and china and stainless with plastic dinnerware.

As far as the human element is concerned, pay cuts, increasing workloads and lower competency levels have taken their toll. Ticket agents

---

The range of travel services offered by the major on-line information providers varies widely and is growing weekly. Below is a brief summary of the services offered by Compuserve, The Source, Delphi, Dow Jones News/Retrieval, and Western Union's Easylink. All services except Delphi offer the Electronic Edition of the *Official Airlines Guide*.

COMPUSERVE

Travel Shopper: TWA's consumer version of its electronic airlines reservations network. Users can browse through listings of flight schedules and fares; however, there is currently no ticketing capability.

ABC Worldwide Hotel and Travel Guide: An electronic edition of the A-Z Guide used by travel professionals that contains a comprehensive listing of more than 20,000 hotels worldwide, with detailed information on location, rates, facilities, and amenities.

The American Express Advance Travel Service: Allows subscribers to order brochures or make reservations for vacation packages in the United States, Mexico, South America, Europe, the Middle East, Africa, and the Far East.

Worldwide Exchange: Provides listings of holiday home rentals and yacht and recreational vehicle charters around the world.

Department of State Travel Advisory: Provides travelers with information on destinations where war, political unrest, medical alerts, hotel or motel shortages, and other international emergencies create travel hazards.

Pan Am Travel Guide: Lists entry regulations, health requirements, banking holidays, and customs regulations for foreign destinations worldwide.

Travel Vision: Provides information for ground transportation planning, including road maps, guides, and atlases for the United States, Canada, and Mexico. Also offers a personalized routing service. *(614) 457-8600.*

THE SOURCE

Airsched: Lists schedules and fares for direct and connecting domestic and international routes.

City Connections: Shows connections between small airports and larger ones listed in Airsched service. For example, City Connections would be used to find the schedules for flights between Washington and Dubuque, Iowa, two cities with no direct flights.

A-Z Travel Service: Offers a comprehensive listing of 23,000 hotels throughout the world. Information includes street address, location (downtown, airport), local and toll-free telephone numbers, telex, number of rooms, regular rates (in U.S. dollars), credit cards accepted, hotel facilities, and business services.

Mobil Hotel Guide: Provides a listing of hotels and inns in North America.

Mobil Restaurant Guide: Lists 6,000 dining establishments in 1,800 cities and towns across the United States and Canada. Users can search by location, type of food, or special features, such as live music or dancing.

The First World Travel Club: A 24-hour travel service that helps users make airline and hotel reservations.

Accu-Weather: A 24-hour weather service used by newspapers, radio, and TV stations across country that provides national and international weather conditions as well as city, regional, and national forecasts. During winter months (November through March), it keeps you informed about major U.S. highway conditions. *(703) 734-7500.*

DELPHI

Delphi's on-line travel service is called The Electronic Connection (TEC), which offers soup-to-nuts travel services, according to a spokesman for Interactive Office Services Inc., which created and maintains the service.

Full reservations capabilities now tie Delphi subscribers to travel agents who can confirm all flight requests, airline seats, car rentals, hotel rooms, and tours. Real-time airline reservations will be offered soon, according to the Interactive Office Services spokesman.

TEC also offers detailed entertainment and business reports on more than 450 cities and every country in the world. All information and reservations capabilities are integrated and cross-referenced, according to the firm, so that all information on a specific topic can be quickly and easily found. *(617) 491-3393.*

DOW JONES NEWS/RETRIEVAL

The American Express Advance Travel Service: Allows subscribers to order brochures or make reservations for vacation packages in the United States, Mexico, South America, Europe, the Middle East, Africa, and the Far East. *(609) 452-2000.*

EASYLINK

Western Union's Easylink also has various other travel services ranging from sophisticated communications services for arranging meetings, seminars, or conferences to domestic and international car rental reservations; weather reports; currency exchange rates; and financial information from on-line electronic versions of Dunn & Bradstreet's *Million Dollar Directory,* Moody's *Corporate Profiles,* and Standard & Poor's *Register of Corporations.* (201) 825-6201.

Fig. 73. On-line Travel Services offered by major information providers.

InfoWorld July 21, 1986

and flight attendants are often rude and inexperienced. In so many cases, price takes precedence over service, and personnel do not derive significant career benefit for going out of their way to be helpful.

Finally, many agree that business class and first class have suffered declines as well.

In certain cases, competition has improved service, as on an important route such as New York–Boston, where airlines fight it out for passengers. Since there is little difference in price, they try to win loyalty with better service. What follows is a list of what you should know about air travel.

OVERBOOKING

Airlines engage in a practice, known as overbooking, that helps them keep the flights as full as possible. Their computers track passenger patterns and determine that a certain percentage of travelers who make reservations on a given flight never show up. Rather than letting the seats of these no-shows go empty, the airlines book more passengers than they have room for, figuring that the no-shows will bring the flight back in line. You really can't blame them for doing this: It makes good business sense, and prices would be even higher if airlines didn't overbook.

Most of the time the airlines guess right. But sometimes a flight has more people than seats. In such cases, the airline will first ask for volunteers to take the next open flight. The reward for this sacrifice is often a voucher for a free round-trip anywhere the carrier flies, good for twelve months. If this doesn't work, the person or persons bumped involuntarily receive cash compensation. Law requires they be paid an amount equal to double the fare plus a seat on the next available flight. The best way to avoid an involuntary bump is to get to the airport early.

WAIT-LIST

This is the list you get put on when you want a seat on a flight that is sold out. When you are "wait-listed" for a flight, don't expect to hear from the airlines unless you are "cleared" for the flight—that is, unless a seat opens up for you. It doesn't hurt to check with the airline periodically; sometimes such persistence improves your chances of getting a seat. According to the rules, the wait-list clears on a first come, first served basis.

It is important to remember that being on the wait-list has no connection with standing by at the airport. If you haven't been cleared for a reservation by the day of the flight, consider it a whole new ball game.

STANDBY

You're on standby when you arrive at the airport without a reservation and "stand by" for the flight, hoping that someone who is booked on the flight won't show up and you'll get the seat. Being wait-listed for the flight won't mean a thing; being first in the standby line *will*. So when you arrive for standby, have the time of check-in and the agent's sign (identification) stamped on your ticket. This will establish priority at the gate.

The rules state that in standby, full fares have priority over the discount standby fares—students, special promotion fares, military personnel, and airline employees. But it ain't necessarily so. Popular employees and airline execs, VIPs, and soldiers on special orders sometimes get seated first. However, on balance, those willing to pay list price will rarely get left behind. In these times of poor fiscal health, the airline biggies have given the word to the gates: Heads will roll if anyone seats a cheapo or a freebie ahead of a full fare.

RESTRICTIONS

Restrictions usually involve (a) the days of the week you can travel, (b) how far in advance you pay for your ticket, (c) specific seats on specific flights.

Some restrictions are simple and logical: the earlier you buy your ticket (*e.g.*, 30 days in advance), the less you pay. Others are more complex (*e.g.*, one fare if you go via Kansas City but you must leave on a Tuesday). Airlines try very hard not to discount seats they can sell at full fare. So they will often offer incentives to fly on the slow days, like Tuesday or Wednesday, and discourage business travelers from flying too inexpensively by requiring one to stay over a Saturday to qualify for lower fares. Most business travelers want to spend the weekends at home.

Now that fares have become so confusing and numerous, airlines have expanded on the simple fare code system. Once there was only F class for first class, and Y class for economy. Now there is Q class for Ultimate Super Saver, B for 14-day advance purchase, and so on. Undoubtedly, you and/or the reservations clerk will someday be confused by the restrictions and the fare structure. Knowing the fare's letter code could be helpful when communicating.

One of the biggest *caveats* to discount travel is the penalty. Penalties are usually imposed if you must change a reservation on a special fare. They can run 25, 50, even 100 percent of the fare (during special promotions) for canceling or merely re-booking. Read the fine print and make sure you are clear on the penalty policy. A cheap fare may cost you more money in the end. You must play the odds that you won't have to change your plans.

When reading fare quotes and advertisements, take note of the difference between *nonstop* (the plane does not touch down between two cities), *direct* (the plane stops one or more times before it reaches your destination), and *connecting* flights (*i.e.*, you must change planes somewhere, making a "connection" to your destination).

Obviously, the connection is the least fun. If there are departure delays on the first leg, you might miss your connection, and/or your baggage may not make it off the first plane and aboard the next. If you arrive on time, the connecting flight might be late, delaying your trip even further. Nonstop is the simplest and the best because it usually takes the least time and there is less of a chance you will lose your bags. Direct flights are a kind of compromise. Once on, you and your bags stand a pretty good chance of making it to your destination, but not as quickly as you would like.

Often, very low fares will involve a direct flight or connection, since the seats on nonstops often fill up first (for that particular route). However, one man's connection is another man's nonstop, so it is not always the case. A New York–Kansas City–Los Angeles connecting flight might be filled with bargain-hunters leaving New York for L.A., but the second leg is a nonstop to those from K.C.

BAGGAGE

The best way to ensure that your baggage arrives with you is to carry it onboard. But between the crowded flights and the FAA safety restrictions, that is often impossible. Here are several tips:

Make sure you can identify your bags. Use an ID tag, preferably the kind which conceals the information until it is needed. If your luggage is common, use tape or some other feature to pick it out from the crowd. Inside, insert a card with your itinerary and other vital information.

Make sure they are tagged properly. Watch the agent or skycap as he tags your luggage. Make sure that it is labelled with the correct destination (airlines use codes; if you are unsure, ask what airport the code stands for). Make sure that you get all your claim stubs. No matter how rushed you are, never leave without them.

Allow enough time. Many airlines won't accept bags if you check-in within fifteen minutes of departure. Others will take late check-in luggage, but at your own risk. Rules differ with the carrier, but don't press your luck; thirty minutes to an hour before is best.

Book connections with care. Each airport sets minimum connecting times, *i.e.*, the least amount of time one can legally allow between the scheduled arrival of a flight and the departure of its connection. If the connection falls within those limits, the airline will accept your baggage to be checked through to your final destination. However, you should allow more than the minimum; air traffic delays shrink those times pretty quickly, and in the case of some carriers, it might be safer to allow enough time to check the bags to the connection point, claim them, and re-check them once more, this time on the connecting flight.

What to do if you lose your luggage. File a claim at once; don't leave the airport until you do. It will usually be traced and recovered within 24 hours. If it isn't located within three days, your chances of retrieving it are slim.

The airline will probably pursue it for thirty days, but in the meantime will ask you for an itemized list of the baggage contents. It is better if you can substantiate the estimated value.

Caught away from home with no luggage? Airlines will usually reimburse you for incidentals such as toiletries and in some circumstances, for essential clothing.

Finally, if forced to reimburse you for lost luggage, the airline will depreciate the value of the contents. Clothes must be less than six months old to be worth their full purchase price. Maximum liability on domestic flights is $1,250 per traveler, unless you purchase additional coverage. Some homeowners insurance policies and credit card insurance services kick in over that amount.

ON-BOARD OPTIONS

FIRST CLASS

When it comes to arriving fresh and well rested, first class is the only way to go. A recent survey indicated that most business travelers still fly coach, but the number of first-class travelers increases with the length of the trip. This shows that the average American business traveler is pretty smart: He travels first class not for its snob appeal, but for its comfort.

In first class, the food and beverage selection is better, the service is better, and, best of all, the seats are bigger. Sometimes there is special check-in for first class, and luggage priority (your luggage is last on, first off); so your waiting time is reduced. The first-class section is smaller than coach. And nothing can drain you faster than being surrounded by rude, loud, and inconsiderate fellow passengers.

First class costs more money, but this surcharge is deductible: As far as the IRS is concerned, first class is no different from coach. The fares have been reduced to about 20 percent above full-fare coach, and as a result the first-class sections are fuller than they used to be. But it is *still* worthwhile to fly first class for comfort.

IN-FLIGHT EXTRAS

First came the stewardess, then the steward, and now the service director. This person is the maitre d' of the flight and can do some special things for you. For example, the service director can make hotel, airline, and rent-a-car reservations, reconfirm flights, and, in certain cases, get seat assignments—all while in flight.

SPECIAL MEALS

Unfortunately, special meals are usually not very special. But then again, neither are the regular meals. And if you have a restricted diet, a little knowledge and a phone call can keep you from starving. A commonly

DIETARY MEALS

Special meal service may be ordered through local reservations offices. Hindu, Kosher, Muslim, Oriental, Soul Food, Weight Watchers and children's meals require confirmation from United's flight kitchen and catering locations if less than 24 hours notice. All other type meals require up to 4 hours notice prior to departure. Dietary meals will be provided using a variety of the components as shown. Specific items (for ethnic, religious, medical or dietary restrictions only) may be requested and will be served as available. Personal preference requests are *not* to be accepted.

NOTE: Passengers traveling with children on flights scheduled for meal service should inquire about children's meals at the time of reservation. These meals are no longer available in-flight if not specifically requested prior to flight departure.

The items listed are only a guide, do not treat them as exact meal components.

DIETARY MEAL	BLAND	CHILDREN'S	DIABETIC
LEAD TIME REQUIRED	4 hours	4 hours	4 hours
CODE	SPML	CSML	SPML
RESTRICTIONS AND REMARKS	Dried beans and peas. Corn, broccoli, brussel sprouts, cabbage, onions, cauliflower, cucumber, green pepper, rutabaga, turnips, sauerkraut. Any fried and highly seasoned item including snacks such as chips or frankfurters, sausages and luncheon meats. Chunky peanut butter Any item containing nuts or coconut.	Listed below are meals available. If any other meal is specifically requested, it may be confirmed with 24 hours notice to appropriate kitchen or catering location.	Commercial hot chocolate Sweetened fruits and juices Pastries, sugar coated cereals. Sugar, syrup, honey, jelly, jam, preserves, marmalade. All candy including dietetic candy. Cakes, cookies, pies. Sweetened soft beverages Sweet pickles.
FOODS RECOMMENDED OR AVAILABLE	Milk and milk drinks. All vegetable and fruit juices. All cereals, breads, rolls, crackers. Fruits Non-fried starches Meats and substitutes not fried or highly seasoned Butter/margarine and mild salad dressings. Smooth peanut butter Decaffeinated coffee and non-cola beverages.	Hot dog and bun Assorted cold sandwiches Franco-American spaghetti and meatballs.	Milk All vegetables Fruits and juices with no sugar added All bread products Potatoes and substitute starches. All meats, eggs, cheese. Peanut butter Butter, margarine, salad dressings including mayonnaise. Soups Artificial sweetener coffee, tea, dietetic pop Spices, nuts, gravies.

Fig. 74. Typical airline guidelines on special meals
(through page 619)
Reprinted by permission of United Airlines.

DIETARY MEAL	GLUTEN FREE	HIGH PROTEIN	HINDU
LEAD TIME REQUIRED	4 hours	4 hours	24 hours
CODE	SPML	SPML	HNML
RESTRICTIONS AND REMARKS	Commercial chocolate milk, malted milk Any creamed or breaded vegetables *Any wheat, rye, oats, barley, buckwheat product.* Cold cuts, sandwich spreads, canned meats prepared with wheat, rye, oats, barley, or buckwheat. Processed cheese Commercial salad dressing Chili sauce, soy sauce, bottled meat sauces with wheat, rye, oats, barley or buckwheat.	General diet with increased protein of high biological value.	Vegetarian Hindu: — Three types eat all vegetables except parts of roots eat only fruit and milk Non-vegetarian Hindu: no beef or veal but will eat all other meat, poultry, fish.
FOODS RECOMMENDED OR AVAILABLE	Milk and milk products other than above. Fresh vegetables All fruits, juices Corn or rice cereals, gluten free bread, breads and rolls made from arrowroot, rice, corn, potato, soybean flour. Potatoes, rice All meat, poultry, fish, shellfish Eggs, nuts, natural cheese, peanut butter Butter, margarine Sugar, cake, ice cream.		Milk and milk products, yoghurt. Fruits Whole grain products, rice. Cheese, eggs, peanut butter. Tea, coffee. Spices, nuts.

DIETARY MEAL	MUSLIM	ORIENTAL	SOUL FOOD
LEAD TIME REQUIRED	24 hours	24 hours	24 hours
CODE	MOML	ORML	SMPL
RESTRICTIONS AND REMARKS	Diet avoids pork products, shrimp, lobster, scavenger fish and shellfish.	Diet typically favors stir fried or slightly undercooked vegetables.	Diet typically favors home cooking and the addition of hot sauce or Tabasco with meal.
FOODS RECOMMENDED OR AVAILABLE			

616

DIETARY MEAL	HYPOGLYCEMIC (Low Carbohydrate)	INFANT	KOSHER
LEAD TIME REQUIRED	4 hours	4 hours	24 hours
CODE	SPML	BBML	KSML
RESTRICTIONS AND REMARKS	Chocolate milk, hot chocolate. Any breaded vegetables Sweetened fruits, juices Pastries, quick breads, sugar, syrup, honey, jam, jelly, preserves, molasses. All candies, cakes, cookies, pies, pudding, ice cream, sherbet, jello Sweet pickles, gravies Cola, coffee, tea, soft beverages.	Special diet for infants 8 months to 2 years of age.	Kosher breakfasts, lunches, dinners and snacks prepared for United Airlines by an approved Kosher caterer. Contains no pork, shellfish or scavenger fish products; milk and meat products prepared separately.
FOODS RECOMMENDED OR AVAILABLE	Whole, lowfat, skim, or buttermilk. All vegetables Unsweetened fruits, juices Breads and cereals Potatoes and substitutes Meats and substitutes Fats Soups Decaffeinated coffee, dietetic soft beverages Nuts.	Typically strained or finely chopped fruit, meats and vegetables.	Reservations should specify "beef" or "chicken" on passenger meal request for lunches or dinners.

DIETARY MEAL	LACTOSE RESTRICTED	LOW CALORIE	LOW CHOLESTEROL
LEAD TIME REQUIRED	4 hours	4 hours	4 hours
CODE	SPML	SPML	SPML
RESTRICTIONS AND REMARKS	Milk and milk products served or used in preparation of any foods.	Chocolate milk or commercial hot chocolate Sweetened fruits and juices. Sugar, jelly, jam, preserves, syrup, honey, molasses, candy. Cakes, pies, puddings, cookies, ice cream, sherbet Sauces, gravies. Regular sweetened pop.	Whole milk and products made from whole milk. Egg breads, butter rolls Breads and cereals made with egg yolks, butter, whole milk, or cream. Fatty meats, duck, bacon, corned beef, spareribs, sausages, canned meats, shellfish. Ice cream, ice milk Chocolate, coconut. Cashews, macadamia nuts.
FOODS RECOMMENDED OR AVAILABLE	All food items which do not have milk or milk products as an ingredient Fortified margarines marked "Kosher" or "Pareve."	Milk, all vegetables, unsweetened fruits, juices. Meats, poultry, fish Cheese, eggs, peanut butter Nuts. Potatoes and substitutes Soups Dietetic pop, coffee, tea.	Skim milk All vegetables Fruits Whole grain breads Potatoes, rice, barley Lean meats, poultry without skin. Corn, safflower, soybean oils, polyunsaturated margarine Sweets made with skim milk, egg substitutes.

DIETARY MEAL	LOW FAT	LOW PROTEIN	LOW SODIUM
LEAD TIME REQUIRED	4 hours	4 hours	4 hours
CODE	SPML	SPML	NSML
RESTRICTIONS AND REMARKS	Whole milk, 2% milk, low fat milk, chocolate milk, evaporated and condensed milk and their products. Broccoli, brussel sprouts, cabbage, corn, cauliflower cucumber, garlic, dried beans and pies, onions, green pepper, rutabaga, turnips, sauerkraut Avocado Breads with large amount of fat Fried potatoes, meats Bacon, sausages, luncheon meats, duck Poultry skin, high fat cheeses, cream cheese Gravies Ice cream, nuts.	Buttermilk Artichokes Glazed fruits Commercial waffles and pancakes Brains, kidneys.	Buttermilk Vegetables prepared with salt Frozen peas, lima beans, mixed vegetables, corn. Sauerkraut, pickles and other items in brine Instant cereal and other dry cereals Salted butter, margarine Any item with salt as an ingredient or has salt needed for preparation. All candies made with chocolate, nuts, coconut.
FOODS RECOMMENDED OR AVAILABLE	Skim milk Vegetables other than above All fruits except avocado Potatoes and substitutes. Lean meat, poultry, fish, shellfish broiled, baked, roasted, stewed.	Milk and milk products other than above. All vegetables All fruits and juices Breads and cereals except quick breakfast breads Meat, poultry, fish, shellfish Cheese, eggs, peanut butter.	All milk and milk products Low salt/sodium items including fruits, juices, whole grain or enriched bread, potatoes, meat, poultry, fish, shellfish.

DIETARY MEAL	VEGETARIAN: LACTO-OVO	VEGETARIAN: PURE	WEIGHT WATCHERS
LEAD TIME REQUIRED	4 hours	4 hours	24 hours
CODE	VGML—Dairy Eggs OK	VGML	SPML
RESTRICTIONS AND REMARKS	Diet eliminates all meat, fish, poultry, but includes eggs, milk, and other dairy products.	Diet excluding all sources of animal protein.	Diet approved for use in Weight Watchers Program and features breakfasts, lunches, dinners and snacks. Prepared for United Airlines by approved caterer following Weight Watchers, Inc. standards.
FOODS RECOMMENDED OR AVAILABLE			Typical meals might be: —Breakfast: Spanish omelette —Lunch: Chicken Chasseur —Dinner: Braised Beef Tips —Snack: Cold breast of Turkey Sandwich

UNITED FOOD SERVICE CODES

MEAL CODES
- **B** Breakfast
- **C** Brunch/Deli Service
- **D** Dinner
- **L** Lunch
- **P** Purchase Snack (Price varies depending upon flight segment)
- **R** Brunch
- **S** Snack

FLIGHT THEMES
- **F** Four Star Service
- **O** Ocean to Ocean Service
- **R** Royal Hawaiian

LIQUOR CODES
- **Q** Cocktails/First Class and Coach
- ***** Cocktails/First Class only

SPECIAL MEAL CODES (SIPP Codes)

BBML	Infant Meal/Baby Food
HNML	Hindu Meal
KSML	Kosher Meal
MOML	Moslem Meal
NSML	No Salt
ORML	Oriental Meal
SPML	Special Meal (Followed by details)
VGML	Vegetarian Meal

UNITED ONLY SPECIAL MEAL CODES

CSML	Child's Meal

held belief is that there are only four or five special meals. This is wrong. United has about 13; Pan Am, 19. And although the basic classifications appear to be industry-wide, each airline has its own interpretation. A couple of sample lists are included here to give you an idea of the range of meals available. If you don't see what you want, ask for it. You may be pleasantly surprised. Just get in your meal request 48 hours in advance. If you can't do that, request your choice anyway. Sometimes an airline can rustle something up on short notice.

SEATING

Anyone who travels by plane knows that getting a good seat can make the difference between a pleasant trip and an unpleasant one. What many people don't know is that seating needn't be left to chance.

Lately the airlines have been engaging in a practice known as "reconfiguring"—a euphemism for adding more seats. How do they do it? They reduce or eliminate lounge space, move the seats closer together, and, in some instances, narrow or eliminate aisles.

You can fight back:

REQUEST A SEATING PLAN   Every airline prints up seating charts for all the planes they fly. Sometimes there are several configurations for each type of aircraft.

WHEN YOU BOOK THE FLIGHT, ASK ABOUT THE TYPE OF AIRCRAFT AND THE CONFIGURATION   It's rather like going to the theater. When you request a seat assignment, you've got a chart in front of you so you have a good idea where 18C is located.

MAKE SURE THAT YOU ALLOW SUFFICIENT TIME TO REQUEST THE SEAT ASSIGNMENT   It's first come, first served. The sooner you request, the greater the choice.

DOUBLE-CHECK   Seat assignments are often incorrectly entered in the reservation computer. They seem to get lost often. My guess is that a besieged reservations agent will sometimes juggle seat assignments to mollify an irate passenger who simply will not book on the flight unless promised a particular seat, say, by the emergency exit. The agent plays the odds and figures that you won't gripe too much about the loss of a little extra leg room. *Is it worth the trouble?* You bet! You'll be in the air for quite a while. If you don't want to hassle with this, get your travel agent to do it.

SMOKING/NONSMOKING SECTIONS   The smoker/nonsmoker feud really heats up on planes. There have even been a few punches thrown over a lit cigarette in the wrong row. The CAB has cracked down hard: The airlines and each cabin crew *must* enforce the restrictions. A new rule says that a nonsmoking seat must be provided for anyone who wants one, even if the whole plane has to be given over to nonsmokers.

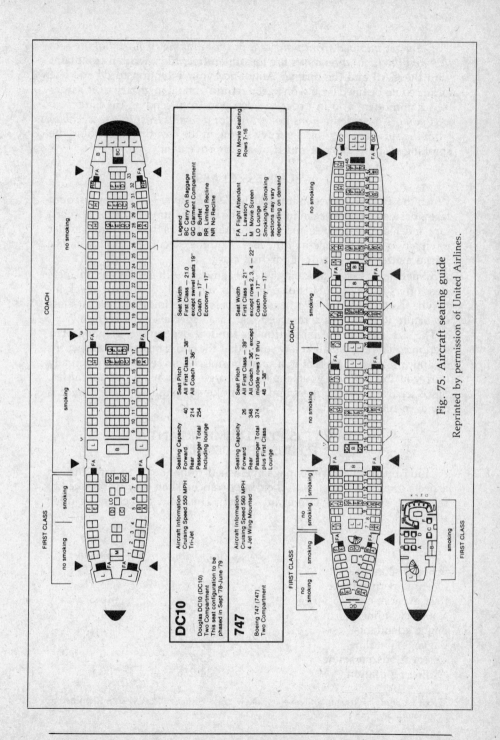

Fig. 75. Aircraft seating guide
Reprinted by permission of United Airlines.

If you get bumped from your seat in the smoking or nonsmoking section and the flight attendants are uncooperative, file a written complaint with the CAB and the airline. Announce your intention to do so. The airline could be fined (you won't get a refund), and it might try a bit harder to accommodate you in order to keep you from sending the letter.

If you are a hardcore nonsmoker, try for a seat at least five rows away from the smoking section. Ever try sitting in the row directly behind the smoking section? It's not much of an improvement.

BUSINESS CLASS

When the air carriers began introducing "super saver" and other discount fares, business people began to revolt. The business traveler pays full coach fare and gets exactly the same service and seating as the discount traveler paying two-thirds or one-half the fare. And the executive has little choice in the matter, except to opt for first class.

Somewhere, some marketing wizard came up with a solution. Business class offers travelers first choice of meals, a special counter for check-in, maybe free drinks and/or a headset, access (sometimes) to the first-class departure lounge, and a reserved seat in a "special coach section."

The size of this "special section" is fluid; it depends on demand. The section could be so small (a few rows) that the entire business-class benefit disappears. Booking a seat in a small business-class section may actually hurt you, by limiting your choice of seats—fewer windows and aisles. Since separating of smokers and nonsmokers is required, your choice is cut even further.

WHAT IS REALLY IMPORTANT
TO BUSINESS PEOPLE?

A study by *BusinessWeek* magazine asked respondents to rate thirteen aspects of airline travel as to their importance. Then they were asked to select the single most important aspect. The eight aspects most often selected:*

	Very important	*Most important*
Schedule convenience	81.8%	30.9%
On-time performance	81.6%	33.7%
Past experience with airline	59.9%	16.3%
Cabin cleanliness	52.5%	1.7%
Flight attendants	51.8%	3.1%
Baggage handling	47.1%	1.8%
Reservations personnel	43.7%	2.1%
Airline reputation	34.2%	3.6%

*From "A Study of Recent Air Travelers" (New York: *Business Week*, 1979). Reprinted by permission.

THE CONCORDE

The Concorde is flown by rich people and business people. The business people deduct the expensive fare, and the rich don't care. Don't fly it for the thrill of breaking Mach 1; there's not much to it. Certainly, the Concorde will save you time. And supersonic travel reduces jet lag, thanks to reduced travel time and better cabin conditions (higher pressure and better temperature and humidity control). But the real reason for flying Concorde is the contacts you might make. As a spokesman for British Airways told me, "Concorde passengers are already successful, so they don't need your book." Let's just say that those who fly this plane place a high premium on their time.

FUTURE CLASS

Although the airlines may be caught in a profit squeeze, there will never be a shortage of people willing to pay for an extra bit of comfort. In fact in air travel, as in automobiles, as the gap between the rich and the middle class widens, there are more and more people willing to pay bigger bucks for more luxury. The airlines want to avoid getting into an "extras war," as they did in the sixties, with each trying to outdo the other by offering unprofitable come-ons to increase ridership. This time, it's different: The engineers and designers have come up with a host of meaningful extras that well-heeled passengers will willingly pay more for. Some of them are already available:

DRESSING ROOMS AND SHOWERS   Boeing already has these on the drawing board and is no doubt awaiting the go-ahead from the carriers.

OFFICE COMPLEX   This will include photocopy machine, stenographer, and dictation machines, as well as other important office equipment. In the near future, office set-ups will be available only on the "all first-class" luxury class airlines.

CLUBS

Airline "clubs" began as an exclusive service for VIPs only. Now, anybody can join. Membership fees are reasonable and can be a darn good investment if you travel a great deal on the same airline. At these prices, it might serve you well to belong to several clubs. The "clubs" are located at the airports, and most have bar service, free soft drinks, special check-in (the best feature of all), and business meeting facilities (they come in handy when two out-of-towners want to meet in transit).

Major airline clubs are summarized in the following table. They all have very silly names:

AIRLINE CLUBS	MEMBERSHIP FEES	NO. OF CLUBS & MEETING ROOMS	SPECIAL BENEFITS
American Admirals Club	$50 initiation, $80 annual, $20 annual spouse, $1,100 lifetime, $350 lifetime spouse.	22 clubs, most with meeting rooms.	Message center. Stereo music centers. Check cashing up to $100.
Continental Presidents Club	$25 initiation, $80 annual, $20 annual spouse, $750 lifetime, $200 lifetime spouse.	9 U.S. clubs, 3 with meeting rooms. Participates in 5 international lounges.	Alcoholic beverages free. Check cashing up to $50. Writing desks in all clubs. 2,500 bonus miles in frequent flyer program (enrollment fee: $25), plus 10 percent mileage bonus on all Continental flights through 1986.
Delta Crown Room Club	No initiation, $85 annual, $30 annual spouse, $200 3-year, $75 3-year spouse, no lifetime.	19 clubs; no meeting rooms.	Free alcoholic beverages. Check cashing up to $50.
Eastern Ionosphere Club	$25 initiation, $70 annual, $20 annual spouse, $280 5-year, $80 5-year spouse, $630 lifetime, $200 lifetime spouse.	32 clubs, 18 with meeting rooms.	Alcoholic beverages free at some clubs. Check cashing up to $50. Free 5-year membership offered at 60,000-mile level in frequent flyer program, lifetime membership at 100,000-mile level. Members eligible to join credit union, with checking, savings, loan and other services offered at preferential interest rates. Automated teller machines at most major airports.
Northwest Orient Top Flight Club	$25 initiation, $50 annual, $200 5-year, $500 lifetime. Spouse card free to all members.	23 clubs; no meeting rooms.	Free alcoholic beverages. Check cashing up to $50. Meeting areas enclosed by partitions. Direct phone lines to National and Thrifty rental cars, often with member discounts. In-club flight monitors. Hotel frequent-guest program tie-ins.
Pan Am Clipper Club	$25 initiation, $150 annual, $45 annual spouse, $390 3-year, $100 3-year spouse, $1,500 lifetime, $350 lifetime spouse, $675 senior lifetime (age 60 or older), $200 senior lifetime spouse.	32 clubs; no meeting rooms.	Free alcoholic beverages. Check cashing up to $100. Free membership in frequent flyer program (normally $25). Hotel frequent-guest program tie-ins.

Piedmont Presidential Suite	$25 initiation, $50 annual, $25 annual spouse, $500 lifetime, $250 lifetime spouse.	10 clubs; no meeting rooms.	Check cashing up to $50. Free annual club membership offered at 50,000-mile level in frequent flyer program. Unenclosed conference tables. Music centers.
TWA Ambassadors Club	No initiation, $100 annual, $25 annual spouse, $1,000 lifetime, $250 lifetime spouse.	28 clubs, 11 with meeting rooms.	Check cashing up to $50 in the U.S. with domestic ticket, up to $100 with international ticket. Automatic enrollment in frequent flyer program with 5,000 bonus miles. At most clubs, electronic news sign providing business, financial and general news updates. Telecommunications centers to be installed.
United Red Carpet Club	$50 initiation, $75 annual, $25 annual spouse, $1,125 lifetime, $375 lifetime spouse.	18 U.S. clubs, 16 with meeting rooms.	Check cashing up to $50. Message center. Desks in most clubs. Direct-dial phones to Westin Hotels at some clubs, to Hertz at most clubs. 9 Pacific clubs due to open early in 1986, purchased from Pan Am.
USAir USAir Club	$25 initiation, $40 annual, $400 lifetime. Spouse card free to all members.	7 clubs, each with meeting room	Check cashing up to $100. 50 percent discount in membership fees offered at 10,000-mile level in frequent flyer program.

Fig. 76. Airline Clubs.
Compiled by Neil Chesanow,
author of *The World Class
Executive: Everything You Need
to Know to Do Business Around
the World*

CLOSED CIRCUIT TV   Boeing and McDonnell Douglas have blueprints for systems that feature high resolution video screens, offering computer-controlled programming.

ON-BOARD COMPUTER   You will be able to send telexes, run computer software, and make hotel and airline reservations.

VENDING MACHINES   Will dispense food and beverages, especially helpful on short flights. And on-board refrigerators will hold fresh food for passengers.

MISCELLANEOUS   More in-flight telephones; hand rails above each seat; fresher cabin air; larger overhead bins; wider aisles.

SHOULD YOUR COMPANY OWN ITS OWN PLANE?

THE PROS

- *Airline service to suburban areas and small cities is decreasing.* Ironically, more and more corporations are shunning the metropolitan areas and setting up headquarters in rural areas.
- *A corporate jet is an excellent "image builder."*
- *You can hold business meetings in the air.*
- *The cabins are very comfortable, so you arrive fresh and well rested.*
- *You are not limited by airline schedules and routes.*
- *You can offset costs by renting out the plane.*
- *Security can be tighter.*
- *Maybe, just maybe, you'll save some money.*

THE CONS

- *There is a serious shortage of airports and parking space.* At present this is a seller's market. Demand is very great, so you probably won't find any bargains.
- *You can never completely eliminate airline travel.*
- *A corporate jet increases "executive visibility."* Some stockholders are extremely sensitive to what they consider abuse of company funds. A jet might increase the level of scrutiny.
- *When a firm owns its own plane, employees tend to use it because it's there.* Not because it makes sense.

When making a decision involving such a large expenditure, careful analysis is obviously required.

HOW TO DO A CORPORATE JET ANALYSIS

TALK TO THE VENDORS Piper and Cessna offer feasibility studies that can be quite helpful. Of course, they are sales come-ons, but they aren't greatly misleading. These aircraft companies depend heavily on reputation. A good feasibility study by a vendor will:

- help you determine whether you really need a plane
- suggest an appropriate model (built by the vendor)
- compare the cost of outright purchase with that of leasing
- estimate operating costs
- analyze the benefits to your company

YOUR FIRM SHOULD ENGAGE IN ITS OWN ANALYSIS Look not only at the costs of owning a plane, but also at the costs of the entire corporate travel operation. Questions to ask:

- Who does the traveling in your company?
- How often?
- Where? What are the most frequently visited and most common destinations?
- Do these executives travel alone? With each other? With clients, attorneys, or others?
- How far (in air miles) are these journeys?

Now pull all the travel vouchers. Look carefully at the travel patterns of the staff, and the total costs. Be sure to include surface transit to and from the airport, meals and lodging, and the value of the executive's time. Many firms decide on the corporate jet option, not so much because the airport-to-airport fare is cheaper than that of a commercial airline, but because the company plane can save enough executive travel time to make it cost-effective. Just compute (with base salary, benefits, and incentives) what an hour of senior management time is worth. It'll make you a believer.

The next step is to compare this with analysis of what it's going to cost to own a plane. The costs can be divided into two categories:

- *fixed.* Includes the purchase price of the plane and finance charges; the cost of the hangar space; the pilot's salary; insurance and depreciation. Fixed costs per hour are reduced as usage increases.
- *operating.* Landing and parking fees; fuel and oil; maintenance. Operating costs increase as usage increases.

At this point it is a good idea to figure out just how much airline travel you can eliminate and how efficiently the corporate jet would operate. Can you fill the seats regularly? Sometimes, efficiency means flying a planeload of executives to a centrally located airport, where they connect with scheduled airlines, and picking them up in the same manner.

Before you buy, you might try chartering a plane in order to gain some hands-on experience. You can either charter on a pay-as-you-go basis or purchase a block of time (so many hours per year or per quarter).

RENTING A PLANE

This alternative is becoming increasingly popular, especially when you've got to go to a place not served by a scheduled airline or want to avoid a stopover, change of plane, or flying out of your way. Prices run from $50 up, for a small one- or two-seater (in addition to the pilot's seat), to $400 per hour and up, for the top-of-the-line six-seat turboprop. A few tips:

CHECK OUT THE RENTAL OUTFIT   If it doesn't come recommended, you can call the FAA to check on its license, safety record, and classification (some charter companies are licensed for photo and sightseeing excursions only).

SPREAD THE WORD   All pilots need to log flight time in order to qualify to operate aircraft. There are always a few around who are in the process of qualifying for a certain type of aircraft. So eager are they that they will often take you where you want to go if you pay only aircraft rental and fuel expenses. Sometimes you'll run into pilots with their own planes who will get you from here to there for just fuel and landing fees—a good way to travel on the cheap.

FEASIBILITY STUDIES

TRANSPORTATION ANALYSIS PLAN (TAP)   From Cessna Aircraft and available through Cessna dealers, the data is then sent to Cessna's headquarters, in Wichita, Kansas, for analysis. Your comptroller might take issue with some of the estimates and figures, but with a little extra work, he should be able to tailor them to your own requirements.
>   Contact:
>   Cessna Aircraft Company
>   P.O. Box 1521
>   Wichita, Kansas 67201

PIPER AIRCRAFT TRAVEL COST/BENEFIT ANALYSIS AND CASH FLOW   Available free through Piper dealers, this analysis is computer generated and written in accountantese. As with Cessna's TAP, the analysis is worthwhile.
>   Piper also offers a detailed lease back cash flow analysis program that generates both cash flow and income projections for an individual lease back package.
>   Contact:
>   Piper Aircraft Corporation
>   820 East Bald Eagle Street
>   Lock Haven, Pennsylvania 17745

BUSINESS AND COMMERCIAL AVIATION FEASIBILITY/JUSTIFICA-
TION STUDY   This study is essentially a do-it-yourself travel analysis
kit. Even if you don't buy a plane, this kit will provide you with invaluable
information on just how the staff gets around. Prepared in 1975, the cost
estimates are out of date, but a little arithmetic can remedy that.
Contact:
Business and Commercial Aviation Magazine
Hangar C-1
Westchester County Airport
New York, New York 10604

HOW TO SURVIVE A PLANE CRASH

It is possible to increase your chances.   Consider these facts: Most crashes
occur on takeoff or landing. The majority of people die not because of
impact, but because of failure to get out of the plane.
You must learn to:
(1) survive the impact
(2) evacuate as quickly as possible

PREPARATION

ACCEPT RESPONSIBILITY   You have no control over the flight, nor
can you even see where you are going, so there is a tendency to simply
put yourself in the hands of the flight crew. But when there is trouble,
how much can several hostesses and stewards do for 75 or more passengers? You'd better be prepared to take matters into your own hands.

READ THE LITTLE PLASTIC CARD AND LISTEN TO THE TAKEOFF
SPEECH   Don't assume you know the layout because you've taken this
kind of plane before; the configuration does change often. Find your seat
on the diagram and locate the nearest exists and an alternate. Find the
closest exists—two front and two rear. Take some time to examine the
doors to see how they work.

BE ALERT DURING TAKEOFFS AND LANDINGS   And do put those
seat backs and tray tables "in their original, upright positions." This
minimizes the possibility of injury and keeps the aisles and rows clear.

LOCATE FLOTATION EQUIPMENT   Longer overwater flights have life
jackets that the attendants will demonstrate. Otherwise, a part of the seat
acts as a flotation device.

WEAR YOUR SEAT BELT   Make sure you know how to work it, and
wear it tight and low. Erect posture is safer.

DON'T BE UNCOOPERATIVE ABOUT CARRY-ONS The temptation is to stick something heavy, like a camera or a bottle of Scotch, in the overhead compartment. Don't. When they say that the carry-on should fit under the seat in front of you, don't flimflam. If it blocks the aisle, it may kill you and the person next to you.

SURVIVING THE IMPACT

ASSUME BRACE POSITION AT THE SIGN OF ABRUPT CHANGE IN ALTITUDE, FIRE, TWISTING OR BREAKING METAL This position will give you some protection against debris: Bend over, placing your arms around your ankles, and your head between your arms against your legs. Or, cross your arms in front of your head, folding them against the seat in front of you. Then lean forward, with your head against your arms.

EVACUATION

GET OUT AS FAST AS YOU CAN Undo your seat belt. Leave everything behind and head for the exit.

At the exit. Open the door and look out. If you see fire, go look for another exit. If not, you want out:

- *Inflatable slide?* Inflate, pull handle, and jump.
- *Escape rope?* Hand over hand, lower yourself until you are low enough to jump.
- *Stairs?* Run down them.
- *Window over wing?* Exit feet first, move toward the back of the wing, and slide off rear wing flap.

GET AWAY FROM THE PLANE Go for a good, safe distance, but don't hail a cab for the nearest Holiday Inn. Stay around. Your assistance will be of immense importance to the authorities. And if you are not there when the head counts are done, your next-of-kin might be in for a pretty distressing phone call.

IF THERE IS SMOKE Smoke, especially from burning jet fuel, is the killer.

Crawl toward the exit, on all fours, but not with your belly on the ground. The crawl should put you under the rising smoke; but if you go too low, you might get your lungs full of some toxic gases that tend to sink rather than rise.

IF THERE IS FIRE Never run into it, unless you absolutely have no other choice. If you know the alternate exits, you have a much better chance to avoid performing a "wall of fire" trick.

WHAT ABOUT EXPLOSIONS? Nothing looks better on film than an explosion, so most of us have seen Hollywood blast a few planes now and then. But the truth is, planes rarely explode. They rely on kerosene, not gasoline, and kerosene is much less explosive. What people often mistake for an explosion is the fire flaring up as the result of being fed by more fuel from ruptured tanks. Airplane survival expert Sarah Uzzell-Rindlaub* compares this flare-up to the one that occurs when we throw another log on the fire. Worry about fire, not explosion. It means that running clear of the plane is worth the effort. Some people think that they will be vaporized by a gigantic explosion just slightly smaller than Hiroshima and never bother to run the hundred yards that could make a difference.

THE HUMAN FACTOR: PANIC   *Negative panic.* This occurs when, in a crisis, people just freeze: no screaming or struggling, just sitting or standing motionless. These people fail to leave the plane in time and often succumb to smoke inhalation.

Regular panic. Not as prevalent as negative panic, but equally deadly, because screaming can cause you to engulf large amounts of smoke and waste your breath. Also, the panic contributes to confused and illogical thinking and action—for example, trying to get off the plane with the stuffed animal you bought for your niece.

PLANES ARE DESIGNED FOR EASY EVACUATION   In order to pass the FAA regulations, the airplane manufacturer must demonstrate that a full load of passengers can get out of the plane within 90 seconds, even with half the exits blocked. Theoretically, this means that you should be able to get off within 90 seconds, provided you know where you're going.

YOUR PAPERS, MONSIEUR?

International travel is becoming physically easier, but bureaucratically more complex and difficult. In some countries, governments change faster than the weather; visa requirements appear to be authored by the Marx Brothers.

Plan ahead. Give yourself lots of time to get the necessary shots and applications in order, especially when traveling outside Western Europe or the industrialized nations of Asia.

Double check. If you have acted in advance, don't assume that your visa is irrevocable. It isn't. Make sure that, in the interim, regulations haven't changed; check just before you go.

---

*For more on this subject, read Sarah Uzzell-Rindlaub's article "Getting Out in 90 Seconds," *Quest*, September, 1979, pp. 18–20.

Consider using a visa agency. Things have gotten so crazy that a hot new service has emerged for travelers—visa agencies. They share the same basic premise of the travel agencies—save the customer the hassle. Of course, visa agencies do not get a commission from the country granting the visa (wouldn't that be a twist); they make their money by charging you.

What visa agencies do. They do the running around. They take care of getting you the visas and passport renewals and extra pages. In some cases, they arrange for vaccinations and/or vaccination certification. And they handle a few quirks. For example, if you want to go to Libya or any other Middle Eastern country of the rabid anti-Zionist persuasion and you have an Israeli stamp on your passport, you are advised to stay on the plane. And Taiwan doesn't want you if you have been to Peking, etc. Any good visa agency is hip to this and will get you a second, "restricted," passport for use in countries that are into this sort of thing. Or it can get you additional passport pages that you can use for the Israeli or South African stamp or that of any other "ostracized" nation; you remove the offending page before you hit the Baghdad airport. Of course, you can do this yourself: Any holder of a valid passport can apply for a "restricted" one or get extra pages. Another bit of weirdness is the requirement by some Arab nations (you guessed it—Libya's in this group too) that your visa application be submitted in Arabic. Unless you took Arabic 101 in college, this means a translation. The visa agencies will provide it for a fee.

Perhaps a visa agency can be most valuable to you by virtue of its location. Most visa agencies are in Washington, D.C., and since a surprisingly large number of countries won't allow you to apply for a visa through their missions or consulates around the country, it can be handy to have a person in Washington, where the embassies are.

Watch out. Visa agencies are not licensed. Try to get the name of one from an associate. Or check with the embassy of the country(ies) you wish to travel to and see whether it has dealt with the agency and found it kosher (don't use that term at the Libyan Embassy).

Countries requiring a business visa (but not a tourist visa)

Dominican Republic	Philippines
Jamaica	Sri Lanka
Mexico	Trinidad/Tobago
Pakistan	Venezuela

Countries not requiring business or tourist visa

Argentina	Great Britain	New Zealand
Austria	Greece	Nicaragua
Bahamas	Grenada	Norway
Barbados	Guyana	Panama
Belgium	Haiti	Paraguay
Botswana	Iceland	Peru
Canada	Ireland	Portugal
Chile	Israel	Singapore
Colombia	Italy	Spain
Costa Rica	Lesotho	Surinam
Cyprus	Luxembourg	Sweden
Denmark	Malawi	Switzerland
Ecuador	Malaysia	Tunisia
El Salvador	Malta	Turkey
Fiji	Morocco	Uruguay
Finland	Netherlands	West Germany

State Department list of countries considered dangerous for Americans (as of February 1980)

Check with the State Department before going to a country of questionable safety. U.S. intelligence may have gone downhill in recent years, but it can still call a dangerous situation. The list:

Afghanistan	Iran	Oman
Algeria	Iraq	Pakistan
Bahrain	Kuwait	Qatar
Bangladesh	Lebanon	Syria
Chad	Libya	United Arab Emirates
El Salvador	Nicaragua	Yemen

Limited warnings have been issued for Uganda and Zimbabwe-Rhodesia. The State Department also puts out bulletins on special situations—a crime wave, a ring of passport thieves, etc.

Regulations concerning currency can be rigorously enforced and failure to comply with them can cause travel delays and severe penalties. Many countries allow free import and export of foreign currency and traveller's cheques, but have strict laws regarding local currency. Other countries allow unlimited import of foreign currency on condition that it has been declared at the point of entry. Usually the amount taken out must not exceed the amount brought in. Even when a country fails to list restrictions on currency, it will rarely permit the unrestricted flow of gold coins or bars.

The phrase "unrestricted if declared" should be interpreted to mean that the import of foreign currency is unrestricted and the amounts declared upon entry may be re-exported.

In some countries it is difficult to cash large traveller's cheques, thus cheques of small denominations are recommended.

The following currency prescriptions were in effect at the time this directory went to press and apply to travellers only.

* The Won is not an international currency and cannot be exchanged outside Korea.
**Visitors are advised to use traveller's cheques.

| Country | Local Currency | | Foreign Currency | |
	Import	Export	Import	Export
Afghanistan	Af. 500		unrestricted if declared	
Albania	prohibited		unrestricted if declared	
Algeria	prohibited		unrestricted if declared	
Angola	prohibited		unrestricted if declared	
Argentina	unrestricted		unrestricted	
Australia	unrestricted I A. $100.		unrestricted if declared	
Austria	unrestricted I Sch. 15000.		unrestricted	
Bahamas	unrestricted		unrestricted if declared	
Bangladesh	Taka 25 I prohibited		unrestricted if declared	
Barbados	unrestricted		unrestricted	
Belgium	unrestricted		unrestricted	
Benin	unrestricted		unrestricted	
Bermuda	unrestricted		unrestricted if declared	
Bolivia	unrestricted		unrestricted	
Brazil	unrestricted		unrestricted	
Bulgaria	prohibited		unrestricted if declared	
Burma	prohibited		unrestricted if declared	
Burundi	unrestricted if declared		unrestricted if declared	
Cambodia	prohibited		unrestricted if declared	
Cameroon	unrestricted I CFA Fr 25000.		unrestricted if declared	
Canada	unrestricted		unrestricted	
Central African Rep.	unrestricted		unrestricted if declared	
Chad	unrestricted		unrestricted if declared	
Chile	unrestricted		unrestricted if declared	
China	prohibited		unrestricted if declared	
Colombia	unrestricted I Pesos imported		unrestricted	
Congo	unrestricted I CFA. Fr. 50000.		unrestricted if declared	
Costa Rica	unrestricted		unrestricted if declared	
Cuba	prohibited		unrestricted if declared	

Fig. 77. International currency regulations
Check with the embassy of the country of destination
before you go for any revisions.
(through page 636)
From *The Multinational Executive Travel Companion* (Cambridge, MA:
Guides To Multinational Business Inc., 1979), pp. 51–53.

Country	Local Currency		Foreign Currency	
	Import	Export	Import	Export
Cyprus	unrestricted		unrestricted	
Czechoslovakia	prohibited		unrestricted if declared	
Denmark	unrestricted I Kr. 3000.		unrestricted	
Dominican Rep.	unrestricted		unrestricted	
Ecuador	unrestricted		unrestricted	
Egypt	E. P. 20 /prohibited		unrestricted if declared	
El Salvador	unrestricted		unrestricted if declared	
Ethiopia	unrestricted I E. $100.		unrestricted if declared	
Finland	unrestricted I Markka 3000.		unrestricted if declared	
France	unrestricted I F. 5000.		unrestricted if declared	
Gabon	unrestricted		unrestricted if declared	
Gambia	unrestricted		unrestricted if declared	
Germany (East)	prohibited		unrestricted if declared	
Germany (West)	unrestricted		unrestricted	
Ghana	unrestricted		unrestricted if declared	
Great Britain	unrestricted I P.Stlg. 25		unrestricted if declared	
Greece	Dr. 750.		unrestricted if declared	
Guatemala	unrestricted		unrestricted if declared	
Guinea	prohibited		unrestricted if declared	
Guyana	unrestricted		unrestricted if declared	
Haiti	unrestricted		unrestricted if declared	
Honduras	unrestricted		unrestricted if declared	
Hong Kong	unrestricted		unrestricted	
Hungary	Ft. 400.		unrestricted if declared	
Iceland	Kr. 500. I Kr. imported		unrestricted if declared	
India	prohibited		unrestricted if declared	
Indonesia	prohibited		unrestricted if declared	
Iran	unrestricted I Rl. 3000.		unrestricted if declared	
Iraq	Din. 25.		unrestricted if declared	
Ireland (Eire)	unrestricted P. 25.		unrestricted if declared	
Israel	IL. 200.		unrestricted if declared	
Italy	LIT 35000.		unrestricted if declared	
Ivory Coast	unrestricted I CFA. Fr. 75000.		unrestricted if declared	
Jamaica	unrestricted I J. $20.		unrestricted if declared	
Japan	unrestricted I Yen 30000.		unrestricted if declared	
Jordan	unrestricted		unrestricted if declared	
Kenya	prohibited		unrestricted if declared	
Korea (North & South)*	prohibited		unrestricted if declared	
Kuwait	unrestricted		unrestricted if declared	
Laos	unrestricted		unrestricted if declared	
Lebanon	unrestricted		unrestricted	
Lesotho	unrestricted		unrestricted if declared	
Liberia	unrestricted		unrestricted if declared	
Libya	L.D. 20		unrestricted if declared	
Liechtenstein	unrestricted		unrestricted	
Luxembourg	unrestricted		unrestricted	
Madagascar	unrestricted		unrestricted if declared	
Malawi**	unrestricted		unrestricted if declared	
Malaysia	M. $500.		unrestricted if declared	
Mali	unrestricted		unrestricted if declared	
Malta	unrestricted I P.M. 20		unrestricted if declared	
Mauritania	unrestricted		unrestricted if declared	
Mexico	unrestricted		unrestricted	

Country	Local Currency		Foreign Currency	
	Import	Export	Import	Export
Monaco	unrestricted		unrestricted	
Morocco	prohibited		unrestricted if declared	
Mozambique	Esc. 2500.		unrestricted if declared	
Nepal	unrestricted		unrestricted	
Netherlands	unrestricted		unrestricted	
New Zealand	NZ. $10.		unrestricted if declared	
Nicaragua	unrestricted		unrestricted	
Niger	unrestricted I CFA. Fr. 75000.		unrestricted if declared	
Nigeria	prohibited		unrestricted if declared	
Norway	unrestricted I Kr. 800.		unrestricted if declared	
Pakistan	P.Rps. 20.		unrestricted if declared	
Panama	unrestricted		unrestricted if declared	
Paraguay	unrestricted		unrestricted if declared	
Peru	unrestricted		unrestricted if declared	
Philippines	P.Pesos 100.		unrestricted if declared	
Poland	prohibited		unrestricted if declared	
Portugal	Esc. 1000		unrestricted	
Rhodesia	R. $10.		unrestricted if declared	
Romania	prohibited		unrestricted if declared	
Saudi Arabia	unrestricted		unrestricted if declared	
Senegal	CFA. Fr. 75000.		unrestricted if declared	
Sierra Leone	Leone 20.		unrestricted if declared	
Singapore	unrestricted I Sing. $1000.		unrestricted if declared	
Somali Rep.	unrestricted		unrestricted if declared	
South Africa	Rand 50.		unrestricted if declared	
Spain	Ptas. 50000 I Ptas. 3000.		unrestricted if declared	
Sri Lanka (Ceylon)	Rps. 50		unrestricted if declared	
Sudan	prohibited		unrestricted if declared	
Surinam	unrestricted		unrestricted if declared	
Sweden	Kr. 6000.		unrestricted	
Switzerland	unrestricted		unrestricted	
Syria	S.100.		unrestricted if declared	
Taiwan	N.T. $4000. I N.T. $2000.		unrestricted if declared	
Tanzania	prohibited		unrestricted if declared	
Thailand	Baht 500.		unrestricted if declared	
Togo	unrestricted I CFA. Fr. 75000.		unrestricted if declared	
Trinidad & Tobago	unrestricted		unrestricted if declared	
Tunisia	prohibited		unrestricted if declared	
Turkey	TL. 1000		unrestricted if declared	
Uganda	unrestricted		unrestricted if declared	
Upper Volta	unrestricted		unrestricted if declared	
U.S.A.	unrestricted		unrestricted	
U.S.S.R.	prohibited		unrestricted if declared	
Venezuela	unrestricted		unrestricted if declared	
Vietnam	prohibited		unrestricted if declared	
Yugoslavia	Y.Din. 1500./Y.Din. 1000		unrestricted if declared	
Zaire	unrestricted		unrestricted if declared	
Zambia	Kw 10 I Kw imported		unrestricted if declared	

GUIDES TO MULTINATIONAL BUSINESS

This company, in Cambridge, Massachusetts, issues several travel guides that rank among the best available for businesspeople. Cheap they are not, but they have the kind of information that matters when you mean business. Most other travel guides are concerned primarily with restaurants, museums, and other diversions.

Take, for example, the *Multinational Executive Travel Companion*. It has information on over 160 countries and features in-depth information on 115 international business centers. Besides the expected data on airlines, cars, embassies, hotels, etc., there are entries for business hours, business customs, trade fairs, holidays, currency regulations, and even important business statistics, such as key market indicators, balance of payments, and the performance of over 1350 companies worldwide.

The publishers mean for you to take this book with you, so it is very small. Even at 624 pages, it is quite light and slim. They do this by making the print very, very small, and the paper is very thin—that's the trick.

The book is updated annually, and it costs $35, $45 if ordering from abroad.

Guides to Multinational Business also publishes a *Global Telecommunications Guide* which includes information about phoning and telexing around the world. Features include time-zone charts, business hours, country codes, access codes, and useful data on making and accepting international collect calls. The cost for the book is $15 US, $25 abroad.

Other booklets from this firm include *Business Travel Costs in Major Cities Worldwide*, a small, comprehensive booklet ($5 US, $7.50 elsewhere), *Business Vocabulary for the Traveling Executive*, a booklet of business terms in French, German, and English ($5 US, $7.50 elsewhere), and the *Airlines Shopping Guide*, an at-a-glance comparison chart of routing and features of major international carriers ($5 US, $7.50 elsewhere).

All the Multinational Guides books are updated annually and are available from:

Guides to Multinational Business
Harvard Square
P.O. Box 92
Cambridge, Massachusetts 02238
(617) 868-2288

If you are ordering, you must enclose a check or money order.

HOW TO GO TO A TRADE SHOW

IF YOU ARE ATTENDING AS A VISITOR

Trade shows are an important medium for companies to make contacts, write business, and show their goods and services to the business community and the press. But often, the difference between being "the talk of the show" and being lost in obscurity has little to do with the quality of the product on exhibit; there is an art to setting up a booth at a show.

Attending a show can be a colossal waste of time if you wander aimlessly, picking up brochures and chatting with ladies in bathing suits or half-drunk glad-handers in polyester suits. Make a game plan based on the size of the show, its duration, and the amount of time you are prepared to commit.

CASE OUT THE SHOW   If it's one you've never attended, talk to someone who has. Find out its primary purpose. Some shows are mainly for writing business. Others are strictly showcases. Still others are merely a chance to trade business cards, talk shop, and gossip. Is the show "to the trade only" or open to customers? Whatever the case, it's up to you to decide whether the show will justify your time and expense. One ambitious young junior executive working for a major communications conglomerate convinced his superiors to retain the services of an outside consultant whose job was simply to advise them on what shows to attend, what shows to place booths in, and what shows to skip. It paid off. The junior executive claims he doubled business in his division simply by following the "road show" schedule proposed by the consultant.

Speak to colleagues who have attended the show in the past. Call the show manager and ask questions about who attends, and for what purpose. Ask for data to be mailed to you. Also, find out how "new" the show is: Shows often take several years to get organized and gain credibility in the industry. The first few computer industry shows were sheer pandemonium. Many are no longer held, but the ones that survive are well attended.

PRIORITIZE   Some exhibitors are musts. Know who they are and where they are. You don't necessarily have to hit them first, but hit them with enough time to do what you have to do. Some of the larger exhibits maintain "hospitality suites," which offer a more intimate setting. Since the shows usually run about three days, that leaves only three evenings—and three dinner engagements. Try to lock the key people into dinner at the start of the show, before the others get to them. Don't be surprised, however, if the exhibitor cancels because there is someone else he wants to have dinner with (someone who has more clout that you have). *C'est la guerre.*

GET A COPY OF THE EXHIBIT DIRECTORY AND SCHEDULE, AND STUDY IT BEFORE EMBARKING   This will help you avoid skipping from floor to floor or searching endlessly for your destination. Exhibition centers are huge.

DON'T BE SUCKED INTO TOO MANY SEMINARS   Seminars given at trade shows are more for insiders than for outsiders. Often, they are PR vehicles for the speakers of the sponsoring companies. But if the idea of a given seminar grabs you, by all means attend. You'll be able to tell after the first few minutes whether you will learn anything worthwhile. If your reaction is negative, don't be embarrassed; get up and leave. Another approach is to have someone tape the seminar for you; then you can listen to the proceedings while soaking in a tub or driving home.

DON'T TRY TO GET FREE MERCHANDISE   It makes you look like a nickel-and-dime merchant. Don't drool; be subtle. If it's a big item and you are not giving the company a big order, the best you can expect is a chance to buy at cost. Selling merchandise out of a booth is usually banned at trade shows, but the exhibitors would rather not pay the shipping charges of returning the stuff to home base. So on the last day of the show, they'll try to get rid of it by selling it to attendees or to a local store that can pick it up. Sometimes you can get them to promise the stuff to you right at the beginning. But don't bug them throughout the show; this is not the primary reason you are there.

PLAN A STRATEGY TO SHOP THE SHOW   Most shows are organized with the larger and more established lines on the lower floors, the newer and often smaller lines and firms on the upper floors. Some buyers refer to "working the show backward" when they are interested primarily in seeing what's new and who's new.

IF YOU ARE AN EXHIBITOR

PLAN WELL IN ADVANCE   There are always problems. And it takes a good 60–90 days to build a display. Beginning a year in advance is not excessive. Talk to the show management for all the details.

FORMULATE OBJECTIVES   What do you hope to accomplish? Are you going to the right show for that purpose? Get demographic and marketing data from the show management before making a final decision. Shows can be quite expensive, with costs encompassing booth rental space, display construction, and the travel and living expenses of personnel.

BUDGET   Decide in advance how much to spend.

DECIDE ON A THEME   You are competing for the attention of the attendees, so the tenets of advertising apply—you've got to get your message across, convincingly, forcefully, and memorably. Don't be afraid to go to your ad agency. And once you have a basic theme, a design consultant can be very helpful in translating it into a display with impact.

GET THE ENTIRE FIRM BEHIND YOU   It helps to have enthusiasm from top management. Since your exhibit will both represent and influence the image of the firm, it should not be regarded as strictly a project of the sales department. Bring in the advertising and PR people. Even product design people benefit, because feedback from buyers about what they want is priceless.

Make sure your booth will be manned by informed, well-mannered personnel. Too often, this is left to the last minute and you wind up with people who can't talk shop and, all too apparently, are just minding the store. Don't let this happen. And don't skimp on personnel: The booth must be attended at all times, and you may want to slip away to talk privately with a client. Some exhibitors rely on the crude method of using bikini-clad or seductively dressed models to lure potential customers to the booth. There is no denying that it sometimes works, but the practice is offensive. (Many women are now buying, and you could lose business.) My advice is to hire intelligent, well-qualified people. Women should wear fashionable business dress.

PUSH   Promote the show and your exhibit *before* as well as during the show. You want to reach the out-of-towners who are here for the show. Take ads in the local papers, and, if you have the bucks, try radio (ideally, run your ad during business news and the stock market report). Other approaches include billboards along main routes (especially to airports), ads in trade papers, and, of course, the exhibitor's stock in trade—premiums, ad specialty items, gimmicks, and other giveaways. Check with exposition management for the rules regarding this.

GO FOR IT   Go after business, whether you are out for orders, looking for contacts, or just desirous of spreading the word.

WHERE TO LEARN MORE ABOUT TRADE SHOWS

The most complete listing of trade shows is the *Exhibits Schedule, the Annual Directory of Trade and Industrial Shows,* published by *Successful Meetings* magazine in cooperation with the Exhibit Designers and Producers Association. It classifies trade shows in three ways: by industry, by geography (city, state, and nation), and by chronology. The listings include the name of each show, its frequency, site, and dates; the names of the exhibition manager and the sponsoring organization; the exhibition's size and number of booths, the location of the sponsor's headquarters, and an estimated attendance for each show. It is invaluable for planning your show schedule, whether you are an exhibitor or an attendee.

Contact:
Exhibits Schedule
633 Third Avenue
New York, New York 10017

The U.S. Department of Commerce publishes the *Overseas Export Promotion Calendar*, which lists U.S. trade promotion events held abroad. The calendar is organized by product classification and gives the name, location, date, and American-based contact for each exhibition, mission, or seminar included.

Contact:
Overseas Export Promotion Calendar
Industry Participation Division, Room 4012
Office of Export Promotion
U.S. Department of Commerce
Washington, D.C. 20230

The Dow Jones-Irwin Business Almanac also lists some of the principal international trade shows and fairs.

Contact:
The Dow Jones-Irwin Business Almanac
Dow Jones-Irwin
1818 Ridge Road
Homewood, Illinois 60430

42

TRAVEL BUMMERS

A vacation spent in a sickbed can leave you depressed. But a business trip thrown out of kilter by an unexpected, unpleasant occurrence can cost your firm a great deal of time and money—and cause a setback in your career.

AIR SICKNESS

Your personal experience may tell you otherwise, but air sickness is much rarer these days. Planes fly higher, and cabin conditions have improved. Still, the presence of turbulence, or just your own natural tendency toward queasiness may result in your being fixated on the air sickness bag in the pocket in front of you.

PRECAUTIONS

- *Loosen tight clothing, or remove it.* Especially tight things—stockings, girdles, garters, neckties, shoes.
- *Stand and stretch periodically.* This is especially important for those who are older or obese, or who suffer from a bad heart or varicose veins.
- *Try to get a seat on the right-hand side.* In holding patterns and approaches to domestic airports, more left turns occur than right.
- *If you anticipate a problem, you might want to take a pill.* Bonamine, Dramamine, and Marezine are very effective. *Caution:* They make you drowsy. You'd better keep this in mind if you'll be driving after you leave the plane, or if you have to be sharp for a business meeting.
- *Sit in a reclining position and keep your eyes closed.* Relaxing this way will help stave off the onset of air sickness.
- *Don't eat anything that is new to you or that you tend not to digest easily.*

JET LAG

JET LAG IS REAL

It is now generally regarded as a disease called circadian dysrhythmia and desynchronosis. This simply means that the body's natural rhythms and cycles—such as sleep, digestion, hunger, and sex—become out of phase with the external world and out of synch with each other. Jet lag can cause insomnia, headaches, irritability, diarrhea or constipation, muscle aches, and excessive fatigue, to name just a few of the more common disorders.

THE PROBLEM

Adjuting to a new time zone takes time; unfortunately, we don't usually have the time we need. Although some rhythms can adjust within 48 hours, the digestive system usually takes about one day to normalize for each time zone crossed (New York to Rome crosses *seven* zones). The heart rate takes five and a half days to normalize; body temperature, seven; urine output, ten; and sleep patterns, up to fourteen.

The body has an internal clock which must be "reset" if there is to be a smooth transition to another time zone. This clock responds to external cues such as light and dark (night and day), eating and exercise patterns.

Many bodily cycles—from cell division and brainwaves to beard growth—are disturbed by jet lag.

Jet lag can seriously impair physical and mental performance. It can leave you with a distorted sense of time, place and well-being.

HOW TO MINIMIZE JET LAG

PREPARE YOUR RHYTHMS IN ADVANCE   Several days before departure, begin gradually to change your eating and sleeping schedule in the direction of the time zone you are traveling to.

DON'T RUSH   Many people start cramming in work in anticipation of a trip. In the days prior, they neglect their diet, exercise and sleep, often boarding the plane in an exhausted and agitated state. This only compounds the problem, and despite the fatigue, it is often difficult to fall asleep on-board under these circumstances.

CHOOSE YOUR FLIGHT   Consider:

- *travel time*. Minimize lengthy stopovers.
- *departure and arrival times*. It's better to leave in the morning and arrive at your destination when it's time to rest, than to fly all night and arrive during early-morning activity.
- *flight load and configuration*. The more space, the better; if it's a long flight, opt for a wide-body craft, and a first-class seat if it's in the budget.

SELECT YOUR SEAT   Seats opposite emergency exits, hatches, or bulkheads have slightly more room. Try to stay on the aisle or at the window; middle seats offer the least room. Arrive early so you can choose the "best" seat. Ask about the load: If it is light, request a seat next to two empty ones so you can stretch across them (the arms of the seats fold up and back) and sleep.

TRY TO AVOID TRAVELING ALONE   Believe it or not, studies show that jet lag is lessened when you travel in a group or with a companion.

DRESS CASUALLY   Wear loose clothing; allow circulation to be free. Tight neckties and tight shoes are out. Better yet, take a carry-on with you and keep your necktie there—you can put it on just before landing, if necessary. Some airlines provide soft slippers. Use them, or bring your own. On a very long flight, it would be wise to bring along your favorite comfortable "dress down" clothing—soft jeans and a sweat shirt, maybe?—and change on the plane, and then back again if you've got a meeting upon landing.

KEEP "FRESHNESS" WITH YOU   Toothbrush and paste, razors, aftershave, mouth wash, eye wash, deodorant, moisturizer (to combat the desert-dry atmosphere aloft). You'll be surprised at how much better they can make you feel.

DON'T DRINK   Okay, okay; if you must drink, drink moderately. The notion of "I had a few drinks, and didn't feel a thing the whole flight" is, for most people, a big mistake. Remember—the higher you are, the higher you'll get. At only 10,000 feet, two or three martinis are as potent as four or five imbibed at sea level. And hangover from in-flight drinking lasts much longer, too. Because the oxygen supply in the planes is reduced, the cells of the body get less of it, and lack of oxygen aggravates the effects of alcohol.

KEEP SMOKING TO A MINIMUM   Excessive smoking in a poorly ventilated area can contribute to nausea, especially when supplemented by the effects of the altitude, turbulence, and lack of exercise and sleep associated with air travel. In addition, the cabin air is not only short on oxygen, but also virtually free of moisture. The dryness and lack of oxygen increase the amount of carbon monoxide absorbed into the blood by the smoker, and this may increase the work load of the heart.

EAT RIGHT   Eat lightly and never at odd hours. It may be lunchtime on the plane, but if your body is set at 3:00 A.M., a steak is hardly the thing. Odd-hours munching will throw your digestive cycle out of whack. And remember, *a plane is not the place to try something new.* Most airline food is extremely predictable. When in doubt about a particular dish, choose the simplest or most familiar one on the menu.

EXERCISE   From time to time, take a walk down the aisle. Some airlines provide suggestions for exercises you can do in your seat. Stretch those muscles. Prolonged sitting is a bigger problem than you might think—the muscles are weakened, the joints get stiff, circulation is hampered—and you notice these effects in the form of tension, fatigue, backaches, cramps, and other annoyances. It is amazing how many of us never miss a day of jogging or pushups at home, and then go on a trip and skip all exercising for days at a time. It may be socially awkward to do some simple calisthenics on a plane or in a flight lounge—but do them. You'll see Japanese and Chinese tour groups doing them wherever you go.

TRY TO AVOID SCHEDULING YOURSELF TOO TIGHTLY   If you want to rest after the flight, you should be able to do so.

CONTINUE WITH PRESCRIBED MEDICATION   Get advice from your doctor concerning timing. For example, if the pill bottle says "before bedtime" and you are traveling, does that mean you take the pill before you go to bed in Hong Kong, or when it's bedtime according to your home time zone? Some medication works better before sleep; in other cases, it's the time between dosages that is important. Get it straight.

AVOID PROLONGED FLYING   The biggest danger is from *accumulated sleep debt.* Then there's the *excessive dryness* in the cabin. Prolonged exposure can cause scratchy throats, itchy eyes, dimming vision, and other signs of dehydration. In extreme cases, cabin conditions, when coupled with alcohol and smoking, can produce brittleness of hair and nails, and hypoxia (oxygen deficiency) leading to temporary anemia and subpar mental ability and perception. So remember to plan your trip to allow time for rest.

A NOTE OF CAUTION   The change in air pressure during landing can cause discomfort in the ears and, in some cases, lead to permanent damage. Serious cases can result in accumulation of fluid or bleeding in the air, which doctors call *aerotitis.* If you notice a problem, chew gum or open your mouth to equalize the pressure in the inner ear with that on the outside. Avoid traveling with a bad cold. If you feel a need for it, take a decongestant about a half hour before landing to clear your respiratory passages. Some people have a chronic problem with their ears at high altitudes. If your ears bother you during a long elevator ride or at the top of a tall building, get them checked before you fly. It's a more serious problem than the airlines are willing to admit.

DR. EHRET'S PROGRAM

Charles F. Ehret, a chronobiologist at the Argonne National Laboratory in Illinois, has conducted extensive research into the causes, effects and prevention of jet lag. His findings have been utilized by the military.

His program, found to be effective by people traveling as many as five time zones in one day, consists of three parts. The *Preflight Step* involves a preparatory period of light eating and fasting, beginning one to three days prior to takeoff. During the *Inflight Step* you reset your body's internal clock using periods of light and darkness, rest and activity, and coffee or tea. During the *Postflight Step*, you follow a diet designed to give you a big energy boost and sound sleep in your new time zone.

For the specifics of the program, read *Overcoming Jet Lag* by Dr. Charles F. Ehret and Lynne Walter Scanlon (New York: Berkley, 1986).

WATER

You've got to be careful about drinking water overseas. But don't overdo your concern. "I have had patients who have become so obsessed with precautions about water or disease that they have actually filled their bathtubs with bottled water," wrote noted tropical medicine expert Kevin Cahill, MD. "This is asinine." Here, in a nutshell, are the rules to follow:

- *In the large cities of industrialized nations, tap water is safe to drink.*
- *Tap water is often safe in many developing countries, but it is advisable not to depend on its potability.*
- *When drinking bottled water, make sure that you or one of your companions breaks the seal.* A common trick of locals is refilling mineral water bottles with the local stuff. Usually, such a bottle will be poorly sealed.
- *Although it seems logical that using locally made ice would defeat your purpose, small amounts of contaminated water almost never do any harm.* So an ice cube or two won't hurt you. Neither will a little water for brushing your teeth or douching. Still, it's a good idea to check first with local health officials, because there are local outbreaks during which the water could become severely contaminated.
- *When in Africa, Asia, or South America, do not swim in inland bodies of water or canals.* They are usually filled with parasites and infectious amoebas.

OTHER LIQUIDS

Beer. When you are hot and thirsty, beer can be a good, safe way to quench yourself. Although beer is better than hard liquor, keep in mind that one gets drunk easier while sweating.

Soft drinks. Stay away from the local stuff when in the tropics. Sugar in liquid provides an excellent culture for bacteria. Imported soft drinks are usually okay. And some soft drinks, such as Coca-Cola, are prepared according to strict standards. Again, watch out for Coke bottles that have been filled with something else.

Wine. Wines do not travel well and are usually not good in the tropics, except in the most plush hotels or industrialized tropical nations.

Milk. Milk is dangerous in many places. Pasteurization is still uncommon in developing nations, and even where it does exist, sterilization is sometimes poor. You could boil your milk first, but boiling also destroys the protein. Another alternative is powdered milk, provided you mix it with safe water.

FOOD

Americans often claim that they got sick from the food in a given country. Very often, it's simply a matter of eating something that didn't "agree" with them. Doctors cite four main factors that contribute to food-related sickness:

Insects. In tropical climates, it is very difficult to keep insects away. Stay away from food that has been sitting out in the open.

Proper hygiene. You must be especially careful when abroad. Wash thoroughly, especially after a visit to the lavatory. This also applies to the domestic help, so you should be conscientious in finding a hotel that has high standards of cleanliness.

Lack of good judgment. If you are the type that likes to do as the locals do, you might get a bit too fearless. Don't eat in dirty places or from dirty dishes, and be sensible when it comes to trying exotic fare.

Contaminated food:
- *vegetables.* Fresh vegetables are usually safe when freshly cooked. Reheated vegetables are a no-no. Stay away from the leafy green variety in the tropics.
- *fruit.* Fresh fruits with unbroken skins are usually okay. Fruit compotes must be fresh, or forget about them. Always wash and peel fresh fruit yourself. If the skin is broken, throw the fruit away.
- *fish.* Avoid clams in strange places. They are hepatitis carriers. Fresh fish is usually safe if well cooked. Be careful with raw or smoked fish.
- *meats.* Should be well cooked and hot.

- *duck.* A poor choice, because it takes a long time to prepare and is often reheated.
- *lamb.* A very safe bet, if freshly killed and cooked on charcoal, as it is in the Arab nations. If you can watch your meal being prepared, you can feel safe even in a dirty restaurant.
- *cold plates, custards, pastries—or anything prepared long in advance.* Watch out; flies can carry disease.

MEDICAL CARE

If you are abroad for a short stay, avoid seeking medical treatment unless it's absolutely necessary. When you begin treatment, you are opening yourself to the possibility of complications, infection, and lack of proper follow-up. Besides, in general, the quality of medical care abroad is far below that available in the United States. Possible exceptions include England, Switzerland, Germany, Scandinavia, Japan, and the Soviet Union. If you are planning to stay around for a while or take up residence, of course you'll have little choice. The best thing to do is get the name of a good doctor *before* you need him. Get a referral from someone you trust. It pays to drop by for a preliminary visit and to provide him with a medical history. This precaution is especially important if you have kids with you.

If you don't know anyone in town, try the American Embassy, British Embassy, an American airline or cruise line, or an American or British missionary organization. All these groups keep lists of English-speaking doctors.

Recently, several firms began offering emergency medical assistance to overseas travelers. The services vary according to type of coverage, payment terms and fees.

American Express and MasterCard offer limited assistance to cardholders; American Express does so in conjunction with Paris-based Europ Assistance Worldwide Services.

Travel Assistance International is the U.S. marketing arm of Europ Assistance (1333 F Street NW, Suite 300, Washington, D.C. 20004 800-821-2828).

International SOS Assistance (1 Neshaminy Interplex, Trevose, PA 19047 800-523-8930).

Access America Inc., a Blue Cross/Blue Shield subsidiary (600 Third Avenue, Box 807, New York, New York 10163, 800-851-2800).

WorldCare Travel Assistance Association Inc. (2000 Pennsylvania Avenue NW, Suite 7600, Washington, D.C. 20006 800-521-4822).

HealthCare Abroad (219 Investment Building, 1511 K Street NW, Washington, D.C. 20005 800-336-3310).

TravMed-Medex (Post Office Box 10623, Towson, MD, 21204 800-732-5309).

International Association for Medical Assistance to Travellers (IAMAT) offers a directory providing information on "Western style" medical services in 450 cities around the world. All the doctors cited in the directory speak English and have fixed rates for office visits, house calls, and Sundays or holidays. In addition to the directory, IAMAT will provide you with a membership card, a "Travellers Clinical Record," and a "World Immunization and Malaria Chart." You can also gain access to IAMAT's "World Climate Charts," which also feature information on food, water, and milk in 1,400 cities around the world.

The IAMAT membership is free, although I recommend a donation. A fixed minimum donation for membership is required if you wish to gain access to the climate charts. Corporate memberships are accepted. You may request as many applications as you like for your traveling employees, but then a donation must be included.

Contact:
IAMAT
417 Center Street
Lewiston, New York 14092
716-754-4883

Before you go. It is a good idea to see a doctor before extensive overseas travel. Get a physical and a fresh supply of prescription drugs that you will need while you are away. Ask for the generic names in case your particular brand is unavailable overseas. And go to the dentist to make sure there is no problem lurking that could ruin your trip.

You can get information about health conditions abroad from Worldwide Health Forecast (800-368-3531) or the Access America Hotline (800-851-2800) A U.S. Government Publication, "Health Information For International Travel," available for $4.75 from the U.S. Government Printing Office, is also useful.

Returning home. It is always a good idea to get a checkup upon returning home from (a) the tropics, (b) developing nations, (c) any long trip, (d) any trip during which you have been sexually adventurous. Or if you have done something risky or simply have a hunch that you might have been exposed to disease.

The world is full of weird strains of VD; even doctors misdiagnose them. So watch out. Most developing nations have VD epidemics. And even in the advanced nations, VD is still very easy to pick up. See a doctor at the first sign of any possible symptoms.

Regarding AIDS, preventive measures should be applied worldwide, even in countries with few or no reported cases.

Tropical diseases are also easily misdiagnosed. And they can linger in a dormant stage for months after you return. If you have been in a tropical or underdeveloped nation, ask your physician to do a blood count, tuberculin test, urine analysis, and stool analysis. Depending on the indications, the doctor may wish to run a liver function test, chest X ray, proctoscopy, serologic test, and/or skin test. Recently, some hospitals have begun offering screening programs for travelers returning home.

WHAT TO TAKE WITH YOU

YOUR BASIC KIT

- *an extra pair of eyeglasses.* Your eyeglass prescription.
- *extra medication,* clearly labeled, and a renewal prescription that gives the generic name and dosage of the medication
- *a brief medical record,* noting blood group, Rh factor, etc., and any drug-related allergies
- *sleeping pills.* These are not recommended for regular use, but if jet lag really throws you out of whack, they might help you get on track again.
- *an antihistamine,* such as Chlortrimeton or Benadryl. Relieves itching from bites or rashes.
- *an antibiotic,* such as *tetracycline.*
- *an analgesic, or painkiller.* If you are ever in a great deal of pain, these could save your life by allowing you to function.
- *a decongestant,* if you suffer from clogged ears on plane flights.

WHEN VISITING TROPICAL OR DEVELOPING COUNTRIES

- *insect repellent.* You can usually buy this locally.
- *water purification tablets.* They often make the water taste awful.
- *chloroquine.* The old standby antimalarial.
- *paregoric.* An antidiarrheal agent, but it is an opiate. Use only if you really have it bad. Otherwise, stick with Kaopectate or Lomotil.
- *snakebite kits.* Well, maybe if you plan to stomp around in the desert or high grass. It is more important to be careful and wear proper footwear where snakes are known to hang around. But snake bite kits don't weigh much or cost much, so what the heck.

LOSING THINGS

The best advice—indeed, the *only* general advice that makes sense—is to prepare for the possibility that you will lose something, somewhere:

Have enough of the right kind of insurance. Make sure that your policy covers luggage. The airlines have limited liability, and it usually isn't enough to cover the full value of the contents of the luggage. Does your policy cover the *loss* of property, or only what's missing as a result of a crime? Is the policy in effect abroad as well as in the United States?

Make copies. When you are away, the only really critical things you can lose are things you need to get back home. Valuables such as jewelry can be insured, but all the insurance in the world won't help you if you lose your passport in Bulgaria. Do this now:

Get your wallet in order. Notice the discrepancy between what is in it and what you *thought* was in it. When you are satisfied that the wallet carries the items you require to be kept on your person at all times, go to the nearest copier. Remove all papers and cards from the wallet and make copies of them. Some copiers will reproduce credit cards and IDs. If yours doesn't, write all the numbers on a piece of paper. File the copies and other records.

It's a good idea to make *two* copies of what's in your wallet: Take the extra copy with you on the trip. This copy will not only aid you in retrieving a lost wallet, but might also serve as ID in the absence of the real thing.

Before you go. Make a record of traveler's cheque numbers. File it. Take on your trip the record that the issuer gives you, but keep it apart from your traveler's cheques—you don't want to lose both your cheques and your record of their numbers.

Carry your plane tickets separately. They are very tough to replace. Overseas, it's more difficult for a thief to cash them in or use them, because he'll need your passport: So don't keep your tickets and passport in the same place. It's also wise not to put them in your wallet.

Guard your passport. A U.S. passport is a super-hot black market commodity. If you lose it, chances are you'll never see it again. Call the American embassy, mission, or consulate immediately. Life without your passport can be a big hassle if you are in a remote area, far from a government office. In some countries, you *are* your passport. Without it, you simply don't exist. And it's not only in the Warsaw Pact nations or the developing countries that you might encounter this attitude. Try losing your passport in Switzerland sometime.

Consider joining a credit card bureau. For a small annual fee, it will insure you against misuse of stolen credit cards, keep on file a record of all your cards and numbers, and notify all the card issuers for you; you just phone the bureau. Some credit card protection services also offer emergency cash advances.

43

ARE YOU A TARGET? TERRORISM AND THE AMERICAN EXECUTIVE

According to the State Department, there were 67 terrorist attacks involving U.S. business staff and facilities abroad. If this seems like a small number considering the amount of business Americans do overseas, consider this. A recent report by Risk International stated that while there were only twenty-one attacks on U.S. business overseas in 1984, they accounted for twenty-eight deaths, sixty-four wounded, and an estimated $22 million in damages. Statistics compiled by the Rand Corporation indicate that the typical terrorist attack has an 87 percent chance of success.

This chapter should be taken quite seriously, because terrorist activity against you or your firm may be a very real threat. Naturally, some will chide you for taking an alarmist or paranoid attitude. Better to appear slightly foolish than dead.

Several basic facts about terrorism help explain why it has become so widespread:

- Terrorism is a tactic used by small groups to call attention to their cause and, sometimes, to force capitulation to their demands and goals.
- For terrorists, the ends justify the means.
- They generally accept the loss of life (both theirs and that of their victims) as a part of the struggle.
- Terrorists are aware that attacks on high-profile individuals and institutions (and their representatives) will bring publicity. Indeed, the Rand Corporation has concluded that a terrorist seeking publicity through kidnapping has a virtual 100 percent chance of success.
- Terrorists have a stake in demonstrating that the "establishment" doesn't work—that it is incapable of protecting its citizens against terrorism and that it is disorderly and weak.
- Terrorists generally run in small groups, but they are often very well organized, well trained, and good at what they do. They may be fanatics, but they are not dumb. More often than not, they outsmart local law enforcement officials.

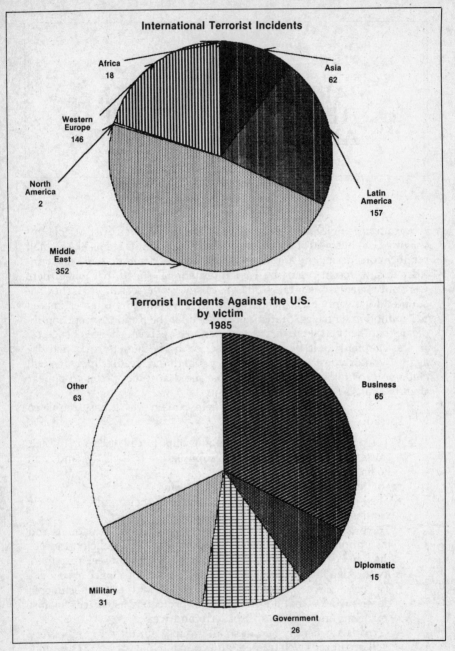

Fig. 78. Latest statistics on
terrorism from the
U.S. Department of State.

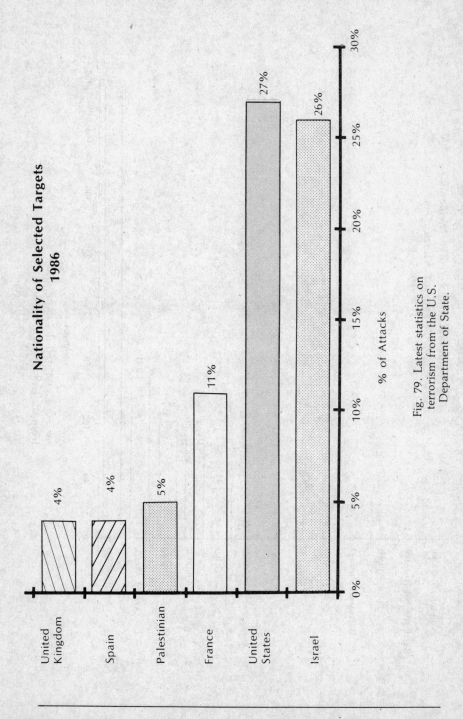

Nationality of Selected Targets 1986

% of Attacks

Fig. 79. Latest statistics on terrorism from the U.S. Department of State.

655

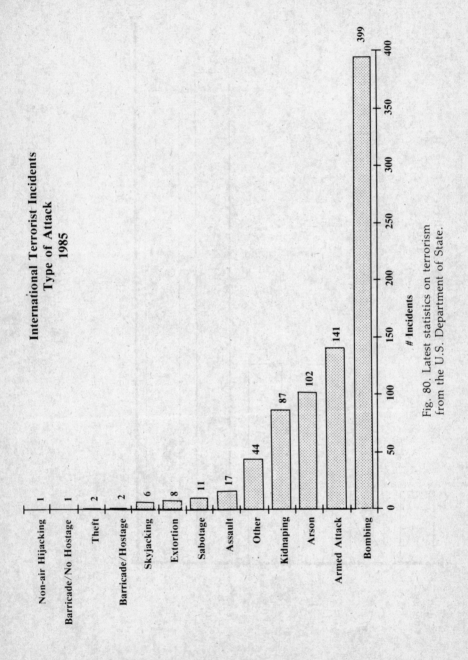

**International Terrorist Incidents
Type of Attack
1985**

Incidents

Non-air Hijacking   1

Barricade/No Hostage   1

Theft   2

Barricade/Hostage   2

Skyjacking   6

Extortion   8

Sabotage   11

Assault   17

Other   44

Kidnaping   87

Arson   102

Armed Attack   141

Bombing   399

Fig. 80. Latest statistics on terrorism
from the U.S. Department of State.

656

- Terrorists do operate inside the United States as well as abroad, although their activity here appears to be more clandestine and less headline-grabbing. In 1976, 26 percent of all bombings in the U.S.A. were against domestic corporations; 12.5 percent were against banks. And 18.3 percent were against foreign companies. That means that over half were directed against private capitalist institutions. Only a small number were against political factions and individuals. And only 26 percent were against federal and state government domestic offices. (Are you squirming yet?)

The terrorist activity around the world is all the more unnerving when one realizes that there are probably fewer than 3,000 hard-core terrorists in fewer than 50 terrorist organizations. The primary threat comes from four or five groups with a total combined membership of about 200. Increasing economic and political instability worldwide could indeed swell the numbers of active terrorists. *American businesspeople are extremely vulnerable, especially when traveling abroad.*

CHECKING OUT THE BASICS

If you work for a large corporation that regularly sends people abroad, find out if it has taken any preventive measures and/or has developed some kind of organized response capability to such a crisis.

Lloyd Singer, Jan Reber, and Paul Shaw, experts on terrorists and terrorism, suggest the formation of a *Crisis Management Team (CMT)* that will be trained in how to handle a crisis generated by terrorists—and any other unforeseen disaster, man-made or natural.

In addition to establishing a mechanism to handle such problems effectively (this may save your life if it's a matter of delivering a ransom in 48 hours—the CMT will have thought it out in advance):

See to it that appropriate defensive measures are taken to protect you and your family. The days of the muscle-bound bodyguards have long been over. What good is a black belt in karate when you're confronted by a student terrorist armed with a Kalashnikov machine gun?

Terrorist groups, financed by Libya, and booty from bank robberies and kidnap ransoms, buy the best equipment they can. The protection program should be realistic and in line with the risks involved.

If you work for a Fortune 500 company, it is fair to request the facts regarding the executive protection program. Often, you will be briefed by a security expert on counterterrorism measures. If you are an entrepreneur, or an executive for a small company, you may be on your own. So here are some basic points to consider before making that swing through Italy (over 2000 terrorist attacks in 1978) or Latin America (nobody knows how many terrorist incidents take place there).

ARE YOU A POTENTIAL VICTIM?

This checklist was compiled with the assistance of Carmine Pellosie Jr., vice president of Communication Control Systems, a New York–based firm specializing in countersurveillance and protection equipment.

1. *How visible is the corporation you represent?* Is it known nationally? Internationally? Is it familiar to the public, or to the trade only? Has it been involved in any well-publicized or controversial ventures? How are relations with local and national governments, and the community? What has been the extent of the press coverage it has received: general and trade press? radio? television? Do terrorists consider your firm exploitive? What about its products? Does the company make a point of appearing to be tough on security? Is this provocative behavior, or does it seem to be a deterrent? Does the firm publicize its wealth?
2. *How visible are you?* Do you have a high or a low profile? Are your movements noted in the general or trade press? Do you "make a splash" among colleagues or in social circles? Are you known to be well-to-do? Are you considered by many to be a key executive in your firm? Are you the subject of coverage daily? Weekly? Just occasionally?
3. *What countries will you be in?* Some countries carry higher risks than others. In each country you'll visit: How stable is the government? How competent and cooperative is the law enforcement? Is there much terrorist activity there?
4. *How desirable are you as a target for terrorism?* A morbid question, but consider what the terrorists could gain by kidnapping you. The types of people terrorists consider victimizing vary, depending on the cause and the country. For example, women and children are prime targets in Israel, a nation struggling to preserve an ethnic group that was very nearly wiped out by the Nazis. A major target among the English is royalty, because of the "symbolic" importance. Attacks against U.S. "imperialism" by leftists often involve American multinational corporations, which are the most visible signs of the American presence abroad.

   In some countries rarely visited by Americans or other Westerners, you may be a desirable target by default. For example, there are so few Americans in Iran and Lebanon that every U.S. citizen is a potential target.

5. *Consider the motives of the terrorists.* Are they primarily monetary? Political? Religious? Or purely tactical? Often, the motive is a combination of several of these factors.

6. *How available are arms and weapons in the country?* In some countries, one can buy a heat-seeking missile, which can be fired from the shoulder, for a mere $15,000. Not much when you consider that the PLO has a budget of $1 million per day. Such a missile could turn your Learjet into a crash statistic. And what about AK–47s, Uzi submachine guns, etc.? In some countries, possession of a handgun is enough to put you behind bars. In others, don't be surprised to see twelve-year-olds armed with high-powered rifles.

7. *How available is information about you and your movements?* Terrorists need information in order to operate. Unless you take precautions, it is easy to discover your personal and business travel plans, mode of travel, movement patterns, and general life-style, as well as facts about your firm and its security measures.

8. *Will your company protect you? To what extent?* What is the nature of insurance coverage for you and your family should something occur? How much is the company willing to do to insure your safety? This usually translates to "How much is it willing to spend?" As with any other business expense, your company will use some type of criteria to determine what amount of cash constitutes a reasonable security expense, given the situation. Just be sure that it has some means of taking into account the risks involved. It is true that the lower level executive is less likely to be a target and, therefore, does not usually require extensive security protection; but that same lower level executive, when traveling abroad, might be the highest ranking executive within striking distance of a terrorist organization. Even salesmen have been targets of terrorism and kidnap over the years.

9. *What is your primary mode of transportation?* Public? Train, bus, or plane? Private? Automobile? What kind—company limo or rented Fiat? Will you have a driver?

10. *Will you have an entourage?* Perhaps a local business associate will be at your side constantly. Or maybe you will be followed by publicity hounds, journalists, and paparazzi. If the entourage includes business people or government officials, consider whether they might be targets.

11. *How will you be transmitting information?* Phone? Telex? What is the possibility that your communications will be monitored or bugged?

12. *Where will you be working?* Will you be spending your time at the local offices of your firm, or those of a subsidiary? At the offices of a firm with which you are doing business? Or at a hotel

conference room or trade show? It is difficult to generalize about which site is safest. In a nation being torn apart by leftist agitators and rioters, a building owned by Ford, GM, IBM, or ITT might not be such a safe place. But if it's a small group of terrorists that you are concerned about, such buildings, equipped with excellent security, might be much safer than your hotel room, where the complicity of one clerk or chambermaid could place you in danger.

13. *Where will you be staying?* Consider the section of the city and the security of the hotel, home, or apartment. Again, how safe a place is depends on the situation. Sometimes the downtown areas are where law enforcement is most efficient and heavily concentrated, while the outskirts of town are danger zones. In other cases the relative obscurity of a rented suburban home or apartment with good protection systems might be more desirable.

REDUCING THE RISKS

Security experts divide "protection strategies" into two basic approaches. The "low profile" approach seeks to eliminate all forms of attention-getting behavior and property. No flashy limousines, luxurious hotel rooms, or corporate aircraft.

The opposite strategy is sometimes called the hard-line (maximum security) approach. This involves providing the highest degree of protection available for the executive and family. Naturally, the armored vehicles and fortified residences involved will attract attention, but the sheer thoroughness and defense capability of the system is thought to serve as a deterrent. The hard-line strategy costs money and is usually used only by large corporations and wealthy individuals. Besides expensive hardware, it calls for specially trained security personnel who will brief the parties to be protected on what to do and what not to do.

The low-profile approach is within the reach of every executive. It just means being aware of the potential dangers and taking precautions to minimize the risks. But even the low-profile approach should be coordinated with a crisis management team in the home office, so that if something does happen, someone, somewhere, will know what to do.

Remember, when you travel abroad, the U.S. Constitution doesn't travel with you. So you might not get the kind of fair treatment and protection you are used to from local law enforcement authorities.

Here is a regimen of preventive measures generally agreed upon by most security and law enforcement experts:

Limit information. Terrorist activities are usually well planned. Attackers must know a great deal about their potential victims. Don't make it easy for them. Control and conceal information regarding:

- your patterns of movement, and your general life-style and that of your family
- business and personal travel plans, itineraries, and modes of travel
- the location, physical layout, and other details about your office or work site and your residence
- facts about your firm, its subsidiaries, and your personal duties and responsibilities
- details concerning security measures and procedures to protect you, your family, and your residence

Be reticent about such details when filling out hotel registration cards, conversing with strangers, filling out forms, and talking on the telephone.

Vary patterns and habits. Terrorists and other criminals are, by necessity, trained observers. The more you fall into daily routines and patterns of behavior, the easier it is for a crime to be planned and executed against you. Some of the most common patterns are:

- your departure time, travel time, and route to work—or, in the case of your family, to school, social activities, and shopping
- children's play patterns
- your work patterns and the times, frequency, and duration of periods you spend alone

Vary these patterns as frequently as possible. Take care that your variation is not a pattern in itself: Monday you leave for work at 9:00, Tuesday at 8:30, Wednesday at 9:15. An observer will quickly catch on, and know what to expect.

Be alert. People who want to observe you or your family on a regular basis risk making themselves conspicuous. Of course, they will attempt to be discreet, but if something seems strange to you, don't be so quick to dismiss your observation as paranoia. Common surveillance techniques used by terrorists include these phenomena:

- a cruising vehicle (car, bike, scooter, truck) passing in front of your residence or office several times a day or night
- a vehicle parked nearby that looks out of place. If it often has occupants who just sit there, be even more suspicious.
- attempts to case out your home or work site using clever disguises—mother with baby carriage, young couple with children, repair crews, etc.
- frequent phone calls in which the caller asks personal questions, or frequent phone hangups
- survey takers, door-to-door salespeople, bellhops, chambermaids, and waiters

- someone tailing you by car or other vehicle, or on foot. This is done while you are riding, walking, or engaged in recreational activity.

Take precautions when you travel.
- Inspect your car.
- Drive a car commonly used in the host country. And make sure that it has common plates.
- If it is a rented car or a company car, change the car frequently. If you own it, switch often with another executive.
- Vary your routes to work. This holds true even if you travel by bus or train.

Make sure your work site is secure.
- If it's an office, be sure that access is limited, that there is an adequate protection system, and that packages and deliveries can somehow be screened.
- Never work alone after hours.
- If you are working in a hotel, leave specific instructions with hotel security: Make sure that neither your name nor your room number is given out, and give the clerks and security guards a list of expected visitors.
- Do not attend meetings in unfamiliar places, especially when the meeting is arranged by someone you don't know well.

Limit information concerning trips.
- Don't buy tickets too far in advance. Get them at the airport or train station on the day of departure, if possible.
- Don't give affiliations and position to hotel check-in people or to travel agents.
- Most of the problems occur during transit to and from airports or train stations, so get there several hours early. This is not the kind of behavior expected of a busy executive.
- Don't have a chauffeured limousine waiting to meet you upon arrival. Take a cab instead.
- If you have a company plane, don't advertise the fact. Make sure the markings on it are discreet and that you have adequate preflight security. When the plane is parked, make sure that it is sitting in a secure hangar in an area that is well patrolled; or see to it that the plane is equipped with a perimeter alarm system.
- If you travel by train, lock your compartment.

Keep your mouth shut. Do not boast, broadcast information about where you are staying, or say why you are visiting, etc.

Prevention Checklist 1: General

1. Instruct family and business associates not to provide strangers with information concerning executive or family.

2. Avoid giving unnecessary personal details to information collectors in response to their inquiries on behalf of publications such as business directories, social registers, or community directories.

3. Review organization's security plans to determine its effectiveness. Make certain all employees are aware of these plans.

4. Establish simple, effective signal systems which, when activated, will alert business associates, chauffeur, or family members of danger.

5. Be alert to strangers who are on business property for no apparent reasons.

6. Vary daily routines to avoid habitual patterns which kidnappers look for. Fluctuate travel, times, and routes to and from the office.

7. Executives should refuse to meet with strangers at scheduled or unknown locations.

8. An executive should always advise a business associate or family member of his destination when leaviing the office or home, and intended time of arrival.

9. Do not accept delivery of packages from unknown persons unless they have been cleared by security.

10. Do not open doors to strangers.

11. Do not hire domestics without a thorough background check.

12. Try to know where every member of the family is at all times, or where they will be.

13. Know all phone numbers — office, home, police, security headquarters.

14. Set up regular telephone check-in contacts between: Executive and family; executive and office; and executive and security base.

15. Use simple code words to confirm that everything is all right. Code words can be used for executive, family, security officer, parts of the city, etc.

16. Be cautious about giving out information regarding family, travel plans, or security measures and procedures. Use the phone with caution.

17. Report all suspicious persons loitering near the residence or the office, with a complete description of the person and/or vehicle to the police or security.

18. Know enough of the language of a foreign country to ask for a policeman or a doctor. Know how to use the telephone, especially pay phones.

19. Corporate press releases announcing promotions of executives should not list the executive's home address; other information releases should not discuss upcoming travel plans or other activities that might provide useful information to terrorists on where an executive might be at a given time, or on his pattern of living.

Fig. 81. Three antiterrorist and security surveys
(through page 665)

From Jan Reber and Paul Shaw, *Executive Protection Manual* (Northbrook, IL: MTI Teleprograms Inc., 1976), pp. 111a-111b, 143-144. Reprinted by permission.

20. Press releases should be either without photographs of the executive, or else should not show the executive in his office or work location. Use a grey or a neutral background for all photographs.

Prevention Checklist 2: Vehicle Protection

1. Inspect the car before entering. Look for:
   a. Evidence of entry
   b. Tail pipe blocked with explosives
   c. Material in the tire wells
   d. Check the back seat
   e. If packages are found near the car, do not move them. Call authorities.
2. Whenever possible, do not park the car unattended or unlocked.
3. Do not have the company or the executive's name on the car.
4. Park the car in a locked garage; never leave it parked on the street.
5. Park in general reserved areas, not in reserve stalls with executive's name.
6. The hood latch should be controlled from inside the car. The hood should also have a lock. The gas cap too, should have a lock.
7. The executive car should always have at least a half tank of gas.
8. Tamper alarms should be installed on the car.
9. The car should be serviced by the organization or by a local service station that has been given a thorough background check.
10. Never leave keys, other than the ignition key, with a service station or parking garage.

Executive Biographical File Checklist

1. Does file contain full name and any nicknames?
2. Are home address and all telephone numbers (home, office, marina, etc.) included?
3. Are names, addresses and telephone numbers of all neighbors included?
4. Are five sets of photographs, fingerprints and palmprints included in each file? (Two photos should be black and white and three should be color.) Are copies of dental charts included in the file?
5. Are blood types, commonly-taken drugs, and sources of supply for both listed?
6. Are names of school, school officials, location, and school schedules for dependents included?
7. Are profiles of special activities (sports, etc.) included as well as location of usual indulgences?
8. Are written physical descriptions included?
9. Are descriptions of favorite articles of clothing and accessories (sunglasses, cane, etc.) included?

10. Are all regular activities such as church listed with schedules and locations?

11. Are all details of vehicles (cars, bicycles, motorcycles, etc.) listed? (Details should include make, model, year, color, license plate, accessories, serial number, etc.)

12. Are full details and photos of servants and drivers included? (Name, address, telephone, photos, schedule, fingerprints.)

13. Are names, addresses, telephone numbers of family and friends noted?

14. Are names, addresses, telephone numbers and schedule of employment for any working dependent included?

15. Are the names, addresses and telephone numbers of personal lawyer, physician, psychologist, and all other professionals included?

16. Are the names, addresses and telephone numbers of relatives included?

17. Are details of all forms of personal insurance included?

18. Are details of all forms of duress signals and codes included?

FOOTNOTES

1. Arthur A. Kingsbury, *Introduction to Security and Crime Prevention Surveys*, C. C. Thomas, Springfield, 1973, p. 6.

2. Adapted from *ibid.*, pp. 24-25.

Harden your heart to hitchhikers. This is tough, especially if you hitched your way through Europe as a student. But times have changed. And don't be victimized by giving into the temptation of having an attractive traveling companion. There is no law that says terrorists have to be ugly.

Don't leave valuable documents in your car or in your hotel room. Remember that U.S. passports are worth cash on the black market.

Believe your eyes and ears. Cops and soldiers in riot gear are a bad sign: Get the hell away from the area. Chances are they are not shooting a movie. You don't rubberneck in Italy, Turkey, or South America.

Foreign cops are often not nice people. They can tend to be trigger-happy in riot-prone or unstable cities. Imagine being an English soldier in Belfast. To them, all rented cars are suspect, and when they ask you to stop, OBEY.

Dress like a native. You shouldn't overdo it, especially in the Middle East. Just don't look like a rich American or dress in any way that will offend the sensibilities of the locals. If you can blend in with the crowd, so much the better.

Stay in touch with someone at home on a regular basis. Keep that person abreast of your plans, and say when you will be calling next.

Make sure that your company maintains a complete, up-to-date biographical file on you. This file should include:

- *all important names, addresses, and phone numbers,* including those of friends and neighbors, relatives (both at home and abroad), people at the office, country club, marina, etc., and doctors and lawyers
- *several sets of fingerprints, palm prints, photos, and dental records for you and your family*
- *physical descriptions and information on hobbies and special activities*
- *medical info,* including blood type and drugs taken
- *activities you engage in regularly.* Sunday mass, etc.
- *insurance records*
- *duress signals.* Code words that you will use to indicate various types of emergencies

Insurance. At least 25 percent of the Fortune 500 companies carry kidnap insurance. It's maintained strictly on the q.t., because if terrorists or other criminals were to get wind of it, it would surely increase the likelihood of a kidnap attempt. The perpetrators figure that their chances of getting a ransom are better if the payment is covered by an insurance company.

Nevertheless, a quiet inquiry with regard to insurance is a sound idea.

HARDWARE: JAMES BOND
IN PINSTRIPES

For those individuals or companies opting for the hard-line approach to security, there is almost no limit to the number and sophistication of security devices available. That is, of course, if you have the cash. Carmine Pellosie, of Communication Control Systems, tells of a certain gentleman who wanted an absolutely burglarproof, snatchproof, fireproof, bombproof attaché for some papers. He called in the morning, and CCS had one ready, custom made, by the afternoon.

For the more typical executive with more modest requirements, CCS also carries a large in-stock selection of protection devices.

Armor for the automobile. Ninety percent of all kidnappings involve an automobile. It is considered a prime target by terrorists because it contains the victims in a small space, is easy to identify and offers them a wide choice of time and location of attack.

Any car can be armored, even VWs, Toyotas, and Fiats; so you can choose a commonly used car instead of a huge, gas-guzzling American car if you want to keep a low profile. However, as some experts point out, in order to protect against high-powered rifles or explosives, you need a car with additional weight, such as a Mercedes, a large Peugeot, or perhaps a Catalina or a Bonneville (not so uncommon in Latin America). Some security experts prefer working with a car that is two or three years old rather than brand-new, because it has a lower profile. Armored cars have several basic elements: power steering, automatic transmission, high performance engines, air-conditioning, stronger chassis, suspension brakes, four doors, automatic locking, special bolts that won't fly off when hit. Advanced communication equipment is a must. The specifics of armoring include:

- *bullet-resistant glazing.* Bulletproof glass. Recent advances have made certain types resistant to common projectiles such as bricks, rocks, hammers, and steel bars.
- *vehicle armor.* There are several ways to go, depending on costs, allowable extra weight, and degree of protection. Fiberglas and ceramic composites have become popular, because they are lighter than plate steel. A new lightweight steel plate adds only about 600–900 pounds to the car.

- *other measures.* There are gas tanks equipped with self-sealing foam that will not only repair leaks, but also prevent the tank from igniting when punctured; special bullet-resistant tires that are treated with foam (a problem at high speeds), steel lines (not a very smooth ride), or plastic (light, absorbs shocks). Then, of course, you can get really heavy by installing a device that squirts a slippery, oily goo from the rear of the car to slow down pursuers. Or you could add a smoke screen device. Or build in machine guns.

Armoring a vehicle is only part of the battle. Your driver should be trained in evasive and defensive driving techniques. If you are doing the driving, it would be worthwhile to take a course on such techniques.

Armor for the home and office. Hardware for this purpose is usually standard, involving the more sophisticated burglar, fire, and intrusion alarms systems, as well as access control. These systems usually employ a motion detection unit (sensitive to sound, light, vibration, heat), a closed circuit TV system, and smoke and heat detection for fire. Companies often issue special cards that must be used to gain access to its premises. In a nation with lots of violence, "site-hardened" residences often are equipped with bullet-resistant windows and security fences with built-in intrusion sensors, as well as other sensors located near and surrounding the home. (For a more thorough discussion of basic alarm systems, see Chapter 37.)

Body armor. Bullet-resistant clothing worn under or over your own threads. You can even buy bullet-resistant underwear. This kind of protection is becoming so popular that I wouldn't be surprised to see Pierre Cardin create a line of bullet-proof fashions.

If you think you need body armor, you would be wise to consult an expert. The selection must take into account the degree of protection required, the types of activities you'll be engaged in while wearing the armor, your height and build, and the specifications of the armor itself. Often you must make certain trade-offs. After the attempt on his life by Squeaky Fromme, Gerald Ford began wearing a bullet-resistant vest designed to match his two-piece suit. Thus, the armor went unnoticed, but his throat was exposed because of the design of the vest. So he wore a "dicky" under his shirt to protect that area. Naturally, the president did not want his armor to look conspicuous; that would have been quite unnerving.

Today, most bullet-resistant clothing is made of DuPont Kevlar® because it is lightweight, cheap, relatively comfortable and effective. Pound-for-pound, it is five times stronger than steel.

Other types include soft fabric armor and rigid. Rigid types are usually made of Fiberglas, ceramics, steel, or titanium. The soft types are usually bullet-resistant nylon, sometimes combined with other materials.

While the highest degree of protection is offered by the rigid armors, some of them cannot withstand multiple hits: Once fractured by bullets, they lose their resistant qualities. Also, they are heavier than the soft type.

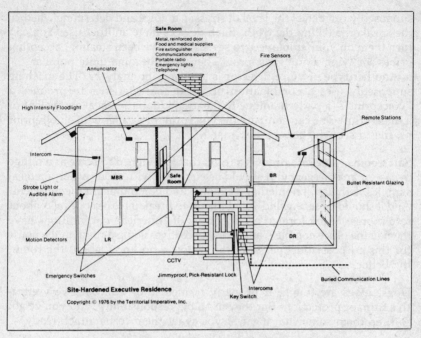

Fig. 82. Executive residence secured against terrorism
The emphasis here is on detection of intrusion.

From Jan Reber and Paul Shaw, *Executive Protection Manual*
(Northbrook, IL: MTI Teleprograms Inc., 1976), p. 125.
Reprinted by permission.

The soft armors are lighter and more comfortable, but some types lose their resistant qualities when they get wet. Soft armor will "give" when hit with a bullet, causing the fabric to "bubble in" toward the wearer, or become stretched or deformed. As a result, the bullet may actually hit the body of the wearer, even though the armor will prevent the body from being punctured by the projectile or fragments. The resulting "bullet trauma" is a drawback of soft armor, since it may involve some injury.

Keep in mind that such armor is not bullet-proof; there is no such thing. Besides, items like jackets and vests offer no protection to the head or limbs, and rarely to the neck. People have been killed wearing body armor. It is a good idea to look at test results for the products you are considering; also take note of the *blunt trauma* figures, *i.e.*, the amount of damage done by the force of the impact of the bullet.

Voice detectors. In the event of a kidnap or extortion attempt, it is helpful to know whether the caller is telling the truth and whether the voice of the hostage is, indeed, the voice of the hostage. There are several voice detectors on the market, portable enough to fit into an attaché case, that supposedly can detect the level of stress in a voice and determine whether the speaker is telling the truth. Such devices have another use: You can turn them on your employees to see if they have been stealing, accepting bribes, or lying about their past. They have become quite popular.

Another type of voice detector is a voiceprint analyzer. The machine supposedly uses a combination of vocal characteristics to produce a "voiceprint"—a pattern unique to the individual; the vocal equivalent of a fingerprint. One can compare the voiceprint of a caller with a voiceprint on file to see whether the two match.

Safe rooms. The safe room is a room that is designed to serve as a refuge in case of an emergency. It should be equipped with food, water, medical supplies, lethal and nonlethal weapons, and communication equipment. And it should be secure and very difficult to break into. No one talks about safe rooms. Many foreign headquarters of American corporations have them in the office complex, and many executives equip a room in the house for this purpose. But the fewer the people who know about the room, the better.

Dogs. Dogs are tough. If properly trained, they will be a very effective form of protection. But they are a big responsibility, and you've got to keep them somewhat mean if you want them to be attack-ready.

Bug alerts. Is there a bugging device in the room? On someone's person? Alerts, which range upward from palm size, may be built into desk sets, humidors, or notebooks. Large-scale sweeping devices are also used.

Tap alerts let you know if your phone is being tapped. Most of these devices are pretty sophisticated, bulky, and costly, but there are a few built into phones, desk units, and even several excellent portable units that are set into attaché cases.

Bomb detectors. Almost all bombs have a trigger device that is hooked to a timer. So a popular type of bomb detector amplifies ticking sounds a thousand times. According to Communication Control Systems (CCS), 90 percent of all bombs involve such time devices, and CCS makes a detector that fits into an attaché. Another type, the *vapor trace detector*, sniffs out the vapors of the gases emanating from explosive devices. (In a demonstration, one of these picked up the cologne on my chin.) Another popular approach is metal detection, which can be very sensitive. X-ray systems are also good, but not very portable.

The letter bomb detector. I love this one. Open the attaché and set up the slide. Just slide the mail through and the sensors will scan the letter for danger. The device usually works by metal or vapor trace detection.

Kidnap prevention. We've all seen Mannix, Bond, et alia use concealed radio transmitters to tail criminals to their hideouts or to rescue kidnap victims. Well, now you too can own your own Kidnap Recovery System. The transmitters are small enough to fit into a pack of cigarettes or on a medallion, or they can be sewn into your suit. Wear several, just in case the terrorists find one. The receiver will indicate relative course, distance, and directional path. An optional alert device will sound an alarm at your "home base" when you activate your transmitter, so someone will know you've been snatched during the first few moments it occurs, rather than when you are noticed missing.

For more information about CCS products and other security services they offer, contact:
Communication Control Systems, Ltd.
World Headquarters
633 Third Avenue
New York, New York 10017

NONLETHAL WEAPONS

The security blanket AL 22 (CCS). This very handy device allows one to immobilize an attacker without doing permanent physical damage. Essentially, it's a flashlight that weighs less than a pound. But it's equipped with what looks like a standard household bulb. But if you look close, you can see that the bulb is really a very oversized version of a flashbulb (photographic type). Even a little olive-pit size flashcube can leave you seeing spots, so imagine what happens when this bulb flashes. "It's as bright," says CCS's Pellosie, "as five suns." It leaves the attacker totally zonked, blind, and disoriented long enough for you to escape. Or, Pellosie points out, you might use the AL 22 as a club. But that would inflict physical harm, no doubt. You can take this device with you when you travel.

Chemicals. You can get spray cans, fountain pens, etc. that squirt CS (a type of tear gas), mace, or some other unpleasant liquid into the face of the attacker, making the person so sick that he will be helpless or will forget all about you, or both.

Stun guns. Electric shock devices. When used properly, a stun gun can knock an assailant flat on his back in an instant by delivering a high-voltage, low-current charge that is immobilizing but nonlethal. Unfortunately, the assailant has to be close enough for you to make direct contact with his body. Several cases of abuses by policemen have created a controversy about the availability of stun guns, and they've been taken off the market in many states.

Stun guns work, and overseas, they could prove very useful.

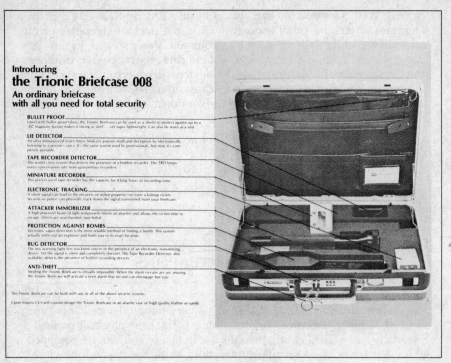

Introducing
the Trionic Briefcase 008
An ordinary briefcase
with all you need for total security

BULLET PROOF
Lined with bullet proof fabric, the Trionic Briefcase can be used as a shield to protect against up to a .357 magnum. Kevlar makes it strong as steel . . . yet super lightweight. Can also be worn as a vest.

LIE DETECTOR
An ultra miniaturized Voice Stress Analyzer assesses truth and deception by electronically listening to a person's voice. It's the same system used by professionals, but now it's completely portable.

TAPE RECORDER DETECTOR
The world's first system that detects the presence of a hidden recorder. The TRD keeps every conversation safe from surreptitious recorders.

MINIATURE RECORDER
This pocket sized tape recorder has the capacity for 4 long hours of recording time.

ELECTRONIC TRACKING
A silent signal can lead to the recovery of stolen property—or even a kidnap victim. Security or police can physically track down the signal transmitted from your briefcase.

ATTACKER IMMOBILIZER
A high powered beam of light temporarily blinds an attacker and allows the victim time to escape. Effects are non-harmful, non-lethal.

PROTECTION AGAINST BOMBS
Electronic vapor detection is the most reliable method of finding a bomb. This system actually sniffs out an explosive and leads you to its exact location.

BUG DETECTOR
The tiny warning light lets you know you're in the presence of an electronic transmitting device. Yet the signal is silent and completely discreet. The Tape Recorder Detector, also available, detects the presence of hidden recording devices.

ANTI-THEFT
Stealing the Trionic Briefcase is virtually impossible. When the alarm circuits are set, moving the Trionic Briefcase will activate a siren alarm that no one can disengage but you.

The Trionic Briefcase can be built with any or all of the above security systems.

Upon request CCS will custom design the Trionic Briefcase in an attache case of high quality leather or suede.

Fig. 83. The incredible "Trionic" briefcase
A traveling security kit modeled after a custom design built
by CCS Communication Control for a special client.

SUGGESTED READING

Executive Safety and International Terrorism: A Guide for Travelers by Anthony J. Scotti (Englewood Cliffs: Prentice-Hall, 1986). This is a practical, well-organized book covering all the basic areas in a comprehensive manner. It is clearly written, sober, but not hysterical. The information is intended to be useful rather than to preach.

The War Against Terrorists: How to Win It by Gayle Rivers (Briarcliff Manor: Stein & Day, 1986). This book is a hybrid. It offers an appraisal of the current terrorist and counterterrorist situations, and offers the author's own suggestions for solving the problem. This makes for interesting reading, and there are some juicy anecdotes included, but it does little for the poor soul who must go to a trade show in Milan. However, Mr. Rivers doesn't let us down. He knows the territory and provides some very useful information on avoiding being victimized by terrorists. He devotes a considerable amount of time to air travel and airport security.

AFTERWORD

PUTTING IT ALL TOGETHER

The last page seems like the logical place to sum up, even though many of you have arrived here without reading the entire book through. My intention was that you *use* this book as a *tool* rather than labor over it as a textbook. I hope that it has provided some assistance so far.

Executive Essentials is about three things: knowledge, experience, and attitude. If I've done my job, you should be more knowledgeable about executive life and methods. You should have a better sense of how, where, and why to get the kind of experience that competitive careers are made of. Finally, you should be inspired to achieve: The difference between the successful and mediocre executive often comes down to the attitude one brings to work, life, and self.

As lengthy as this book is, I've only been able to tell part of the story through it. There are other "executive essentials"—those that are yours alone. I urge you to find them.

INDEX

A

A.A.C.S.B. Membership Directory, 310
ABC News, 199
Absenteeism, excessive, 171
Absolute Theory of
   Management, 2, 284-85
Academics, self-help books by,
   235-36
Accelerator boards, 509
Access America Hotline, 650
Access America Inc., 649
Access control systems, 549,
   552
Accounting firms, executive
   search departments of,
   382
Across the Board, 87-88
Acupuncture, 216
Added costs: 519-21
   drums, 520
   toner, 519
Add-on boards, 509-10
Administrative Management,
   485,521
Admission Council for
   Graduate Study, 311
Adultery, 166
Advertising:
   in periodicals, 104
   for trade show exhibitions,
      639-41
Advertising industry, 454
Aerobic exercise, 192
Aerotitis, 646
Affirmative action, 244, 405
Africa, 373, 647
Agenda for meetings, 16
AIDS, 650-51
Air:
   fresh, 223
   negative-ion environment,
      219
   plants and, 570-71
Airline tickets, 652, 662
Airplanes, company, 626-28,
   662
   analyzing the need for, 627-
      28
   feasibility studies, 628-29

pros and cons of, 626
renting, 628
Air travel, 603-41
   air sickness, 643
   baggage, 613-14
   company plane, 626-28, 662
   connecting flights, 612-13
   countries of questionable
      safety, 633
   cutting down on, 603-604
   direct, 613
   fares, 606-607
   flight book, 607-608
   ground rules for, 606-607
   guides to international, 637
   international currency
      regulations, 634-36
   jet lag, 644-45
   on-board options, 614-26
      business class, 622
      clubs, 623-25
      on-board computer, 626
      Concorde, 623
      first class, 614
      future class, 623-26
      in-flight extras, 614
      nonstop, 612-13
      seating, 620-21, 645
      special meals, 614-20
      user study, 622-23
   on-line travel service, 609-
      10
   overbooking, 608-11
   penalty policy, 612
   planning, 604-608
   reservations, 607
   restrictions, 612-13
   standby, 611-12
   surviving a plane crash,
      629-31
   trade shows, 638-41
   vending machines, 626
   visas, 632-33
   wait-list, 611
   see also Travel problems and
      solutions; Terrorism
AL, 22, 671
Alarms, 25
Alcohol, 157, 176, 216, 645

Allergies, 179
All-News Radio, 68-69, 106-
   107
   listing of U.S. stations, 148-
      49
Altitude and job performance,
   219
American Assembly of
   Collegiate Schools of
   Business, 310
   study conducted by, 315-18,
      320-22
American Cancer Society, 215
American Embassy, 650
American Express, 649
American Management
   Association, 297, 306,
   307, 314
American plan for office
   space, 562
American Society of Travel
   Agents (ASTA), 605
Ammer, Christine and Dean
   S., 111
Amplifiers, telephone, 473
AMR International, 298, 307
Anderson, Bob, 186,230
Angina, 178
Annual reports, 400
Antibiotics, 651
Anticipation and stress, 167
Antihistamines, 651
Anti-terrorism training, 453
Anxiety, 157, 163, 167, 174-75,
   201
   see also Stress
Apartment(s):
   executive, 451
   as hideout, 20
Appearance:
   executive wardrobe, 591-99,
      666
   at job interview, 401
Appetite, 174, 176
   see also Diet; Eating
Apple computer, 511
Appointment calendars, *see*
   Planners, diaries and
   appointment calendars

Appointments:
  being on time for, 25-27
  reconfirming, 26
Aptitudes, *see* Cognitive skills
Arbitration, 261
Argentina, 372
Arguing skills, 266-77
Armor:
  body, 668-69
  for cars, 667
  for the home and office, 668
Arthritis, 179
Arthur Brown & Co., 590
Artificial intelligence, 510
Artificial light, 213-14
Art of Japanese Management:
  Applications for Amercian
  Executives (Pascale and
  Athos), 284
Asia, 647
Assertiveness training, 31
Association as memory tool,
  100
Association of Executive
  Recruiting Consultants,
  Inc., member firms of,
  382-88
Association of professional
  Sleep Societies, 223
AT&T, 533, 539
Athos, Anthony G., 284
Atlas of corporate careers, *see*
  Corporate career atlas
Atlas Van Lines, 363
Atmosphere and your body,
  221
Attache cases, 582-84, 672
Atypical behavior and stress,
  171-73
Audience, public speaking and,
  263, 264, 265
Audio cassettes, *see* Cassettes
Australia, 372, 373
Authority:
  delegating, 285
  power derived from, 289
  risk taking and, 256
Authors, 71, 106
  of self-help books, 233-37
  see also names of individuals
Autocratic manager, 253
Autogenic training, 186
Automated office, 465-81
  computers, 471-73, 475-88,
    525, 527
  convincing your boss to
    automate, 573-74
  copiers, 37, 39, 49, 515-25
  cost trends, 576-77
  electronic mail, 535-45, 604
  environment of, 559-70
  micrographics, 527
  the office of the future,
    467-74

definition of, 467
equipping the, 473-74
importance of, 468
reasons for growth in
  office automation,
  468
reasons for its necessity,
  469-71
what you need to know
  about, 471-73
personal accessories and
  appointments, 581-99
  business case, 582-84, 672
  calculators, 584-87
  pens, 587-90
  stationery, 581-82
  wardrobe, 591-99
security and, 547-57
smart typewriters, 511-14,
  486
surviving in style, 573-80
  adjusting to the office of
    the future, 575-76
  implications of automated
    office, 577-79
  introducing automation,
    573-75
  signs of a "class" office,
    580
  trends to watch in office
    automation, 576-77
word processors, 480-88
see also Data bases
Automatic document feeders
  (ADF), 518
Automatic document feed
  semi-automatic (SADF),
  518
Automatic duplexing, 518
Automatic telephone dialers,
  20, 529
Automobile, *see* Car;
  Limousine
Autosuggestion, 185-87, 243
Aversion therapy, 216

B

Back pain, 176, 178-79
Baker Library, Harvard
  Business School,
  publications of, 109
Balance-sheet method, 23
Bargaining, *see* Negotiating
Beards, 592-93
Beepers, 26
Beer, 647
Behavior modification, 216,
  251-53
Belts, 597
Bennis, Warren, 77-78

Bentley, Trevor, 39
Berendt, John, 403
Best, Fred, 454*n.*
Biases, listening skills and
  your, 91
Biofeedback, 184-85
Biographical file, 666
Biorhythms, 217-18
  scheduling and, 33-36
Birkman, Roger, 245-47
Bliss, Edwin, 22-23, 61
Blood pressure, 191
Bloomfield, Harold, 184
Blunt trauma, 669
Body armor, 668-69
Body language, 92, 260, 402
Body Time: Physiological Rhythms
  and Social Stress (Luce), 33*n.*
Boeing Corporation, 623
Bolles, Richard, 330-31
Bomb detectors, 670
Bonelli, Robert Allen, 481*n.*
Bonoma, Thomas, 8, 11, 253
Bonus wizard, 497
Bonuses, 432, 461
Book(s), 68
  contents page, 71
  dust jacket of, 72
  index of, 72
  personal reference library,
    78, 108-12
  preface or introduction to,
    72
  screening of, 71-72
  self-help, for success, 233-
    44
  suggested readings, *see*
    under individual subjects
Book copying, 517
Bookmark, 491
Book units plan, 447
Boredom:
  automation and, 469-70
  listening and, 92, 94
Boss(es), 289
  company politics and, 296
  convincing your, to
    automate, 573-74
  going over or around the,
    258
Bowker Company, R.R., 110
Braces, 229
Braiker, Harriet B., 157
Brain, human, 83-84, 200
  capacity of the, 83
  improving information
    capabilities of, 83-101
Brain Book, The (Russell), 83,
  242*n.*
Brain/Mind, 78
Breaks:
  permissible, 21, 98-99, 217
  in public speaking, 264
Breaktime: Living Without Work in

a Nine to Five World
(Lefkowitz), 455
Breathing deeply, 187
Breathing exercises, 90
Breathplay, 186
Briefcases, 582-83, 584, 672
British Airways, 623
British Embassy, 650
Brokerage house analyses, 79
Brown, Cecil, 590
Brown, Warren, 590
Brownstone, David M., 108
"Bug" detection, 553
  bug alerts, 670
Bulgaria, 373
Bullet-proof clothing, 668-69
Bureau of National Affairs,
  156, 390
Burnout, 181
Business and commercial
  aviation feasibility/
  justification study, 629
*Business and Commercial Aviation
  Magazine,* 629
Business case, 582-83, 672
*Business Intelligence and Strategic
  Planning and Executive
  Compensation,* 109
"Business Management in
  Japan," 282*n.*
*Businessman's Guide to the Arab
  World,* 637
Business periodical, 69
  major English-language, 137
  selection criteria, 103-104
  see also individual titles
*Business Reference Sources: An
  Annotated Guide for Harvard
  Business School Students,* 109
Business schools, *see*
  Universities
*Business Services and Information:
  The Guide to the Federal
  Government,* 109
Business Week, 51, 69, 72, 78,
  236, 308, 360*n.,* 622-33
Business Week Executive
  Planner, 53, 54-55
Buyer's Laboratory, Inc., 524
Buzan, Tony, 99, 100*n.*
By-pass, 517
Byrd, Richard, 257-58

C

Caffeine-intake, 178, 221, 223
Cahill, Dr. Kevin, 647
Cain, Michael, 184
Calcium, 203
Calculators, pocket, 584-87
  alarm devices on, 25
  features worth looking for,
    586-87

programmability of, 586
  selecting, 584-86
  sizes of, 585
Call-back systems, 553
Call timers, 20
Camus, Albert, 327
Canada, 372
Cancer, 179, 213
Candido, Anthony, 586
Capital Gains, 446
Car:
  company, 451
  leaving valuable documents
    in, 666
  terrorist attacks on,
    protecting against, 662,
    667-68
  working in your, 20
  see also Limousines
CAR (computer assisted
  retrieval), 527
Carbohydrate loading, 199
Carbohydrates, 199
Cardiovascular disease, 206
  see also Heart disease
Career mobility, 351-54
Career paths, 327-416
  corporate career atlas, 343-
    50
    watershed, 347-49
    formative stage, 346-47
    key, 344
    negotiating the heights,
      349-50
    preparatory stage, 344-45
  corporate snoop and your
    privacy, 406-407
  deciding to become an
    executive, 329-32
    charting a course, 330-31
    self-analysis, 331-32
    types of work performed
      by executives, 329-30
  interviews, *see* Interviews,
    job
  job hunt, 377-93
    creative, 392-93
    headhunters, 377-88
    philosophy of, 377
    tactics for, 389
    zeroing in on
      opportunities, 390-91
  narrowing the field, 333-41
    job outlook for the 1980s,
      333-41
    prospects for the
      executive, 335-41
  résumés, see Résumés
  roadblocks in, 355-76
    corporate mergers, 359-
      62, 360*n.*
    getting fired, 355-58
    quality of life and, 365-76
    transfers, 363-64

working abroad, 372-76
trends in, 350-54
  age of specialization and,
    353
  compact careers, 352-53
  current, 351
  in the past, 351
  reasons for mobility, 351-
    52
  women in the work force,
    352
Carnegie-Mellon University,
  314
Carruth, Gorton, 108
Cash control and automation,
  471
Cash value and cash needs,
  determining your, 420
Cassettes, 68, 239
  for memos, 49
  screening audio, 76-78
Cassidy & Davis, 453
Catalogs, 47, 69
Catalyst, 390
Cathode ray tube (CRT), 545
Cattell Press, Jacques, 111
CD/ROM, 499
Cellular phones, 531
Certified Travel Counselor,
  605-606
Cessna Aircraft Company,
  628
Challenge, need for, 245
Challenger, Gray, and
  Christmas, 358
Change, need for, 247
Character assassination, 268
Charitable contributions, 452
Charles Letts (USA) Ltd., 57
Chase Manhattan Bank, 470
Checker, the, 39
Checklist(s), 24, 58-60
  copier, 523-24
  to determine if you're a
    potential victim of
    terrorism, 658-60
  how to make a, 58
  media, 81
  for meeting preparation, 16
  moving policy, 366-67
  as time-saver, 58
Cheeks, James E., 421, 425
Chemistry test, job interview
  and, 403-406
Chief Executive Officer
  (CEO), compensation of,
  and your compensation,
  430-31
Child care, 453
Chloroquine, 651
Cholesterol, 205, 206-207
Cigarette smoke, 215-16
  see also Smoking
CIM (computer input

microfilm), 527
Circular reasoning, 267-68
Civil Aeronautics Board
  (CAB), 611, 620-22
Classification systems, 100
Classifieds, 390, 431
"Class" office, signs of a, 580
Clerical workers, paperwork
  problem and, 38
Clipping services, 70
Clocks, 509
Clothing, see Wardrobe,
  executive
Club memberships, 452-53
  airline, 623-25
Coaching, 253, 391
Coca-Cola, 648
Coffee, see Caffeine-intake
Cognitive skills:
  analyzing your, 331
  success and, 324
  see also Success, skills and
    concepts important for
Colker, David, 230
Collectibles, pens as, 590
Color copying, 518
Columbia University, 312, 313
COM (computer outside
  microfilm), 527
Committees, 15
Communication Control
  Systems, 658, 667, 670,
  671, 672
Communications software,
  488-489
Company-offered seminars,
  308
Company politics, 294-96, 356
Comparewrite, 492
  compatibility, 501
Compensation, 379, 417-64
  abroad, 376
  in Japan, 283
  bargaining for, 459-64
  cash or incentive bonus,
    432-38, 461
  computing your, 430-31
  the corporation's objectives,
    420-21
  job mobility and, 351-52
  perks, 439-57, 461
    deferred compensation
      plans, 445, 462
    insurance plans, 443-44,
      452, 659, 666-67
    miscellaneous, 452
    pension plans, 442-44,
      461
    product, 452
    profit sharing plans, 444-
      45
    stock plans, 446-48, 461,
      462
    top-of-the-line, 451-52

vacations, 454-57
salary factors, 423-29
  in new job, 461
salary range desired on
  résumé, 36
severance, 356-58, 461
taxes and, 421-22, 425-27,
  439-54 passim, 462
your goals, 419-20
Competition:
  need for, 246
  sizing up the, 294
Computer(s), 475-88, 525
  basic advantages of, 476
  capabilities of, 471-72
  communicating, 537-38, 539
  components of, 477-78, 481
  computer output microfilm,
    527
  programs, 478-81
  security, 553
  uses for, 472-73
  see also Automated office
Computer assisted retrieval
  (CAR), 527
Computer based message
  systems (CBMS), 539,
  541-42
Computer input microfilm
  (CIM), 527
Computer output microfilm
  (COM), 527
Comsat General, 542
Concentration, listening skills
  and, 92
Concorde, 623
Conference Board, Inc., 307-
  308
Conference calls, 472, 603-604
Conferences, 469
  as news source, 70
  teleconferencing, 472, 539,
    603-604
  see also Meetings; Seminars
Confrontation, 23, 258
  avoiding, 31
Consensus manager, 254
Consultant News, 382
Consultive autocrat, 254
Consumer magazines, 69
Consumer trends and job
  outlook, 334
Contacts, cultivating for job
  openings, 392
Contaminated food, 648-49
Contingency plans, 22, 257,
  259
Continuing Education Units,
  309
Contracts, 261
  employment, 461
  health club, 197
Contributions, 452

Control:
  of information and
    resources, 291
  lack of, and stress, 168
Control Center, 58
Conventional office space
  plans, 559-60
Converter, the, 39
Cooper, Kenneth, 230
"Copier Review," 524
Copiers, 515-24
  checklist, 523-24
  consciousness of use of, 37,
    49
  copier freak, 39
  survey of what users look
    for, 521-22
  word processors and, 485
Copies per minute, 516
Cordless phones, 531
Corporate career atlas, 343-50
  critical stage of watershed,
    347-49
  formative stage, 346-47
  key, 344
  negotiating the heights,
    349-50
  preparatory stage, 344
"Corporate Moving Policy
  Manual," 366n.
Correspondence, 47, 469
  cover letter for résumé,
    397-98
  defense of paper, 544-45
  junk mail, 48
  with key executives, for job
    hunt, 393
  résumé vs. the letter, 397-
    98
  see also Automated office;
    Electronic mail;
    Typewriters; Word
    processors
Cost of living of major
  international cities, 375-
  76
Counseling and counselors:
  financial, 451
  job, 390-92
  outplacement, 358
  travel, 605-606
Country club memberships,
  452
Cousins, Norman, 601
CP/M, 478-79
Creator, the, 39
Credit cards, 472
  credit card bureau, 652
  telephone, 532
Crises, see Urgent matters
Crisis Management Team
  (CMT), 652
Critical issues in office
  automation, 579

CRT (cathode ray tube), 545
Crystal, John C., 392, 393, 395
Currency regulations,
    international, 634-36
"Customized"
    correspondence, 483
Custom-tailored periodicals,
    104-106
Cutbacks, firing due to, 356
Czechoslovakia, 373

D

D & B Reports, 363
Daisywheel, 506
Dalton Communications, Inc.,
    579
Data bases, 70, 107, 108, 112-
    37, 472
  advantages of, 113
  data base services, 114-37
    sample listings, 117-21,
      122
  disadvantages of, 113-14
  in the future, 137
  software, 493
  uses of, 114
  see also Automated office
Data management, 488
Data transmission,
    automated, 472
Dayrunner, 56
Daytimers, 53-56
Deadlines
  setting, 24, 280
Death benefits, 452
Decision making, "ringi"
    system, 282
Decongestants, 651
Defensiveness, 171
Deferred compensation plans,
    445, 462
Delegation of work, 27-30,
    248-51
  ability to delegate, 246
  daily to do list and, 33
  how to delegate, 27-30,
    248-51
  how not to delegate, 248
  negative, 251
  reverse, 27, 28
  volunteering for
    everything, 251
  when you are the delegate,
    250-51
Denier, the, 66
Denmark, 372
Dependency, job-related, and
    power, 287-92, 293
Depression, 167, 174, 201
Desk:
  organizing your, 41-47

uncluttering your, 40-44
  see also Office space plans
*Deskbook of Business Management
    Terms, A* (Wortman), 109
Desk fatigue, 217
Desk management utilities,
    480
Destroyer, the 40
Diabetes, 179
Dialog, 115, 117*n*.
*DIALOG Information Retrieval
    Service*, 115-116
Diaries, *see* Planners, diaries,
    and appointment
    calendars
Dictating machines, 49
Dictionaries, 78, 109, 110, 111
*Dictionary of Business and
    Economics* (Ammer and
    Ammer), 111
Diebold Group, 137, 475, 577,
    579
Diet, 153, 182, 189-90, 192,
    199-211
  analysis chart, 208-209
  carbohydrates, 199
  cholesterol, 206-207
  of executive women, 156-
    57, 193
  fats, 200
  forgetting food, 223
  minerals, 203-204
  programs, 453
  proteins, 199-200
    analysis chart, 211
  salt, 205-206
  sugar, 204-205
  vitamins, 200-203
  water, 204
  see also Eating
Dieting, 193
"Dimensions of Executive
    Positions," 330*n*.
Dines, Jim, 105
Dines Letter, 105
Dining room, executive, 451
Direct mail, 301
Directories compiled by word
    processors, 485
*Directory of Management Education
    Programs*, 314
*Directory of Management
    Enhancement Programs*
    (Brickner), 314
Disability insurance, 442
Diseases, 213
  diet and, 202-207 *passim*
  heredity and, 178, 206
  stress-related, 178-81
  tropical, 651
  venereal, 650
  see also Health, executive;
    specific diseases

Distractions:
  listening skills and avoiding,
    92
  see also Time management
Distribution, 471
Disturbance bonuses, 453
Divide and conquer method,
    23
Divorce, 166
Doctoral programs in
    business, 312
Documents:
  copying important, before
    traveling, 652
  leaving, in a car, 666
  paperwork problems and,
    38
Dogs, 670
Domestic partners, 453
Donations, 452
Dos shells, 480
Dot matrix printers, 506
Dow Jones-Irwin, 61
Dow Jones-Irwin Business Almanac,
    108, 641
Dow Jones-Irwin Business Papers
    (Tate et al.), 59*n*., 61
Dow Jones News/Retrieval
    Service, 116, 134-37
Drafts, word processors and,
    483
Drake-Beam and Associates,
    353
Dreams, 222
Dress, 591-99
  abroad, 666
  jet lag and, 645
  for job interview, 401
  for men, 592-98
  for women, 598-99
Dress for Success (Molloy), 589
Drinking, *see* Alcohol; Water;
    specific beverages
Drive to action, 247-48
Drivers, 498
Drucker, Peter F., 242, 281
Drug Abuse, 154, 176
Drug Abuse Warning
    Network (DAWN), 216
Drugs, 216, 223
  see also Medication when
    traveling
Drugs in the workplace, 154-
    55
Drum, 520
Dun's Review, 308
Dupont de Paris Chinese
    lacquer coated pens, 588
Dyer, Wayne W., 240

E

Eagle Three Star locks, 547
Ear damage and flying, 646

Earnings, *see* Compensation; Income
Earnings per share (EPS), 435
Eating, 401, 645
  on airplanes, 614-20, 643, 645
  dieting, 193
  executive dining room, 451
  overseas, 647-49
  stress and, 174, 176
  see also Diet
Eaton-Swain Associates, 358, 402
Economist, The, 69
Edge-to-edge copying, 516
Editing, electronic, 473
Education, 2, 297-325
  correlation between success and formal, 324-25
  important knowledge areas, 315-22
    noncognitive skills, 319-22
  overseas, 372
  in public speaking, 265-66
  selecting a school and program, 309-14
    degree options, 311-14
    planning your courses, 310-11
    the school, 310
    the teachers, 310
  seminars, 243, 297-309
    attending, 300
    company approval for, 299-300
    holders of, 297-98, 306-309
    reasons for popularity of, 298
    returning from, what to do after, 300-301
    selecting, 298-99
    sources of information on, 301-305
  study of who gets ahead, 323-35
Educational Testing Service, 329, 330
Ehret, Dr. Charles F., 646-47
  Dr. Ehret's Program, 646-47
Electric Power Research Institute, 373
Electric Wastebasket, 550
Electronic conferencing, 472
Electronic mail, 535-45, 604
  computer based message systems (CBMS), 541-42
  in defense of paper, 544-45
  facsimile ("fax") equipment, 538-39
  TELEX, 537
  trends in, 542

Ellig, Bruce R., 463
EMBA degree, 312
Emergencies, *see* Urgent matters
Emergency medical assistance, 649-50
Emerson Electric, 219
Empathy, ability to balance objectivity and, 246
Employment agencies, 390-92
Employment contracts, 461
Encyclopedia of Associations, 110
Ending meetings and engagements, 16, 25-26
Encryption, 553
Encyclopedic Databases, 115
Energaire, 219
Energy levels, awareness of patterns in, 33
  see also Biorhythms
Energy savings, 539, 565-66
Energy systems, electronic monitoring of, 473
England, 650
Engraving, 582
Environment, 68
  office, 559-71
    office space plans, 559-69
    plants, 569-70
    quality of life and, 372
Escape From Stress (Lamott), 179n.
Esquire, 104, 335, 403
est, 31
Estate planning, 451
Evaluation Interview, The (Fear), 398-99
Executive dining room, 451
Executive Health (Goldberg), 174n., 186, 230
Executive Health Examiners Group, 153, 158-60
Executive Money Map, The (McLaughlin), 420, 445n., 462, 463
Executive Safety & International Terrorism: A guide for Travellers, 672
  (Reber and Shaw), 663n.
Executive Survival Manual, The (Bonoma and Slevin), 8n., 253-54
Exercise, 153, 182, 187, 203, 223, 645-46
  Aerobic, 192
  balanced program of, 189-93
  calories, 192
  endurance, 191
  flexibility, 190
  mood and, 183
  muscle mass, 190-91
  strength, 190

stretching, 190
  weight control, 192-93
Exhibit Designers and Producers Association, 640
Exhibits Schedule, 112
Exhibits Schedule, the Annual Directory of Trade and Industrial Shows, 112, 640
Expectations, 242-43
Experience:
  analyzing your, 331
  on your résumé, 397
Experience/knowledge paradox, 137
Experts, arguing and citing, 268
Exxon, 538
Eye contact, 264
Eye glasses, 229, 593, 651
Eyeguards, 229

F

Facsimile/computer interfaces, 535, 538-40
Facsimile machines ("FAX") 538-39
Fair Credit Reporting Act, 407
Family background, 323-24
"Faster, Faster," 87-88
"Fat-Free Daily Reading Diet," 77-79
Father's occupational status, 323, 324
Fatigue, 201, 202, 203
  desk, 217
Fats, 200, 206-207
"FAX," 538-39
FCC, 531
Fear, Richard A., 398-99
Fear Method of interviewing, 398-99, 402
Federal Aviation Administration (FAA), 631
Federal Communications Commission (FCC), 474
Feedback, 250-51
  biofeedback, 184-85
  Management by Objectives and, 278
  on seminars, 300
Feel Younger, Live Longer, 177n.
Fiber optics, 515
Fichet locks, 547
Fight-or-flight response, 170, 178
Filer, the, 39-40
Files and filing, 469

paperwork problem and, 38
word processors and, 484
Financial calculators, 585-86
Financial counseling, 450
Financial Executives Institute, 424
Finkin, Eugene, 431
Fire(s):
on airplanes, 630
detection and suppression, 554
"Fired! Recoup, Recover and Re-enter!," 402n.
Fire extinguishers, 554
Firing (getting fired), 355-58
the facts, 355
severance compensation package, 357-58
signs to look for, 356
what to do, 356-57
who gets fired, 355-56
Fitness, see Diet; Exercise; Fitness facilities, 452
Health, executive; Physical fitness
Flanagan, William, 396n.
Flax, Isabelle, 589
Flexible benefit programs, 455-56
Fliess, Wilhelm, 217
Flight Simulator, 500
Floppy disk drives, 498
Florida State, 312
Flynn Stationers, M. C., 590
Food, see Diet; Eating
Forbes, 69, 72, 78, 308
Ford, Gerald, 668
Ford Corporation, 660
Foreign travel, see International travel
Form(s):
executive compensation planning, 464
letters, 484
overuse of, 37
Form Generators, 497
Formatting by word processor, 483
Formula value stock options, 447
Fortune, 69, 72, 78, 377, 539, 576
Fountain of knowledge, the, 40
Four-day week, 454
France, 373
Free Enterprise, 78
Free Press, 111
Freud, Sigmund, 217
Frew, Dr. David, 183, 285
Friedman, Myra, 335n.
Fringe benefits, see Perks
Frustration relief, self-help books on, 240

Fuchs, Cuthrell and Company, 358
Full-spectrum light, 213
Future, the:
automated office, see Automated office
information management and, 137
Future Shock (Toffler), 65
Future Shock theory, 162

G

Gale Research Company, 110
Gallup poll, 155
Game ports, 510
Gantz, George, 539
Geis, Irving, 286
General Electric, 219, 548
Generalization, 278
General Motors, 183, 660
Geographical location:
executive prospects and, 336-41
Salary levels and, 424
see also Moving; Relocation, corporate
Georgia Tech, 312
Gerberg, Robert, 390
Germany, 650
"Getting Out in 90 Seconds," 631
Getting Things Done (Bliss), 61
Giegold, William C., 9, 281
Gilbert, Michael A., 266n., 267
Gittleson, Bernard, 218
Glamour courses in management, 312-14
Glasses, eye, see Eye glasses
Glazing protection, 548
bullet-proof, 667
GNP, see Gross National Product
Goggles, 229
Goldberg, Philip, 174n., 184, 186, 230
Golden Handcuff, 448
Golden Parachutes, 436-38
Government:
budget cuts by, 334
business and, 282
regulation by, 334, 471
"Government takes a new look at word processing, The," 487n.
Graduate Study in Management, 311
Graphics Cards, 509
Graphic Sciences, 538
Graphics Software, 489
Graphnet, 482

Greenfield, Meg, 286
Griesinger, Frank K., 534
Grooming, 264
Gross National Product, 333, 365
Growth Resources, 439
Guides to Multinational Business, 637
Guide to American Directories, 110
Guide to Personal Risk Taking, A (Byrd), 257
Gunslingers, self-help books by, 237
Gutmann, M., 375n.-76n.
Gyms, see Health clubs

H

Hair style, 592
Hand-held input devices, 508
Hands, public speaking and, 264
Hanson, Richard, 524
"Hanson's Guidelines...Best Copier Buys for the Small User," 524
Hard disks, 498-99
Harper's, 78
Harper House, 56
Harris, Thomas A., 240
Harris polls, 199, 336-39
Harvard Business School, 237, 287, 311
Harvard University, 251
Advanced Management Program, 313
Program for Management Development, 314
Haskell & Stern Associates, 335
Hatha yoga, 187
Hats, 592
Headaches, 178
Headhunters, 377-88, 431
directly approaching, 380-82
how to talk to, 378-79
locating, 382-88
reasons executives are lured by, 389
services of, 389
targets of, 389
ways to attract, 379-80
Health, executive, 160-230
diet, see Diet
healthy hardware, 197, 225-29
overseas conditions, 372, 649
physical examinations, 158-60, 167, 169, 452, 650
physiology of job performance, 213-23
programs, 452
stress and, see Stress

suggested reading, 229-30
travel and, 643-51
    air sickness, 643
    food, 648-49
    jet lag, 644-46
    medical care, 650-51
    water and other liquids,
        647-48
of women executives, 156-
    57
see also Diseases
Health clubs:
    company, 452
    selecting, 194-96
HealthCare Abroad, 649
Heart attack, 206
Heart disease, 178
    diet and, 204-205, 206, 207
Heart rate, 192
Heat, 214
Hemphill, John K., 329, 330n.,
    409
Heredity, 292
    disease and, 178
    sleep and, 222
Hewlett-Packard, 586
Hideout from interruptions,
    20-21
High blood pressure, see
    Hypertension
High Volume, 521
Hill, Napoleon, 239, 243
Hilton, Jack, 265
Hitchhikers, 666
HMO Plan (Health
    Maintenance Org.), 441-
    42
Hobbies, 307
Hoffman, Marshall, 230
Holmes, T.H., 170-71
Home, 389
    armor for, 668
    working at, 20, 473, 578-79
Home/career conflict, 244
Homosexuality, 166
Honeywell, 548
Hotel and Travel Index, 605
Hotels, 532, 662
    company suite, 451
    as hideout, 20
Housing as perks, 451
Howe, Michael, 98
How to Compensate Executives
    (Cheeks and Wolf), 421,
    425
How to Cut Costs and Improve
    Service of Your Telephone,
    Telex, TWX and Other
    Telecommunications
    (Griesinger), 534
"How to Figure Out Executive
    Compensation," 431
How to Get Control of Your Time
    and Your Life (Lakein), 22

How To Lie With Statistics (Huff
    and Geis), 286
How to Win an Argument
    (Gilbert), 266n., 277
Hubbard, Frank McKinney,
    417
Huff, Darrell, 286
Humidity and plants, 570
Hummel, Charles, 21
Humor, saying "no" and, 32
Hypercalcemia, 203
Hyperresponsivity, 30
Hypertension, 178, 184, 205-
    206
Hypnosis, 216
    self-, 185
Hypoglycemia, 205

I

IAMAT, 650
IBM, 660
Idemitsu, Saizo, 283
Idemitsu Kosan Co., 283
Identification devices, 553
Illinois Duo locks, 547
Image editing, 517
Imagination, 243
I'm O.K., You're O.K. (Harris),
    240
Impact printers, 506
Inc., 78
Income:
    cognitive skills and, 324
    family background and,
        323-24
    IRS's classification of, 421
    see also Taxes
    personality and, 324
    schooling and, 324-25
    see also Compensation;
        Quality of life
Income averaging, 462
"Income, Energy
    Requirements, and the
    Quality of Life Indicators:
    An International
    Comparison, 1979,"
    374n.
Independence, 246, 249, 289
Indexes:
    book, 72
    microform, 526
Industrial Research Laboratories in
    the United States, 111
Industry(ies):
    prospects for executives in,
        335-36
    salary levels in various, 423-
        24, 425-30
Industry Week, 69
Inflation, 373
Infomaster, 124
Information Bank, The, 115

Information Communication and the
    Paperwork Explosion
    (Bentley), 39
Information control, 291
"Information ecologist," 67
Information explosion, coping
    with the, 1-2, 63-158
    data deluge, 65-70
        coping, ways of, 67-68
        negative reactions to
            "information
            overload," 66-67
    improving brain's
        information
        capabilities, 84-101
        memory aids, 68, 98-101
        note-taking skills, 67-68,
            94-98
        reading better, 68, 84-90
    information and the future,
        137
    information ecology, 71-81
        developing your own
            media mix, 79-81
        "Fat-Free Daily Reading
            Diet," 77-78
        screening nonprint media,
            75-76
        screening printed matter,
            71-75
        using your intuition, 77
    information gathering, 103-
        137
        choosing a business
            magazine, 103-104
        choosing a newsletter,
            104-106
        data bases, 112-137
        monitoring All-News
            Radio, 106-107
        personal reference library,
            77-78, 107-112
        research skills and
            resources, 107-137
    news courses for
        executives, 68-70
    see also Automated office;
        Record retention
        timetable
Information-gathering
    techniques, 68
Information junkie, 67
Information Overload Anxiety
    (I.O.A.), 77-78
Information retrieval,
    automated, 472
    CAR (computer assisted
        retrieval), 527
Information sources, principal,
    68
Information storage, see
    Computers;
    Micrographics; Record
    cabinets; Typewriters;

Word processors
Information Utilities, 115
Ink-jet printers, 507
Input devices, 508
Insect repellent, 651
Insects, 648
Insiders, self-help books by, 235
Insight, 247
Insomnia, 174, 176
Inspirational self-help books, 239-240
Insurance, 652
    company plans, 439-442, 452, 659, 666-667
Integrated security systems, 550
Integrity, 293
Interests, analyzing your, 331
Intermedic, 650
Internal Revenue Service, 419, 421-422, 425-427, 439-452 passim, 462-463, 614
International Association for Medical Assistance to Travellers (IAMAT), 650
International Data Corporation, 576
International Directory of Published Market Research, 111-112
International living condition, 372-376
International Meditation Society, 183
International SOS Assistance, 649
"International Terrorism In 1978," 654-656
International travel:
    countries of questionable safety, 633
    currency regulations, 634-636
    eating and drinking precautions, 647-649
    guides to, 637
    jet lag, 644-646
    losing things during, 651-652
    medical care, 650-651
    visas, 632-633
    see also Air travel; Terrorism
Interrupting a speaker, 93
Interviews:
    with headhunters, 380
    job, 398-406
        appearance and, 401
        being aware at, 402-403
        being clear at, 401-402
        chemistry test, 403-406
        coaching for, 391
        Fear Method, 398-99
        learning ins and outs of professional, 398-99

preparing for, 400-01
        questions that may not be asked, 403
        salesmanship, 398
        ten favorite questions of interviewers, 399
    termination, 355-57
Intrusion detection systems, 549-53
Intuition:
    information ecology and using your, 77
    power and, 292
    risk taking and, 256-57
Investory, 470
Ion counter, 219
Ions, negatively charged, 219, 223
Israel, 372,373
"Is This Any Way to Make a Living," 335
Italy, 373, 658
ITT, 483, 591, 660
IVDT, 531-32

J

Jack Hilton, Inc., 265
Jackson, 186
Jackson, Reggie, 218
Jacobson, Edmund, 185
Jaffe, Betsy, 390
Jaffe, Dennis, 184
Japan, 650
    management system in, 281-84
        elements of, 281-84
        suggested reading, 284
    quality of life in, 372
Jencks, Christopher, 247, 323-25
Jennings, Dr. Eugene, 350
Jet lag, 644-46
Jets, *see* Air travel
"Job-Changing Game, The," 390
Job hunt, 377-93
    creative, 392-93
    headhunters, 377-88
    philosophy of, 377
    tactics for, 389
    zeroing in on opportunities, 390-92
Job interviews, *see* Interviews, job
Job mobility, 350-54
Job outlook for the 1980s, 333-34, 377
    prospects for executives, 335-42
        expertise, 335
        by industry, 336
        location and, 336-41

Job-related dependency and power, 287-92, 293
Job-related stressors, 162-66
    good management, 164
    success, 164
    workaholism, 164-65
Job security, 282-83
    corporate mergers, 359-62
    getting fired, 355-58
    transfers, 363-64
Johnson, Samuel, 103
Journals, 236
Joysticks, 508
J.S. & A. Electronics, 219, 587
Junk mail, 48, 484

K

Kaopectate, 651
Kaplan, Heidi, 298
Keso locks, 547
Kevlar, 668
Key words in note-taking, 94, 95, 98
Keyboard, 481, 498, 508
Keys and Locks, 547-48
Kidnap and Extortion Insurance, 453
Kidnap insurance, 666-67
Kidnapping, *see* Terrorism
Kidnap Recovery Systems, 671
Klein Publications, B., 110
Knowledge Index, 115
Korda, Michael, 237, 238, 567
    advice on executive wardrobe, 591-98
Kory, Robert, 184
Kotter, John P., 238-39, 287, 288n., 289, 292n., 293
Kruck, Dr. A., 375n.-76n.
Kuwait, 373

L

Labels, arguing over, 268
Labor force:
    outlook for the 1980s, 334
        see also Job outlook for the 1980s
    women in the, 352
    see also Career paths
Ladies Home Journal, 104
Lakein, Alan, 22-23, 61
Lamott, Kenneth, 170n., 179n.
LAN, 510
Laptops, 510
Larkin, David, 486, 487
Laser copiers, 517
Laser printers, 507
Lateness, 24-27
    how to be on time, 25-26

tips for chronic offenders,
26-27
Latin America, 373, 647, 658,
667
Leadership methods, 253-54
*Leadership: What Effective
Managers Really Do...And
How They Do It* (Sayles),
242
Leathersmith of London
planners and diaries, 57
LeBoeuf, Michael, 23, 61
Lefkowitz, Bernard, 455
Left-handers, pens for, 590
Legal rights:
  airline overbooking and, 611
  to inspect your employment
    records, 406, 407
  interview questions, 403
  to privacy, 406
Letts of London planners and
  diaries, 57
Levine, Sumner N., 108
Lexan, 548
Library(ies), 107, 108
  business, 68
  of the future, 130, 137
  as hideout, 20
  personal, *see* Reference
    library, personal
Libya, 373, 657
Life insurance, 441
Lighting, 213, 548, 569, 570,
  571
Light pens, 508
Light therapy, 213-14
Limitless copying, 517
Limousines, 662
  see also Car
Lipoproteins, 206
Listener, The, 77
Listening skills, 68, 90-94
  arguing and, 266-67
  critical listening, 88
  at job interview, 401-02
  ways to avoid common
    listening traps, 93-94
  ways to be a better listener,
    91-93
Lists:
  compiled by word
    processors, 485
  mailing, 484
  of daily activities, 32-33
  see also Checklists
Loans, company, 451
Local area networks, 510, 535,
  541, 542, 543
Location:
  prospects for executives
    and, 336-41
  salary levels and, 424
  see also Moving; Relocation,
    corporate

Locks and keys, 547-48
Logos, 582
Logs:
  daily time, 8-13, 222
    analysis of, 9-13
  media, 80
  of meetings, 15
  of telephone calls, 18, 533
Lomotil, 651
Longevity, 153
Looking Out For Number 1
  (Ringer), 238
Lorayne, Harry, 240
Lotus Development, 488, 542
Lotus Hal, 488
Lotus Metro, 58
Louis, Arthur M., 218
Low volume copiers, 521
Lower mid-volume, 521
Lucas, Jerry, 240
Luce, Gay Gaer, 33*n*.

M

Mace, 603, 671
Machinery, electronic
  monitoring of, 470, 473
Machlowitz, Marilyn, 164-65
MacIntosh, 479, 509, 511
MacKenzie, R. Alec, 8, 12*n*.-
  13*n*., 61
McLaughlin, David J., 329,
  343, 353*n*.
  on compensation, 420, 421,
    422, 439, 444, 462, 463,
    464*n*.
Macmillan, 111
Macro utility, 480
Magazines, *see* Periodicals
Magnesium, 203-04
Maharishi International
  University, 285
Maharishi Mahesh Yogi, 284
Mail:
  correspondence, *see*
    Correspondence
  direct, 301
  electronic, 535-544
  junk, 48-484
  sorting by ZIP code, 484
Mailing lists, 484
Main points, 92
  in note-taking, 94, 95, 98
Major medical insurance,
  excess, 452
  see also Medical insurance
Maltz, Maxwell, 240
Management:
  books on, 242
  education for, *see* Education
  good, stress and, 164
  see also Success, skills and
    concepts important for
Management accounting, 335

Management by Objectives
  (MBO), 277-81
  definition of, 277
  further information sources
    on, 281
  process of, 278
  requirements for effective,
    280-81
Management by Objectives
  (Giegold), 281
Management by Objectives
  (Odiorne), 277*n*.
Management consultants, *see*
  Headhunters
Management Information
  Exchange, Inc., 109
*Management of Stress: Using TM
  at Work* (Frew), 184
*Management: Tasks, Practices,
  Responsibilities* (Drucker),
  242, 281
Managerial skills, *see* Success,
  skills and concepts
  important for
*Manager's Guide to Copying and
  Duplicating, A* (Hanson),
  524
*Managing Stress: A
  Businessperson's Guide*
  (Yates), 163*n*., 177*n*.,
  180*n*., 186
Manas, 78
Manhattan Office Products,
  586
Mantread, Inc., 302-05
Marcus, Jay B., 184
Margin shift, 517
Marketing, 470, 544, 576-77
Maslow, Abraham, 246
Massage, 186
Master Card, 649
Masters in Business
  Administration, *see* MBA
  degree
Matsushita, 284
Mattlin, Everett, 230
MBA degree, 311
  part-time study, 311
MBO, *see* Management by
  Objectives
MCI, 532, 533
MCI Mail, 123
Medeco, 547
Media checklist, 81
Media log, 80
Mediation, 261
Medical care while traveling,
  650-51
Medical examinations, 158-60,
  167, 169, 452, 650
Medical history, 153, 651
Medical insurance, 441-42,
  452
Medication when traveling,

646, 651
see also Drugs
Meetings, 15-17, 662
  improving, 16-17
  preparing for, 16
  reducing number and
    duration of, 15
Megabyte, 501
Megginson, Leon C., 59n.,
    60n., 61
Mela locks, 547
Memory:
  aiding your, 68, 98-101, 240
  for information and data, see
    Automated office
Memory Book (Lorayne and
    Lucas), 240
Memory expansion boards,
    509
Memory Made Easy
    (Montgomery), 240
Memory typewriters, 513-14,
    486-87
Memos, 282, 587
  on cassettes, 49
Mendeloff, Dr. I., 179
Mergers, 356, 359-62
Merrill Lynch Relocation
    Management, 363-64
Message switching, 535, 542
Metronome training, 90
Metropolitan Life Insurance
    Company, 78
Michigan State University,
    350
Microbook fiche, 526
Microfilm/microfiche, 38, 68,
    526
  COM (computer output
    microfilm), 527
Microforms, 526-27
Micrographics, 525-27
Mid-volume copiers, 521
Midwest Research Institute
    (MRI)
  quality of life study, 365-71
  international, 372-76
Migraines, 178
Milk, 648
Millionaires, self-made, books
    by, 234-35
Mind map, 95-98, 263
Minerals, 203-04, 205-06
Mini-copiers, 520
Miracle Magnetic locks, 547
Mirkin, Dr. Gabe, 230
M.I.T., 311, 313-14
Mnemonics, 100-01
Models, 520
Modems, 477, 488-489, 502,
    507
Modular (work station)
    systems, 562

Molloy, John, 589
  advice on executive
    wardrobe, 591-98
Money books, 239
Money chests, 548
Monitor, 492, 505-506
Mont Blanc Diplomat pen,
    588-89
Montgomery, Robert L., 240
Monthly Economic Report, 78
Moods:
  awareness of patterns in, 33
  exercise and, 193
Morgan Guaranty Trust Co.,
    78
Motels, 20
Motherboard, 509
Motivation, 247
  books on, 239-40
Motivational training, 90
Mouse, 502, 508
Moving:
  costs of, 363-64, 461
  transfers and, 363-64
  willingness to move, 379,
    397
MS/DOS, 479, 490
MS in business, 312
MTI Teleprograms, Inc., 672
Multifunction boards, 509
Multinational Business Yearbook
    and Marketing Guide, 637
Multinational Executive Travel
    Companion, 634n.-636n.,
    637
Muscle cramps, 203
Mustaches, 593

N

National Association of
  Accountants, 301, 308
National Directory of Addresses and
  Phone Numbers, 78, 112
National Information Center
  for Educational Media
  (NICEM), 110-11
National Personnel
  Associates, 391, 405
National Personnel
  Association, 351
"National Recruitment
  survey," 396n.
National Reporter of Job Openings,
  390
National Research Council,
  201
National Science Foundation,
  539
Natural History, 78
Nautilus machines, 197
Neck pain, 176

Negative ion generator, 219,
  223
Negotiating, 258-62
  alternatives to, 261
  for compensation package,
    459-64
    the bottom line, 462-463
    compensation
      planning form, 464
    further reading on, 463
    in a new job, 461
    preparation for, 459-60
    protocol for, 460
    taxes and, 462-63
    time for, 459
    your bargaining position,
      459
  contract stage, 261
  determining if it's
    negotiable, 258
  planning stage, 258-59
  for severance compensation,
    357
  tactics at the bargaining
    table, 259-61
  tips on, 261-62
Nervousness, 176
  public speaking and, 264
Netherlands, 372
Net worth goals, 420
New Aerobics, The (Cooper), 230
New England Energy
  Conference, 78
New Job, see Career paths;
  Compensation
Newman, Edwin, 265
New-product development,
  470
New Products and Processes, 78
New Scientist, 78
Newsflash, 116
Newsletters, 47
  cost of, 104-05, 106
  screening of, 73
  selection criteria, 104-06
Newsnet, 115, 116
Newspapers, 68, 77
  custom-tailored, 137
News sources for executives,
  68-70, 106-07
  for job hunt, 393
  see also specific sources
Newsweek, 68, 77, 286
New Yorker, 78
New York Management
  Center, 298, 308-09
New York State, 403
New York Times, The, 68, 77,
  334n., 336, 390, 395
  National Recruitment
    Survey, 396n.
New York Times Information Bank,
  The, 115, 124

New York University, 297, 308
New Zealand, 372
Niceness, overdoing, 31
Nightinggale, Earl, 239
"No," inability to say, 31-32
Noda, Mitz, 281n.
Noise, 217, 563-64
Noise levels, 568
Noncognitive skills, important, 319-22
Non-impact printers, 506
Non-lethal weapons, 671
Non-print media, *see* Information explosion, coping with; *specific media, e.g.* Radio; Television
Non-qualified pensions, 443
Non-qualified stock options, 446
Nonverbal communication, 92, 260, 402
North American OAG Pocket Flight Guide, 608
Northwestern University, 312, 314, 405
Norton Utilities, 491-92
Norway, 372
Note-taking, 20, 24
reasons for inefficient, 94
skills, 94-98
the mind map, 95-98
sharpening, 68, 95-98
Nutrition, *see* Diet
Nutrition Almanac, 208n., 209n., 211n., 230
Nutrition Search, Inc., 208n., 209n., 211n., 230

O

OAG Pocket Guide, 608
OAG Publications, 607-08
Obesity, 177
Objectives:
delegation of work and, 249
employment, 389
Management by Objectives, 277-81
Objectivity, ability to balance empathy and, 246
Obstinacy, 258
Occupational status:
cognitive skills and, 324
family background and, 323-24
personality and, 324
schooling and, 324-25
OCRS (optical character readers), 527
Odiorne, George S., 277
Office:

on airplanes, 624-25
armor for, 668
automated, *see* Automated office
empty, as hideout, 21
physical working conditions, 213-17
see also Office space plans
security, *see* Security, office
support system, 358
Office landscape, 560-61
Office security, 473, 547-57
Office space plans, 559-68
conventional, 559-60
open, 559-68
design approaches, 562
further information on, 567-68
how to set yourself up in, 566
if one might be coming, 566-68
pros and cons, 562-65
reasons for growth in, 565-66
your needs vs. the company's, 567
Official Airlines Guide, 124, 605, 607-608
Offset printing, 483, 582
Ogilvy and Mather, 265
Ohio State, 312
On-line special services 115-124
Open Office Planning (Pile), 560n., 561n., 567
Open office space plans, *see* Office space plans, open
Operating systems, 478-480
Opportunity(ies), 247, 294, 390-92
Optical character recognition, 508
Optical scanners, 477
Oral communication, 100
job interviews and, 401
public speaking, 262-66
see also Negotiating; Telephone(s)
Ouchi, William, 284
Outplacement counseling, 358
ORBIT, 124
Organization:
of your desk, 41-47
as memory tool, 100
O'Shea, Michael, 197
Overbooking of flights, 608-11
Overburdening yourself, 30-31
Overseas Export Promotion Calendar, 641

P

Packagers, seminars offered by, 308-09
Painkillers, 651
Palestine Liberation Organization, 659
Panel or component systems, 562
Paper(s):
copying important, before traveling, 652
defense of, 544-45
size, 516
for stationery, 581
trays, 517
weight, 516
see also Documents
Paperwork problem, *see* Time management, paperwork problem
Paregoric, 681
Parker pens, 590
Pascale, Richard Tanner, 284
Pay for Performance Policies, 434-35
Payerlee, Laura, 598
Passports, 632, 652
see also Visas
Peale, Norman Vincent, 240
Peat, Marwick, Mitchell & Co., 308
Pellosie, Carmine, Jr., 658, 667
Pens, 587-90
Pension plans, 421, 442-43, 461
Pep talk, psychological basis of, 242-43
Perfectionism, avoiding trap of, 24
Performance appraisals, 435
Performance Dynamics International (PDI), 390
Performance review, 278
Performance shares plans, 448
Performance standards, 24, 249, 280
Performance stock options, 447
Performance units plans, 448
Periodicals, 47, 78, 79
advertising in, 104
business, 69
major English-language, 134-41
selection criteria, 103-04
consumer magazines, 69
custom-tailored, 130
directory to, 110
as news sources, 68, 69, 77-78
publishers of, seminars offered by, 308

screening of, 71-72
trade, 301
Peripheral vision, 88
Peripherals, 505-514
Perks, 439-57, 461
    deferred compensation
        plans, 445, 462
    insurance plans, 441-42,
        452, 659, 666-667
    miscellaneous, 452
    pension plans, 421, 442-44,
        461
    product, 452
    profit sharing plans, 421,
        444-45
    stock plans, 446-51, 461,
        462
    tax advantage of, 451, 462
    top-of-the-line, 451-52
    vacations, 454-57
Personal computer, 475-76
Personal computing, 473
Personal fulfillment, career
    mobility and, 352
Personal strategies for
    Managing Stress, 187
Personality:
    effect on occupational
        status and earnings,
        324
    individual differences in,
        and stress-response,
        167-68
    of successful executive, 245-
        47
Personality problems:
    of others, 17
    your:
        getting fired and, 356
        inability to say "no" and,
            31
Personality testing, 167
Personal reference library, see
    Reference library,
    personal
Personal stressors, 166
Personnel, 485
Personnel agencies, 390-92,
    431
Personnel Journal, 430
Personnel managers, 335
Peter, Henry, 63
Phantom stock plan, 447
PhD in business, 312
Photoreceptor, 520
Phototypesetting, 485
Physical examinations, 158-60,
    167, 169, 452
Physical fitness, 153, 206
    see also Diet; Exercise;
        Health, executive
Physical restraint systems,
    553
Physiological difference,

scheduling and, 33-36
Physiology of job
    performance, 213-23
    aids to staying alert, 223
    air quality, 223
    cigarette smoke, 215-16
    desk fatigue, 217
    drugs and alcohol, 216, 223
    exercise, eliminating, 223
    "far-out" factors, 217-220
        altitude, 220
        atmosphere and your
            body, 220
        biorhythms, 217-18
        pollen, 219
        smog, 219
        weather, 218-19
    food, forgetting, 220
    heat, 214
    light, 213-14
    noise, 217
    seating comfort, 214
    sleep, skipping, 221-22
Pile, John, 560n., 567
Piper Aircraft Corporation,
    627, 628
    travel cost-benefit analysis
        and cash flow, 629
Planners, diaries, and
    appointment calendar, 51-
    57
    features looked for in, 51-52
    features not wanted in, 52-
        53
    pocket planners, 53
    recommended, 57
Planning:
    business trips, 604-08, 644-
        45
    Management by Objectives,
        277-81
    poor, 30
    for trade show exhibiting,
        639
    urgent matters and, 22
Plants, indoor, 569-71
Platen, 516
Playboy, 104
Pocket planners, 53
Poe, Randall, 87
Poland, 373
Police in foreign countries,
    666
Politics, company, 294-96, 356
Pollen, 219
Portfolios, 582-83, 584
Positive thinking, 242-43
Postal Service, 542
Posture, 264
Potassium, 203
Power, 287-96
    abuses of, 293
    books on, 237-38
    company politics,

294-96, 356
    illusion of, 290
    and job-related dependence
        on others, 287-92
    need for, 245, 293-4
    power games, 289, 293-94
    risk taking and, 256-57
    tactics of, 290-93
Power! How to Get It, How to Use
    It (Korda), 237, 238
Power in Management (Kotter),
    237-38, 288n., 292n.
Power Management, 569
Power of Positive Thinking, The
    (Peale), 240
Power structure, corporate,
    428
Practice of Management, The
    (Drucker), 242
Pre-select capacity, 516
Preference income, 421
"Preferences on worklife
    scheduling and work
    leisure tradeoffs," 454
"Prescription for Information
    Overload Anxiety," 77n.
Prejudices, listening skills and
    your, 91
Previewing technique, 73-74
"Prices and Earnings Around
    the Globe," 375n.-376n.
Prime Time, 57-58, 490-91
Printed matter, see
    Information explosion,
    coping with; specific types of
    printed matter, e.g., Books(s);
    Newspapers; Trade
    journals
Printers, 506-07
Printer spoolers, 509
    see also Engraving; Offset
        printing;
        Phototypesetting;
        Thermography
Priorities:
    analyzing your personal,
        331-32
    computer based message
        systems and, 541-42
    setting, 23-24
    in daily to do list, 32
    overburdening yourself
        and, 31
    at trade shows, 638-39
Pritikin, Nathan, 206-07
Privacy, 455
    corporate snoop and the job
        hunt, 406-08
    in open office, 563
Privacy: How to Protect What Is
    Left of It (Smith), 406-08
Procrastination, 22-24, 171
Productivity, 467, 468, 469,
    485, 486, 574

open office and, 564-65
Productivity experts, 473
Product perks, 452
Product testing techniques, advanced, 547
Professional associations, 301
  dues, 452
  seminars offered by, 308
Professional Job Changing System, The, 390
Profit sharing plans, 444-445
Programming, 471, 478-81
  calculators, 586
Progressive Relaxation, 185-86
Promotions, 461
  in Japan, 283
  transfers and, 363, 364
Project management, computers and, 473
Project management software, 489
Proteins, 199-200
Proxy statements, 431
Psycho-cybernetics (Maltz), 240
Psychological problems:
  lateness and, 27
  of open office, 564
Psychology Today, 78, 454
Public speaking, 262-66
  after the talk, 265
  giving the talk, 264-65
  preparing for, 262-64
  professional advice on, 265-66
Publishing industry, 454
Pulse rate monitors, 229
Publishers:
  reference book, 107
  seminars offered by, 308
  see also names of specific publishers
Punctuality, 24-27
  how to be on time, 25-26
  tips for chronic lateness, 26-27
Punishment, behavior modification and, 252-53
Purchasing agents, 473
Pygmalion effect, 242

Q

Qualified stock options, 446
Quality of life, 365-76
  components of, 365, 368
  transfers and, 363-66
  within the U.S., comparisons, 365-71, 372, 373
  working abroad, 372-76
  see also Compensation; Income

Quality of Life Indicators in the U.S. Metropolitan Areas, 1970, 365-71
Quality of printed matter, evaluating, 74-75
Quality of work, decline in, 171
Quest, 78
Questionnaire on activities and responsibilities of the executive, 409-16
Quitting, threat of, 257
Quiz, workaholic, 165-66
Qwip, 538

R

Race, 323, 405
Radio, 68
  All-News, 68-69, 106-07
  screening of, 76
Rahe, R. H., 170-72
RAM resident, 490
Rand Corporation, 653
Random House Dictionary, 78
Rapid reading, *see* Reading, rapid
Reader, the, 39
Reader's Digest, 219
Reading, 68, 84-90
  myths and truths about, 84-85
  problems associated with, 85-86
  rapid, 86-90
    basic principles of, 88-90
    pros and cons of, 86-88
  screening materials, 71-76
  skimming technique, 73
  see also Information explosion, coping with the
Reading courses, 86, 90
Real estate brokers, 515
Reality avoidance, 171
Reber, Jan, 589, 597n., 604
Recirculating Document Handlers (RDH), 519
Recommended Dietary Allowances (RDAs), 201
Record cabinets, 554
Records retention timetable, 42-46
"Records Retention Timetable," 46n.
Recruiters, *see* Headhunters
Redbook, 104
Redoing projects, doing it right the first time, 24
Reduction/enlargement, 516
Reedy, George, 265
Reference book publishers, 108-112

see also names of individual publishers
Reference library, personal, 78, 108-112
Reference services, 68
Regulation, 334, 471
Rehearsing:
  for negotiating, 259
  for public speaking, 263-64
Reinforcement, 251-53
Relaxation techniques, 167, 180-87
Religion, 323, 324
Religious retreats, 21
Relocation, corporate, transfers and, 363
  see also Moving
"Relocation Blues," 364n.
Relocation policy, corporate, 364
REM, 222
Reminders, 32
Rene Plessner Associates, 454
Reputation, 290-91
Research Centers Directory, 111
Researcher's Guide to Washington, A, 109-110
Research organizations, 108
  directories to, 111-12
Research skills, 107
Research sources, 107-137
  see also specific sources
Research Triangle Institute, 154
Reservations, airline, 607
Resource control, 291
Responsibility, 289
  delegation of work and, 28, 246, 248, 249
  Management by Objectives and, 280
Restricted stock plans, 448
Rest room, 20-21
Résumé(s), 395-98
  copy and layout, 395-97
  cover letter for, 397-98
  for headhunters, 380-82
  sample, 396
  targeting companies for, 393
  vs. the letter, 397-98
Retention of information, *see* Memory; Records retention timetable
Retirement, 282-83, 443
  see also Pension plans
Return on equity (ROE), 435
Reversionist, the, 66
Reviews of television programs, 75
Rewards, behavior modification and, 251-52
Richard Hanson & Associates, 524

Ringer, Robert, 238
"Ringi" system of decision making, 282
Risk analysis, 445
Risk international, 653
Risk taking, 249, 255-58, 291, 294
    examination of, 255-56
    four major risks, 257-58
    how to take risks, 256-58
Roadblocks in career paths, 355-76
    corporate mergers, 359-62
    getting fired, 355-58
    quality of life and, 364-76
        working abroad, 372-76
    transfers, 363-364
Role conflict and ambiguity, 166
Role playing, 259
Royal Canadian Air Force Plans for Physical Fitness, 230
Ruff, Howard, 105
Ruff Times, 105
Running Away From Home (Colker), 230
Russell, Peter, 83, 99, 214, 242n.
Russell, Richard, 105
"Russian Know How," 254

S

Sabbaticals, 455
Safe rooms, 670
Safes, 548
Salary, *see* Compensation
Sales, 470
Sales and Marketing Magazine, 112
Salt, *see* Sodium
Sam Flax, Inc., 589
S. A. M. Management Journal, 247
San Diego State, 312
Sarcasm, 32
Sargent locks, 547
Sarnoff, Dorothy, 265
Satellite Business Systems (SBS), 542
Satellite communications, 130
Saudi Arabia, 373
Savvy, 598
Sayles, Leonard, 242
SBS (Satellite Business Systems), 542
Scandinavia, 650
Scanners, 508
Schedule(ing):

leaving room in, 26, 30, 646
    physiological differences and, 33-36
    the to do list, 32-33
    word processors used for, 483-86
Schiff, Robert, 485
Schools, *see* Education; Universities
Schuller, Robert, 240
Schultz, Johannes H., 186
Schuster, Jay, 457
Schwartz, Tony, 90
Schweitzer, Albert, 160
Science, 78
Scientific American, 78
Scientific calculators, 584-86
Scott, Charles R., Jr., 60n., 62
Scotti, Anthony J., 672
Screening:
    of nonprint media, 75-76
    of printed matter, 71-75
    of telephone calls, 18
Scurvy, 202
SDC Search Service of System Development Corporation, 124
Search firms, *see* Headhunters
Seating comfort, 214
Secretary, 485, 486
    appointments and, keeping you on schedule, 26-27
    office politics and, 296
    screening of phone calls by, 18
Securities and Exchange Commission, 106
Security:
    job, *see* Job security
    national, 372-73
    office, 473, 547-49, 662
        buying, 553-554
        basic points about, 547
        equipment, 547-49
        fire detection/supression, 554
        guide to security organizations, 555-57
        types of systems, 549-550, 551-52
    telephone, devices, 531-32
    terrorism, 653-671
Sedentary life-style, 157
See You at the Top (Ziglar), 240
Self-analysis, 331-32, 389
Self-confidence, saying "no" and, 31
Self-help books, 233-44
    authors of, 233-36
        gunslingers, 237
        insiders, 235
        school boys, 235-36
        self-made millionaires, 234-35
        technicians, 236

categories of, 237-42
    inspirational, 239-40
    on money, 238
    on power, 237-38
    on relief from frustration, 240
    on specific skills, 240-242
    about success, 238, 241
    common errors of, 244
    psychological basis of the pep talk, 242-43
    women's success materials, 243-44
Self-hypnosis, 185-86
Self Love (Schuller), 240
Selye, Dr. Hans, 161, 174, 175, 177, 180
Semiconductor memory chips, 477
Seminars, 297-309, 639
    attending, 300
    company approval for, 299-300
    geared to women, 243
    holders of, 297-98
        big names in, 306-08
        others in the field, 308-09
    as news source, 70
    reasons for popularity of, 298
    returning from, what to do after, 300-301
    selecting, 298-99
    sources of information on, 301-05
Serial copying, 517
Serotonin, 219
Service:
    copy kit, 520
    on call, 520
    contract, 520
Service industries, prospects for executives in, 336-37
Set, 242
Severance compensation, 356-57, 461
Sexual dysfunction, 179
Sexual harassment, 244
Shared offices, 579
Shareholder manager, 254
Shaw, George Bernard, 287
Shaw, Paul 657, 663n., 671
Sheaffer pens, 589
Shirts, 595-96
Shockley, William, 268
Shoes, 597-98
Shredders, 550
Sick pay, 442
Sidekick, 58
Singer, Lloyd, 657
16mm Educational Films Index, The, 110
Skimming, 73, 86
Skinner, B. F., 251

Skirts, 598
Sleep, 174, 176, 203, 401
  insomnia, 174-76
  jet lag and, 644-45, 646
  -reduction program, 222
  skipping, 221-22
Sleeping pills, 651
Sleep Less, Live More (Mattlin),
  230
Slevin, Dennis, 8, 11, 253
"Small things" syndrome,
  32-33
Smart buildings, 578
Smart copiers, 393
"Smart" information systems,
  470
Smart People (Spooner), 290
Smith, Robert Ellis, 406
Smithsonian, 78
Smog, 219
Smoke alarms, 554
Smokenders, 215
Smoking, 157, 176, 215-16,
  222
  on airplanes, 620-22, 645
  stress and, 176
Smolowe, Jill, 395, 397
Snake bite kits, 651
Social context of a situation
  and stress, 168
Social Readjustment Rating
  Scale, 172-73
"Social Readjustment Rating
  Scale, The," 172*n.*
Social Security benefits, 442
Socks, 597
Sodium, 204, 205-206
Soft drinks, 647-48
Software, *see* Programming
Solar power, 587
Sorters, 518
Souped-up phones, 531
Source Telecomputing
  Corporation, 123-25
South Africa, 373
Soviet Union, 372, 373, 650,
  657
Spas, *see* Health clubs
Speaker phones, 20, 530
Specialist, the, 66
Specialization and career
  planning, 353-54
Specialized databases, 114
Speech Dynamics and
  Communications
  Services, Inc., 265-66
Speeches, *see* Public speaking
Spock, Dr., 268
Spooner, John, 290
Sport jackets, 594
Sports, 153
Sports Illustrated, 78
Sportsmedicine (Mirkin and
  Hoffman), 230

Sports Training Institute, 197
Spouse, transfers and, 364
Spreadsheets, 487-88
Sprinklers, 554
Sprint, 532
Staff, news gathered by, 69
Standards of performance, *see*
  Performance standards
Standard and Poor's Register, 393
Standby, flying, 611-12
Stanford Graduate School of
  Business, 311, 312-13
Standard Metropolitan
  Statistical Areas
  (SMSAs), comparisons of,
  365-71
Standard of living, 365, 372
  see also Compensation;
    Income; Quality of life
Static electricity, 569
Stationery, 581-82
Statistical Bulletin, 78
Statistics, 286
Steelcase, 567
"Steelcase National Study of
  Office Environments,
  The," 567
Stein, David Lewis, 5
Stewart Baeder Associates, C.,
  405
Stock appreciation rights
  (SARs), 447
Stock plans, 445-48, 461
Stock purchase plan, 447-48
Storage media, 498
*Strategic Planning and the MBO
  Process* (Giegold), 9
Streaming Tape Backups, 499
Stress, 68, 154, 161-87, 189,
  206
  causes of, 162-67
    anxiety and depression,
    167
    job-related stressors,
    162-66
    personal stressors, 167
  definition of, 162
  disease and disorders
    related to, 178-80
  effects of, 169
  misconceptions about, 162
  physical and mental distress
    signals, 174, 175
  poor solutions to, 176-77
  primary symptons of, 174-
    76
  reasons situations become
    "stressors," 167-68
  secondary symptoms of,
    174-76
  stress reduction and
    relaxation techniques,
    182-87
    autogenic training, 186

    biofeedback, 184-85
    breathing deeply, 186
    massage, 186
    progressive relaxation,
    185-86
    self-hypnosis and
      autosuggestion, 185
    stretching, 186
    transcendental
      meditation, 182-84
    yoga, 187
  warning signs, 169-173
    atypical behavior on the
    job, 171, 173
    fight-or-flight response,
    169-70, 178
    life changes, 170-71
Stretching, 186
Stretching (Anderson), 186, 230
Stroke, 178
"Study of Recent Air
  Travelers," 623*n.*
Stun guns, 671
*Subliminal suggestions and self-
  hypnosis programs,* 497
Success, 231-325
  education and, 2, 273-301
    Continuing Education
    Units, 309
    important knowledge
    areas, 315-322
    in public speaking, 264-66
    selecting a school and
    program, 309-314
    seminars, 297-309
    study on who gets ahead,
    323-25
    teaching, 314-15
  power and, *see* Power
  self-help books, 233-44
    authors of, 233-237
    categories of, 237-242
    common errors of, 244
    psychological basis of the
    pep talk, 242-43
    women's success
    materials, 243-44
  skills and concepts
    important for, 245-86,
    315-22
    Absolute Theory of
    Management, 2,
    284-85
    arguing, 266-77
    behavior modification,
    251-53
    delegating, 248-51
    Japanese management
    system, 281-84
    leadership methods,
    253-54
    Management by
    Objectives, 277-81
    negotiating, 258-62

noncognitive, 319-22
personality traits of
    successful executives,
    245-47
public speaking, 262-66
risk taking, 254-258
statistics, 286
stress and, 162-67
Success!(Korda), 238
Successful Meetings magazine,
    640
Success Motivation Institute,
    640
Sugar, 204-05
Suicide, 454
Sunlight, 213
    see also Lighting
Supportiveness, 250
Suskin Koyo, 282-83
Supersimplifier, the, 66-67
Surgeon General, 155
Surveillance intrusion
    systems, 549
Surveillance techniques of
    terrorists, 661-62
Survey of Buying Power, 112
"Survey of Corporate Moving
    Practices," 363
Suspiciousness, excessive, 171
Sutcliffe, Jon, 457
Swain, Madeleine, 402
Sweden, 372
Switchboards, 532
Switzerland, 372, 373, 650
System box, 500

T

Ta, 31
Tactfulness, risk taking and,
    257
Taiwan, 372
Talents, analyzing your, 331
Tap alerts, 670
Targets of creative job hunt,
    393
Tate, Curtis E., Jr., 60*n.*, 61
Taxes, 614
    compensation packages and,
        419, 421-22, 425-27,
        439-52 *passim*, 462-63
    "shelters," 462
Tax-offset stock options, 447
Tax Reform Act of 1986, 446,
    447
Teachers:
    selection of, 310
    teaching business courses,
        314-15
Technical publications,
    selection criteria, 105
Technicians, self-help books
    by, 236
Technology, *see* Automated

office
Telecomputing Corporation of
    America, 124
Teleconferencing, 472, 539,
    603-604
Telematique, 137
Telephone(s), 17-20, 469, 473,
    529-34, 580
    abuse of, 17-18
    answering devices, 20,
        529-30
    automatic dialers, 20,
        529-30
    conference calls, 472, 603
    data base involving, 137
    electronic conferencing, 472
    service, things to remember
        about, 532-34
    souped-up , 531
    suggested reading, 533-34
    tap alerts, 670
    timing devices, 530-31
    using, to eliminate
        paperwork, 37, 49
    ways to cut time on, 18-20
    wireless, 20
Telephone call log, 18, 532
Telephone consultants, 533
Teletex, 535, 537
Teletext, 136-37
Television, 68
    on airplanes, 626
    data bases involving, 136-37
    public speaking, training
        for, 265-66
    screening, 75-76
Telex, 537
Temper, controlling your, 94
Temperature, room, 214, 570
Termination interview, 356-
    57
Terrorism, 653-71
    antiterrorist and security
        surveys, 663-65
    basic facts about, 653-57
    checking out the basics,
        657-58
    checklist to determine
        likelihood of being a
        victim, 658-60
    hardware for security
        against, 667-71
    reducing the risks, 660-67
Texas Instruments, 549-586
Text editing typewriters, 513-
    14, 480, 486
Thacker, Dr. Steven, 215
*Theory Z: How American Business
    Can Meet the Japanese
    Challenge* (Ouchi), 284
Thermal printers, 506
Thermography, 582
TH Inc. Consulting Group,
    358

Think and Grow Rich (Hill), 239
3M, 538
Thrift or savings plans, 444
Ties, 596-97
Time/design, 54-55, 57
Time, poor estimation of, 30
Time logs, 8, 9, 10, 33, 222
    planner and, 53
Time magazine, 68
Time management, 1, 5-62,
    469, 473
    books on, suggested, 61-62
    intangibles in, 11
    paperwork problem, 39-49
        the cluttered desk, 40-41
        the culprits, 39-40
        cutting down on, 49
        organizing your desk,
            41-47
        the paper test, 38-39
        personal paperflow
            system, 47-48
        symptoms of, 37-38
    time wasters, tackling,
        15-36
        the break, 21
        daily to do list, 32-33
        the hideout, 20-21
        inability to say no, 31-32
        ineffective delegation,
            27-30
        lateness, 24-27
        meetings, 15-17
        physiological differences
            and your schedule,
            33-36
        poor planning, 30
        procrastination, 22-24
        taking on too much, 30-
            31
        telephones, 17-20
        urgent matters, 21-22
    tangibles in, 11
    tools to save time with,
        51-61
        checklists, 58-61
        planners, diaries and
            appointment
            calendars, 51-58
        suggested reading, 61-62
        word processors, 485
    see also Automated office
Time management software,
    52, 57-58
Time Trap, The (MacKenzie),
    12*n.*-13*n.*, 61
Time wasters, *see* Time
    management, time
    wasters, tackling
TM, *see* Transcendental
    Meditation
TM and Business (Marcus), 184
*TM: Discovering Inner Energy and
    Overcoming Stress*

(Bloomfield et al.), 184
TM Program: The Way to Fulfillment, The (Goldberg), 184
Toffler, Alvin, 65, 66-67
Toiletries, 645
Toner, 515, 519
Toner replacement, 515
Tornado Notes, 58, 491
Toshiba, 523*n*.
Touchpads, 508
Trade associations, 301, 308, 431
  dues, 452
Trade journals, 301, 431
  screening of, 73
  selection criteria, 104
Trade shows, 638-41
  information sources, 640-41
Training offices, company, 277
Transactions, electronically processed, 472-73
Transcendental meditation, (TM) 182-84, 285
  suggested reading, 184
Transfers, 363-64
  circumstances of, 363
  responding to notice of, 362-64
Transportable computers, 510
Transportation, Analysis Plan (TAP), 628
Travel, 3, 601-71
  air, 603-41
  alternatives to, 544, 603-604
  problems and solutions, 643-52
  terrorism and, 653-71
  vacations, 454-55
Travel agents and agencies, 604-606, 607
Travel Assistance International, 649
Traveler's cheques, 632
Travel guides, 637
Travelling Sidekick, 58, 491
Travmed-Medex, 650
Trends in Employee Benefits, 454-55
Tressider, Jack, 177*n*.
Triglycerides, 206
Trim and Mask Features, 517
Trueblood, Lyle R., 60*n*.
Trust, 28, 250
TWX, 535, 537
Type E-Stress Cycle, 157
Typewriters, 511
  electronic, 511-13, 514,
  memory, 511-13, 514
  purchasers of, 514
  vs. word processors, 486-87
Typing, backlog of, 37

Tyranny of the Urgent (Hummel), 21*n*.

U

Ulcers, 176, 179
Ulrich's International Periodicals Directory, 110
Undine Corporation, 111
United Airlines, 620, 621*n*.,
United States:
  quality of life in, 365-71, 372, 373
  standard of living in, 365
UNIX, 479
Upper Mid/Volume copiers, 521
U.S. Department of Commerce, 641
  Office of Administrative Services and Procurement, 486
U.S. Labor Department, 334
U.S. News and World Report, 68, 72
U.S. State Department, 633
Universal machines, 197-98
Universities:
  graduate programs of, 311-14
  seminars offered by, 297, 301, 308-309
  see also Education; *names of individual institutions*
University of California at Berkeley, 314
University of Chicago, 308, 314
University of Massachusetts, 312
University of North Carolina, 314
University of Pittsburgh, 253
University of Southern California, 312
University of Virginia, 314
Unpredictability and stress, 168
Updating capabilities of word processors, 484
Urgent matters, 21-22
Use Both Sides of Your Brain (Buzan), 96*n*.-97*n*.
User friendly, 511
U.S.S.R., *see* Soviet Union
Utilities programs, 489-90
Uzzell-Rindlaub, Sarah, 631

V

Vacations, 454-57
Vanocur, Sander, 265

Variable-priced stock options, 447
VCRs, *see* Videotape recorders
Venereal diseases, 650-51
Venezuela, 373
Venture, 78
Vibration sensor, 548
Video cassettes, *see* Cassettes
Video teleconferencing, 535, 539-40
Videotape recorders (VCRs), 76, 79
Viewdata, 137
Visa agencies, 632
Visas, 631-32
Viscott, David, 174
Visibility, 267, 380, 658
Visuals for a speech, 263, 264
Visualizing, 243
  as memory aid, 100-101
Vitamin B12, 202-03
Vitamin C, 202
Vitamin D, 203, 213
Vitamin E, 202
Vitamins, 200-203
  the "in" vitamins, 201-203
Vogue, 77
Voice Mail, 540-41
Voice Memo, 540-41
Voice, public speaking and, 264
Voice detectors, 669-70
Voltaire, 67

W

Wait-list, airline, 611
Wall Street Journal, 68, 69, 72, 254, 364, 390, 446, 587
Want ads, 390, 431
War Against Terrorists: How to Win It, The, 672
Wardrobe, executive, 591-99
  abroad, 666
  jet lag and, 644-45
Wardrobe consultants, 591-92
  for job interview, 401
  for men, 592-98
  for women, 598-99
Washington Post, The, 68
Washington Researchers, 109-110
Wats, 532
Water, 204, 647
  purification tablets, 651
Watson-Guptil, 567-68
Weather and job performance, 218-19
Western Union, 123, 535, 537, 541
West Germany, 372
Wharton School of Business, 297, 308, 311, 314

What Color is Your Parachute? (Bolles), 330-331
"What Sets an Executive Apart From His Peers," 245*n.*, 248
What to Buy for Business, 525
Where to Find Business Information (Brownstone and Carruth), 108
Whitehead, Alfred North, 465
Who Gets Ahead? The Determinants of Economic Success in America (Jencks), 247, 323, 324*n.*
Whyte, Anthony, 298
Wilson, Earl, 231
Wine, 648
Winning Through Intimidation (Ringer), 238
Wireless telephones, 20, 473
Wolf, Gordon D., 421, 425
Wolff, Dr. Harold, 178
Wood, Evelyn, 86, 90
Women, 405
  dieting, 193
  executive:
    health and, 156-57
    job outlook for, 335

success materials for, 243
wardrobe for, 598-99
in the work force, 352-53
Word Processing, 483-87
Word Processing Utility Programs, 489-96
Word processors, 480-88
  vs. automatic typewriters, 486-87
  components of, 477-78
  the bottom line, 488
  capabilities of, 480
  case for, 483-86
  companies that need, 486
Workaholics (Maclowitz), 165-66
Workaholism, 164-65, 221
Work environment, 68
Work overload, 165-66
Work stations, 510
Working Smart (LeBoeuf), 61
Working Woman, 598
Workmen's compensation, 442
Work performed by executives, 329-30, 409-16
World Plan Executive Council, 285

WorldCare Travel Assistance Association Inc., 649
Worldwide Health Forecast, 650
Wortman, Leon A., 109

X

Xenophobia, 171
Xerox, 515, 538
XTEN (Xerox Telecommunications Network), 539

Y

Yale University, 311
Yellow Pages, 61, 70, 393
Yates, Jere E., 162, 163, 175*n.*, 177*n.*, 180*n.*, 186, 230
Yoga, 187
Your Erroneous Zones (Dyer), 240

Z

Zeigarnik effect, 21
Ziglar, Zig, 240
ZIP codes, mail sorting by, 484